Introduction to
Psychology

Introduction to
Psychology

EDITOR
LIONEL NICHOLAS

UCT
PRESS

Introduction to Psychology

First published 2003

PO Box 24309, Landsdowne, 7779

ISBN 1-91971-379-4

Copy editing by Alex Potter
Indexing by Ethne Clarke
Design and typesetting by New Leaf design
Cover design by Catherine Crookes
Illustrations in Chapter 3 by Lyn de la Motte

Typeset in Sabon and Rotis
Printed and bound in South Africa by Formeset

Contents

Contributors

Lionel Nicholas
Deputy Vice-Chancellor
University of Durban Westville

Norman Duncan
Institute for Social and
Health Sciences
University of South Africa

Jane Mufamadi
Department of Psychology
University of Venda

Ashley van Niekerk
Institute for Social and
Health Sciences
University of South Africa

Martin Jooste
Department of Psychology
Rand Afrikaans University

Nhlanhla Mkhize
Department of Psychology
University of Natal,
Pietermaritzburg

Charles Malcolm
Department of Psychology
University of the Western Cape

Beate von Krosigk
Department of Psychology
University of South Africa

Basil Pillay
Department of Psychology
University of Natal, Durban

Umesh Bawa
Department of Psychology
University of the Western Cape

Patrick Sibaya
Department of Psychology
University of Zululand

Don Foster
Department of Psychology
University of Cape Town

Dolores Luiz
Department of Psychology
University of Port Elizabeth

Mark Eaton
Department of Psychology
University of Port Elizabeth

Inge-Marie Schwellnus
Department of Psychology
University of Port Elizabeth

Darin de Klerk
Department of Psychology
University of Port Elizabeth

Jessica Singh
Department of Psychology
Rand Afrikaans University

Ann Watts
Clinical Neuropsychologist

Theo Lazarus
Department of Psychology
University of Natal, Durban

Anthony Naidoo
Department of Psychology
University of Stellenbosch

Nokuthula Shabalala
Department of Psychology
University of the Western Cape

Fatima Abrahams
Department of Industrial
Psychology
University of the Western Cape

Russel Ruiters
Department of Industrial
Psychology
University of the Western Cape

Terry Mashego
Department of Psychology
University of the North

Karl Peltzer
Department of Psychology
University of the North

Tyrone Pretorius
Vice-Rector, Student Affairs
University of the Western Cape

An Introduction to Psychology

L.J. Nicholas

Objectives

After studying this chapter you should:
- know how the field of psychology developed internationally and in South Africa
- understand the contributions of the main figures in psychology
- understand psychology in the South African context.

Introduction

For thousands of years, philosophers from many cultures have grappled with many of the basic problems of psychology, such as physiological influences on behaviour, learning, motivation and personality. Records of the systematic study of human behaviour are evident from about two to three thousand years ago. The most recognised of these philosophers are Confucius (551–479 BC) and his successor Mencius (372–289 BC) in China, Siddharta Sakyamuni (560–480 BC), also known as Buddha (enlightened one), in India, and Plato (437–347 BC) and Aristotle (384–322 BC) in Greece.

Within the belief system of ancient Polynesians, a secret knowledge kept by *kahunas* ('keepers of the secret') presented humans as having a subconscious that is the locus of emotions, the conscious, intellectual reasoning and a super conscious, the repository of past and present experiences and planning. These were also presented as a low self *unihipili*, a middle self *uhane* and a high self *aumakua*. In Polynesian folklore, they trace their origins to 12 tribes from the Sahara desert who initially moved to North Africa (Long 1991).

The Greek philosophers, however, were considered to be the first to offer natural instead of supernatural explanations for natural phenomena and the mind. Aristotle presented the first systematic discussion of

basic psychological issues in *De Anima* ('On The Soul'), which is considered to be the first book of psychology. His writings include 'On sensation
and that which is sensed', 'On memory and forgetting', 'Concerning sleep
and awakening', 'Concerning dreams', 'Interpretation of dreams', 'About
a long life and a short life', 'Concerning youth and old age', 'Concerning
life and death' and 'About respiration'.

   While the many definitions of psychology may have varying emphases,
all agree that psychology is the scientific study of behaviour. 'Psychology'
is derived from the Greek words *psyche* ('the soul') and *logos* ('study'). In
Europe, Philip Melancthon (1497–1560) is credited with coining the term
psychology, which was popularised by Christian von Wolff (1679–1754)
but only gained more than rare usage by the early eighteenth century. In
1874, Wilhelm Wundt (1821–1894), a professor of physiology and philosophy, stated his intention to mark out a new domain of science in his
Principles of Physiological Psychology (1904). In 1879, he established a
psychological laboratory at Leipzig University with a few rooms and some
equipment for psychological demonstrations. In 1875, William James also
had a room set up for psychological experimentation at Harvard
University. Wundt has been generally acknowledged as the founder of
modern experimental psychology. Wundt also trained those who became
leaders in psychology around the world, including Emil Kraepelin
(Germany); Stanley Hall and James McKeen Cattell (USA); E.B. Titchener
(England); Georgy Chelpanov and Niseolgy Lange, founders of Russian
psychology; Matataro Matsumato (Japan); and Cai Yuanpei (China).

   Wundt's emphasis on experimental methodology gave psychology a
strong scientific basis and his system of structuralism tested the method
of introspection. Wundt was preceded by Hermann von Helmholtz (1821–
1874), known for his contributions on sight and hearing, who was the first
to measure the speed of a nerve impulse; Gustav Fechner (1801–1887),
known for developing mathematical principles to explain the relationship
between a physical and a mental event; Ernst Heinrich Weber (1795–
1878), known for his research on the sense of touch; and Johannes Muller
(1801–1858), who formulated a theory of sensation that helped to explain
how nerve cells transmitted information to the brain.

   E.B Titchener (1867–1927), an Englishman who emigrated to the
USA, was the foremost proponent of **structuralism**. He studied with
Wundt at Leipzig. Structuralism proposed that the task of psychology was
to analyse consciousness into its basic elements and investigate the relationships among them. Most of the work of structuralists focused on
touch, sensation, perception, vision and hearing. Trained normal adults
made descriptive reports of how stimuli appeared to them, which allowed

Structuralism:
School of psychology that
proposed that the task
of psychology was to
analyse consciousness.

researchers to interpret the **structure** of the mind and how it worked. According to Titchener, the structure of the mind consists of 30 000 separate sensations, feelings and images (Papalia & Olds 1985).

William James (1842–1910) was the foremost proponent of functionalism, which proposed that psychology should investigate the function or purpose of consciousness rather than its structure. Functionalists adopted a broader view of psychology, which allowed them to study all age groups and a range of subjects. The new areas of investigation included child psychology, motivation and emotion. The contestation of ideas between structuralism and functionalism continued for many years, but neither could claim a decisive victory. The influence of both faded as new schools of thought emerged. However, the practical orientation embedded in functionalism encouraged the development of behaviourism and applied psychology.

Structure:
The way in which something is organised.

Psychoanalysis

Sigmund Freud (1856–1939) was born in Freiberg, Czechoslovakia, but spent most of his life in Vienna, Austria. He fled from the Nazis in 1938 and died in England in 1939. His interest in neuroanatomy led to his discovery that many 'nervous diseases' had a psychological rather than organic origin. He showed that mental illness may result from psychoneuroses and developed a special therapeutic approach called **psychoanalysis**. Psychoanalytic therapy involves exploration of the unconscious to bring into consciousness inner conflicts that may originate in the earliest infantile experiences. Freud also demonstrated the importance of the unconscious in human motivation. The unconscious determines our thinking, feeling and actions, yet we have no immediate awareness of it. Freud's work with Josef Breuer (1842–1925) in treating the 21-year-old Anna O alerted him to the possible links between her childhood experiences and neurotic symptoms. Breuer and Freud jointly published *Studies in Hysteria* in 1895. The same year is considered the birthyear of psychoanalysis. Freud's intolerance of those who questioned his ideas led to a series of estrangements. Breuer, a close friend and financial supporter, did not accept Freud's early theory that early sexual experience was the cause of every case of hysteria – a theory that he later abandoned and replaced with infantile **sexual fantasies** that interfered with sexual maturation. Even when Breuer wanted to reconcile, Freud remained unforgiving (Fuller 1995). Members of the inner circle of the psychoanalytic movement broke away and formed their own schools, initiating new psychoanalytic trends, much to Freud's dismay. Among them were Alfred Adler, Wilhelm Stekel, Carl Jung and Otto Rank.

Psychoanalysis:
System of therapy based on exploration of the unconscious mind.

Sexual fantasies:
Sexual imaginings

Behaviourism

John B. Watson (1878–1958) founded behaviourism, whose theoretical goal is the prediction and control of behaviour. Watson's series of lectures at Columbia University in 1912 was the first public exposition of behaviourism. He followed this with an article in *Psychological Review* (Watson 1913). Behaviourism took up cudgels against the whole of existing psychology, believing it to be a dismal failure in establishing itself as an undisputed natural science. The fault was in its adherence to consciousness and introspection. Behaviourism would therefore exclusively study behaviour, which, simply put, is the reaction of the organism to a stimulus. Initially behaviourism was characterised by investigating the muscular movements and glandular responses of subjects. Watson's doctoral thesis in 1903 was on the neurological and psychological maturation of the white rat. Watson's contribution to psychology lies in turning it in the direction of objectivity and precision of methodology. Watson was forced to resign from Johns Hopkins University after a heavily publicised divorce in 1920. Subsequently, he became a pioneer in advertising. The leading figures in behaviourism were E.C. Tolman (1886–1961), C.L. Hall (1884–1952), E.R. Gulthrie (1886–1959) and B.F. Skinner (1904–1990).

Stimulus:
Any detectable input from the environment.

Gestalt psychology

Max Wertheimer (1880–1943) founded the school of Gestalt psychology. *Gestalt* means 'shape' or 'configuration' in German. It began as the study of the visual perception of motion, and developed as a system based on a holistic view of mental and behavioural processes (Misiak & Sexton 1968). The strength of the theory derives from experimental investigations verifying the dynamic whole, which could neither be reduced to the sensory elements, nor explained as a sum or succession of sensations. 'The whole is greater than the sum of its parts.' This **phi phenomenon**, which is the illusion of movement induced by presenting visual stimuli in rapid succession, presented the basis for a challenge to the influential structural psychology. The Gestaltists also made the figure-ground relationship an important component of the theory. The 'figure' is that which is clear and the object of attention, and the 'ground' is what is not being attended to. Figure and ground can be changed by shifting one's attention (Hergenhahn 1992). Christian von Ehrenfels (1859–1932) first proposed the notion of *Gestalqualität* ('form-quality'). The Gestaltists extended this to mean any integrated, organised whole greater than the sum of its parts. Wertheimer attended some of Von Ehrenfels' lectures while attending the University of Prague. Other leaders in the Gestalt

Phi phenomenon:
The illusion of movement induced by presenting visual stimuli in rapid succession.

movement were Kurt Koffka (1886–1941), who concentrated on developmental psychology; Wofgang Köhler (1897–1967), who focused on psychophysics and learning; and Kurt Lewin (1890–1947), who focused on motivation and social psychology.

Humanistic psychology

Carl Rogers (1902–1987) and Abraham Maslow (1908–1970) were the most prominent leaders in humanistic psychology, which emphasised optimism, unique human qualities and the unbounded potential of growth in humans. Maslow is often credited for making humanistic psychology a formal branch of psychology. Its tenets are:

- Little of value can be learned about humans by studying nonhuman animals.
- Subjective reality is the primary guide for human behaviour.
- Studying individuals is more important than studying what groups of individuals have in common.
- A major effort should be made to discuss those things that expand and enrich human experience.
- Research should seek information that will help solve human problems.
- The goal of psychology should be to formulate a complete description of what it means to be a human being. Such a description would include the importance of language, the valuing process, the full range of human emotions, and the ways humans seek and attain meaning in their lives.

(HERGENHAHN 1992: p. 510)

The international development of psychology

Vladimir M. Bekhterev founded the first Russian psychological laboratory in Kazan in 1885, and in 1912, the Russian Psychological Institute was opened. Lev S. Vygotsky and Alexander R. Luria worked at this institute. Yujiro Motora established the first psychology laboratory in Japan in 1900; Chen Daqi established China's first psychological laboratory in 1917; and N.N. Sengupta established India's first psychological laboratory in 1915. On 8 July 1892, in the study of G. Stanley Hall, the American Psychology Association (APA) was formed with a membership of 31. The APA now has over 130 000 members (Pawlik & Rozenzweig 2000). The first International Congress of Psychology took place in Paris in 1889. Currently, women psychologists number about

53% in European countries, 70% in South America and Caribbean countries, 25% in Asian countries and 63% in South Africa (Jing, 2000).

Overall gender representation by practice category in South Africa

Clinical psychology	Female	1 108
	Male	710
Counselling psychology	Female	698
	Male	423
Educational psychology	Female	693
	Male	354
Industrial psychology	Female	333
	Male	524
Research psychology	Female	120
	Male	122
Total		**5 085**

(SOURCE: PROFESSIONAL BOARD FOR PSYCHOLOGY 2002)

Overall gender representation of psychologists, masters students and interns in South Africa

Registered psychologists	Female	2952
	Male	2 133
M1 students	Female	539
	Male	154
Interns	Female	634
	Male	328

(SOURCE: PROFESSIONAL BOARD FOR PSYCHOLOGY 2002)

Psychology across the world

Country	GNP/ capita $	Total number of psychologists (1998)	Membership of national society (1998)	Population (million) (1995)	Psychologists per million population
Argentina	8 100	37 000	100	34.6	1069.4
Australia	18 000	12 000	12 500	18.1	663.0
Austria	24 630	4 000	1 500	8.0	500.0
Belgium	22 870	3 987	500	10.1	394.8
Bulgaria	1 250	4 500	500	8.8	511.4
Canada	19 510	16 000	4 300	29.5	542.4
China	530	3 500	3 500	1 221.5	2.9

Country	GNP/ capita $	Total number of psychologists (1998)	Membership of national society (1998)	Population (million) (1995)	Psychologists per million population
Colombia	1 670	12 000	900	35.1	341.9
Croatia	2 560	1 200	–	4.5	266.7
Czechoslovakia	3 200	1 060	1 000	10.3	102.9
Estonia	2 820	600	58	1.5	400.0
Finland	18 850	4 300	1 500	5.1	843.1
France	23 420	30 000	1 100	58.0	517.2
Georgia	580	780	–	5.5	141.8
Germany	25 580	45 000	22 000	81.6	551.5
Greece	7 700	1 600	260	10.5	152.4
Israel	13 530	1 039	850	3.6	288.6
Italy	19 300	30 000	2 600	57.2	524.5
Japan	34 630	12 000	5 800	125.1	95.9
Korea	8 260	1 100	1 200	45.0	24.4
Mexico	4 180	11 500	1 025	93.7	122.7
Netherlands	22 010	20 000	8 000	15.5	1 290.3
New Zealand	13 350	1 700	700	3.6	472.2
Norway	26 390	3 200	3 526	4.3	744.2
Portugal	9 320	8 000	252	9.8	816.3
Romania	1 270	2 000	500	22.8	87.7
South Africa	1 930	4 341	1 337	44.6	97.3
Singapore	22 500	1 700	120	2.8	607.1
Slovenia	7 040	1 300	420	1.9	684.2
Spain	13 440	30 000	500	39.6	757.6
Uganda	190	100	100	21.3	4.7
USA	25 880	174 900	114 000	263.3	664.3
Venezuela	2 760	6 145	3 938	21.8	281.9

In South Africa, psychology was taught in philosophy departments until 1918, when R.W. Wilcocks was appointed Professor of Logic and Psychology at the University of Stellenbosch. After his appointment, Wilcocks established the first experimental psychology laboratory in South Africa at the University of Stellenbosch. He modelled it along the lines of Wundt's laboratory, having received his doctorate on the analysis of productive thought at the University of Berlin in 1917. Through his work in the Carnegie Commission into the Poor White problem and his mentorship of H.F. Verwoerd he was responsible for the entrenchment of apartheid legislation (Nicholas 1990). Hugh Reyburn was appointed to a chair in psychology at the University of Cape Town in 1920, and other universities followed. The first psychology association was established in 1948 in Bloemfontein, with a membership of 34. When a black psychologist was admitted as a member of the South African Psychology Association (SAPA) in 1962, five years after the initial application, a sizable group of SAPA members resigned to form a whites-only organisation, the Psychological Institute of the Republic of South Africa (PIRSA). A.J. la Grange, a Stellenbosch University professor, was the first president of SAPA and later PIRSA. SAPA and PIRSA merged in 1983 to form the Psychological Association of South Africa (PASA), after T.M.D. Kruger, the leader of the pro-apartheid action committee that took the lead in establishing PIRSA, indicated that two separate psychology associations did not serve the best interests of the profession and the science of psychology.

Racism has been the most enduring and significant problem in South Africa, and elsewhere, and psychology's achievements could be measured by the extent of its contribution to its eradication. The professional societies seem to have played a role in exacerbating racism and making psychology an unpalatable option for potential black psychologists (Nicholas 1990). A new society, the Psychological Society of South Africa (PSYSSA) was established in 1994, as a direct result of the neglect of racism and the perceived acceptance by PASA of the status quo. (See Nicholas 1990 for a detailed history of professional psychology associations and apartheid.) Historically, the record of psychology is poor both locally and internationally on the issues of race and gender.

Intelligence quotient testing and twin studies were initially used to promote racial agendas in England and North America. Kamin (1981: p. 93) illustrated how far-reaching the effects of these investigations were:

> The uncritical belief in the power of heredity, linked to the advocacy of eugenic ideas, was already widespread when Binet's test appeared. More than 30 American states followed the lead taken by Indiana in 1907 in passing eugenic sterilisation laws which provided for the compulsory sterilisation of, among others, criminals, idiots, imbeciles, epileptics, rapists, lunatics, drunkards, drug fiends, syphilitics, moral and sexual perverts, and 'diseased and degenerate persons'. The laws declared as a matter of legal fact, the various defects of all these offenders were transmitted through the genes. The wholly unscientific fantasies of the eugenicists encouraged the naïve claim that sterilisation of offenders would eliminate these undesirable traits from the population. Fortunately, the sterilisation laws were not often enforced. When they were, the victims were poor.
> (EYSENCK & KAMIN 1981: p. 93)

G. Stanley Hall, a leading US psychologist, believed that most 'savages' in most respects are children, and that women are primitive and men more modern in 'body and soul' (Gould 1981). He received what may be regarded as the world's first psychology doctorate from Harvard University, for work done with William James. He was Wundt's first US student and also studied with Helmholtz, from whom he felt he learnt more than Wundt (Hergenhahn 1992).

Sir Cyril Burt, a leading British psychologist, faked his data and invented collaborations to substantiate hereditarian claims. Leon Kamin noticed that, while Burt increased his samples of twins from fewer than 20 to more than 50 in a series of publications, the average correlation between pairs for IQ remained unchanged to the third decimal place (Gould 1981). Some of his other studies were also found to be fraudulent. South African psychologists R.W. Wilcocks, H.F. Verwoerd, J.A.J. van Rensburg and L.M. Fick all contributed to the entrenchment of racism in South Africa. Other psychologists have expended considerable resources in debunking racist claims, including Hussein Abdilahi Bulhan, N. Chabani Manganyi, Saths Cooper and Don Foster.

The draft professional practice framework for psychology in South Africa

A new professional practice framework has been adopted by the Professional Board of Psychology, which extends the training of psychologists to a doctoral degree. Post-doctoral specialisation will be incorporated later. Registered counsellors who qualify at a fourth year level will be able to practice in the following areas: psychometrics, career, trauma, primary mental health, family, school, sport, HIV/AIDS, human resources, pastoral, and employee relations and well being.

- Post-Doctoral specialisation
  Ad hoc specialisations will be considered once the new practice framework is in place.
- Psychologist
  A doctorate, involving a one-year internship after completion of course work requirements. A professional doctorate at NQF level 8, with at least a 50% research component (including a thesis) is integral to the degree.
- Registered counsellor
  A masters degree, involving six months of practical work per practice area, with registration in up to three practice areas. As a structured

masters degree, this qualification involves research component/s comprising at least 120 credits.

- **Registered counsellor**
  This career-focused qualification/vocational degree could be a B.Psych degree or an Honours degree in psychology, and will be the entry point to a career in psychology. The Honours degree involves six months of practical work per practice area, with registration in not more than two practice areas.
- **Bachelors degree**
  This degree cannot result in a professional registration. The degree, with a major in psychology, will lead to entry to the Honours degree in psychology and may permit entry to the fourth year B.Psych degree.

Current scopes of practice of psychologists

Psychologists and registered counsellors are trained and registered in particular practice areas, and are ethically obliged to work only in their area of expertise.

Industrial psychologists apply the principles of psychology to issues related to the work situation of relatively normal and well-adjusted adults in order to optimise individual, group and organisational well-being and effectiveness.

Clinical psychologists assess, diagnose and intervene in order to alleviate or contain relatively serious forms of psychological distress and dysfunction, particularly psychopathology, or what is commonly referred to as 'abnormal' behaviour.

Counselling psychologists assist relatively healthy people in dealing with normal problems of life, concerning all stages and aspects of a person's existence, in order to facilitate desirable psychological adjustment, growth and maturity.

The primary role of **educational psychologists** is to facilitate the healthy development of the child towards adulthood, within the educational contexts of the family, the school, and social or peer groups.

Research psychologists may address any of the above four fields – not to render services to the public, but to apply research methods and techniques purely in order to contribute to the knowledge base of a particular field.

Registered counsellors may address more formalised, structured and short-term interventions at the primary curative/preventative levels across the scope of psychology. These interventions require the application of concrete and pre-determined decision-making rules, and are likely to comprise the bulk of services offered in psychology in the future.

Summary

- Psychology is the scientific study of behaviour.
- The late 19th and early 20th century saw the emergence of different schools of psychology.
- Wilhelm Wundt established the first laboratory for psychological experimentation.
- E. B Titchener named Wundt's work structuralism and was its foremost proponent.
- William James was the foremost proponent of functionalism, which proposed that psychology investigate the function of consciousness.
- Sigmund Freud developed a therapeutic approach called psycho-analysis, which involves bringing into consciousness inner conflicts in the unconscious.
- Behaviourists focus on observable behaviours and events.
- Humanistic psychologists emphasise healthy human behaviour and the potential for growth in humans.
- Psychology in South Africa fell prey to the racism that affected society prior to 1994.
- Psychologists in South Africa practice in five distinct areas: industrial, clinical, counselling, educational and research.

Further reading

Brown, L.B. (1981) *Psychology in Contemporary China*. Oxford: Pergamon Press.

Bulhan, H.A. (1985) *Frantz Fanon and the Psychology of Oppression*. New York: Plenum Press.

Eysenck, H.J. & Kamin, L. (1981) *The Intelligence Controversy*. New York: John Wiley.

Fuller, R. (1995) *Seven Pioneers of Psychology, Behaviour and Mind*. London and New York: Routledge.

Gould, S.J. (1981) *The Mismeasure of Man*. Harmondsworth: Penguin Books.

Hergenhahn, B.R. (1992) *An Introduction to the History of Psychology* (2nd edition). Belmont: Wadsworth.

Jing, Q. (2000) International psychology. In K. Pawlik & M.R. Rosenweig, *The International Handbook of Psychology*.

Long, M.F. (1991) *The Secret Science behind Miracles: Unveiling the Huna Tradition of the Ancient Polynesians*. Marina del Rey: De Vorss.

Louw, D.A. & Edwards, D.J.A. (1995) *Psychology: An Introduction for Students in Southern Africa*. Johannesburg: Lexicon.

Misiak, H. & Sexton, V.S. (1968) *History of Psychology: An Overview*. New York and London: Grune & Stratton.

Nicholas, L.J. (1990) The response of professional psychology associations to apartheid. *Journal of the History of the Behavioral Sciences*, 26, pp. 58–63.

Papalia, D.E. & Olds, S.W. (1985) *Psychology*. New York: McGraw-Hill.

Pawlik, K. & Rosenzweig, M.R. (2000) *The International Handbook of Psychology*. London: Sage.

Professional Board of Psychology (2002) Unpublished report.

Watson, J.B. (1913) Psychology as the behaviorist views it. *Psychological Review,* 20, pp. 158–77.

Weiten, W. (1998*) Psychology: Themes and Variations* (4th edition). Pacific Grove: Books/Cole.

Wittig, A.F. & Belkin, G.S. (1990) *Introduction to Psychology*. New York: McGraw-Hill.

2 Developmental Psychology: A life-span perspective

N. Duncan, A. van Niekerk and J. Mufamadi

Objectives

After studying this chapter you should:

- know how to define developmental psychology
- be able to describe the key tasks of developmental psychology
- be able to describe the life-span approach to human development
- be able to describe in broad terms the development of the individual from conception to late adulthood and death
- know how to describe some of the key obstacles to optimal human development in South Africa.

Introduction

This chapter has been written within a critical social science framework. In simple terms, critical social science endeavours to analyse, understand and explain social phenomena in a manner that will lead to the transformation of extant social inequalities (Neuman 1997). In other words, critical social science does not attempt to be neutral. Instead, it attempts to uncover obstacles to optimal human development, so as to empower people (largely through the knowledge it produces) to challenge these obstacles.

What is developmental psychology?

The last three to four decades have witnessed an increasing awareness of the importance of developmental psychology for a variety of professions that deal with human development in one capacity or another, professions such as social work, education, nursing and physiotherapy. Within psychology, developmental psychology is recognised as a vital foundation for the acquisition of knowledge in the other sub-disciplines of psychology. For example, a thorough grounding in developmental psychology is viewed as essential for an adequate understanding of psychopathology, psychotherapy, organisational psychology, health psychology, etc. (LaBarba 1981). The last few years have also witnessed a recognition of the importance of a critical knowledge of developmental psychology in enabling people to understand their own functioning and to lead more fulfilling lives.

Defining developmental psychology

Butterworth and Harris (1994: p. 3) defined developmental psychology as the 'scientific [study] of age-related changes in experience and behaviour'. Hurlock (1980: p. 2), along similar lines, but with a greater degree of specificity, defines developmental psychology as that 'branch of psychology that studies intra-individual changes' in terms of cognitive, psychosocial and physical processes, as well as 'the inter-individual differences within these intra-individual changes'. According to Hurlock, in this branch of psychology we are primarily concerned with the study of the changes that occur within the individual over time and how the individual differs from others in terms of these changes.

Maturation:
More or less automatic unfolding of a genetically or biologically determined sequence of behaviours or behaviour patterns.

Learning:
A process of relatively permanent change in the individual's behaviour that results from experience or practice.

From the definitions presented above, one can deduce that developmental psychology is primarily concerned with the study of change. Indeed, as Piaget (in Hurlock 1980: p. 2) is reported to have remarked, the human organism is 'far from static and given from the start'. Instead, from birth to death, largely because of **maturation** and **learning**, the individual undergoes continued and progressive change.

Maturation, learning and human development

Most developmental psychologists today agree that development is a consequence of two related processes: maturation and learning.

Maturation can be defined as the more or less automatic unfolding of a genetically or biological-ly determined sequence of behaviours or behaviour patterns (Huffman *et al.* 1994; Morris 1979; Papalia & Olds 1995). Behaviours that depend primarily on maturation include grasping, crawling and walking. These behaviours normally only appear when the individual is biologically 'ready' to perform them and not earlier (Papalia & Olds 1995). Thus, no matter how much parents attempt to train their children to walk, children will only be capable of walking when their bodies are capable of performing this action.

Learning refers to a process of relatively perma-nent change in an individual's behaviour that results from experience or practice (Papalia & Olds 1995). Developing the ability to cycle or to kick a ball, or acquiring the capacity to read, are examples of learning. It is important to note that many forms of learning can generally only take place once the individual is maturationally ready and if the conditions conducive to learning exist. For example, a young child will only be able to learn to kick a ball once his or her sensory and motor capacities have developed to the point where he or she is capable of executing all the actions required to actually kick the ball, and if the conditions necessary for such learning to take place exist.

Hurlock (1980) distinguished two ostensibly antagonistic forms of change that, according to her, constitute the essence of development: on the one hand, there is growth or evolution, and on the other, atrophy or involution. Both forms of change begin at conception and both end at death. Even though evolutionary processes are dominant during the early years, involutionary processes can occur as early as during prena-tal life (Hurlock 1980; Meyer 1991). For example, skin cells are produced and die during the foetal stage. In the latter stages of life, invo-lutionary processes continue even though evolutionary processes predominate. For example, even when a person is 80 years old, his or her hair continues to grow and skin cells continue to be replaced (Craig 1989; Hurlock 1980; Meyer 1991).

Craig (1989) emphasised two further forms of change that typify human development: **quantitative** and **qualitative change**. Very simply put, quantitative change refers to a change in quantity, such as a change in height or weight, or the size of a child's vocabulary. **Qualitative change,** however, refers to a change in quality or complexity, such as changes in the complexity of the thinking processes and the types of sentences children are capable of at different ages.

Quantitative change:
A change in the number or amount of an attribute, such as height or weight.

Qualitative change:
A change in the structure or complexity of an attribute, such as the way the mind functions.

When we use the term 'development' in developmental psychology, we generally refer to all the forms of change described above. Obviously there is considerable overlap and a complex interaction between these different types of change. Evolutionary and involutionary changes are interconnected, and both forms of change can be qualitative and quantitative in nature.

Domains of development

Many developmental psychology textbooks divide the field of development into three principle categories:

- physical development, which includes physiological changes and motor development;
- cognitive development, which includes the development of language and thought processes; and
- psychosocial development, which includes emotional development, personality development and the development of interpersonal relations (Clarke-Stewart *et al.* 1988; Hook & Cockcroft 2002).

Whereas dividing the development of the individual into three domains might facilitate the study and explanation of developmental processes, people's behaviour and development, in reality, cannot be divided into such neat categories. People are integrated or 'whole' beings, and their development involves 'interconnected changes across all [three] domains' (Clarke-Stewart *et al.* 1988, p. 24).

Tasks of developmental psychology

Developmental psychology has four major objectives: the description, explication, prediction and modification of human behaviour and development. To illustrate these tasks we will consider the case study 'Jenny'. However, before we do so, two points must be stressed. Firstly, while prediction is one of the key objectives of human development, this objective can never be met completely, simply because people are unique and their behaviour so variable. Secondly, developmental psychologists are generally interested in the developmental patterns detectable among groups of individuals. However, since each individual is unique, developmental psychologists often also focus on changes that occur within individuals (Clarke-Stewart *et al.*, 1988).

Jenny

Jenny Hendricks (not her real name), a six-year-old girl about to enter a primary school in Valhalla Park in the Western Cape, was recently referred to the psychological services unit at a local children's hospital. She was born in this urban ghetto. Though her family has always struggled to make ends meet, about a year ago, matters took a turn for the worse when her father was killed by gangsters on his way from work one Friday evening. This forced Jenny's mother, Fairoza Hendricks, to go to work to support her children. After the birth of her youngest son, who was born physically disabled, Fairoza had given up working.

However, after her husband's murder, Fairoza had no alternative but to find employment outside the home. As her eldest son was attending school, Fairoza left her two youngest children in Jenny's care while she was at work.

When Jenny was admitted to the children's hospital, her presenting problems were severe abdominal pains, extreme separation anxiety and recurring nightmares. In her initial interview with the resident psychologist at the hospital, when she was asked whether she was looking forward to going to school, her vehement reply was, 'No! I do not want to go to school! I want to stay at home!'

While concerning themselves with the descriptive aspects of this case, developmental psychologists will typically also be interested in explaining Jenny's behaviour. For example, why is Jenny unwilling to go to school? And why is she so anxious? The developmental psychologist will attempt to understand how Jenny's current context and her past experiences might have influenced her behaviour and well-being. Based on her past and present experiences, the psychologist might try to predict Jenny's future behaviour. For example, how will the fact that Jenny lost her father at such an early age influence her future development? And how will the fact that she is the primary caregiver to her siblings for the better part of the day affect her in future? If the psychologist's predictions hint at problems in Jenny's future development, he or she could make certain suggestions that would enable the modification of Jenny's environment or behaviour, to ensure her optimal development.

The way in which developmental psychologists will describe and explain Jenny's behaviour, the predictions they will make about her future development and the suggestions they might make to ensure her optimal development, will largely depend on the human development theories that they subscribe to, or the theories that will enable them to make sense of Jenny's experiences and behaviour. Currently, there are several theories of human development that inform the work of developmental psychologists and structure the subject matter of developmental psychology. These include Sigmund Freud's psychosexual theory of development, Erik Erikson's psychosocial theory of development, social learning theories of development, Piaget's theory of cognitive development, and ecological theories of development. What we present here is an outline of six basic assumptions that inform our thinking, research and writings on human development. These assumptions are based on some of the principal ideas contained in the theories referred to above, as well as the extant research in the field of developmental psychology.

Assumption 1: Development is a function of the interaction between innate and environmental factors

One of the oldest – and some would say, rather misguided (Bulhan 1992) – debates in developmental psychology revolves around the question: To what extent is development a product of innate or internal factors, and to what extent is it a function of external or environmental factors? In the past, some psychologists adopted fairly rigid and extreme positions on this question. For example, Sigmund Freud (1933) and Arnold Gesell (in Butterworth & Harris 1994) maintained that development is primarily a product of innate factors (nature). Gesell posited that development is a result of maturational processes. Specifically, he held that development occurs according to a fixed biological time clock – in other words, automatically.

In contrast, other psychologists, such as John B. Watson and Albert Bandura (in Clarke-Stewart, *et al.* 1988), argued that development is largely determined by environmental factors and learning (nurture). Watson was so convinced of the pre-eminent influence of environmental factors on development that he wrote:

> *Give me a dozen healthy infants ... and my own specified world to bring them up in, and I'll guarantee to take any one at random and train him*[1] *to become any type of specialist I might select – doctor, lawyer, artist, merchant-chief and, yes, even beggar man and thief, regardless of his talents, penchants, tendencies, abilities, vocations and race of his ancestors.*
> (in Butterworth & Harris 1994: p. 12)

In recent years, however, developmental psychologists have tended to adopt a more nuanced position than the likes of Gesell and Watson in relation to the nature/nurture question. More specifically, most contemporary developmental psychologists are of the opinion that the nature and nurture positions offer only part of the truth, and that a 'synthesis of the two would possibly be much nearer the truth' (Louw 1991: p. 203). In other words, development is a result of both innate and environmental factors. This position is illustrated in the case studies: 'Teaching Yoni to talk' and 'Wolf children'. These case studies collectively demonstrate that both innate human phylogenetic capacities (nature) and appropriate environmental conditions (nurture) are essential for adequate human development to take place.

Teaching Yoni to talk

Several years ago, Ladygina-Kots, an animal psychologist, conducted an interesting experiment in which she reared a chimpanzee, Yoni, in her home. Raised as a member of Ladygina-Kots' family from the age of one-and-a-half to four years, Yoni was exposed to all the toys, attention and human interaction that a young child would normally be exposed to. While his foster 'mother' allowed him complete freedom, she did her utmost to teach him to use the objects in his environment appropriately and to relate to others through the medium of language. Throughout Yoni's stay with her, Ladygina-Kots carefully recorded the chimpanzee's development.

Some years later, the researcher had a son, Rudi, whose development to the age of four was monitored just as carefully. When she compared the development of Yoni and Rudi, Ladygina-Kots noted several similarities in their play and emotional behaviours. However, their development also reflected several important differences. Firstly, the chimpanzee, unlike the human child, could neither walk upright nor correctly use instruments such as household utensils and tools. Secondly, despite the regular special speech training he received, Yoni, unlike Rudi, was unable to imitate human speech and speech sounds.

As Mukhina (1984) observed, it is impossible for human qualities such as the ability to utilise language to emerge in the absence of those phylogenetic attributes that are uniquely human (for example, the human brain and voice).

(MUKHINA 1984)

Wolf children[2]

At the beginning of the twentieth century, two strange beings were discovered in a forest near a village in India. While resembling humans, they moved about on all fours, howled like wolves, and ran away from or snapped at people who ventured too close. They were later identified as two girls of approximately eight and two years of age, who apparently had been abandoned and presumably reared by wolves. After being caught, they were placed in a human environment, and a concerted effort was made to teach them human behaviours. Unfortunately, the younger of the two girls died a year after being placed in human care. The other girl lived several years longer. While attempts to wean the older child of her lupine behaviours appeared to be relatively successful, she only managed to learn 40 words and could never speak fluently. Indeed, her linguistic abilities never surpassed that of the average two-year-old child raised in a 'normal' human environment.

More than anything else, this case illustrates that human development is likely to be retarded in environmental conditions that are not conducive to optimal human development.

(MUKHINA 1984)

Assumption 2: People contribute to shaping their own development

While genetic and environmental factors condition human development, people are not passive beings completely at the mercy of the influence of these factors. For example, people, through their actions, have an impact upon and shape their environment. In turn, the environment that they help to transform impacts on their subsequent actions and the expression of their developmental potential (Craig 1989; Mukhina 1984). Thus, the young child who is verbally 'gifted' might, through his or her performance in the classroom, inspire the teacher to interact with him or her more frequently and at a more advanced level than with other students. In turn, this attention might further enhance his or her verbal capabilities.

Assumption 3: Human beings are resilient

Another key assumption is that human beings are extremely resilient. Humans generally have the remarkable capacity to recover from difficult life circumstances and traumatic experiences. Research has shown that exposure to traumatic events does not necessarily cause irreversible damage (Wessels & Monteiro 2000). In South Africa, for instance, there are many examples of individuals who were exposed to the cruellest forms of abuse and trauma during the apartheid period, but today are well-adjusted and lead very productive lives, some occupying influential positions in society. However, while acknowledging the resilience of the individual, one needs to emphasise the responsibility of developmental psychologists and students of developmental psychology to advocate and work towards the creation of conditions that will enhance human development (Macleod 2002). Ultimately, optimal environmental conditions are a surer and more effective way of ensuring optimal human development than relying on the potential resilience of the individual (Papalia & Olds 1989).

Assumption 4: Development follows a fairly predictable pattern

Various writers argue that development takes place according to a fairly orderly and predictable pattern (Clarke-Stewart et al. 1988; Craig 1989; Hurlock 1980). To an extent, this position is supported by the fact that physical development, for example, generally occurs according to the cephalo-caudal and proximal-distal developmental principles. The cephalo-caudal (head-to-tail) principle posits that development generally proceeds from the head to the lower limbs. Thus, we find that infants generally acquire control over the top parts of their bodies before they can exercise control over the lower parts. The proximal-distal (near-to-far) principle predicates that development generally occurs from the centre of the body to the extremities. Consequently, we note that babies generally acquire the ability to control their upper arms and upper legs before they acquire control over their hands and feet and, ultimately, their fingers and toes (Craig 1989).

Hurlock (1980) held that, unless environmental conditions prevented it, development in terms of cognitive and psychosocial processes might occur according to similar predictable patterns. Given the complexity of cognitive and psychosocial processes, however, there is not much consensus among developmental psychologists regarding the nature of these patterns. Some psychologists even contest the usefulness of trying to identify patterns of development. Berger (1994) and Hook and Cockcroft (2002) note that, in view of the variability of the contexts in which development occurs, there are always bound to be many exceptions to whatever normative patterns of development are identified.

Despite Berger's and Hook and Cockcroft's reservations about the value of identifying development trends, there are certain broad development trends. Indeed, if we accept that development does not occur according to any identifiable trends, developmental psychology loses much of its explanatory and (limited) predictive value and, consequently, its overall value as a sub-discipline of psychology that can be harnessed to advocate the improvement in living conditions of particularly lower-income communities. Even though we might accept that development in some respects occurs according to certain broad patterns, it should be stressed that these patterns of development differ from one socio-cultural context to another, and from one time-period to the next. For example, the socio-emotional pattern known as the midlife crisis, which is precipitated by dramatic life changes and characterised by an identity crisis of sorts, seems to be much more evident in post-World War II youth-oriented societies, such as North America and Europe, than in societies that revere old age (Berger 1994). Furthermore, it should be stressed that the tempo of developmental change in physical, cognitive and psychosocial processes varies from one person to another (Butterworth & Harris 1994; Schiamberg 1985). For example, while we know that most children generally crawl before they walk, not all children start crawling and walking at the same time. This leads us to the next assumption.

Assumption 5: **Every individual is unique**

Every individual is unique and his or her development takes a distinctive course (within certain limits). This is largely because every human being is born with a unique set of biological and genetic potentialities, and is exposed to a unique environment. Moreover, there is evidence that the differences between individuals increase from infancy to late adulthood. As Clarke-Stewart *et al.* (1988) and Hook and Cockcroft (2002) observe, adults are not only more complex than children, but they are also more different from one another than children, and they become increasingly different as they move towards late adulthood. Although 'every individual human being is born, lives and dies, no two of us are alike. And the further we develop, the more individual – the more like ourselves – we become' (Clarke-Stewart *et al.* 1988: p. 25). This is partly because, as we grow older, we are exposed to an increasingly unique repertoire of environmental influences.

Assumption 6: **Development is a life-long process**

Consistent with the life-span perspective of human development, development is considered a life-long process. As such, we acknowledge the human potential for growth from conception to old age and/or death. In keeping with the life-span perspective, we do not consider any period in life to have an overriding or pre-eminent influence on the development of the individual. This is obviously in contrast to earlier psychoanalytic perspectives of human development, which tended to represent the end of childhood as effectively constituting the end of significant psychological development in human beings. Here we are reminded specifically of Sigmund Freud's views on human development. According to Freud, the psychological constitution of the human being is decisively formed during the first five to six years of life. Furthermore, he posited that the developmental experiences of childhood laid the basis for most adult behaviour (Freud 1933; Cloninger 1996).

While childhood experiences often influence later development in important ways, this does not mean that all significant development occurs during the childhood years. If we consider the many significant and life-altering events typical of adolescence and adulthood – events such as entering university, entering the job market, marriage, becoming a parent and retirement – then we must acknowledge that significant development continues long after childhood (Butterworth & Harris 1994).

Many developmental psychology textbooks subdivide the human life span into periods or stages, and the criteria for this subdivision are usually chronological age and biological markers such as **puberty** and **menopause** (Butterworth & Harris 1994; Hurlock 1980). While subdividing human development into stages may facilitate the description, explication and prediction of human development, it has two important shortcomings. Firstly, it tends to homogenise or gloss over the differences in development within stages, and in the process, therefore, negates the uniqueness of individual development (Berger 1994). For Berger, actual development is much more complex than the 'stages of development' narrative would lead us to believe, for individuals 'grow in leaps and bounds, sometimes step by step, and sometimes with such continuity that they do not seem to change at all' (Berger 1994: p. 17). Secondly, as observed by Laubscher and Klinger (1997), the focus on the age- or biology-determined unfolding of development typical of the 'stages of development' approach frequently leads to the crucial role of the environment in human development being underplayed.

While taking cognisance of Berger's (1994) and Laubscher and Klinger's (1997) views, this chapter considers the life span in six broad stages. These stages reflect broad approximate trends of development and do not reflect the actual development of every individual in every context. The life span stages are:

- prenatal development;
- infancy;
- childhood;
- adolescence;
- adulthood; and
- late adulthood.

Puberty:
The point at which an individual attains sexual maturity and is able to reproduce.

Menopause:
Period in later life in which women cease to be fertile.

Alfred Adler

Alfred Adler, the second of six siblings, was born in 1870. As a young child, Adler suffered from various ailments, including rickets. At the age of five, he contracted pneumonia and overheard the family doctor telling his father that his illness was so severe that he would certainly die. The doctor suggested that treatment would be useless. On the advice of another doctor, however, treatment was administered and Adler recovered from his illness. Owing to the role of medical science in his recovery, and to overcome his fear of death,

Adler at that point decided to become a doctor when he grew up. He qualified as a medical practitioner at the age of 25 and later became one of the most influential psychologists of the twentieth century. Specifically, he developed an important theory of personality development that *inter alia* underlined the importance of social factors in human development.

By his own account, Adler's early childhood experiences had a profound impact on the direction of as well as his orientation to his life.

(Bem 1997; Cloninger 1996)

South Africa as context of human development

Even the most optimistic would have to admit that the South African context poses many obstacles to the optimal development of the individual (Dawes & Donald 2000). The high levels of HIV/AIDS infection, violence and poverty are of greatest concern (Reconstruction and Development Programme 1996) and those most affected by these obstacles are women, children and members of lower income groups.

Prenatal development and the birth process

Fertilisation:
The process whereby an egg cell fuses with a sperm cell.

Zygote:
The product of the fusion of an egg and sperm cell.

The prenatal period begins with conception, or **fertilisation**, and ends at birth. Fertilisation occurs when a sperm cell fuses with an egg cell. The fusion of the sperm and egg cells leads to the formation of a new cell, referred to as a **zygote**. In essence, fertilisation marks the beginning of a new life. The prenatal period usually lasts for nine months and is generally divided into three phases: the germinal, embryonic and foetal phases.

The **germinal phase** begins with conception and lasts approximately one to two weeks. The germinal phase is also called the period of the zygote or the period of the ovum. Soon after its formation, the zygote starts dividing through the process of mitosis. After two weeks, the zygote has developed into a ball of cells, known as a blastocyst, which attaches itself to the uterine wall. The implantation of the blastocyst in the uterine wall signals the end of the germinal phase and the beginning of the embryonic phase (Craig 1989).

The **embryonic phase** starts towards the end of the second week after conception, and ends at about eight weeks after conception. During this period, the basis for the development of all the major human organs, such as the arms, legs, heart and brain, is laid. During the embryonic phase, the embryo's life-support system – the umbilical cord and the placenta – are also formed.

The placenta, which is connected to the embryo via the umbilical cord, breathes, digests and excretes for the multiplying cells of the embryo. While the bloodstreams of both the embryo and the mother have contact with the placenta, they are separated by the cell walls within the placenta. The placenta consists of semi-permeable membranes with pores large enough to permit the passage of gases and other substances of small molecular structure, but too small to allow blood cells to get through (Mussen *et al.* 1974). The placenta's primary functions are to serve as the conduit for nutrients to the developing **conceptus**, while preventing harmful substances from reaching it. However, research shows that many

Conceptus:
The unborn child.

viruses, noxious gases and drugs can pass through the placenta from the mother to the embryo (Craig 1989).

The **embryonic period** is characterised by extremely rapid development, so much so that, by the end of the eighth week after conception, the embryo has assumed a distinctly human form (Louw *et al.* 1993). The commencement of the formation of bone cells in the developing organism at the end of the eighth week after conception announces the third prenatal period (Mussen *et al.* 1974).

The **foetal phase** is the longest of the three prenatal phases and lasts from the ninth week after conception until birth. The developing organism is now known as a foetus. Many of the major organs and organ systems that the foetus will need in order to survive begin to function during this phase. For example, at seven months, the foetus' nervous system is mature enough to control its breathing and swallowing. At this point too, the foetus' brain forms the tissues that are important for the functioning of the senses and motor activities (Clarke-Stewart & Friedman 1987; Craig 1989).

Factors affecting prenatal development

The development of most conceptuses follows a fairly similar and predictable pattern. However, there are various factors related to the mother's well-being and the environment in which she finds herself that may disturb this pattern of development. Some of these factors, which are often collectively referred to as environmental factors, are briefly discussed below.

The mother's age

Many authors have indicated that mothers younger than 15 or older than 35 have a greater chance of experiencing difficult pregnancies and childbirth complications. Bee and Mitchell (1980) and Mussen *et al.* (1974) have found that young mothers are more susceptible to obstetrical complications, toxaemia and childbirth problems. They are also more likely to give birth to stillborn infants. Some of these problems occur because young mothers often are psychologically ill prepared for pregnancy, physically immature and inadequately nourished. They frequently also do not have access to adequate medical care. These risk factors may impact quite adversely on both the mother and the unborn child (Clarke-Stewart & Friedman 1987).

In view of the above, the high levels of unplanned teenage pregnancy in South Africa are obviously a cause for concern. In 1997, according
to De la Rey and Carolissen (1997), the mothers of no less than 15% of
all children born in South Africa were teenagers.

According to Louw (1991), older women are also more likely to give
birth to Down's syndrome babies. Verp (1993) has also found that older
women have a greater chance than women aged between 20 and 35 of
experiencing spontaneous abortions. One possible explanation for this is
that the reproductive systems of older women no longer function at optimal levels (Louw *et al.* 1993).

Maternal nutrition

A healthy and balanced diet is important for the normal development of
the conceptus. This is because the conceptus is dependent on the mother
for all of its nutritional needs. Several studies (see Craig 1989) indicate
that infants born to chronically malnourished mothers are less active, less
alert and more likely to be born prematurely than the babies of mothers
who were adequately nourished both before and during pregnancy.
Furthermore, infants born to mothers on an inadequate diet are more
likely to be underweight at birth and more susceptible to diseases, such
as pneumonia and bronchitis, than infants born to adequately nourished
mothers (Bhatia *et al.*, in Clarke-Stewart & Friedman 1987; Mussen *et
al.* 1974; Craig 1989). However, these are merely the most obvious and
immediate consequences of maternal malnutrition. As the following quotation indicates, the effects of maternal malnutrition can be more serious
and long lasting than the discussion thus far suggests:

> *A foetus malnourished in the womb may never make up for the brain
> cells and structures that never came properly into being [as a result of
> maternal malnutrition]. Malnutrition before ... birth virtually dooms
> a child to stunted brain development and therefore to considerable
> diminished mental capacities.*
>
> (CRAIG 1989: p. 98)

Maternal malnutrition before and during pregnancy also increases the
risk of congenital defects, retarded growth and infant mortality (Bee
1989; Liebert *et al.* 1986; Shaffer 1966).

In view of the above, and the high levels of poverty and malnutrition
in South Africa, it can be argued that a large proportion of South African

children, particularly black children born in rural areas, start out life at a decided disadvantage (May 1998; Seedat 1984; Wilkinson 1996). In a recent study, May (1998) found that 61% of Africans and 38% of coloureds live in abject poverty, leaving them susceptible to malnutrition.

Maternal diseases

As the placental barrier between the mother and the conceptus' blood-streams is only partially effective in preventing harmful substances from reaching the conceptus, some maternal diseases can also affect the development of the conceptus. Among the diseases known to affect the developing conceptus are syphilis, rubella and the human immuno-deficiency virus (HIV). It has been found that syphilitic infection of the foetus four to five months into the pregnancy can lead to various developmental abnormalities, including blindness, deafness and mental retardation. If contracted during the first three months of pregnancy, rubella may result in a range of developmental problems for the child. These include visual and hearing impairment, and heart defects (Louw *et al.* 1993). It is estimated that up to 40% of infants born to HIV-infected mothers will themselves be infected (Pauw & Brener 1997). Because of their weakened immune systems, HIV-infected infants have only a 50% chance of reaching the age of two. Few survive beyond the age of five (Louw *et al.* 1993; Pauw & Brener 1997). The fact that 68% of South African mothers tested in a 1999 study were HIV-positive (Dorrington *et al.* 2001) does not bode well for the overall health and well-being of many South African children.

The story of Nokephu

In 1992, Nokephu started an intimate relationship with a male partner that was to last for two years. When she became aware that her partner was having relationships with other women, she tried to convince him to use condoms. He always refused. As a result, Nokephu fell pregnant and gave birth to his child. From birth, her baby was persistently ill. At the age of four months, he became so severely ill that Nokephu had to take him to hospital. At the suggestion of the medical personnel at the hospital, Nokephu and her son were tested for HIV. Both tested HIV-positive. Struggling with the news of this diagnosis, Nokephu became severely depressed. She decided to reveal her status to her family and friends. Fortunately for her, they were not judgemental and supported her unconditionally. Tragically, however, her son died at the age of 14 months due to AIDS-related symptoms.

(PAUW & BRENER 1997)

Drugs

Over the last few decades, as the many dramatic cases involving maternal drug consumption both before and during pregnancy have shown, drugs may cross the placenta just as easily as nutrients. The most dramatic of these cases is that of Thalidomide – a tranquilliser prescribed for many pregnant women, particularly in Germany and Great Britain in 1959 and 1960, as a treatment for morning sickness. While the drug might have been effective in treating morning sickness symptoms, it also led to the birth of countless babies with various gross anatomical deformities, including missing limbs (see Berger 1994; Craig 1989).

The effects of maternal drug consumption on the development of the conceptus largely depend on factors such as the type of drug consumed and the stage of the conceptus' development when it is exposed to the drug. The first three months of pregnancy are the most critical. Drugs generally known to have an adverse effect on prenatal development include narcotics (e.g. heroin), certain types of barbiturates, alcohol and certain types of over-the-counter medications.

In general, infants born to mothers who use narcotics are smaller than the norm. These infants may also experience withdrawal symptoms, including extreme irritability, constant shrill crying and tremors. Research has also shown a link between maternal barbiturate consumption during pregnancy and childhood learning disabilities (Clarke-Stewart & Friedman 1987; Craig 1989).

Research shows that, while safe for the mother, birth-control pills and other over-the-counter drugs may not always be safe for the developing conceptus. Indeed, injudicious consumption may lead to a range of developmental problems for the conceptus, in particular neurological problems (Clarke-Stewart & Friedman 1987; Craig 1989).

Pregnant women who consume alcohol risk giving birth to infants suffering from foetal alcohol syndrome (FAS). These children may suffer mental retardation, slow motor development and a range of other problems (Craig 1989; Van der Zanden 1989).

In summary, there are ranges of factors that have the potential to compromise the development and well-being of a child before birth. Those most at risk of these developmental impediments are the socio-economically disadvantaged, which, in South Africa, most frequently are black people and the rural poor (Reconstruction and Development Programme 1996).

Infancy

Infancy lasts from birth to the end of the second year. Infancy includes the neonatal period, which lasts from birth to approximately four weeks after birth. The neonatal period is an important period of adjustment. At birth, the newborn moves from a sheltered environment, where breathing and feeding are automatic, into an environment where his or her body has to function relatively independently. Specifically, once the umbilical cord is cut, the neonate's circulatory, digestive and respiratory systems have to function on their own if he or she is to survive.

Physical development

The first year of life is characterised by extremely rapid physical growth. For example, by four months, an average infant has doubled in birth weight and size. On average, infants double their mass every four to five months. Skeletal and muscular growth also proceeds very rapidly. The fact that the child's brain attains four-fifths of its eventual adult size by the age of two serves as indication of the rapid development of the nervous system during infancy (Louw *et al.* 1993).

Motor development

A child's motor development depends on his or her total physical development. In order to crawl, walk and grasp, he or she must first have reached a certain level of skeletal, neural and muscular development (Louw 1991). As indicated earlier in this chapter, motor development occurs according to the cephalo-caudal and proximal-distal developmental trends. At three months, infants can turn their heads and lift their chins as they lie on their backs. Within four to six months, they can grasp and hold things between their fingers or palms with reasonable facility. Six-month-old infants can sit on their own for short periods. At about 13 months, most infants take their first steps (Louw *et al.* 1993). Although motor development follows more or less the same pattern in all infants, some researchers have found that babies born in certain African, Asian and Latin American socio-cultural contexts appear to be more advanced in terms of motor activities than other babies (Clark 1987; Killbride 1977; Wober, in Louw *et al.* 1993). The reasons for this trend are not clear, but are certainly worth exploring.

Reflexes

Reflex:
An inborn, involuntary
reaction to a stimulus.

Reflexes are inborn, unlearned, involuntary reactions to stimuli (Louw 1991). Most infants possess a large repertoire of reflexes at birth, including the sucking, stepping and grasping reflexes. Some reflexes, such as sucking and grasping, have clear survival value. Others, however, have no apparent value and may be related to the behaviour patterns of the human species' ancient ancestors (Craig 1989). Many reflexes disappear during the sixth month. This is because the infant's ability to control its actions increases as its brain develops. Consequently, the persistence of certain reflexes is generally perceived as an indication of neurological problems (Clarke-Stewart & Friedman 1987).

Sensory capacities

Although all human sensory capacities are present at birth, most are not fully developed. For example, certain parts of the eye and visual cortex are not fully developed at birth. As a result, a newborn is near-sighted, has poor visual acuity and cannot focus properly. However, soon after birth, infants can discriminate between sounds. For example, it has been suggested that they can distinguish between their mother's voice and that of a stranger within a few hours of birth (De Casper & Fifer, in Louw *et al.* 1993). Hearing reaches the adult level over the first two years of life. Newborns are also able to distinguish between smells. For example, they tend to turn towards the source of pleasant odours (such as the smell of milk) and away from strong, noxious odours (such as the smell of ammonia). Infants can also distinguish between salty and sweet substances (Craig & Kermis 1995).

Cognitive development

Cognitive development refers to changes in the processes of thinking, learning, perceiving, understanding and recall (Craig 1989). Largely because of its pervasive influence in psychology and related disciplines (Clark 1987), Piaget's theory of cognitive development will serve as framework for the discussion of cognitive development from infancy to adolescence. This does not mean that Piaget is the sole or most important authority on cognitive development. There are other important theorists, such as Bruner and Vygotsky,[3] who have produced an important body of work on the cognitive development of the individual.

Piaget (1970) suggested that children proceed through a series of four stages of cognitive development (see Table 2.1, on the next page). According to him, the period of infancy coincides with the first of these stages – the sensorimotor stage of cognitive development (Piaget 1977). The label 'sensorimotor' derives from Piaget's belief that, during infancy, children's cognitive abilities are reflected and developed primarily through their sensory and motor capacities (Craig 1989).

Object permanence

According to Piaget (in Craig 1989), the acquisition of the notion of **object permanence** is one of the child's key accomplishments during the sensorimotor stage. We say that the child has acquired a sense of object permanence when he or she has learnt that an object can continue to exist, even when the object is no longer visible (Craig 1989). For example, during the first months of life, an infant will not search for an object that has moved out of sight. So, if you hide the toy a six-month-old child is playing with, he or she will in all likelihood immediately focus attention on something else – as if the object has ceased to exist. However, if you hide a toy that a two-year-old is playing with, he or she might become upset and start looking for the toy. This means that the child has developed a sense of object permanence – a sense that an object exists even when it is not visible. This ability is linked to the child's ability to retain mental images of objects. Most infants acquire a full sense of object permanence at approximately 18 months (Craig 1989). However, it should be noted that infants generally have a sense of **person permanence** between five and eight months (Craig 1989). In other words, the acquisition of a sense of person permanence precedes the acquisition of object permanence. Thus, we find that children of eight months frequently become distressed or anxious if their caregivers leave them (Craig 1989). This anxiety is known as separation anxiety.

Object permanence: The realisation that an object continues to exist even when it is no longer visible.

Person permanence: The realisation that a person continues to exist even when he or she is no longer visible.

Life stage	Stage	Approximate age	Major characteristics
Infancy	Sensorimotor	Birth to 2 years	The infant learns through sensory and motor activities and has little capacity for symbolic representation.
Childhood	Pre-operational	2 to 7 years	The child develops a representational system and uses symbols such as words to represent things.
Childhood	Concrete operational	7 to 12 years	The child can solve problems logically if they relate to the here and now.
Adolescence and adulthood	Formal operational	12 to adulthood	The individual can now think in abstract terms.

TABLE 2.1: Piaget's stages of cognitive development (Papalia & Olds 1995).

Language development

The acquisition of language is another key developmental task that starts unfolding in infancy. Generally, there is a wide range of individual variation in the rate at which language is acquired. However, 'delayed' or 'accelerated' language acquisition during this stage does not indicate a permanent trend, or indicate delayed or accelerated progress in other areas of development. It is interesting to note, though, that the sequence of language acquisition appears to be similar across most languages (Clark 1987; Louw *et al.* 1993).

In general, the sequence of language acquisition during infancy is as follows. At birth, all infants produce pre-verbal, vowel-like sounds called cooing. At approximately five months after birth, the infant starts producing what are known as babbling sounds. These sounds consist of consonants and vowels (e.g. ma, da, me, ta). By their first birthdays, most infants have produced their first recognisable words. Some children may, however, produce their first words earlier or much later. At one year of age, children generally cannot yet combine words and their speech is referred to as holophrastic. What this means is that the one-word utterances produced by the child at this stage are really substitutes for sentences. In other words, the child expresses in only one word an idea that an adult would have expressed with a full sentence. By the age of two years, children start producing two-word sentences (Clark 1987). These sentences, which consist primarily of nouns, verbs and adjectives, are generally referred to as telegraphic sentences.

It is important to point out that the child's expressive ability at this stage is not reflective of all his or her language abilities. Children generally understand language before they are able to speak. In other words, language comprehension precedes language production (Louw 1991).

Psychosocial development

Whereas development takes place throughout life, it is generally accepted that the foundation of most aspects of psychosocial development are laid during infancy (Hurlock 1980).

Researchers such as Campos and his associates (in Louw *et al.* 1993) believe that emotions such as happiness, anger, fear, interest and sadness are present during the first weeks of the baby's life. Other researchers, such as Izard (in Louw *et al.* 1993), however, argue that, during the first few weeks of life, the infant experiences a much less nuanced repertoire of emotions. According to Izard, the infant's emotions during the first few weeks of life are restricted to displeasure, aversion and disinterest

(Louw *et al.* 1993). Whatever the case may be, reactions that are regarded as indicators of emotion, such as smiling, laughter and crying, are present from early in life.

Attachment

Texts on the psychosocial development of the infant have traditionally tended to focus on the development of attachment during infancy (Clark 1987). **Attachment** can be defined as the strong emotional bonding that occurs between the infant and the primary caregiver. This relationship is characterised by the infant seeking out and constantly wanting contact with the primary caregiver. Typical behaviour expressed by the infant in relation to the person to whom he or she is attached includes directing his or her vocalisation primarily at that person and being more readily pacified by that person when upset.

Attachment:
The strong emotional bonding that occurs between an infant and his or her primary caregiver.

The quality of the attachment relationship between an infant and his or her caregiver differs from one infant-caregiver dyad to another. Various factors contribute to the quality of the attachment relationship, including the personality of the caregiver, poverty and the basic temperament of the infant. For example, poverty could lead to the primary caregiver being less available, both physically and emotionally, for the child. This will certainly have an effect on the quality of the attachment relationship.

Various personality theorists attribute great importance to the attachment relationship. Erikson (in Cloninger 1996), for example, posited that a failed primary attachment would ultimately lead to the individual later in life doubting his or her self-worth and being unable to invest trust in his or her relationships with others. Research also seems to indicate that the quality of the attachment relationship could have an enduring effect on the child (Craig 1989; Louw *et al.* 1993). Weiten (1989) has, for example, found that children who experienced a secure attachment with their primary caregivers displayed greater endurance and self-assurance later in life (see also Louw *et al.* 1993).

Childhood

The period of childhood stretches from the end of infancy to adolescence. Three facets of childhood development will be discussed in this section: physical, cognitive and psychosocial development. However, it must be borne in mind that these facets of development are interdependent and take place simultaneously.

Physical development

The rate of physical growth is substantially slower during childhood than infancy (Clark 1987). Changes in the proportions of the body are very noticeable, particularly during early childhood. After three years, the child's body loses its round 'baby' appearance and increasingly assumes the proportions of the adult body. For example, the body becomes more cone-shaped, with the abdomen becoming increasingly flatter and the arms and legs becoming longer in relation to the rest of the body. In sum, the child's body assumes an increasingly slender, 'athletic' appearance. Furthermore, at this stage of development, children show a variety of individual and sex-related differences, with boys developing more muscle per kilogram of body weight than girls (Louw *et al.* 1993; Papalia & Olds 1995). During this stage, children also become significantly stronger because of rapid muscle and bone development.

Motor development

Motor development proceeds at a very rapid rate during childhood. For example, by four years of age, the average child can assemble elementary puzzles and draw pictures. By the time children enter pre-school, they can competently dress themselves and tie their shoelaces. Other skills they would have acquired by the age of six years include jumping rope, roller-skating, balancing on beams and swimming (Hurlock 1980; Louw *et al.* 1993). Play offers children a valuable opportunity to practice and perfect many of their motor skills.

Cognitive development

The period of childhood corresponds with Piaget's pre-operational and concrete operational stages of development. According to Clark (1987), advances in cognitive development during the period of childhood are best exemplified by development in the areas of symbolic activity, scientific reasoning and social thinking.

Symbolic activity

According to Piaget, the ability to use symbols is one of the major attainments of early childhood (Clark 1987). Symbolic thought is very clearly reflected in children's 'pretend' play, when they, for example, pretend that a box is a car, or that pieces of cardboard are sandwiches. Such instances, where the objects of play are representations of the 'real' thing, serve as clear indications of children's ability to use symbols. This ability to use symbols is best reflected in their increasing facility in the use of language, because words are symbols for things and ideas. Louw *et al.* (1993: p. 517) argue that symbolic thinking is an important aspect of the cognitive development of the child, for it enables him or her 'to think, to speak and to act in terms of the past, the future and objects which are not present at that moment'.

Scientific reasoning

Piaget held that children are like young scientists and he consequently explored children's capacity for scientific reasoning in a number of innovative experiments. In one of his experiments to test children's ability to conserve quantity in liquids, Piaget showed children two containers, Container 1 and Container 2, filled with the same amount of liquid. The children were then asked if the two containers contained the same amount of liquid. If the children agreed that they did, Container 2 was emptied into a third container, Container 3, which was shorter and wider. The children were then asked if Container 1 and Container 3 contained the same amount of liquid. It was found that children's responses to this question varied with their age. Some of the younger children in Piaget's pre-operational stage often said that Container 1 contained more liquid because the level of the liquid in this container was higher. Other children in the pre-operational stage said that Container 3 contained more liquid because the container was broader. In both cases, the children focused only on one dimension and failed to understand that the two containers contained the same amount of liquid. Only the older children in the stage of concrete operations were able to reason that because no liquid was added or taken away, Container 1 and Container 3 contained the same amount of liquid. Based on experiments such as this, Piaget concluded that older children are capable of many forms of logical thinking of which younger children are incapable (Clark 1987). Here it should be noted that, while children in Piaget's stage of concrete operations are capable of utilising logical thinking to solve problems, they are generally only able to do so in terms of concrete phenomena, hence the label Piaget attached to this stage.

Social thinking

According to Piaget's theory, one of the major advances in a child's thinking, which occurs during late childhood, relates to the child's increasing ability to consider other people's perspectives. In early childhood, according to Piagetian theory, children's thinking is generally

Egocentricism:
In Piaget's theory,
the inability to consider
another person's
perspective.

egocentric, which means that young children tend to view everything from their own perspective only (Clark 1987). This is aptly illustrated by the following anecdote recounted by Craig (1989):

> When a four-year-old child was asked, 'Do you have a brother?' he responded, 'Yes'. Asked what his brother's name was, he replied, 'Jim'. However, when he was asked, 'Does Jim have a brother?' he answered, 'No'.

According to Louw (1991), older children assimilate information and shift their attention from one task to another faster than younger children. Older children also develop the capacity for selective attention. In addition, they have a greater attention and memory span (Lane & Pearson 1982). Although older children, in general, remember more items than younger ones, some children remember better than others. Papalia and Olds (1995) suggest that the way adults explain events and phenomena will influence how well a child remembers them.

Language development

At about six or seven years of age, children begin to use all parts of speech and construct grammatically correct compound and complex sentences. Although they speak fluently, they still fail to follow certain irregular language rules. For example, they frequently fail to understand that '-ed' is not always added to a verb in the present tense to form a past tense verb. Thus, statements such as 'I hurted her' are common at this age.

Psychosocial development

Children, particularly younger children, tend to express their emotions spontaneously. However, in many cultures, children are frequently taught not to express emotions such as anger and jealousy. Consequently, when they feel these emotions they often experience fear and anxiety (Craig 1989). As a result, as children grow older, they generally tend to become less spontaneous in expressing their emotions.

In socio-cultural contexts marked by sharp gender role differentiation, certain gender differences in social behaviour start manifesting after the third year. For example, boys start to be more aggressive and domineering, whereas girls cooperate more with their parents, avoid conflicts and help younger children (Maccoboy 1980). According to some writers, such as Clark (1987), these gender-related differences are largely due to socialisation.

Socialisation, the process whereby children learn acceptable or socially appropriate behaviour and values, differs from one socio-cultural context to another. Schell and Hall (in Louw 1991) identify four basic factors central to the process of socialisation:

- the desire for affection, regard, acceptance and recognition;
- the urge to avoid the unpleasant feelings that result from rejection or punishment;
- the tendency to imitate the behaviour of others;
- the desire to be like specific people whom the child has come to respect, admire or love: a process known as identification.

Socialisation:
The process of acquiring the behaviours considered appropriate in a specific culture.

Adolescence

Adolescence is characterised by profound physiological, psychological and social changes. In most societies, adolescence is regarded as a period that allows for the preparation for adulthood. Some societies celebrate the onset of puberty with a so-called rite of passage, such as a religious celebration (Bernstein *et al.* 1994; Gerdes 1988; Kaplan & Sadock 1998; Papalia & Olds 1995).

Adolescence is variable in age of onset, duration, and in rates of growth, sexual maturation and psychosocial development. The onset of adolescence is, however, commonly indicated to be about age ten-and-a-half years for girls (with a range of 8 to 13 years) and about 12 years for boys (with a range of 10 to 14 years). Developmental theorists have tended to divide adolescence into three phases: early (ages 11 to 14), middle (ages 14 to 17) and late adolescence (ages 17 to 20). In many societies, the end of adolescence is understood as coinciding with the start of legal maturity. These divisions are arbitrary, but assist conceptualisation and discussion. As indicated earlier in this chapter, growth and development occur along a continuum that varies from person to person (Bernstein *et al.* 1994; Kaplan & Sadock 1998).

Physical development

The onset of puberty is triggered by the maturation of the hypothalamic-pituitary-adrenal-gonadal cluster of glands, and the subsequent secretion of sex steroids. This hormonal activity produces the manifestations of puberty: the primary and secondary sexual characteristics. The development of the **primary sex characteristics** is focused on the maturation of the reproductive organs and the external genitalia. Males are able to produce semen and females experience **menarche** or first menstruation.

Primary sex characteristics:
The physiological features directly related to reproduction, specifically the male and female reproductive organs.

Menarche:
The first menstruation.

Secondary sex characteristics:
The physiological characteristics of the sexes that develop during adolescence but do not include the sexual organs.

From the onset of puberty, the approximate time to reach sexual maturity is three years for girls, and between two and four years for boys. The **secondary sex characteristics** include pubic hair, axillary (underarm) hair, and changes in the voices and skin of both girls and boys. In addition, girls develop enlarged breasts and hips, and boys facial hair and a broadening of the shoulders (Kaplan & Sadock 1998; Papalia & Olds 1995).

These physical changes, as well as the general increases in height and weight, occur earlier in girls. Some research has indicated a general trend towards an earlier puberty onset, particularly in communities where individuals manifest an improved health status and nutrition, and better prenatal and postnatal care. The puberty growth spurt is accompanied by significant psychological, familial and social development. Although adolescence has, in the past, been described as a period of intense interpersonal upheaval and distress, research has suggested that this is the case for only approximately 15% of teenagers (Peterson, in Bernstein *et al.* 1994). Typically, girls express distress in higher rates of depression, whereas for teenage boys, difficulties in adjustment tend to translate into anti-social conduct (Kaplan & Sadock 1998). However, the majority of adolescents are able to effectively negotiate the challenges posed by their changing physical and psychosocial status, and report experiencing the period as relatively trouble free.

Cognitive development

The period of adolescence coincides with Piaget's highest level of cognitive development: the formal operational period. The stage is marked by the ability to engage in abstract or hypothetical thinking, the ability to think in terms of what is possible, and thus beyond what is only concrete and apparent (Papalia & Olds 1995). The teenager is able to hypothesise a range of potential solutions to a problem, and systematically test possible explanations, eliminating false explanations until a true one is found. The ability to engage in abstract matters, such as moral or political issues, is acquired, enabling the individual's ability to process decisions about a career, individual values and ideologies, in order to construct a value system, social roles and his or her own identity. This emerging ability to think and reason about abstract concepts is associated with increased self-scrutiny and self-awareness – abilities that facilitate the consolidation of the teenager's personal identity (Kaplan & Sadock 1998).

Psychosocial development

According to Erikson's psychosocial theory of development, a central task for the adolescent is the formation of a unique and secure sense of personal and social identity. Identity may be defined as 'an internal, self constructed, dynamic organisation of drives, abilities, beliefs, and individual history' (Marcia, in Papalia & Olds 1995). Whereas the process of identity development begins in early childhood, puberty poses the emerging adolescent with a range of physical, interpersonal and social dilemmas, the effective resolution of which precedes the formation of satisfactory adult roles and long-term personal, social and occupational objectives (Kaplan & Sadock 1998; Papalia & Olds 1995).

Identity formation and consolidation

With the onset of puberty, precipitating a period of personal and social transition, comes an increased self-consciousness and awareness, and a growing autonomy from parents. During this period, adolescents increasingly begin to refine their personal and social identities, and begin to think of themselves in terms of general, stable psychological and social attributes (Bernstein *et al.* 1994). While there is an initial reliance on the traditional, usually parental notions about appropriate appearance and personal conduct, sex-appropriate appearance, an ideal physical concept and understandings of relationships, this may be rapidly expanded upon and altered as the teenager reviews and addresses issues about his or her individual, especially sexual, identity. There may be dissatisfaction, anxiety and depression because of the changes in bodily status, particularly in early adolescence. This dissatisfaction may be exacerbated by inadequate parental support during this period. Hill (in Papalia & Olds 1995) suggests that authoritative parenting may provide the necessary warmth, acceptance, willingness to listen, explain and negotiate, and the assertion of values, rules and norms to the adolescent.

The adolescent's experience of aspects of the physical and interpersonal changes of adolescence may also be complicated by negative social opinion – for example, the persistence in some societies of shameful views about menstruation, which may colour girls' experiences and comfort with their bodies (Bernstein *et al.* 1994). Social, especially peer, opinion gains importance during this period. This shift is associated with the increasing independence from parental norms and rules, and openness to new experiences and relationships. The peer group increasingly serves as a reference or guide to perceived appropriate appearance,

dress code and behaviour (Kaplan & Sadock 1998), and serves as a vehi-
cle for exposure to alternative lifestyles, conduct and activities. At an
emotional level, the peer group also serves as a source of empathy and
affection, and a supportive setting for achieving autonomy and independence from parents (Papalia & Olds 1995).

Exposure to risk taking

The increased contact with the peer group, and receptivity to new social
experiences, behaviour and activities, may be associated with an increased
exposure to several activities that are linked to negative health and
psychosocial outcomes. In particular, cigarette smoking, alcohol consumption, drug use and high-risk sexual relationships, all with widely described
deleterious effects, are widely reported among South African adolescents
(Flisher et al. 1993a, 1993b; Flisher et al. 1993). According to several
accounts, the teenage consumption of alcohol is increasing in South Africa
(Morejele 1997), as is the experimental use of various illegal substances
(Flisher et al. 1993). According to Love Life (2002), increasing numbers of
South African teenagers are becoming sexually active at younger ages.
Generally, it has been concluded that adolescent sexual activity is charac-
terised by multiple partners with a low incidence of contraceptive use.
Consequently, the rates of unwanted pregnancies and sexually transmitted
diseases are relatively high (Flisher et al. 1993b).

The rate of HIV infection is also a source of concern for South
African adolescents and young adults. HIV mostly affects younger people, with approximately half of all adults who acquire HIV becoming
infected before age 25. The organisation Love Life has indicated that over
50% of these young people will die of AIDS-related illnesses before they
turn 35. Gender differences are also pronounced, with women at highest
risk between the ages of 15 and 20, while men achieve their highest
incidence some years later (Love Life 2002). There is an overwhelming
concentration of AIDS-related deaths among young adult South African
women (in 1998/9, AIDS rates in the 25–29 years age range were 3,5
times higher than in 1985), with some studies indicating high rates of
infection among teenage girls and young adult women (Dorrington et al.
2001). A recent survey undertaken at the University of Durban-Westville
indicated high rates of infection among tertiary education students, especially female students. The survey showed that approximately 26% of
women and 12% of men aged between 20 and 24 were infected with
HIV. In South Africa, where 53% of the population is under 25, teenage
infection levels are rising at an alarming rate (Love Life 2002).

Exposure to social instability, conflict and violence

The multitude of psychosocial transitions, which the majority of teenagers are reported to transverse effectively, may be complicated by an array of stressors from within the family, the local neighbourhood or community, and broader social processes. Familial stressors may include the conflict generated by increasingly divergent rules, values and decision-making processes, all of which may be exacerbated by, for example, poor communication, authoritarian rule and decision-making systems, resulting in turmoil and distress. With 53% of South Africans (approximately 18,1 million people) estimated to be living in poor households (National Institute for Economic Policy 1996), there are a number of attendant stressors resulting from the current adverse macro-economic climate. These include parental unemployment and related home and social instability, overcrowding and the threat of increasingly poor living circumstances.

These conditions are implicated in the ongoing epidemic of violence in the country, despite the remarkably peaceful political transition marked by the first democratic elections in 1994. Reports indicate South Africa to be among the most violent societies in the world (Butchart *et al.* 1996; Burrows *et al.* 2001). Butchart *et al.* (1996: p. 4) indicate that 'the South African incidence rate for violent death is ... nearly six times that of the US rate, which, in turn, is considered to be among the world's more violent societies'. In South Africa, males between the ages of 10 and 30 are at a particularly high risk for exposure to violent incidents (Butchart *et al.* 1996). Over and above the immediate physical consequences of exposure to violence, in particular death, disability and injury, there are a range of economic, social and psychological consequences. Recent reports have indicated that homicide is the single major cause of fatalities among male adolescents in South Africa (Burrows *et al.* 2001). In 2002, Human Rights Watch indicated that thousands of South African girls regularly encounter sexual violence and harassment, much of which takes place in schools. The report also indicates that school authorities rarely challenge perpetrators, with many girls consequently interrupting their education or leaving school altogether because they feel vulnerable to sexual assault (Human Rights Watch 2002).

Adulthood

In Northern (i.e. developed) societies, adulthood is usually the longest phase of human life. It is defined as the stage when people are expected to reach full biological and psychosocial maturity. Although the exact onset of adulthood varies across individuals and societies, some texts describe adulthood as traditionally constituting three distinct phases: early (20–40 years), middle (40–64 years) and late adulthood or old age (65 years and older) (Kaplan & Sadock 1998). These estimates are based on Northern models of human development and, because of the relatively shorter life span estimated for South Africans, estimated to be 54 years in 1997 (Dorrington *et al.* 2001), are considered inappropriate for use in the South African context. The periods ascribed to each phase are likely to be somewhat shorter when applied locally. Again, the processes ascribed to these developmental periods are not precisely determined, but serve as a general description of human development.

Physical development

Early adulthood is characterised by a peaking of biological development. During this period, physical growth continues, especially shoulder width, height and chest size, with muscular strength peaking at around 25 to 30 years (Papalia & Olds 1995). Manual dexterity is also most efficient during the early years of adulthood. The middle and later phases of adulthood, however, see a gradual decline in physical attributes, such as a decrease in muscle size, a decline in dexterity and flexibility, an increase in fat retention, and a decline in sensory and perceptual abilities (Bernstein *et al.* 1994; Kaplan & Sadock 1998; Papalia & Olds 1995). A gradual hearing loss typically begins before age 25; after age 25, the loss is more apparent. Visual and perceptual declines are prominent from about the age of 40, while taste, smell and sensitivity to pain and temperature generally only decline from about 45 years (Papalia & Olds 1995). The older adult becomes increasingly susceptible to the risk of illness and various diseases (cardiovascular and cancers), a decline of the digestive system, a shrinking of brain size, and a decrease in the flow of blood to the brain. During this period, women reach menopause and males experience a decline of sexual response.

Cognitive development

Several development theorists have proposed models of cognitive development that include a greater consideration of the context to cognitive challenges, the utilisation of past experiences, and the acquisition and application of knowledge towards individual life goals (Papalia & Olds 1995). During this period, thought is more complex, global and adaptive in new ways that go beyond logic. This kind of post-formal or mature thought allows thinkers to merge logic with feelings, intuition and personal experience: 'Wisdom can now flower, as more flexible thought enables people to accept inconsistency, contradiction, imperfection and compromise, so that they can solve real-life problems' (Papalia & Olds 1995: p. 384).

Psychosocial development

Adulthood is generally characterised by the assumption of major social roles and responsibilities. The satisfactory entry into adulthood depends on an effective resolution of childhood and adolescent demands. Erik Erikson described the central psychosocial challenge of the earlier adulthood period as the resolution of an intimacy versus self-absorption or isolation tension. The key developmental task of middle adulthood involves a process of reviewing aspirations and personal progress over the past years, and the refining of future objectives (Papalia & Olds 1995).

Marriage and partnerships

A number of major social milestones are negotiated during this period. Most young adults may seek and find marriage partners in their mid-twenties, although this varies considerably across settings, with a growing trend of marriages taking place later in life (Papalia & Olds 1995). People get married for a variety of reasons, including emotional, religious, social, economic and political reasons (Bernstein et al. 1994). This is particularly so in South Africa, with its diverse religious and social formations. For many people, this transition is smooth and satisfactory, resulting in warm and caring friendships, and intimate relationships. Studies have indicated that married people are happier and more satisfied than single people, with the most happy being married women in their early twenties without children. Many other married people may, however, experience significant upheaval, manifested by intimacy and relationship conflicts, disillusionment with attachments, partners and the individual's ideals and relationship expectations, and retreat into isolation or to limited, although functional, attachments (Kaplan & Sadock 1998). In South Africa, women continue to face extraordinarily high levels of family violence. South African women's organisations report that domestic violence and sexual assault are pervasive, and directed almost exclusively against women. As many as one in every four women report sexual abuse at some point in their life, often within relationships or by ex-partners (Jewkes et al. 2001). Women victims of violence often face an indifferent judicial and police system that routinely denies them redress. In addition, black women continue to face racial prejudice in their interactions with the authorities (Nowrojee & Manby 1995; Suffla et al. 2001).

Parenthood

The formalisation of partnerships is often followed by parenthood. In many societies, child rearing is still perceived to be the domain of women, although this appears to be changing. In South Africa, where economic imperatives often demand that both parents work, the extended family tends to play a central role in child rearing and in the maintenance of family systems. For both women and men, pursuing fulfilling occupations is widely recognised as a priority activity. For women, the opposing demands of career and child rearing may, however, generate a great deal of conflict, frustration and anxiety. Conversely, the successful negotiation of these tasks may result in a feeling of independence and achievement (Bernstein *et al.* 1994).

Occupational achievement

A range of factors, including socio-economic status and gender, affect the choice and timing of an individual's occupation. Access to certain occupations requires an expensive university education and a time and energy commitment that few families and individuals can make without considerable support. A healthy adaptation to work, however, provides an outlet for creative accomplishment, stimulating relationships with colleagues and increased self-esteem. Finding a stable source of income is a matter of considerable stress in contemporary South Africa. At least 23,7% of the South African population (mainly black people) are said to live on less than R11,00 a day. The Development Bank of South Africa (1991) has reported that the majority of the poor are women. It estimates that 56,4% of women aged 15 years and older are without any form of income (Kinsella & Ferreira 1997).

Some research has indicated that the loss of employment and income places individuals at a high risk for alcohol dependence, violence, suicide and psychological illness (Kaplan & Sadock 1998). The intense competition and instability in the job market also leaves many South Africans vulnerable to exploitation, with conditions in the formal workplace being less than optimal.

Late adulthood

Senescence:
The period in the life span where people experience a decline in bodily functioning that is ascribed to ageing.

The onset of late adulthood coincides with **senescence** – the decline in bodily functions associated with ageing. The onset of ageing may vary greatly among individuals. The general increase of living standards and improvement in medical technology has led to an increase in longevity in many societies and, therefore, a significant number of older persons.

However, for many low-income countries, this is not the case. South Africa has reported a decline in life expectancy because of the HIV/AIDS epidemic (Dorrington *et al.* 2001).

Physical changes

With senescence, there is a marked decline in sensory and psychomotor abilities, although there is a great deal of individual variation (Papalia & Olds 1995). Losses of vision and hearing are common, and may have particularly serious psychological impacts, since they deprive people of a range of daily living and social activities, and their independence (Papalia & Olds 1995). There may also be a sharp drop in the sensitivity to a range of tastes and smells, with older people often complaining that food is less tasty and, consequently, eating less. Older people's bodies adjust more slowly to cold and heat, and are vulnerable to over-exposure to extreme temperatures. Although older people can do most of the physical activities that younger people can, these are conducted more slowly. They have less strength and coordination, and slower reaction times, resulting in high proportions of home and traffic accidents (Papalia & Olds 1995). With senescence, there is a shortening of the spinal column, a consequent decrease in height, and an increased vulnerability to osteoporosis. Generally, the organs, especially the heart, become less efficient. There is also a decline in the immune system, with greater susceptibility to infectious illnesses. For both men and women, there is a decline in sexual function and response. Finally, there is a decrease in melanin production, resulting in a decline in the texture and elasticity of skin, and increased greying (Papalia & Olds 1995; Kaplan & Sadock 1998).

Cognitive development

The older adult may experience a decrease of some cognitive abilities, in particular his or her ability to rapidly and flexibly manipulate ideas and symbols. Reasoning, mathematical ability, comprehension, novel problem-solving and memory all decline. However, repetition and some memory-based activities remain intact, although there may be a decrease in the complexity of thought (Papalia & Olds 1995; Kaplan & Sadock 1998). Despite this physical and cognitive decline, many psychologists have asserted that a general intelligence decline in old age is a myth, and argue that new abilities, such as wisdom, emerge to compensate for the decline in others. Others have described this position as optimistic (Papalia & Olds 1995). Many people over the age of 65 report a decline in cognitive functioning (between 6 and 10%), and even more over the age of 85 (20 to 50%), because of Alzheimer's disease alone. Alzheimer's disease is a degenerative brain disorder that results in a decline in intelligence, awareness and the ability to control bodily functions. There are various theories as to the cause of this disease, which is the most prevalent and feared of the **dementias** that may affect older people (Papalia & Olds 1995).

Dementia:
The intellectual and personality deterioration sometimes associated with old age.

Psychosocial development

For many, old age is a period of continued intellectual, social and emotional growth. However, during this period, the older adult has to deal with a host of physical difficulties and often a number of trying social circumstances. These include declining independence, retirement and often a reduction in financial resources, the death of spouses and friends, transitions in the relationships with siblings, and the task of constructing a meaningful understanding of one's life achievements.

Retirement and economic adjustments

Older adults may continue to live socially active and politically influential lives. During this period, the older adult is likely to have retired from a full-time occupation. There may be a range of economic adjustments. In South Africa, 4,5% of the population receive a government pension. Most households with at least one elderly member are poor by most standards, and rely on state-funded social and medical support. These households are often dependent on the pensions of its elderly members. While the South African government has focused on women and children in terms of social security, the concerns of the elderly have had limited recognition, although there has been growing support of the pension system as an important social security net (Kinsella & Ferreira 1997).

Family and social roles

Healthy older adults often maintain a level of social activity much as they did before. For many, old age remains a period of continued emotional and social growth (Kaplan & Sadock 1998). For others, late adulthood often becomes a more inward-looking, cautious and conforming time. Family roles appear more **androgynous**, with males appearing more nurturing and females becoming more assertive. This may be especially apparent in grandparenting roles (Papalia & Olds 1995; Kaplan & Sadock 1998).

For the older adult, long-standing relationships may end with the death of a partner or others from the friendship circle or peer group. The older adult has to cope with the pain of mourning loved ones and, with the death of married partners, widowhood. Men and women tend to have different styles of adjusting and dealing with these losses. During this period, family and other support systems play a vital emotional role in the adjustment to these deaths (Kaplan & Sadock 1998). It appears that those who adjust best to widowhood keep themselves busy, develop new roles (for example, by taking on volunteer work), visit friends often, and take part in community organisations and activities (for example, religious organisations and activities). Men may find new partners and remarry, although widowed women are more likely to make friends with other widows and are less likely to form new relationships with men (Papalia & Olds 1998).

Androgynous:
A status characterised by the integration of characteristics considered typically masculine and feminine.

Death and dying

Late adulthood is characterised by the re-examination and integration of past events and experiences. The awareness of death precipitates a review of achievements and failures, and may result in possible depression and despair. Erikson asserted that older people needed to confront a tension around integrating their life experiences and stories versus a despair over the inability to relive their lives differently (Papalia & Olds 1995). People who succeed in resolving this tension are able to meaningfully integrate their past experiences, often into a wisdom that Erikson described as an 'informed and detached concern with life itself in the face of death itself' (in Papalia & Olds 1995: p. 501). When death is imminent, people generally wish to die with dignity, love, affection, physical contact and no pain. As they think about death, they may wish to be comforted by their religious faith, their achievements and the love of their friends.

Questions for discussion

1. Is development a result largely of nature factors or nurture factors?
2. It is frequently argued that children from low-income communities are doomed before birth. Explain why you would agree or disagree with this statement.
3. What are the major challenges to optimal development currently confronting adolescents and adults in South Africa?
4. What should be done to enhance the development of children from low-income communities in South Africa?

Summary

In this chapter you were introduced to some of the basic concepts in
developmental psychology, including developmental change, life-span
development, human resilience, learning and maturation. Several basic
assumptions guided the content of the chapter:

- Human development is a function of the interaction between innate
  and environmental influences.
- Development follows a fairly predictable pattern.
- Individuals contribute significantly to their own development.
- Human beings are resilient.
- Every individual is unique.
- Development is a life-long process.

Further reading

Bee, H.L. (1989) *The Developing Child*. New York: Harper & Row.

Bee, H.L. & Mitchel, S.K. (1980) *The Developing Person: A Lifespan
Approach*. New York: Harper & Row.

Bem, P.A. (1997) *Personality Theories: Development, Growth and Diversity*.
Boston: Allyn & Bacon.

Berger, K.S. (1994) *The Developing Person through the Life Span*. New
York: Worth.

Bernstein, D.A., Clarke-Stewart, A., Roy, E.J., Srull, T.K. & Wickens, C.D.
(1994) *Psychology*. Boston: Houghton Mifflin.

Bulhan, H.A. (1992) Imperialism in studies of the psyche: A critique of
African psychological research. In L.J. Nicholas (ed.), *Psychology and
Oppression*. Johannesburg: Skotaville, pp. 1–34.

Burman, E. (1994), *Deconstructing Developmental Psychology*. London:
Routledge.

Burrows, S., Bowman, B. Matzopoulos, R. & Van Niekerk, A. (2001)
*A Profile of Fatal Injuries in South Africa 2000: Second Annual Report
of the National Injury Mortality Surveillance System*. Tygerberg:
Medical Research Council.

Butterworth, G. & Harris, M. (1994) *Principles of Developmental
Psychology*. Hove: Erlbaum.

Butchart, A., Nell, V. & Seedat, M. (1996) Violence in South Africa:
Its definition and prevention as a public health problem.
Paper prepared for inclusion in Seager and Parry (1996).

Clark, P.M. (1987) Developmental psychology. In G.A. Tyson (ed.),
    Introduction to Psychology: A South African Perspective.
    Johannesburg: Westro Educational Books, pp. 141–81.

Clarke-Stewart, A. & Friedman, S. (1987) *Child Development: Infancy
    through Childhood.* New York: John Wiley.

Clarke-Stewart, A., Perlmutter, M. & Friedman, S. (1988) *Lifelong Human
    Development.* New York: John Wiley.

Cloninger, S.C. (1996) *Theories of Personality: Understanding Persons.*
    Englewood Cliffs: Prentice-Hall.

Cockcroft, K. (2002) Theories of cognitive development: Piaget, Vygotsky
    and information-processing theory. In D. Hook, J. Watts & K.
    Cockcroft (eds), *Developmental Psychology.* Cape Town: UCT Press,
    pp. 175–99.

Craig, G.J. (1989) *Human Development.* Englewood Cliffs: Prentice-Hall.

Craig, G.J. & Kermis, M.D. (1995) *Children Today.* Englewood Cliffs:
    Prentice-Hall.

Dawes, A. & Donald, D. (2000) Improving children's chances.
    In D. Donald, A. Dawes & J. Louw (eds), *Addressing Childhood
    Adversity.* Cape Town: David Philip, pp. 1–25.

De la Rey, C. & Carolissen, R. (1997) Teenage pregnancy: A contextual
    analysis. In C. de la Rey, N. Duncan, T. Shefer & A. van Niekerk (eds),
    Contemporary Issues in Human Development: A South African Focus.
    Johannesburg: International Thomson, pp. 25–37.

Dorrington, R., Bourne, D., Bradshaw, D., Laubscher, R. & Timaeus, I.M.
    (2001) *The Impact of HIV/AIDS on Adult Mortality in South Africa.*
    Technical report: Burden of Disease Research Unit. Tygerberg: Medical
    Research Council.

Flisher, A.J., Ziervogel, C.F., Chalton, D.O., Leger, P.H. & Robertson, B.A.
    (1993a) Risk-taking behaviour of Cape Peninsula high-school students,
    Part 4: Alcohol use. *South African Medical Journal,* 83 (7), pp. 480–2.

Flisher, A.J., Ziervogel, C.F., Chalton, D.O., Leger, P.H. & Robertson, B.A.
    (1993b) Risk-taking behaviour of Cape Peninsula high-school
    students, Part 8: Sexual behaviour. *South African Medical Journal,*
    83 (7), pp. 495–7.

Flisher, A.J., Ziervogel, C.F., Chalton, D.O. & Robertson, B.A. (1993)
    Risk-taking behaviour of Cape Peninsula high-school students, Part 7:
    Violent behaviour. *South African Medical Journal,* 83 (7), pp. 490–4.

Freud, S. (1933) (translated by R. Zeitlin, 1984) *Nouvelles Conferences
    d'Introduction à la Psychoanalyse.* Mayenne: Gallimard.

Gerdes, L.C. (1988) *The Developing Adult.* Durban: Butterworths.

Hook, D. & Cockcroft, K. (2002) Basic concepts and principles in developmental psychology. In D. Hook, J. Watts & K. Cockcroft (eds), *Developmental Psychology*. Cape Town: UCT Press, pp. 25–37.

Huffman, K., Vernoy, M. & Vernoy, J. (1994) *Psychology in Action*. New York: John Wiley.

Human Rights Watch (2002) http://www.ippf.org/resource/gbv/chogm99/foster.html. 1 June 2002.

Hurlock, E.B. (1980) *Developmental Psychology: A Life Span Approach*. New York: McGraw-Hill.

Jewkes, R., Penn-Kekana, L., Levin, J., Ratsaka, M. & Schrieber, M. (2001) Prevalence of emotional, physical and sexual abuse of women in three South African provinces. *South African Medical Journal*, 91, pp. 421–8.

Kaplan, H.I. & Sadock, B.J. (1998) *Synopsis of Psychiatry: Behavioral Sciences/ Clinical Psychiatry* (8th edition). Baltimore: Williams and Wilkins.

Kelly-Buchanan, C. (1988) *Peace of Mind during Pregnancy: An A-Z Guide to the Substances that could Affect your Unborn Baby*. New York: Facts of Life Publications.

Killbride, J.E. (1977) Mother infant interaction and infant sensorimotor development among the Baganda of Uganda. Dissertation. *Abstract Dissertations International*, 37 (10–13), pp. 5326–7.

Kinsella, K. & Ferreira, M. (1997) Aging trends: South Africa. International Brief: United States Department of Commerce. http://www.census.gov/ipc/prod/ib-9702.pdf. 1 June 2002.

Kozulin, A. (1990) *Vygotsky's Psychology: A Biography of Ideas*. New York: Harvester Wheatsheaf.

LaBarba, R.C. (1981) *Foundations of Developmental Psychology*. New York: Academia.

Lane, D.M. & Pearson, D.A. (1982) The development of selective attention. *Merrill-Palmer Quarterly*, 28, pp. 317–45.

Liebert, R.M., Wicks-Nelson, R. & Kail, R.V. (1986) *Developmental Psychology*. New York: Prentice-Hall.

Laubscher, L. & Klinger, J. (1997) Story and the making of the self. In C. De la Rey, N. Duncan, T. Shefer & A. van Niekerk (1997) *Contemporary Issues in Human Development: A South African Focus*. Johannesburg: International Thomson, pp. 58–79.

Louw, D.A. (1991) *Human Development*. Pretoria: Haum.

Louw, D., Louw, A. & Schoeman, W. (1993) Developmental Psychology. In D.A. Louw & D.J.A. Edwards (eds), *Psychology: An Introduction for Students in Southern Africa*. Sandton: Heinemann, pp. 487–560.

Love Life (2002) http://www.lovelife.org.za. 1 May 2002.

Maccoboy, E.E. (1980) *Social Development: Psychological Growth and the Parent-Child Relationship*. New York: Harcout Brace Jovanovich.

Macleod, C. (2002) Theory and South African developmental research and literature. In D. Hook, J. Watts & K. Cockcroft (eds), *Developmental Psychology*. Cape Town: UCT Press, pp. 379–96.

May, J. (1998) *Poverty and Inequality in South Africa*. Report prepared for the Office of the Executive Deputy President and the Inter-Ministerial Committee for Poverty and Inequality. http://www.polity.org.za/govdocs/reports/poverty.html. 3 February 2002.

Meyer, W.F. (1991) Basic concepts of developmental psychology. In D.A. Louw (ed.), *Human Development*, pp. 3–48.

Morojele, N. (1997). Adolescent alcohol misuse. In C. de la Rey, N. Duncan, T. Shefer & A. van Niekerk, *Contemporary Issues in Human Development: A South African Focus*. Johannesburg: International Thomson, pp. 207–32.

Morris, C. (1979) *Psychology: An Introduction*. Englewood Cliffs: Prentice-Hall.

Mott, S.R., Fazekas, N.F. & James, S.R. (1985) *Nursing Care of Children and Families: A Holistic Approach*. Reading, Mass.: Addison-Wesley.

Mukhina, V. (1984) *Growing up Human* (translated by M. Sydney). Moscow: Progress.

Mussen, P.H., Conger, J.J. & Huston, A.C. (1974) *Child Development and Personality*. New York: Harper & Row.

National Institute for Economic Policy (1996) *Children, Poverty and Disparity Reduction: Towards Fulfilling the Rights of South Africa's Children*. Report commissioned by the Minister in the Office of the President (Reconstruction and Development Programme).

Neuman, W. L. (1997) *Social Research Methods: Qualitative and Quantitative Research Approaches*. Boston: Allyn & Bacon.

Nowrojee, B. & Manby, B. (1995) *South Africa: The State Response to Domestic Violence and Rape*. Human Rights Watch. www.hrw.org/reports/1995/Safricawm-02.html. 1 May 2002.

Papalia, D.E. & Olds, S.W. (1995) *Human Development*. New York: McGraw-Hill.

Pauw, I. & Brener, L. (1997) Women & AIDS in South Africa. In C. de la Rey, N. Duncan, T. Shefer & A. van Niekerk (eds), *Contemporary Issues in Human Development: A South African Focus*. Johannesburg: International Thomson, pp. 250–73.

Piaget, J. (1970) A conversation with Jean Piaget. *Psychology Today*, 3, pp. 25–32.

Piaget, J. (1977) *The Origin of Intelligence in the Child*. London: Penguin Books.

Reconstruction and Development Programme (RDP) (1996) *Children, Poverty and Disparity Reduction*. Pretoria: RDP.

Schell, P.E. & Hall, E. (1979) *Developmental Psychology Today* (3rd edition). New York: Random House.

Schiamberg, L.B. (1985) *Human development*. New York: Macmillan.

Seager, J. & Parry, C. (eds) (1996) *Urbanisation and Health in South Africa*. Tygerberg: Medical Research Council.

Seedat, A. (1984) *Crippling a Nation: Health in Apartheid South Africa*. London: IAF.

Shaffer, D.R. (1966) *Developmental Psychology: Childhood and Adolescence*. New York: Brookes/Cole.

Suffla, S., Seedat, M. & Nascimento, A. (2001) Evaluation of medico-legal services in Gauteng: Implications for the development of best practices in the after-care of rape survivors. MRC policy brief, no. 5. Tygerberg: Medical Research Council.

Van der Zanden, J.W. (1989) *Human Development*. New York: Knopf.

Verp, M.S. (1993) Environmental causes of pregnancy loss and malformations. In C. Lin, M.S. Verp & R.E. Sabbagha (eds), *The High-Risk Fetus: Phatho-physiology, Diagnosis and Management*. New York: Springer-Verlag.

Weiten, W. (1989) *Psychology: Themes and Variations*. Pacific Grove: Brooks/Cole.

Wessels, M. & Monteiro, C. (2000) Healing wounds of war in Angola: A community-based approach. In D. Donald, A. Dawes & J. Louw (eds), *Addressing Childhood Adversity*. Cape Town: David Philip, pp. 176–201.

Wilkinson, B. (1996, April 4). Malnutrition – cause of massive stunted growth. *The Argus*, p. 4.

[1] See Burman (1994) for an incisive critique of the 'masculine-centredness' of developmental psychology during the twentieth century.

[2] See Hook and Cockcroft (2002) for a discussion of a similar case.

[3] Interested readers are referred to Craig (1989), Cockcroft (2002) and Kozulin (1990) for useful discussions of these theories.

3 Sensation and Perception

M. Jooste

Objectives

After studying this chapter you should
- be able to distinguish between the processes of sensation and perception
- be able to describe the nature of psychophysics
- be able to distinguish between the absolute and differential thresholds in sensation
- be able to distinguish and explain the three laws of psychophysics
- be able to explain signal detection theory and the application of the information from an ROC curve
- be able to explain the sensation processes of each of the sensory systems
- be able to explain the major theories linked to each sensory system
- be able to explain all aspects of visual perception
- be able to explain all aspects of auditory perception.

Introduction

We obtain information about ourselves and our environment through our senses. We can distinguish between obtaining basic information through our senses and processing this information to obtain a more meaningful picture. For example, if we look at the printed characters and numbers on this page, we obtain basic sensory information in the form of the lines, squiggles and signs that we see, from which we need to create a meaningful message. Our **perception** and interpretation of this sensory information as being part of a certain language system of letters, numbers, words and punctuation marks informs us about the content of this chapter.

Perception:
Process of organising sensory information into a percept.

Sensation:
Also known as subception. The process during which the sense organs and brain are physiologically processing unorganised bits of sensory information of which we are unaware or only vaguely aware.

This example illustrates the difference between **sensation** (or subception) and perception. We obtain the basic building blocks of information through our sensory channels (sensory processes) and then use this information to construct meaningful perceptual experiences (perceptual processes). The information we obtain through these processes is therefore partly given to us by our sensory system and partly constructed when we process the information and find meaning in it.

We have to be critical about the information we obtain, as we often make mistakes while sensing, perceiving and remembering information. This holds true both for physical objects and events, and perceiving people or the contents of their communication. Information is often unwittingly distorted when it is communicated during social interaction. It is important, therefore, that people question or clarify and validate the information they have, to avoid premature conclusions, especially in relation to interpersonal and inter-group relations.

The main processes involved in the sensing and perceiving of information are summarised in Figure 3.1.

Stimuli Sense organs and brain Attributing meaning in a socio-cultural context

FIGURE 3.1: Sensing and perceiving model

Stimuli:
Some form of physical energy impinging on a specific type of sense organ suited for that specific form of energy.

Subcepts:
Also called sensations. Information of which we are unaware or only vaguely aware.

Percept:
Sensory information that has been organised, interpreted and systematically integrated into a hierarchically comprehensive image of which an observer is clearly aware.

Stimuli constitute some form of physical energy impinging on a specific type of sense organ suited for that specific form of energy.

The sense organs and brain are critical in the physiological sensing of initially unorganised bits of information of which we are unaware or only vaguely aware, called sensations (or **subcepts**). These basic sensations are interpreted and systematically integrated into hierarchically more comprehensive units called **percepts** (perceived images). An observer is clearly aware of his or her own percepts.

The more complex processes of attributing meaning in a socio-cultural context are also involved in perception. Learnt meanings are experienced as valid if people in a specific social or cultural context accept them. These socially or culturally learnt meanings provide an overarching symbolic framework for interpreting and integrating a variety of percepts into hierarchically more holistic meaning systems, e.g. language, values and other beliefs that link the person to the social or cultural group.

The arrows in the sensing and perceiving model (Figure 3.1, above) indicate interaction among all three aspects.

Sensation

Sensory organs are activated by a special energy form in the environment. These energy forms can activate sensory organs to provide information about objects or events at a distance or in direct contact with the perceiver. The eyes, ears and nose are distance sensors, while the tongue and skin senses are contact sensors. Our sensory organs are activated by only a limited variety of energy forms:

- eyes: light waves (electromagnetic energy);
- ears: sound waves (mechanical energy);
- nose and tongue: various scents and tastes (chemical energy); and
- skin senses: movement (kinetic energy), temperature (heat energy entering or leaving the body) and pressure (mechanical energy).

Humans are only directly aware of a limited range of sensory information in their environments, as they do not have the sensory organs for various other energy forms. Sometimes we need to use equipment such as an X-ray machine, a radio, radar, a compass, an infrared camera or an ultraviolet viewer to transform certain energy types into a form that our sense organs can become aware of.

Psychophysics

Psychophysics is a specialist field in psychology that focuses on the relationship between the physical characteristics of the stimuli impinging on our sensory organs and the perceived characteristics that we experience. Psychophysical research is usually carried out in a research laboratory utilising experimental research methods. A researcher in a psychophysics experiment might, for example, try to determine the effect of sound intensity on a person's experience of the volume of the sound. Many psychophysical experiments have been done since researchers started this line of investigation in the nineteenth century. Some prominent psychophysicists were E. Weber, G. Fechner (Weber's brother-in-law), H. von Helmholtz, E.G. Boring, S.S. Stevens and H.R. Schiffman.

The intensity of a stimulus – like a sound or a visual image – must exceed a certain minimum energy level for a person to sense it in full awareness. If the stimulus intensity remains below this minimum level, it is known as a subliminal stimulus (under-the-threshold stimulus). To some extent, information can be processed on the subliminal level. This process is called subception and its products are known as subcepts. The process of subception assists a person's automatic (i.e. routine) behaviour like walking, talking, playing a musical instrument or driving a car.

Psychophysics:
Specialist field focusing on the relationship between the physical characteristics of the stimulus impinging on our sensory organs and the perceived characteristics that we experience.

Various studies have confirmed the existence of subliminal perception or subception (Bar & Biederman 1998; Greenwald *et al.* 1991; Merikle & Daneman 1998; Whalen *et al.* 1998). Subliminal messages can be associated (primed) with positive or negative feelings about a person, an object or a thought (Westen 2002). Subliminal positive or negative associations with a person's face have been demonstrated at a physiological level in the functioning of the amygdala in the limbic system, a brain structure that is important for emotional learning (Morris *et al.* 1998). In an intriguing phenomenon called blindsight, a person can describe the form of an object or give its location in space relative to the viewer, but does not know what object it is or cannot recall that he or she has ever seen it (Sahraie *et al.* 1997). However, subception has not been empirically found to provide a coercive means of influencing someone. It cannot be used to compel a person to engage in a specific act. In addition, people cannot be coerced (forced) at the subliminal level to commit acts against their convictions (Weiten 2001).

All sensory experiences have thresholds (minimum intensity levels) for full awareness, which is a prerequisite for planned or deliberate actions. As these sensory thresholds can vary, lack of awareness has a disruptive effect on intentional planning or responsible behaviour. We therefore need to discuss how sensory thresholds can be influenced by stimulus characteristics and psychological factors. Before this, we need to examine the types of thresholds that have been identified and the threshold laws (general principles) to which they are linked.

Thresholds

Absolute threshold:
The minimum intensity level at which a stimulus, under controlled conditions, can be sensed correctly for 50% of the time.

The **absolute threshold** of a stimulus is the minimum intensity level at which the stimulus, under controlled conditions, can be sensed correctly for 50% of the time. The absolute threshold varies from person to person and from situation to situation, depending on a variety of factors affecting our perceptual sensitivity in any given context. The absolute threshold is more indicative of an average or typical sensory sensitivity value for sensing various stimuli. Our sensory abilities vary around this typical value for each sensory system. Furthermore, the absolute threshold indicates that sometimes we can be aware of events or behaviours in our situation and at other times we can be unaware of them, even though other people might be aware of these events or behaviours that we manifest. Social interaction enables us to clarify whether we are aware or unaware of certain behaviours, and whether our perceptions and interpretations of these behaviours or intentions are accurate or inaccurate.

Often there is more than one stimulus impinging on the same sensory organ. Sometimes we become aware of two or more stimuli activating the sensory organs sequentially. We may experience the intensity levels of these stimuli as the same and, at other times, as being of different intensities.

The **differential threshold**, also known as the just-noticeable-difference (jnd), refers to the minimum difference in intensity levels between two stimuli, presented under controlled conditions, that is sensed correctly 50% of the time.

We automatically tend to expect that our environment remains constant, a phenomenon called **perceptual constancy**. If we think critically about our habitual expectations, which often happen automatically, we realise that experiences do not remain constant. The jnd is a reminder that people and events change. We therefore need to be perceptually sensitive to these changes in our environment and in ourselves.

Weber's, Fechner's and Stevens' laws on thresholds

According to Weber's law, there exists a constant ratio (relationship) between the intensity of a stimulus and the additional intensity required for comparison purposes, in order to experience a jnd (Westen 2002). Each sensory system has its characteristic set of ratios, also known as Weber fractions (W-fractions). As the W-fraction decreases, the more sensitively that sensory system tends to function in human behaviour. For example, an electric shock could have a W-fraction = 0,01, which is indicative of high sensitivity to a possibly dangerous stimulus. A W-fraction = 0,05 is characteristic of **loudness** and indicative of our sensitivity for aversive stimuli, e.g. noises (Teghtsoonian 1971). We have an extremely high sensitivity to the **pitch** of a sound: a W-fraction = 0,003 (Woodworth & Schlosberg 1954). This may be because the pitch of a sound is often linked to danger to ourselves or to others when other sounds can also be heard, e.g. when we hear someone screaming for help while we are having a conversation with friends.

According to Fechner's law, sequentially larger increases in the intensity of a stimulus are necessary for awareness of sequential increases in sensory experiences (Coren *et al.* 1994). If, for example, a sound is already quite loud, it requires more intensity in the physical stimulus to create a psychological awareness of increased loudness.

Stevens' research on the jnd resulted in a general law that applies to all stimuli and all sensory systems. It is an improvement on Fechner's law, which only applies to certain sensory systems and stimuli. According to **Stevens' law**, as the perceived intensity of a stimulus increases arithmetically, the actual magnitude of the physical stimulus has to increase according to a power function (Coren *et al.* 1994). For instance, if the rating of loudness on an experiential scale of 1 to 10

Differential threshold: The minimum difference in intensity levels between two stimuli, presented under controlled conditions, that is sensed correctly 50% of the time. Also known as the just-noticeable-difference (jnd).

Perceptual constancy: Our belief that our environment remains constant.

Loudness: The extent to which an auditory stimulus is experienced as soft or loud. Linked to the amplitude (intensity) of the sound wave.

Pitch: The experience of how high or how low a sound is, based mainly on the frequency of the sound stimulus.

Stevens' law: Law stating that as the perceived intensity of a stimulus increases arithmetically, the actual magnitude of the physical stimulus has to increase according to a power function.

increases from one point to the next, the physical intensity will have to increase by some power (it will have to be squared, or cubed, etc.). This can be illustrated using an imaginary example. For loudness to be increased from 6 to 7 on a loudness experiential scale and if the physical intensity of the sound at a loudness level of 6 is equal to 3 decibels, the physical intensity of the stimulus may have to be squared – i.e. increased to 9 decibels (3 × 3 = 9 decibels) – before a loudness level of 7 is experienced. The power function (the increase in the intensity of the physical stimulus in relation to the experienced increase) will vary for different sensory systems. For brightness, the power is 0,33, and for estimated length, it is a linear ratio (relationship) of 1,00 (Stevens 1961: p. 11). The linear ratio implies that a unit of increase in the physical length of an object corresponds to the unit of increase in the experienced length of an object. Sometimes smaller increases in the intensity of a stimulus are associated with larger increases in the experience. For instance, a high level of experienced pain requires a smaller additional increase in the intensity of a pain stimulus to produce a jnd. This finding illustrates that increases in a danger signal (e.g. pain) evokes proportionately larger increases in our need to attend to the problem being experienced, in order to avoid serious consequences for ourselves.

All three laws indicate that sensory experience manifests an orderly and systematic relationship to the intensity of the stimulus. As a psychophysical researcher knows the nature of this relationship, he or she can predict the one from the other. There is mostly a non-linear relationship between the stimulus and the sensation experienced. This is because the physical characteristics of stimuli are insufficient in determining perception. Physiological and psychological factors are co-determinants of perception. This fact led to the rise of **signal detection theory** as a way of studying the complex relationship between physical stimuli and physiological and psychological processes.

Signal detection theory

Besides the physical energy characteristics of a stimulus, sensory processes and psychological factors are important determinants of sensory thresholds. Signal detection theory tries to distinguish between the sensory and the psychological determinants of sensory thresholds (Green & Swets 1966; Swets 1992).

A signal (stimulus) is always sensed against a background of some type of noise, e.g. neurological activity, blood flowing through one's veins, environmental visual images or noises, etc. In order to sense a signal, it must be distinguished from background 'noise', otherwise it is viewed as part of the 'noise'. In Figure 3.2, on page 59 there are four options when

Signal detection theory: Psychophysiological theory postulating that the perception of stimuli involves certain psychological factors and decision-making processes, besides the physical stimuli and sensory processes. Particularly, it involves distinguishing background noise from a stimulus.

a person needs to decide whether a signal can be distinguished from background noise.

	Person's response	
Signal condition	Yes (signal + noise)	No (noise only)
Signal present	Hit	Miss
Signal absent	False alarm	Correct rejection

FIGURE 3.2: Response options in deciding whether a signal is present

The percentage of the total number of choices allocated to each option is used in signal detection theory. For instance, one could compare the percentage of hits in relation to the percentage of false alarms to distinguish between a perceiver's sensory sensitivity and his or her psychological criteria for the certainty level required to decide whether a signal is present or absent.

The probability that a person will answer 'yes' or 'no' depends, among other things, on the following factors:

- The intensity of the stimulus: This will impact largely on a person's sensory sensitivity.
- The expectations that constitute a person's subjective criteria for the presence or absence of the signal.
- A person's subjective criteria regarding the consequences of making a decisional mistake (a miss or a false alarm).
- A graph known as the **receiver operating characteristics curve** (ROC curve) can be drawn of the ratio of hits to false alarms. It enables one to distinguish between the sensory sensitivity of the perceiver and the influence of psychological factors on his or her perceptual performance (see Figure 3.3).

Receiver operating characteristics curve: Also known as a ROC curve. A graph allowing one to distinguish between the sensory sensitivity of the perceiver and the influence of psychological factors on perceptual performance.

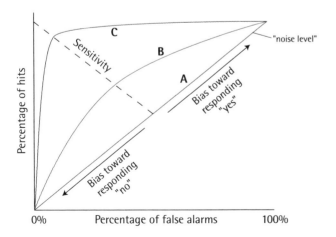

FIGURE 3.3: Example of an ROC curve

SOURCE: WESTEN 2002: p. 108

The ROC curve is the diagonal line from the left lower corner to the right top corner. It is arched if the signal can be successfully distinguished from the noise. In this case, the percentage of hits is greater than the percentage of false alarms. When an extremely flat curve, or particularly a straight line, is obtained, the perceiver shows very little or no success in accurately perceiving the signal from the noise.

Personal criteria that emphasise obtaining hits and avoiding false alarms lead to an accumulation of the majority of responses on the left half of the arched graph. In this case, the arch is skewed to the left. Criteria that emphasise the identification of a signal without much regard for the accuracy of a response lead to an accumulation of the majority of responses on the right half of the arched graph. In this case, the graph is skewed to the right.

Signal detection theory helps us to understand perceptual defence and perceptual vigilance. When people would like to avoid perceiving information linked to a very unpleasant stimulus (e.g. a traumatic experience), they manifest an insensitive perceptual set by increasing the minimum threshold for any information linked to the unpleasant stimulus (experience). They would then manifest many 'misses' in their ROC curve. In the phenomenon of perceptual vigilance, the reverse happens. A person may feel very threatened about an experience that he or she has had. This person then develops a perceptual set that makes them hypersensitive by decreasing the minimum threshold for any information that may forewarn him or her about the topic linked to the feeling of threat. These hypersensitive perceptions are not necessarily more accurate. On the contrary, they often include a host of false alarms, i.e. perceptions of danger where, in reality, none exists.

Signal detection assessments can assist a psychologist in personnel selection, e.g. of airline or air force pilots, radar personnel and air traffic controllers. It can be used in clinical settings to distinguish between different psychological, psychiatric and medical conditions, e.g. between psychological deafness or blindness and real cases of deafness or blindness. Many other uses of signal detection theory have also been developed.

Physiological properties common to all senses

Certain sensory processes are common across all the sensory systems.

Transduction is the process of converting the physical energy of a stimulus into a nerve impulse. Sensory receptors are specialised cells in the sense organs that respond to the physical energy of a stimulus and generate action potentials. These action potentials are then neurologically conducted to the brain.

Transduction:
The process of converting the physical energy of a stimulus into a nerve impulse.

Sensory coding refers to the way in which sensory receptors in the sense organs code information electrochemically so that information about the stimulus can be conducted to the brain. Coding patterns and rates of firing in neuron groups send neural impulses from a sense organ to the brain, which then utilises these impulses to interpret more detailed information about the characteristics of the stimulus. For example, coding in the visual receptors can provide critical information to enable a person to distinguish between gestures indicating that he or she is being approached and about to be physically attacked or congratulated.

Sensory adaptation refers to a decrease in sensory sensitivity resulting from constant stimuli and an increased sensitivity to variable stimuli. Sensory adaptation focuses the sense organs on variations or changes in events that convey new information, rather than on constant trends in events that communicate only familiar or obvious information.

Each of the sensory systems involved in the various sensation processes will now be discussed in detail.

Sensory coding:
The way in which sensory receptors in the sense organs code information electrochemically so that information regarding the stimulus can be conducted to the brain.

Sensory adaptation:
A decrease in sensory sensitivity to constant stimuli and an increased sensitivity to variable stimuli.

The visual sensory system

Most of the information of which we are aware can be obtained through vision. Visual perception is therefore the most intensely studied sensory system in psychology. A very complex relationship exists between the physical stimulus and the sensory processes involved in vision.

The nature of light

Visible light is a form of electromagnetic radiation (i.e. a type of energy). Only a small section of that energy form can be directly sensed by the sensory receptors in the eye. Electromagnetic energy is radiated in a varying patterned form, known as waves, at a speed of approximately 300 000 kilometres per second (Westen 2002). Different forms of electromagnetic radiation have different wavelengths. This means that the energy waves radiate with a higher or lower number of waves per nanosecond (one-billionth of a second). As this period is so minute, scientists rather focus on the wavelengths of light in studying visible light. The wavelength of electromagnetic energy is measured in nanometers (one-billionth of a metre or one-millionth of a millimetre). The human eye is only capable of seeing wavelengths between approximately 350 and 750 nanometers (Coren *et al.* 1994). The visible spectrum constitutes a very small portion of the electromagnetic spectrum, as indicated on the next page in Figure 3.4.

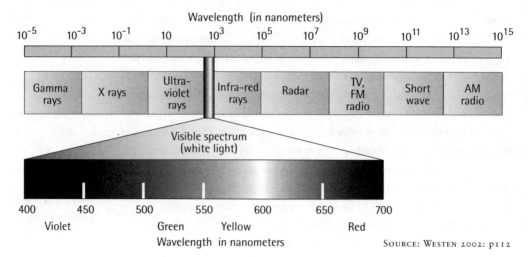

SOURCE: WESTEN 2002: p112

FIGURE 3.4: The electromagnetic spectrum indicating the range of visible light waves

Light can only activate the sensory receptors in the eye from two sources: either by being emitted by a light source – e.g. a television set – and then falling directly on the eye; or by being reflected from an object before activating the sensory receptors in the eye.

All visible light waves manifest three important interrelated characteristics: wavelength (length in nanometers), wave complexity (either one wavelength, or a combination of different wavelengths) and wave amplitude (the intensity of the energy present in the light wave). These three dimensions of light waves interact to provide our experience of colours.

Physical and correspondent psychological characteristics of light waves

The psychological links for the three main physical dimensions of visible light are:

- **wavelength:** colour hue (type of colour – red, green, blue, etc.);
- **complexity:** colour saturation (pureness of a colour hue versus how much it is diluted with 'whiteness', 'greyness' or 'blackness'); and
- **amplitude:** colour brightness (the intensity with which a colour can be experienced as light or dark).

Anatomy and physiology of the eye

Two basic processes are involved in vision. Firstly, the light has to be focused on the sensory receptors in the back of the eye for transduction purposes. This is followed by sensory coding and conduction of the neural impulse to the brain so that the visual information can be interpreted.

Focusing light on the sensory receptors

Light enters the eye through the cornea, a concave transparent tissue that converges (bends) the light to some extent (see Figure 3.5, below). Thereafter, the light goes through the pupil, an opening in the centre of the iris. The iris consists of pigmented tissue that determines the colour of the eye. The muscle fibres of the iris reflexively regulate the size of the pupil and, therefore, the amount of light entering the eye. Finally, the light passes through the lens, which focuses it on the retina at the back of the eye. The ciliary muscles around the lens can contract to make the lens flatter for distant objects, or expand to make it more convex (spherical) for closer objects. This function of the lens is known as **accommodation**. The light is then focused on the retina, a light-sensitive thick layer of tissue containing the receptors that transduce the light into a nerve impulse. The eye is filled with a clear liquid (the aqueous humour) between the cornea and the lens to let the light pass through efficiently. Between the lens and the retina, the eye contains a clear gelatinous liquid (the vitreous humour) through which the light passes to the retina.

Accommodation: Capacity of the lens to change shape in order to focus.

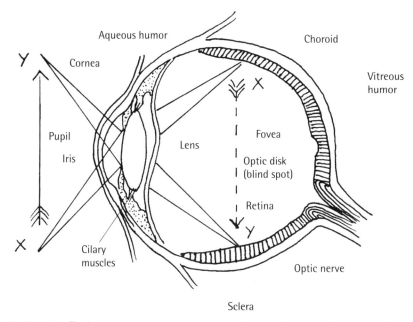

FIGURE 3.5: The human eye   SOURCE: COREN *et al.*, 1994: p. 68

Light passes through layers of neurons to eventually activate two types of receptors called rods and cones (named because of their to their appearance) at the back of the retina. These photoreceptors respond to different wavelengths of light. The rods and cones are connected to bipolar cells that relay nerve impulses to ganglion cells whose axons make up the optic nerve. The rods are more sensitive to a very low intensity level of light. They enable one to see in dim light or darkness (as in night vision), as well as providing black, white and grey sensations. The cones require more light to be activated, and provide more detail and colour hues.

The central region of the retina, called the fovea, is the most sensitive region for small detail, whereas no photoreceptors are found in the region where the optic nerve leaves the eye, called the blind spot. Rods are concentrated on the retinal periphery (off the centre of the retina), while the cones are mostly concentrated in the fovea.

Transduction and sensory coding of visual information

The total information that one can see at any specific moment is defined as the **visual field**. This field can be divided into a left half and a right half. Information from the left half of the visual field is focused on the right half of the retina, and information from the right half of the visual field activates the rods and cones on the left half of the retina.

Visual field: The total information that one can see at any specific moment.

When the rods and cones are activated by light waves, certain photosensitive chemicals are bleached, creating an action potential. It takes a while before the photosensitive chemicals are restored again, which is why it takes time for our eyes to adapt when we enter a dark room. The photosensitive chemicals in the cones adapt quicker than rods to the dark, but the cones are not activated by dim light as quickly as the rods. This phenomenon causes a short period of discomfort before general adaptation takes place. The rods and cones adapt more quickly during adaptation to light than during adaptation to the dark (Westen 2002).

After transduction, action potentials are relayed to the bipolar cells. Each bipolar cell combines action potentials from many photoreceptors and produce graded (varying) potentials in ganglion cells to which they are connected by synapses (Weiten 2001). Each ganglion cell integrates action potentials from various bipolar cells, thus forming a graded potential. The long axons of the ganglion cells collectively constitute the optic nerve along which the action potentials are conducted to the brain.

The ganglion cells are involved in important neural coding processes. Each of the ganglion cells has a concentric receptive field (Hubel & Wiesel 1959, 1979). A ganglion cell is activated by a sensory stimulus within this region. The combination of action potentials from certain groups of ganglion cells, and the absence of action potentials from other groups of ganglion cells, are forwarded to higher neurological centres.

This concentric pattern of neural 'on' and 'off' impulses is maintained up to the various brain centres where decoding takes place and visual sensations are experienced in the visual cortex.

In the visual cortex, decoding takes place in terms of a hierarchical system of **feature detectors** (Hubel & Wiesel 1959, 1979). Feature detectors are neurons and ganglion cells that are activated only when stimulation of their receptive fields corresponds to a specific pattern that is relayed from the retina to the visual cortex. Simple feature detectors in the retina are activated by lines of a particular orientation – e.g. horizontal, vertical or diagonal – at a specific position in the receptive field. They also react to slow movement by an object. Complex feature detectors cover a larger receptive field and receive input from the simple feature detectors. They are activated when a stimulus of a specific orientation or faster movement enters their receptive fields at any location. Hyper-complex feature detectors receive input from the complex feature detectors and require that stimuli exhibit only certain combinations of features, e.g. a particular length, form and colour, or a certain form, colour and movement.

Feature detectors:
A hierarchical system of neurons and ganglion cells that function as form, colour and movement detectors from the retina to the visual cortex.

Neural pathways to the brain and neurological interpretation of the visual information

The central section of the visual field, where most of the images are focused on the fovea, is over-represented by receptor cells on the retina. This over-representation is maintained in the neural decoding levels in the visual cortex.

The nerve impulses in the optic nerve first pass through the optic chiasma, where the nerve splits into two main routes (see Figure 3.6, overleaf). Nerve impulses from each left half of the retina (conveying information from the right half of the visual field), travel to the left cerebral hemisphere, while nerve impulses from each right half of the retina (conveying information from the left half of the visual field) are conducted to the right cerebral hemisphere. This implies that those neurons in the retinal half of each eye closest to the nose cross over to the opposite cerebral hemisphere (Sternberg 1995). The neurons from the other half of each retina stay on their respective sides of the brain. From the optic chiasma onwards, the combined nerve impulses from the same side of the two retinas travel along the two optic tracts to the corresponding side of the brain.

FIGURE 3.6:
The visual field
linked to the neural
pathways from the
eye to the brain

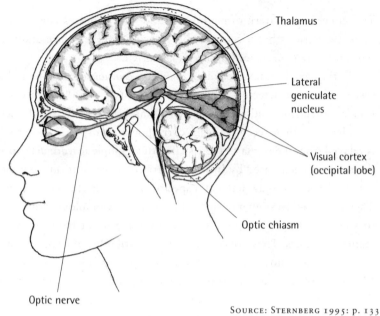

Thalamus

Lateral
geniculate
nucleus

Visual cortex
(occipital lobe)

Optic chiasm

Optic nerve

SOURCE: STERNBERG 1995: p. 133

Right visual field

Left visual field

Optic nerve

Optic chiasm

Optic tract

Nuclei of the thalamus

Lateral geniculate nucleus

Lateral geniculate nucleus

Tectopulvinar system:
Optic tract pathway
that provides information
about the functioning
of the iris and the
lens muscles.

In one optic tract pathway, the **tectopulvinar system**, some neurons branch off and travel through the superior colliculus in the tectum to the lateral posterior nucleus and pulvar nucleus in the thalamus (Coren *et al.* 1994). From here, the neurons fan out to the secondary visual areas in the occipital lobe (see Figure 3.7, opposite). The function of this system is to provide information about the functioning of the iris and the lens muscles, and for the co-ordination and guidance of eye movements. This system is also linked to the neurons of the reticular formation for the regulation of general arousal level and information selection on the sub-cortical and secondary association levels (Jordaan & Jordaan 2000). This pathway prepares the visual cortex for the decoding of the incoming visual impulses.

The other neural pathway, the **geniculo-striate system**, relays impulses to the lateral geniculate nucleus in the thalamus, before fanning out to the visual areas in the cortex (see Figure 3.6, opposite). The pattern of neural coding of impulses that originated in the ganglion cells of the retina is preserved and relayed to the primary and secondary visual areas in the occipital lobe and other related areas in the cortex (see Figure 3.8, below). The function of the geniculo-striate system seems to be the provision of detailed information on the meaning of visual forms, patterns and colours. Efferent (feedback) pathways from the visual cortex to the lateral geniculate nucleus are also set up, in order to select information by enhancing awareness of certain visual information while suppressing awareness of other visual information (Coren *et al.* 1994).

In both visual systems, the visual areas in the cortex are structurally organised in such a way that the patterns of neural impulses travelling from the retina to the cortex are maintained for decoding purposes, even though the hierarchical levels of neural processing progressively become more complex.

Geniculo-striate system:
System that relays impulses from the retina to the lateral geniculate nucleus in the thalamus, before fanning out to the visual areas in the cortex. Provides detailed information on the meaning of visual forms, patterns and colours.

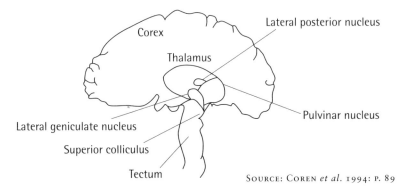

SOURCE: COREN *et al.* 1994: P. 89

FIGURE 3.7: The tectopulvinar neural pathways for vision

After the primary area, information is decoded along two important pathways: the 'what' and the 'where' pathways. The 'what' pathway to the memory areas in the temporal lobes determines the visual details of geometric shapes, patterns and colours of objects. These details are integrated to provide more comprehensive meaning to the percepts. The 'where' pathway to the parietal lobes provides information on the spatial localisation of objects and body movements in relation to objects in three-dimensional space.

Neural decoding of the patterns of neural impulses takes place in the primary and secondary areas in the occipital lobes and the relevant tertiary association areas in other lobes, especially the temporal and parietal lobes, before visual percepts are experienced (Coren *et al.* 1994). Integration of all the visual information from the left and right visual fields takes place via the corpus callosum, which connects the left and right cerebral hemispheres.

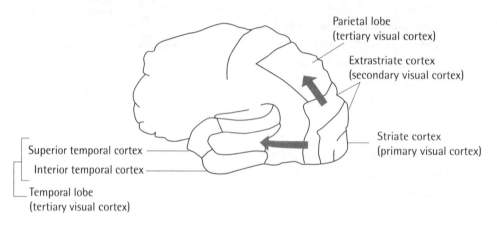

Parietal lobe
(tertiary visual cortex)

Extrastriate cortex
(secondary visual cortex)

Striate cortex
(primary visual cortex)

Superior temporal cortex

Interior temporal cortex

Temporal lobe
(tertiary visual cortex)

FIGURE 3.8: The primary, secondary and tertiary areas involved in vision

Myopia:
Also called near-sightedness. Visual disability in which the lens contracts too much, shifting the focus-point of the light waves to a position before the retina, thus blurring the image on the retina.

Hyperopia:
Also called hypermetropia (far-sightedness). Visual disability in which the lens contracts too little, moving the focus-point to a position beyond the retina, thus blurring the image on the retina.

Visual acuity

The cornea, iris, lens and fovea are very important structures in the eye in determining visual acuity. Any problems present in the functioning of these structures can cause certain visual defects. Frequently experienced problems are near-sightedness and far-sightedness (Weiten 2001). In **myopia** (near-sightedness), the lens contracts too much, shifting the focal point of the light waves to a position in front of the retina, thus blurring the retinal image. In **hyperopia**, also known as hypermetropia (far-sightedness), the lens contracts too little, moving the focal point to a position beyond the retina, also blurring the retinal image.

The classification of colours

Colours are classified according to whether they are monochromatic (containing one wavelength of light), as for example the colours in the colour spectrum, or multichromatic (containing more than one wavelength of light). Monochromatic colours are also known as **spectral** colours. The colours that are not included in the spectrum are called non-spectral colours (Coren *et al.* 1994). The dimensions of hue, saturation and brightness are demonstrated by means of the **colour solid** (see Figure 3.9, below). We can distinguish more than seven million colours by varying hue, saturation and brightness (Sternberg 1995).

Spectral colours:
All the monochromatic colours of the visible spectrum.

Non-spectral colours:
Colours not included in the visible spectrum.

Colour solid:
A model illustrating how colour varies along three perceptual dimensions, i.e. hue, saturation and brightness.

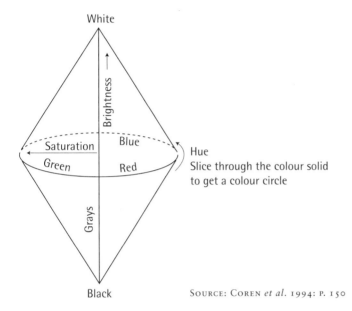

SOURCE: COREN *et al.* 1994: P. 150

FIGURE 3.9: The colour solid

Hue is indicated on the circle in the middle of the figure. Saturation is increased as a colour moves from the centre of the circle to the edge. A vertical line through the centre of the circle indicates brightness. An increase in brightness is experienced as the colour moves from the middle of the figure up towards white. This is, however, associated with a decrease in saturation, as white is in the centre of the circle. An increase in grey in a colour indicates a decrease in brightness until a total absence of chromatic colour is experienced. This achromatic colour is what we call black. It is clear from the colour solid that saturation and brightness are very closely linked to our sensing of colour hues.

Colour mixing
There are basically two ways in which colours can be mixed: by using additive or subtractive colour mixing processes (Westen 2002). **Additive colour mixture** is obtained by mixing direct light sources, e.g. different coloured lights or light from a television screen impacting directly on the retina. Any colour can be obtained by the additive colour principle, if different combinations of the three primary colours (red, blue and green

Additive colour mixture:
The mixture of colours obtained by mixing direct light sources.

light sources) are used. Red includes some of the yellow range of wavelength sensations.

Subtractive colour mixture:
Formation of colours by removing certain reflected wavelengths of light.

Subtractive colour mixture is limited to light reflected from a surface before impacting on the retina. The surface of an object absorbs some of the wavelengths before reflecting the light that activates the retina, e.g. looking at a work of art. When an artist mixes paints, different wavelengths of light are subtracted (eliminated) from the reflected light and only the reflected wavelengths are seen (Coren *et al.* 1994). So blue absorbs all the wavelengths except those which give blue, which are reflected into the eye. Any colour can be obtained by the subtractive colour principle if different combinations of the three primary colours (yellow, blue and green paints) are used. Yellow includes some of the red range of wavelength sensations.

After images

Positive after image:
Visual image that persists even after the visual stimulation has ceased.

Negative after image:
The complementary colours that are seen in a visual image after visual stimulation has ceased.

Constant stimulation by a visual stimulus causes visual adaptation to occur. If one stares at a coloured visual stimulus for a long time and then focuses on a blank piece of paper, the image will still be seen for a few seconds. This is called a **positive after image**, as the neurological processes are still relaying the same information to the visual cortex. However, this positive after image soon stops, and is replaced by a visual adaptation process, during which the sensory pigment of the image is exhausted and needs to be re-synthesised. As the bipolar neurons cannot keep sending an inhibitory signal to the opposing colour neurons during the exhaustion period, complementary colours are seen in the image, called a **negative after image** (Westen 2002). In such an image, for example, red will be replaced by green, yellow by blue and white by black.

Defective colour vision

Defective colour vision:
A deficiency in the ability to distinguish between various colours.

People with defective colour vision tend to manifest mostly a deficiency in the red or green type of cones, or sometimes in the yellow or blue type (Westen 2002). Remember that red-dominant cones include some yellow sensitivity and yellow-dominant cones include some red sensitivity. Sometimes two types of cones can be deficient, e.g. red and green or blue and yellow cones. A few people are deficient in blue, green and yellow-red cones. They are totally colour blind and only see achromatic colours, i.e. various shades of grey and black.

All of the above aspects of visual sensation have been experimentally studied along with various other visual phenomena. These studies have had an important impact on the two main types of theories on colour vision.

Explanatory theories for colour vision

Research on vision has been influenced by two main theories: trichromatic theory and opponent-process theory (Coren *et al.* 1994). Trichromatic theory focuses on three types of receptors in the retina as an explanatory principle for vision, whereas opponent-process theory emphasises three types of colour systems on a higher neural processing level.

Trichromatic theory of vision: Two researchers developed this theory independently, Thomas Young (in 1802) and Hermann von Helmholtz (in 1857). It is therefore called the Young-Helmholtz theory (Westen 2002). According to this theory, the eye contains three types of cones, each one being especially sensitive to a specific range of wavelengths that are linked to either blue, green or red sensations, although they can also be activated by some of the other visible wavelengths. Together, the three types of cones cover all the visible wavelengths of light. Any colour can be seen by means of relative mixes of neural information from the three primary colour cones.

Opponent-process theory of vision: In 1878, Ewald Hering proposed an opponent-process principle in his explanation of the processes involved in colour vision. His views were modified and more clearly formalised in a theory proposed by Leo Hurvich and Dorothea Jameson in 1957 (Sternberg 1995). Subsequent research by DeValois and Jacobs (1968) and DeValois and DeValois (1975) indicated that the modified theory was well supported by empirical evidence. This theory proposes two opposing sets of basic chromatic colours: red versus green and yellow versus blue. A third set, black versus white, was added to emphasise the achromatic dimension (white, grey or black) that is important in understanding the brightness of colours. There are cones for blue, green and yellow-red wavelengths. The yellow-red cones are sensitive to a range of wavelengths, but some are more sensitive to the yellow, while others are more intensely activated by the red wavelengths (DeValois & Jacobs 1968). Separate neurons link the cones in each type of colour to its corresponding bipolar cells. In addition, each of the neurons from the basic chromatic colours has an inhibitory link to its opposing colour bipolar neuron and bipolar ganglion cell. The graded potentials arising in all the ganglion cells are then conducted to the lateral geniculate nucleus. There are four types of neurons in the lateral geniculate nucleus (DeValois & Jacobs 1968):

- excitatory for red but inhibitory for green;
- excitatory for green but inhibitory for red;
- excitatory for blue but inhibitory for yellow; and
- excitatory for yellow but inhibitory for blue.

Trichromatic theory of vision:
Theory stating that the eye contains three types of cones, each one being especially sensitive to a specific range of wavelengths that are linked to either blue, green, or red sensations.

Opponent-process theory of vision:
Theory proposing two opposing sets of chromatic colour cones: 'red' versus 'green' and 'yellow' versus 'blue' to explain colour hue. A third set, 'black' versus 'white' rods explains the achromatic dimension that is important in understanding the brightness of colours.

The patterns of nerve impulses from the optic nerve determine which combination of geniculate neurons are excited or inhibited or remain unaffected. In the case of white light, all the cones are activated and the nerve impulses mutually inhibit each other. This combination of gener-alised excitation and mutual inhibition of opponent pairs is decoded in the visual cortex as the colours in the spectrum – white light. Hue is the result of patterns of excitation and inhibition of the chromatic opponent cells and their resultant graded potentials. The achromatic geniculate cells are broadband cells that receive input from neurons relaying infor-mation from both the cones and the rods for all wavelengths of light. They are organised in opponent pairs, with one of the pair being excited by an increase in the intensity of a light stimulus and inhibited by a decrease in light intensity. The other cell in each pair functions in the opposite way, i.e. it is excited by a decrease in light intensity and inhibit-ed by an increase. These achromatic cells provide information on the brightness of colours (DeValois & Jacobs 1968). Finally, saturation is viewed as the result of the ratio of activated chromatic cells to achromat-ic cells. The more the chromatic cells are activated, the purer the colour sensation; the more the achromatic cells are stimulated, the less saturat-ed the colour sensation.

An integrated theory of colour vision will have to include the core features of both theories.

The auditory sensory system

Whereas vision is based on the information obtained from electromag-netic energy waves, the auditory system focuses on becoming aware of changes in mechanical energy waves in the environment. In this regard, the sensory systems are complementary. They are both important in mak-ing us aware of crucial processes in the environment that affect our survival, personal development and general well-being.

Physical and correspondent psychological characteristics of sound waves

The sound waves created by mechanical energy in the environment spread outward in all directions, like ripples in a pond, at a speed of approximately 340 metres per second (Westen 2002). This is very slow in comparison to light waves. That is why one sees a lightning flash before hearing the thunderclap. Sound can be reflected off a hard surface, or it can be absorbed by a soft surface. Unlike visible light waves, sound waves can move through objects, e.g. a human body, wooden objects or a wall.

Sound waves manifest three important properties: frequency, complexity and amplitude (see Figure 3.10, overleaf). The mechanical energy in an object – e.g. a ringing bell – compresses the air molecules and then expands them in a wave-like manner. There are different ways of measuring this wave-like activity of sounds. The method most often used determines a wave as starting from the middle point of one compression to the middle point of the next (Coren *et al.* 1994). This is defined as one cycle (or one wavelength). As sound travels slowly enough to study sound waves in terms of time parameters, researchers usually link sound waves to time dimensions. The two time parameters most often used are a second and a millisecond (one-thousandth of a second).

The number of cycles (wavelengths) per second determines the frequency of the sound. The frequency of a sound stimulus is psychologically experienced as **pitch** (how high or how low a sound is experienced). Frequency is measured in hertz (Hz). One cycle per second is one Hz and 1 000 cycles per second is one kilohertz (one Khz). As in the case of visible light, humans can hear only a very limited frequency range in the sound spectrum. The audible range for humans is limited to frequencies of approximately 20 Hz to 20 Khz (Jordaan & Jordaan 2000; Weiten 2001). The human voice ranges from approximately 100 Hz to about 3 500 Hz. The human ear is most sensitive to sounds in the range of two Khz to four Khz. Elephants can easily hear frequencies lower than 20 Hz, while dogs and bats can hear frequencies much higher than 20 Khz (Westen 2002).

Pitch:
How high or low a sound is experienced.

Sounds are most often of mixed wavelength. The degree to which a sound wave is composed of different wavelengths is indicated by the complexity of the wave. This is psychologically linked to the **timbre** (quality) of the experienced sound. A complex sound wave consists of a dominant frequency and one or more additional frequencies (Westen 2002) (see Figure 3.10, overleaf, for pure and complex wave patterns). Timbre has to do with the pureness of a sound, or how many additional qualities are experienced besides the basic tone of a sound. The same musical note (for example, middle C) on a piano, clarinet or violin produces the same basic tone, but produces different musical qualities, which are due to the different overtones (harmonics) produced by each musical instrument (Schiffman 1996).

Timbre:
The psychological quality of an experienced sound, related to the complexity of a sound wave.

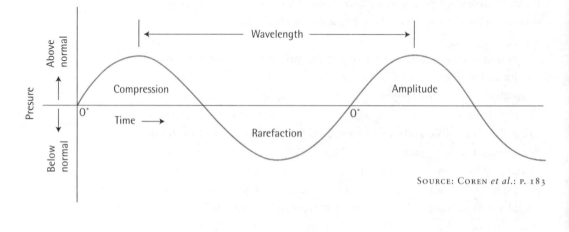

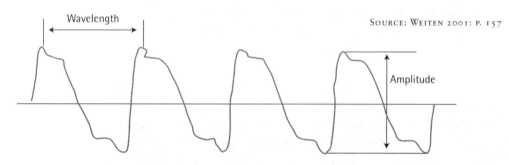

FIGURE 3.10: Physical properties of a sound wave

Loudness:
How soft or loud a sound
is experienced

The intensity of the energy involved in the compressions and expansions of a sound wave is indicated by the amplitude of the wave. The amplitude of a sound stimulus is psychologically experienced as **loudness** (how soft or loud a sound is experienced). Amplitude is measured in decibels (dB). Zero decibels is the absolute threshold above which most people can hear a sound of 1 Kz (Westen 2002). Amplitudes of different sounds are provided in Figure 3.11, opposite. Conversation is typically conducted at 50 to 60 dB. The pain threshold is somewhere between 120–130 dB. The harmful effects of sounds increase drastically from 120 to 180 dB (see Figure 3.11). Surprisingly, the human ear is very sensitive to a very broad range of loudness variations. It can hear sounds with an amplitude energy that differs ten billion times between the softest and the loudest sound (Westen 2002).

The characteristics of the sounds we experience are the result of a complex combination of three physical dimensions of sound waves. Furthermore, what sounds are perceived by some people as pleasant and by others as unpleasant is determined by the interpretation of the sounds as defined by the meaning systems of one's social and cultural group.

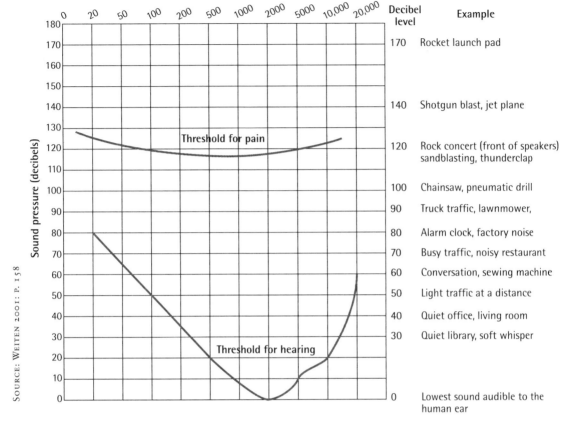

FIGURE 3.11: Typical amplitude of various sounds

The anatomy and physiology of the ear

The ear consists of the outer, the middle and the inner ear (see Figure 3.12, below). The pinna (outer ear) collects sounds in the environment and focuses them on the channel called the auditory canal, where they are amplified before reaching the tympanic membrane (ear drum). Sound waves (air pressure waves) set the tympanic membrane in motion. In the middle ear, the vibration of the tympanic membrane is relayed and further amplified by the mechanical movements of three auditory bones, called the hammer, the anvil and the stirrup, which conduct the movements to the oval window of the inner ear. The Eustachian tube is a channel from the back of the throat to the middle ear that regulates the air pressure in the middle ear when we yawn, equalising it with the air pressure outside (Coren *et al.* 1994). Middle ear infection blocks the Eustachian tube and, therefore, hamper our sense of hearing. In the inner ear are two types of fluid-filled canals: the semi-circular canals and the cochlea, where auditory receptor cells are located.

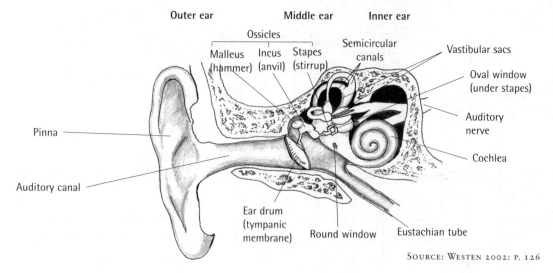

SOURCE: WESTEN 2002: P. 126

FIGURE 3.12: Anatomy and physiology of the ear

The cochlea is a fluid-filled tube that appears curled up like a snail shell. In order to understand its structure and functioning, imagine that it is uncurled and stretched out straight. At the oval window, the mechanical movements of the auditory bones are transformed into wave-like movements inside the fluid of the cochlea (see Figure 3.13, opposite). These pressure waves activate vibration movements in the basilar membrane, which is located in the middle, along the length of the cochlea, creating two main canals: the vestibular canal and the tympanic canal. A smaller canal is located in the middle, between the basilar membrane and tectorial membrane. The vestibular and tympanic canals are connected to each other at the apex (end) of the cochlea by an opening called the helicotrema (Schiffman 1996). This wave-like movement continues until it reaches the round window at the end of the tympanic canal, where it is extinguished (stopped) by the shock-absorbing effect of the round window.

Transduction and sensory coding of the information

Protruding from the basilar membrane is another membrane known as the tectorial membrane (see Figure 3.13, opposite). It consists mostly of a structure called the Organ of Corti, where the hair-like auditory receptor cells are located. The receptor cells link the Organ of Corti with the basilar membrane, much like the strings on a harp. Movements in the basilar and tectorial membranes that are activated by the pressure waves in the cochlear fluid bend the receptor cells, activating action potentials in the neurons (Schiffman 1996). The basilar membrane is narrow close to the oval window and is at its widest close to the helicotrema. Activation of the basilar membrane closer to the oval window elicits higher pitch experiences, while movement of the basilar membrane closer to the apex evokes lower pitch sensations.

After transduction, action potentials are relayed to the bipolar cells. Each bipolar cell combines action potentials from many receptor cells to produce graded (varying) potentials on ganglion cells to which it is connected by means of synapses (Weiten 2001). The long axons of the ganglion cells together make up the auditory nerve, along which action potentials are conducted to the brain.

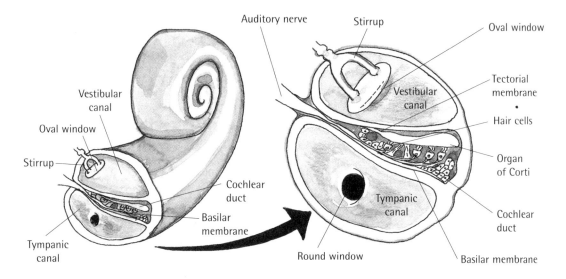

FIGURE 3.13: The process of auditory transduction in the cochlea   SOURCE: WESTEN 2002: P. 127

Neural pathways to the brain and the neurological interpretation of the auditory information

The auditory nerve impulses from each ear first go to the cochlear nucleus in the medulla, where the neurons split up (see Figure 3.14, opposite). The minority of neurons from the left ear go to the left olivary nucleus in the medulla, while the majority of neurons from the left ear cross over to the right olivary nucleus in the medulla (Coren *et al.* 1994; Schiffman 1996). The opposite happens to the neurons from the right ear. Only a minority of neurons go to the right olivary nucleus in the medulla, while the majority cross over to the left olivary nucleus. Efferent (feedback) neurons from each olivary nucleus to the ear on the same side regulate the sensitivity levels of the hair cells reflexively, as well as the sensitivity of the eardrum and oval window (Coren *et al.* 1994; Schiffman 1996). People who have psychological blockages for certain messages manifest a conditioned reflex 'not to hear' these messages.

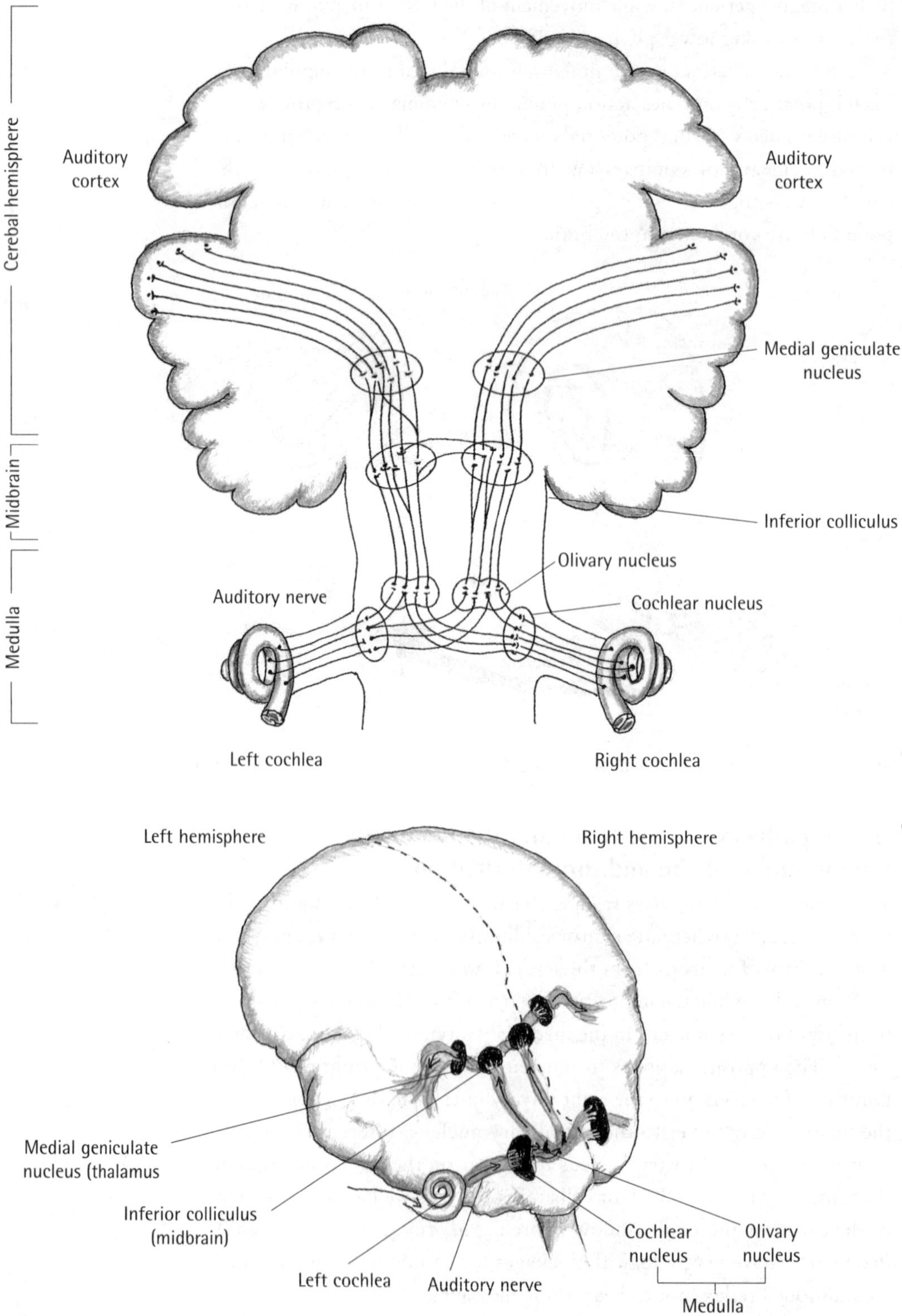

SOURCE: SCHIFFMAN 1996: P. 74

FIGURE 4.22 FROM WESTEN 2002, P. 129

FIGURE 3.14: Neural pathways from the ear to the brain

From the olivary nuclei, the neural impulses go to the inferior colliculi in the tectum, where more criss-crossing of neurons from one side to the other side of the brain takes place (Coren *et al.* 1994; Schiffman 1996). Each cerebral hemisphere therefore receives auditory input from both ears, the majority being nerve impulses from the opposite ear. The inferior colliculi regulates sound volume reflexively, and the attendant startle reaction that accompanies an unexpected sound (Jordaan & Jordaan 2000). It is also linked to the neurons of the reticular formation for the regulation of auditory arousal levels and information selection (Jordaan & Jordaan 2000).

After the inferior colliculi, a few neural impulses travel to the superior colliculi of the tectum for integration of visual and auditory information for direction and distance. The rest of the impulses go to the medial geniculate nuclei of the thalamus. From here, the neural impulses travel to the auditory areas in the temporal lobe that have specific sections focused on specific frequencies. The auditory areas in the temporal lobe manifest a tonotopic organisation. This implies that certain sections of the basilar membrane are connected to specific sections of the auditory cortex.

The region in the primary auditory area that is tuned in to speech is disproportionately large in comparison to the cortical areas for the other frequencies (Westen 2002). This emphasises the important role of auditory communication in our psychological functioning.

Auditory problems

Auditory problems can arise from two main types of problem categories. They can be caused by conduction problems in the relaying of sound waves to the auditory receptors, or by malfunctioning receptors or neural relaying circuits to the brain. The first problem category is called **auditory conduction loss**, and the second category is known as **sensori-neural loss** (Schiffman 1996; Westen 2002). The first type of problem is related to the conduction of the sound wave through the outer and middle ear to the auditory receptors of the inner ear, while the latter type of loss arises from problems in transduction in the Organ of Corti and neural conduction to the brain. While both categories occur with increasing age, conduction loss tends to predominate in old age due to ossification of the auditory bones. A noisy lifestyle or environment, as well as noisy working conditions, can also cause hearing loss or make it worse.

Auditory conduction loss: Problems in conducting sound waves through the outer and middle ear to the auditory receptors of the inner ear.

Sensori-neural loss: Problems in transduction in the Organ of Corti and neutral conduction to the brain.

Explanatory theories for auditory perception

Frequency theory of auditory perception: Theory holding that the basilar membrane acts much like a diaphragm in a microphone, by vibrating as a whole. The frequency of a sound correlates with the frequency of nerve impulses travelling to the brain.

In 1931, Wever and Bray proposed the **frequency theory of auditory perception** (Schiffman 1996). It holds that the basilar membrane acts much like a diaphragm in a microphone, by vibrating as a whole. The frequency of a sound correlates with the frequency of nerve impulses travelling to the brain. The brain then analyses the frequency of nerve impulses and determines the pitch of the sound.

Research indicates that this explanation for pitch perception was oversimplified. The maximum neural transmission rate is 1 000 impulses per second, as a neuron has a minimum recovery rate of one millisecond (one-thousandth of a second) during the absolute refractory period, before it can continue transmitting a neural impulse. Thus, the frequency theory could not explain how we hear pitches for sound frequencies higher than one Khz. Wever and Bray then proposed the notion that neurons do not conduct nerve impulses for all frequencies at the same time. Neural conduction takes place in neuron groups, and each group of neurons conducts impulses in succession for a specific range of frequencies. According to their **volley principle**, for all frequencies above one Khz, nerve impulses are relayed to the brain in sequential volleys. The overall effect is that the neural pattern of nerve impulses is spread over the whole frequency of a sound wave for sounds above one Khz. Loudness is explained by an increase in the rate of nerve impulses within certain volleys while maintaining a constant rate across other volleys.

Volley principle: Theory stating that, in the case of sound frequencies above 1 Khz, nerve impulses are relayed to the brain in sequential volleys.

In 1863, Hermann von Helmholtz proposed a **place theory of hearing**. According to this view, the basilar membrane functions very much like a harp – wider at one end and shorter at the other end. The longer 'strings' near the helicotrema generate lower frequencies, while the shorter ones near the oval window evoke higher frequencies. The position of the neural 'strings' that are activated in the basilar membrane will determine the sound that is heard (Sternberg 1995).

Place theory of hearing: Theory that the basilar membrane functions very much like a harp, with the longer 'strings' near the helicotrema generating lower sounds and the shorter ones near the oval window evoking higher sounds.

In 1961, Georg von Békésy received the Nobel Prize for his pioneering research on the perception of pitch and loudness. According to his findings, these two dimensions of sound in turn explain the experience of timbre. His version of place theory is known as the **travelling wave theory of auditory perception** (Coren et al. 1994; Schiffman 1996). According to this theory, a travelling wave is generated at the oval window by the action of the stirrup. This wave-like movement travels along the vestibular canal and through the helicotrema into the tympanic canal, before it is extinguished at the round window, which acts as a shock-absorber.

Travelling wave theory of auditory perception: Theory stating that wave-like movements are created by the stirrup, and travel along the vestibular canal and through the helicotrema into the tympanic canal, before the movement is stopped at the round window acting as a shock-absorber.

The wave-like motion stimulates movement in the basilar and tectorial membranes that bend the hair-like receptor cells in the Organ of

Corti, inducing action potentials in the neurons of the auditory nerve. Although the whole basilar membrane tends to vibrate, most vibration is focused on a specific section or sections of the membrane. According to the tonotopical links between the basilar membrane and the auditory cortex, the neural impulses at the section or sections on the basilar membrane where the most concentrated vibration occurs are relayed to their counterpart sections in the temporal lobe. This is subsequently decoded as a certain basic pitch. Maximal vibration of the basilar membrane closer to its base at the oval window produces higher pitches, whereas maximal vibration of the membrane closer to the helicotrema is linked to lower pitches. Concerning loudness, Von Békésy maintained that the number of activated hair-like cells and neurons determines the loudness of a sound. The experience of timbre is determined by the number of places on the basilar membrane that are stimulated very intensely, as well as the number of hair-like cells and neurons activated at each of these places.

It appears that, to some extent, both theories have empirical support. The frequency theory has a better explanation for frequencies below 50 Hz. The place theory is better than the frequency theory for frequencies above three Khz. For frequencies between 50 Hz and three Khz, the explanations of both theories seem to play a role.

The chemical sensory system (taste and smell)

Smell is mainly a distance receptor, whereas taste is a contact receptor. In combination, these two chemical senses can warn against approaching danger, e.g. toxic gases, or poisonous and putrefying substances in food. The chemical senses can also contribute to our quality of life experiences in terms of fragrant odours and gourmet food tastes.

The chemical senses mostly function as one sensory system. What we call 'tastes' are often odours, as, for example, in the case of food. When we have flu, we discover that food does not taste as good as usual because we can't smell it. Conversely, if we were unable to taste food, the result would also be less appetising to us.

Anatomy and physiology of the sensory organs

Although taste and smell function as one sensory system, there are various distinct physiological differences in the functioning of the two chemical senses. Therefore they will be dealt with separately in this subsection.

Taste: Chemical stimuli and location of receptors

Taste sensations (also called gustatory sensations) can only be acquired through molecules soluble in liquid form, e.g. in saliva. There are four basic types of gustatory sensations: sweet, salt, sour and bitter (Coren *et al.* 1994). Cross-cultural studies indicate that these four tastes are apparently universal (Westen 2002). Other tastes can be obtained by combining two or more of the basic tastes in varying degrees. Taste combinations can be extrapolated using Henning's taste pyramid with each of the four basic tastes at the corners of the pyramid (see Figure 3.15, below). This taste pyramid has been demonstrated to have substantial empirical support (Schiffman 1996).

The gustatory buds are located in the papillae (bumps) on the tongue. Sweet taste receptors are most sensitive on the front tip of the tongue, while the most sensitive salt taste receptors are located on both sides of the tongue, next to the sweet ones (see Figure 3.15). Sour gustation areas are concentrated on the left and right sides of the tongue, behind the salt ones. Bitter tastes are located far back in the middle of the tongue. General chemical receptors are located in the throat and palate of the mouth (Coren *et al.* 1994). Gustatory buds have a very short life span and the body replaces them every ten days. There is a progressive decrease in the number of taste buds as one ages, and very old people tend to have a weak sense of taste. Sensory adaptation is also found in gustation. Repeated tasting of the same substance results in decreased sensory sensitivity. However, rinsing the mouth with water can restore full sensitivity, as for example in the practice of wine-tasting professionals (and some students I have known!).

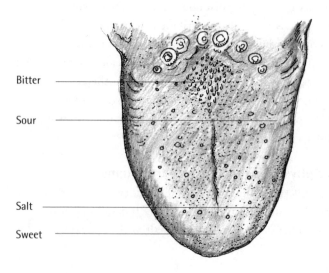

Bitter

Sour

Salt

Sweet

SOURCE: SCHIFFMAN 1996: P. 128

FIGURE 3.15: Maximum sensitivity areas on the tongue for the four basic tastes

Taste: Transduction and neural pathways to the brain

Soluble chemicals enter the taste pores inside the taste buds and stimulate the receptor cells through various electrochemical reactions (Coren *et al.* 1994). Neural impulses are relayed to the medulla and pons, whereupon the neurons split into two pathways. One pathway has no access to consciousness but functions at the subcortical (subconscious) level. This pathway leads to the limbic system for immediate emotional responses, e.g. reflexively spitting out a substance previously associated with poison or feelings of nausea. The second pathway goes to the thalamus and the gustatory area in the temporal lobe where the different tastes are decoded. Neural links also exist with the somatosensory area (skin senses area) in the parietal lobe (Jordaan & Jordaan 2000; Westen 2002).

Smell: Chemical stimuli, receptors and explanatory models

Olfactory sensations can only be activated by gaseous substances like food odours, perfume, etc. Absolute thresholds for identifying odours are extremely low (Westen 2002). Only a small number of molecules from a gaseous substance are required to activate an olfactory sensation at conscious level. Nevertheless, much of our sense of smell happens automatically at the subcortical (subconscious) level (Coren *et al.* 1994; Westen 2002). Olfactory sensations are closely linked to associations in long-term memory, as both are chemically based (Coren *et al.* 1994). Often, long-term olfactory memories cannot easily be recalled in words, but can quite easily be reactivated by the same odour.

Olfactory stimuli can enter either the nose or the mouth. In the case of food, the odours enter the nasal cavity through the back of the mouth. Olfactory adaptation happens within approximately 30 seconds for most odours. The adaptation lasts until the gaseous substance has gone, but sensitivity returns immediately when the substance is reintroduced (Louw & Edwards 1993). This enables a person to become aware of a variety of odours and recurring odours in the immediate environment that may be significant.

No generally accepted classification system or explanatory model exists for odours, although **Henning's odour prism** and Amoore's three-dimensional stereo-chemical lock-and-key model feature prominently (Schiffman 1996; Sternberg 1995). Olfactory receptors have various templates (shapes) and can also generate new templates that can be matched to the molecular shape of known or new odours entering the nose. When the template matches the molecular shape of an odour, electrochemical impulses are activated. More recently, there has been **Wright's vibration theory**. It postulates the notion that each distinctive odour is linked to a specific type of vibrating molecular structure of the

Henning's odour prism: System for classifying odours.

Wright's vibration theory: Theory stating that each distinctive odour is linked to a specific type of vibrating molecular structure of the stimulus. The frequency of vibration of the molecules characterises the eventual interpretation of the type of odour.

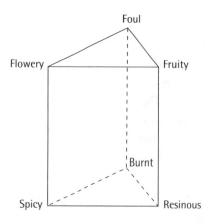

FIGURE 3.16:
Henning's classification
model for odours

SOURCE: COREN *et al.*
1994: P. 277

stimulus. The frequency of vibration of the molecules
characterises the eventual interpretation of the type of
odour (Sternberg 1995).

No generally accepted classification system exists for
odours. However, olfactory combinations are often based
on Henning's odour prism (see Figure 3.16). It comprises
six main categories of odours – flowery, foul, fruity, burnt,
resinous and spicy – arranged at the six corners of the
prism. Each corner represents an odour that differs clearly
from those at the other corners of the model. Henning's
model can be used to indicate the nature of combinations
of odours (Sternberg 1995).

Smell: Transduction and neural pathways to the brain

Gaseous molecules enter the olfactory epithelium at the top of the nasal
cavity, where they activate the oval-shaped receptor cells electrochemically (Westen 2002). The receptor cells only function for approximately
four to eight weeks before the body replaces them (Coren *et al.* 1994).
The nerve impulses travel to the olfactory bulb, immediately below the
frontal lobe (see Figure 3.17, below). From here, they are relayed via the
thalamus to the primary olfactory areas in the temporal lobe. Neural
pathways stay on the same side of the brain as the respective nostril.
Another group of neurons travels from the olfactory bulb to the limbic
system, a structure that is involved in the (often) subconscious experience
of emotion and associated positive or negative memories.

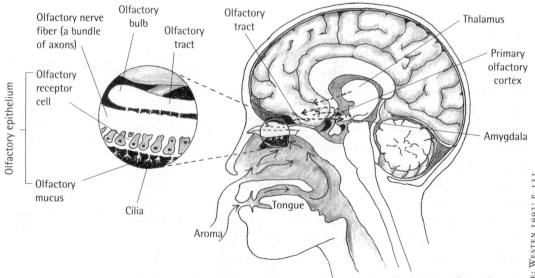

FIGURE 3.17: Olfactory neural pathways to the brain

SOURCE: WESTEN 1992: P. 131

The link between the chemical senses and emotions

Gustatory sensations associated with the tastes of poisonous substances can evoke intense nausea. Even one traumatic experience – e.g. food poisoning – is sufficient to create an extreme emotional aversion to the odour of foods or other substances associated with or resembling those involved in the experience. In addition, positive and negative experiences with various kinds of food can create strong emotional associations with food odours or tastes, which may also create strong drives to eat those kinds of food. In extreme cases, it may lead to compulsive eating behaviour.

Odours can also be positively or negatively associated with social interaction. Good personal hygiene is important in avoiding eliciting unpleasant associations and reactions from others. People attempt to avoid such problems by the appropriate use of cologne or fragrant perfume or aftershave, and car and room fresheners (although some people claim that the solution can be worse than the problem!). This also applies to the odours of objects, e.g. a keepsake or a bouquet of flowers, and buildings like one's home, a restaurant or a bakery.

Olfactory sensations seem to play a somewhat less important role in human interaction than in animal behaviour. Olfaction is central to animals' capacity for biological survival and reproduction. Animals secrete and sense chemical messages, which they use during the communication of herd-related and reproductive messages to one another, and for marking territory (Westen 2002). The ability of humans to use olfaction as a distance and contact sensory system has greatly been inhibited by urban lifestyles and environmental pollution. Nevertheless, even when people maintain good hygiene practices, human bodies have natural odours that seem to be distinctly different for the sexes. Various studies have reported that humans secrete and sense olfactory messages that have distinct biological functions, although this happens mostly on the subcortical (subconscious) level, or in a very subtle, consciously controlled way, due to social learning (Coren *et al.* 1994; Schiffman 1996; Westen 2002).

The chemical substances that affect human behaviour are called **human pheromones**. Studies carried out on humans' olfactory sensitivity have indicated that people can accurately identify odours associated with both sexes (Coren *et al.* 1994; Westen 2002). Furthermore, most colognes, female perfumes and other toiletries that are regarded as important in promoting passion in heterosexual relationships are manufactured from substances that also contain the sexual pheromones of various animals (Schiffman 1996). According to some studies, body odour may be involved in mother-baby bonding, e.g. six-day old babies

Human pheromones: Chemical substances secreted by humans that affect certain types of behaviours.

can respond to the smell of their own mother's breasts, but not to the smell of other mothers' breasts (Coren *et al.* 1994). In addition, each person has a distinct odour. For instance, people who have been blindfolded and prevented from using their touch sense can accurately distinguish the odour of their own clothing from clothing belonging to others.

The chemical sensory system is a biologically less-advanced system in humans than in animals. Nevertheless, it is still important for humans. Other biologically less-advanced systems are the somatosensory and proprioceptive sensory systems.

The somatosensory and proprioceptive sensory systems

The somatosensory and proprioceptive sensory systems provide closely related yet complementary sets of information that are very important for carrying out actions or performing very complicated movements.

The somatosensory system

This is the sense of touch. The approximately two square metres of body skin can be viewed as one complex sense organ constituting a variety of sensory receptor cells. What we call 'touch' is actually a mixture of at least three types of sensory experiences: pressure, temperature and pain. Besides protecting the body from possible harm by avoiding painful actions, the skin senses also help us to identify objects by touching them, or determining the type of texture of an object, e.g. furry, metallic, rough or smooth. Touch verifies the contact characteristics of an object. If we are uncertain of the reality of an object or a person, touching can confirm this. Furthermore, the skin senses regulate comfortable temperature levels and facilitate interpersonal interaction through physical contact, e.g. greeting or congratulating a person, or communicating love to someone.

Physiology of the somatosensory receptors, neural pathways to the brain and explanatory model for pain

The somatosensory receptor cells are specialised for each sensory modality: pressure, heat or pain. Mostly, however, they function in a multimodal way by providing information on most or all of the skin senses simultaneously (Westen 2002). The skin senses also have receptive fields that can identify the location and intensity of a stimulus. The receptors for the skin senses are indicated in Figure 3.18.

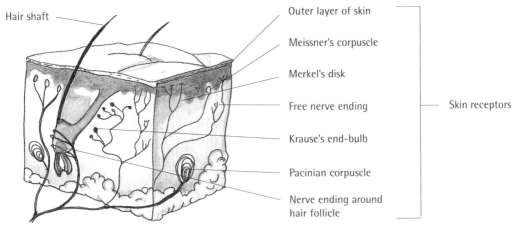

FIGURE 3.18: Receptors of the skin senses

Touch (pressure) sensitivity varies across the body. The most tactile sensitive areas are the face and fingers, while the least sensitive are the back and legs (Westen 2002). The hands and fingers are tactile active sense organs for exploring the environment. Fingers are crucial sense organs for blind people to actively sense detailed tactile information about objects – e.g. coins – and to obtain information by 'touch reading' documents printed in Braille. Sensory neurons synapse on interneurons in the spinal cord and then relay nerve impulses along the spinal cord to the medulla. In the medulla, the neurons from both sides of the body's skin senses cross over to the other side of the brain. The afferent (sensory) information is relayed via the thalamus to the somatosensory areas in the parietal lobe.

Temperature sensations are based on the difference between the temperature of the skin and that of an object. Hot sensations indicate that heat is entering the body at the contact point, while cold sensations indicate that heat is leaving the body at the contact point. Temperature may be viewed as relative, as the temperature of an object can be experienced as either warm or cold, depending on the temperature of the skin touching the object. This relativity of temperature sensations is illustrated in the phenomenon of **paradoxical heat**. When 'hot' and 'cold' receptors are stimulated simultaneously with very hot and very cold stimuli, the overall sensation experienced is hot (Schiffman 1996; Westen 2002). The cold sensations are paradoxically interpreted as being hot. **Paradoxical cold** refers to the opposite, where very hot sensations are interpreted as cold (Schiffman 1996). Yogi who walk barefoot across very hot coals describe the coals as being 'very cool'. The neural coding of the impulses result in a different impulse pattern to those in either normally hot or cold sensations (Westen 2002).

Paradoxical heat:
Phenomenon when 'hot' and 'cold' receptors are stimulated simultaneously with very hot and very cold stimuli, the overall sensation experienced being hot.

Paradoxical cold:
Phenomenon where 'cold' receptors relay very hot stimuli as if they are very cold.

Pain sensations are important for a person's physical security, as they indicate tissue damage to the body. Those who are neurologically or medically incapable of sensing pain often suffer serious injuries. Persistent pain can cause enormous suffering that may need to be dealt with both medically and psychotherapeutically. There are various types of pain, e.g. sharp, dull, pricking and burning pain (Schiffman 1996). Surprisingly, there are no specific stimuli for pain. Any stimulus that damages body tissue, or is too intense, can activate pain impulses (Weiten 2001). The most important pain receptors are the free nerve endings in the skin. Damage to cells in the body elicits substance P, a chemical about which little is known (Westen 2002). This substance activates neural impulses in the free nerve endings that transmit pain impulses to the brain. However, much research has been done on the neural processing of pain impulses to the brain. **Melzack and Wall's gate-control theory** emphasises the role of the brain and spinal cord in the regulation of pain sensations (Melzack 1993; Melzack & Wall 1965; Weiten 2001). When sensory neurons transmit pain impulses to the spinal cord, neural input from other sensory neurons and from efferent neural impulses (messages descending from the brain) can inhibit or amplify pain impulses (see Figure 3.19, opposite). Gate-control theory distinguishes between two types of sensory neurons that open and close spinal gateways for pain impulses to the brain. Large diameter fibres (A-fibres) have low activation thresholds for stimuli. They are easily activated and transmit neural information for various skin senses, as well as light and sharp pains, very quickly to the brain. Once they transmit a neural impulse, they inhibit (close the neural gate) for other pain impulse pathways with which they may synapse. Their feedback loops inhibit the A-fibres from repeatedly relaying the same pain message after a short period. Small diameter fibres (C-fibres) have higher activation thresholds. They need more intense stimulation before they are activated (Coren *et al.* 1994). Once activated, they inhibit the less intense A-fibre pain pathways on which they synapse in the spinal cord, while relaying information on dull pains and burning feelings to the brain. They can relay these pain impulses for a long period. However, any sensory input from other sensory receptors or efferent messages from the brain can inhibit pain impulses relayed by C-fibres. For instance, lightly massaging an area around a burn or wound can reactivate the A-fibres that partially close the pain gate for impulses from C-fibres (Westen 2002). Messages from the brain – e.g. anxiety or depression – can increase the opening of the pain gate and therefore the intensity of the pain, while other messages – e.g. relaxing visualisations, positively focused thoughts, interesting distractions and calm exhortations – gradually close the pain gate and eventually alleviate most or all

Melzack and Wall's gate-control theory: Theory emphasising the role of sensory nerves, large diameter A-fibres, small diameter C-fibres, the brain and the spinal cord in the regulation of pain sensations.

of the experienced pain. Furthermore, it has been found that the body manufactures its own analgesic chemicals – enkephalins and endorphins – that inhibit the sensation pathways for pain to the brain, creating relief from all suffering (Coren *et al.* 1994). Also, the Chinese practice of acupuncture appears to elicit the functioning of endogenous analgesics in relieving pain and suffering (Coren *et al.* 1994).

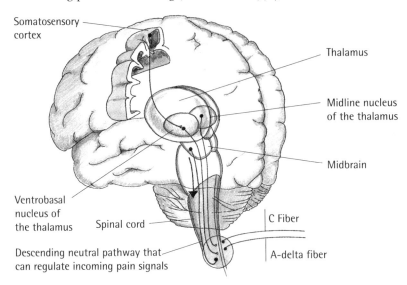

FIGURE 3.19: The gate-control theory of pain   SOURCE: WEITEN 2002: P. 166

Tactile and pain sensations can combine to create somatosensory illusions. This is illustrated in the **phantom limb** phenomenon. Phantom limbs are misleading sensations of experiencing real limbs when they in fact no longer exist, e.g. after an amputation (Westen 2002). After an arm has been amputated, a patient may experience a painful hand attached to the shoulder. Usually it takes some time for the body image areas in the somatosensory cortex to reorganise themselves around the new reality. The experience of pain is a very complex phenomenon. Cultural and personal beliefs, social and personal expectations, as well as emotions, can have a huge effect on whether pain will be experienced or not and, if so, on the nature and the reality of the pain that a person experiences.

Phantom limb:
The misleading sensations of experiencing a limb or part of a limb as still existing when it in fact no longer exists.

The proprioceptive system

Some people enjoy the swings and the roller coasters at fairs. Babies like to be gently rocked to sleep. Gymnasts and acrobats enjoy carrying out very complex coordinated movements. This is all made possible by vestibular and kinesthetic reflexes and the associated sensations we experience.

The vestibular sense includes awareness of balance, the orientation of the body in space, and changes in body movement, e.g. acceleration or stopping. Kinesthesis includes the awareness of one's own movements and body posture. The proprioceptive system is crucial in controlling any coordinated body movements in space, such as when circus acrobats exert control over their body movements during a performance.

Physiology of the proprioceptive organs and the neural pathways to the brain

The physiology and neural pathways of the vestibular and kinesthetic senses differ to some extent and are discussed separately.

Vestibular sense, or a sense of balance, is determined by the position of the head in relation to the ground, which is the usual point of reference for gravity and movement of the body. We are mostly unaware of our vestibular sense. However, when it is overstimulated – e.g. on a roller coaster or a merry-go-round – we experience dizziness and sometimes nausea (Sternberg 1995). Middle ear infection also makes us feel dizzy, due to the effects of the infection on the vestibular sense. The receptors are located in the inner ear, along with the auditory system, as part of the cochlea (see Figure 3.20, opposite). The vestibular system comprises the two vestibular sacs and three semicircular canals (Schiffman 1996). Each of the two sacs contains fluid and a hard object called an otolith (stone). The three semicircular canals are positioned at a 90 degree angle to one another. They contain fluids that move when the head moves. Movement changes the position of the otoliths, which, with the fluid movement, cause the ciliary cells inside the canals to bend, activating nerve impulses. The nerve impulses are relayed to the cerebellum, where balance and spatial orientation are reflexively regulated. Some neural impulses are also relayed to the superior colliculi in the tectum for reflexive coordination of balance and eye movements (Coren *et al.* 1994). Other neural pathways travel to certain areas in the temporal lobe and the somatosensory cortex in the parietal lobe for interpretation of the direction of any head movement and its spatial orientation, as well as interpreting the rate of acceleration and slowing of movements. In the parietal tertiary areas, information from the proprioceptive, auditory and visual systems are coordinated to provide an integrated approach to spatial perception and orientation in space (Sternberg 1995).

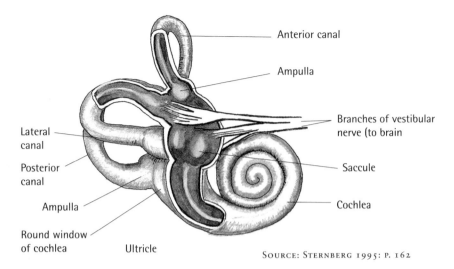

Anterior canal

Ampulla

Branches of vestibular
nerve (to brain

Lateral
canal

Posterior
canal

Ampulla

Round window
of cochlea

Ultricle

Saccule

Cochlea

SOURCE: STERNBERG 1995: P. 162

FIGURE 3.20: The vestibular system

Kinesthetic sense or kinesthesis is important for being aware of the position of any limb or mobile part of the body in relation to other limbs and
the rest of the body during voluntary movements. Kinesthesis enables
one to know the position, posture and direction of movement of any
limb at any moment. Kinesthetic receptors are located in the joints,
tendons, muscles and skin (Coren *et al.* 1994). When they are activated
by pressure being exerted on them, they encode information about speed
of movement changes, the angle of bones and joints, and muscle tension
(Sternberg 1995). These neural impulses from each side of the body
travel along the spinal cord to the medulla, where they cross to the other
side of the body before reaching the brain. Some neurons travel to the
cerebellum for reflexive control over body movements, while the rest
travel via the thalamus to the somatosensory cortex in the parietal lobe,
where decoding of movement, posture and the spatial position of the
body takes place.

The physiological decoding of sensory information in order to
obtain the basic information of our sensory experiences has now been
finalised. In the remainder of this chapter, the discussion will focus on
the process for the hierarchical integration of these basic sensations into
more comprehensive units called percepts, which are linked to social
and cultural meaning systems.

Perception

Non-focused attention:
Passive attention in which the environment is scanned in a general, random manner in order to detect something of interest.

Focused attention:
An active form of attention required for obtaining all the relevant sensory information that is available on a topic, while the observer is still aware to some extent of other types of sensory information.

Concentration:
The combined psychological effect of selecting information and focusing intently on it, while blocking out all irrelevant information.

Sensory register:
Also called memory. Type of 'neural' memory that holds different sensory modalities of information automatically for approximately two seconds because of neural impulses still being relayed to the brain.

For more elaborate interpretation and meaningful integration of sensory information in social and cultural meaning systems, various perceptual-cognitive processes closely linked to perception need to be considered.

Attention is a prerequisite for conscious perception. The environment can be scanned in an act of general, passive, **non-focused attention**, to detect something of interest – e.g. when a person does window-shopping or goes for a walk in a park. However, **focused attention** is an active form of attention, required to obtain all the relevant sensory information that is available on a particular topic – e.g. choosing an interesting video or magazine – while the observer is still aware of other types of sensory information. In the case where a topic of interest is of paramount importance – e.g. a conscientious student studying a prescribed book for an exam – the student would naturally focus intently on the topic, while simultaneously blocking out any irrelevant information about the exam. This combination of selecting and focusing intently on a topic while blocking out irrelevant information is called **concentration**. Non-focused or focused attention is important during sensory scanning activities for objects or topics that are of interest to an observer generally. However, concentration is a prerequisite for high priority topics, where optimal observation levels are crucial for obtaining specific sensory information. Factors that promote attention and concentration will also facilitate the quality of perceptual processes. Novel, variable, intense and enduring types of stimuli tend to attract an observer's attention. These are called physical determinants of attention. Psychological factors are also important in determining attention and concentration. Personal and social expectations, values, goals, emotional states and needs could have a crucial effect on the types of stimuli a person attends to.

Information also needs to be focused on and stored for a short period while the sensory and perceptual processes are finalised. The **sensory register** (memory) holds different sensory modalities of information automatically for approximately two to three seconds because of neural impulses still being relayed to the brain (Westen 2002). This period is sufficient for sensation and for only the most basic perceptual interpretations. Thereafter, the sensory information needs to be transferred and actively stored in a temporary storage facility, or the sensations are lost forever, unless the sensory receptors are reactivated by identical stimuli. This implies that no percepts can be developed out of any sensations that are lost from the sensory register.

Perceptual organising and conceptual categorising of any unorganised sensations are prerequisites before the complex formation of percepts can be finalised. These percepts also need more elaborate symbolic interpretation and integration with social and cultural meaning systems, e.g. social conventions and language and value systems, as well as previous experiences stored in long-term memory. The effects of psychological and socio-cultural meaning systems on the perceptual process imply that percepts are not only physiological products, but can, to some extent, also be viewed as psychosocial constructs. As this construction process is a complex process, an active temporary storage mechanism is necessary while perceptual and conceptual processing takes place. The complexity of the perceptual information determines the time required for perceptual processing.

The required temporary storage facility is provided by **working memory** for approximately 30 seconds. It can last longer if the information is repeated several times (Westen 2002). There is an interaction process between working memory and long-term memory for the meaning and integration of these attributions to complete the perceptual process. The process is only finalised when the percepts have been adequately processed in working memory in order to be stored in long-term memory.

Working memory:
A temporary storage facility provided by working memory for approximately 5–10 seconds. Lasts longer if the stimulus is repeated.

Perceptual information in long-term memory manifests a stable or constant structure. This phenomenon, mentioned earlier and called perceptual constancy, provides psychological stability and security despite quite drastic changes in the sensory information that we sense. It enables us to experience our world as relatively stable and predictable, so that we can plan and execute our actions. Perceptual constancy applies to all sensory modalities.

Types of perception

We will focus on visual and auditory perception systems, where extensive research has already been carried out. Nevertheless, much of what is said about the principles of **form perception**, perceptual constancy and Day's theory for the explanation of visual illusions can be applied to most of the other senses.

Form perception:
The organisation of sensory experiences into meaningful shapes and patterns.

Visual perception

Most research on perception has been focused on visual perception. The predominance of the visual sensory system in perceptual research is also manifested in the trend sometimes to wrongly equate perception with vision. As most of our perceptual information about our environment originates from visual perception, this section is somewhat comprehensive in its scope.

Form perception

Form perception refers to the organisation of sensory experiences into meaningful shapes and patterns (Westen 2002). Visual, kinesthetic and tactile sensory information all play an important role in the perception of the form or shape of objects.

Contours (lines) in visual information enable the viewer to see shapes and patterns. The Gestalt psychologists were the first researchers to study the role of contours and the principles underlying the perceptual organisation of information. Although these principles also apply to other sensory systems, they are discussed within the context of vision, as most research has focused on this sensory system.

FIGURE 3.21:
Figure-ground
relationship

- **Figure-ground perception:** Perception is always in terms of a figure in relation to a background. Contours enable people to distinguish automatically between a figure and its background, e.g. words (figure) against a white page (background). In some situations, the figure and ground can be reversible, as seen in Figure 3.21.

There are also other principles of visual organisation of information that were detected by the Gestalt psychologists. The following are examples of some of these principles:

- **Similarity:** Similar elements of information are grouped together. See Figure 3.22 (a), below.
- **Proximity:** Objects close to each other are grouped together. See Figure 3.22 (b), below.
- **Good continuity:** Smooth flowing patterns or continuous forms are more easily perceived than disrupted patterns or disrupted lines. See Figure 3.22 (c), below.
- **Simplicity:** Existing patterns in information are combined as simply as possible to identify two or more shapes or objects. See Figure 3.22 (d), below.
- **Closure:** Incomplete patterns or shapes are perceived as complete. See Figure 3.22 (e), below. This applies to both physical lines and subjective contours.

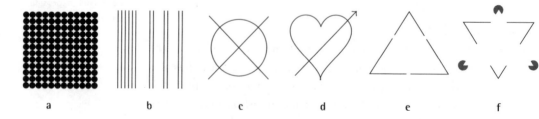

a   b   c   d   e   f

FIGURE 3.22: Gestalt principles for the visual organisation of sensory information
SOURCE: WESTEN 2002: P. 140

Besides identifying the basic features of objects using the Gestalt laws, we often use these basic images or shapes to scan and identify more complex symbols or objects among other diverse objects or symbol types. To do this quickly, in less than a second, we have to combine certain basic shapes that characterise that symbol or object.

According to the **recognition by components theory** of Biederman (1987, 1990), shapes of symbols and objects are categorised by breaking them down into a few elementary component images called geons (geometric icons). These geometric shapes, and the way the icons are arranged, constitute an 'alphabet' of standard shapes that are matched with familiar images stored in memory. A geon or combinations of geons enables a viewer to identify images or symbols in less than a second. That is why fast-forwarding a videotape for 20 seconds can provide sufficient meaningful information for the viewer to decide whether or not to watch the whole video. Recognition-by-components also explains the phenomenon of scanning the unknown contents of a book in order to obtain an overview, or learning to do speed reading while maintaining comprehension of the content that has been read.

Recognition by components theory: Theory that categorises the shapes of symbols and objects by breaking them down into a few elementary component images called geons (geometric icons), constituting an 'alphabet' of standard shapes that are matched with familiar images stored in memory.

Spatial perception

Spatial perception refers to the ability to perceive the environment in a three-dimensional way, in order to position ourselves in space and the objects relative to the viewer. The image registered on the retina is two-dimensional, but we interpret spatial information in the visual cortex in a three-dimensional way. Although three-dimensional perception relies mainly on vision, we also rely on hearing, the vestibular sense and kinesthesis to provide information on the three-dimensional characteristics of space. In the visual perception of space, the viewer focuses on depth or distance and direction, using a variety of cues from one or both eyes. Visual artists are skilled in using both types of cues to create the impression of three-dimensional space in their paintings.

Monocular cues are cues that only require visual information from one eye. Monocular cues are not only of innate origin, but can also be acquired through cultural learning processes (Berry *et al.* 1992). A viewer can utilise one cue or a combination of the following monocular cues to perceive three-dimensional space (Coren *et al.* 1994; Schiffman 1996; Westen 2002):

Monocular cues: Spatial cues that only require visual information from one eye.

- **Interposition:** When one object partially obscures another object, the complete object is seen as closer and the obscured one is seen as more distant. See Figure 3.23 (a) on page 97.
- **Elevation:** The horizon is conventionally viewed as vertically 'higher' than the foreground in a person's visual field. The difference in

elevation of objects between the foreground and the horizon is used as an indication of distance. Any objects appearing 'lower' are perceived to be closer, while those that are 'higher' in the viewer's visual field are perceived to be further away. See Figure 3.23 (b), opposite.

- **Linear perspective:** The point where apparent parallel lines seem to be maximally 'divergent' is viewed as the closest to the viewer, while the point where the lines are maximally 'convergent' is seen as the furthest away from the viewer. Linear perspective applies to both the horizontal and the vertical plane for the three dimensions of objects in the visual field. See Figure 3.23 (c), opposite.

- **Texture gradient:** Textured surfaces – e.g. cobblestones or the gravel in a gravel road – seem to be coarser nearest to the viewer, while progressively becoming finer at greater distances from the viewer. See Figure 3.23 (d), opposite.

- **Shading and lighting:** A viewer assumes that light shines from a certain angle on an object. Therefore, the section of an object that is closer to the angle of the light ray is viewed as brighter and nearer, while the section furthest away from the angle of light is viewed as dimmer and consequently further away from the light source. Brighter objects are also seen as nearer the viewer, while dimmer objects are seen as further away. Differences in brightness in reflected light from hollow entities provide depth cues. See both Figures 3.23 (e), opposite.

- **Relative size:** If two objects known to be of similar size appear to be different in size, the larger one is seen as closer and the smaller one is perceived to be further away. See Figure 3.23 (f), opposite.

- **Motion parallax:** When an observer moves – e.g. a passenger in a train looking out of the window – images of nearby objects cross the visual field at a faster speed than objects further away. In addition, objects below the visual focus point outside the train will be perceived to travel in the opposite direction to the train, while objects above the visual focus point seem to travel in the same direction. See Figure 3.23 (g), opposite.

- **Accommodation of the lens:** The lens muscles of the eye have to contract minimally for distant objects, but maximally for very close objects. See Figure 3.23 (h), opposite.

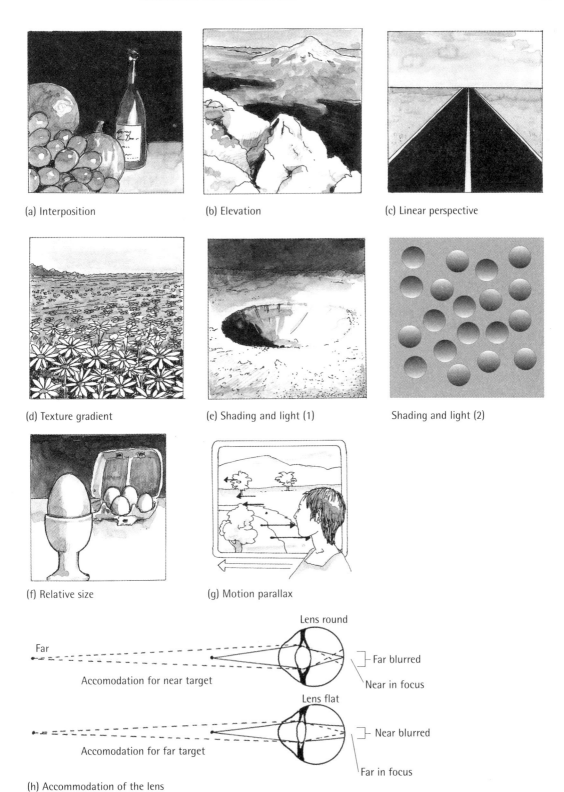

(a) Interposition

(b) Elevation

(c) Linear perspective

(d) Texture gradient

(e) Shading and light (1)

Shading and light (2)

(f) Relative size

(g) Motion parallax

(h) Accommodation of the lens

Figure 3.23: Monocular cues used in spatial perception.

SOURCES: COREN *et al.* 1994: P. 70; COREN 2002: P. 331; WEITEN 2001: P. 150

Binocular cues:
Visual spatial
cues sensesed by
using both eyes.

We also make use of **binocular cues** that are physically innate. Like other visual sensory cells, the binocular cells in the visual cortex require environmental stimulation early in life in order to function normally. Sensory information from both eyes is essential for binocular cues to provide three-dimensional percepts. The two most important binocular cues are retinal disparity and convergence.

Retinal disparity: This innate depth cue is also known as stereopsis (Coren *et al.* 1994). As the eyes view an object, they are horizontally separate from each other. The images registered on the two retinas are therefore slightly different. This disparity is maximal for close objects and minimal for distant ones. The binocular cells in the primary visual cortex compare the disparate information and provide a distance interpretation of the percepts.

Eye convergence: The eyes are turned slightly towards each other in order for the retinal image to be focused on the fovea for optimal depth perception. The more the eyes converge, the closer the object. Minimal convergence is required for distant objects.

Perceptual constancy in vision

Perceptual constancy in the visual system provides important cues for psychological stability and security, despite quite drastic changes in the retinal images we experience. The real environment, as it activates the sensory organs, is vastly different to the perceived environment. Under specific conditions, perceptual constancy may not be obtained, e.g. the hue and brightness of an item of clothing in certain types of fluorescent light. Mostly, however, perceptual constancy is maintained in the way we experience our world. There are four important types of visual constancy: size, shape, colour and movement (Coren *et al.* 1994; Schiffman 1996; Westen 2002).

- **Size:** Objects are perceived to be the same size, even though the size of the retinal image changes. A person walking away from the viewer is seen to remain the same size although the retinal image progressively becomes smaller.
- **Shape:** Objects are perceived to be the same shape, even though the shape of the retinal image changes continually. When you watch someone playing soccer, the shape of the retinal images changes drastically, but that player is seen to remain the same person (i.e. maintain the same shape) and stays identifiable in comparison with the other soccer players.
- **Colour:** Objects are perceived, within certain limits, to be the same colour in terms of hue, brightness and saturation, even though the sensory information from the retinal image may be vastly different.

The colour of a person's clothes is seen to remain the same, even when he or she enters a dimly lit room.

- **Movement:** When we detect a moving object in the environment, we fix our vision on it. To be able to fix on a specific object, we need to maintain perceptual constancy in the percept of the moving object.

Visual perception of motion

The perception of moving objects is crucial for one's effective psychological and physical functioning in the environment. Although the perception of motion relies mainly on vision, we also rely on hearing, the vestibular sense and kinesthesis to provide information on the three-dimensional characteristics of motion.

The visual perception of motion starts with graded action potentials in certain ganglion cells in the retina called motion detectors (Coren *et al.* 1994; Schiffman 1996; Westen 2002). These motion detectors have large receptive fields, are concentrated outside the fovea on the retinal periphery, and tend to respond or to stop responding very quickly to motion or lack of motion in an object. The graded potentials from the ganglion cells are relayed to the thalamus and, from there, to the primary areas in the visual cortex where basic form and colour is decoded. From here, neural information is relayed along the information pathway for motion that leads to the medial area of the temporal lobe, where speed and visual detail are interpreted. It eventually reaches the parietal lobe for spatial decoding of the moving object.

According to the two-system model of motion perception (Gregory 1978), visual perception of motion requires the co-ordination and comparison of both visual and kinesthetic information on movement sensations. Sensory information on any movement by the perceiver has to be coordinated with information about any sensation of motion of an object, before conclusions can be made whether an object is moving or only appears to be moving (Schiffman 1996).

The two movement-detection systems are the image-retina system and the eye-head movement system. In the image-retina system, a stationary viewer can detect movement in an object if the image of the object moves across the retina. Detecting movement across the retina in the retinal image of an object, while there are no kinesthetic indications of movement by the muscles of the eyes, head or body, indicates real movement of an object. In the eye-head movement system, a combination of an absence of movement in the retinal image of an object while kinesthetic information from the body muscles shows the presence of movement is indicative of real movement by an object. The viewer visually stabilises the image of the object when tracking it, while the viewer and the object are both moving.

Any detection of movement in the retinal image of an object and in the kinesthetic information from the eye, head or body indicates no real movement by an object. In this case, the viewer's own movement is inducing movement in the retinal image of the object, e.g. by moving his or her head. The presence of movement sensations in both sensory systems is therefore indicative of no real movement. A detection of movement sensations in either the visual or the kinesthetic sensory system, while the other system senses no movement, is an indication of real movement by an object in the environment (Gregory 1978; Schiffman 1996).

Perceptual illusions in form and motion

The phenomenon of perceptual constancy indicates that a discrepancy often exists between our sensory information and our perceptions, the latter being interpretations of our sensory experiences. Our perceptions are often illusionary in nature, as we need to maintain stability in our experiencing of the world. It is therefore important for us to be critical about our interpretation of our sensory experiences (especially in inter-personal or inter-group situations), as we might misperceive the facts or intentions of what people are doing or saying, because we might wish to maintain a fixed point of view on a specific matter.

Psychological researchers have discovered various types of form and motion illusions based on visual sensory information. These optical illusions tend to be habitual – even after people have been informed that they are sensory distortions. Optical illusions, as in the case of various other psychological illusions, are part of daily life. Different living contexts influence the type of perceptual learning processes people are exposed to. The specific nature of the learning experiences people have had make them susceptible to specific types of visual illusions.

Day (1972) provided a general explanation for most visual illusions of form and motion. Perceptual constancy requires that visual corrections are automatically made in the changing sensory information from the retina about an object. These corrections are based on visual spatial cues. However, if the retinal image of an object remains constant, any correction of the retinal information will lead to a visual illusion. Day's explanation of illusions implies that we can easily fall prey to all types of psychological illusions if we remain fixed in our expectations of people or events based on our previous experience of them.

Form illusions:
Various optical discrepancies between the perceived characteristics of visual forms and their real physical attributes.

Form illusions: A variety of optical form illusions have been reported (Coren *et al.* 1994; Louw & Edwards 1993; Schiffman 1996). The Möller-Lyer, Ponzo, horizontal-vertical and Sander parallelogram illusions have often been used in empirical research on the variables that affect visual illusions in general. Visual illusions are still perceived in an illusionary way even though viewers are provided incontrovertable evidence regarding the nature of the illusion. In the Möller-Lyer illusions the length of the vertical lines are all actually identical (see Figure 3.24 (a), below). The horizontal lines of the Ponzo illusion and the vertical and horizontal lines of the horizontal-vertical illusion, as well as the left and right sides of the Sander parallelogram, are actually of identical length if measured (see Figures 3.24 (b), (c) and (d) respectively, below). Some logically impossible figures based on visual illusions have also been included (see examples in Figures 3.24 (e)). In the impossible figures, certain contradictory elements in the drawings prevent them from being a portrayal of real objects. The same principle applies to 'impossible art', for example Escher's paintings of continuous motion and water flowing uphill.

SOURCE: STERNBERG 1995: P. 186

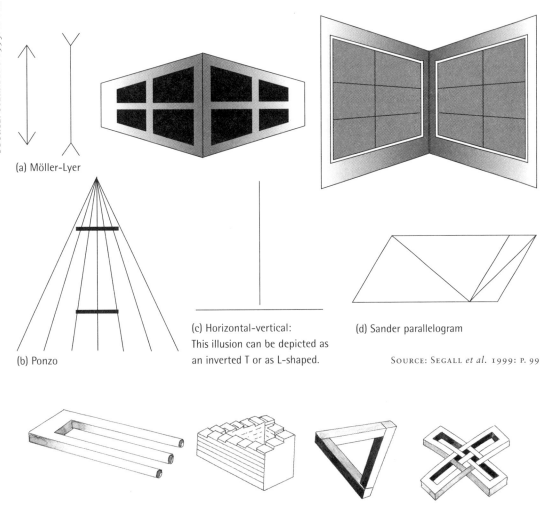

(a) Möller-Lyer

(b) Ponzo

(c) Horizontal-vertical:
This illusion can be depicted as
an inverted T or as L-shaped.

(d) Sander parallelogram

SOURCE: SEGALL *et al.* 1999: P. 99

(e) Impossible figures

FIGURE 3.24: Visual form illusions

SOURCE: WEITEN 2001: P. 173

Visual illusions have been closely related to the type of ecological context we live in and the nature of the socio-cultural and perceptual learning experiences we are exposed to. As these conditions change, we may become less susceptible to these illusions in an increasingly familiar ecological context. However, we still experience susceptibility to other types of illusions when we move to less familiar or totally unfamiliar contexts, necessitating new perceptual learning in the new eco-cultural environment.

Visual illusions, depth perception and cultural context

Much interest has been expressed by researchers in the role of culture in determining susceptibility to visual illusions (Segall *et al.* 1999). To what extent does culture influence perception? Do cultural differences determine the ability for three-dimensional perception? If so, can these differences be changed over time?

Hudson (1960, 1967) researched some aspects of pictorial depth perception using a test that he constructed at the National Institute for Personnel Research in Johannesburg. The pictures were similar to the one shown in Figure 3.25, below. He carried out extensive research on participants from different cultural groups who varied in age, educational level and job type. He found small but significant differences in representational depth perception between participants from developing and developed communities. These findings were supported by research carried out by other researchers (Deregowski 1972). However, the research methodologies on which these findings were based contained certain flaws, as was later indicated by Hagan and Jones (1978).

SOURCE: WEITEN 2001: P. 151

FIGURE 3.25: Cultural influences in pictorial depth perception

Pictorial depth representation is closely associated with perceptual inference cues found in developed countries. People in these cultures show a susceptibility to visual illusions in a 'carpentered' eco-cultural environment, where large buildings manifesting sharp angles are usually found. Segall *et al.* (1966) studied the Möller-Lyer, horizontal-vertical and the Sander parallelogram illusions in order to determine the level of susceptibility to these illusions in different cultures. They found substantial cross-cultural differences between participants living in Western 'carpentered' cultures and participants from other cultures who were minimally exposed to a 'carpentered' environment. As expected, Westerners were more susceptible to the Möller-Lyer and parallelogram illusions because of the sharp angular appearances of the figures, which implied a need to correct for depth perspective. Participants from the non-Western cultures were more susceptible than Western participants to the horizontal-vertical illusion. The perceptual learning of these participants took place in a very different eco-cultural context. They were more exposed to living in open plains where correction for foreshortening of distance and for the effect of an open horizon on the vertical line was necessary in daily life. These people had few experiences of large sharp-angular objects in their immediate environments. The researchers concluded that people learn perceptual inference habits that facilitate adaptation to a cultural group's ecological environment.

The Segall *et al.* (1966) study spurred a number of other studies on illusion susceptibility across various cultures in the developing and developed world (Segall *et al.* 1999). The latter authors concluded that subsequent research generally confirmed the hypothesis that illusion susceptibility is a reflection of learned habits of perceptual inference, which are ecologically valid for effective functioning of the people living in a specific eco-cultural environment (Segall *et al.* 1999). The cues used in pictorial depth representation on a two-dimensional plane are only conventional signs and can be learned by people from other cultures, even though, in the past, their eco-cultural environment may have shaped their perceptual habits very differently from the environment in which they are presently living. This implies that people can learn to perceive differently if life in new eco-cultural contexts requires them to do so.

Visual steepness, size and distance illusions that have been reported in the literature and have aroused much interest are:

- the **steepness illusion** in perceiving geographical slant;
- the effect of an unfamiliar context in creating illusions;
- the **moon illusion**; and
- the **Ames distorted room illusion** (Coren *et al.* 1994; Schiffman 1996; Sternberg 1995).

Steepness illusion:
The illusion that a slope is steeper than it really is.

Moon illusion:
Tendency to see the moon as much larger on the horizon than at its zenith.

Ames distorted room illusion:
A room built in such a way as to create a size illusion based on a distortion of spatial cues.

- **Steepness illusion:** We tend to view a slope as steeper than it really is, while the kinesthetic estimate of the steepness of a slope is more accurate (Weiten 2001). For instance, Profitt *et al.* (1995) found that kinesthetic estimates of a slope were most accurate, that visual ratings were less accurate, and that verbal estimates (which included visualising) least accurate. According to Profitt *et al.* (1995), visual estimation is focused on the anticipated challenge a slope would be for a climber. Therefore, from an adaptive point of view, a person would rather overestimate a slope than underestimate it. However, kinesthetic information is important in determining the progress a climber is making. From an adaptive point of view, kinesthetic estimation should be as close as possible to the real challenge a slope would be for a climber.

Unfamiliar perceptual context illusions: Illusions created by unfamiliar contexts.

- **Unfamiliar perceptual context illusions:** Unfamiliar contexts have a radical effect on perceptual constancy and, therefore, on the creation of visual illusions. Turnbull (1961) reported that he was accompanied by a pygmy (who had lived his whole life in a dense jungle) onto the open plains for the first time. The pygmy had no experience of open plains and of long distances in the jungle. When the pygmy saw the distant buffaloes (which pygmies usually viewed at a maximum distance of 30 metres), they appeared as insects to him. As Turnbull drove closer to the buffalo, the 'insects' became 'small' buffalo that were magically growing larger and larger until they were eventually their 'normal' size to the pygmy. Viewing an object in an unfamiliar context can elicit the breakdown of learned perceptual constancy and evoke strange interpretations and anxiety from the viewer.

- **Moon illusion:** We tend to see the moon as much larger on the horizon than at its zenith, i.e. in the middle of the sky (Figure 3.26, opposite). The retinal image of the moon is the same whether viewed on the horizon or at the zenith. The difference in the perceived size of the moon can be attributed to the presence or absence of distance cues for the viewer. When the moon is at the horizon, we use such distance cues – e.g. linear perspective, texture and other familiar objects – to correct the retinal image for distance. At its zenith, however, there are no distance cues to correct for distance. So while distance cues are used to correct the retinal image of the moon on the horizon, the retinal image of the moon at its zenith remains uncorrected.

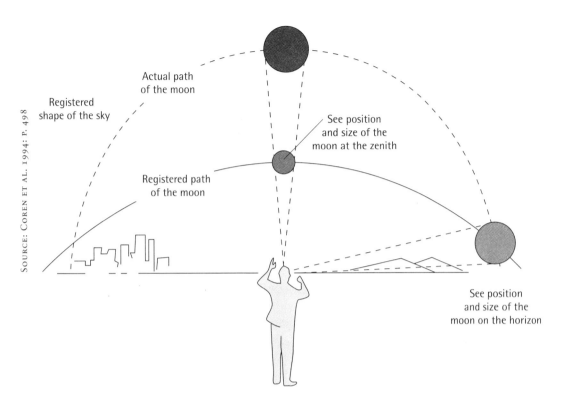

SOURCE: COREN ET AL. 1994: P. 498

FIGURE 3.26: Explanation of the moon illusion

- **Ames distorted room illusion:** The Ames distorted room is a room built in such a way as to create a size illusion. This type of room has been extensively used in research on visual illusions and visual problems, and in the film industry to create impressions of dwarfs or giants. A visual context is created in such a way that visual cues for distance and space are distorted. These cues are utilised erroneously to correct the retinal image for distance and three-dimensional space, resulting in illusions of size concerning the perceived objects (see Figure 3.27, overleaf). Being informed that it is a distorted room does not change the illusion. The only way to adapt perceptually to these distortions is to use kinesthetic indications in combination with visual information – e.g. using a rod to touch the participant, or walking inside the room to correctly judge the distance of the person in that room.

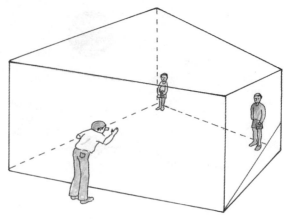

Source: Weiten 2001: p. 155

FIGURE 3.27: The Ames distorted room

Besides form illusions, we also experience visual motion illusions. These refer to apparent movement or 'movement' that does not really take place. Various visual motion illusions have been reported (Coren *et al.* 1994; Schiffman 1996; Sternberg 1995). The main apparent movement illusions that will be discussed here are autokinetic movement, stroboscopic movement and induced movement.

Autokinetic movement:
Phenomenon in which a small dot viewed against a large, plain background of a different colour or a small light source viewed in the dark seems to move in an irregular way and at different speeds after a while.

Stroboscopic movement:
Also called the phi phenomenon. Illusion created when two stationary lights close to each other are alternately flashed on and off at a certain rate, giving the impression that there is only one light alternately moving from one position to the other.

Induced movement:
Illusion of movement of a stationary object created by the movement of contextual elements.

- **Autokinetic movement:** A small dot viewed against a large, plain background of a different colour, especially a contrasting colour, seems to move if it is stared at long enough. This also applies at night. A small light source viewed in the dark seems to move in an irregular way and at different speeds after a while. This happens because the eye muscles automatically start moving slightly after a time of fixed viewing, in order to prevent visual adaptation and due to fatigue. As there are no spatial cues in the background to compensate for the eye movement, an illusion of 'real' movement is perceived in the light source.

- **Stroboscopic movement:** This is also known as the phi phenomenon. When two stationary lights close to each other are alternately flashed on and off at a certain rate, an illusion is created that there is only one light alternately moving from one position to the other. The stroboscopic movement effect is used in neon advertisements and in films to create an illusion of movement. This is usually obtained at a rate of 24 images per second in a film.

- **Induced movement:** The perception of movement is highly influenced by the spatial context within which it occurs. We have all seen the moon to be 'moving,' while the clouds are 'stationary'. The moving object (e.g. the clouds), called the inductor object, is perceived as stationary, while a stationary object (e.g. the moon), called the inductee object, is perceived as moving. An inductor object is erroneously viewed as constant because it has a dominant contextual influence, while the inductee object is seen as variable and therefore the moving object. For example, as Figure 3.28, below, indicates, a light surrounded by a large luminous rectangle that is moving to the right of the viewer will be seen in a dark room to 'move' to the left while the rectangle remains 'stationary'.

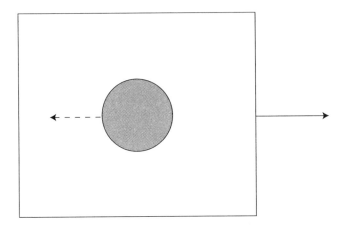

SOURCE: SCHIFFMAN 1996: P. 265

FIGURE 3.28: Induced movement and spatial context effects

The role of visual perception in written language and communication

In our modern multicultural world, visual symbols are often used in public signboards and notices. Visual perception plays an increasingly important role in mass communication, in cognitive (intellectual) problem solving and in education, to name but a few examples. It is therefore important to understand how language symbols and written text are visually perceived.

The perception of written or printed information during reading is a rather complex process. The following account of this process should therefore be seen as somewhat oversimplified in order to describe the main features concisely. Reading involves both multimodal (multiple sensory), afferent (perceptual-receptive) and efferent (motor-expressive) processes. This discussion focuses only on the visual perceptual aspects of reading a text written from left to right in a Western-type language system and alphabet, as most research is focused on a Western-type language system.

The focus in this section will be on silent reading of a written text, as well as the visual analysis of a written text and the synthesis of the letters into meaningful graphemes – a combination of letters corresponding to a phoneme, a basic speech sound, that will be discussed in the auditory perception section (Rayner *et al.* 2001). In addition, this section will include the combination of graphemes into meaningful words and the syntactical integration of words into meaningful sentences according to grammatical rules. The process of learning to read and the integration of visual perception with auditory and motor processes, as well as reading comprehension, will not be discussed in this chapter.

When a person starts reading, it is important that the written information is focused on the fovea in the retina as clearly as possible, as the fovea is most sensitive to information from the central visual field (Westen 2002). The cornea, iris and lens are very important structures in the eye in determining a perceiver's visual acuity, in the process of focusing visual information on the fovea.

From the retina to the visual cortex, decoding takes place in terms of the hierarchical system of feature detectors: simple, complex and hyper-complex detectors (Hubel & Wiesel 1979). Feature detectors receive input from the neurons and ganglion cells in the retina and require at the highest detection level that letters, words, numbers and punctuation marks exhibit only certain combinations of features, e.g. a particular form, size and sequential pattern.

Visual sensations of language are processed on the subcortical level as well as on the cortical level in the visual cortex and secondary areas of various lobes, and in certain tertiary association areas that include various multimodal neural pathways (Coren *et al.* 1994). The function of the tectopulvinar neural system is to ensure optimal visual acuity during reading, as well as information for the coordination and guidance of eye movements during text perception. This system is also linked to the neurons of the reticular formation for the regulation of the sensory arousal level on the subcortical level and in the secondary association areas of the visual cortex. The tectopulvinar pathway therefore prepares the visual cortex for the decoding of the patterns of neural impulses activated by the reading material, by increasing visual alertness and activating the memories in the visual association areas.

The functions of the geniculo-striate neural system seem to be the provision of detailed information on the recognition of visual forms, patterns and even the colours of the words and sentences being read (Rayner *et al.* 2001). Efferent (feedback) pathways from the visual cortex to the lateral geniculate nucleus also exist, in order to select information for cortical decoding by enhancing awareness of certain relevant information being read, while suppressing awareness of other less important information in the construction of a particular sentence at a specific position in the text.

After the primary area, the decoding of reading material takes place along two important multimodal pathways: the 'what' and the 'where' pathways. The 'what' pathway from the occipital to the temporal lobe determines the visual details about the semantic meaning of letters or graphemes, the patterns of words, and punctuation of the text (Rayner *et al.* 2001). These details are integrated to provide more comprehensive semantic meaning to the complex pattern of words and sentences. The 'where' pathway to the parietal lobe provides information on the spatial location and sequencing of letters, numbers, words and sentences in the text (Rayner *et al.* 2001). During the 'what' and 'where' processing of the text, information from the left and right visual fields can be integrated in the tertiary areas for language by means of the corpus callosum, which connects the left and right cerebral hemispheres (Jordaan & Jordaan 2000). Multimodal integration of all the occipital, temporal and parietal information takes place in tertiary association areas between the occipital, parietal and temporal lobes. The angular gyrus in the left cerebral hemisphere is an example of a high-level integrative area for language perception (Louw & Edwards 1993). The final semantic and syntactical integration of the relevant perceptual information related to understanding what is read is carried out in the tertiary association areas for language.

Social and cultural meaning systems provide psychological contexts for comprehensive interpretation of textual information in terms of social attitudes towards the content being read, norms determining what is acceptable reading material, central beliefs about what can be accepted as true and valid in the reading material, and normative guidelines for evaluating whether the contents have a positive or negative influence on the reader's views and beliefs (Mboya 1999; Segall *et al.* 1999). Ideas expressed in written text format are very influential in persuading readers to change their views on the topics under discussion. This influential power dimension often has important implications for interpersonal and inter-group or inter-cultural communication and relationships.

Besides the visual aspects of written language, we also perceive visual signals in terms of body 'language' in attempting to understand interpersonal messages. We attend to and 'read' a person's non-verbal 'messages' to us, e.g. their posture, their approaching towards or distancing from us, their making or avoiding of eye contact, grimacing, frowning, indicating surprise, or showing signs of shock. The impressions we obtain from body language are compared with what we perceive from their spoken words. The visual non-verbal messages are compared to the spoken messages to determine what the nature of the real messages are that the communication produces, e.g. vague or conflicting messages, or aggressive, rejecting attitudes towards the listener, or clear, affirmative and congruent messages expressed towards the listener/viewer.

Auditory perception

The auditory perceptual channel provides us with our second largest source of information. We are able to hear something even when we are unable to see it. Auditory perception is a very important distance sensory channel and an inherent part of our daily lives in terms of communication, education and for an appreciation of music.

Location of sounds

Localisation means identifying the location of sound in space in terms of direction, distance and movement. There are two main categories of spatial cues used in auditory localisation: monaural or single ear cues, and binaural cues, where both ears are needed (Coren *et al.* 1994; Schiffman 1996).

In general, the loudness level or changes in the loudness of a stimulus can be used as **monaural location cues** for distance, direction and motion perception. An important monaural spatial cue is known as the Doppler shift (Schiffman 1996). It refers to the changes in pitch by a moving object as experienced by a listener. When an object moves, the sound waves in front of it are more compressed than in a static position, while the sound waves behind it are less compressed. This phenomenon elicits a higher pitch than usual by an approaching object, followed by a sudden lower pitch than usual by a passing object. Spectators at a grand prix initially hear the high pitch of a car's engine as it approaches the listener, followed by a sudden much lower pitch as the car passes them.

Monaural location cues: Cues that only require auditory information from one ear to locate sounds during distance, direction and motion perception.

Both humans and animals make use of **binaural spatial cues** (Schiffman 1996). The difference in time for a sound to reach each ear is an indication of direction. The same applies to the phase of the sound wave. At one ear, it may be at the most compressed phase, but when it is received at the other ear, it is in a different phase of the sound wave. This also applies to differences in the pitch, timbre and loudness of a sound. Echolocation cues are also used both by humans and animals to locate objects and to orient themselves in a situation. Sounds elicited during walking, or by a deliberate act (e.g. tapping with a walking stick by people experiencing visual problems), are reflected off objects and used by people to determine the presence of objects, animals or other people, as well as their distance or direction, and sometimes their movement.

Binaural spatial cues: Auditory spatial cues sensed by using both ears.

The role of auditory perception in speech

Hearing and speaking are interdependent aspects of human communication. Hearing provides an auditory feedback channel in the process of learning to speak a language competently. If auditory perception is seriously impeded, a person is obliged to utilise other sensory systems, e.g. visual, somatosensory and kinesthetic perception, to provide a feedback channel for learning to speak a language and to communicate effectively. Auditory perception of spoken language is based on the perception of basic speech sounds called phonemes. These basic sounds mostly comprise consonants and vowel sounds (Sternberg 1995). A phoneme is the smallest auditory component of spoken language. Some phonemes are combined to form a word, and a large number of phonemes in a systematic sequential pattern make up a sentence. The number of phonemes used varies from language to language. Some languages use as few as 20 phonemes, while others use as many as 60. English speakers use approximately 40 phonemes in speech, depending on where they live (Schiffman 1996).

Auditory neural impulses concerning speech are decoded in the temporal lobe, where the phonemes are analysed. Thereafter, comprehensive interpretation of the patterns of spoken (phonetic) information takes place in Wernicke's language area in the left cerebral hemisphere. The corresponding brain area in the right cerebral hemisphere is involved in the interpretation of non-verbal sounds, including those paralingual sounds that accompany speech (Jordaan & Jordaan 2000). Social and cultural meaning systems provide psychological contexts for a more comprehensive interpretation of speech, and indicate power relationships, attitudes, beliefs and values, during interpersonal and inter-group or inter-cultural communication.

According to Massaro's speech stage theory, speech sounds are analysed into their constituent phonemes. In the following stage, these phonemes are subsequently analysed for patterns of meaning (Massaro 1987). Liberman and Mattingly (1985) argue that a perceiver does not only rely on the analysis of what is heard. In their motor theory of speech perception, they state that speech perception depends both on what a speaker says and on what the listener infers the intention of the speaker to be. According to Pisoni *et al.*'s (1985) phonetic-refinement perception theory, phonetics provide cues for a progressive refinement of the possible alternative choices for the words being communicated to the listener, within the context of each sentence. The perceiver's previous phonetic experiences provide cues for the elimination of most of the alternative choices of each new word as the words are being spoken.

The context of the already identified words and the perceived expectations of the intended meaning by the speaker finalise the listener's choice of each probable word in a sentence as they are spoken.

Besides the phonetic aspects of language, we also perceive and analyse para-lingual sounds to understand a message. We attend to the 'punctuation' in the speech, e.g. pausing, exclaiming, shouting, whispering, emphasising, mumbling, or articulating slowly and clearly in a formal manner. The para-lingual aspects are compared to the phonetic aspects to determine whether the communication produces a vague, confusing, or conflicting message, or one that is clearly comprehensible, accurate and congruent to the listener. Visual and kinesthetic aspects of body language are also important, but are not discussed in this subsection of the chapter.

Researchers have been curious about the effects of subliminal auditory messages from audiotapes on people's psychological functioning. One recent study in this regard appears below.

Subliminal auditory perception, memory and self-esteem

Can the use of audiotapes during sleep assist a student in improving his or her memory of material significantly before a test or an exam? Can subtle subliminal messages on an instrumental music self-help audiotape improve one's self-confidence and general self-esteem significantly? Subliminal auditory perception (subception) implies the processing of sensory information without a person being aware of these auditory subcepts. Subliminal self-help tapes are widely marketed for weight control, improvement of sleep, memory, self-esteem, interpersonal skills and love relationships, to name but a few (Weiten 2001). In the majority of cases, little if any scientific validation of the value of these subliminal tapes is provided.

Greenwald *et al.* (1991) investigated certain commercially available tapes for the improvement of memory and self-esteem. Volunteers (full-time students and full-time employed people) who were interested in buying these audiotapes were involved as research participants. A total of 149 female and 88 male participants completed the one-month research project. Three different subliminal tapes for the improvement of memory and three different tapes for the enhancement of self-esteem (but not for both conditions) were obtained from different commercial organisations. The auditory content consisted of instrumental music or recorded sounds of nature.

Each participant was given a tape to which a memory or self-esteem label had been randomly assigned. This implies that approximately half of the tapes had intentionally been mislabelled. No participant could identify the purpose of his or her tape purely by listening to it, as the tapes only contained instrumental music or natural sounds. Participants who received a memory tape labelled as a 'self-esteem' tape served as an experimental subject for the memory tape and a control subject for the 'self-esteem' tape. In the same way, those who received the self-esteem tape labelled as a 'memory' tape served as experimental subjects for the self-esteem tape and control subjects for the 'memory' tape.

The participants were tested using a battery of established memory and self-esteem tests before receiving the tapes. They were retested after one month. The independent variables were the real purpose of the tapes and the nature of the label on the tape: accurately labelled or mislabelled. The dependent variables were the memory and self-esteem improvement scores between the testing and re-testing sessions, as well as the participants' beliefs about whether they had improved or not.

The researchers found that self-esteem was not significantly enhanced by the self-esteem audiotapes. In testing for the extent of self-esteem improvement above the memory scores (the latter being the control condition), it was found that the memory improvement scores were actually higher than the self-esteem scores. It should have been the other way round for the experimental condition if the self-esteem audiotapes had really worked. In testing for the extent of memory improvement (the experimental condition) above the self-esteem scores (the control condition), only negligible differences were found between those participants who listened to the memory tapes and those who did not (the control condition).

Despite these objective findings, approximately half of the participants believed that the tapes were functioning as well as they were expected to function. This is indicative of the expectancy effect of a novel experience. It sometimes happens that people believe a new programme for solving a personal problem like weight control or memory improvement is actually working for them, even if it does not produce the significant results claimed by the promoters of the product.

The authors concluded that the six subliminal audiotapes they investigated were not effective in improving either memory or self-esteem. Of course, this research needs to be replicated with other subliminal audiotapes with music and verbal subliminal messages for the same and different treatment conditions, as well as for a variety of other audiotape users.

Summary

Initially we distinguished between sensation (the physical experience of information from the external world) and perception (internally making sense of these sensations).

Sensation

The chapter discussed psychophysics, which focuses on the relationship between the physical characteristics of a stimulus impinging on our sensory organs and the perceived characteristics that we experience. Thresholds define the degree of our awareness of a stimulus, while signal detection theory studies how we deal with background 'noise'.

Certain sensory processes are common across all sensory systems, namely transduction, sensory coding and sensory adaptation. The chapter then went on to discuss the various human senses.

The visual sensory system is the most important for humans. We discussed the qualities of light, and how the eye detects them, including the anatomy and physiology of the eye. We looked at the neural pathways to the brain, and how the brain interprets visual information, and discussed explanatory theories for colour vision.

We then moved on to the auditory sensory system, discussing the qualities of sound, the anatomy and physiology of the ear, neural pathways to the brain and the way in which the brain interprets auditory information. We looked at hearing problems, and some explanatory theories for sound perception.

We then looked in less detail at the chemical (taste and smell), somatosensory (pressure, heat and pain), proprioceptive (balance and three-dimensional spatial orientation) and kinesthetic (movement) sensory systems.

Perception

Initially, we distinguished between non-focused and focssed attention and concentration. We then pointed out that perception is closely linked to memory, especially the sensory register and working memory. We then discussed the different types of perception.

Under visual perception, we discussed form perception, using Gestalt principles, and recognition-by-components theory, monocular and binocular cues that determine visual perception of space, perceptual constancy and visual perception of motion. We then looked at form and motion illusions.

Under auditory perception, we looked at various monaural and binaural location cues that determine our auditory perception of space. We then examined various explanatory theories that have proposed a link between auditory perception and speech, namely speech stage theory, motor theory of speech perception and the phonetic refinement perception theory.

Further reading

Bar, M. & Biederman, I. (1998) Subliminal visual priming. *Psychological Science*, 9, pp. 464–9.

Berry, J.W., Poortinga, Y.H., Segall, M.H. & Dasen, P.R. (1992) *Cross-cultural Psychology: Research and Applications*. New York: Cambridge University Press.

Biederman, I. (1987) Recognition by components: A theory of human image understanding. *Psychological Review*, 94, pp. 115–47.

Biederman, I. (1990) Higher-level vision. In D.N. Osherson, S.M. Kosslyn *et al.* (eds), *Visual Cognition and Action: An Invitation to Cognitive Science*, Vol. 2. Cambridge, Mass.: MIT Press, pp. 41–72.

Coren, S., Ward, L.M. & Enns, J.T. (1994) *Sensation and Perception*. New York: Harcourt Brace.

Day, R.H. (1972) Visual spatial illusions: A general explanation. *Science*, 1972, p. 175.

Deregowski, J.B. (1972) Pictorial perception and culture. *Scientific American*, 227(5), pp. 82–8.

DeValois, R.L. & DeValois, K. (1975) Neural coding of colour. In E.C. Carterette & M.P. Friedman (eds), *Handbook of Perception*. New York: Academic Press.

DeValois, R.L. & Jacobs, G.H. (1968) Primate colour vision. *Science*, 162, pp. 533–40.

Green, D.M. & Swets, J.A. (1966) *Signal Detection Theory and Psychophysics*. New York: Krieger.

Greenwald, A.G., Spangenberg, E.R., Pratkanis, A.R. & Eskenazi, J. (1991) Double-blind tests of subliminal self-help audiotapes. *Psychological Science*, 2, pp. 119–22.

Gregory, R.I. (1978) *Eye and Brain: The Psychology of Seeing*. New York: McGraw-Hill.

Hagan, M. & Jones, R. (1978) Cultural effects on pictorial perception: How many words is just one picture really worth? In R.D. Walk & H. Pick (eds), *Perception and Experience*. New York: Plenum Press.

Hubel, D.H. & Wiesel, T.N. (1959) Receptive fields of single neurons in the cat's striate cortex. *Journal of Physiology*, 148, pp. 574–91.

Hubel, D.H. & Wiesel, T.N. (1979) Brain mechanisms of vision. *Scientific American*, 241, pp. 150–62.

Hudson, W. (1960) Pictorial depth perception in sub-cultural groups in Africa. *Journal of Social Psychology*, 52, pp. 183–208.

Hudson, W. (1967) The study of the problem of pictorial perception among unacculturated groups. *International Journal of Psychology*, 2, pp. 89–107.

Jordaan, W. & Jordaan, J. (2000) *People in Context*. Johannesburg: Heinemann.

Liberman, A.M. & Mattingly, I.G. (1985) The motor theory of speech perception revised. *Cognition*, 21, pp. 1–36.

Louw, D.A. & Edwards, D.J.A. (1993) *Psychology: An Introduction for Students in Southern Africa*. Johannesburg: Lexicon.

Massaro, D.W. (1987) *Speech Perception by Ear and Eye: A Paradigm for Psychological Enquiry*. Hillsdale: Erlbaum.

Mboya, M.M. (ed.) (1999) *Culture and Self: Theory and Research from an African Perspective*. Pretoria: Illitha.

Melzack, R. (1993) Pain: Past, present and future. *Canadian Journal of Experimental Psychology*, 47, pp. 615–29.

Melzack, R. & Wall, P.D. (1965) Pain mechanisms: A new theory. *Science*, 150, pp. 971–9.

Merikle, P.M. & Daneman, M. (1998) Psychological investigations of unconscious perception. *Journal of Consciousness Studies*, 5, pp. 5–18.

Morris, J.S., Oehman, A. & Dolan, R.J. (1998) Conscious and unconscious emotional learning in the human amygdala. *Nature*, 393, pp. 467–70.

Pisoni, D.B., Nusbaum, H.C., Luce, P.A. & Slowiaczek, L.M. (1985) Speech perception, word recognition and the structure of the lexicon. *Speech Communication*, 4, pp. 75–95.

Pollnac, R.B. (1977) Illusion susceptibility and adaptation to the marine environment: Is the carpentered world hypothesis seaworthy? *International Journal of Cross-Cultural Psychology*, 8, pp. 425–33.

Proffitt, D.R., Bhalla, M., Gossweiler, R. & Midgett, J. (1995) Perceiving geographical slant. *Psychonomic Bulletin & Review*, 2, pp. 409–28.

Rayner, K., Foorman, B.R., Perfetti, C.A., Pesetsky, D. & Seidenberg, M.S. (2001) How psychological science informs the teaching of reading. *Psychological Science in the Public Interest: Supplement to Psychological Science*, 2(2), pp. 31–71.

Sahraie, A. Weiskrantz, L., Barbur, J.L., Simmons, A., Williams, S.C. & Brammer, M.J. (1997) Pattern of neuronal activity associated with conscious and unconscious processing of visual signals. *Proceedings of the National Academy of Sciences of the United States of America*, 94, pp. 9406–11.

Schiffman, H.R. (1996) *Sensation and Perception* (4th edition). New York: John Wiley.

Segall, M.H., Campbell, D.T. & Herskovitz, M.J. (1966) *Influence of Culture on Visual Perception*. New York: Bobbs-Merrill.

Segall, M.H., Dasen, P.R., Berry, J.W. & Poortinga, Y. (1999) *Human Behavior in Global Perspective: An Introduction to Cross-cultural Psychology* (2nd edition). Boston: Allyn & Bacon.

Sternberg, R.J. (1995) *In Search of the Human Mind*. New York: Harcourt Brace.

Stevens, S.S. (1960) *Handbook of Experimental Psychology*. New York: John Wiley.

Stevens, S.S. (1961) Psychophysics of sensory function. In W. Rosenblith (ed.), *Sensory Communication*. Cambridge, Mass.: MIT Press, pp. 1–33.

Swets, J.A. (1992) The science of choosing the right decision threshold in high-stakes diagnostics. *American Psychologist*, 47, pp. 522–32.

Teghtsoonian, R. (1971) On the exponents in Steven's law and the constant in Ekman's law. *Psychological Review*, 78(1), pp. 71–80.

Turnbull, C. (1961) Some observations regarding the experiences and behavior of the Bambuti pygmies. *American Journal of Psychology*, 74, pp. 304–8.

Weiten, W. (2001) *Psychology: Themes and Variations* (5th edition). London: Wadsworth/Thomson Learning.

Westen, D. (2002) *Psychology: Brain, Behavior, and Culture* (3rd edition). New York: John Wiley.

Whalen, P.J., Rauch, S.L., Etcoff, N.L., McInerney, S.C., Lee, M.B. & Jenike, M.A. (1998) Masked presentations of emotional facial expressions modulate amygdala activity without explicit knowledge. *Journal of Neuroscience*, 18(1), pp. 411–18.

Woodworth, R.S. & Schlosberg, H. (1954) *Experimental Psychology*. London: Methuen.

Learning

N. Mkhize

Objectives

After studying this chapter you should:
- be able to define learning
- be able to distinguish between classical and operant conditioning
- be able to apply classical and operant conditioning to human problems
- be able to explain the contributions of cognitive and biological factors in human learning.

Introduction

Learning has been defined as a relatively permanent change in behaviour that occurs as a result of experience (Goldstein 1994; Mwawenda 1995; Hilgard & Bower 1975). These changes may manifest cognitively, in the way a person thinks; behaviourally, in the way a person acts; or affectively, in the way a person feels. Non-lasting changes resulting from fatigue, motivation, maturation, or any other temporal state of an organism do not qualify as learning. For example, some drugs bring about changes in a person's behaviour (e.g. drowsiness), but such behaviour is not the result of experience. Similarly, behaviours that are part of an organism's normal biological or maturational processes do not qualify as learning.

Of all the schools of thought in psychology, **behaviourism** has had the most profound influence on learning research and theory. According to behaviourism, the study of human behaviour should be concerned with observable events rather than hidden mental processes. However, not all psychologists believe that principles derived from behaviourism are sufficient to understand human learning. Most notably, cognitive psychologists and social learning theorists object to the omission of mental processes, arguing that 'learning is not so much a change in behaviour as a change in knowledge that has the potential for affecting behaviour'.

(GOLDSTEIN 1994: p. 245)

Learning:
A relatively permanent change in behaviour that occurs as a result of experience.

Behaviourism:
School of thought that believes that the study of human behaviour should be concerned with observable events rather than hidden mental processes.

This chapter discusses three main approaches to learning: classical conditioning, instrumental conditioning and observational learning. Given the resurgence of interest in cognitive approaches, these are briefly discussed at the end of the chapter.

Classical conditioning

Russian physiologist Ivan Pavlov (1849–1936) was the first person to systematically study classical conditioning. His interest in the subject was aroused accidentally, while he was studying salivation in dogs as part of a larger research study on digestion. His investigative procedure involved making a small surgical incision in the dog's cheeks, through which a tube was connected to the salivary glands. As the dog salivated, saliva flowed through the tube and into a container, where it was measured (see Figure 4.1). Placing meat powder or some titbit on the dog's tongue induced salivation and the salivary flow was measured as the dog chewed and swallowed. Having gone through this experimental procedure with the dog many times, Pavlov noted that the dog began to salivate even before the meat powder was placed in its mouth. This observation marked the beginning of work on classical conditioning.

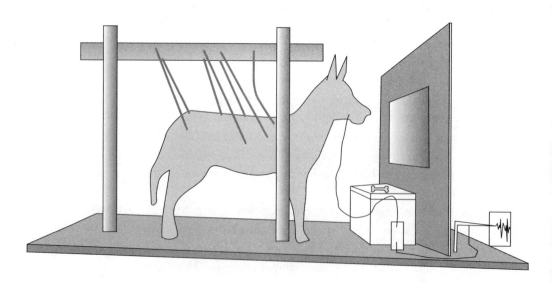

FIGURE 4.1: Apparatus for classical conditioning experiments

The dog, restrained in a harness, is presented with meat to elicit salivation. A tube is inserted through the dog's cheeks. The amount of saliva is recorded on the revolving paper drum, via the tube.

Pavlov also observed that the dog salivated in response to other stimuli associated with food. It salivated when it saw him entering the room, on sight of the food dish, and in response to the sound of the closing door when the food was brought in. Pavlov wanted to know why such neutral stimuli elicited salivation, which is a reflex response. A perusal of the literature on reflexes led him to the realisation that he had stumbled on an important principle underlying animal and human learning. Reflexes are automatic stimulus-response connections; they are natural and unlearned. Behaviours such as withdrawing one's hand when accidentally touching something hot, shivering when cold and salivating upon presentation of food are all reflexes. For the dog to salivate in response to cues associated with food, some form of learning must have taken place, whereby the previously neutral stimulus becomes associated with the food itself. Pavlov called this phenomenon 'conditioning'.

To study the phenomenon, Pavlov devised a series of experiments, using the procedure shown in Figure 4.1. Having noted that meat powder elicited copious salivation, he presented a **neutral stimulus**, a ringing bell, which prompted no salivation. He then varied the experimental procedure. When the bell and the food were paired, with the ringing of the bell preceding the presentation of the food by a few seconds, the dog learned to associate the sound of the bell with the food. It began to salivate at the sound of the bell, even if no food was given. Through further experimentation, Pavlov showed that numerous other neutral stimuli, such as the vibrating sound of a buzzer or the ticking of a metronome, elicited salivation when paired with food. In the language of learning theory, an innate, non-learned response such as salivation is called an **unconditioned response** (UR). For example, we blink automatically when air is blown onto our eyes. Blinking is an unconditioned response. An event or stimulus that automatically (reflexively) elicits a response, without prior learning, is called an **unconditioned stimulus** (US). Pavlonian conditioning contends that learning occurs because the neutral (bell) and unconditioned (food) stimuli have been paired repeatedly. When the neutral stimulus begins to elicit the same behaviour previously produced by the unconditioned stimulus, it becomes a conditioned (learned) stimulus (CS), and the resultant behaviour a conditioned (learned) response (CR). The relationship between the various stimuli and responses is presented in Figure 4.2, overleaf.

Neutral stimulus:
Stimulus that produces no response.

Unconditioned response:
An innate, non-learned response.

Unconditioned stimulus:
An event or stimulus that automatically elicits a response.

Before conditioning:
Food = Salivation
(US)   (UR)

Conditioning:
Bell + Food = Salivation
(NS)   (US)   (UR)

Post conditioning:
Bell = Salivation
(CS)   (CR)

FIGURE 4.2: The relationship between stimuli and responses during the conditioning procedure

Classical conditioning:
An associative form of learning that involves pairing a neutral stimulus with one that elicits the desired response naturally.

Classical conditioning is an associative form of learning. It involves pairing a neutral stimulus with one that elicits the desired response naturally (the unconditioned stimulus). When learning has occurred, the neutral (conditioned) stimulus is capable of eliciting a conditioned response independently of the unconditioned stimulus. We use the principles of classical conditioning in our daily lives, without being aware of the process or the specialist vocabulary.

Principles of classical conditioning

We will now look at some of the main principles governing learning in the classical conditioning paradigm.

Acquisition

What are the processes involved for a learned response to occur? The time interval between a conditioned stimulus and an unconditioned stimulus is one of the most important determinants of whether learning will occur (Weidermann *et al.* 1999). The timing of a conditioned stimulus and an unconditioned stimulus determines the degree of association or contiguity between the stimuli. This is known as the contiguity hypothesis. Let us reconsider Pavlov's experiments. If the bell is sounded 15 minutes before the presentation of the unconditioned stimulus (food), it is highly unlikely that the dog will associate the sound of the bell with the food, and thus conditioning will not occur.

Pavlov experimented with a number of temporal pairing relationships between the neutral stimulus and the unconditioned stimulus, in an attempt to determine both the rate and the strength of the conditioned response. In simultaneous conditioning, the neutral and unconditioned stimuli are presented together. Thus, the bell is sounded at the same time as the meat powder is presented to the dog. In backward conditioning, the sequence is reversed: the unconditioned stimulus (food) is presented first, followed by the neutral stimulus (the bell). In delayed conditioning, the onset of the neutral stimulus precedes the unconditioned stimulus, but continues while the unconditioned stimulus is being presented. Finally, in trace conditioning, the neutral stimulus precedes the uncondi-tioned stimulus, but is terminated before its onset (for example, the bell is sounded briefly, followed by the presentation of the meat powder). The four types of temporal arrangements between the neutral stimulus and the unconditioned stimulus are represented in Table 4.1, on the next page.

Both simultaneous and backward conditioning produce very weak responses (Rescorla 1981). It has been argued that if the neutral stimulus and unconditioned stimulus occur simultaneously, the neutral stimulus is overshadowed by the unconditioned stimulus, and therefore goes unnoticed (Schwartz 1978). In backward conditioning, the dog is already satiating its hunger and the neutral stimulus is no longer relevant; in other words, it does not signal anything. A much stronger effect is produced by trace conditioning, provided the interval between the neutral stimulus and the unconditioned stimulus is very brief (between 0,5 and 5 seconds) (Schwartz & Robbins 1995). This makes sense because, if the neutral stimulus precedes the unconditioned stimulus, it serves as a signal for the unconditioned response (saliva-tion), with which the dog prepares for digestion. It has been established that learning is most effective in delayed conditioning (with the neutral stimulus presented first and maintained for the duration of the uncondi-tioned stimulus). Using Pavlov's studies as an example, we would first ring the bell, and continue ringing as the dog is fed the meat powder. Ross and Ross (1971) have further shown that optimal conditioning occurs when the neutral stimulus precedes the unconditioned stimulus by about half a second. Conditioning is most effective under trace and delayed temporal arrangements, with the latter superior to the former. Simultaneous and backward temporal arrangements, however, produce an extremely weak effect.

TABLE 4.1: Temporal relationship between neutral stimulus and
unconditioned stimulus ·

Type of conditioning	Time elapsed between NS and US
Simultaneous	The NS (bell) and the US (meat) are presented together. No time elapses between the two. Conditioning effect is weak.
Backward	The US (meat) is given first, and the NS (bell) is rung thereafter. Conditioning effect is weak.
Delayed	NS (bell) is sounded first, and continued while US (meat) is given. Best conditioning effect.
Trace	NS (bell) is presented shortly and stopped, and the US (meat) is given. Good conditioning effect.

Extinction and spontaneous recovery

For conditioning to occur, the neutral stimulus and the unconditioned stimulus are paired repeatedly, until the neutral stimulus alone is capable of producing the desired response (i.e. until it becomes a conditioned stimulus). To determine the effect of repeated presentations of the conditioned stimulus alone, without the unconditioned stimulus (after conditioning had occurred), Pavlov varied his experimental procedure slightly. A bell was sounded, but no meat was forthcoming. Would the dog continue to salivate to the sound of the bell alone? Pavlov noted that the conditioned response (salivation) decreased gradually as the number of trials in which the conditioned stimulus was not paired with the unconditioned stimulus increased. Eventually, the conditioned response was extinguished (the dog stopped salivating at the sound of the bell). The gradual weakening and eventual cessation of the conditioned response following repeated presentations of the conditioned stimulus without the unconditioned stimulus is known as **extinction**. The relationship between the dog's response, as measured by salivation, and the number of trials the conditioned stimulus was not followed by the unconditioned stimulus, is shown in Figure 4.3, on the next page. As the figure indicates, the power of the conditioned stimulus to produce the conditioned response is lost if the conditioned stimulus is no longer associated with the unconditioned stimulus.

Extinction:
The gradual weakening and eventual cessation of the conditioned response following repeated presentations of the conditioned stimulus without the unconditioned stimulus.

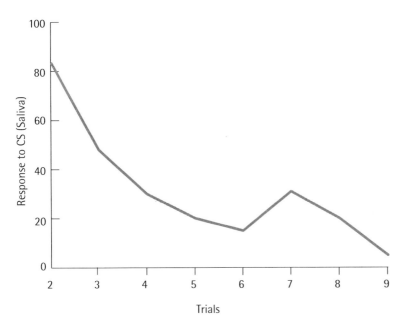

FIGURE 4.3: Extinction

The conditioned response (salivation) declines gradually, and is eventually eliminated, if the conditioned stimulus (bell) is presented without the US (food) repeatedly.

Upon further experimentation, Pavlov noted that, although it appeared as if extinction had been achieved if the conditioned stimulus (the bell) was repeatedly unpaired with the unconditioned stimulus, salivation occurred upon resumption of trials the following day, even though no conditioned stimulus/unconditioned stimulus pairings had been presented in the interim. The reappearance of a conditioned response following a brief period of extinction is known as **spontaneous recovery**.

Figure 4.4, on the next page, depicts the sequence of extinction and spontaneous recovery. It indicates that the strength of the conditioned response during spontaneous recovery is weaker than it was during the acquisition phase. Although spontaneous recovery can occur a number of times, the conditioned response is eventually extinguished if the experimenter continues to present the conditioned stimulus alone. In other words, the organism learns to respond to the environment. Salivation to the sound of the bell, even if there is no food forthcoming, is of no adaptive value, and the response ceases to occur.

Spontaneous recovery: The reappearance of a conditioned response following a brief period of extinction.

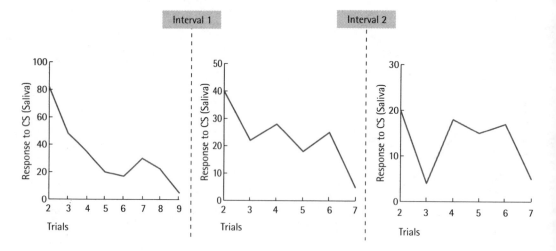

FIGURE 4.4: Extinction and spontaneous recovery

Spontaneous recovery is the re-emergence of a conditioned response following extinction. It gets weaker if the conditioned response is presented repeatedly without the unconditioned stimulus.

What happens if the conditioning process is resumed after a period of extinction? Is the conditioned response lost forever? It has been established that the conditioned response reappears if the conditioned stimulus and unconditioned stimulus are paired again. In fact, should the experimenter continue pairing the conditioned stimulus and unconditioned stimulus, a stronger response is produced. This indicates that the response was not lost, but merely inhibited because the conditioned stimulus no longer signalled food (i.e. it was no longer of adaptive value) (Hannon 1987).

Stimulus generalisation and discrimination

Having been conditioned to salivate at the sound of the bell, suppose the dog begins to salivate in response to other similar sounding stimuli, such as a ringing doorbell or telephone. **Stimulus generalisation** refers to the tendency to respond with a conditioned response to a stimulus similar to the conditioned stimulus. This depends on the degree of similarity between the new stimulus and the conditioned stimulus: the greater the similarity, the greater the response.

Stimulus generalisation:
The tendency to respond with a conditioned response to a stimulus similar to the conditioned stimulus.

The value of stimulus generalisation is that learning is extended to related situations, making the response more adaptive. Consider a baby who was bitten while playing with a puppy, and whose fears have generalised to cats. By retreating to the comfort of her mother at the mere sight of a cat, the chances of being bitten again are reduced. Stimulus generalisation plays an important role in our daily lives. For example, advertisers often associate their products with role models who are already known to elicit positive feelings and attitudes. They are counting on the positive feelings toward the models generalising to their products.

The counterpart of stimulus generalisation is **discrimination**. In classical conditioning, this occurs when an organism learns to respond differently to stimuli resembling the conditioned stimulus. For example, Pavlov's dog would respond to the sound of the bell only, and not a ringing telephone.

Discrimination: When an organism learns to respond differently to stimuli resembling the conditioned stimulus.

Higher-order conditioning

When a neutral stimulus is paired with an established conditioned stimulus to produce a conditioned response, the procedure is called **higher-order conditioning** (also known as second-order conditioning). For example, the conditioned stimulus (the bell) may be paired with a neutral stimulus, such as a flash of light. The light (neutral stimulus) and the bell (first conditioned stimulus or CS1) are presented repeatedly until the dog learns to salivate at the presentation of the light alone. The light becomes the second conditioned stimulus (CS2). This occurs without the CS2 ever being paired with the unconditioned stimulus (food). This procedure is illustrated in Figure 4.5.

Higher-order conditioning: When a neutral stimulus is paired with an established conditioned stimulus to produce a conditioned response.

Before conditioning:

Bell (CS1) = Salivation (CR1)

Conditioning

Light (NS) + Bell (CS1) = Salivation (UR1)

Post conditioning

Light (CS2) = Salivation (CR2)

FIGURE 4.5: The procedure of higher-order conditioning

Higher-order conditioning is a means through which learning is extended to situations other than by generalisation (Goldstein 1994). It may explain many of our reactions, including emotional responses (Chance 1999). Consider a child who has developed a fear of a doctor's consulting room (where he received a painful injection (unconditioned stimulus), now associated with the consulting room (conditioned stimulus)). In the waiting room, the child meets his mother's friend. Suppose that friend visits the child's family the following day, and the child runs away in fear. The anxiety associated with going to the doctor has been extended to his mother's friend. Higher-order conditioning is neither strong nor long lasting, however. Responses elicited by the CS2 are easily extinguished.

Classical conditioning: Traditional and modern explanations

Three main theoretical approaches have been advanced to explain how learning in classical conditioning takes place: stimulus substitution, the contiguity hypothesis and information theory.

Stimulus substitution

Pavlov's explanation of classical conditioning hinged on the association between the neutral stimulus and the unconditioned stimulus (Plotnick 1996; Santrock 2000). He maintained that, upon repeated presentation of the neutral stimulus, together with the unconditioned stimulus, the neutral stimulus eventually becomes a conditioned stimulus. The conditioned stimulus was thought to eventually substitute for the unconditioned stimulus. According to substitution theory, the conditioned stimulus should elicit a response similar to the one produced by an unconditioned stimulus. However, empirical findings have not supported this view. Organisms have been observed to respond by jumping and flinching when shocked (unconditioned stimulus), but remain immobile when a light (conditioned stimulus) is presented (Santrock 2000). Similarly, Zener (in Plotnick 1996) showed that dogs always salivated and chewed following the unconditioned stimulus, and salivated but rarely chewed following the conditioned stimulus. The fact that responses elicited by the conditioned stimulus often differ slightly from those elicited by the unconditioned stimulus means that stimulus substitution cannot adequately account for how learning occurs in classical conditioning.

The contiguity hypothesis

This hypothesis holds that learning in classical conditioning results from contiguity (nearness in time) between the neutral stimulus and the unconditioned stimulus during the pairing trials. Any neutral stimulus could become a conditioned stimulus and elicit a conditioned response, provided it is contiguous with the unconditioned stimulus.

Information theory

Rescorla's (1966, 1988, 1996) research led to findings that challenged the contiguity hypothesis, the most dominant explanation of classical conditioning in the 1960s. He hypothesised that conditioning occurred because the conditioned stimulus provided the subject with information to reliably predict when the unconditioned stimulus would follow in time. In the case of extinction, the conditioned stimulus provides the subject with information that no unconditioned stimulus (e.g. food) was forthcoming. Information theorists would argue that the dog salivated at the sound of the bell (conditioned stimulus) because it had learnt that it reliably predicted food (the unconditioned stimulus). If the conditioned stimulus and the unconditioned stimulus were unpredictable – for example, the conditioned stimulus is sometimes followed by the unconditioned stimulus, and sometimes preceded by the unconditioned stimulus – Rescorla hypothesised that association would not occur.

To test the predictiveness hypothesis, Rescorla (1966) randomly assigned rats into two groups: a contiguity-only group (neutral stimulus always paired with unconditioned stimulus), and the contiguity-plus-random group (neutral stimulus sometimes paired with uncondi-tioned stimulus, and unconditioned stimulus sometimes appearing without neutral stimulus). On average, the groups were subjected to an equal number of tone-shock pairs, except that for the contiguity-only group, the tone (neutral stimulus) always occurred with the shock (unconditioned stimulus). In the contiguity-plus-random group, the shock sometimes occurred without the tone. The effect of pairing the tone and the shock was tested by training rats to press a bar for food. A tone sounded as they pressed the bar. If conditioning depended on contiguity only, both groups should refrain from pressing the bar when the tone is sounded – a response known as conditioned suppression. Rats in the contiguity group immediately stopped pressing the bar when the tone sounded. In other words, the tone had an inhibitory effect. The contiguity-plus-random group, however, continued pressing the bar despite the tone being sounded. Rats in the contiguity-only group learnt to associate the tone with an unpleasant event (shock); rats in the contiguity-plus-random group did not. Rescorla argued that this was because, in the contiguity-only group, the tone reliably predicted being shocked. The contiguity-plus-random group failed to associate the tone with being shocked because the relationship between the two was unpredictable.

Evidence questioning the contiguity hypothesis has also come from taste aversion studies (Garcia & Koelling 1966). **Taste aversion learning** is the tendency to associate sensory cues, such as smells, tastes or sounds, with unpleasant responses (e.g. vomiting). At the time Garcia conducted his studies, it was believed that taste aversion was not due to classical conditioning, as it violated the established view that the neutral stimulus and the unconditioned stimulus must be paired repeatedly for the conditioned response to occur. Garcia showed that taste aversion learning could occur after only one trial. He also observed that conditioning nausea in rats was easily effected if stimuli involving taste cues were used, and rarely if stimuli involving light cues were used. This contradicted the long-held view that stimuli had equal potential for becoming conditioned stimuli. This indicates that conditioning does not depend on contiguity only. Information about the extent to which the organism is biologically prepared to detect stimuli ought to be considered. The reason rats acquire taste aversion easily if taste cues are used is because of their superior olfaction (smell). Cues involving light do not work well for them because of their poor vision. The biological predisposition to associate some combinations of stimuli more readily than others has been called **preparedness** (Seligman 1970).

The importance of information in classical conditioning has also come from studies by Kamin (1968). Kamin produced a conditioned fear response in a rat by repeatedly pairing a tone (conditioned stimulus) with a shock (unconditioned stimulus). When a conditioned fear response had been established, the pairing of the tone and the shock was continued, but a light (second conditioned stimulus) was turned on each time. Although the light and the shock were paired repeatedly, the rat did not develop a conditioned fear response to the light. Kamin argued that the tone signalled to the rat that it was going to be shocked. Adding a light as a second conditioned stimulus provided no additional information. In other words, information provided by the light was redundant. The study thus indicated that the relevance of information provided by the conditioned stimulus is important in classical conditioning.

The studies mentioned above transformed psychologists' understanding of classical conditioning. It is no longer conceived of only in terms of contiguity. Instead, an organism's preparedness and ability to draw meaningful relationships between stimuli are now considered, bringing classical conditioning closer to biological and cognitive approaches to human behaviour.

Taste aversion learning:
The tendency to associate sensory cues with unpleasant responses.

Preparedness:
The biological predisposition to associate some combinations of stimuli more readily than others.

Classical conditioning: Human applications

Classical conditioning is of great survival value to humans. Consider what would happen if we did not learn to associate fire with pain. Many phobias are acquired through classical conditioning. The reasons why people may fear a dental surgery is because they associate it with pain. Classical conditioning has been successfully applied to understand phobias. A **phobia** is a fear of a stimulus or situation that is disproportional to the danger posed. Excessive fear of heights and meeting new people are a few examples of commonly observed phobias. Many phobias, psychologists believe, are conditioned emotional responses (CERs) to previously neutral stimuli.

Phobia:
A fear of a stimulus or situation that is disproportional to the danger posed.

In one of the most often cited, but ethically questionable studies, American psychologist John Watson conditioned a nine-month-old boy, Albert, to fear a white rat. Initially, the boy was not afraid of the rat; he played with it freely. As he was playing with it, a loud banging noise was sounded behind his head, which caused him to cry. After about seven pairings of the rat and the noise, Albert began to fear the rat, even though the noise was not sounded. This fear generalised to a dog, a rabbit and other furry creatures.

It should be noted that Watson's study was conducted before stringent ethical requirements were in place. Such a study would not gain ethical approval today (assuming there are functional ethics committees in the country or university where approval for the research is being sought).

The good news is that phobias can be unlearned. If a fear-arousing stimulus is repeatedly paired with another stimulus incompatible with the fear, the conditioned fear response is eliminated. This procedure is known as **counter conditioning**. Mary Cover Jones (1924) used it to successfully treat a boy named Peter who was afraid of rabbits. The rabbit was repeatedly paired with one of Peter's pleasurable activities: eating. To avoid upsetting him, the rabbit was first placed within sighting distance as the boy was fed his favourite food. Each day, the rabbit was brought closer and closer and Peter's reaction monitored. Eventually, his fears were eliminated and the boy and the rabbit became friends.

Counter conditioning:
When a fear-arousing stimulus is repeatedly paired with another stimulus incompatible with the fear, eliminating the conditioned fear response.

In the 1950s, Joseph Wolpe extended Jones's work to develop a therapeutic technique known as **systematic desensitisation**, used to treat anxiety. This involves pairing anxiety-provoking stimuli with relaxation. The logic is that a conditioned anxiety response will be eventually extinguished because it is incompatible with relaxation. Because anxiety

Systematic desensitisation:
Pairing anxiety-provoking stimuli with relaxation.

is often accompanied by muscle tension, and its absence by muscle relaxation, clients or subjects are first trained in progressive muscle relaxation. They are also asked to construct a list of about 20, thematically related, anxiety-proving stimuli. The list is ordered hierarchically, from the least anxiety-provoking to the one that provokes the highest level of anxiety. For example, a person who has a fear of heights could begin by standing next to a ladder, holding it, then climbing onto a roof, being on top of a roof, up to the most feared stimulus (for example, being on the roof of a skyscraper). Although the therapist could help the client to construct the hierarchy, the primary responsibility is the client's because it should be based on his or her life experiences. Once muscle relaxation has been learned, and the hierarchy has been constructed, the client is asked to visualise the first item in the hierarchy, while remaining relaxed. For example, the person who fears heights would be asked to visualise him or herself standing next to the ladder. The therapist takes the client gradually up the hierarchy, while monitoring his or her level of anxiety. The procedure is successful when the client can imagine the last item without feeling anxious.

Systematic desensitisation is based on classical learning principles, in particular counter conditioning. Classical conditioning has been used to treat other health-related problems, such as smoking.

Operant conditioning

Having discussed classical conditioning, we will now turn to the principles of operant conditioning. Similarities and differences between the two types of conditioning are highlighted.

What is operant conditioning?

Learning in classical conditioning involves establishing a relationship between the conditioned stimulus and the unconditioned stimulus. The animal or subject does not operate in or act on the environment as such. Consequently, classical conditioning is considered a passive process. Consider a child who is given praise for doing his or her homework. By being praised, the likelihood that he or she will do homework in future is increased. In this case, the child is not a passive recipient of environmental stimuli; he or she is actively engaged in the process. To be praised, the child had to operate or act on the environment in some way. In the language of learning theory, an event that increases the probability that the behaviour will occur in the future is known as an **operant reinforcer**. In some instances, the consequences of one's actions are such that the

Operant reinforcer:
An event that increases the probability that the behaviour will occur in the future.

probability of the behaviour occurring again is decreased. If a child is denied a lunch break for talking during a lesson, this decreases the likelihood that he or she will talk during a lesson again. An event that lowers the chances that the target behaviour will occur again is known as a **punisher**. Thus, **operant conditioning**, also known as instrumental conditioning, is a kind of learning in which the consequences of one's actions increase or decrease the probability (chances, likelihood) that the behaviour will occur again. Unlike classical conditioning, it involves an association between a response and its consequences.

Punisher:
An event that lowers the chances that the target behaviour will occur again.

Operant conditioning:
A kind of learning in which the consequences of one's actions increase or decrease the probability that the behaviour will occur again.

Thorndike and the Law of Effect

Although B.F. Skinner coined the term 'operant conditioning', B.L. Thorndike was the first to conduct experiments to determine the relationship between behaviour and its consequences. Thorndike was interested in animal problem-solving behaviour. To study animal behaviour, a cat that had been deprived of food was placed inside an experimental apparatus known as a 'puzzle box' (see Figure 4.6, below). A piece of fish was placed outside the box. The cat could escape from the box if it opened a latched door by pulling a string or depressing a lever. The number of trials before the cat learned how to open the door was monitored. At first, the cat engaged in random, ineffective behaviour. It tried to squeeze through the openings of the box, clawed at the walls, paced in agitation from corner to corner, etc. Eventually, and by pure accident, it stepped on the lever, releasing the latch. It escaped from the box and was rewarded with the piece of fish.

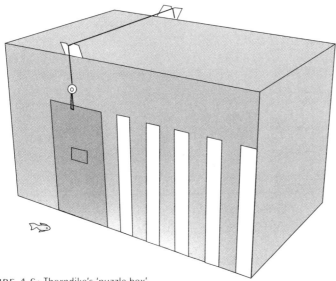

FIGURE 4.6: Thorndike's 'puzzle box'

When the cat had been fed, it was placed in the box. It engaged in the same sort of random behaviour as before, until the lever was accidentally depressed, allowing it to escape. After a number of trials, the random behaviours decreased, and the time taken to escape was significantly reduced. For example, Thorndike noted that it took approximately 448 seconds to escape during the first trial. By the fortieth trial, this had been reduced to about 15 seconds. Behaviours that were unnecessary to escape from the box were gradually eliminated. Eventually, the cat would depress the lever to open the box immediately. Figure 4.7 shows the typical learning curve observed by Thorndike. The gradual slope indicates that learning occurred in small, successive steps. Thorndike labelled this process trial-and-error learning. By trial and error, the cat learned that some behaviours did not produce the intended outcome and stopped engaging in them. Behaviours that led to a pleasant effect (food) were strengthened. Thorndike formulated the **Law of Effect** to explain this process. It states that learning is determined by the effect the response produces. If a response is followed by a positive outcome, this increases the probability that it will occur again. Behaviours followed by undesirable consequences are weakened. According to Thorndike, the relationship between the correct stimulus (S) and the response (R), strengthens or weakens depending on the actions of the organism. It should be noted, unlike classical conditioning, that the response comes first.

Law of Effect:
Law that states that learning is determined by the effect the response produces.

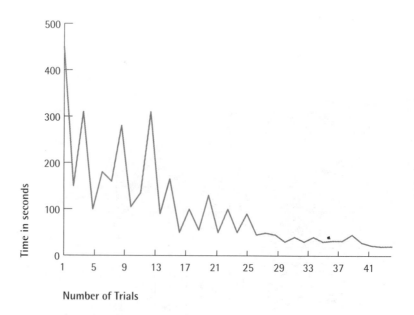

FIGURE 4.7: Thorndike's trial-and-error learning curve

The time the animal takes to escape from the box decreases as the number of trials increases.

Skinner's approach to operant conditioning

Although Thorndike pioneered studies on instrumental conditioning, B.F. Skinner highlighted most of the principles of learning known today. To study learning processes, Skinner designed a special, cage-like apparatus, which he called a conditioning chamber. This instrument is now widely known as the Skinner box. The box is transparent and soundproof, with a grid floor. The box is empty, apart from a lever (when the subjects are rats) or a disk (when the subjects are pigeons), and a tray into which food can be received. Depressing the lever or pecking at the disk activates a feeder mechanism, which dispenses a pellet of food into a tray. To automatically record the animal's responses, Skinner devised a mechanism known as a cumulative recorder (see Figure 4.8, below). It consists of a pen that records responses on a continuously moving paper strip. A response (e.g. pecking) causes the pen to move upward, creating a 'step' in the record. Thus, responding at a faster rate creates a steep slope. When the animal is at rest (not responding), a horizontal line is created. This instrument makes it possible to trace both the rate and patterns of responding.

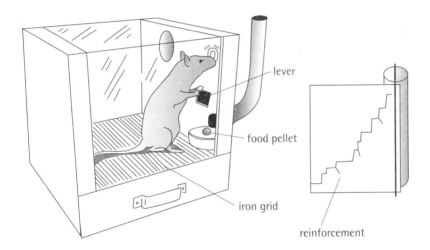

FIGURE 4.8: The Skinner box and cumulative recorder

Using the conditioning chamber and the cumulative recorder, Skinner noted that rats depressed the lever more rapidly if their actions were rewarded (the delivery of food). To describe behaviours in which the animal operates in its environment, Skinner coined the term 'operant behaviour'. Until his death in 1990, he studied how consequences of an organism's actions influence future behaviour.

The elements of operant conditioning

Before the elements of operant conditioning are discussed, two terms need to be reviewed briefly: reinforcement and contingency. **Reinforcement** refers to a consequence that follows a behaviour and increases the likelihood that the behaviour will be repeated. It is important to note that the consequence must be **contingent** upon the desired behaviour. This means that it is dispensed only following an appropriate response. For example, if we wanted to eliminate out-of-seat behaviour in the classroom, children would be given attention (reinforced) only when they were seated.

Although the words 'reinforcer' and 'reward' are sometimes used interchangeably, Skinner preferred the former. This is because the latter implies a subjective, unobservable effect within the organism. For example, we can say that the animal found the food 'rewarding' because it satisfied hunger, but this refers to an unobservable internal state. It is inconsistent with the cardinal behavioural principle: the study of observable behaviour. As Skinner was more concerned with measurable outcomes, he defined reinforcers in terms of observable consequences in future behaviour, rather than their reward value.

To objectively measure the conditioned response, its baseline level should first be established. The baseline level is the frequency or infrequency of the behaviour in question before the introduction of a reinforcer. For example, we may want to know how many times the rat presses the bar in the Skinner box before the reinforcer (food pellets) is introduced.

Reinforcement:
A consequence that follows a behaviour and increases the likelihood that the behaviour will be repeated.

Contingent:
When a consequence is dispensed only following an appropriate response.

Positive reinforcement

When a presentation of a stimulus increases the likelihood that the behaviour will recur, this is known as **positive reinforcement**. A positive reinforcer could be an event, a privilege, a material object or a behaviour that strengthens the response (Driscoll 1994; Masters *et al.* 1987). If a teacher nods approvingly after a shy child has volunteered to answer a question during a lesson, the nodding behaviour is a positive reinforcer. It strengthens the child's response (volunteering). In the Skinner box, the food pellet delivered after the rat had pressed the lever is a positive reinforcer. The more the response is reinforced, the more it will be emitted.

Positive reinforcement:
When a presentation of a stimulus increases the likelihood that the behaviour will recur.

Negative reinforcement

This type of reinforcement increases the probability that the response will recur because it is followed by the removal of an unpleasant or aversive stimulus. In other words, the response allows the subject to avoid a negative consequence. Consider a rat in a Skinner box, into which a low level shock is delivered via the metal grid. Initially, the rat behaves randomly: it runs about, squeals, urinates, etc., until it presses the lever by chance. When depressed, the lever acts as a switch that terminates the shock. Depressing the lever is thus followed by the removal of an unpleasant stimulus (shock). In other words, it is negatively reinforced. This increases the probability that the behaviour (pressing the lever) will recur.

Sometimes, students have problems distinguishing between positive and negative reinforcement. It should be noted that both increase the probability of a response. The difference is that, in positive reinforcement, something is given or added (e.g. praise, food), whereas negative reinforcement strengthens the response by removing an aversive (unpleasant) stimulus (e.g. pain, scolding). Table 4.2 illustrates the difference between the two reinforcement procedures.

Negative reinforcement: Reinforcement that increases the probability that the response will recur because it is followed by the removal of an unpleasant or aversive stimulus.

TABLE 4.2: Positive and negative reinforcement

Positive reinforcement	
Behaviour:	Shy child volunteers to answer a question.
Consequence:	Teacher smiles, nods approvingly (something is given).
Future behaviour:	Volunteering is strengthened.

Negative reinforcement	
Behaviour:	Boy returns cattle to kraal before sunset.
Consequence:	Mother stops scolding him (something is taken away).
Future behaviour:	Boy returns cattle to kraal before sunset.

Types of reinforcers

We can distinguish between two types of reinforcers in positive reinforcement: **primary reinforcers** and secondary reinforcers. The rat that received a food pellet on depressing a lever was rewarded with a primary reinforcer. Primary reinforcers are unlearned; they are innately pleasurable because they are related to our biological needs. Examples are food, sex and water. These types of reinforcers are present at birth. For example, we do not have to be taught that food is pleasurable. Apart from the biologically necessary reinforcers, researchers have established another category: sensory reinforcers. Butler (1954) established that monkeys would work to be allowed to look through a window into an experimental room. Similarly, Jones *et al.* (1961) noted that humans would engage in a button-pushing task to turn on the lights in a dark room. Sensory reinforcers are apparently unlearned, and therefore regarded as primary reinforcers. Lieberman (1990) has suggested that social reinforcers, such as smiles and praise, are also primary reinforcers.

Unlike primary reinforcers, **secondary reinforcers** are learned. They acquire their reinforcing power by being paired with a primary reinforcer or another secondary reinforcer. Examples of secondary reinforcers are grades and money. Grades gain their reinforcing power by being associated with other reinforcers, such as gaining entry into an esteemed university or getting a well-paid job. Similarly, the power of money lies in its ability to buy food and shelter, to attract a desired sexual partner, etc. The system of token economies, which uses secondary reinforcers to manage behavioural problems in psychiatric and educational settings, is discussed below.

The timing of reinforcers

Timing is crucial in operant conditioning. Learning is maximised if the interval between a behaviour and its consequences is a few seconds, rather than hours. In the Skinner box, the rat's behaviour (depressing a lever) is strengthened if the food pellet is delivered immediately after each bar press. If the reinforcement is delayed, the rat will not establish the relationship between its actions and the reinforcer.

What happens if the reinforcement is delivered at regular time intervals, irrespective of the animal's behaviour? To explore this question, Skinner (1948) delivered food to pigeons at regular intervals, no matter what they were doing. He found that each pigeon developed its own peculiar behaviour, coinciding with whatever it happened to be doing at the time the first reinforcement was delivered. For example, one rocked back and forth like a pendulum, while another turned around in a circle two or three times, between reinforcements. Skinner labelled this **superstitious behaviour**. The term refers to a situation in which subjects behave as if there is a causal relationship between two coincidental events.

Sportspeople are known to engage in similar ritualistic acts, which they believe will influence the course of their game. Often, these acts coincide with their best performance in the past, where a 'causal' relationship was established. For example, a footballer who insists on stepping on to the field of play with his left foot first, because previously he scored a hat trick after doing so, is behaving superstitiously. Another example of superstitious behaviour among sportspeople has to do with dress code. A sportsperson may insist on wearing a particular colour of underpants whenever he or she competes. Students too can become superstitious about taking examinations or tests.

The timing of the interval between a response and its reinforcement explains many aspects of behaviour other than superstition. Martin and Pear (1999) explored the role of immediate versus delayed consequences in the development of self-control behaviour. They maintained that, when reinforcers are small but immediate, and punishers strong but delayed, the immediate, pleasurable consequences override the latter. Immediate, small reinforcers sometimes compete with stronger, but delayed ones. For example, it may be more tempting to spend one's money on clothes and entertainment (immediate, small reinforcers) than investing it in a retirement scheme (a delayed stronger reinforcer).

Self-control may also involve competition between an immediate punisher and a delayed reinforcer. Beginning an exercise programme or taking up a new sport, for example, often involves immediate punishers (body aches, looking stupid because you don't know the correct sequence of moves, etc.). Thus, long-term reinforcers (for example, looking slim, athletic, sexy and healthy), may be overridden by immediate punishers.

Finally, in the event of immediate weak punishers competing with strong delayed punishers, the former takes precedence over the latter. Thus, we may put off minor surgery for fear of the associated pain. The delayed consequences (major surgery) may, however, be more severe.

The cited examples point to the importance of the timing of the interval between a response and its consequences in real life situations. We have seen that immediate consequences tend to interfere with self-control. Fortunately, behavioural strategies can be employed to help us manage our behaviour effectively (Martin & Pear 1999).

Superstitious behaviour: A situation in which subjects behave as if there is a causal relationship between two coincidental events.

Behavioural shaping

In operant conditioning, the subject is reinforced for emitting a desired response. However, what if the base rate of the desired behaviour is zero? Rewarding the subject for doing nothing, or for random behaviour, will strengthen these behaviours, as we have already seen with superstitious behaviour. A procedure that rewards successive approximations of the desired behaviour is called **shaping** (or response differentiation) (Bandura 1969). Consider the rat in the Skinner box. At first, the rat roams the cage restlessly, sniffing about, standing on its hind legs. When it turns its head in the direction of the lever, a food pellet is dropped into the tray. After a few trials, the rat learns that the food pellet is contingent upon facing the lever, so it spends more time looking in that direction. Next, it is rewarded for taking a few steps in the direction of the lever. Once we get the rat closer to the lever, the food pellet is delivered only if the rat places a paw on it. Finally, it is rewarded for putting a paw on the lever and depressing it. Thus, rewarding responses that approximate the desired outcome eliminates random behaviours.

Shaping:
A procedure that rewards successive approximations of the desired behaviour.

Behavioural shaping has been applied successfully to human problems. Werle *et al.* (1993) reported using this technique with a child who refused to eat certain foods (or would not eat enough to maintain a healthy diet and weight). The goal of shaping was to make the child notice, taste, chew and swallow a food – for example, vegetables. The mother was trained to reward the child for behaviour that successively approximated the desired response (noticing the food, keeping it in his mouth, chewing and swallowing). These behaviours were awarded with smiles, praise and attention, until the child's habit of refusing food was overcome.

Shaping is commonly applied in our daily lives, even without conscious awareness of the principles involved. Consider the procedure commonly applied to encourage babies to walk. First, the child, who may be seated a few paces away from the mother, is showered with praise for standing on two feet (or attempting to do so). Thereafter, a single step taken towards a beckoning mother is rewarded with smiles, praise and social approval. The procedure continues until the child can move the full distance to the mother (to be rewarded with smiles and kisses).

Schedules of reinforcement

Continuous reinforcement:
Operant conditioning procedures in which every response is followed by a reinforcer.

So far, we have considered operant conditioning procedures in which every response is followed by a reinforcer. This is known as a **continuous reinforcement** (CRF) schedule. Learning under a continuous reinforcement schedule occurs rapidly. It is often used in the initial stages of the conditioning procedure. Extinction also takes place very quickly in a CRF schedule if the conditioned response is not reinforced. Although a CRF schedule may be useful in shaping a particular behaviour, other forms of reinforcement may be necessary to sustain it. Another disadvantage of the CRF schedule is that the natural environment rarely reinforces every appropriate response. Often some instances of appropriate behaviour are reinforced, and others not.

In a **partial** (or intermittent) **reinforcement** schedule, some instances of behaviours are reinforced, and others not. Skinner discovered this schedule accidentally, when he ran short of food pellets. He decided to conserve the food by reinforcing the rat for only some of its responses. Partial reinforcement is usually denoted by the letters FR (Fixed Ratio) and FI (Fixed Interval), followed by a number indicating how often the reinforcement occurred. FR-2, for example, indicates that every second response is reinforced. It should be noted that FR-1 is the same as continuous reinforcement (every response is rewarded), and is therefore rarely used.

Partial reinforcement: Situation in which some instances of behaviours are reinforced, and others not.

If partial reinforcement is used from the start, the result is less rapid acquisition of the desired behaviour. Since not every response is reinforced, it takes longer to establish the relationship between the action and its consequences. The rate of response tends to be unsteady: sometimes the subject responds at a rapid rate, but slows down at other times.

Behaviours established using partial reinforcement take longer to extinguish than those established using continuous reinforcement. This is known as the partial reinforcement effect. Ferster *et al.* (1975) tested this effect by assigning one pigeon to a partial reinforcement schedule and another to a CRF schedule. When both pigeons were placed on extinction trials, the pigeon exposed to the CRF schedule pecked about 200 times after the reinforcement had been terminated. The one on the partial reinforcement schedule, however, pecked about 5 000 times following termination. This indicates that partial reinforcement is more resistant to extinction than continuous reinforcement.

What lies behind the partial reinforcement effect? One plausible explanation is that subjects in a continuous reinforcement schedule are used to being reinforced for every response. When their responses are no longer reinforced, they are quick to establish that the relationship between their actions and consequences has changed, and extinction sets in. Subjects on a partial reinforcement schedule, however, take longer to recognise the onset of an extinction procedure because they are used to responding without being reinforced. Longer exposure to the new conditions (responding without contingent reinforcement) is necessary before extinction sets in (Masters *et al.* 1987).

Ratio schedule:
Situation in which the subject is reinforced only after making a certain number of responses.

Interval schedule:
Situation in which reinforcement is based on the amount of time that elapses in between reinforcers.

Fixed ratio schedule:
Situation in which the subject is reinforced after a fixed number of responses.

There are two main types of partial reinforcement schedule: ratio and interval. In a **ratio schedule**, the subject is reinforced only after making a certain number of responses. In an **interval schedule**, reinforcement is based on the amount of time that elapses in between reinforcers. Both the ratio and the interval schedules may be fixed or variable.

Fixed ratio (FR) schedule

In a **fixed ratio schedule**, the subject is reinforced after a fixed number of responses. A subject on an FR-10 schedule will be reinforced every tenth time the desired response is emitted, independently of how long it took to do so. Thus, in the Skinner box, the pigeon would be rewarded with food for every tenth peck. This schedule is sometimes used in business. The rate of the subject's response can be manipulated by changing the ratio. The larger the ratio, the faster the subject will work for the same amount of reinforcement. For example, salespeople are rewarded for making a predetermined number of sales. If they are changed from an FR-5 to an FR-8 schedule, they are working harder for the same amount of reinforcement.

Fixed ratio schedules usually produce a high responding rate, followed by a post-reinforcement pause. The length of the pause before the subject starts responding again is dependent on the size of the ratio. The larger the ratio, the longer the post-reinforcement pause (Hannon 1987). Fixed ratio schedules result in very steep response slopes, as shown in Figure 4.9.

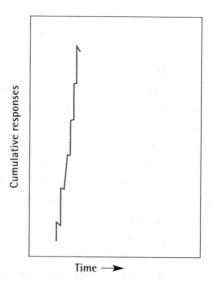

FIGURE 4.9: The learning curve in an FR schedule

A fixed ratio schedule produces a high response rate (note steep slope), but is lower on resistance to extinction. Reinforcement is usually followed by a short pause.

Fixed ratio schedules require very close monitoring of the subject's behaviour, and tend to be uncharacteristic of the natural environment. Hannon (1987) reported on the use of this schedule to teach under-achieving children simple arithmetic. Initially they were given three cards with arithmetic problems printed on them. Successful completion of the task (all three problems solved) earned them a token, which could be exchanged for other reinforcers. The number of correct responses per token was increased gradually, until 20 correct responses were required to earn a token. Hannon reported that the children's arithmetic skills not only improved, but that they also worked harder on the problems.

Variable ratio (VR) schedule

This form of reinforcement is more common in the natural environment. In a **variable ratio schedule**, the number of responses and the delivery of reinforcement changes from time to time. Reinforcement may occur after ten responses, then after the next five, and then after the next fifteen. Although the number of responses per reinforcement is not fixed, they are averaged to a certain value. Thus, a VR-10 schedule indicates that, on average, every tenth response is reinforced. VR schedules produce a very high rate of responding, without the post-reinforcement pause associated with FR schedules. The response rate is high because the subject cannot reliably predict which response will be reinforced. Examples of VR schedules are selling insurance and gambling. The insurance salesperson keeps on phoning potential clients because it is not possible to predict which call will be rewarded. Similarly, slot machines are programmed on a variable ratio schedule. On average, they may pay out after every 25th response, but this is unknown to the gambler. Typical response patterns associated with VR schedules are shown in Figure 4.10.

Varaible ratio schedule: Situation in which the number of responses and the delivery of reinforcement changes from time to time.

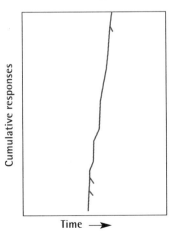

FIGURE 4.10: The learning curve in a VR schedule. This schedule produces a steady and fast response rate, without pauses. It offers high resistance to extinction.

A variable ratio schedule produces a steady and fast response rate without pauses. It offers higher resistance to extinction.

Variable ratio schedules are more resistant to extinction, because the next reinforcement is unpredictable. They also give training in responding to delayed reinforcement, which is more common in real life (Masters *et al.* 1987).

Fixed interval (FI) schedule

Fixed interval schedule:
Situation in which the first response to occur after a fixed amount of time has elapsed is reinforced.

Reinforcement in interval schedules is not tied to the subject's behaviour. In a **fixed interval schedule**, the first response to occur after a fixed amount of time has elapsed is reinforced. For example, a pigeon on an FI-60 schedule will be reinforced for the first response occurring after an interval of 60 seconds. Responses that occur in the interim period are not reinforced, no matter how many there are. Two conditions must be satisfied for an FI schedule: the prescribed interval must have elapsed and the subject must make a response. FI schedules tend to produce very slow responding at first. The response rate accumulates gradually as the time for reinforcement approaches. It is at its highest immediately before reinforcement, then slows down again. This response pattern, known as scalloping, is most noticeable with longer, rather than shorter intervals. The typical response rate associated with FI schedules is shown in Figure 4.11.

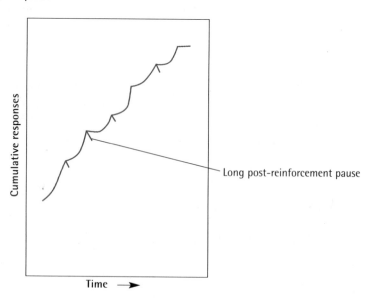

FIGURE 4.11: The learning curve in an FI schedule

Fixed interval schedules offer lower resistance to extinction. Note the long pause following reinforcement. Shorter intervals tend to generate higher rates overall.

Fixed interval schedules are rare. The way students behave before and immediately after tests or examinations is a good example. Usually, examinations are scheduled at regular intervals (quarterly, half-yearly). Most students do not study much at the beginning of the interval. This changes gradually as the exam period approaches, with the greatest effort occurring just before the exams. Effort is reduced again after the exam.

Variable interval (VI) schedules

In a **variable interval schedule**, reinforcement follows the first response after a variable amount of time has elapsed. Although the interval in between reinforced responses is not fixed, it is averaged to a certain value. Thus, a subject may be rewarded for every first response that occurs after 5 minutes, 12 minutes, 15 minutes, 8 minutes, etc., with the average interval being 10 minutes. Because reinforcement is unpredictable, a VI schedule results in a steadier rate of responding, without pauses in between. The response rate is slower than the one associated with a VR schedule. However, it has been shown that the rate of responding is affected by the size of the average interval between reinforcements. Shorter average intervals produce higher response rates, while longer average intervals produce slower response rates (Hannon 1987). The typical response curve associated with VI schedules is shown in Figure 4.12, below.

Fishing is a good example of a VI schedule. One never knows when the next catch will come – it could be in 5 minutes, 10 minutes or 30 minutes. Because it is difficult to predict the occurrence of the reward, VI schedules produce a steady but consistent response.

> **Variable interval schedule:** Situation in which reinforcement follows the first response after a variable amount of time has elapsed.

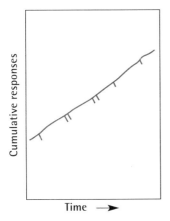

FIGURE 4.12: The learning curve in a VI schedule

Variable interval schedules produce steady responses, without pauses. They are high on resistance to extinction.

Extinction, generalisation and discrimination

Extinction in operant conditioning:
The gradual weakening and disappearance of the conditioned response if it is not reinforced.

In operant conditioning, **extinction** refers to the gradual weakening and disappearance of the conditioned response if it is not reinforced. Skinner noted this principle by accident when the pellet dispenser jammed. Thus, the rat's responses (pressing the bar) produced no reinforcements. On inspecting the cumulative recorder, Skinner found that the rat briefly increased its response after the jam. Thereafter, it pressed less frequently, and eventually stopped. Extinction had occurred. When the rat is removed from the box, and returned later, bar pressing is resumed, even though no reinforcement has been given since extinction. As in classical conditioning, this is known as spontaneous recovery. However, responding during the spontaneous recovery period is not as strong as before extinction. Exposure to further extinction sessions leads to fewer spontaneous recoveries, until the animal stops responding altogether.

Extinction procedures may be used to eliminate undesirable human behaviour. Williams (1959, in Masters *et al.* 1987) reported on the use of this technique to extinguish a young boy's aggressive, demanding and dependency behaviours. The boy had developed these behaviours when he was severely ill, during which time he received a lot of attention and care from his parents. Upon his recovery, the parents tried to withdraw some of the attention, but their actions were met with intense protests, forcing them to continue giving him special attention. This inadvertently reinforced the boy's actions. The therapists instructed the parents to take the boy to bed, complete traditional bedtime rituals, and to ignore his subsequent calls. It is reported that his tantrums disappeared in a matter of days. As Masters *et al.* (1987) point out, extinction procedures must be consistently applied to be effective.

Generalisation in operant conditioning:
A process in which the subject emits the same response to similar stimuli or situations.

Generalisation in operant conditioning refers to a process in which the subject emits the same response to similar stimuli or situations. (Note how this differs from generalisation in classical conditioning: the tendency for a stimulus resembling a conditioned stimulus to elicit a conditioned response.) In one example of generalisation, pigeons trained to peck at a disk of a particular colour were most likely to peck at a disk in a colour closest to the original one (Guttman & Kalish, in Santrock 2000). The importance of generalising behavioural changes to appropriate new situations cannot be overemphasised. For example, if mentally challenged children have been trained to display socially appropriate behaviours in the therapeutic context (saying 'thank you', 'please', etc.), generalisation of these behaviours to the school and home environment is highly desirable. Using multiple contingency managers during training may maximise generalisation. For example, therapists may train teachers and parents to reinforce appropriate behaviours (Masters *et al.* 1987).

Discrimination in operant conditioning occurs when the response is emitted in the presence of a stimulus that signals that the behaviour will be rewarded, and not in the presence of a stimulus that is not rewarded. A cue that signals whether behaviour will be reinforced is known as a discriminative stimulus. How does a discriminative stimulus work? In a laboratory setting, for example, a pigeon may be reinforced for pecking when a green light is on, and not when a red light is on. Thus, the green light signals that pecking will be rewarded. This procedure is known as differential reinforcement.

Discriminative stimuli play an important role in the control of human behaviour. Consider the child who developed dependency following a period of illness. If he throws his temper tantrums in the presence of his parents, and not his siblings, stimulus discrimination has occurred. His parents' presence signal that temper tantrums will be rewarded.

Careful application of a differential reinforcement schedule (also known as differential reinforcement of other behaviour, or DRO) can help eliminate unwanted behaviours. The procedure involves careful reinforcement of target behaviours (or types of behaviours) when they occur, and non-reinforcement of problem behaviours (Masters *et al.* 1987). For example, a mother who ignores her child when she is too loud and insistent, but attends to her as soon as she makes gentle, polite requests, is applying a differential reinforcement schedule. This is likely to eliminate the child's impolite requests.

> **Discrimination in operant conditioning:**
> A process in which the response is emitted in the presence of a stimulus that signals that the behaviour will be rewarded, and not in the presence of a stimulus that is not rewarded.

Punishment

Punishment refers to the application of an aversive (unpleasant) stimulus or the withdrawal of a rewarding stimulus. For example, a teacher scolds a child who reports to school without his or her home-work (an aversive stimulus is applied). As a result, the child is unlikely to come to school without homework in future. Punishment also occurs when a rewarding stimulus is removed. For example, a child may be denied the privilege of playing soccer with friends if he or she has damaged toys belonging to a younger sibling.

Punishment should not be confused with negative reinforcement. Reinforcement, whether positive or negative, increases the probability

> **Punishment:**
> The application of an aversive (unpleasant) stimulus or the withdrawal of a rewarding stimulus.

that the response will occur. We saw that a rat in the Skinner box will press the bar to avoid being shocked (negative reinforcement). Punishment, however, decreases the probability of a response. The child denied playing soccer for damaging the toys should engage less in that behaviour in future, if the punishment was effective.

Contingent punishment procedures

Most of us are familiar with this form of punishment, which involves the application of an unpleasant stimulus following the behaviour to be eliminated. Adams *et al.* (1973) applied this technique successfully to treat an epileptic girl's self-injurious behaviour. The child repeatedly fell on the floor in a pseudo-seizure that could be clearly distinguished from the real seizures she suffered from. Pseudo-seizures were punished by intense verbal scolding. The child was required to wear a helmet, an aversive stimulus for her, but it was made clear that the helmet would be removed in the absence of constant falling. Reportedly, the seizures were eliminated within five days. In a follow-up 30 days after discharge, the gains had been maintained. Note that the success of this programme hinged on the successful distinction between real and pseudo-seizures. Alternative behaviour (absence of falling) was also clearly specified.

Response cost

Response cost:
A punishment procedure involving the withdrawal of a positive reinforcer following inappropriate behaviour.

This punishment procedure involves the withdrawal of a positive reinforcer following inappropriate behaviour. The reinforcer that is withdrawn must have been accrued or earned. For example, individuals may be given tokens for behaving appropriately. An agreed upon number of tokens is then withdrawn if they misbehave. Wolf (1970, in Masters *et al.* 1987) reported on the use of a similar response cost procedure to control the hyperactive behaviour of a child in a classroom. Before class began, points were allocated non-contingently. They were then deducted for out-of-seat behaviour. It was reported that out-of-seat behaviour ceased rapidly. The response cost was even more effective when the points remaining at the end of the programme were divided equally among the members of the class.

In another study, Ross (1974) used response cost to treat a client's nail-biting behaviour. First, the client was contracted to contribute money to a strongly disliked organisation if nail-length did not increase. Periodic measurements of nail-length were taken. It is reported that nail-length increased. The gains were maintained at three- and six-month follow-ups.

Timeout procedures

Response cost clearly specifies which reinforcers will be withdrawn for problem behaviour. In a **timeout procedure**, an individual is isolated from as many reinforcers as possible. For example, a child may be deprived of social contact by being put in a timeout room for a specified period. It should be noted that the room should have no items of reinforcing value, such as toys or television, or the procedure will not work. Like most punishment procedures, timeout programmes need to be scrutinised carefully, for ethical reasons.

Timeout procedures:
A procedure in which an individual is isolated from as many reinforcers as possible.

Considerations when using punishment

Many factors need to be taken into account when using aversive punishment in particular (the application of an unpleasant stimulus). Contingent punishment involves a degree of physical and mental discomfort. Ethical considerations thus come into play. Masters *et al.* (1987) noted that informed client approval is necessary, though not sufficient, in deciding on the use of aversive punishment. Professional judgement should also indicate whether punishment would be effective in changing inappropriate behaviour, without leaving residual mental and physical ill effects. Further, there needs to be evidence that alternative treatments are ineffective or unavailable.

If aversive punishment is to be used, it should be administered immediately after problem behaviour. The longer the delay between a behaviour and punishment, the less effective the punishment will be. Effectiveness is also maximised if alternative models of behaviour are available and pointed out to the individual.

There are other reasons why psychologists prefer to use reinforcement or timeout procedures rather than aversive punishment:

- There are instances in which punishment may exacerbate rather than eliminate problem behaviours. For example, aggressive children may interpret punishment as counter-aggression. It could serve as an inappropriate model, resulting in escalation of undesired behaviour (Masters *et al.* 1987).
- The effects of punishment do not necessarily generalise to other contexts. A child who is punished for aggression at home may be well behaved in that context but aggressive toward peers at school (Masters *et al.* 1987; Santrock 2000).
- Punishment may result in conditioned emotional responses. For example, if children are punished at school, they may develop school anxiety and stay away from school. Even if they do not, the teacher responsible for administering the punishment may be feared. This creates an atmosphere that is not conducive to learning.

- What is regarded as punishment may not be punitive at all. For example, a child who is ignored by her parents when playing quietly, but scolded when she misbehaves, may prefer the attention she gets from being scolded, rather than being ignored (Goldstein 1994; Santrock 2000).
- Punishment may be used prematurely because it is reinforcing to the individual administering it. For example, a parent may use punishment as an outlet for anger and frustration (Masters *et al.* 1987).

Operant conditioning: Applications

Applications of operant conditioning principles have been referred to throughout this chapter. The basic principle underlying these applications is that behaviours that are reinforced are strengthened, while those that are followed by unpleasant consequences are weakened and extinguished.

Token economies

Token economy:
A programme in which an individual or group earns points or tokens for behaving appropriately.

A **token economy** is a programme in which an individual or group earns points or tokens (e.g. coins, tickets, stars) for behaving appropriately. The tokens are later exchanged for other reinforcers, such as food, privileges or enjoyable activities (Kazdin 1994). In using the token economy system, it is important that the tokens be established as conditioned reinforcers, as they have no reinforcing value on their own. For most populations, it is sufficient to explain that tokens can be exchanged for goods and services. The target behaviours subject to change need to be specified, and the number of points earned for each behaviour (Kazdin 1994). A system then needs to be established to keep track of tokens or points (Barkley 1990). Most importantly, the rewards to be exchanged for the tokens must be motivating or meaningful for the person or group. For example, riding a bicycle may be of rewarding value for one child, but not for another.

Token economies have been used to modify behaviours in institutional and educational settings (Masters *et al.* 1987; Barkley 1990). Fixsen *et al.* (1976, in Kazdin 1994) reported on the use of a token economy to rehabilitate pre-delinquent boys who had committed various offences, such as theft, school truancy and fighting. The programme was run in a cottage-style home. The boys earned points for behaviours such as reading newspapers, receiving good grades at school, and remaining neat and clean. Disruptive behaviour, such as fighting, lying or stealing, led to loss of points. It was reported that boys who participated in the programme committed fewer offences and had fewer contacts with law enforcement officers than delinquent boys who did not participate in the programme. However, long-term evaluations indicated that the gains were not maintained (Kazdin 1994).

Jones (1982) reported on the use of a token economy to teach basic handwriting to a group of predominantly black children. The children were taught skills such as holding a pencil and drawing straight lines, curved lines and shapes. Tokens were given for correct responses, which could be exchanged for reinforcing activities (snacks, access to a play-room and a movie room). Achievement tests were administered at the beginning of the programme. A control group (not on token economy) was also tested. At the end of the programme, the experimental group (on token economy) had made significant gains over those of the control group.

The advantage of token economies is that tokens are powerful reinforcers. For example, they can develop behaviours at a higher level than reinforcement procedures that rely on praise. Thus, to obtain higher levels of performance, it is useful to begin a reinforcement programme with a token economy system. Once desired behaviours have been established, they can be maintained with other reinforcers (e.g. praise). Further, tokens are less subject to satiation (loss of value) because they are backed by a variety of reinforcers. Reinforcers can be changed when they are no longer of value. A potential disadvantage of the system is that it may be difficult to withdraw tokens once the target behaviours have been established. Thus, the gains may be lost if tokens are not given. Kazdin (1994) discusses procedures that can be employed to minimise loss of behavioural gains once the token system is withdrawn.

Classical and operant conditioning: Comparisons and overlaps

Classical and operant conditioning represent two forms of learning based on different principles. Table 4.3, overleaf, captures some of the differences between the two.

Although classical and operant conditioning are based on different assumptions, strict distinctions between the two have been questioned. It has been shown that each paradigm shares many properties of the other. For example, Zimmerman (1957) exposed rats to a buzzer for a period of two minutes, and then gave them some water. The pairing of the buzzer and the water is an example of classical conditioning. After repeatedly pairing the buzzer and the water, Zimmerman noted that the rats would press a bar to hear the buzzer. This illustrates operant conditioning. The buzzer had become a secondary reinforcer (a stimulus that gains its reinforcing power by being associated with a primary reinforcer). Before the buzzer was paired with water (classical conditioning), the rats would not press the bar to hear it. The study shows an interaction between classical and operant conditioning.

The overlap between classical and operant conditioning is also illustrated by studies combining elements of the two. For example, when we reviewed Rescorla's (1966) conditioned suppression studies, we noted that rats that had been subjected to a tone and a shock (classical conditioning) stopped engaging in an operantly conditioned response (pressing the bar for food) when the tone was sounded. What was learned through classical conditioning (tone-shock) 'interfered' with an operantly conditioned response (pressing the bar). In a similar study, Estes and Skinner (1941) initially trained rats to press a lever for food using an FI-4 minute schedule (operant conditioning). An FI schedule produces steady, bar-pressing behaviour. Thereafter, a tone was sounded for three minutes at a time. When the tone ended, the rats were subjected to a brief shock, which they could not avoid. Meanwhile, reinforcement was continued on an FI-4 schedule, independently of the tone and the shock. They observed that bar pressing was reduced when the tone was on. However, the rats resumed pressing the bar when the shock was over, until the next tone was sounded. The study, like Rescorla's (1966), showed that what was learnt during classical conditioning (tone-shock) influenced operantly conditioned behaviours (pressing the bar), illustrating the interaction between classical and operant conditioning.

TABLE 4.3: A comparison of classical and operant conditioning

Classical conditioning	Operant conditioning
Key figures	
Pavlov, Watson	Thorndike, Skinner
Nature of response	
Involves involuntary, reflexive behaviour, such as salivation and withdrawing one's hand when burnt.	Involves voluntary behaviour, such as pressing a bar, remaining quiet in a classroom, etc.

Classical conditioning	Operant conditioning
How does response come about?	
The response is elicited; it is triggered by an unconditioned stimulus.	The response is emitted; the organism acts or operates on the environment.
How does learning occur?	
A neutral stimulus (NS) is paired with an unconditioned stimulus (US). Learning occurs when the NS becomes a conditioned stimulus (CS) (i.e. capable of eliciting a conditioned response).	Learning results from reinforcement (negative or positive) or application of an aversive stimulus (punishment), following behaviour. Reinforced behaviours are increased and punished behaviours decreased or eliminated.
Examples	
Albert cries upon seeing a white rabbit, because it has been paired with banging the door.	A rat learns to press a bar to get food (positive reinforcement).
An emotional response, such as joy, is elicited by music associated with one's honeymoon.	A child does homework to avoid being scolded by a teacher (negative reinforcement).
A fear-arousing stimulus (for example, public speaking) is paired with relaxation to eliminate the phobia (systematic desensitisation).	A teacher rewards a child's attending behaviour in the classroom with stars, which are later exchanged for the privilege of seeing a movie at the weekend (token economy).
Comparison of common terms	
Extinction occurs because the CS is no longer accompanied by the US. The dog no longer salivates to the bell because it has been repeatedly presented alone (without food).	**Extinction** occurs because the behaviour is no longer reinforced. The boy stops behaving appropriately in the classroom because he is no longer rewarded with tokens.
Discrimination: Subjects learn to respond differently to stimuli resembling the CS (e.g. the dog salivates to the sound of the bell, not the ringing telephone).	**Discrimination:** Subjects learn to distinguish between cues signalling that a response will be reinforced or not reinforced. For example, a baby cries hysterically only when his or her mother, and not a sibling, is in sight.
Generalisation: Subjects respond with a conditioned response to stimuli similar to the CS (e.g. a child who was bitten by a puppy runs away at the sight of a cat).	**Generalisation:** Subject emits the same response in a similar situation. For example, a mentally challenged child trained to behave socially (to say 'thank you', 'please') in a clinical setting, does the same at school and at home.

Learning: Cognitive and biological factors

Classical and operant conditioning do not pay much attention to cognitive and biological factors. Cognitive processes such as thinking, memory and expectations do not feature in these approaches. This is because behaviourists (Skinnerians in particular) were more interested in observable and measurable behaviour than in what was going on inside the organism's mind. Recently, there has been a resurgence of interest in cognitive and biological approaches to learning. These approaches to psychology are discussed in other chapters, but are reviewed briefly here in relation to learning.

Social learning theories

Social learning theorists maintain that learning results from observing other people in the social context. Most social learning theorists accept the role played by conditioning in human learning. They also argue, however, that human beings have expectations, beliefs and attitudes. Our expectations and beliefs influence the way we acquire information, including perceptions of what is considered a reinforcer. A reciprocal relationship between the organism and the environment is postulated: the environment influences our behaviour, but we are also actively involved in shaping the environment. This is known as **reciprocal determinism** (Bandura 1994). Social learning theories do not represent a single, unified approach to human behaviour. They are united, however, by the emphasis they place on observational learning and cognitive factors in human learning.

Reciprocal determinism: Interactive relationship in which the environment influences our behaviour, but we are also actively involved in shaping the environment.

Observational learning

Observational learning: Learning by observing and imitating another person.

Model: Person observed and imitated in observational learning.

Observational learning is the view that we learn by observing and imitating another person, known as a **model**. The term modelling is often used generically to explain both the learning that occurs from observing others and the resultant imitative change in behaviour. Specifically, the term refers to the behaviours of the person being observed. Imitation, however, refers specifically to the person who observes and copies the actions of another (Masters *et al.* 1987). Observational learning can occur without immediate imitation of the model. For example, children often observe the behaviour of peers or adults, but do not imitate or behave in that fashion until a later period, when they find themselves in a similar situation, or reach a stage when the behaviour is appropriate (Masters *et al.* 1987).

According to Bandura (1986), four main processes must be present for observational learning to occur: attention, retention, motor reproduction and reinforcement.

Firstly, we need to pay attention to what the model is doing or saying. How is the attention of the observer attained and secured in modelling? Two primary factors are involved: the characteristics and behaviour of the model, and the characteristics of the observer. For example, models who are similar to the observer in terms of sex, age group and ethnicity are likely to be effective compared to models who differ from the observer on these variables. Competent models are more effective than those who lack expertise. With regard to the characteristics of the observer, he or she must be able to attend to the model. For example, hyperanxious individuals may be too excited to note the model's characteristics and message.

Secondly, the observer must be able to symbolically code and retain the information observed (retention). Symbolic coding refers to procedures employed to organise information so that it can be retained with ease. Verbal rehearsal (describing the events in words) and practice assist information retention.

Thirdly, observational learning involves motor reproduction. The observer must have the physical capabilities to repeat the model's actions. For example, watching an ice-skating competition does not mean that a child will be able to reproduce the required movements.

The final process in Bandura's modelling analysis is reinforcement. This refers to conditions that will motivate the observer to reproduce the acquired behaviour pattern. In one study, Bandura (1965) showed children a film depicting an adult behaving violently toward a life-size plastic doll called Bobo. One group saw a version of the film showing the model rewarded for aggression. Another group saw the model punished for violent behaviour. A third group saw the model behaving violently, followed by no consequences. The last group was not shown the film at all. Thereafter, all the children were taken to a playroom containing a variety of toys, including a life-size Bobo doll. Their free play was monitored. Children who had seen the model rewarded for violence were the most aggressive, while those who had seen the model punished were the least aggressive. Children who had not seen the film, and those who had seen no consequences following the model's aggression, did not display any aggression. However, when the groups exposed to the film were offered incentives for violence (a prize), it was noted that all three had learnt the model's actions. The study shows the facilitative and inhibitory role of reinforcement and punishment in observational learning.

The immediate applications of observational learning pertain to the influence of television and the film media in influencing children's behaviour. Many children spend thousands of hours watching television. In many instances, television and movie models are heroes: they are rewarded for violent behaviour. Does this mean that this will cause children to engage in violent acts? Researchers had an opportunity to study the impact of television on behaviour when a Canadian town that did not have television began receiving broadcasts. It was reported that, after the broadcasts began, children's reading levels declined (Corteen & Williams 1986) and their perceptions of sex roles became more stereotyped. Increases in verbal and physical aggression were also noted among both boys and girls (Joy *et al.* 1986). Although one cannot conclude that there is a direct causal relationship between television and violence based on this study alone due to other factors involved – for example, individual identification with aggressor, reinforcement for aggression – it does point at a relationship between television violence and aggression.

In summary, observational learning, unlike classical and operant conditioning, pays attention to the processes involved in transforming information received into cognitive representations that are used to guide our behaviour.

Cognitive maps

Cognitive map:
An internal, cognitive representation of physical space.

A **cognitive map** is an internal, cognitive representation of physical space, such as a city or a maze. Tolman (1948) argued that cognitive maps play an important part in animal learning. In one experiment, Tolman and Honzik (1930) had rats run through a maze from a starting point to a point where food was located. There were three possible pathways to the food: the shortest path, the intermediate path and the longest path. First, the rats were given an opportunity to explore the maze. Thereafter, the most direct (shortest) path to the food was blocked. The rats chose the second most direct route to the food source, rather than the longest one. Tolman and Honzik argued that rats had developed an internal representation of the maze, hence the choice of the second most direct route. The idea of cognitive maps also applies to human learning. For example, we are likely to have an internal representation of where things are located in our house or office. It is another aspect of learning that is not covered by classical and operant conditioning.

Biological factors in learning

This refers to an organism's innate biological predispositions that may facilitate or inhibit learning. Biological determinants of learning were hinted at previously, when Seligman's (1970) notion of preparedness was introduced. The importance of biological factors in learning is also illustrated by a phenomenon known as **instinctive drift** (Breland & Breland 1961). The term refers to an organism's tendency to revert to instinctive behaviour that interferes with learning. It was accidentally discovered by the Brelands, who used operant conditioning principles to train circus animals. In one of these sessions, a pig was trained to carry large wooden coins and deposit them in a piggy bank. It was rewarded with food. At first, everything went well, but then, suddenly, the animal's behaviour broke down. It began to use the coins to perform activities that it would normally perform with food. For example, it would drop the coin on the ground and shove it with its snout repeatedly. These behaviours delayed reinforcement (food) and, hence, should have been eliminated. The Brelands labelled this 'misbehaviour', as it violated the operant conditioning principle that non-reinforced behaviours are eliminated. In this case, the pig's rooting instinct took over. It associated the coin with the food. The example indicates that not all behaviours can be shaped by operant conditioning and that the organism's biological predisposition ought to be considered.

Instinctive drift:
An organism's tendency to revert to instinctive behaviour that interferes with learning.

Summary

Two main approaches to learning have been reviewed: classical and operant conditioning. In classical conditioning, a neutral stimulus (NS) is repeatedly paired with a stimulus that elicits a desired response (US). Learning occurs when the neutral stimulus becomes a conditioned stimulus (i.e. capable of producing a conditioned response).

The organism remains passive in classical conditioning. An approach to learning in which the organism is actively involved in manipulating the environment is called operant (or instrumental) conditioning. It involves an association between an organism's responses and its consequences. The consequences either increase or decrease the likelihood that the behaviour will be emitted again.

Traditional distinctions between classical and operant conditioning have been questioned. It has been shown that behaviours established through classical conditioning may 'interfere' with operantly conditioned responses (Rescorla 1966). This points to an interaction between the two forms of learning.

Both classical and operant conditioning do not account for biological and cognitive factors in learning. Three such approaches were briefly reviewed. Social learning theories emphasise observational and cognitive factors in learning. There is also the view that we learn by creating cognitive maps, consisting of an internal representation of objects in space. Finally, the notion of preparedness maintains that learning may be facilitated or inhibited by innate biological predispositions.

Further reading

Adams, K.M., Klinge, V.K. & Keiser, T.W. (1973) The extinction of self-injurious behavior on an epileptic child. *Behavior Research and Therapy*, 11, pp. 351–6.

Barkley, R.A. (1990) *Attention Deficit Hyperactivity Disorder: A Handbook for Diagnosis and Treatment*. New York: Guilford.

Bandura, A. (1965) Influence of models' reinforcement contingencies on the acquisition of imitative responses. *Journal of Personality and Social Psychology*, 1, pp. 589–95.

Bandura, A. (1969) *Principles of Behavior Modification*. New York: Holt, Rinehart & Winston.

Bandura, A. (1986) *Social Foundations of Thought and Action*. Englewood Cliffs: Prentice-Hall.

Bandura, A. (1994) Social cognitive theory of mass communication. In J. Bryant & D. Zillman (eds), *Media Effects*. Mahwah: Erlbaum.

Breland, K. & Breland, M. (1961) The misbehavior of organisms. *American Psychologist*, 16, pp. 681–4.

Butler, R.H. (1954) Incentive conditions which influence visual exploration. *Journal of Experimental Psychology*, 48, pp. 19–23.

Chance, P. (1999) *Learning and Behaviour* (4th edition). Belmont: Wadsworth.

Corteen, R.S. & Williams, T.M. (1986) Television and reading skills. In T.M. Williams (ed.), *The Impact of Television: A Natural Experiment in Three Communities*. Orlando: Academic.

Driscoll, M.P. (1994) *Psychology of Learning for Instruction*. Boston: Allyn & Bacon.

Estes, W.K. & Skinner, B.F. (1941) Some quantitative properties of anxiety. *Journal of Experimental Psychology*, 29, pp. 390–400.

Ferster, C.B., Culbertson, S. & Boren, M. (1975) *Behavior Principles* (2nd edition). New York: Prentice-Hall.

Garcia, J. & Koelling, R.A. (1966) Relation of cue to consequence in avoidance learning. *Psychonomic Science*, 4, pp. 123–4.

Goldstein, E.B. (1994) *Psychology*. Pacific Grove: Brooks/Cole.

Hannon, A. (1987) Learning and conditioning. In G.A. Tyson (ed.), *Introduction to Psychology: A South African Perspective*. Johannesburg: Westro Educational Books.

Hilgard, E.R. & Bower, G.H. (1975) *Theories of Learning* (4th edition). Englewood Cliffs: Prentice-Hall.

Huesmann, L.R., Moise, J.F. & Podolski, C. (1997) The effects of media violence on the development of antisocial behavior. In D.M. Stoff, J. Breiling & J.D. Maser (eds), *Handbook of Antisocial Behavior*. New York: John Wiley.

Jones, M.C. (1924) The elimination of children's fears. *Journal of Experimental Psychology*, 7, pp. 382–90.

Jones, R.T. (1982) Academic improvement through behavior modification. In S.M. Turner and R.T. Jones (eds), *Behavior Modification in Black Populations: Psychosocial Issues and Empirical Findings*. New York: Plenum Press.

Jones, A., Wilkinson, H.J. & Braden, I. (1961) Information deprivation as a motivational variable. *Journal of Experimental Psychology*, 62, pp. 126–37.

Joy, L.A., Kimball, M.M. & Zabrack, M.L. (1986) Television and aggressive behavior. In T.M. Williams (ed.), *The Impact of Television: A Natural Experiment Involving Three Communities*. New York: Academic.

Kamin, L.J. (1968) Attention-like processes in classical conditioning. In M.R. Jones (ed.), *Miami Symposium on the Prediction of Behavior: Aversive Stimuli*. Coral Gables: University of Miami Press.

Kazdin, A.E. (1994) *Behavior Modification in Applied Settings* (5th edition). Pacific Grove: Brooks/Cole.

Lieberman, D.A. (1990) *Learning: Behavior and Cognition*. Belmont: Wadsworth.

Martin, G. & Pear, J. (1999) *Behavior Modification* (6th edition). Upper Saddle River: Prentice-Hall.

Masters, J.C., Burish, T.G., Hollon, S.D. & Rimm, D.C. (1987) *Behavior Therapy: Techniques and Empirical Findings* (3rd edition). Washington, DC: Harcourt.

Mwawenda, T.S. (1995) *Educational Psychology: An African Perspective* (2nd edition). Durban: Butterworths.

Plotnick, R. (1996) *Introduction to Psychology*. Pacific Grove: Brooks/Cole.

Rescorla, R.A. (1966) Predictability and number of pairings in Pavlonian fear conditioning. *Psychonomic Science*, 4, pp. 383–4.

Rescorla, R.A. (1981) Simultaneous associations. In P. Harzem & M.D. Zeiler (eds), *Predictability, Correlation, and Contiguity*. New York: John Wiley.

Rescorla, R.A. (1988) Pavlonian conditioning: It's not what you think it is. *American Psychologist*, 43, pp. 151–60.

Rescorla, R.A. (1996) Spontaneous recovery after training with multiple outcomes. *Animal Learning and Behavior*, 24, pp. 11–18.

Rosen L., Taylor, S., O'Leary, S. & Sanderson, W. (1990) A survey of classroom management practices. *Journal of School Psychology*, 28, pp. 257–69.

Ross, J.A. (1974) The use of contingency contracting in controlling adult nail-biting. *Journal of Behavior Therapy and Experimental Psychiatry*, 5, pp. 105–6.

Ross, S.M. & Ross, L.E. (1971) Comparison of trace and delay classical conditioning as a function of interstimulus. *Journal of Experimental Psychology*, 91, pp. 165–7.

Santrock, J.W. (2000) *Psychology* (6th edition). Boston: McGraw-Hill.

Schwartz, B. (1978) *Psychology of Learning and Behavior*. New York: Norton.

Schwartz, B. & Robbins, S.J. (1995) *Psychology of Learning and Behavior*. New York: Norton.

Seligman, M.E.P. (1970) On the generality of the laws of learning. *Psychological Review*, 77, pp. 406–18.

Skinner, B.F. (1948) 'Superstition' in the pigeon. *Journal of Experimental Psychology*, 38, pp. 168–72.

Tolman, E.C. (1948) Cognitive maps in rats and man. *Psychological Review*, 55, pp. 189–208.

Tolman, E.C. & Honzik, C.H. (1930) Introduction and removal of reward, and maze performance in rats. *University of California Publications in Psychology*, 4, pp. 257–75.

Weidemann, G., Georgilas, A. & Kehoe, E.J. (1999) Temporal specificity in patterning of the rabbit nictitating membrane response. *Animal Learning and Behavior*, 27, pp. 99–109.

Werle, M.A., Murphy, T.B. & Budd, K.S. (1993) Treating chronic food refusal in young children: Home-based parent training. *Journal of Applied Behavior Analysis*, 26, pp. 421–33.

Zimmerman, D.W. (1957) Double-secondary reinforcement: Method and theory. *Psychological Review*, 64, pp. 373–83.

Psychopathology

5

L.J. Nicholas, C. Malcolm, B. von Krosigk and B.J. Pillay

Objectives

After studying this chapter you should:

- understand the full range of psychological disorders described in the *Diagnostic and Statistical Manual of Mental Disorders: Text Revised* (4th edition) (DSM-IV-TR)
- be able to identify the major clusters of psychological disorders described in DSM-IV-TR
- be able to recognise the core symptoms of psychological disorders
- understand the etiological factors involved in psychological disorders
- understand the role of culture in the expression of psychological disorders.

Psychological disorders

Defining abnormal behaviour is difficult, since it is based on a number of definitions from various perspectives. The biopsychosocial approach to abnormal behaviour defines it as the persistent manifestation of seriously different behaviour that impairs the individual's everyday functioning, is distressing to the individual concerned and contrary to the individual's well-being and/or that of the community of which the individual is a member. DSM-IV-TR bases its assessment of whether behaviour is abnormal on the criteria of personal distress and impairment of everyday functioning.

Thousands of years ago, illness, disease and abnormal behaviour were believed to be a curse or punishment from the gods. Demons were believed to have been sent by the gods to torment the afflicted individual. Much later, Christianity transferred the belief in demons as the originators of disease to the Devil, and spirit beings were also assigned powers for causing illness and disease. Around 550 BC, the Persian King Kyros required physicians to have practised medicine for at least 20 years among the king's enemies before treating the king and his family. The king wanted to establish the number of patients who recovered and the number who died under their care. Many millennia before Christ, some form of medicine was already being practised, largely based on a combination of science, superstition, religion and art. Explanations for abnormal behaviour were mostly aligned with the then scientific status of life on Earth and related beliefs about natural and supernatural phenomena.

The ancient world

The Greek physician Hippocrates (460–377 BC) was the first to assume that all disease was the result of natural causes rather than the result of invasions of demons in the brain or body. He proposed that the body contained four humours: blood, black bile, yellow bile and phlegm, and that while they were properly balanced the individual would be healthy. He also proposed that, when the balance was disturbed, there was a natural tendency for balance to be regained (Hergenhahn 1992).

Galen (130–200), a Greek physician, contributed towards our understanding of the nervous system by dividing the causes of mental disorders into physical and mental categories. Plato (429–347 BC) and Aristotle (384–322 BC) were two Greek philosophers who believed that the mentally ill should be treated humanely, that various agents within the body were responsible for mental disorders, and that the mentally ill should therefore not be held responsible for their actions.

The Middle Ages

The Middle Ages and fifteenth- and sixteenth-century Europe spawned many damaging views and beliefs about abnormal behaviour. Witchcraft was deemed a plausible explanation for such behaviour, resulting in people being ostracised and sometimes killed.

Lebakeng *et al.* (2002: p. 211) contend that 'witchcraft accusations flourish in communities that entertain supernatural cosmologies and gain ascendance at times of socio-historical upheaval, and individual and collective adversity'. They quote Minnaar *et al.*'s (1997) figures that from 1990 to 1995, 455 witchcraft-related cases were reported to the police in Northern Province (now Limpopo Province), with 55% being reported in the year of South Africa's transition to democracy, 1994/1995. The cases usually involved elderly women who were targeted by young men.

The German theologian Martin Luther (1483–1546) believed that those who were mentally ill were possessed by the devil. Avicenna

(980–1037), an Islamic physician, rejected the belief in demonology and acted contrary to the Western belief of his time by treating the mentally disturbed in a humane way. The Swiss physician Paracelsus (1493–1541) also rejected demonology as a cause for mental disturbances, and he introduced the belief in psychic causes for mental illness. He speculated that hysteria had sexual origins and that mania was caused by bodily substances influencing the brain. Johann Weyer (1515–1588), a German physician who argued against demonology, was subsequently ostracised by his peers and the church.

The eighteenth to early twentieth centuries

In the eighteenth century, a resurgence of scientific questioning in Europe led to the development of more humanitarian approaches to understanding and treating abnormal behaviour through the establishment of asylums. Individuals who behaved abnormally were understood to be mentally ill, and the superstitious beliefs that had impeded the treatment of mental disorders were challenged. William Tuke (1732–1822), an English Quaker, housed the mentally ill in his newly established York Retreat in a humane way. At the same time, French physician Philippe Pinel (1745–1826) established humane and moral conditions for caring for the mentally ill at the La Bicître and La Salpîtriëre hospitals in France.

In the United States, Dorothea Dix (1802–1887), an American teacher, started the mental hygiene movement by focusing on the physical well-being of mental patients in hospitals. During the nineteenth century, Victorian attitudes about sexuality, mood and brain functioning influenced the understanding of mental illness. Victorian morality was thus hailed as an essential feature for good mental health. Women were considered physically inferior to men, and women's minds were subsequently considered inferior to the minds of men. Despite this, the foundations of twentieth and twenty-first century attitudes towards abnormal behaviour were laid in the nineteenth century, and the roots of abnormal behaviour were explored by studying organic factors that were believed to be the cause of such behaviour. A scientific breakthrough occurred between 1825 and 1917, when brain pathology was found to be the causal factor in general paresis.

In 1883, Emil Kraepelin (1856–1926) published a list of mental disorders that was adopted worldwide. His system of classification was based on causation, the degree of involvement of the brain and nervous system, and symptoms and their treatment (Hergenhahn 1992).

Classification of psychological disorders

The *Diagnostic and Statistical Manual of Mental Disorders* (DSM-I), first published by the American Psychiatric Association (APA) in 1952, became the dominant classification scheme for mental disorders around the world and in South Africa. Revisions were published in 1968 (DSM-II), 1980 (DSM-III) and 1987 (DSM-III-R), to improve the diagnostic consistency of psychologists by making diagnostic guidelines more explicit, detailed and concrete. DSM-IV was published in 1994 and the revision was based on empirical research rather than the consensus of experts (Weiten 1998). DSM-V is not expected to appear before 2006 and a text revision, DSM-IV-TR, was published in 2000 in order to bridge the span between DSM-IV and DSM-V. DSM-IV-TR was published to:

- correct factual errors in the previous edition;
- review the DSM-IV text to ensure up-to-date information;
- update DSM-IV literature reviews that had been completed in 1992;
- improve the educational value of DSM; and
- update ICD.9 CM codes that had been changed since 1996 (APA 2000).

Classification

DSM-IV-TR uses a multiaxial system of classification that was first introduced in DSM-III. The multiaxial system evaluates the individual on five axes or dimensions, and facilitates a comprehensive and systematic evaluation.

Axis I   This is used to report clinical disorders and other conditions that may be a focus of clinical attention. This is obtained by observing the symptoms and syndromes that an individual with features of abnormal behaviour displays, for example, anxiety disorder, undifferentiated schizophrenia, dysthymia disorder, etc.

Axis II   The name of the diagnostic category is indicated, which corresponds to features of a personality disorder or mental retardation. Symptoms and syndromes of a particular disorder are obtained by observing the individual and by questioning others who are and have been close to the individual, and who have some knowledge of his or her past and long-term functioning, for example, paranoid personality disorder and obsessive-compulsive personality disorder.

Axis III   The name of medical or physical problems that may be related to the diagnosis on Axis I and/or Axis II are indicated, for example, diabetes mellitus or concussion.

Axis IV   Any environmental and social problems that the individual
           has at the moment of diagnosis, and which may affect the
           diagnosis, treatment and prognosis of the Axis I and/or Axis
           II disorder are indicated. These problems could fall into the
           realm of the individual's social functioning, such as death of
           a spouse; job-related problems, such as retrenchment; educa-
           tional problems, such as incomplete education due to school
           pregnancy; family problems, such as an alcoholic and abu-
           sive father; problems with the law; and economic and
           housing problems.

Axis V   The Global Assessment of Functioning Scale (GAF) reflects
           the overall mental, social and career functioning of a person
           expressed as a percentage. Scores range from 1 to 100, where
           1 indicates poor functioning and that the individual is a
           threat to him- or herself and/or others, and 100 indicates
           superior functioning with no symptoms.

This classification of abnormal behaviour is based on scientific theory,
which proposes that observable symptoms of abnormal behaviour are
the result of biological, psychological and social influences, which is
known as the **biopsychosocial approach** to understanding, diagnosing
and classifying abnormal behaviour. Possible biological influences are
indicated on Axis III; the result of biological, psychological and social
influences are indicated on Axes I and II; current social influences are
indicated on Axis IV; and the current functioning of the individual on
the biological, psychological and social levels is indicated on Axis V.

Biopsychosocial approach:
Theory that observable syptoms of abnormal behaviour are the result of biological, psychological and social influences.

Types of psychological disorders and their main diagnostic features

Note that the diagnostic criteria are only guidelines for diagnoses.

DSM-IV-TR classification of disorders
Disorders usually first diagnosed in infancy, childhood or adolescence:

Disorder	Examples
Mental retardation	Mild, moderate, severe, profound
Learning disorders	Reading
Motor skills disorder	Developmental coordination
Communication disorders	Stuttering
Pervasive developmental disorders	Autism

Attention deficit and disruptive behaviour attention deficit and hyperactivity (ADHD) disorders	
Feeding and eating disorders of infancy or early childhood	Pica
Tic disorders	Tourettes
Elimination disorders	Encopresis
Other	Separation anxiety

Delirium, dementia, amnestic and other cognitive disorders:

Disorder	Examples
Delirium	Substance withdrawal
Dementia	Alzheimer's type
Amnestic	Substance induced

Substance-related disorders:

Disorder	Examples
Alcohol use	Dependence/Abuse
Alcohol induced	Withdrawal
Amphetamine use	Dependence/Abuse
Amphetamine induced	Withdrawal
Caffeine induced	Caffeine intoxication
Cannabis use	Dependence/Abuse
Cannabis-induced disorder	Intoxication
Cocaine use	Dependence/Abuse
Cocaine-induced disorder	Intoxication
Hallucinogen use	Dependence/Abuse
Hallucinogen-induced disorder	Intoxication
Inhalant use	Dependence/Abuse
Inhalant-induced disorder	Intoxication
Nicotine use	Dependence
Nicotine-induced disorder	Withdrawal
Opoid use	Dependence/Abuse
Opoid-induced disorder	Intoxication
Other substances	(Use/Induced)

Schizophrenia and other psychotic disorders:

- Paranoid type
- Disorganised type
- Catatonic type
- Undifferentiated type

- Residual type

Mood disorders:

- Major depressive disorder
- Dysthymic disorder
- Bipolar disorder

Anxiety disorders:

- Panic disorder – with/without agoraphobia
- Agoraphobia without history of panic disorder
- Specific phobia
- Social phobia
- Obsessive-compulsive disorder
- Post-traumatic stress disorder (PTSD)
- Acute stress disorder
- Generalised anxiety disorder

Somatoform disorders:

- Somatisation disorder
- Conversion disorder
- Pain disorder
- Hypochondriasis
- Body dysmorphic disorder

Dissociative disorders:

- Dissociative amnesia
- Dissociative fugue
- Dissociative identity disorder
- Dissociative depersonalisation disorder

Sexual and gender identity disorders:

- Sexual dysfunctions disorder
- Sexual desire disorders
- Arousal disorders
- Orgasmic disorders
- Sexual pain disorders
- Sexual dysfunction due to general medical condition
- Paraphilias
- Gender identity disorder

Eating disorders:

- Anorexia nervosa
- Bulimia nervosa

Sleep disorders:

- Primary insomnia
- Primary hypersomnia
- Narcolepsy
- Breathing-related sleep disorder
- Circadian rhythm sleep disorder
- Nightmare disorder
- Sleep terror disorder
- Sleepwalking disorder
- Insomnia or hypersomnia related to another mental disorder
- Substance induced sleep disorder

Impulse control disorders:

- Intermittent explosive disorder
- Kleptomania
- Pyromania
- Pathological gambling
- Trichotillomania

Adjustment disorders:

- With depressed mood
- With anxiety
- With disturbances of conduct

Other conditions that may be a focus of clinical attention:

- Psychological factors affecting medical condition
- Medication-induced movement disorders

Personality disorders

Personality disorders are enduring patterns of inner experience and behaviour that deviate markedly from the expectations of an individual's culture. They are pervasive and inflexible, have an onset in early adulthood or adolescence, are stable over time, and lead to distress or impairment (DSM-IV-TR).

Paranoid personality disorder

- Pervasive distrust and suspiciousness on the basis of little or no evidence.
- Preoccupation with unjustified doubts about the loyalty of friends and associates.

- Persistently bear grudges and unwilling to forgive the insults that they believe they have received.
- Reluctance to confide in others because of baseless fears that the confidences will be used against her or him.

Schizoid personality disorder
- Neither wants nor takes pleasure in close relationships.
- Almost always chooses solitary activities.
- Appearance of indifference to praise or criticism.
- Emotionally cold and detached.

Schizotypal personality disorder
- Acute discomfort with and reduced capacity for close relationships.
- Cognitive or perceptual distortions and eccentricities of behaviour, including bodily illusions.
- Suspiciousness or paranoid ideation.
- Odd beliefs or magical thinking.
- Odd behaviour and appearance.

Anti-social personality disorder
- Disregard for and violation of the rights of others occurring since age 15.
- Lack of remorse.
- Consistent irresponsibility.
- Deceitfulness.
- Impulsivity.
- Reckless disregard for safety of self and others.

Borderline personality disorder
- Unstable and intense interpersonal relationships with extremes of idealisation and devaluation.
- Unstable self-image or sense of self.
- Impulsivity.
- Recurring suicidal behaviours, gestures or threats, or self-mutilating behaviour.
- Inappropriate intense anger or problems controlling anger.

Histrionic personality disorder
- Uncomfortable when not the centre of attention.
- Inappropriate sexually-seductive or provocative behaviour.
- Rapidly shifting and shallow emotional expression.
- Suggestible.

Narcissistic personality disorder

- Grandiose sense of self.
- Fantasises about unlimited success, power, etc.
- Requires excessive administration because of his or her 'specialness'.
- Has unreasonable expectations of special treatment.
- Lacks empathy.

Avoidant personality disorder

- Avoids work activities that involve significant interpersonal contact with people unless certain of being liked.
- Avoids new activities because they might be embarrassing.
- Preoccupied with being rejected or criticised in social situations.
- Views self as socially inept or inferior.

Dependent personality disorder

- Requires an excessive amount of advice and reassurance to make everyday decisions.
- Leaves the responsibility for major areas of life to others.
- Expresses disagreement with difficulty because of fear of loss of approval.
- Excessively seeks nurturance and support.
- Is uncomfortable or helpless when alone because of exaggerated fears of inability to take care of him- or herself.
- Lack of self confidence in judgement or abilities.

Obsessive-compulsive personality disorder

- Pervasive preoccupation with orderliness, perfectionism, and mental and interpersonal control.
- Perfectionism interferes with task completion.
- Over-conscientious, scrupulous and inflexible about morality, ethics or values.
- Has a miserly spending style.
- Rigid and stubborn.
- Excessively devoted to work and productivity.

Contemporary models of psychopathology

Normality:
A biochemical balance of the mind and body, usually determined by an objective expert.

Normality is viewed as a biochemical balance of the body and mind, which is usually determined by an expert who is, in most instances, objective, neutral and value-free. Some practitioners, mainly psychiatrists (medical doctors trained in psychiatry), who adhere to these models, would look for certain clues when they investigate the cause of the individual's abnormal behaviour. They may check if the family has a history of that behaviour, which will lend a possible genetic predisposition. Does the disorder seem to be related to past illness or accident (biological trauma), or follow its own course, irrespective of situational changes? They may also assess the patient's mental status. **Mental status** refers to the intactness of memory, orientation to reality with regard to time, place and person (whether the patient knows who he or she is, what day of the week it is, and so forth), state of consciousness (whether the person is clear and alert), reasoning ability, and the ability to think rationally and abstractly. For example, a patient who tends to use words incoherently may be suspected of presenting with a mental disorder. Clinicians adhering to this orientation might then inquire if the patient hears voices or sees things that are not there. They may further focus on particular areas of presumed organic dysfunction to come up with an appropriate course of biological treatment.

Mental status:
Intactness of memory, orientation to reality with regard to time, place and person, state of conciousness, reasoning ability, and the ability to think rationally and abstractly.

In brief, biological models focus on five categories of biological factors that are considered significant in the development of abnormal behaviour:

- biochemical imbalances in the brain;
- genetic defects;
- constitutional liabilities;
- brain dysfunction; and
- physical deprivation or disruptions.

Evaluation of biological models

Although several criticisms have been levelled against biological models, they have affected the way we think about human behaviour and have undoubted virtues. They have enabled us to recognise the significant role of biochemical factors and innate characteristics that are genetically determined in the development of abnormal behaviour.

They have often been used concurrently with most therapeutic interventions, and thus complement the latter in the treatment of more serious mental disorders, such as major depression and schizophrenia. Although biological processes affect our thoughts, behaviour and emotions, they are also affected by the latter in a circular way. Abnormal behaviour, therefore, is a result of the interplay of biological and non-biological factors (social and cultural) and, as such, can be explained by exploring that interplay instead of focusing exclusively on biological factors.

Biological models have been criticised for their overemphasis of internal causes, equating organic dysfunction with mental dysfunction, and assuming biochemical differences are the cause of the disorder when they may be its result.

Substance-related disorders

Substance-related disorders:
Disorders related to the use of substances in excess and their after-effects.

Substance:
A drug of abuse, medication or toxin.

Substance-related disorders include a broad category of disorders that are related to the use of substances in excess and their after-effects. A **substance** within this context refers to a drug of abuse, a medication or a toxin. Over time, most individuals have used substances: legal, illegal or prescription drugs in moderation and for short-lived effects. However, some individuals abuse substances to such an extent that it has far-reaching consequences on different levels of human functioning.

Any substance can be dangerous if taken in excessive amounts. It is important to define substance abuse, and when moderate use become abuse. Excessive use of any substance can lead to either substance abuse, which according to the DSM-IV-TR classification system is a maladaptive pattern of substance use of over a 12-month period, despite recurrent and significant adverse consequences or substance dependence, which is a maladaptive pattern of substance use and results in significant impairment, manifested by three or more of the following:

- The person develops tolerance, indicated by either a need for larger doses of the substance to produce the desired effect, or markedly diminished effect with continued use of the same amount of the substance.
- Withdrawal symptoms develop, as manifested by negative physical and psychological effects, which develop when the person stops or reduces intake of the substance.
- The substance is often taken in larger amounts or over a longer period than intended.
- The person recognises excessive use of the substance: he or she might have had a persistent desire or made unsuccessful efforts to cut down or control substance use.
- Much of the person's time is spent on activities necessary to obtain the substance.
- Significant social, occupational or recreational activities are given up or reduced because of substance use.
- Substance use continues despite the knowledge of having persistent psychological or physical problems caused or aggravated by the use of the substance.

For one to make a diagnosis of substance abuse, the person must experience at least one of the following:

- recurrent substance use resulting in failure to meet major role obligations at school, at work or at home (e.g. absence from work, neglect of children, poor school performance related to the substance abuse);
- recurrent substance use in situations in which it is physically hazardous (e.g. driving while intoxicated);
- recurrent substance-related legal problems (e.g. traffic violations or arrests for disorderly conduct); and
- continued substance use despite having persistent or recurrent social and interpersonal problems (e.g. physical fights or arguments with a spouse).

Substance intoxication is diagnosed when the ingestion of a substance affects the central nervous system and produces maladaptive cognitive and behavioural effects (e.g. impaired judgement, mood liability, cognitive impairment, impaired social and occupational functioning) that develop shortly after the use of the substance.

Substance intoxication: Condition when the ingestion of a substance affects the central nervous system and produces maladaptive cognitive and behavioural effects that develop shortly after the use of the substance.

Biological causation of alcohol-related disorders

Biological factors
Alcohol may produce a morphine-like substance in the brains of certain individuals, which may increase the potential for addiction.

Genetic factors
Primary alcoholism especially tends to run strongly in families. The rate of concordance in identical twins is higher than in non-identical twins or same-sex siblings. Adoption studies, where children had no knowledge of their parents' alcohol status have shown that:

- there is a higher rate of alcoholism in children removed from homes of alcoholic parents; and
- children from non-alcoholic parents who are adopted into alcoholic homes do not exhibit an increase in alcoholism rates in adult life.

A number of potential genetic markers have been isolated and are now under further scrutiny. These are associated with alcoholism directly and the factors that influence the patterns of alcohol consumption. However, due to the fact that there is no adequate screening test, it is uncertain whether some of these changes have occurred as a result of the alcohol abuse or whether they were present prior to the development of the behaviour. Therefore, researchers are now looking at the children of alcoholics before alcoholism develops in the hope of identifying some consistent pathology. Some of the findings include a decreased intensity of reaction to ethanol and changes in electroencephalograph (EEG) readings.

It has been accepted that there is no one causative factor responsible for the pathogenesis of alcohol abuse. Certain genetic and biological factors may place the individual at increased risk, but only when there is an adequate interplay with environmental and social factors is the disorder manifested and sustained.

Anxiety disorders

DSM-IV-TR presents six main categories of anxiety disorder: panic disorder, phobia, obsessive-compulsive disorder (OCD), post-traumatic stress disorder (PTSD), acute stress disorder, and generalised anxiety disorder (GAD). Someone with one anxiety disorder often meets the criteria of another – a situation know as co-morbidity. A **panic disorder** is characterised by a sudden inexplicable onset of a cluster of symptoms, such as heart palpitations, nausea, chest pain, dizziness, sweating, trembling, terror and feelings of impending doom.

A **phobia** is a disruptive, fearful avoidance of an object or situation that is out of proportion to the potential threat thereof, and recognised by the sufferer as groundless.

An **obsessive-compulsive disorder** is marked by persistent and uncontrollable thoughts and compulsion to repeat senseless acts, causing distress and interference with everyday functioning.

Post-traumatic stress disorder develops after exposure to an extreme traumatic stressor and involves re-experiencing the event, avoiding stimuli associated with the event, and symptoms of increased arousal. Acute stress disorder is marked by anxiety, and dissociative and other symptoms, which occur within one month of exposure to an extreme traumatic stressor.

Generalised anxiety disorder, sometimes referred to as free-floating anxiety, is characterised by persistent uncontrollable anxiety about all manner of things, frequently accompanied by somatic complaints.

'Phobia' is derived from the name of the Greek god Phobos, who frightened his enemies (Davison & Neale 1998). DSM-IV-TR lists the following subtypes.

Animal type:
This subtype should be specified if the fear is cued by animals or insects.

Panic disorder:
Condition characterised by a sudden inexplicable onset of a cluster of symptoms, such as heart palpitations, nausea, chest pain, dizziness, sweating, trembling, terror and feelings of impending doom.

Phobia:
Condition characterised by a disruptive, fearful avoidance of an object or situation that is out of proportion to the potential threat thereof, and recognised by the sufferer as groundless.

Obsessive compulsive disorder:
Condition marked by persistent and uncontrollable thoughts and compulsion to repeat senseless acts, causing distress and interference with everyday functioning.

Post-traumatic stress disorder:
Condition that develops after exposure to an extreme traumatic stressor.

Generalised anxiety disorder:
Condition characterised by persistent uncontrollable anxiety about all manner of things, frequently accompanied by somatic complaints.

It generally has a childhood onset.

Natural environment type:
This subtype should be specified if the fear is cued by objects in the natural environment, such as storms, heights or water. It generally has a childhood onset.

Blood-injection injury type:
This subtype should be specified if the fear is cued by seeing blood, or an injury, or by receiving an injection or other invasive medical procedure.

Situational type:
This subtype should be specified if the fear is cued by a specific situation, such as public transport, tunnels, bridges, elevators, flying, driving or enclosed places. This subtype has a bimodal age-at-onset distribution, with one peak in childhood and another in the mid-20s. This subtype appears to be similar to panic disorder, with agoraphobia in its characteristic sex ratios, familial aggregation pattern and age of onset.

Other type:
This subtype should be specified if the fear is cued by other stimuli. These stimuli might include the fear of choking, vomiting or contracting an illness; 'space' phobia (i.e. the individual is afraid of falling down if away from walls or other means of physical support); and children's fears of loud sounds or costumed characters.
(DSM-IV-TR 2000: p. 445)

Etiology of anxiety disorders

Biological factors
Anxiety appears to run in families. Genetic studies show that almost 50% of patients with panic disorder have at least one affected relative. There is a higher incidence in first-degree relatives. Twin studies also implicate a genetic component. New studies have attributed a percentage of anxiety to a polymorphic variant of a gene for the serotonin transporter, which is the site of action for many serotonergic drugs. Patients with the variant gene produce fewer transporters and have higher levels of anxiety.

Biochemical theories implicate neurotransmitters in the development of anxiety disorders. In considering noradrenaline (NA), it is suggested that patients with anxiety disorders may have an abnormal noradrenergic system that is poorly regulated, with outbursts of activity. Stimulation of the locus ceruleus (where the main cell bodies of the NA system are found) causes anxiety, while ablation (removal) of this area destroys the fear response. Therefore, drugs such as beta-adrenergic agonists and alpha-2 antagonists can provoke a panic attack. Concerning serotonin, it was found that anxiety improved in patients who received serotonergic anti-depressants. This is an area of controversy, as data obtained from human studies have been inconclusive. The use of serotonergic hallucinogens and stimulants (lysergic acid diethylamide – LSD) is associated with the development of acute and chronic anxiety disorders. The role of gamma-aminobutyric acid (GABA), an important brain transmitter, is supported by the use of benzodiazepines, which increase the effect of GABA at the GABA2 receptors. The use of GABA antagonists has been implicated in the development of anxiety symptoms. It has been proposed that patients with anxiety disorder may have abnormal functioning of their GABA receptors.

The limbic system (especially the septohippocampal pathway and cingulated gyrus due to its generation of anticipatory anxiety) and the cerebral cortex, in particular the frontal lobe, are implicated. They receive a rich supply of adrenergic, serotonergic and GABA receptors, and are implicated in anxiety disorder, possibly due to the generation of anticipatory anxiety.

In brain-imaging studies, it has been noted that in patients with anxiety disorders, scans have shown an increase in the size of cerebral ventricles and cerebral asymmetry.

Patients with panic disorder appear to have increased sympathetic tone, adapt more slowly to repeated stimuli, and respond more excessively to moderate stimuli. Certain substances (panicogens) have been implicated in the production of panic attacks. These include carbon dioxide, sodium lactate, bicarbonate, certain serotonergic-releasing drugs, alpha adrenergic receptors, caffeine and cholecystokinin. These drugs may act on areas such as the respiratory centre or baroreceptors.

General medical conditions may present with anxiety-like symptoms. These include:

- neurological conditions (cerebral neoplasms, trauma, post-concussive syndromes, cerebrovascular disease, subarachnoid haemorrhage, migraine, encephalitis, neurosyphilis, and multiple sclerosis and Wilson's disease);
- endocrine conditions (pituitary, thyroid, parathyroid, adrenal, pheochromocytoma and in virilisation of females);

- toxic conditions (alcohol and drug withdrawal, amphetamines, sympathetomimetic agents, vasopressor agents, caffeine and caffeine withdrawal);
- systemic illnesses (hypoxia, cardiovascular disease and respiratory disease); and
- other conditions such as hypoglycaemia, carcinoid syndrome, systemic malignancies, febrile illnesses and chronic infections, porphyria and uraemia.

Other factors

These include personality, where certain personality traits, such as neuroticism, appear to be related to developing anxiety disorders. Cognitive factors include misinterpreting harmless situations as threatening, focusing excessive attention on perceived threats, and selectively recalling seemingly threatening information. An association between stress and the development of generalised anxiety disorders has also been found. Behavioural approaches emphasise the acquisition of anxiety responses through classical conditioning and maintaining them through operant conditioning.

Counter-conditioning is a widely used behavioural technique for phobias – relearning through eliciting a new response in the presence of the anxiety-provoking stimulus. This principle is used in the popular behaviour therapy technique of systematic desensitisation, developed by South African psychiatrist Joseph Wolpe (1958).

Mood disorders

Mood disorders are divided into depressive and bipolar disorders. The **depressive disorders** feature persistent feelings of sadness and despair, and loss of interest in previous sources of pleasure. In **bipolar disorders**, people experience both depressed and manic periods.

- Depressed mood is experienced most of the day, nearly every day, as indicated by either subjective report (e.g. feels sad or empty) or observation made by others (e.g. appears tearful).
- Markedly diminished interest or pleasure is experienced in all, or almost all, activities most of the day, nearly every day (as indicated by either subjective account or observation made by others).
- Significant weight loss when not dieting or weight gain (e.g. a change of more than 5% of body weight in a month), or decrease or increase in appetite nearly every day is experienced.
- Insomnia (inability to sleep) or hypersomnia (excessive sleeping) is experienced nearly every day.

Depressive disorders: Conditions featuring persistent feelings of sadness and despair, and loss of interest in previous sources of pleasure.

Bipolar disorders: Conditions characterised by both depressed and manic periods.

- Psychomotor agitation or retardation is experienced nearly every day (observable by others; not merely subjective feelings of restlessness or being slowed down).
- Fatigue or loss of energy is experienced nearly every day.
- Feelings of worthlessness or excessive or inappropriate guilt (which may be delusional) are experienced nearly every day (not merely self-approach or guilt about being sick).
- Diminished ability to think or concentrate, or indecisiveness, is experienced nearly every day.
- Recurrent thoughts of death (not just fear of dying), or recurrent suicidal ideation without a specific plan, or a suicide attempt or a specific plan for committing suicide is experienced.

Manic episode:
State characterised by abnormally and persistently elevated, expansive or irritable mood.

The **manic episode** is characterised by abnormally and persistently elevated, expansive or irritable mood, and is accompanied by symptoms that include inflated self-esteem, grandiosity, decreased need for sleep, pressure of speech, flight of ideas, distractibility and psychomotor agitation.

Criteria for a manic episode

A A distinct period of abnormally and persistently elevated, expansive, or irritable mood, which lasts at least one week (or any duration if hospitalisation is necessary), is experienced.

B During the period of mood disturbance, three (or more) of the following symptoms have persisted (four if the mood is only irritable), and have been present to a significant degree:
- inflated self-esteem or grandiosity;
- decreased need for sleep (e.g. feels rested after only three hours of sleep);
- more talkative than usual or pressure to keep talking;
- flight of ideas or subjective experience that thoughts are racing;
- distractibility (i.e. attention too easily drawn to unimportant or irrelevant external stimuli);
- increase in goal-directed activity (either socially, at work or school, or sexually) or psychomotor agitation; and
- excessive involvement in pleasurable activities that have a high potential for painful consequences (e.g. engaging in unrestrained buying sprees, sexual indiscretions or foolish business investments).

Etiology of mood disorders

Biological factors

The development of mood disorder, particular bipolar disorder, appears to be inherited. Family studies have shown that first-degree relatives of patients with major depressive disorder have a 1,5–2,5 times greater risk of developing a bipolar disorder and 2–3 times greater risk of developing a major depressive disorder. It is estimated that 50% of patients with depressive disorder have a parent with a mood disorder. The rate of incidence increases as the gap between the relatives widens. Adoption studies have also shown a genetic component, as children born of patients with depressive disorder have been shown to have a higher incidence of depression, even if they were reared in non-affected families. Twin studies have shown a 33–90% concordance rate in monozygotic twins and a 10–25% concordance rate in dizygotic twins. Numerous genes have been implicated in depressive disorders. Some genetic studies have implicated specific receptors (e.g. D2 (D = dopamine)).

Neurotransmitters

Anti-depressants act on beta adrenergic receptors, which are associated with the release of noradrenaline and serotonin. A number of antidepressants may target a specific neurotransmitter and, therefore, further implicate these neurotransmitters. Dopamine is reduced in patients with depression. Drugs that act by decreasing dopamine levels – for example, Reserpine Æ, which is used in the treatment of hypertension – are known to cause depressive symptoms.

Numerous hormonal abnormalities have been implicated in depressive disorder. These include altered cortisol production and decreased growth hormone release during sleep. Many patients with depression have an abnormal dexamethasone suppression test.

Thyroid function is a recognised contributing factor towards depressive disorder, such that patients presenting with depressive symptoms have a thyroid function test performed. It has even been noted that a subset of depressed patients may have an underlying auto-immune disorder.

General medical conditions also commonly cause depressive symptoms. These include abnormalities in thyroid and adrenal function, infectious mononucleosis (Ebstein barr virus infection) and AIDS. The drugs that should be considered are cardiac drugs, anti-hypertensives, sedatives, hypnotics, anti-psychotics, anti-epileptics, anti-Parkinsonians, analgesics, anti-bacterials and anti-neoplastics. In addition, neurological conditions such as Parkinson's disease, dementias (e.g. Alzheimer's disease), pseudodementia, epilepsy, cerebrovascular disease and tumours cause depressive symptoms.

There is no doubt that mood disorders involve biochemical changes in the nervous system. The unresolved question is whether such changes are the cause or the result of psychological changes.

Cognitive factors

Aaron Beck (1976) proposed that depressed individuals feel the way they do because their thinking is biased towards negative interpretations. A negative triad of negative views of the self, the world and the future is maintained by subscribing to some of the principal cognitive biases of the depressed individual, for example:

- **Arbitrary inference:** Drawing a conclusion in the absence of sufficient or any evidence.
- **Selective abstraction:** Drawing a conclusion based on only one of the many elements in a situation.
- **Overgeneralisation:** An overall sweeping conclusion based on a single, perhaps trivial event.
- **Magnification and minimisation:** Exaggerating the evaluation of performance.

(DAVISON & NEALE 1998)

Schizophrenia

Phenomenology

The schizophrenias represent either a group of disorders or perhaps one disorder with variable presentations. Although there is a range of symptoms and signs, there are no clear boundaries to the concept, and there is no single defining or diagnostic characteristic. However, a core feature of schizophrenia is a disturbance of the privacy or integrity of the self, with an associated loss of the autonomous sense of being in control or having a degree of mastery over oneself and the environment.

Schizophrenic disorders are a class of disorders marked by a primary disturbance of thought, with secondary disturbances in perceptual, social and emotional processes.

How common is schizophrenia in the population? International prevalence studies suggest that about 1,0 to 1,5% of the population suffer from schizophrenic-spectrum disorders. That may not sound like a lot, but it means that in South Africa alone there may be 500 000 people troubled by schizophrenic disturbances. Schizophrenic disorders usually emerge during adolescence (mainly in women) or early adulthood (mainly men), and only rarely after 45 (Weiten 1998). They emerge either gradually or rapidly and, once they emerge, their course is variable. About 30% of sufferers enjoy full recovery, 25% experience partial recovery, and the remaining 45% endure chronic illness. For a variety of reasons, including high suicide rates, poor health behaviours, social neglect and poverty, patients with schizophrenia tend to have shorter life spans than the general population (Weiten 1998).

Four subtypes of schizophrenic disorders are recognised in DSM-IV-TR.

- **Paranoid schizophrenia** is marked by delusions of persecution alternating with delusions of grandeur. These patients believe themselves to be the victims of harrassment, conspiracies, stalking and assassination attempts. They often attribute their persecution to unknown individuals or groups such as the CIA. They often believe they are being sent cryptic messages via radio or television. Allied to this, they often believe they are highly important people, usually of a political or religious nature. A good example was the physicist John Nash, portrayed in the film *A Beautiful Mind*. John Nash was a Princeton 'wunderkind' who believed he was enlisted by the CIA to break Russian codes being infiltrated into American newsprint. Most mental hospitals have numerous patients claiming to be God, Christ or Mohammed. An interesting example is of two patients at Valkenberg Hospital, Cape Town, who developed a shared delusion that she was Princess Diana, he was Prince Charles, and they were inseparable. The knowledge that the real Diana and Charles were separated and that Diana had died did not shake their delusion.

- **Catatonic schizophrenia** is characterised by marked motor disturbances, ranging from muscular rigidity to random motor activity. Some patients go into an extreme withdrawal called catatonic stupor, where they go into a state of complete immobility for long periods, even years. This can alternate with periods of catatonic excitement, marked by incoherent speech known as 'word salad'. The catatonic subtype is the least common.

- **Disorganised schizophrenia** is characterised by a sharp deterioration in adaptive behaviour. Symptoms include emotional withdrawal and indifference, random babbling and inappropriate giggling, and somatic delusions. A good example of the latter was a patient admitted to Valkenberg Hospital, Cape Town, who had a fixed delusion that 'my head is full of semen, not a brain'. Even when presented with a brain scan plate, he could not be convinced otherwise. Another famous example was that of Dimitri Tsafendas, the assassin of apartheid's architect, Hendrik Verwoerd. Tsafendas ultimately never went to trial because psychiatrists declared him schizophrenic with a fixed delusion of a giant tapeworm eating away at his organs. He lived out his days in Sterkfontein Psychiatric Hospital, Krugersdorp.

- **Undifferentiated schizophrenia** is a mixed presentation and is used as a diagnosis for people who do not fit clearly into the other types. This is fairly common, and is characterised by idiosyncratic features of schizophrenic symptoms.

Contemporary theorists (Andreasen 1990) have questioned the usefulness of this typology, given that there are so many overlaps in etiology, prognosis and treatment response. Consequently, they have proposed an alternative to subtyping schizophrenia. This new schema divides schizophrenia into two subtypes dependent on the presence of positive or negative symptom clusters. This schema is fast gaining international approval.

Positive symptoms of schizophrenia

Positive symptoms include delusions or false beliefs, hallucinations (which are perceptions in the absence of external stimuli), and various forms of thought disorders (Baumann 1998). Thought disorders take various forms. A general feature, however, is that the patient is unable to communicate in a clear and effective way because of the interference of the thought disorder. The patient's manner of speaking is imprecise, and answers are either tangential and irrelevant or vague. The mood disturbance in these positive syndromes tends to be inappropriate. Thus, a patient describing terrifying persecutory delusions may seem emotionally unaffected. It is this division of mood from thought, rather than the popular conception of a split personality, that is central to the concept of schizophrenia (Baumann 1998). This 'split ' between thought and emotion is apparent in a patient with schizophrenia who might cry when watching a cartoon on television, and laugh or giggle inappropriately when watching a tragic documentary about, for example, a child's death.

An important qualification in the assessment of delusions, particularly in a multicultural setting such as South Africa, where there are many culturally-specific modes of expressing distress, is that the beliefs expressed do not correspond with the patient's social, cultural, linguistic or spiritual background. In other words, people from the patient's own cultural group would find the beliefs odd or unusual. Hallucinations usually take the form of hearing voices that may talk about the person, issue instructions (command hallucinations), or comment on his or her behaviour. The voices are perceived as being external to the person rather than inner voices often described in religious states. Often the voices are perceived to be emanating from the radio or television, or from some other appliance. Other perceptions, such as visual or tactile hallucinations, are more likely to be symptoms of organicity (neurological dysfunction), such as substance abuse withdrawal.

Case study

During her third year at college, Thandi's behaviour and personality changed dramatically. She refused to come out of her residence room for meals, stopped attending class, stopped socialising and seemed emotionally 'cut off' to friends who tried to get her to come for meals. These behaviours escalated in intensity and, after six months, she was overtly ill. She was terrified of being hunted by the secret police, she complained of taunting voices mocking and denigrating her, and her speech was confused and disorganised.

Negative symptoms of schizophrenia

In contrast to the florid cognitive positive symptoms, the negative forms of schizophrenia represent deficits in cognitive, social and adaptive functioning. Features include social withdrawal, loss of drive, motivation or volition, a blunting of affect, and a restriction of the mood state. The onset of these forms of schizophrenia tends to be more insidious and gradual. The negative states may also persist after the resolution of the positive symptoms. The affected person tends to avoid contact with friends or family, isolates him- or herself, and ceases to be goal-directed or productive in any way. The range of emotional expression becomes restricted, speech loses its complexity, and thinking is impoverished and becomes literal. The associated behaviour is characteristically detached, slow and apathetic. This should not be confused with the social withdrawal and psychomotor retardation of a depressive illness (Baumann 1998).

Case study

Jayne was a sociable and reasonably attractive 17-year-old. She had friends, played sport and was expected to complete her matriculation year and go on to study at university. At age 18, she was a very different person. She began to neglect her appearance, appearing unkempt and dishevelled. She withdrew from her friends, neglected her studies, started skipping school, and her manner was apathetic and detached. She isolated herself in her room, sleeping most of the time or curled up under her duvet. All attempts by her worried parents to get her back on track were met with hostile resistance and short outbursts.

Clinical features of schizophrenia

Positive	Negative
● delusions	● social withdrawal
● hallucinations	● blunted or restricted emotions
● thought disorder	● loss of drive or volition

There are numerous etiological theories for schizophrenia, but the most accepted explanation is that there is some form of biological disorder underpinning the bizarre and tragic deterioration of the patient with schizophrenia. Let us consider some of these theories.

Biological perspective

There is increasing evidence that there is a hereditary predisposition for developing schizophrenia. A definitive genetic component has been demonstrated, but with variable inheritance patterns. The risk in the general population is 1%; to a sibling of someone suffering from schizophrenia 8%; to a child with one parent with schizophrenia 12%; and to a child with two parents with schizophrenia, 40%. The risk to a dizygotic twin of a person with schizophrenia is 12% and to an identical twin 47%. However, fewer than half of the identical twins of individuals who suffer from schizophrenia have schizophrenia themselves, even though they share the same genes. This shows the importance of environmental factors in the expression of genetic vulnerability. The chromosomes that have been implicated in schizophrenia are the long arms of 5, 11 and 18, and the short arms of 19 and X. The dopamine receptor genes are also hypothesised to play a role in schizophrenia vulnerability.

Although the exact cause of schizophrenia is unknown, most research has shown that the major pathology is located in the limbic system, the frontal cortex and the basal ganglia, thalamus and midbrain. Since these cortical areas are interlinked, the pathology in one area also manifests in the other areas. The limbic system is especially implicated. It is thought that a lesion arises in the brain and that this interplays with stressors. The lesion may arise due to abnormal development (abnormal migration of neurons) or degeneration (abnormal cell death). However, the cause is as yet uncertain. Many neurological diseases are implicated in this disease, but patients with a certain neurological disorder may not develop schizophrenia, whereas other patients do. Patients have been shown to have decreased brain volume, especially the limbic system. The basal ganglia are involved in the coordination of movement and implicated in non-medication-induced movement symptoms. Patients have shown a disorganisation of neurons in this area.

Currently, the dopamine hypothesis of schizophrenia is probably the most widely accepted theory. It is postulated that the disease arises from excessive dopaminergic activity. This view is supported by the efficacy of anti-psychotic drugs used, which are D2 receptor antagonists, and the fact that drugs that increase dopamine activity are also known to cause psychotic effects. It is unknown whether this is due to increased dopamine production, increased D2 receptors, or hypersensitivity of receptors to dopamine, or a combination of these three. The mesolimbic and mesocortical tracts are the ones most implicated. The cell bodies of the dopaminergic receptors project to various areas, such as the limbic system and the cerebral cortex. The metabolites of dopamine measured also correlate with the currently held view (increased during the disease and decreased with therapy). The dopamine theory is still under much research, which is always being expanded. D1 may be involved in negative symptoms of schizophrenia.

Certain studies have, however, shown that patients with long-term anti-psychotic therapy may show increased firing of dopaminergic neurons (indicating a hypo-dopaminergic state to begin with). The newer anti-psychotics may not target dopamine receptors and yet have shown to be effective. It is important to note that increased dopamine activity is not unique to schizophrenia, but to all psychotic disorders. Other transmitters that are being studied include:

- **Serotonin:** Serotonin antagonists reduce psychotic symptoms and do not cause the movement disorders associated with dopamine antagonists.
- **Noradrenaline:** Abnormalities in this system are thought to increase the relapse rate of such patients.
- **GABA:** Some patients with schizophrenia have decreased receptors in the hippocampus. This could lead to increased dopaminergic activity.

Somatoform disorders

Somatoform disorders are reported physical ailments that, on examination, prove to have no organic basis and are due to psychological factors. These must be distinguished from psychosomatic diseases/ailments that are genuine physical complaints caused in part by psychological factors such as stress. The latter would include ailments like ulcers, chronic headaches and high blood pressure. Somatoform disorders are more imaginary than real. However, the patient is unaware of the psychological origins of the complaint and is convinced it has an organic basis. There are three such disorder types.

Somatoform disorders: Reported physical ailments that prove to have no organic basis and are due to psychological factors.

- **Somatisation disorder:** This is a disorder marked by a history of diverse physical complaints that appear to be linked by being psychological in origin. Such patients, over time, present to the doctor with a range of cardiovascular, gastrointestinal, pulmonary, neurological, and genitourinary symptoms that lack clear physical markers. Often the psychology underpinning the regular doctor's appointments is the patient's need for attention or reassurance.
- **Conversion disorder:** In conversion disorder, there is a serious or marked loss of physical function in a single organ system. Typical presentations are muteness (inability to speak), sudden blindness, paralysis of one of the major limbs, partial or complete loss of hearing, or even false pregnancy.

Case study

Michael was a 32-year-old Catholic priest who developed a stiffness or seizure of his knees such that he could not bend them. The implication was that he could not genuflect and thus conduct his duties as a priest. He felt his 'disability' meant he could not continue as a priest. Orthopaedic examination revealed nothing of note. Michael was referred for counselling. What emerged was extreme ambivalence about his religious vocation. In counselling, Michael resolved to leave the priesthood and pursue a secular life. Soon thereafter, his knees spontaneously returned to normal function.

Case study

Janet was a 15-year-old schoolgirl who injured her right ankle slightly playing hockey. Soon this injury escalated into her leg buckling when she attempted to walk. She claimed complete paralysis of the leg from the thigh down. Physical examination revealed no organic pathology, in that she had full reflexes and appropriate sensation. Also, the paralysis and sensation loss were arbitrary, in that they did not correspond to any pattern of nerve pathways in the leg. Janet was notably blasé about her predicament and revelled in the attention. Due to her illness, she became the centre of attention in the family and was waited on hand and foot by her parents. In counselling, it emerged that she was envious of the attention her younger brother received from her parents. The counsellor speculated that the 'conversion paralysis' was a way of regaining parental attention.

- **Hypochondriasis:** Individuals diagnosed with hypochondriasis are constantly monitoring their bodies and sensations, looking for signs of illness. Despite the lack of physical evidence, they are convinced they have developed or contracted a disease such as cancer, leukaemia, diabetes, HIV, ulcers, chronic fatigue due to a viral infection, or a tumour. They often press the doctor to conduct innumerable tests and, when told they have a clean bill of health, disbelieve the doctor. They often doctor-hop in search of a professional who will confirm their personal theory of illness. Professionals often refer to them as the 'worried well'. People suffering from hypochondriasis often are anxious and obsessive worriers, and are likely to have histrionic personality features (Slavney 1990).

Case study

Peter was referred to a local psychiatric out-patient clinic by his general practitioner. He was convinced he had contracted HIV from a casual sexual encounter. Several HIV tests conducted over 12 months indicated he was HIV-negative. Peter, however, could not accept this outcome. He continually monitored his body, convincing himself that he had early-stage AIDS-related ailments. He read avidly on the subject and this reinforced his bodily preoccupation and his conviction that he had certain HIV-related symptoms. He would interpret minute somatic or physical changes and events as confirmation of his self-diagnosis.

Biological markers

There is some evidence to indicate that this class of disorders has a genetic link, as it tends to run in families, but the mode of transmission is not entirely understood. It is estimated that 10–20% of first-degree female relatives will also suffer from this disorder. Interestingly, first-degree male relatives are also more prone to substance abuse and anti-social personality disorder.

Cytokines are now being increasingly implicated in the disorder. Cytokines are messenger molecules that convey information between the immune system and the nervous system. It is thought that these substances may play a role in the development of the non-specific signs and symptoms of the disease (but especially the infections) such as hypersomnia, anorexia, fatigue and depression. However, the exact nature of the cytokine system abnormality is not yet clear.

Brain-imaging studies have demonstrated decreased metabolism in the frontal lobe and the non-dominant hemisphere. In conversion disorder, brain imaging has shown decreased metabolism in the dominant hemisphere and hypermetabolism of the non-dominant hemisphere. Impaired communication between the two hemispheres has also been implicated. It is thought that there may be excessive cortical arousal, which sets up negative feedback loops between the cerebral cortex and the brainstem reticular formation. Patients may have subtle impairments in verbal communication, memory, vigilance, affective incongruity and attention. It is also thought that there is increased corticofugal output (from the brain to the peripheral nervous system), which makes the patient more aware of his or her bodily symptoms.

In body dysmorphic disorder, there tends to be a genetic basis to this disorder, as family members are also affected. However, this may also indicate prevalent cultural norms in the family. These patients also have a higher incidence of co-morbid psychiatric illnesses, such as mood disorders and obsessive-compulsive disorder. Patients may respond to serotonin-specific drugs, and this has led to the belief that serotonin could play an important part in the etiology of the disease.

Research on pain disorder has demonstrated that the cerebral cortex has the ability to inhibit the firing of afferent pain fibres. Serotonin has been implicated as the main neurotransmitter in the descending inhibitory pathway. Endorphins play a role in the modulation of pain in the central nervous system. Endorphin and serotonin deficiency may therefore play a role in the development of this disorder. Abnormalities in the chemistry and/or structure of the limbic or sensory system may predispose a patient to the development of pain disorder rather than other disorders.

Culture and abnormality

There is mounting evidence that the majority of the disorders described in DSM-IV-TR are found in virtually all cultures. For example, schizophrenia and other psychotic states seem to be equally common in all societies. Similarly, research is pointing to the universal incidence of depression, whereas it was previously thought not to occur in Africa. Thus the form of disorders such as schizophrenia are considered universal, but the content will vary depending on the individual's cultural background. For example, a person with schizophrenia in a modern urban culture may believe that the television is giving him or her commands, whereas a rural patient may believe that his or her ancestors are giving him or her commands. Practitioners must be aware of local cultural variations in content that represent the same form as disorders described in DSM.

DSM-IV-TR uses the term 'culture-bound syndromes' (CBS) to refer to symptom clusters that are limited to specific societies or cultural groups. These syndromes are localised, folk, diagnostic categories that frame coherent meanings for certain repetitive, patterned and troubling sets of experiences and observations (Drennan 1998). Linked to this is the concept of local idioms of distress. These are culturally sanctioned modes of expression of distress that are understood by members of the same cultural or language group. These idioms of distress provide a meaning for the afflicted person and their family as to why the person became ill. They can explain the moral and social cause of illness, not just the biological or psychological cause. One of the weaknesses of the Western diagnostic process is that it is an insufficient explanatory model in cross-cultural settings where a social causative explanation is expected. In South Africa, numerous local idioms of distress exist. For example, among the Xhosa and Zulu cultural groupings there are, to name a few, *Amafufunyane*, *Ukuthwasa*, *Ukuphaphazela* and *Isimnyama Eskoli*.

Local idioms of distress:

- provide a conduit for communication;
- provide a coherent meaning; and
- elicit helping responses.

Ukuthwasa is probably the most common among Nguni peoples. It is commonly believed to be a calling by the ancestors to become a healer. The descriptions vary widely, but what is common are fears of madness, wild and turbulent dreams, tearfulness, social withdrawal, anti-social behaviour and anxiety symptoms. Western interpretations of people with *Ukuthwasa* range from psychotic to manic to hypomanic. However, caution should be exercised in mapping Western psychiatric diagnostic categories onto local idioms of distress such as *Ukuthwasa*.

Ukuthwasa

- calling by ancestors
- feelings/fears of madness
- vivid dreams
- social withdrawal
- anxiousness and tearfulness

Amafufunyane is also a well-known traditional illness of the Nguni peoples. Traditional healers consider it due to possession by evil spirits. Drennan (1998) notes that it is believed to be contracted when soil and ants from graves are mixed into a *muti* (traditional medicine) and ingested. The ants are believed to carry the spirits of the dead, who create internal disturbance in the form of symptoms such as listlessness, appetite loss and social withdrawal. The acute presentation is ritualised episodes of faintness, grunting and collapse to the ground. Following this, the afflicted person speaks in one or more foreign languages. The person is usually amnestic for the event. *Amafufunyane* occurs at social gatherings, is episodic, and is not considered a mental illness. It is a local category or idiom of distress.

Amafufunyane

- possession by evil spirits
- ingestion of soil/ants
- grunting and falling
- speaking in other languages/voices
- altered consciousness and amnesia

Ukuphaphazela occurs among children and involves nervousness and agitation during the night, often accompanied by visual hallucinations and rapid motor activity. Traditional healers explain it as the child being frightened by seeing evil spirits who want the child dead. The phenomenon is very similar to the Western descriptions of night terrors that commonly occur in children.

Ukuphaphazela

- affects children
- nervousness/agitation at night
- hallucinations
- attempts to run away
- seeing evil spirits

Isimnyama Eskoli is a syndrome described among the Xhosa. The predominant symptoms are the inability to see a book or paper, and the afflicted person's eyes are red and sore. Associated symptoms are hearing difficulties, dizziness, weak fingers and cardiac palpitations. In psychiatric terms, this is considered an anxiety disorder in the context of academic performance pressure.

Isimnyama Eskoli

- inability to see or read
- red, painful eyes
- headaches
- weakness

Summary

In this chapter we have outlined all of the psychological disorders encountered by psychologists and described in DSM-IV-TR. The disorders are presented according to their clustering in DSM-IV-TR. Each disorder is presented according to its core symptomatology, and biological and psychosocial etiological and predisposing factors. Particular attention is paid to the role of culture in the expression of psychopathology and southern African local idioms of distress are described.

Further reading

American Psychiatric Association (APA) (2000) *Diagnostic and Statistical Manual of Mental Disorders: Text Revised* (4th edition) (DSM-IV-TR). Washington, DC: American Psychiatric Association.

Andreasen, N.C. (1990) *Positive and Negative Symptoms: Historical and Conceptual Aspects.* In N.C. Andreasen (ed.), *Modern Problems of Pharmaco-psychiatry: Positive and Negative Symptoms and Syndromes.* Basel: Karger.

Baumann, S.E. (1998) *Odd Ideas, Voices and the Loss of Insight: The Psychotic Patient.* In S.E. Baumann (ed.), *Psychiatry and Primary Health Care.* Cape Town: Juta.

Beck, A.T. (1976) *Cognitive Therapy and the Emotional Disorders.* New York: International Universities Press.

Davison, G.C. & Neale, J.M. (1998) *Abnormal Psychology.* New York: John Wiley.

Drennan, G. (1998) *Southern African Categories of Distress.* In S.E. Baumann (ed.), *Psychiatry and Primary Health Care.* Cape Town: Juta.

Hergenhahn, B.R. (1972) *An Introduction to the History of Psychology.* Belmont: Wadsworth.

Hook, D. & Eagle, G. (eds) (2002) *Psychopathology and Social Prejudice.* Cape Town: UCT Press.

Lebakeng, T., Sedumedi, S. & Eagle, G. (2002) Witches and watches: Witchcraft beliefs and practices in South African rural communities of the Northern Province. In D. Hook and G. Eagle (eds), *Psychopathology and Social Prejudice.*

Minnaar, A., Wentzel, M. & Payze, C. (1997) Witch-purging in the Northern Province. *Focus Forum*, 4(56), pp. 25–9.

Slavney, P.R. (1990) *Perspectives on Hysteria.* Baltimore: Johns Hopkins University Press.

Weiten, W. (1989) *Psychology: Approaches and Variations* (3rd edition). Pacific Grove: Brookes/Cole.

Wolpe, J. (1958) *Psychotherapy by Reciprocal Inhibition.* Stanford: Stanford University Press.

Psychotherapy

6

L.J. Nicholas, U. Bawa,
C. Malcolm and B.J. Pillay

Objectives

After studying this chapter you should:

- understand the various psychological theories that inform the practice of psychology
- be able to describe the various modalities of psychotherapeutic interventions
- understand the importance of psychotherapy in addressing emotional difficulties and ensuring well-being
- be able to identify the different psychotherapeutic models.

Introduction

Sigmund Freud is widely regarded as having launched modern psychotherapy (Smith 1982). In a survey of clinical and counselling psychologists, Smith (1982) found that Freud was still regarded as the third most influential psychotherapist according to current trends. Carl Rogers was selected as the most influential, with Albert Ellis second. Interestingly, two South Africans – Joseph Wolpe and Arnold Lazarus – were selected as fourth and fifth most influential. The full list is given in Table 6.1.

TABLE 6.1: The ten most influential psychotherapists based on weighted scores

Psychotherapist	% of respondents assigning a rank	Weighted score
Carl Rogers	37,35	363
Albert Ellis	27,23	229
Sigmund Freud	10,84	117
Joseph Wolpe	11,08	87
Arnold Lazarus	9,40	84
Fritz Perls	8,19	54
Aaron Beck	5,78	49
Jay Haley	6,02	46
Milton Erickson	4,58	40
Donald Meichenbaum	4,34	37

(SOURCE: SMITH 1982: p. 807)

Smith (1982) noted that three of the therapists were deceased (Erickson, Freud and Perls), since joined by Rogers and Wolpe, and that cognitive behavioural and/or rational therapy dominated. While 'Rogerian therapy had passed its most popular days in the early 1980s, a trend which continued to date, Rogers was still regarded as a major influence' (Smith 1982: p. 807). The existence of multiple trends in contemporary psychotherapeutic practice was endorsed by the diversity among the top ten therapists.

Wolpe, whose brother Harold was a well known political activist and professor at the University of the Western Cape, was trained as a psychiatrist at the University of the Witwatersrand (Wits). Lazarus was trained as a psychologist at Wits and, like Wolpe, has spent most of his professional life in North America. In the mid 1980s, Lionel Nicholas wrote to both, enquiring about their views on psychology and South Africa. A reply was received from Lazarus which highlighted a somewhat closed mindedness to new ideas in psychology among certain South African psychologists:

ARNOLD A. LAZARUS, Ph.D.
Clinical Psychologist
56 Herrontown Circle • Princeton, N.J. 08540 • (609) 924-8450

October 11, 1985

Mr. L.J. Nicholas
90 Brainero Rd.
Apt #2
Allston, MA 02134

Dear Mr. Nicholas:

   I have been out of South Africa for more than 20 years and my
views therefore have to be out of date vis-a-vis the issues raised
in your letter to me. Back in 1964, having just spent a year at
Stanford University, I returned home and offered to give free
talks and lectures on some of the (then) current thinking in the
areas of personality theory and psychotherapy. The reaction was
underwhelming. As the head of the Johannesburg Child Guidance put
it: "We are quite satisfied with our ideas and have no need to listen
to your ideas." I think that says it all!

   Thank you for your interest in multimodal therapy. If you have
read the basic materials on MMT and have had a year-long course, you
are probably in a better position to offer courses, seminars, and
lectures yourself than to learn much from others. I do not know
anyone in the Boston area whom I would regard as a "multimodalist."
I am due to give several lectures, but I will cover pretty much the
same ground as I did in Stellenbosch. Have you seen the new CASEBOOK
OF MULTIMODAL THERAPY which I edited this year, published in New York
by Guilford Press?

   Good luck with your studies.

   Sincerely,

   Arnold A. Lazarus

FIGURE 6.2: A letter from Arnold Lazarus to the editor in reply to an enquiry about his views of psychology in South Africa and multimodal therapy training.

The influence of strategic therapy, perhaps the least known of the therapies included in the top ten, was acknowledged by the inclusion of Milton H. Erickson and Jay Haley, who were the most closely associated with the use of hypnosis in psychotherapy. Doyle (1987) claimed that the discovery of hypnosis led to the first structured psychotherapy: psychoanalysis.

Jean-Martin Charcot (1825–1893), considered one of the most brilliant physicians in Europe, drew well-known psychologists like Alfred Binet and William James to his lectures, and gave popular demonstrations where he hypnotised hysterics. Freud studied with him from October 1885 to February 1886, and was so impressed with Charcot that he named his first son Jean-Martin, after him. Freud found that he could not hypnotise some of his patients, that symptoms removed during trance would recur, and that patients resisted integrating material revealed under hypnosis. He visited another school to improve his hypnotic skills and learned about post-hypnotic suggestion. Freud still found hypnosis to be ineffective, and tried a technique he had previously observed, where he would place his hand on the forehead of a reclining patient and say 'Now you can remember' (Hergenhahn 1992). He later found that he need not use this 'pressure technique' and that what worked was simply encouraging patients to speak freely about whatever came to mind; thus free association was born (Hergenhahn 1992).

Milton Erickson developed strategic therapy directly from a hypnotic orientation. A strategic therapist identifies solvable problems, sets goals, designs interventions, alters his or her approach as new information is received, and examines the outcome of therapy. The therapist takes responsibility for directly influencing clients consciously and unconsciously. (For a more detailed explanation, see Haley 1973.)

Behaviour therapy

Behaviour therapy:
The use of experimentally established principles of learning to overcome maladaptive behaviour.

Behaviour therapy is the use of experimentally established principles of learning to overcome maladaptive behaviour. The therapist helps the client unlearn maladaptive behaviour and learn new behaviour in line with therapeutic goals. Behaviourists are interested in past experiences only to the extent to which they maintain current undesirable behaviour and make no attempt to have clients gain deep insights about themselves in order to resolve problems. Knowledge about past experiences would only be used to design a behaviour therapy programme.

Systematic desensitisation

Desensitisation:
Therapy aimed at desensitising clients to anxiety-provoking stimuli.

This technique was developed by Joseph Wolpe and involves **desensitisation** by reciprocal inhibition or counter conditioning. It is assumed that most anxiety responses are acquired through classical conditioning. An anxiety hierarchy is developed – a list of stimuli from least anxiety provoking to most anxiety provoking. The client is then taught a relaxation technique and works through the hierarchy, learning to remain relaxed while imagining each increasingly anxiety-provoking stimulus. Wolpe extended this procedure to accompanying his patients into the world outside his office, encouraging them to remain relaxed while encountering anxiety-provoking stimuli (Doyle 1987).

Behaviour therapists developed a range of other techniques, such as aversion therapy, pairing an aversive stimulus with one that elicits an undesirable response. Alcoholics have had the drug Antabuse paired with drinking alcohol, which would then cause nausea and vomiting, creating a conditioned aversion (Weiten 1998). Flooding is an intensive exposure to a feared stimulus while supporting the client through the initial panic reaction as a means of alleviation.

Psychoanalysis

Sigmund Freud was the founder of the tradition of psychoanalysis that serves as the foundational theory underpinning most insight therapies. Since Freud, there has been a proliferation of insight-oriented approaches to therapy. However, they all share the assumption that personal, attitudinal, affective and behavioural changes occur via the process of the client arriving at renewed insight into him- or herself. This insight theoretically gives the client greater awareness and thus choice in psychological adjustment. The *modus operandi* of insight therapy is that client and therapist talk about the client; the therapist makes comments and interpretations about the client's functioning from what he or she is told and observes about the client; and the client gains insight from these comments and is able to change. Although this is a simplification, it captures the essential process of all insight therapeutic processes.

Freud theorised that most anxious neurotic problems were the result of unconscious conflicts between the id, the ego and the superego, usually over sexual and aggressive drives. He proposed that these drives are unacceptable in the social world and that people, through their early development, develop a scaffolding of defences to manage, contain and neutralise these unacceptable impulses from breaking out into conscious expression. Symptoms are the consequence of these defences being either overdeveloped or underdeveloped. The therapeutic technique emphasised the recovery of unconscious conflicts, motives and defences through the application of techniques such as free association, transference, hypnosis, dream analysis and working through.

Free association was a technique Freud developed, alongside hypnosis and dream analysis, to access the unconscious and bypass conscious defences. In free association, clients are encouraged to spontaneously express their thoughts and feelings without censoring them. The therapist analyses the patterns of association and weaves together a coherent understanding of the client's unconscious/conscious conflicts.

Freud considered dreams a more direct unconscious expression, calling them the 'royal road to the unconscious'. In **dream analysis**, the therapist interprets the symbolic meaning of the client's dreams and attempts to link this interpretation to the client's symptoms.

Interpretation is the process whereby the therapist puts into words his or her understanding of the client's inner motivations and provides an account of the unconscious dimensions of the client's psychological

Free association:
Therapy in which clients are encouraged to spontaneously express their thoughts and feelings without censoring them.

Dream analysis:
Therapy in which the therapist interprets the symbolic meaning of the client's dreams and links this intertpretation to the client's symptoms.

life. Interpretations are offered in a sequence that edges the client towards insight. This slow incremental process of gaining from insight is called working through the unconscious conflict.

Transference occurs when clients start relating to the therapist in ways that resemble or mimic critical relationships from their past and present. Take, for example, a client who enters therapy where one of her manifest problems is that she is having conflicts with her female boss, whom she experiences as critical and stifling of her autonomy and career development. After a period of therapy, the client starts experiencing the therapist as critical and simultaneously overprotective. In particular, the client interprets the therapist's clarifying comments as critical and dismissive. The therapist becomes aware that this was how the client experienced her mother during her adolescent years. The client would thus be unconsciously transferring her conflicted feelings and perceptions of her mother onto the therapist. The therapist's task is to encourage this transference, identify it, explain it to the client, and thereby facilitate the client's working through of the unconscious conflict.

Transference:
Process whereby clients relate to the therapist in ways that resemble critical relationships in their past or present.

Contemporary psychoanalysis

Contemporary psychoanalysis has moved on somewhat from Freud's days, although classical Freudian psychoanalysis still thrives in the United States and Britain. Freud and his followers were, in large part, of the Jewish diaspora from Germany and Austria before the Second World War. As they spread to different parts of the world, they found it necessary to adapt psychoanalysis to changing times, cultures and economic circumstances. These revisions have broadly become known as psychodynamic or psychoanalytic psychotherapy, as opposed to classic psychoanalysis.

Some of the major revisionists have been Carl Jung in Switzerland, Alfred Adler in Germany, Melanie Klein in London and Heinz Kohut in Chicago. All of these theorists developed new theoretical schools of psychoanalysis, although their roots lay in classical Freudian ideas of the structure of the unconscious. Although these schools and others have distinctive theoretical claims, there are some commonalities to the modern approaches to psychodynamic psychotherapy.

Firstly, modern approaches lay greater emphasis on the interpersonal world in shaping unconscious life and de-emphasise unconscious sexual and aggressive drives. As a result, therapists probe less into clients' sexual fantasies and more into their experiences of their primary developmental relationships with parents, grandparents, siblings and peers.

Secondly, modern therapists are more interested in conscious processes than the exclusive emphasis put on the unconscious by classical Freudian analysts.

Thirdly, client-therapist interactions have become more direct. Clients often sit in a chair rather than lie on a couch. The therapist now faces the sitting client rather than sitting behind him or her on the couch. The therapist is also verbal and candid in communication, rather than relying on listening to the free association of the client. In sum, therapy has moved from an investigative to a more dialogical and collaborative approach to treatment.

Fourthly, modern approaches are shorter. They can be brief-term (five to ten sessions), short-term (40 sessions) or long-term (two to three years). Various new brief- and short-term approaches have been proven effective for particular problems. As such, analysts are more precise in their matching of the client to the type of treatment, unlike the classical Freudians, where 'one treatment fits all'.

Fifthly, psychodynamic ideas have informed an array of treatment approaches for specific populations such as family therapy, couples therapy, group therapy, child psychotherapy, and therapy for adolescents and young people. The range of applications has become varied and population-specific models have emerged.

Client–centred therapy

Client-centred therapy is an insight therapy that emphasises the therapist providing a non-interpretive, empathically supportive environment for the client, with the client determining the pace of insight and change. The school was founded by Carl Rogers (1951, 1986) in California.

Rogers sees the root cause of neurosis being a lack of 'congruence' between a person's self-concept and reality. Incongruent self-perception cannot tolerate realistic feedback. As a result, the person experiences anxiety and engages defences to ward off the reality feedback coming from the environment. For example, if someone grew up with parental messages that they were hopeless and bad, any messages from the environment to the contrary later in life would invoke anxiety and defences that block out the contradictory messages. As a result, the person continues perceiving him- or herself as unworthy or bad. The opposite could also happen. A client could grow up feeling entitled, having been waited on hand and foot by his or her parents. Later feedback that he or she is not special but rather ordinary could invoke considerable anxiety and defensiveness to ward off the reality feedback.

Empathy, genuineness and unconditional positive regard are the client-centred therapist's 'techniques', compared to the psychoanalytic

Client-centred therapy: Therapy in which the therapist provides a non-interpretive, empathetically supportive environment for treatment, and in which clients determine the pace of insight and change.

reliance on interpretation. Client-centred therapists provide clients with the experience of total acceptance of their being and, as such, encourage clients to identify, claim and respect their own feelings and values. They also help clients recognise that they do not have to continually seek to please others and gain acceptance as they did when they were children. They help clients restructure their self-concept to correspond more to adult reality and thereby foster self-acceptance, realistic self-evaluation and, ultimately, growth.

There is great emphasis on creating the correct interpersonal climate in therapy for growth to occur. The therapist and the client collaborate on a more equal footing in the therapeutic process. The therapist's primary task is to help the client identify and clarify his or her feelings by reflecting back the client's statements and feeling tones. This enhances the client's awareness of his or her subjective experiences. Further, therapists help clients better understand their contribution to interpersonal patterns and to become more comfortable with their genuine selves.

The basic principles of client-centred therapy have been incorporated into other therapeutic approaches. As such, a purely client-centred approach has become a rarity, with pressure for results and outcomes being determined by health insurers, particularly in America.

Cognitive therapy

Cognitive therapy:
Therapy aimed at changing the client's cognitive style.

Cognitive therapy has been the fastest growing modern therapeutic approach. It is now the most popular and accepted therapeutic approach in the United States and Britain. The most influential cognitive-oriented therapies have been Aaron Beck's (1976, 1987) cognitive therapy, Albert Ellis' (1973, 1989) rational-emotive therapy, and Anthony Ryle's (1988) cognitive-analytic therapy. These three pioneers have spawned a range of derivative therapies, all with an emphasis on the role of cognitions in maladjustment and adjustment. The most influential has been Aaron Beck's cognitive therapy model.

Beck originally developed a treatment for depression, which he believes is the direct result of 'errors in cognition' or 'distorted cognitions'. His model holds that depressed people have a predominant cognitive set where they:

- tend to personalise setbacks in life by attributing them to personal inadequacies as opposed to circumstances;
- focus selectively on negative events and outcomes at the expense of positive ones;
- entertain pessimistic views on future outcomes; and
- self-evaluate themselves negatively despite evidence to the contrary.

This cognitive style is likely to have developed in childhood because of negative parental injunctions or insufficient self-esteem-boosting interactions with significant caretakers.

The goal of cognitive therapy is to alter the clients' cognitive style. Clients are first taught to identify their cognitive errors. Secondly, the therapist helps clients to develop realistic cognitive evaluations of themselves and their circumstances. Thirdly, the therapist explores the cognitive errors to identify the error assumptions that underline the clients' negative thinking and cognitive style. To this end, cognitive therapists play an active role in directing the therapeutic process. They challenge the clients' thinking and assumptions, and actively suggest alternative modes of thinking.

Cognitive therapy started as a treatment for depression, but has been applied and tailored to fit most client problems. It has also been well researched and is considered the treatment of choice for many disorders today. One of its greatest advantages is that it is focused on symptoms and is time-limited.

TABLE 6.2: Beck's theory of cognitive errors in depression

Cognitive error	Descriptor	Overgeneralisation
If it is valid in one situation, then it applies to all other vaguely similar situations.	Dichotomous thinking	Everything is perceived in extremes (good or bad; love or hate).
Everybody's eyes are focused on me, particularly when it comes to personal attributes or bad personal performance.	Self-referencing	Selective abstraction
The events that matter are failures, embarrassments and errors.	'Catastrophising'	The worst-case scenario is always the one considered first.
I am responsible for all negative outcomes such as failures.	Personal causation	Assuming temporal causality. If it has been true in the past, then it will recur and be true again in the future.

(SOURCE: BECK 1976)

Biological approaches to therapy
ECT therapy

Biological approaches to therapy:
Approaches that assume that mental illness is caused by biochemical or physiological dysfunction of the brain.

Electroconvulsive therapy (ECT), known as shock therapy, is a non-pharmacological intervention used for patients suffering from certain severe neuropsychiatric disorders, such as major depression, mania, catatonia and schizophrenia. While psychotropic medication produces improvement in most patients, in some, these medications do not appear effective: they suffer from adverse side effects or require urgent intervention. ECT is used for such patients.

The procedure involves passing an alternating current across the patient's temples for a fraction of a second. The goal of ECT is to induce a generalised seizure of adequate duration in the central nervous system. During the procedure, the patient is anaesthetised and administered a muscle relaxant. The shock produces a convulsion that lasts for a short duration, usually 30 to 90 seconds. The patient experiences amnesia, which can last for an hour or so following ECT. Although there can be a favourable response to treatment quite rapidly, the patient usually benefits from several treatments over a few weeks.

However there are several adverse reactions and risks associated with ECT. These include cardiovascular effects, cognitive impairment, brain damage, spontaneous seizures and even death. Other effects include pain from contractions, muscle soreness and headaches. While ECT is a source of controversial debate and is often associated with negative perceptions because of bad publicity, adverse side effects are minimised by new advances in its administration.

Drug therapy

A biological approach assumes that mental illness is caused by biochemical or physiological dysfunction of the brain. Since the early 1950s, the discovery of drug therapy has revolutionised patient treatment and management. Aggressive and agitated patients were no longer straight-jacketed and were less likely to be institutionalised. Management of the mentally ill in hospitals was easier and the rapid response to treatment meant shorter hospital stays. Patients with disturbing psychotic behaviour, such as hallucinations, delusions and other bizarre psychotic symptoms, were able to be more functional and productive. The development of anti-depressant and anti-anxiety drugs followed, and the new advances have significantly contributed to treatment and management of most mental disorders.

Anti-depressants are drugs that improve mood. Three major classes of anti-depressant drugs are used in the treatment of depression. The so called 'new generation' of drugs are the selective serotonin reuptake inhibitors (SSRIs). They act at the pre-synaptic neurones and selectively block the reuptake of serotonin. They have the added advantage of causing fewer anti-cholinergic and cardiovascular side effects and drug interactions than the older drugs, such as the tricyclics. The first of the SSRIs, Fluoxetine (Prozac®) was introduced in the United States in 1988. Since then, other SSRIs, such as Sertraline (Zoloft®) have been introduced and, subsequently, more selective SSRIs, such as Citalopram (Cipramil®) and Fluvoxamine (Luvox®) are available for use. The availability of these new agents and new-generation anti-depressants, such as Venlafaxine (Effexor®), has markedly changed the treatment of depression and anxiety disorders. However, these drugs do cause side effects, which include induction of mania in certain patients, lowering of seizure threshold, headache, dry mouth, central nervous system effects (nervousness, insomnia, etc.), sexual dysfunction and hypoglycaemia.

Another class of anti-depressants is the tricyclic anti-depressants. They are older generation drugs, but still in use today. They are usually indicated for the treatment of depression, especially major depressive disorder and depression with anxiety and/or somatic complaints. Some may have sedative effects for inducing and maintaining sleep. They may be used in the depressive phase of bipolar disorder. These drugs are also used in low doses in the treatment of pain disorder and conditions that cause chronic pain. They may act by blocking the activation of certain pain pathways. Some of these drugs have the ability to cause considerable anti-cholinergic side effects (dry mouth, dry eyes, constipation, urinary retention, blurred vision), sedation and orthostatic hypotension. Examples of tricyclics are Amitriptyline (Tryptanol®) and Imipramine (Tofranil®).

The third class is monoamine oxidase inhibitors (MAOI). These act by irreversibly inhibiting the enzyme monoamine oxidase, so that there is an increase in the biogenic amines such as noradrenaline, dopamine and serotonin in the brain and the peripheries. These drugs are infrequently used nowadays because of the adverse side effects that occur when they are combined with certain other drugs and foods. The effects of the drugs last for a long period and frequently cause a hypertensive crisis.

Anti-psychotics are indicated for psychotic conditions such as schizophrenia, mania and organic psychoses. These drugs are sometimes used for other conditions, such as nausea and vomiting, intractable hiccups, Tourette's syndrome, behaviour disorders, anaesthesia and alcohol withdrawal syndrome. These drugs may cause severe side effects, such as Parkinsonian features, and anti-cholinergic side effects. Depot (long-acting) preparations are available for patients who need long-term therapy but do not adhere to treatment. These drugs may cause extra pyramidal side effects, such as acute dystonia (torticollis, facial grimacing, laryngeal spasm, truncal dystonia); Parkinsonian syndrome (slow movements, rigidity and tremor); or akathisia (motor restlessness). Tardive dyskinesia is also common, with development of odd movements of the face, lips, tongue and extremities. Examples of these drugs are Chlorpromazine (Largactil®), Fluphenazine (Modecate®) and Haloperidol (Serenace®).

Anti-anxiety drugs are referred to as anxiolytics. They are by far the most widely prescribed class of drugs, and include barbiturates, non-barbiturate sedative hypnotics, benzodiazepines and buspirone. They reduce tension and cause drowsiness. Currently benzodiazepines and buspirone are widely used and recommended for the treatment of anxiety because of their superior safety. The drugs are generally prescribed for short periods because patients may become dependent on them. Although widely prescribed, they have the potential for abuse. Examples include Diazepam (Valium®), Lorazepam (Ativan®), Midazolam (Dormicum®) and Clonazepam (Rivotril®).

While drug therapy has proven useful, it also has limitations. For example, side effects can be quite undesirable and distressing to patients. Another problem is that this mode of therapy requires compliance on the part of the patient. Failure to take medication regularly will result in relapses. However, many psychologists believe that drugs alleviate symptoms and do not treat the 'cause' of the problem or help the patients assume personal responsibility for their behaviours. It is generally considered helpful to combine drug therapy with psychotherapy.

Culture and therapy

The importance of culture in the therapeutic milieu cannot be over-emphasised. An awareness of the religious, social and cultural background of the client by the therapist is often the most crucial factor that contributes to the development of a facilitative atmosphere within which a meaningful and sustainable outcome can be reached. A psychological intervention that does little to understand the world view of clients who do not share the culture of the psychology practitioner runs the risk of failure.

205

The dominant view of mental illness has been that of a scientific and Western view of physical ailments embedded in natural causes that are amenable to a medicalised intervention (Dana 1993). However, other competing explanations for mental illness are not based on the natural cause-physical manifestation duality. This largely non-Western view sees psychological disorders as being rooted in the spiritual, ancestral and supernatural world. Possession by demons and angry gods, and being cursed by jealous others, are often cited as reasons for mental illness. The solution to these problems is often first sought from priests, spiritual healers and shamans (Wittkower & Warnes 1984; Swartz & Gibson 2001), before traditional Western medical practitioners are consulted. The sangoma or traditional healer is often seen as culturally sensitive, and a better medium for understanding and resolving the patient's troubling psychological reactions than the Western medical doctor or psychologist. Research into the consultation of traditional healers for illness in South Africa has shown that many urban people may consult both traditional and Western medical practitioners to assist them with their difficulties (Swartz 1996; Lifschitz & Oosthuizen 2001).

Among the difficulties encountered by South African clients seeking assistance from mainstream psychologists for their emotional problems have been language barriers. Most of the currently trained psychologists do not offer services in the majority of indigenous South African languages. The problem of access due to the high cost of psychotherapy is also prevalent. However, the increasing focus within health-care settings of providing affordable and primary health care has resulted in the training of community mental-health workers (CMHWs) to provide culturally appropriate mental-health services (Swartz & Gibson 2001).

The Professional Board for Psychology within the Health Professions Council of South Africa (HPCSA) has suggested that training institutions recruit and train psychologists who would be more sensitive to the mental-health needs of the majority of South Africans, who, in the main, have an indigenous and non-Western world view. Mental-health services would then more readily meet the requirement of providing a relevant, appropriate and affordable mental-health intervention in a culturally diverse South Africa. Research in the United States found that clients who received psychological help from a mental-health practitioner from their own cultural background reported better therapy outcomes than those for whom a cultural match was not available (Wade & Bernstein 1991; Mays & Albee 1992).

Treatment in mental hospitals

Mental hospital:
Medical institution providing in-patient care for psychological disorders.

A **mental hospital** is a medical institution specialising in providing in-patient care for psychological disorders. It may also provide out-patient services for patients on therapeutic maintenance programmes, both at the institution and in community health-care services.

Critique of mental institutions

Public mental hospitals have been criticised for not fulfilling their intended goal of curing pathology, but rather contributing to the development of further mental difficulties. Overcrowding, lack of adequately trained staff, and racial segregation due to apartheid legislation left many mental hospitals as dumping grounds for the mentally ill, and 'custodial warehouses' (Scull 1990; Freeman 1998). Patient reintegration into the community following treatment has been difficult, raising further questions about the fundamental policy of institutional mental-health services.

The availability of mental-health services in South Africa has improved since 1994, but these services are still severely under-resourced compared to their international counterparts. Many communities remain under-serviced by state mental-health services. Many in-patient psychiatric treatment programmes have, with the current health legislation that prioritises primary health care, been severely curtailed.

A community mental-health model

The disenchantment with public mental-health services that were primarily located in mental hospitals has led to the emergence of a community mental-health movement. This approach emphasises local community-based care, prevention of psychological disorders, and decreased dependence on mental hospitals for the provision of care. Comprehensive mental-health services are provided in community health-care centres. Services range from short-term in-patient care, out-patient therapy, and emergency services based on crisis intervention models, to education and consultation with other agencies.

Mental illness and the poor

Despite the fact that mental-health services are more readily available today, many of the poor, homeless and chronically mentally ill fail to receive adequate care. The high cost of hospitalisation and inadequate community reintegration programmes for those with chronic, severe disorders have created a population of mentally ill who are discharged into an unprepared community, poorly equipped to provide adequate out-patient services. They are unsuccessfully treated by drug therapies and are inevitably readmitted to the hospital. Public mental-health services for the poor have nevertheless improved with the training of CMHWs, who are providing care despite the lack of adequate resources. In South Africa, much still needs to be done.

Managed health care

The demands of a health-care system burdened with immense medical costs has led to many innovative strategies to meet the health needs of the population. The managed health-care system has been successful in promoting awareness of medical difficulties and has emphasised the prevention of health problems by encouraging a healthy lifestyle. People are encouraged to take care of their bodies and minds in order to live better lives. An awareness of the importance of stress reduction, relaxation and exercise are promoted as health ingredients for positive mental health. Thus, the prevention of mental disorders is emphasised.

Critics of the managed health-care system emphasise that this system primarily benefits the private health-care provider at the expense of the consumer with limited medical aid cover. It does nothing for the poor and those who cannot afford private health care. Nevertheless, the managed health-care system does emphasise the importance of providing time-limited solution-based interventions with high efficacy for those seeking psychological help. Mental-health practitioners are thus encouraged to provide appropriate services with a high cost-efficacy ratio (Gore 2002).

Is psychotherapy important?

When you have a psychological or emotional difficulty, seeking help from a professional source is very important. The kind of professional, the type of therapy, and an individual or group counselling modality all become very important questions. The complexity of the problem often determines the choice of therapy. The crucial factor remains: when you think you need help, talk to someone. Many people talk to their friends, family, religious advisors and even their hairdressers. All of these people are both caring and can offer assistance in times of distress. It is also useful to seek help from an independent trained counsellor who may be able to offer you a different perspective on the personal and emotional problem that you are experiencing. Professional treatment is also valuable when you wish to improve your life, to feel more content and motivated – and even if you wish to study better. There are many options, of which psychotherapy is one. In a recent survey of the kinds of assistance first-year students preferred for personal, career and learning-skills needs, the following results were reported (Nicholas 2002).

TABLE 6.3: Desired counselling options of first-year university students

	N	%
Individual counselling	929,8	46,5
Group counselling	667	62,7
Workshop	899	53,5
Lecture	767	23,4
Professional help outside university	336	6,3
Indigenous helper	90	27,1
Religious helper	389	15,4
Other	22 164,8	

OF THE RESPONDENTS, 22,8% SPOKE AN AFRICAN LANGUAGE.

Psychological services in South Africa

Therapeutic services in South Africa include psychologists trained in clinical, counselling, educational or industrial settings. These psychologists would be trained in psychology and many may specialise in offering services for specific problems – for example, scholastic problems, study difficulties, work-related problems, or family or couple counselling. Only psychologists registered with the Health Professions Council of South Africa (HPCSA), a statutory body mandated to protect the public and maintain standards of training, are licensed to offer psychological services. Psychologists cannot currently prescribe medication for the treatment of psychological problems. However, together with a psychiatrist, the best possible treatment can be offered by blending drugs and 'talk therapy'.

Where can I find therapeutic services?

Private practitioners, institutional settings such as community mental-health centres, hospitals, university counselling centres, and non-governmental organisations (NGOs) such as Lifeline, Childline, Rape Crisis and FAMSA are all resource agencies offering psychological services. The local health-care clinic and Department of Health office can direct you to the nearest service.

Therapist language and sex

The foundation of any therapeutic relationship is empathy, trust, rapport and a sense of being understood. Thus, if you feel more comfortable with a therapist of a particular sex, choose appropriately. A therapist who shares your language may help you to feel more understood. It is therefore important for psychologists offering services in South Africa to be proficient in more than one South African language.

Cost

The cost of seeking professional help may be a problem. Private psychotherapeutic services are expensive for those who do not have medical aid. Nevertheless, services offered by community clinics, university counselling centres and NGOs are more affordable and as good as any other service. Many private practitioners are willing to negotiate treatment rates with their patients. Though cost may be a prohibitive concern when seeking psychological assistance, it is important to remember that adequate mental-health services are available in all hospitals and community clinics.

Ethics

Treatment for personal and emotional problems is both intense and confidential. The demand for high standards of ethical behaviour from psychologists is therefore crucial. The Professional Board for Psychology is adamant that all psychologists conduct their practices in the best interest of their clients. This means adhering to the stringent requirements of confidentiality, competence and professional conduct. If you find a therapist behaving unethically, you have the right to terminate treatment and report the person to the Professional Board for Psychology.

Will I like therapy?

The therapeutic experience is different for everyone. Many people report that it is very helpful, thought provoking, and often emotionally painful and distressing. All of these are true. It is important to have realistic expectations about therapy. It will not solve long-standing problems overnight. Therapy can be a slow process, and the more motivated you are to resolve your problems, the more likely it is that you will experience a positive outcome. You are the only person who can eventually overcome your problem. Your therapist can help you, encourage you and support you in confronting the issues, but only you can finally overcome them. The benefits of psychotherapy are best when you have high motivation, adequate support and perseverance.

Summary

In this chapter, we have presented an overview of psychotherapy, its history, its theoretical background and the various intervention modalities that can be utilised to address individual social and psychological well-being. Some of the different types of therapy have been described, and their appropriateness to the South African cultural context examined. The advantages and disadvantages of institutional care have been elaborated upon. Finally, the chapter examined the issue of culture and therapy in some depth.

Further reading

Adler, A. (1927) *Practice and Theory of Individual Psychology.* New York: Harcourt, Brace & World.

Beck, A.T. (1976) *Cognitive Therapy and the Emotional Disorders.* New York: International Universities Press.

Beck, A.T. (1987) *Cognitive Therapy.* In J.K. Zeig (ed.), *The Evolution of Psychotherapy.* New York: Brunner/Mazel.

Dana, R.H. (1993) *Multicultural Assessment Perspectives for Professional Psychology.* Boston: Allyn & Bacon.

Doyle, C.L. (1987) *Explorations in Psychology.* Pacific Grove: Brooks/Cole.

Ellis, A. (1973) *Humanistic Psychotherapy: The Rational-emotive Approach.* New York: Julian Press.

Ellis, A. (1989) *Rational-emotive Therapy.* In R.J. Corsini & D. Wedding, (eds), *Current Psychotherapies.* Itasca: F.E. Peacock.

Freeman, M. (1998) *Providing Mental Health Care for all in South Africa: Structure and Strategy.* In L. Swartz (ed.), *Culture and Mental Health: A Southern African View.* Cape Town: UCT Press.

Gore, A. (2002) Editorial. In *Discovery Health News,* May.

Haley, J. (1973) *Uncommon Therapy: The Psychiatric Techniques of Milton H. Erickson, M.D.* New York: Ballantine.

Hergenhahn, B.R. (1992) *An Introduction to the History of Psychology.* Belmont: Wadsworth.

Jung, C.G. (1917/1953) *On the Psychology of the Unconscious.* In H. Read, M. Fordham & G. Adler (eds), *Collected Works of C.G. Jung*, Vol. 7. Princeton: Princeton University Press.

Klein, M. (1948) *Contributions to Psychoanalysis.* London: Hogarth.

Kohut, H. (1971) *Analysis of the Self.* New York: International Universities Press.

Lifschitz, S. & Oosthuizen, C. (2001) *Discovering Agape: Forming and Re-forming a Healing Community.* In M. Seedat, N. Duncan & S. Lazarus (eds), *Community Psychology: Theory, Method and Practice.* Cape Town: Oxford University Press.

Mays, V.M. & Albee, G.W. (1992) *Psychotherapy and Ethnic Minorities.* In D.K. Freedheim (ed.), *History of Psychotherapy: A Century of Change.* Washington, DC: American Psychological Association.

Nicholas, L.J. (2002) Unpublished survey of student needs and preferences for assistance.

Rogers, C.R. (1951) *Client-centred Therapy: Its Current Practice, Implications and Theory.* Boston: Houghton Mifflin.

Rogers, C.R. (1986) *Client-centred Therapy.* In I.L. Kutash & A. Wolf (eds), *Psychotherapist's Casebook.* San Francisco: Jossey-Bass.

Ryle, A. (1988) *Cognitive-analytic Therapy.* London: London University Press.

Scull, A. (1990) Deinstitutionalisation: Cycles of despair. *Journal of Mind and Behaviour*, 11(3/4), pp. 301–12.

Smith, D. (1982) Trends in Counseling and Psychotherapy. *American Psychologist*, 37, pp. 802–9.

Swartz, L. (1996) Culture and mental health in the rainbow nation: Transcultural psychiatry in a changing South Africa. *Transcultural Psychiatric Research Review*, 33, pp. 119–36.

Swartz, L. & Gibson, K. (2001) The 'old' versus the 'new' in South African community psychology: The quest for appropriate change. In M. Seedat, N. Duncan & S. Lazarus (eds), *Community Psychology: Theory, Method and Practice.* Cape Town: Oxford University Press.

Wade, P. & Bernstein, B. (1991) Culture sensitivity training and counsellor's race: Effects on Black female clients' perceptions and attrition. *Journal of Counselling Psychology*, 38, pp. 9–15.

Weiten, W. (1989) *Psychology: Themes and Variations* (3rd edition). Pacific Grove: Brooks/Cole.

Wittkower, E.D. & Warnes, H. (1984) *Cultural Aspects of Psychotherapy*. In J.E. Mezzich & C.E. Berganza (eds), *Culture and Psychopathology*. New York: Columbia University Press.

7 Personality

P.T. Sibaya and C. Malcolm

Objectives

After studying this chapter you should:

- be able to appreciate individual differences
- understand why people behave the way they do
- understand psychological theories about people's behaviour
- be able to explain how personality develops
- understand personality and cultural correlates.

Introduction

No person is exactly like another in terms of personality. **Personality** is that aspect of a person that renders the individual unique to others who know him or her. A way of understanding personality is to consider it analogous to a person's thumbprint. Everyone has whorls on their thumb that are similar, but the composition, or configuration, of the whorls is unique for every individual. Thus, each person can, quite clearly, be identified by his or her thumbprint. Similarly, all personalities are composed of the same dimensions, but the configuration renders each personality unique. Unlike the thumb, the personality has more dimensions and aspects to it. As a result, the variation in personality is greater than the minute variations detected in thumb printing. Each personality has its unique configuration of aspects that give the person distinctiveness in all facets of expression. Personality is the person's psychological and behavioural 'thumbprint'.

Although people may share many personality features, they are individually configured. This is partly understandable given that no two people live the same lives or are exposed to identical life experiences from the day of birth. Even identical twins, although similar in most physical characteristics, never have identical personalities. To the outsider, identical twins bear an uncanny resemblance in many of their behaviours, characteristics, life choices, likes and dislikes. However, when one comes

Personality:
That aspect of a person that renders the individual unique.

to know identical twins well, their differences become more apparent, such that their differences are as great as their sameness. Later in this chapter, we will look at the relative contribution of genetics and upbringing in shaping the personality of identical twins.

What exactly are the ingredients of personality? A summary of definitions that have evolved over the years is presented in several textbooks (Ross 1992: p. 4; Möller 1995: p. 5). These definitions have one thing in common: they define personality as the unique blend or composition of characteristics of the individual that renders the person distinctive from others. Personality is a term that encompasses the unique composition of a person's likes and dislikes, attitudes, perceptions, behavioural patterns, thoughts and emotions. Personality is stable over time and yet dynamic in the sense that it characterises one's adjustment to any given situation. Personality is the enduring and repetitive modes of thinking, feeling and acting that a person resorts to over time and context. For example, suppose we have all know Bill from our primary school years. One of his enduring characteristics was that he stood far above everybody else when it came to achievement. However, he was also competitive to the point where he even perceived friends as competitors rather than allies. Assume we meet up with Bill 15 years later. It is likely that, when he recounts his achievements since our last meeting, he will similarly have excelled relative to his peers and that his achievement drive will have been fuelled by a large dose of ruthless competitiveness that lost him friends along the way.

Among the definitions of personality listed by Möller (1995: p. 5) and Ross (1992: p. 4) are:

- the dynamic organisation within the individual of those psycho-physical systems that determine his or her characteristic behaviour and thought:
- a person's unique pattern of traits; and
- the relatively permanent patterns of repetitive interpersonal situations that characterise a person's life.

Personality therefore refers to the enduring nature of a person, his or her psychological make-up, temperament, character, intelligence, sentiments, attitudes, interests, disposition, likes and dislikes. Personality is an individual's unique constellation of consistent behavioural traits. Let us take a closer look at some of the terms embedded in this definition.

Disposition:
A person's tendency to behave in a particular way.

A **disposition** is a term closely related to personality that refers to a person's tendency to behave in a particular manner. An enduring disposition is referred to as a trait. A **trait** is a durable disposition to behave in a particular manner across different contexts. Adjectives such as aggressive, reliable, dishonest, kind and friendly describe personality traits. Traits will be discussed more fully in the section on dispositional theories.

Trait:
A durable disposition to behave in a particular manner across different contexts.

An interesting feature of personality is **temperament**, which is an inborn disposition to emotional responsiveness. Many emotional expressions are regulated by temperament. That someone is short-tempered is an expression of his or her temperament. Thus, temperament refers to the repetitive emotional tone with which a person reacts to the environment. Temperaments can vary from phlegmatic and laconic to easily-aroused and irritable.

Temperament:
An inborn disposition to emotional responsiveness.

Broad aspects of temperament apparent in infancy remain stable throughout the life-span. Chess and Thomas (1984) described three infant temperament types: easy, slow-to-warm-up and difficult. They followed up the same cohort of infants into adulthood and found that temperament in adulthood was fairly closely related to temperament style in infancy. This suggests that, in part, temperament is enduring and likely to be biologically determined to a significant degree.

That someone is a pious, kind, honest, generous and dependable person is a statement of his or her **character** disposition – one's moral standards or value systems. This aspect is related to the quality of an individual and is broader than a description of a discrete behavioural trait.

Character:
One's moral standards or value system.

Conscience refers to internalised cultural attributes that regulate behaviour according to socially acceptable norms. Personality is the sum total of all attributes or characteristics. Personality refers to distinctive/unique patterns of behaviour, thoughts, attitudes, emotions, likes and dislikes that characterise an individual's adjustment to life situations. Conscience refers to the enduring thinking style of the person and his or her adoption and enactment of moral and ethical values.

Conscience:
Internalised cultural attributes that regulate behaviour according to socially acceptable norms.

Theories of personality

A theory is a model, a paradigm or a framework that helps us to explain phenomena. The study of personality has led to the development of theories or models to explain personality. This study has been dominated by 'grand theories', which have attempted to explain the rich tapestry of facets that comprise personality. These separate theories use different theoretical constructs in an attempt to explain personality, yet can be grouped into a number of classes using different criteria. One system establishes three such groups: the conflict approach, the fulfilment approach and behaviourism (Lefton 1982). Another system identifies the following categories: dispositional theory, psychodynamic theories, learning theories and phenomenological theories (Bourne & Ekstrand 1982). Other broad categories of theories include the trait-and-type approach, the dynamic approach, the behavioural approach and the phenomenological approach (Morgan, *et al.* 1979).

Dispositional theories

We often use statements that reflect a dispositional theory of personality, such as 'Gloria is a kind-hearted person', 'He is a workaholic', etc.
Dispositional theories define or explain personality in terms of essential or
inborn tendencies. These theories also assume a large genetic contribution
to personality.

Sheldon's somatotype theory associates human physique with certain personality characteristics or temperament (Bourne & Ekstrand,
1982; Halonen & Santrock 1999; Möller 1995). The somatotype theory
classifies people into three broad groups, represented in Table 7.1.

Physique	Body type	Temperament	Emotion type
Endomorph	Large stomach, round overdeveloped body, plump	Viscerotonic	Relaxed, gregarious, food-loving, tolerant extraverted.
Mesomorph	Muscular, strong, athletic	Somatonic	Energetic, assertive, courageous.
Ectomorph	Thin, fragile looking, slender	Cerebrotonic	Fearful, restrained, introverted.

TABLE 7.1: The relationship between physique and personality

The somatotype theory of personality has been subjected to scientific
scrutiny for some time. Whatever the nature of such results, this theory
does provide us with a framework to classify people. However, people may
not fit neatly into these categories: one personality type may show characteristics of another classification. These three physique classifications are
not watertight compartments, but serve as broad overlapping types.

Trait theories of personality developed as a reaction to type theory.
These theories assume that behaviour is not determined by, or a direct
correlate of, physique, but that those stable and enduring personalities
traits are a substrate of manifest behaviour. The two concepts describe
the two ends of the scale or continuum that comprises the dimension.

Physique ⟶ Personality ⟵ Trait

FIGURE 7.1: The relation between trait and physique theories of personality

Both theories are helpful in describing human behaviour and personality –
for example, 'June is a friendly person', 'John is a diligent person', 'Mum is
an outgoing but impulsive person'. The task of trait theorists is to identify
all words that can be used as adjectives to describe personality. However,
words in themselves can be misleading or have various interpretations.

Allport (Ross 1992: p. 101; Möller 1995: p. 261) defined personality as 'the dynamic organisation within the individual of those psychophysical systems that determine his or her characteristic behaviour and thoughts'. An analysis of this definition shows that personality is a fusion of both the physical and the mental aspects of the personality. The phrase 'dynamic organisation' implies that personality aspects are not static – that they constantly undergo transformation through the life cycle and as a response to exposure to environmental experiences. An individual's personality has the capacity to change to a certain degree while remaining relatively constant over time. Furthermore, the various components of personality do not exist independently and thus change or remain static in concert with one another.

A further distillation of Allport's trait theory reveals that personality is deterministic in nature. An inbuilt or inborn mechanism controls and influences personality, behaviour and thought. Furthermore, the dynamic organisation takes place within the individual. However, this definition does not consider the relative influence of the environment in the shaping of personality.

Allport distinguishes between common and individual traits. A disposition that is shared by many people is called a **common trait**. Friendliness and aggressiveness are examples of traits that appear to some extent in everyone. **Individual traits**, however, are those that are unique to the individual. What determines uniqueness in this instance are the frequency, intensity and degree of manifestation of the trait.

Individual traits have several dimensions. An individual trait that is the most pronounced and pervasively evident in behaviours is a person's **cardinal disposition**. This cardinal disposition is a dominant trait that occurs in the widest range of settings. Not every individual has a cardinal trait. The **central traits/dispositions** are manifested more frequently than cardinal ones. Every person has a few central dispositions. These are adjectives or other forms of descriptors you often use to describe a friend: talkative, friendly, sociable, hard working, shy, insecure, etc. Individual traits have also a third dimension: the **secondary disposition**. Individuals rarely manifest these secondary traits and, only under special circumstances, are they displayed. For example, a person whom you know as shy may suddenly jump up and cheer when a player scores a goal in a soccer match. In this setting, the person is displaying a secondary trait. This characteristic is more peripheral and not crucial in the distinctive organisation of the person's personality. It is more likely to be expressed less frequently and only under particular circumstances, such as an emotive soccer match.

The use of the word 'determination' in this theory implies motivation.

Common trait:
A disposition shared by many people.

Individual traits:
Traits unique to the individual.

Cardinal disposition:
A dominant trait that occurs in the widest range of settings

Central traits/ dispositions:
Traits/dispositions manifest more frequently than cardinal ones.

Secondary disposition:
Disposition only displayed under special circumstances.

Allport used the term traits as synonymous with motives. According to Allport, motives have four characteristics: contemporaneity, diversity, purposefulness and uniqueness. The concept of the functional autonomy of motives means that the process of motivation is self-sustaining and has no roots in basic biological or social needs (Ross 1992: p. 103).

Subsequent trait theorists were faced with the problem of reducing Allport's plethora of traits to a manageable number. A statistical technique called factor analysis provided an efficient way of reducing 18 000 traits into clusters. Traits that have high factor loadings are extracted and put together to form a cluster. Raymond Cattell (Halonen & Santrock 1999) extracted 16 stable personality factors and constructed a questionnaire to measure personality. This became the popular 16PF (personality factor) scale.

Hans Eysenck (Halonen & Santrock 1999) developed a personality model that proposed two dimensions (as opposed to traits) of **neuroticism-stability** and **extraversion-introversion**. Later, he added a third dimension: **psychoticism. Extraversion** involves being social, assertive, active and lively. **Neuroticism** involves being anxious, tense, moody and low in self-esteem. **Psychoticism** involves being egocentric, impulsive, cold and anti-social. Eysenck theorised that core personality traits were determined largely by a person's genes.

Eysenck's model was a precursor to the 'five-factor' model developed by Costa and McCrae (1992, 1995). This is the most recent trait approach to personality. The model proposes that there are five core personality traits (see Table 7.2). The mnemonic OCEAN is internationally used as a way of remembering the five factors: Openness to experience; Conscientiousness; Extraversion; Agreeableness; and Neuroticism.

Extraversion:
Personality dimension involving being social, assertive, active, lively.

Neuroticism:
Personality dimension involving being anxious, tense, moody and low in self-esteem.

Psychoticism:
Personality dimension involving being egocentric, impulsive, cold and anti-social.

Trait	High score	Low score
Openness	Curious, seeks novel and unfamiliar experiences	Conventional, predictable, unimaginative
Conscientiousness	Organised, dependable, goal-directed	Careless, aimless, unreliable
Extraversion	Sociable, optimistic, fun loving.	Quiet, reserved, retiring, unassuming
Agreeableness	Trusting, straightforward, good-natured	Irritable, suspicious, rude
Neuroticism	Emotional, worrisome, insecure, nervous	Unemotional, calm, secure, relaxed

TABLE 7.2: Costa and McCrae's five personality factors

Cross-cultural and cross-national studies indicate that these five factors are widely identifiable in the ordinary language and discourse of people in different cultures around the world. This supports the view that these traits represent universal personality factors. Costa and McCrae, similar to Eysenck, concluded that personality is largely determined by genetics.

Support for a genetic contribution to personality comes from studies conducted on twins. The University of Minnesota Center for Twin and Adoption Research has been investigating the personality resemblance of identical twins reared apart. They have tested over 40 pairs of identical twins separated early in life. The findings reveal many remarkable similarities. One example is that of twins Jim Lewis and Jim Springer. Separated four weeks after birth, in 1940, they grew up 70 km apart in Ohio, and were reunited in 1979. They discovered they drove the same model car, chain-smoked the same brand cigarettes, chewed their fingernails and owned pet dogs named Toy. Both spent their vacations at the same beach in Florida. More important, when tested for personality traits such as flexibility, self-control and sociability, the twins responded almost exactly alike (Weiten 1989: p. 492). Not all the twin pairs have been found to be as similar as Jim and Jim. Tellegen *et al.* (1988) conducted a similar set of studies and concluded that their results support the theory that genetic blueprints shape personality and that the heritability of personality is approximately 50%. They conclude that 'personality differences are more influenced by genetic diversity than they are by environmental diversity'.

Plomin (1990), however, warned against overestimating the influence of genetics and argued that the effects of nature (genetics) and nurture (environment) are twisted together in complicated interactions that cannot be easily separated.

Psychodynamic theories

This theoretical approach to personality assumes that personality and its development are determined by intrapsychic developmental events and conflicts. The psychodynamic theory is also called the conflict approach. Sigmund Freud (1856–1939) developed the most influential theory of personality in this domain, and all psychodynamic theories are derivative of Freud's foundational concepts of unconscious mental life and conflict. Freud's disciples include his daughter Anna Freud, Erick Erikson (ego psychologist), Carl Jung (transpersonal perspective), Alfred Adler, Karen Horney and Erich Fromm (social psychological perspectives).

Personality structure

Freud believed that the personality or the mind is composed of three interrelated parts: the id, the ego and the superego. The threefold structure arises out of two classes of unconscious drives: life instincts and death instincts. An instinct has four aspects – its source, its aim, its object and its intensity. Personality structure and the conflict among the different instinctual domains induce dynamic forces within the personality.

Id:
The unconscious part of the personality.

Pleasure principle:
Primary process demanding immediate fulfillment of primary needs.

The **id** is the unconscious part of the personality and has no contact with the outside reality. The id is driven by the **pleasure principle**; it seeks gratification or pleasure and avoids pain. It cannot postpone gratification. It wants satisfaction now! The pleasure principle is a primary process that can be construed as a demand to take care of primary needs or drives and to do so immediately. It takes no heed of priorities. The infant throws temper tantrums when hungry or has a wet nappy. The id can therefore be regarded as the psychic representative of biological drives. Thus, the infant will put everything in his or her mouth to gratify the id or instinct. The instinct is the reservoir of psychic energy.

The id seeks to rid itself of all discomfort and to immediately satisfy all of its desires. One way the id can rid itself of discomfort is through wish fulfilment, which Freud called **primary process thinking**.

Ego:
That part of the personality in touch with reality.

A second personality structure develops during the first years of a child's life, which is called the **ego**. The ego is responsible for postponing gratification of impulses, desires, needs or drives until an appropriate time and object is found. Therefore, the actions of the ego in preventing a person from indiscriminately satisfying the id's desires are in accordance with the **reality principle**. The ego represents reality, the executive branch, the preconscious part of personality structure, problem-solving activity, reasoning, rational decision-making and, therefore, the **secondary process**. The reality principle enables the ego to control pleasure instincts to conform to the norms of society. Freud calls the type of intelligent reasoning that the ego employs **secondary process thinking**.

Superego:
The moral part of the personality.

The conscious part of the personality that develops as a person, incorporating or introjecting the moral code of parents and significant persons in the environment, is known as the **superego**. It is not fully consolidated until about seven years of age. This is the moral branch of the personality, which represents what is wrong or right. It is not present at birth, but develops as a direct result of parental socialisation and acculturation. There are two aspects of the superego: the **conscience** and the **ego ideal**. The conscience consists of prohibitions learned from parents and is often overly strict. It condemns as wrong certain things that might slip through the ego's vigilance. The superego also keeps a person striving towards ideals (ego ideals).

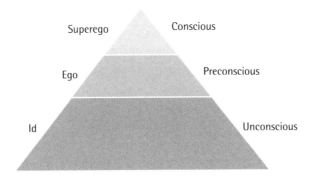

FIGURE 7.2:
The id, the ego
and the superego

Personality dynamics

An individual's personality is often compared to an iceberg, with just its peak visible (the conscious part) and the greater part (the unconscious dimensions) submerged. The preconscious is partly conscious and partly unconscious. Its function is to relegate to the unconscious level the id's impulses and other painful memories. These impulses, however, are easily retrievable and/or triggered by associations or conscious memories. As such, they inadvertently reach the conscious level of the mind/personality. This explains experiences such as Freudian slips or slip-of-the-tongue phenomenon.

There is a life instinct and a death instinct. Freud felt that the dynamic forces of personality arise from unconscious forces, which he called instincts. The life instincts lead toward survival and fulfilment, and the death instincts lead towards aggression and self-destruction. Consequently, human nature is as inherently destructive as it is survival seeking. The energy generated by sexual instincts is called libido. The instinct has four characteristics: source, aim, object and intensity. Freud believed that the source and aim of our instincts remained the same throughout life. However, the object and intensity can change greatly.

Anxiety is produced by unresolved conflict within the personality and can lead to the activation of defence mechanisms in the psyche's attempts to deal with it. Unconscious defence mechanisms then come into play.

A **defence mechanism** is a mainly unconscious device – a person's way of behaving that protects or defends him or her against anxiety. Here are some examples of defence mechanisms:

Defence mechanism: Method of protecting the self against anxiety.

- **Repression** occurs when we relegate to the unconscious any thoughts that arouse anxiety and are therefore painful to the conscious mind. These unconscious urges continue to seek expression and sometimes do in various ways, including dreams. We consciously suppress painful memories at a preconscious level but unconsciously repress them at the unconscious level, for example, an adult sex abuse survivor who has no recollection of her childhood abuse.

- **Reaction-formation** is a defence mechanism whereby unacceptable desires or emotions or motives are replaced with their opposites, often characterised by excessiveness of the expressed emotion. People often try to cope with conflict by using motive reversal. The following examples are not uncommon:
  - a sexually frustrated person becoming a leader of a religious revival or a reformer of moral standards; and
  - excessive love for an unwanted child.
- **Projection** involves attributing one's shortcomings or personality deficiencies to someone else. In other words, another person is made the scapegoat for one's own shortcomings. For example, a young man who has homosexual feelings towards a classmate thinks that the classmate has such feelings for him.
- **Rationalisation** occurs when a socially acceptable reason is given for unacceptable behaviour. For example, an employee takes sick leave without being sick, saying 'Everybody does it'.
- **Intellectualisation** enables one to keep emotions separate from thoughts. A person detaches or insulates him, or herself from the feelings aroused by a situation. An example is a medical practitioner who remains calm and renders services at the scene of a road accident.
- **Displacement** is a psychic mechanism whereby we transfer psychic energy from one object choice to another when satisfaction cannot be derived from the original. In this situation, the motive remains unaltered but a different goal is substituted for the original one. For example, after parental scolding, a young girl takes out her anger on her little brother.
- **Compensation** occurs when a person substitutes an activity to satisfy a motive. A person overdevelops his or her abilities in order to overcome inferiorities or weakness.
- **Sublimation** enables us to, for example, redirect sexual impulses to socially valued activities and goals. An example is a person who does painting to satisfy frustrated sexual urges.
- **Denial** is a subconscious process whereby the ego relegates anxiety-provoking reality to the unconscious . An example would be a young person refusing to recognise the risks of HIV infection from unprotected sex with strangers. He or she might say 'This only happens to other people'.
- **Regression** happens when a person engages in behaviour characteristic of earlier development in order to reduce anxiety. An example would be a young person who is anxious about leaving home and regresses to a more immature dependence on his or her parents.

Psychosexual stages of personality development

According to Freud, an individual goes through five critical developmental stages during childhood, called psychosexual stages. The first stage is the **oral period** (birth to 1 year), in which the libido finds gratification around the mouth. During the **anal period** (± 2 years to ± 3 years), in learning bowel control, a child has his or her first significant encounter with authority and social pressure. After the age of three, children characteristically discover their genitals and masturbation. This is known as the **phallic period**. The Oedipus complex and Electra complex occur during the phallic stage (± 4 years to ± 5 years). The **latency period** streches from 6 years through to puberty (12 years). From 13 years, the **genital stage** sets in. During this stage, heterosexual interests appear, marking the period of adolescence and beyond. The avoidance of intimate contact with the opposite sex is characteristic of the latency period and phallic periods (±13 years).

During these developmental stages, the libido moves from one erogenous zone to another. Fixation of the libido in any of these erogenous zones leads to persistent manifestation of behaviour characteristic of the stage. For example, oral stage fixation could manifest in an unhealthy preoccupation with food; anal stage fixation could manifest as an excessive need for control; phallic stage fixation could manifest as a pronounced concern with physical prowess and competitiveness; and a latency stage fixation could manifest as a pathological anxiety over contact with the opposite sex. The genital stage is said to be a period during which normal heterosexual interests emerge and therefore has no excessive genital behaviour to warrant fixation.

Stage	Ages	Erotogenic focus/ Erogenous zones	Developmental tasks
Oral	0-1	Mouth (sucking, biting)	Weaning and digestion
Anal	2-3	Anus (expelling or retaining faeces)	Toilet training and bowel control
Phallic	4-5	Genitals (masturbating)	Identifying with same-sex adult models
Latency	6-12	None (sexually repressed)	Expanding peer relations and core identity
Genital	13+	Genitals (sexual intimacy)	Establishing intimate relationships and work productivity

TABLE 7.2: Freud's stages of psychosexual development

The key tenets of psychodynamic theory are:

- that unconscious forces shape behaviour;
- that internal conflict plays a key role in generating psychological distress; and
- that early childhood experiences can influence the nature of adult personality.

While these ideas have greatly influenced our understanding of human nature, Freudian theory has received much criticism in recent years. In particular, the theory is criticised for being unscientific and lacking in validity, as resting upon shaky and unproven ideas, as overvaluing the role of the unconscious at the expense of conscious lived experience, and as being characterised by a sexist bias against women.

The behaviour-learning theory of personality

The school of thought known as behaviourism emerged as a reaction to the Freudian psychodynamic model, with its exclusive emphasis on the unconscious dimensions of personality development. The proponents of the behaviouristic school argued that the method of introspection was an unsuitable scientific tool, as was the method of free association. These methods were designed to study the mind or the consciousness of the individual and did not give an adequate account of the behaviour of an individual.

Behaviorists believe that only observable and measurable behaviour is the relevant domain of psychology. Behaviour is a real thing that can be studied (Sprinthall *et al.* 1994: p. 213). The study of behaviourism is not a personality theory but a study of principles of learning. In this context, personality can be viewed as the sum total of reactions acquired through learning. Individuals' behaviour differences are the result of their different learning histories. Each person has a unique learning history and, as such, a unique 'personality' affective, perceptual and behavioural repertoire.

According to this perspective, personality is a function of environmental and situational determinants. People learn to respond to the environment and, as such, a process of learning is established. Personality is therefore seen as something that is always changing, as the person's responses to the environment become more varied and complex. In this way, repetitive modes of responding become established and these become the person's characteristic response repertoire or personality.

Personality structure

Personality structure is not as clearly defined as in the case of the psycho-dynamic model. The basic structural unit of personality is the response that is often made in relation to a stimulus. To establish a connection between a stimulus and a response, a third element comes into play: reinforcement. Thus the three elements or units – **stimulus, response** and **reinforcement** – can be regarded as forming the structure of personality.

Personality can be viewed from different angles within the behavioural-learning theories framework. There is a classical conditioning approach, an instrumental or operant conditioning approach, and an observational learning approach. In classical conditioning, neutral and natural stimuli are paired for a number of joint presentations until the neutral stimulus becomes an effective substitute for the natural stimulus. Classical conditioning or learning occurs when a neutral stimulus elicits the same response as the natural stimulus. Unlike classical conditioning, operant conditioning is expensive in terms of time. A response is emitted by the learner rather than elicited by the experimenter – something that may take hours to occur. Whether elicited or emitted, a response is followed by reinforcement. Responses that are reinforced mould personality. A behavioural principle stipulates that learning is the process that shapes personality.

Young people learn new behaviours by observing others who they feel are important, powerful or influential. Observers imitate behaviours of models. Older children model good behaviour for their younger siblings. In this case, a person learns by watching and there is no reinforcement.

Psychologists maintain that aspects of cognition, such as thought processes, must be added to these forms of learning because human personalities are diverse.

Personality development

In this theory, no stages of development are suggested, but mention is made of a gradual growth process. The main change that occurs with development is the sequence and complexity of scheduled reinforcements.

People grow up in different environments and under different experiential conditions. This accounts for individual differences in behaviour and personality. Rewards and punishments shape personality. People learn through experiences, observation and modelling, with or without reinforcement. However, reinforcement is crucial for learning behaviour performance (Hilgard *et al.* 1979).

Personality is manifested differently in different situations. A response to a situation is gained both by the acquired disposition and the individual's experiences. These experiences dictate appropriate behaviours in different situations. Individuals learn to discriminate between different contexts in terms of appropriateness of behaviour for a specific situation.

Through reinforcement, personality develops relatively stable characteristics. A response that is consistently rewarded in different situations tends to reappear with greater regularity across situations. The principle of generalisation of learned response ensures that appropriate behaviour occurs in a variety of settings. According to the behavioural perspective, this is the essence of personality development. A personality that is characterised by pervasively aggressive behaviour might be suspected of having consistently received rewards for this behaviour as a child. In the case of observational learning, however, personality develops as a function of imitating the behaviours of others.

Personality dynamics

Certain personality characteristics interact with the environment to determine people's reactions in various situations. Hilgard *et al.* (1979: p. 387) mentioned the following acquired personality attributes that influence behaviour: competence, cognitive strategies, expectancies, subjective-outcome values, self-regulatory systems and plans. These personality variables interact with the conditions of a particular situation to determine a person's response.

Thus, for behaviourists, behaviour is driven or directed by the core tendency or motive to reduce or satisfy social or biological needs. This is accomplished through reinforced responses.

Humanistic theories of personality

The proponents of this movement reject basic assumptions made by psychodynamic, trait and behaviourist theorists. Humanistically oriented theorists maintain that personality is unique because each person perceives the world in a manner that is peculiarly his or her own. Behaviour is the outward or manifest reflection of this perception. Perception is not determined by one's personality traits, or ego development or reinforcement history. Each person perceives differently.

In this section, we will consider Carl Rogers' theory of personality. The individual subjective experience (self) is the focus of phenomenological theories of personality. The phenomenological approach to personality includes some theories that have been called humanistic because they emphasise the uniquely human characteristics of people.

Each person is seen as having an innate tendency to grow and develop into a fully mature person. Human nature is inherently good and strives for self-actualisation. The phenomenological approach to personality emphasises subjective experience: the individual's own perception and interpretation of events or reality.

Personality structure

Carl Rogers' theory of personality has as its main structures the concept of self, ideal self, self-regard and self-concept. The self is the main structural component of personality. According to Rogers, the self consists of all the ideas, perceptions, concepts and values that characterise the individual.

Your self-concept influences both your perception of the world and your behaviour. If you do something that is inconsistent with your self-concept, you feel uncomfortable and anxious, and may even deceive yourself to preserve your self-concept. Rogers proposes that we all have an ideal self in addition to our self-concept. The closer our self-concept is to our ideal self, the more fulfilled and happy we are. This congruence implies that we have also come close to self-actualisation.

According to humanistic theories of personality, **self-actualisation** is the basic force motivating or driving behaviour. Self-actualisation is the ongoing, continuous expansion of the self toward the ideal self. Self-actualisation is an innate tendency toward growth and the fulfilment of one's potential.

Self-actualisation: Continuous expansion of the self toward the ideal self.

Personality development

A quotation from Bourne and Ekstrand (1982: p. 349) summarises development or growth as seen according to the self theories:

> Every individual exists in a continually changing world of experience of which he is the centre. The organism reacts to the field as it is experienced and perceived. This perceptual field is, for the individual, 'reality'. The organism reacts as an organised whole to this phenomenal field.

Rogers' theory of personality has no stages of development. The world of the infant is his or her own experience. As the infant develops, he or she learns to discriminate among experiences, thus acquiring a sense of self. This explains how self-concept is formed. It is a dynamic process in which perception plays a significant role. Perception of experiences is influenced by the need for positive regard – a universal need that is pervasive and persistent.

Through complex experiences in life, an individual develops a sense of self-regard – a learned sense of self, based on the perception of the regard a person receives from others. With parental discipline, a child develops conditions of worth.

As children develop, parents and other authority figures react to their behaviour. Parental reactions can be positive, negative or neutral. Consequently, children learn to view some of their actions as unworthy or worthy. The development of a positive self-concept is central to personality development, with the goal of development being self-actualisation.

Personality dynamics

A degree of congruence between the real self (self image) and the ideal self leads to happiness. Lack of congruence between the real self and the ideal self leads to discomfort and unhappiness. This theory does not propose stages of development and does not use the construct of internal conflict for the explanation of observable behaviours.

The basic principle or core tendency in this theory is self-actualisation. This simply means the development of potential to approximate the ideal self, which is a continuous process. Anxiety tends to motivate people to work hard on self-actualisation.

Culture and personality

Theories of personality have made a significant contribution to the expansion of knowledge about understanding people's behaviour, development and psychology in general. Most of the theories of psychotherapy, counselling and other intervention procedures are based on these theories. Like many theories, theories of personality are fallible. Many assumptions and concepts cannot be operationalised, and are therefore not measurable. Nevertheless, contemporary models of personality and research studies into the nature of personality suggest that there are certain universal dimensions or traits that are evident across a range of cultural, ethnic and linguistic contexts. This tends to support the idea that personality variation is a universally uniform thing, and that the content or expression of personality is dependent upon cultural particularities.

For instance, when scales that tap the 'big five' personality traits have been administered and subjected to factor analysis cross-culturally, the usual five traits have typically emerged. Thus, the indication is that the basic structure of personality is invariant, irrespective of cultural and contextual variation.

However, when researchers (Markus & Kitayama 1991) looked at specific personality aspects or facets across cultures they noted culture-specific variations. For example, culture-specific variations have been found in locus of control, where samples from Western cultures show evidence of a more internal locus of control than samples from Asian cultures. Similarly, American children evidence a more independent view of self than their Asian counterparts. The suggestion is that Asian cultures foster a more interdependent view of self. Markus and Kitayama (1991) speculate that this interdependent view of self may also be the norm in many African and Latin American cultures. More research is needed on this aspect of personality, particularly within the multicultural South African setting. The Xhosa concept of *ubuntu* suggests that Xhosa culture too may foster an interdependent view of self. Current cross-cultural research on personality presents more fascinating questions than answers.

Summary

This chapter has attempted to:
- define personality;
- group theories of personality into types, traits, dynamic, behavioural and humanistic models;
- show how personality develops;
- show how personality copes with challenges and life realities; and
- throw light on research in the field of personality psychology.

Further reading

Apter, S.T. & Conoley, J.C. (1984) *Childhood Behavior Disorders and Emotional Disturbance.* Englewood Cliffs: Prentice-Hall.

Bourne, L.E. & Ekstrand, B.R. (1982) *Psychology.* New York: McGraw-Hill.

Brammer, L.M. (1993) *The Helping Relationship: Process and Skills.* Boston: Allyn and Bacon.

Brammer, L.M., Abrego, P.J. & Shostrom, E.L. (1993) *Therapeutic Counselling and Psychotherapy.* Englewood Cliffs: Prentice-Hall.

Chess, S. & Thomas, A. (1984) *Origins and Evolution of Behavior Disorders: From Infancy to Early Adult Life.* New York: Brunner/Mazel.

Corsini, R.J. (1979) *Current Psychotherapies.* Illinois: F.E. Peacock.

Costa, P.T. & McCrae, R. (1992) *Revised NEO Personality Inventory: NEO-PI and NEO Five Factor Inventory (Professional Manual)*. Odessa: Psychological Assessment Resources.

Costa, P.T. & McCrae, R. (1995) Set like plaster? Evidence for the stability of adult personality. In T.F. Heatherton & J.L. Weinberger (eds), *Can Personality Change?* Washington, DC: American Psychological Association.

Edwards, S.D., Grobbelaar, P.W., Makunga, N.V., Sibaya, P.T., Nene, L.M., Kunene, S.T. & Magwaza, A.S. (1983) Traditional Zulu theories of illness in psychiatric patients. *The Journal of Social Psychology*, 121, pp. 213–21.

Egan, G. (1994) *The Skilled Helper: A Problem-Management Approach to Helping*. Pacific Grove: Brooks/Cole.

Gillis, H. (1992) *Counselling Young People: A Practical Guide for Parents, Teachers and Those in Helping Professions*. Saxonwold: Lynn Publications.

Halonen, J.S. & Santrock, J.W. (1999) *Psychology: Context and Applications*. Boston: McGraw-Hill College.

Hilgard, E.R., Atkinson, R.L. & Atkinson, R.C. (1979) *Introduction to Psychology*. New York: Harcourt Brace Jovanovich.

Hjelle, L.A. & Ziegler, D.J. (1976) *Personality Theories*. New York: McGraw-Hill.

Lefton, L.H. (1982) *Psychology*. Boston: Allyn & Bacon.

Levy, L.H. (1970) *Conception of Personality: Theories and Research*. New York: Random House.

Maddi, S.R. (1969) *Personality Theories: A Comparative Analysis*. Homewood: Dorsey.

Markus, H.R. & Kitayama, S. (1991) Culture and the self: Implications for cognition, emotion, and motivation. *Psychological Review*, 98, pp. 224–53.

Morgan, C.T., King, R.A. & Robinson, N.M. (1979) *Introduction to Psychology*. Tokyo: McGraw-Hill, Kogakusha.

Morgan, C.T., King, R.A., Weisz, J.R. & Schopler, J. (1996) *Introduction to Psychology*. New York: McGraw-Hill.

Möller, A.T. (1995) *Perspectives on Personality*. Durban: Butterworths.

Plomin, R. (1990) *Nature and Nurture: An Introduction to Human Behavioral Genetics*. Pacific Grove: Brooks/Cole.

Reid, W.H. & Wise, M.G. (1995) *DSMIV Training Guide*. New York: Brunner/Mazel.

Ross, A.O. (1992) *Personality: Theories and Processes*. New York: Harper Perennial.

Sibaya, P.T., Hlongwane, M.M., Maphumulo, N.C. & Zwane, E.X.S. (1994) *Advance with Guidance*. Cape Town: Maskew Miller Longman.

Sprinthall, N.A., Sprinthall, R.C. & Oja, S.N. (1994) *Educational Psychology: A Developmental Approach*. New York: McGraw-Hill.

Tellegen, A., Lykken, D.T., Bouchard, T.J., Wilcox, K.J., Segal, N.L. & Rich, S. (1988) Personality similarity in twins reared apart and together. *Journal of Personality and Social Psychology*, 54, pp. 1031–39.

Van Niekerk, E. & Prins, A. (2001) *Counselling in Southern Africa: A Youth Perspective*. Sandown: Heinemann.

Weiten, W. (1989) *Psychology: Themes and Variations* (3rd edition). Pacific Grove: Brooks/Cole.

Woolfolk, A.E. (1995) *Educational Psychology*. Boston: Allyn & Bacon.

Social Psychology

8

D. Foster

Objectives

After studying this chapter you should:
- be able to define social psychology
- be able to describe four different levels of explanation
- be able to understand, describe and compare three different perspectives or viewpoints on social psychology
- be able to define social psychology
- be able to describe some of the key studies and theoretical constructs
- be able to understand the dynamics underlying racial and gender oppression
- be able to describe some of the key studies in social psychology
- be able to understand racism, prejudice and stereotyping from the three perspectives
- be able to provide some understanding of the problems of racism and violence in South Africa
- be able to describe some recent South African research in discourse analysis.

What is social psychology?

Most textbooks regard social psychology as a sub-branch of the wider field of psychology, a sub-area concerned with the study of how individuals interact with and are influenced by other individuals or groups. A standard definition would be:

> ... *the scientific field that studies the manner in which the behaviour, feelings, or thoughts of one individual are influenced and determined by the behaviour and/or characteristics of others.*

(BARON & BYRNE 1981: p. 7)

However, the view in this chapter is that all psychology is social. As human beings, we are intrinsically social, cultural and political creatures whose actions are also deeply shaped by historical events. In growing up, we only become fully human in and through interactions with others and so become clothed in cultural forms. We are intrinsically social and cultural beings largely because we use language: we are users and bearers of sign systems. Language and other forms of symbolic communication play a significant role in understanding social interaction.

Despite the claim that we are intrinsically social beings, for some centuries, theorists have artificially separated two major realms – the 'individual' on the one hand and the 'social system' on the other. Even everyday explanations of human actions tend to split these two realms. We explain peoples' actions as either due to the 'individual' (for example, dysfunctional personalities or odd attitudes) or to the 'social' realm (for example, a bad childhood or pressures brought to bear by others). Therefore, this 'individual'-'social' dualism constitutes a central problem and set of questions. How should we think about the relation between the individual and the social? Are we predominantly subjects or victims of social circumstances? Are we driven by individual forces and desires, such as genes, personality types or inner sentiments? Are we active agents or are we determined by wider social actors, institutions and structures? Questions of this sort form the 'big' problems and dilemmas for social psychology. A further problem relates to the question of social change. How do people change their beliefs, attitudes, prejudices and behaviours? For example, currently it is pertinent to work out how to change the actions of people in the face of a life-threatening issue such as HIV/AIDS.

Four levels of analysis

Cognition:
Thoughts.

Affective processes:
Feelings and emotions.

Conative processes:
Motives, desires and drives.

It is useful to propose a scheme of four differing levels of explanation that are commonly employed in social psychology (Doise 1986). At the individual level, explanation is given in terms of individual states or processes, such as thoughts (**cognition**); feelings or emotions (**affective processes**); or motives, desires and drives (**conative processes**). At the interpersonal or situational level, we explain actions as due to interactions among people – for example, seeing divorce as due to poor communication between couples – or as due to the demands of particular situations, such as in church or at weddings, parties or funerals. If there is one major lesson emerging from roughly a hundred years of study in social psychology, it is that people are more under the influence of immediate situations and social roles than we usually assume.

At the group or positional level, people's actions are accounted for in terms of group membership and/or status within a social order. We are deeply affected by being male or female and members of large groupings, such ethnic, religious, cultural or national categories. As individuals, we are also bearers of the social status and privileges that membership of these large groupings confers. For example, in South Africa, whites and males have in the past been in a position of high status, although the situation is to some extent changing.

The ideological level examines the influence of widely shared systems of ideas and social practices that in turn serve to maintain domination of one group over another. For example, **patriarchy** (or androcentrism, or sexism) is a system of practices and beliefs that enables men to dominate women via actions such as rape, sexual harrassment and domestic labour. **Racism** is an ideology that enables people of one skin colour to dominate people of a different colour through forms such as prejudice, stereotyping, discrimination, segregation, job reservation and the like. If men say they have the right to beat or sexually coerce women, then such behaviours are understood as being shaped by sexist **ideology**.

Patriarchy:
System in which males are dominant.

Racism:
System in which one race dominates another.

Although all four levels (others would claim there are more, including a biological or evolutionary level) are equally important in explaining human actions, social psychology has tended to favour the first two levels (individualistic and interpersonal) to the neglect of the others. A social psychological theory – that is, a set of statements about the relationships between component sub-parts of a phenomenon – should take into consideration all four levels of analysis to be an adequate theory, but this has not always occurred. The plea in this chapter is for a wider focus that considers each of these levels of analysis and their interrelationship.

Ideology:
Way of thinking or system of ideas and theories about some aspect of life.

Since psychology has been predominantly a Western and modern project, it tends to carry a cultural bias and set of assumptions. A central problem for modern Western thought is that of individual-social dualism – the tendency to explain human actions either in terms of individual processes or in terms of societal and group-based ideological processes. For the discipline of psychology, this problems looms large. Western cultural bias tends to favour individualistic levels of explanation, because individualism is a Western cultural value and a level of analysis. Psychology itself faces the danger of being part of a system of ideological domination if its explanatory forms are only one-sided. We would do well to look to wider aspects, such as social power, status and ideology, to escape from the traps of a modern, masculine, Western and, indeed, mainly American cultural heritage.

Cultural and historical dimensions

We live in a rapidly changing world: the racist laws of apartheid have been swept away; South Africa has a positive new set of laws; and we are all part of a globalising new era. The historical dimension means that we live quite differently in various historical epochs. Similarly, cultures (different ways of being or doing) influence our beliefs and actions. In South Africa, there are three broad cultural streams – from Africa, from East Asia and from Western Europe – and many languages that shape our ways of being, feeling, thinking and doing. Furthermore, there are other cultural dimensions in South Africa common to all three main cultural streams, including male dominance. Both cultural and historical dimensions are crucial for understanding how people act, but they have often been neglected by mainstream psychology.

Historical and cultural dimensions combine and intertwine, which means that cultures are never static but are constantly shifting and changing to produce new hybrid identities. For example, people in South Africa are being influenced by both modernisation (electricity in townships and rural areas) and Westernisation (McDonald's, fast foods, denim jeans, and Western movies and television). Yet simultaneously, the legacy of the historical past lives on in many ways: black people in general are poorer than white people; in rural areas, some African cultural traditions still hold sway. It is clear from these examples that an adequate social psychology should take most seriously both cultural and historical dimensions, but due in part to the predominance of experimental methods and to Western ways of thinking, such aspects have often been glossed over. The social constructionist movement of recent years gives greater attention to historical and cultural factors, and to the notion that our self-identities are more fluid, multiple and hybrid than claimed by most of mainstream social psychology.

A fragmented field: The three main approaches to social psychology

In the remainder of the chapter, after a brief history of the field, social psychology will be regarded as a fractured and divided field, characterised by three main approaches or positions:

- individualistic approaches or 'mainstream' social psychology;
- social identity theory; and
- social constructionism and discursive psychology.

These approaches do not necessarily agree with one another, which makes for a fragmented field, but they have all contributed to our understanding of social personhood. Nor should they be understood as entirely separate and apart: they may well share some ideas and methods but not others; they might overlap and agree on the centrality of particular topics, but differ in their understanding; and even in sniping at one another they may well bring new insights. These three positions could be regarded as akin to cultures, with their own beliefs and customs, but of necessity having to interact and argue with one another, and often wholly interdependent on one another, with the exciting possibilities of producing new hybrid forms. In decades hence, we may well have a more encompassing 'hybrid socio-psychology', but for the present we will examine the three separate streams, taking racism, particularly in South Africa, as a common 'social problem' to see the differences in the approaches.

A brief history of social psychology

Although its roots lie in the world of earlier philosophers, it is common to date the origins of contemporary social psychology in the 1890s. In France, Gustav le Bon wrote an influential book on *The Crowd* in 1895, while in America in 1898, Triplett conducted one of the earliest experiments. 1908 saw the first two textbooks in this fledgling field authored by E.A. Ross in America and by William McDougall in Britain. In 1924, Floyd Allport published an influential textbook, and during the 1920s, Sigmund Freud wrote extensively on the psychology of groups, while Wundt produced works on 'folk psychology'. It was also during the 1920s that researchers developed various techniques for measuring concepts such as attitude, prejudice and stereotyping.

In 1935, Carl Murchison published the first *Handbook in Social Psychology* and further handbooks appeared in 1954, 1968, 1985 and 1998, charting the developments of a rapidly growing field. Muzafer Sherif conducted important studies on the psychology of norms in 1936, while during the 1940s, the Gestalt-oriented Kurt Lewin was the most influential figure in the field, giving a boost to the fledgling study of group dynamics. Many European scholars fled the Nazi horrors and, working in conjunction with American colleagues, introduced new topics and 'techniques'. One such collaborative effort by Adorno and colleagues produced the influential publication on the authoritarian personality in 1950. The atrocities of the Holocaust intensified the study of prejudice and stereotyping and, in 1954, Gordon Allport wrote an important volume, *The Nature of Prejudice*.

Social psychology has been and remains largely an American endeavour. While the study of attitudes, prejudice, group dynamics and social influence remained central (Asch on conformity in the 1950s;

Milgram on obedience to authority in the 1960s; and Sherif on inter-group dynamics in the 1950s and 1960s), American research gradually turned inwards from the 1960s onwards, with a focus on inner mental calculations in an area known as 'social cognition' (topics such as cognitive consistency and attribution theory) and has predominantly remained in the sway of congnitive perspectives to the present.

In Europe, American dominance was challenged in the form of social identity theory (Henri Tajfel) and social representations (Serge Moscovici) from the late 1970s onwards. From the late 1980s, all of mainstream psychology was challenged by the alternative metatheories known variously as social constructionism, post-modernism or discursive psychology.

'Mainstream' or individualistic social psychology has been the focus of development over the past century. Let us examine some of its key terms and concepts over that period.

Individualistic approaches

Individualistic approaches take the individual as the primary unit of analysis. They tend to look for explanations inside the person and, when investigating group dynamics, forces on the individual person are regard-ed as primary. The social sphere is regarded as outside, as external to the unity of the individual. It is a view that has been described as 'self-conained individualism' (Sampson 1988). The person is regarded as a bounded entity and unit, largely rational and as acting in a totalistic way to the pushes and pulls of outside social forces and inner processes such as thoughts or feelings. While the person may be 'self-contained', he or she is regarded as having three different kinds of processes 'inside', which combine to produce particular actions or behaviours. The three sets of processes or 'mechanisms' are:

- **Cognition:** beliefs, thoughts, ideas, judgements, decisions, perceptions and all other elements regarded as 'higher' mental processes.
- **Affect:** feelings, emotions, sentiments, mood.
- **Conation:** will, drive, purpose, intentions, and other elements that may be regarded as 'motivational' processes.

Often it is assumed that these components or sub-processes act in a linear fashion to produce the outcome of an action – cognitive, affective, conative behaviour – but in more recent thinking (Zajonc 1998; Deaux & Lafrance 1998) the relations between these components are seen as bi-directional and more complex. There are no neat models to describe how these component processes 'work' to produce actions.

Insofar as the 'self-contained individual' is concerned, some concept of a central, overarching organising principle is required; something that pulls together the component parts into a unified whole. Towards this end, the concept of a 'self' has frequently been proposed since William James (1890) made good use of the term. For psychologists in the main, the concept of the self is equivalent to the idea of a self-contained individual, since both imply a sense of unity and a sense of separateness from others and the social or wider society. However, other cultures, and different historical epochs and theoretical views, such as post-modernism, do not agree that the 'self' is equivalent to a self-contained individual. Nevertheless, since Floyd Allport's influential text in 1924, where he maintained that only individuals think, feel and act, it has been difficult to get away from the dominant view of individualism.

The other characteristic of 'mainstream' social psychology is its reliance almost exclusively on the laboratory experiment as the source to produce 'empirical' data and evidence. The term **'empirical'** properly means reliance on evidence through our sensory systems (we know because we can see, or hear, or feel, or touch). While there is no difficulty with reliance on this empirical form of knowing, it does become a problem when it is regarded as the only form of knowledge, rather than knowledge via theoretical speculation, creative writing, the arts in all their forms and so on.

Empirical: Experienced through the five senses.

Attitudes

Gordon Allport repeatedly argued that attitude was the central concept for social psychology. As early as 1935, Allport gave a comprehensive definition of attitude that has not changed much since then. Allport (1935: p. 810) in Murchison's first *Handbook of Social Psychology* defined attitude as a:

> ... *mental and neural state of readiness, organised through experience, exerting a directive or dynamic influence upon the individual's response to all objects and situations with which it is related.*

An attitude, therefore:
- is an inner process that cannot be seen, and therefore must be inferred from what a person says or does;
- is learned;
- is able to direct action in one direction or another;
- is organised; and
- is evaluative: it judges objects or persons in either a positive or a negative manner.

One way of measuring an attitude is to list a series of statements and ask people to agree or disagree with them on a five-point response scale, known as a Likert scale. An example could be:

Q: Women should be able to decide for themselves whether to have an abortion or continue with a pregnancy.

Strongly disagree	2
Disagree	1
Undecided	0
Agree	+1
Strongly agree	+2

Notice that a response to such a statement reflects three aspects of attitudes: whether a person agrees or not indicates direction; how strongly a person feels indicates strength; and how important a person feels about that attitude compared with other attitudes indicates centrality. If an attitude has clear direction, greater strength and higher centrality it will be more difficult to change. Alternatively, it is possible for a person to hold no attitude at all towards an issue that is neutral. It has long been assumed that, by measuring attitudes among a population, psychologists could assist in solving social problems.

Attitudes and behaviour

Allport's (1935) definition claimed that attitudes exerted a directive influence on responses, which meant that one could expect a strong positive relation between attitudes and behaviour. If there was no relation, there would be little point in measuring attitudes. However, numerous studies by the late 1960s reported only two positive correlations, usually around 0,3 (where 0,6 or 0,7 would be regarded as a good relation), between measured attitudes and reported behaviours. This is a problem. Perhaps there were other links in the chain between attitudes and actions, or perhaps the concept of attitudes needed more precise definition. Drawing on the long-held trilogy notion of mind (cognitive, affective and conative processes), two American researchers defined an attitude only in terms of the affective – the evaluative or feeling components – and proposed further links in the chain (Fishbein & Ajzen 1975; Ajzen 1988). In their theory of reasoned action, they proposed that intentions (conative processes) were the levers for action. Neither beliefs (cognitions) nor attitude (feelings) directly produce actions, since we are often pressured to conform to beliefs of significant other people in our groups that may be different from our own. Drawing on these group normative beliefs, an individual forms a subjective norm. An intention to perform an action is, in turn, formed out of the interaction between attitudes and subjective norms, as illustrated in Figure 8.1.

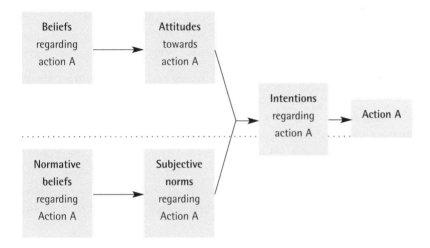

FIGURE 8.1: Theory of reasoned action

To illustrate, using an example from HIV/AIDS risk issues, a person may believe that condoms protect against AIDS and therefore has a positive attitude toward condom use when having sex, but may be influenced by people in the peer group who believe that condoms are a useless form of protection against AIDS. Intentions regarding condom use for sexual encounters depend upon the relative strength of these two factors: an individual's attitude and the internalised beliefs of significant others. Many studies over the past 20 years have shown strong support for the link between intentions and behaviour, and for the theory of reasoned action in general. Furthermore, if an individual's attitudes to perform a specific action are strong, central and meaningful, and are not challenged by conflicting normative influences, then attitudes have been shown to be positively correlated with behaviour (Ajzen 1988).

In a study using this theory of reasoned action to investigate AIDS risk among Malawian students, Bandawe and Foster (1996) found that attitudinal factors played a greater role than normative factors in predicting two major HIV-risk issues: intention to use condoms and intention to remain with a single sexual partner. It is important to be able to tease out these potentially competing factors in order to plan appropriate health preventive campaigns – for example, to target individual beliefs or to work with groups to change group-based feelings, and to find out which groups of significant others are likely to be influential.

Changing attitudes

Many social problems, such as environmental issues, health risks or violence towards women, could be solved or at least improved by changing people's attitudes. However, what are the processes involved in attitude changes? Social psychology has suggested at least three routes: persuasive communications, cognitive dissonance and the contact hypothesis.

In the persuasive communications approach, researchers have proposed a chain of factors or variables that are likely to influence change. They include:

- **Source of message:** This includes the credibility or expertise, as well as the attractiveness, likeability or status of the message giver. In recent HIV campaigns in South Africa, high-status and well-known figures, such as Deputy President Jacob Zuma, Archbishop Desmond Tutu and radio/television presenter Tim Modise have been used as the source for safer-sex messages.
- **Message:** This turns on the style of the message. For example, should messages be high or low in terms of fear arousal; should they be one- or two-sided; and how discrepant from the target's position should the message be pitched?
- **Channel:** What is the best medium of communication – radio, television, press, magazine, group meetings? And what is the best modality – written or face-to-face spoken messages? In the HIV campaign, actor Pieter-Dirk Uys has gone to hundreds of schools to give a spoken message and some straight talk about sex.
- **Factors in the target or receiver:** This depends on issues such as the ability to be persuaded, commitment, participation, or even whether the target person is paying attention to the message: we all tend to 'switch off' during television advertisements.

- **Context:** This depends upon the area or domain of the message (politics/health/advertising) and any other contextual issues, such as being distracted, the timing of the message (a week or a month before an election, for example) and accidental factors – for example, was there a television blackout on the night?

While this tells us about the many steps and factors that could be involved, the approach produced results in the form of isolated bits and pieces, and told us very little about psychological processes. Later, McGuire (1969) proposed a two-factor model, which states that the likelihood of a persuasive message resulting in attitude change is the joint product of the probability of reception and acceptance of the messages. While this model is elegant and simple, it is lacking in principles that tell us what affects reception and acceptance – questions taken up by Petty and Cacioppo (1986) in their elaboration likelihood model (ELM).

The ELM is a model of factors that determine the acceptance or rejection of a message. On receipt of a message, a person may process it according to two different cognitive routes. In the central route, people spend considerable time and effort on evaluating the content and issues of a message. The term 'elaboration' is used to indicate the extent to which a recipient thinks about the issue-relevant arguments in a message. In the second route, the peripheral route to persuasion, people are less motivated and, instead, use **heuristic** processing, making decisions on peripheral factors such as credibility or attractiveness of the source. It also refers to other fast-track processing devices, such as classical conditioning (you like the jingle, you like the product) and modelling (imitating what others do). Persuasion is a product of both the amount of processing and the favourability of the message. If a message, due to high quality, is favourably received, more elaborate processing will increase attitude change. If a message is weak and unconvincing, persuasion should be greater insofar as recipients are unable or not motivated to use elaborate processing.

Heuristic:
Taking a short cut in processing information.

The ELM and similar models that distinguish between almost automatic as opposed to more thoughtful processing of information have received a great deal of support and attention in recent years (Wegner & Bargh 1998). It is a good example of the current trends in social cognition – that is, understanding the routes and processes of information processing, drawing on the analogy of a computer. While a person may at times be computer-like, and understanding how humans process information is likely to be fruitful, the question is: Is a person only like a computer?

Another way to set about changing attitudes is not to try to change people's ideas, but, paradoxically, to try and change their behaviour first. According to Leon Festinger's (1957) influential cognitive dissonance theory, the cognitive system is organised (as Allport suggested earlier) around a principle of consistency. Individuals want consistency between different parts of their cognitive system, as well as between beliefs and their own behaviours. When people act in a way that is inconsistent with their attitudes, they experience an internal state of cognitive dissonance. Since dissonance is uncomfortable, individuals are motivated to reduce this inner state. If a person has already behaved in a certain manner, the easiest way to reduce dissonance is to change the attitude in line with the action, a solution similar to the defence mechanism of rationalisation. For example, it is likely that active smokers will support the line that smoking is not harmful, claiming that the evidence is not all in.

This view suggests that changing attitudes might occur more readily by first trying to change behaviour, for example, forbidding smoking in classrooms, buildings, meetings and restaurants, and changing laws about smoking in public. Cognitive dissonance is wary of this over-heavy approach. If an individual feels he or she has no free choice, he or she will explain away the dissonance by suggesting 'I was forced into this', rather than changing attitude. Following many experimental examples, a more minimalist approach to inducing behaviour changes (forced compliance) with low rewards would create a greater degree of dissonance and increased degree of attitude change. This sets up an interesting conundrum for the activist who wishes to shift attitudes: how to find the optimal degree of behavioural forced compliance to effect the maximal degree of cognitive dissonance.

A warning, however: later research indicates that cognitive dissonance is only significant if the overall self-concept is involved in the issue. If not, people have the remarkable ability to ignore or bypass dissonance, inconsistency and contradictions. Yet, this tendency towards cognitive consistency has been shown to be an important process in the organisation of cognitive systems and is another example of the social cognition approach to social psychology. Cognitive systems are not passive, but are organised in certain ways to process information in order to shape subsequent action.

A third way of thinking about attitude change involves the 'contact hypothesis'. This notion, originally proposed by Gordon Allport (1954), suggests that a person, by being in contact with members of a negatively evaluated out-group, could change attitude towards that out-group in a positive way. But this is not so simple. Actual contact with members of a despised out-group, if anything, could confirm existing prejudices and external hostility. Research over many years has shown that, for positive outcomes to occur, certain conditions of contact should be met (Foster & Finchilescu 1986). Optimal conditions should:

- allow for genuine friendship and knowledge of the other;
- be supported by the social group or institution to which people belong;
- involve people of roughly similar status (e.g. educational, socio-economic, etc.);
- involve cooperation to achieve shared goals; and
- the co-operative activity should lead to rewarding outcomes.

Some 50 years of research has generally confirmed the contact hypothesis, but in racist situations it is difficult to find people of equal status, and social identity theory approaches have found that participants often do not generalise their more positive attitudes to other situations. This is because the contact hypothesis is governed by principles that operate at the individual and interpersonal levels, but do not lead to changes in the wider intergroup arrangements or the ideologies on which power inequalities reside.

Racialised attitudes in South Africa

In the early 1930s, I.D. MacCrone, at the University of the Witwatersrand, began research on racial attitudes and published a major book on the topic (MacCrone 1937). Realising that white people's negative attitudes to black people was a central part of 'the problem' in South Africa, he developed various measures and conducted studies at regular intervals, thus providing an invaluable historical record. The racialised attitudes of white South Africans to black people from 1934 to 1944 are presented graphically in Figures 8.2 and 8.3, using two different measures: the Thurstone scale and social distance measures.

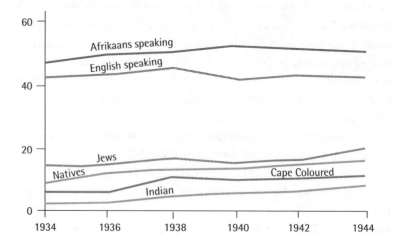

FIGURE 8.2

Research findings were clear-cut. Afrikaans-speaking whites held the
most negative attitudes, then English-speakers, and Jewish whites were
the least prejudiced (perhaps because Jews also faced discrimination,
both in Europe and in South Africa). Both English and Afrikaans-speaking whites held negative attitudes to all categories of black people and
towards Jews (MacCrone 1949).

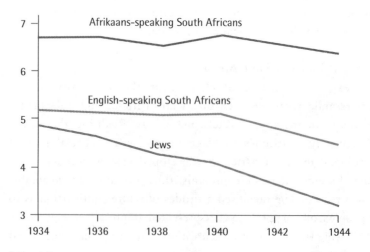

FIGURE 8.3

Numerous other studies over the years revealed similar and relatively
unchanging patterns of negative racial attitudes of whites towards
blacks, although from the 1950s onwards, there were more positive
attitudes towards Jews and some studies reported very unfavourable

attitudes towards Russians, undoubtedly due to the anti-communist ideology rampant in South Africa at that time. (See Foster & Nel (1991) for a detailed review of these studies.) However, black attitudes towards whites were not a mirror-image of prejudice. Blacks consistently showed positive attitudes towards English-speaking whites, but held more negative attitudes towards Afrikaans-speaking whites, undoubtedly blaming the predominantly Afrikaans-speaking National Party government for the dreadful policy of apartheid.

In response to the unchanging prejudicial attitudes of whites and the openly racist laws of the apartheid state, the African National Congress responded with a non-racial policy, developed in the 1950s, in the form of the Freedom Charter (which stated that South Africa belongs to all who live in it). In the 1970s, the black consciousness movement, under the leadership of Steve Biko and Barney Pityana, urged black people to throw off the psychological shackles of oppression (see Manganyi 1973).

Black consciousness

Steve Biko, who was killed by security forces while being held in detention on 12 September 1977, was a leading figure in the black consciousness movement, which was highly influential, particularly among black youth in the 1970s and 1980s. He wrote in the book *I Write What I Like*, published posthumously, about the concept of black consciousness:

> The first step is to make the black man come to himself; to pump life back into his empty shell; to infuse him with pride and dignity; to remind him of his complicity in the crime of allowing himself to be misused and therefore letting evil reign supreme in the country of his birth ... . This is the definition of 'Black Consciousness'.
> (1978: p. 29)

> ... to infuse the black community with a new found pride in themselves, their efforts, their value systems, their culture, their religion and their outlook on life.
> (1978: p. 49)

Have racial attitudes changed in the 1990s in South Africa, along with all the positive developments on the political front? Sadly, it appears not. A number of studies have shown that the deeply embedded patterns have persisted. Sennett and Foster (1996), in a study among Western Cape students following the 1994 democratic election, found that

English-speakers were more positive than Afrikaans-speaking students towards the new government and national symbols, but that both samples were rather wary of the new situation. In a large and important study conducted among 14- and 17-year-old adolescents in the Western Cape and KwaZulu-Natal, over two sampling times, 1992 and 1996, Finchilescu and Dawes (1999) reported results that indicated continuity of racial attitude patterns rather than change.

This study found that English and Afrikaans-speaking youth scored higher on anti-African measures than Coloured or Indian youth, with the Afrikaans-speaking group scoring the highest. In a disquieting result, racism scores were higher among white youths in 1996 than in 1992. Class in the main was not a factor, while males scored higher than females. Scores for white youth were above the midpoint of the scale. However, blacks showed the most negative anti-white attitudes, followed by Coloured and Indian youth. Here, none of the scores was above the midpoint, indicating that among all categories of black youth, anti-white attitudes 'were, in general, low' (Finchilescu & Dawes 1999: p. 124). Class was not a factor, but gender was, with females scoring higher than males.

Similar patterns of results were found with more subtle sets of measures, scoring written essays for positive and negative sentiments about other groups. Overall, there was a significant decrease in the number of essays expressing sentiments about other groups at all between 1992 and 1996, suggesting a gradual development of a norm in which 'expressing inter-group orientations openly is not acceptable' (Finchilescu & Dawes 1999: p. 127). Nevertheless, the racialised patterns persisted. While all categories of black youth showed some measure of positive attitude to whites, neither English- nor Afrikaans-speaking white youth showed any positive attitudes towards any of the black categories. Further, among black youth, anti-white sentiment decreased sharply between 1992 and 1996, whereas among white youth, negative tendencies were far greater towards blacks than positive views, and 'the number of essays expressing positive sentiments towards blacks drop to almost nothing in 1996' (Finchilescu & Dawes 1999: p. 125). Overall, these are grim results and suggest that, in a social order in which intergroup racialised views have been so deeply entrenched for so long, attempts to change attitudes may be difficult and at best gradual.

Social influence

We are most often only vaguely aware of the powerful influences exerted on us by the people around us and the groups or social categories (female/male) we belong to. Yet there are also common everyday terms and phrases that take note of such influences: people talk of 'peer pressure', of 'mob violence' and of 'keeping up with the Joneses'. Social influence has always been one of the central topics of social psychology. In one of the earliest experiments conducted in 1898, Triplett showed that task performance was better in conditions of co-acting with others than when alone. In England, Bartlett (1932), in an early study of 'remembering', showed that peoples' cultural backgrounds formed key frames of reference for interpreting events. Sherif (1936), in a famous study, found that, when with others, an individual's judgements converged towards a group norm. When tested alone, the individual retained the group-based norm of judgements. Later studies showed that such group-based norms were retained over a series of generations of successive groups when none of the original group members were present. Indeed, if there were one major finding in a century of social psychology, it would be this: that people are far more susceptible to group and situational influences than is usually accorded.

Conformity

Conformity means going along with other members of a group and shifting actions to follow the group's norms. In the USA, Solomon Asch (1955) did elegant and now famous studies that demonstrated the power of conformity. Participants, usually numbering seven, sat around a table and were asked to judge the lengths of lines presented on cards. On one card was a single line (the standard); on another card, three comparison lines, as indicated below.

Conformity:
Shifting one's actions to follow a group's norm(s).

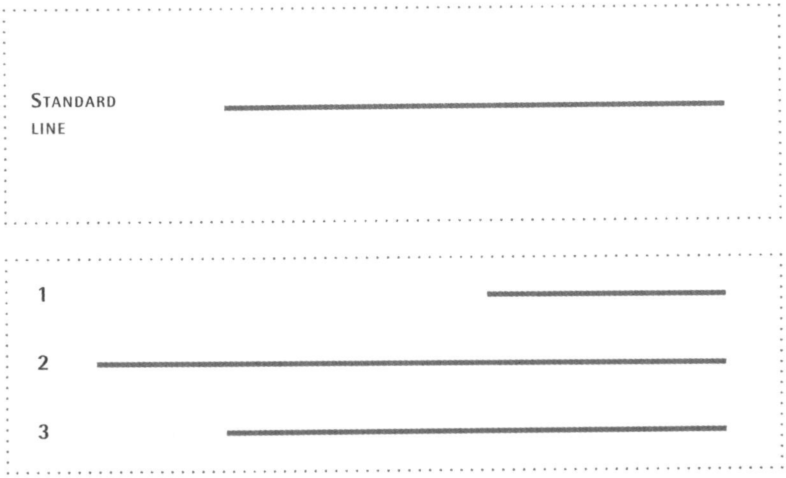

FIGURE 8.4: The Asch experiment

Participants had to say which of the three comparison lines were the same length as the standard line. The task was clearly so simple that nobody could make a mistake. Participants called their responses out loud. However, the trick was that all the other participants were confederates of the experimenter and, on certain critical trials, they were instructed to call out a wrong answer ahead of the one real experimental subject. What would these subjects do? Yield to the others or give the correct answer? Of 123 subjects at three American universities, the overall rate of conforming was 37%. In addition, 75% of the individuals yielded on at least one trial. About a quarter were completely independent and never conformed, whereas the others almost always did – a finding of individual differences. Notably, if one of the confederates gave a different answer from the others (even if it was wrong) the conformity rate dropped to 9%.

Although many studies have confirmed the persuasive power of conformity to majorities, both historical and cultural dimensions also have an effect. For example, lower conformity rates were reported in Britain and the USA in the 1980s, and the highest rates have been reported in collective cultures that stress a 'we' consciousness, group solidarity and decisions, sharing and obligations, and an interdependent view of the self – a set of principles captured by the term **ubuntu** in South Africa. Interestingly, there have been almost no studies of conformity done in South Africa.

Ubuntu:
The defining value of community and loyalty to the group in indigenous African society. Emphasis and value are placed on family, clan and community-oriented functions and customs, such as cooperation and collective decision making.

Why do people conform? There are two lines of understanding. According to the notion of normative influence, we do so because we want to be accepted; we do not want to 'stick out' and risk shame or ridicule. However, according to the notion of informational influence, we depend on others for our very notion of reality, for the perception we hold of the world. Particularly in situations of ambiguity, we rely on information from others.

Obedience to authority

In the wake of the grim revelations of the Truth and Reconciliation Commission of South Africa (1998), we may justifiably ask the question: How did such atrocities occur? Why were political detainees tortured so regularly? (See Foster *et al.* 1987.) Work done by the American researcher Stanly Milgram during the 1960s (Milgram 1974) suggests some insights.

Milgram conducted a lengthy series of experiments, with many variations, that used the same situation in which an experimental participant was required to give increasing 'doses' of electric shocks, spaced at 15 V intervals ranging from 15 V to a maximum of 450 V, to a 'learner', when the learner gave incorrect answers to a word-pairing test. In fact, the 'learner' was a confederate of the experimenter who was instructed to cry loudly at 120 V, shout 'Get me out of here!' at 150 V, give an agonised scream at 270 V and, at 315 V, after a violent scream, fall silent. The experimenter, the authority figure in this procedure, when faced with worried queries from the subject, gave various instructions, such as 'Please go on', or 'The experiment requires you to continue', or 'It is absolutely essential that you continue'. When the learner had collapsed into silence and no longer replied, the experimenter explained, 'No answer is the same as a wrong answer', and 'You have no choice, you must go on'. If individuals went to the maximum, 450 V was administered three times before the experiment ended. When this scenario was put to a group of psychiatrists, they predicted that most people would not go beyond 150 V.

Milgram ran multiple variations for each condition using a new cohort of 40 men: non-students, aged between 20 and 50 years, who responded to advertisements. What were the results? In the baseline conditions, where there were no shouts or screams, 26 participants (65%) went to the maximum. In the voice-feedback condition, 63% went to the maximum. In a further condition, when the learner said he had 'a slight heart condition', 65% went to the maximum. Milgram repeated the study with 40 women and the results were the same: 65% gave the maximum shocks. Other researchers conducted a similar study using puppies as victims. No deception was required, since the puppies howled and struggled. Women were more compliant than men: all women participants went to the maximum. In a later study done in Jordan, children aged from six to 16 years showed greater obedience than the baseline. Other studies replicated the findings in Australia and Germany.

However, the most important findings were due to other variations, giving some insight into the processes involved. Firstly, if the authority conditions were weakened, obedience dropped sharply. If the subject was told he or she was free to select any shock level on any trial, most administered very low levels – averaging below 60 V. Secondly, proximity to the victim was varied. When the victim was in the same room as the teacher, obedience dropped to 40%, and when the teacher had to make physical contact with the victim, forcing his hand onto a shock plate, obedience dropped to 30%. Thirdly, as in the Asch conformity studies, compliance was reduced when there were other dissenting voices. In one variation, two other teachers were in attendance, one refusing to continue at 150 V and the other at 210 V. In this scenario, only 10% went to the maximum. These variations give us some idea of the situational variables involved in obedience; it is not merely a mechanical process.

Few could doubt the power and importance of these studies. Milgram explicitly undertook this work, building on Asch's early work, to understand the events of the Holocaust. They also provide us with some insight into the South African atrocities unearthed by the Truth Commission (see Foster 1997, 2000). At the time, however, the Milgram studies caused an outcry and were criticised on ethical grounds. Although participants were fully debriefed, there is little doubt, as Milgram (1974) reported, that many were distressed during the experiment. These days it would probably not be feasible to conduct such studies, due to the more stringent ethical codes required of psychological research.

Minority influence

While the Asch and Milgram studies show the persuasive influence of majorities and authorities over minorities, it is rarely observed that their work also pointed to the possibilities of resisting such influence. If there was more than one dissenting voice, conformity and obedience reduced sharply. Solidarity among dissenters can clearly facilitate resistance. The French scholar Serge Moscovici (1976) took these ideas further by showing that, under certain circumstances, minorities could indeed facilitate change in majorities. In a series of sophisticated experiments in which a minority of two faced a majority of four, he demonstrated that the minority did exert a reasonable degree of influence as long as the minority remained consistent or unanimous. Consistency is a key 'behavioural style' in minority influence because of the effect it has on a majority. A consistent and firm minority that holds a coherent line creates the impression that it is competent and confident, and the majority attributes such characteristics to the minority itself. Later work by another French researcher, Mugny (1982), showed that another key behavioural style in minority influence is, paradoxically, flexibility. Merely to adopt a rigid position could lead to the attribution of a minority as dogmatic and narrow-minded, as simply hacking out the 'party line'. Flexibility, making some concessions, seems to operate best when the two parties concerned are far apart on an issue, whereas more rigid consistency is better when the two parties are closer on an issue.

Overall, the importance of the work by Moscivici, Mugny and subsequent others is that it demonstrates that social influence is not simply 'one-way traffic' flowing from majorities and dominant authorities. Minorities, both in terms of smaller numbers and in terms of weaker power positions, are able to show resistance and, even more important, are able to initiate innovative social changes. Indeed, that has been precisely the pattern of recent historical events in South Africa: a minority (in power terms) is able to first resist, then produce far-reaching social change.

Racism as prejudice and stereotyping

Since the 1920s, when psychology first became interested in prejudice and stereotyping, and developed techniques to measure such topics, the discipline of psychology has overwhelmingly regarded racism and other similar phenomena, such as sexism, anti-Semitism and homophobia, as problems inside the heads of individuals, rather than located in large-scale intergroup relations, power relations or ideologies.

Describing large-scale problems as due to mechanisms 'inside the minds' of individuals is to reduce a complex set of phenomena to individualism and to perpetrate the individual-social dualism described earlier. With the arrival of measuring scales, it was possible to give an individual a single score on a continuous scale, ranging from most to least prejudiced. However, exactly where to draw the line on a continuous scale is difficult to determine. In redefining racism as due only to prejudice and stereotyping, locating the mechanisms inside the mind of individuals, social psychology has generally taken two explanatory routes – firstly, due to particular cognitive mechanisms and, secondly, due to particular personality types.

Social cognition

The tone was set in Gordon Allport's (1954) influential book, where he explained prejudice as being due to an 'erroneous generalisation', a faulty system in our thoughts, which he stated was 'a natural and common capacity of human mind' (1954: p. 17). Since then, many explanatory models have located the problem as due to faulty information processing.

> Many terms have been used such as 'bias', 'heuristics' (taking a shortcut in processing information), 'schemas', 'categorisation', 'scripts', 'templates' and 'peripheral routes', but all of these terms share the following explanation. The world out there is a complex place and, in dealing with such complexity, the 'self-contained' individual has to be efficient. However, individuals (like computers) have limited information-processing capacities, which mean that the cognitive system has to take shortcuts in order to process all the information efficiently. These shortcuts and biases are seen, in turn, as built into the cognitive system, are treated as universal, a common property of all individuals, and therefore 'natural'. If prejudice and stereotyping are based on normal and universal properties of individuals' cognitive processing operations, then prejudice would seem to be inevitable, and not much could be done to change it.
>
> (FOSTER 1999)

Personality theories

The most influential of a cluster of approaches is that of the theory of the authoritarian personality (Adorno *et al.* 1950). The authoritarian personality type, consisting of a set of nine personality traits, emerged from a harsh and rigid family upbringing with strict rules. Ambivalent towards such authoritarian parents (love them and hate them), such children learn to project the negative feelings outwards onto other, usually weaker, groups in order to maintain harmony in the family. Adorno *et al.* developed a questionnaire measure called the F-scale (F for fascism) to assess the personality type and found that it was highly correlated (+0,7 which is a high correlation statistic) with other questionnaire-type scales measuring ethnocentrism (in-group favouritism) and prejudice (negative evaluation of the out-group).

In South Africa, there has been a considerable amount of research on the authoritarian personality and although, in its original form, it fared poorly (there were criticisms of the psychometric qualities of the original scales), research conducted by John Duckitt (1992) with revised scales did find positive support (correlations varied between 0,53 and 0,69). However, Duckitt explained the phenomena in terms of social identity theory (see next section) and not as a personality type.

The central point is that many theories claim that particular personality types are prone to prejudice. Examples are theories such as rigidity of mind, 'dogmatism', 'closed-mindedness' and 'intolerance of ambiguity'. In such views, prejudice is located within the self-contained individual in the form of particular personality types that are seen as faulty or semi-pathological. It is easy for 'us', the 'normal' types, to blame 'them', the 'rotten apple' personality types, for the ills of prejudice and stereotyping.

In attempting to explain racism or sexism, mainstream or 'individualistic' versions of social psychology can be criticised for locating the explanation only at the first two levels of analysis. They can therefore be criticised as reductionist, and by explaining racism as due to faulty social cognition or faulty individuals ('rotten apples') they perpetuate the problem of individual-social dualism. To examine how other approaches may deal with the missing levels of analysis we turn first to the European rather than the American view of social identity theory (SIT).

Social identity theory

Developed initially by Henri Tajfel and his colleague John Turner at Bristol University, England (Tajfel & Turner 1979; Tajfel 1981) in the late 1970s as a theory to explain intergroup relations, SIT has spread over the past 20 years to provide an understanding of other phenomena, such as conformity and social influence, group dynamics, speech accommodation, gender issues, organisational behaviour, the self, stereotyping and crowd violence (Hogg & Abrams 1988; Foster & Louw-Potgieter 1991). In this respect, it can be regarded as an alternative theory in its own right, and one that challenges some of the shortcomings of mainstream or individualistic approaches. From the outset, Tajfel was aware of this challenge to mainstream views, since he argued for a more relevant and 'socially' oriented social psychology.

The basic principles and processes of SIT can be laid out quite simply in terms of three 'individual' propositions, three 'social' principles, and a further central assumption. In explicitly covering both individual and social components, SIT makes an effort to overcome the problem of individual-social dualism, as well as incorporating understandings at all four of the levels of analysis described earlier.

Individual components

The theory sets out three main components that cover the first and second levels of analysis, which could be thought of as the three Cs: categorisation, social comparison and self-concept.

Categorisation
SIT regards social categorisation as a central and dynamic system of information processing. The complexity of information is reduced through the operation of the principle of accentuation: similarities within a group or category and differences between groups or categories are accentuated or exaggerated. We tend to perceive members of our own group as more similar to one another than they actually are, and to perceive members of an out-group as both similar to one another and more different or differentiated from our own group. This cognitive organising principle is the same for everyday objects (animals, flowers, furniture, etc.) and people, but SIT proposes that perception of human groups is characterised by an additional evaluative (positive/negative) and an emotional (feelings of like/hate) component. This results in a more emphatic accentuation of perceived intergroup similarities and intergroup differences that forms the basis for social stereotyping.

Social comparison
As humans, we compare ourselves with other individuals, as Festinger suggested in the 1950s – an interpersonal level of analysis. However, SIT

pushes this further and states that we also make social comparisons on an intergroup level. The outcome of such comparative processes is an evaluation of the self: the notion of a positive or negative sense of self or self-esteem.

Self-concept

In an area where SIT attempts to go beyond individualistic approaches, the self is regarded as the sum of two sub-systems: a personal identity and a social identity. Personal self consists of aspects unique to that individual: likes and dislikes, personal characteristics, etc. Social identity refers to aspects of the self as a member of various groups: a woman, a gay male, a mature student, etc. The social is regarded as a constituent part of the self and not external to the self-contained individual, as in mainstream views.

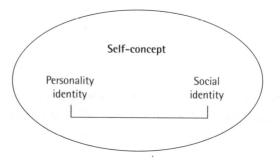

FIGURE 8.5: The self in terms of the social identity theory

Personal and social identities are regarded as end-points of a continuum. The self is seen as shifting along this continuum according to varying social situations. With a lover, one may show unique aspects of personal identity; interaction with a shop assistant may be somewhere in the middle, where the rules say we should act in terms of particular roles; and warfare illustrates the extreme end, where the social identity of the enemy is the only thing that counts.

The process of shifting from the personal to the social end of the continuum is known as **depersonalisation**; that is, becoming less of an individual person and more of a social person governed by membership of a social category. In any given situation, a different part of the self-concept may become 'switched on' or salient. The crux of the theory is that interpersonal and intergroup actions are controlled or governed by different psychological processes: they are motivated by different parts of the self-concept. Unlike self-contained individualism, SIT proposes that we consist of multiple selves, and that actions are dependent upon which sense of self is salient at any given moment.

Depersonalisation: Becoming less of an individual and more a member of a social category.

Social components

The three social 'legs' of SIT may be described as status hierarchy; permeability of group boundaries; and legitimacy of group status hierarchies.

Status hierarchies

All societies are characterised by various groups that are arranged in layers or hierarchies according to status, according more privileges, wealth, importance, power or life opportunities to some groups rather than others. In some societies, these status hierarchies may be highly differentiated; in others, the arrangements might be somewhat flatter and less demarcated. We draw our social identities from these groups.

Permeability of group boundaries and status security

Societies vary in the degree to which individuals are able to shift across the boundaries that separate categories. This has to do with the social process known as **social mobility**. In societies in which upward social mobility is seen as possible, barriers or boundaries are seen as permeable or porous. A social order such as South Africa under apartheid rule made it almost impossible for people to cross the racialised divides. In addition, some categories are more permeable than others: consider the boundaries between gender categories. Permeability also ties in with the notion of security of social identity.

Social mobility: The ability to shift across the boundaries that separate social categories.

SIT made a distinction between secure and insecure social identities. Secure identities occur when there is an absence of cognitive alternatives, which refer to perceptions that status relations between groups are potentially unstable and thus changeable. An insecure social identity results from perceptions that the present intergroup relationship arrangement is potentially changeable; that there are cognitive alternatives to the status quo.

Legitimacy/illegitimacy

This refers to perceptions of the current status hierarchy system as fair, reasonable and just, or their opposites. Legitimacy intertwines with stability. In situations where people perceive possibilities for change (instability), and that existing group relations are unjust and unfair (illegitimate), cognitive alternatives will be readily available. However, if the group system of stratification is regarded as fixed, stable and just (legitimate), there will be no cognitive alternatives and, therefore, no possibilities for a change in social identities. Reference to questions of legitimacy could be seen as incorporating the fourth level of analysis: ideological issues.

Key assumption: Positive social identity

The central motivational assumption that ties together the individual and the social 'legs' of SIT is that individuals are motivated to strive for a positive self-concept – in particular, a positive sense of social identity. Since social identity derives from group membership, people from low-status groups are likely to have a negative social identity and will be motivated to do something about it, to enhance their group-based sense of self-concept. In turn, the sense of positive or negative self-concept derives from social comparison processes.

Social change and intergroup relations

A person's reaction to a negative social identity depends on the availability of cognitive alternatives. When there are no perceived alternatives (secure identity), SIT predicts that people are likely to adopt an individualistic strategy to achieve a more positive self-concept. Social mobility is the strategy for a person to move from a low status to a higher status group – for example, by hard work, obtaining qualifications and getting a better job. It is held to be an individualistic strategy because, while the individual may benefit, it leaves the existing group status hierarchy unchanged. A woman may become chief of the army, but that does not necessarily change the situation for other women.

In some situations, however, group boundaries are impermeable and the system of stratification does not easily permit social mobility. This was the situation for most black people under apartheid. It was difficult to get education, job-reservation laws barred access to higher status jobs, and one could not move out of a designated 'group area'. Where social mobility is not possible and there are few cognitive alternatives, psychological mobility may occur. This is expressed as a preference for the values and standards of a higher status out-group, sometimes referred to as the 'mark of oppression' (Foster 1993). In South Africa under apartheid, this evidenced as a wish among some black people to 'pass for white', using skin lighteners and hair-straightening devices, for instance.

If lower status group members perceive the existing social order as unstable and illegitimate, then social change (rather than social mobility) strategies are predicted. **Social change** refers to collective (thus genuinely social) efforts to change the existing social system. There is a range of such strategies, clustered into two categories. Strategies that are intended to shift negative social identities into more positive images are labelled as forms of social creativity. The black consciousness movement, with the slogan 'black is beautiful', is one such example. Feminism has actively attended to providing a more positive view of women, as have gay and lesbian lobby groups. SIT uses the term '**social action**' to depict more radical actions intended to disrupt, transform or overthrow the existing order. Social action may include strikes, marches, boycotts, protests, campaigns, guerrilla warfare and armed struggle. All of these were evident in South Africa under apartheid and, indeed, are still present. In 2002, the Treatment Action Campaign adopted various protest actions to get the government to change its policies regarding HIV/AIDS.

Even higher status groups, particularly when the social order is seen to be illegitimate, will have to employ various strategies to maintain a positive sense of identity. Imagine you are a white person living under apartheid rule, but aware that there are worldwide protests against apartheid. One strategy may be to become defensive of the system. That is what many white people did, arguing that outsiders just didn't understand the complexities of the system. Another tactic is to increase discrimination and blame the victims for the ills in the system – for example, arguing that black people didn't 'deserve' better jobs or houses since they were idle and lazy and not up to the demands of the modern world. Alternatively, some high-status members may genuinely believe that their own privileged status is wrong because the system is illegitimate. Such people may psychologically dis-identify with their own groups and adopt, for instance, 'ethnic' identity styles of lower-status groups. In a more radical strategy, high-status members may leave their group altogether. Under apartheid, many whites just left the country to take up a new life and identity elsewhere. Others may regard the system as so illegitimate that they leave their own group and join the oppressed

Social change:
Collective efforts to change the existing social system.

Social action:
Radical action to change the existing order.

group, as was the case for a number of whites who left the country to join the liberation movement.

It is clear from the above that SIT proposes a range of intergroup strategies depending on the particular circumstances of group arrangements, comparisons, perceived legitimacy, and spaces and tactics to manoeuvre. The actions of individuals are dependent in this view upon large-scale group configurations, status and power, and ideologies. SIT argues that personal and social phenomena are governed by quite different psychological processes. The complete framework showing the range of identity strategies involved in intergroup relations is given in Figure 8.6.

	Higher status or power	Lower status or power
	CELL A	CELL B
Higher perceived legitimacy	Not a common situation	Ingroup self-aggrandisement
Secure identity	Paternalism	Self-disparagement
	CELL C	CELL D
Low perceived legitimacy	Defensive distinctiveness	Social creativity
	Increased discrimination	– redifinition
	Disidentification	– new comparisions
Insecure Identity	Leave group	Social competition
		– protest
		– strikes, boycotts
		– revolution

FIGURE 8.6

Stereotyping

Social stereotypes:
Shared, widely-held views of larger groups in societies.

Stereotypes:
Sets of images or ideas held in common, derived from and structured by relations between large-scale social categories.

It is interesting to note that SIT has virtually no use for the classic concept of attitude. The term does not appear in the index of Tajfel's (1981) book. An important distinction is drawn by SIT between an individualistic notion of stereotype (increasingly based on cognitive theory) and a notion of **social stereotypes**, which are shared and widely held views of larger groups in societies, such as gender, class, race or nationalities. **Stereotypes** are seen as sets of images or ideas held in common, derived from and structured by relations between large-scale social categories. SIT specifies four functions of stereotypes:

- **Cognitive functions:** These serve to simplify, systematise and order perceptions and information to make sense of a complex world and facilitate action. Categorisation leads to accentuation of difference between groups.

- **Preservation of an individual's value system:** Social stereotypes fulfil a powerful function of protecting the value system that underlies a person's division of the social world into various categories. We do not merely hold ideas or images of others: they are part of wider value systems.

- **Ideologising collective action:** Stereotyping is not only the attitude held by an individual towards others as groups, but also involves group-based images that serve to justify dominations. Stereotyping thus serves the function of maintaining group-based ideologies. Studies of the contents of stereotypes are therefore important.

- **Positive distinctiveness of group identity:** This is part of the general phenomenon of **ethnocentrism** (favouring one's own group), but is only fully understandable in terms of relations between social groups. As we have seen above, under certain situations people may favour out-groups, depending on particular power configurations. Changes in stereotypes (of self and of others) occur under two conditions – firstly, when group identity is negative in comparison with others and, secondly, when group identity is insecure or under threat.

Ethnocentrism: Favouring one's own group.

In the above scheme, the first two refer to individual functions, and the last two to group functions. SIT suggests that the functions of stereotyping should not be analysed in individual terms alone, but also in terms of power and competitive relations between groups. SIT suggests that one should start with the group functions because stereotyping starts with our anchoring in groups. Think of the stereotypes held by men of women, or the images that women hold of men. It is not only abstract individuals who hold stereotypes, but also those anchored in particular social categories.

Explaining racism

Racism, seen through the lens of SIT, could not be explained adequately by individualistic concepts such as attitude, prejudice or cognitive stereotyping. Cognitive processes, such as categorisation and perception, as well as interpersonal processes, such as comparison between self and other, have an important role to play in SIT. However, it clearly goes beyond this. Above all, racialised or genderised stereotyping serves the larger function of maintaining group domination. Negative gender stereotypes held by men (e.g. men are rational, women are emotional) serve a wider function of group domination (e.g. women need to be protected by men). Racialised stereotypes serve the function of exaggerating differences between black and white and promote ethnocentrism.

In short, racism is seen primarily as an intergroup phenomenon and not merely as a matter of individuals holding erroneous ideas. The particular images, ideas and actions that constitute racism are viewed as flowing out of the status and power configurations of large-scale social categories, and the perceived fairness and justice of such relationships. Ultimately, according to SIT, to change racism would require change in the power and status relationships between groups as well as racial ideologies. The reason that racism persists in South Africa is that, in many respects, such as economic status, occupations, educational attainments and housing, the status and power relations between black and white have not changed.

Regarding the contact hypothesis that many commentators have taken to be a useful tool to improve hostile racialised relations, SIT has a rather different view. Many studies have found that contact, even when positive, does not generalise to positive change in wider racialised relations. Why? Because the dynamics that make for positive change in face-to-face contact are primarily those at individual and interpersonal levels, whereas the problem, racism, is mainly an intergroup phenomenon. People say things like: 'Well I get along fine with these particular black or white people, but I don't really trust black or white people in general.' One solution posed by SIT would be to get genuine representatives, people who fight for the cause of that group to debate how to change the nature of the relationships between their groups. The South African political settlement in protracted negotiations in the early 1990s may have worked out quite well because contact took place between genuine representatives and leaders of groups, and because there was some measure of agreement to change group relationships in, for example, agreement on full electoral power and introducing an entirely new constitution for South Africa.

In summary, SIT is a vibrant and relatively new approach to social psychology that attempts to go beyond the limited perspectives of mainstream views, by introducing constructs and measures at the group, intergroup and ideological levels of analysis. SIT agrees with mainstream views that cognitive and other internal processes are important, and acknowledges that most research in SIT still favours experimental methods. However, it goes well beyond mainstream efforts in attempting to overcome the individual-social dualism that still gives us headaches. It is an approach still very much in-the-making that has been extended and revised (only the basics are given here), pushed into many new topics, and is most active in generating new research. Not least, it has been useful in the last decade in guiding research in South Africa (Foster & Louw-Potgieter 1991; Campbell 1995a, 1995b).

Social constructionism and discursive psychology

These are developments that have take place over the last 15 years or so, but have far longer historical roots -- some as far back as the early Greek philosophical tradition of rhetoric (Billig 1987). They are more than a different approach or theory; rather, they are an alternative metatheory or a different philosophy of science. Social constructionism (SC) and discourse analysis (DA) were sprung on a largely unsuspecting psychology community in the mid-1980s through the writings of Ken Gergen (1985, 1994) and Sampson (1993) in the USA, as well as Potter and Wetherell (1987), Shotter (1993), Billig (1987) and Parker (1992) in the UK. But these writers, in turn, drew on recognised writers, usually outside of psychology and stretching throughout the twentieth century, such as Saussure, Wittgenstein, Foucault, Derrida, Kuhn, Harré and Goffman, and on new movements such as feminism, post-colonialism, post-modernism and post-structuralism. These are not easy or comfortable ideas and, at times, they have been sharply contested. However, they are present and provide us with a challenging alternative world view.

What is meant by social constructionism and discourse analysis?

They consist of a cluster of alternative positions that are not neatly bounded, but do have some shared and common strands that will be outlined here.

As a metatheory

SC attempts to go beyond the two grand ways of knowing, i.e. rational (knowing by logic, thinking, reasoning, calculating) and empirical (knowing by sensory data such as seeing, touching, observation, experiences). It is opposed to the philosophy of science known as positivism, which proposes that the only worthwhile knowledge is built on iron laws, objective truths, statistical connections, measuring scales and law-like relationships between fixed entities. Rather, it proposes that people work through meaning and that psychology should be based on an interpretive rather than a positivist-empirical metatheory.

As a focus on language

Consistent with the 'linguist turn' among philosophers of the human and social sciences, SC gives primary attention to language, signs and symbolic and signalling systems of all kinds: talk, non-verbal signals, writing, conversation, signs, icons and representational devices. It proposes that language should be viewed as a representational device to re-present a world already existing 'out there', and as constituent – constructing and making reality. It provides a focus on the pragmatic use of language or sign systems, with the claim that language does things: it gets the salt passed, doors opened and relationships started (I love you) or broken (please go away). It takes the view that language is action and a social practice. It creates, invents, shapes, stores, sculpts and literally 'moves' people, situations and events. If a person swears at you in a foreign language, there would be no meaning and you could not be 'moved' to retaliate: you may even grin in return.

As focusing on historical and cultural phenomena

Since meaning is only established in terms of shared, commonly held conventions and customs, all meaning is both historical, formed over time, and cultural: embedded in shared, traditional ways of being and doing. The very concept of the 'individual' has changed historically and varies culturally.

As a psychological form

SC proposes that psychological forms and states are not inside but rather formed between and among people, constructed in and through shared meanings. The trilogy theory of mind proposes that we have thoughts, emotions, motives or drives, which are separate 'entities' inside us that 'move' us to behave. Instead, SC suggests that psychological notions like attitudes or drives are neither inside nor outside, but exist between people: they are constituents of social practices.

As theory-methods

It is sometimes taken that social constructionism is the theory, and discourse analysis is the method, but that is not quite the case. True, discourse analysis, which involves detailed analysis and the dissecting of texts, talk, conversations, signs and symbolic systems to unravel how language does things or achieves things, is a method. However, DA is so intertwined with SC that they cannot be prised apart. Rather, both SC and DA are better seen as theory-methods aimed at unravelling meaning. There are a host of 'methods', which may have different emphases but are all intertwined with the broad assumptions and propositions of SC. These include terms such as narrative analysis, conversation analysis, rhetorical analysis, hermeneutics, grounded theory, critical theory and critical discourse analysis. Sometimes termed 'reflexive methodologies'

(Alvesson & Skoldberg 2000), they are all theory-methods for interpreting and understanding meaning.

As anti-foundationalism and anti-essentialism

Both SC and DA are anti-foundational in terms of knowledge, in that they claim there can be no certain or accurate or true knowledge. This is because all knowledge is perspectival – in other words, coming from a certain point of view, such as a feminist perspective, or a twentieth century perspective. Knowledge is always being revised, weighed up and is frequently contested, such as the furore and contesting claims about AIDS in South Africa. Knowing is from a point of view, since, according to SC, there can be no 'God's-eye' view, no all encompassing foundation for making truth claims. SC is also anti-essentialist in claiming that there is no fundamental bedrock essence in human variation, despite the claims of some to find the essence or the core in our genes or in biology. SC therefore stands against both environmental and biological determinism. Feminists who take an SC view propose that neither sex nor gender are entities or essences, but are rather constructed through language, signs, performances and actions. People do not have masculinity/femininity but rather do femininity by wearing earrings, putting on stockings, and talking and walking in certain ways.

As metaphor

The core metaphors underlying SC are those of 'building construction' or, alternatively, 'making things up', such as in story-telling (narrative), film-producing or dance construction. People are active agents in jointly building up structures and forms in which we have to live. We negotiate in building these things up – should it be like this or like that? However, when we have built up these 'forms of life', they constitute the rules, norms, grammars, conventions and cultures in terms of which we are required to act and perform. Like a building or a narrative, they can be taken apart, with some effort. They can be taken apart or de-constructed to see how they work and how they were constructed initially, so that they can be built or made up better the next time around. SC is clearly also a construction.

As rhetorical and dialogical

Both Billig (1987) and Shotter (1993) propose that human actions are inherently rhetorical and in dialogue. Rhetoric comprises arguments that are intended to persuade. The notion of argument has two meanings: any piece of reasoned discourse, as in 'I put forward the following argument'; and a dispute or controversy, as in 'These two had an angry argument'. The two meanings are intertwined. Arguments are always two-sided. In an intense argument there are two protagonists: it is two-sided – for and against. There are always two sides to an argument, and rhetoric, as a set of devices to persuade people, is therefore dialogical. Because of this two-sided character of discourse, Billig (1987) maintains that we can never fully know others, or ourselves, but that this lack of certainty (anti-foundationalism) nevertheless gives us choices. This dialogical lack of certainty in both self and others implies that all we do is to constantly negotiate a shared understanding among people through joint action (Shotter 1993). Shotter regards this new vision as a 'knowing of a third kind' (neither rational nor empirical) and as an 'open, incomplete, negotiated form of life' and 'a non-systematic, two-sided form of knowledge' (1993: p. 11).

As transcending binaries

SC and DA attempt to transcend deep binary opposites and dualisms that have characterised modern systems of thought, such as individual-social, body-mind, subject-object, male-female, nature-culture, internal-external, self-other, etc. SC claims that the pairs should not be regarded as separate essences, as they are often thought of, but rather as deeply interdependent linguistic devices with the one term only defined by its absence in the other. Instead of asking whether people are 'caused' by internal or external 'forces', SC suggests that we should look at cause as dialogical, as joint activity, as 'between', or as 'both-and'.

As political intent

As Durrheim (1997) has suggested, the broad political aims of SC and DA are to disrupt, disturb and upset the taken-for-granted, institutionalised discourses and practices that maintain and reproduce oppressive and exploitative relations among people. In this regard, they are critical enterprises and forms of ideology critique. They aspire not to truth, which is held to be questionable, but rather towards change. Analysis of discourse and meaning is not a new road to truth, but rather a 'cutting tool', a means of social change.

The self, identities and subjectivities

Having some idea of what social constructionism, as a broad movement, stands for, we turn to a central topic of social psychology – the self – to see where SC differs from other approaches. SC is certainly opposed to the 'self-contained individualism' that is the hallmark of mainstream psychology, claiming instead that people are multiple and less coherent or rational than we assume. SC shares with SIT the notion that self-identity is multiple, constantly shifting and situationally responsive, changing as different aspects of identity become 'salient' in varying contexts. However, SC is wary of the SIT view of identity shifting along a 'personal-social' continuum, since this reinforces in another guise the problem of individual-social dualism, that we either act as an individual or as a collective being, and that the two acts are governed by different processes. For SC, there are no *a priori* elements labelled 'individual' and 'social'. They are indivisible. We are social persons. Furthermore, for SC, people are firstly taken as far more fluid, fragmented, incoherent, inconsistent and contradictory, and, secondly, as more dialogical, co-produced and co-jointly embedded-with-others than is the view of either mainstream or SIT approaches. We are saturated with the voices of others via television, radio, cellphone, letters, faxes, e-mails, movies, newspapers, magazines, dreams, notices, advertisements and propaganda, as well as conversations and arguments with those close to us (Gergen 1991). Discourse is dialogical: we argue back, we resist, we give our own point of view.

Different terms and labels are used to represent that elusive figure, which is supposedly the very object matter of psychological enquiry. Mainstream approaches tend to use the term 'the self' or 'the individual', which bolsters the image of a self-contained, bounded, universal, coherent and rather isolated figure. Yet, this figure suddenly becomes a 'subject' (a victim if you like) when plunged into a psychological experiment. SIT generally uses the term 'identity' to depict a figure that identifies with a range of groups and could be more multiple than the self-contained individual. In contrast, SC and DA tend to favour the term 'subjectivity' and 'subjectivities' to catch the sense of both reflexive shifting and fluidity, as well as varying senses of subjectivity – that is, both an active agent (the subject of a sentence) and acted-on-by-others (as in 'subjects of the queen'). If SC resorts to the term 'self', it frequently uses the plural form 'selves', as in the phrase 'gendered selves', to catch the plural, multiple and ideological sense that is favoured. In this, it is apparent that the different approaches do not even use the same language: different terms and different discourses create rather different objects. As Foucault (1972: p. 49) has put it, discourses 'form the objects of which they speak'.

Mainstream views of self

Potter and Wetherell (1987) suggest that there are three dominant views of the self in mainstream psychology. The first is that of a personality type, which is usually seen as a collection of traits, such as extraversion/introversion, or internal/external locus of control, to form a coherent type. The picture is one of a rather fixed and cemented inner coherence that determines the person's actions, irrespective of situations. The second is that of social roles, which is a set of expectations, demands and norms set by society, as in concepts such as 'sex roles' or the 'mothering role'. The picture is of particular performance roles set up by society, to which the person rather passively conforms. It is criticised by SC as too passive, static and rigid a concept. Discourse analysts prefer the more active and negotiating concept of 'positioning'. The third view is that of a humanistic self, which assumes a deep inner core known as a true or authentic self in contrast to a false or outer self we wear in public. Humanistic notions suggest that we strive towards the authentic self through a process known as self-actualisation. SC holds that there is no such thing as a true inborn self, but rather that we constitute ourselves through language in interaction with others.

Alternative views of self

Emphasising at all times the view that selves are constructed through language – interacting, negotiating and positioning in relation to others – discourse analysts have suggested alternative views. Grammatical selves suggest that, in part, we come to have particular senses of our selves, because of grammatical forms, for example, pronouns such as 'I' and 'me', or collective terms such as, 'us' and 'them' and 'we' and 'they'. Indigenous or folk selves suggest that different cultures have quite different pictures of selves. There has been much talk recently of individualistic and collectivist cultures, as well as ideas of modern and traditional selves. The concept of indigenous selves raises possibilities of an African concept of selves. Ideological selves suggest that various forms of subjectivity are manufactured through ideological domination and oppressive discourses. Hence, gendered selves are forms of subjectivity constructed by disscourses of patriarchy, while racialised selves are positions of racist discourses. Positional selves suggest that in everyday conversations we actively position ourselves and, in turn, are positioned by others in sequences of interactions. Suppose someone blames you for forgetting his or her birthday. You are positioned as blameworthy, but not entirely stuck. You can accept the position, show remorse and tender an apology with a dash of humour, or argue back, saying 'while a bit late' (apology), 'the birthday card is in the mail'. While the notion of positioning as a negotiating device is common to all these alternative depictions of subjectivity, the operation of power would render the sense of activity and initiative (agency) rather different in the examples given above. For instance, ideological selves might have less agency to negotiate and actively position than is the case in everyday conversation with friends.

Fragments of South African research

Discourse analysis and social constructionism have been influential in South Africa over the past decade or so. While some may argue that this is another form of subjection to Western ideas, critical notions in psychology are hard to come by and South African scholars have added to the field by studying oppression in local circumstances. Ann Levett (1988) probably conducted the first discursive study in South Africa in her doctoral thesis. In a study on trauma and childhood sexual abuse, she showed firstly that mechanical accounts, claiming that abuse always leads to trauma, were not well founded and that the situation was far more complex. She went on to show that widespread discourses on child sexual abuse had the unintended consequences of reproducing patriarchal positions of male sexuality while positioning women as victims. Young women, growing up with talk and warnings of male abuse were simultaneously positioned in ways that shaped traditional gendered selves and sexualities. Given the rampant, and quite justified concerns over childhood sexual abuse into the twenty-first century, we could do well to re-examine Levett's pioneering studies. Levett *et al.* (1997) also produced the first major book in South Africa based on discourse analytic research, showing among many other aspects that South African scholars could work with European colleagues rather than merely subordinate themselves to them. Since then, a considerable flow of research has ensued. A few studies have been selected here to illustrate the DA approach and contributions.

In a study on HIV risk, Wood and Foster (1995) interviewed 20 young, heterosexually active students, half men, half women, in order to answer the question of when and why people would not use condoms as a protection against AIDS. Interview material showed that unequal power relations between women and men considerably influenced non-use of condoms. Male discourses limited women's ability to protect themselves. If women carried condoms with them, men were likely to accuse them of being 'too keen', of being 'slags', or of spoiling the passion and spontaneity of sex. Women often felt powerless to negotiate with men who refused to use condoms. During longer-term relationships, after partners had abandoned condom use because of mutual trust, it became difficult for women to reinstate condom use, even when they suspected their partners were sleeping around, since asking a partner to use a condom unexpectedly would disrupt apparently harmonious relations.

These are rather delicate 'findings' about negotiated selves and gendered power positions, and have little to do with standard notions that people take risks because they lack knowledge or have the wrong attitudes to condom use. Wood and Foster concluded that gendered power relations (ideological issues) would have to be changed rather than society following a simple policy of giving information. Information would be insufficient to transform the gendered selves and power inequality underpinning acts such as condom use.

How do men talk about women? Harris *et al.* (1995) conducted focus-group interviews with well-educated male students and staff at the University of Cape Town, asking questions about gender interaction in situations such as initiating sexual encounters, domestic responsibilities and family roles, as well as vignettes regarding sexual aggression. Two dominant discourses emerged in the men's talk on gender. Firstly, gender was talked of in terms of social/cultural norms: these pressures or exter-nalised forces were 'just there', probably learned. Secondly, gender roles were depicted as natural – as innate, stable, inherited and universal: men had to initiate sexual encounters because that was the natural way. Of more importance, this study investigated rhetorical strategies, which is how these positions of patriarchal power were 'achieved' in talk. The study reported three major strategies:

- **Power:** Ironically, women were positioned in talk as more powerful, but this was covert, subtle and hidden power. Men claim that they 'probably get a vibe, whether they realise it or not, from this woman' (p. 178). This rhetorical move reassigns the responsibility to women.
- **Preference:** Talk of this sort by men proposes that women prefer the current gender positioning – for example, of not initiating sexual encounters. Talking of women in general, a male participant argued that: 'They'd rather sit on their barstool, buying themselves a drink, showing a length of leg, hoping that someone else will trap over and say "Can I buy you a drink" type of thing' (p. 179).
- **Marginalisation:** Men's talk here argued away women's resistance as due to a minority of women who are 'raging feminist stormtroopers', 'watch bitches' or women who had a 'bad experience with men' – in other words, a marginal and minority segment of women, and not ordinary, 'normal' women. Talking about women campaigning against sexual harrassment, a male participant marginalised them as follows: 'they are ugly ... the women who are bitching about it are dif-ferent. They can't get themselves laid, they can't even find themselves a steady boyfriend, um, so they just making it difficult for guys. I mean call them guy haters if you want' (p. 180).

Most disquieting, this study showed that these rhetorical strategies were also used to normalise sexual aggression against women. Men's talk indicated that women preferred to be sexually subdued, and that women subtly lead men on, but then shout 'rape'. Research such as this shows subtle and complex discourses at work in constructing gender inequalities as normal, and women's resistance as marginal and abnormal. Such talk constructs particular positions for men and women that reconstitute traditional gender sexualities and male power.

A recent study examined a large corpus of texts from the Truth and Reconciliation Commission hearings in order to understand the 'causes, motives and perspectives' of perpetrators of atrocities under apartheid. Foster (2000) illustrated a 'magnitude gap' in perspectives, in terms of which perpetrators tended to give comprehensible accounts of their actions, whereas, for victims of gross abuse, acts were spoken of as either utterly incomprehensible or as deliberately malicious. This gap is a discrepancy between two quite irreconcilable positions. Accounts from perpetrators revealed four clusters of arguments and justifications:

- intentional military actions, as in the argument 'we were at war';
- denial, argued as a gap between authorities and followers, in which claims were made that 'things happened that were not authorised', or of insecure and faulty lines of communications between command and followers;
- what went wrong? 'we made mistakes', as an argument in which all parties in the conflict conceded errors, mistakes and unintended consequences; and
- lack of discipline and restraint: 'us' and 'them'. Most parties conceded that they did not discipline their own ranks, since they were part of 'us', part of our own family. Indeed, there were frequent expressions of pride in the overzealous actions of their followers.

The study concluded by arguing against psychological reductionism in understanding atrocities of this magnitude, and claimed that multiple ideologically-linked identities, such as masculinity, nationalism, religion and militarism, as well as racialised subjectivities, 'intertwine and res-onate to generate violent propensities'
(FOSTER 2000: p. 9).

In another area, a study from a feminist perspective examined power inequalities in negotiations of heterosexual sexuality. Growing up as heterosexual is seen as a key site for the reproduction of patriarchy and male dominance. A discourse analysis was conducted on transcripts of focus-group discussions held with over 100 women and men students at the University of the Western Cape, speaking about their sexual experiences with the opposite sex (Shefer & Foster 2001). The study reported a lack of positive discourses regarding women's sexual desires, as well as continuing double standards in the construction of feminine and masculine sexualities. Specifically, discourses depicted men as positively sexual, with women as expressing love and relationships. Women's sexualities were further silenced through representations of women's desires as dangerous (Shefer & Foster 2001: p. 380). Despite a minority of voices challenging male-defined heterosexuality, the study concluded that there was greater 'adherence to traditional versions of masculinity/femininity and less evidence of feminist resistance to male power' (Shefer & Foster 2001: p. 385) among this sample of students. It would appear that patriarchal culture is still deeply embedded in South African communities.

These few studies illustrate research from discursive perspectives and indicate a range of areas in which power operates and continues to craft differences and oppressive practices.

For other similar research in South Africa, see the special issues of the *South African Journal of Psychology* on 'Postmodern perspectives' (September 1996), and papers from the first Annual Qualitative Methods Conference (June 1997), and on 'Black scholarship' (December 1997). The book *Culture, Power and Difference* (Levett *et al.* 1997) also provides interesting contributions, while there are further volumes emanating from the continuing Qualitative Methods Conferences, and similar offerings in the journals *Psychology and Society* and *Agenda*. A related area of 'critical psychology' is just beginning to start up in various parts of South Africa.

Racism and social constructionism

While mainstream views invoke inner states such as faulty cognitions and personality functioning to explain racism, and while SIT favours intergroup relations as the predominant influence, SC and DA locate the workings of racism in discourse (Wetherell & Potter 1992; Foster 1999). This is because neither categories nor groups are 'simply there': they are brought into being in and through discursive practices. Through talk of 'them' and 'us', we bring categories into being and link these to particular rights, spaces, places and privileges.

Wetherell and Potter (1992: p.70) define racist discourse as 'discourse (of whatever content) which has the effect of establishing, sustaining and reinforcing oppressive power relations between those defined as "differing labels in varying contexts" in New Zealand as Pakeha and Maori'. This definition offers a shift from the study of ideology *per se* to the study of ideological practice and outcomes. They go on to show that racist discourse is complex, shifting, shaped into argumentative patterns and often contradictory, unlike the notion of having a single and consistent attitude proposed by mainstream views.

A number of studies in South Africa have examined racism through the lens of discursive approaches. Duncan (1996) looked at 186 articles on violence in the 'liberal' newspaper *The Star* during 1993, and showed that the media aided in the production of the ideology of racism. Duncan reported six dominant themes that depicted black persons as:

- apparently innately violent;
- not to be trusted;
- non- or sub-humans that should be 'tamed';
- racist or the cause of racism, as in the 'racist killings of whites';
- child-like as in 'not acting responsibly'; and
- unreasonable.

He argues that these themes are racist in having the effect of justifying continued asymmetrical power relations.

Stevens (1998) interviewed seven Coloured adults on their views towards Africans in the Western Cape, and described dominant discourses casting the 'other' as a source of threat. Africans were talked of in terms of:

- economic threats, particularly due to affirmative action, which, in turn, was fanned by media discourse on the topic;
- a physical threat in terms of rioting, violence, crime and gangsterism: 'they just break and take'; and
- a socio-economic threat in terms of 'them' having a sense of entitlement and being overly demanding in the new social order: 'blacks ... on top of the list' for everything.

Alternatively, their own group was talked of as marginalised in the new order, as 'left out in the cold' and as the 'real victims'. Stevens accounted for this in terms of an internalisation of a dominant racial ideology.

In 1991, a community of black people were granted rights of legal residence and formed a new township, Imizamo Yethu, in the former white area of Hout Bay. Protest from residents ensued in the media. Dixon *et al.* (1997) studied press letters and reports. Residents faced a 'dilemma'; on the one hand, in the 'new South Africa', they did not want to be accused of being old-style conservatives and racists, yet, on the other, they clearly wanted the removal and exclusion of the 'squatters'. Analysis showed how this 'dilemma' was discursively solved. First, there was little use of the labels 'black' or 'white', and little use of old-fashioned racist talk. Instead, they employed a more neutral and

impersonal language of spatial forces, in which the township was depicted as 'out of place' in Hout Bay, and that squatters were 'foreign' and
akin to 'alien' vegetation that would destroy the local environment. A
language was crafted that classified Hout Bay as 'beautiful', 'picturesque'
and 'unspoiled', while the township was a 'scar', an 'eyesore', a 'festering
sore', 'squalid' and a 'sprawl'. Analysis reported three further rhetorical
strategies:

- an appeal to the tradition of place: an idyllic past against a
  despoiled present;
- naturalisation, which depicted the beauty of Hout Bay as natural, an
  incontestable fact, therefore it would be quite reasonable to conserve
  this natural beauty; and
- a defensive rhetoric, which made an appeal to the role of Hout Bay
  as a tourist site, with eviction of the squatters as merely economic
  good sense, and therefore in the interests of all.

This study shows an example of 'modern' or 'subtle' racism, where there
is no direct denigration of black people, but subtle discourses of aesthet-
ics, economic facts, nature and aliens have the effect of justifying a
practice of racial exclusion.

In a set of conversational interviews with white, English-speaking
students at the University of Cape Town, Lea (1996) also showed
the operation of 'modern' or 'symbolic' racism. Firstly, talk was
constructed to establish the 'facts' of difference, such as 'whites want
progress whereas blacks do not'. This move enabled students to deny
being racist but to be only supporting the 'facts'. Secondly, students drew
on scientific discourses, particularly from social cognition and SIT, to
form three arguments:

- Categorisation is a necessary process that 'provides order'.
- Categories are neutral and 'quite innocent'.
- Categorisation has positive benefits in terms of identity: it 'defines
  who we are'.

These students were able to claim that universal cognitive processes
predispose all people to ethnocentrism, thus discriminating against
others is natural. They were therefore only 'realists' dealing with 'facts'
and 'scientific evidence', not irrational bigots or racists. This study shows
nicely the potentially dangerous role that academic theories can play in
the discursive reproduction of racism.

Conclusion

The preceding pages have set out three viewpoints on social psychology, described as mainstream, social identity theory and social constructionism. They have also illustrated a range of topics, traced some 'classic' experiments, charted the progress in the field, given some examples of South African research, and set out a recent critical stance in the form of discourse analysis.

What are we to make of this? Firstly, let us look at the dominance of the three views in the field of social psychology as a whole. There is little doubt that the mainstream or cognitive approach is the most widely accepted and dominant strand. In many textbooks, it is the only approach discussed. One way to deal with competition is to wish it away by giving it no voice. SIT is a more recent slant. Some mainstream textbooks have incorporated SIT views largely because they have a common method of experimentalism and a similar focus on cognitive approaches, but when included, SIT has often been given just a few pages and regarded as a mini-theory within the mainstream. SIT certainly has a minority relation to the mainstream, but it is now sufficiently solid, soundly researched, established and different from social cognition to warrant status as an alternative position. SC has been the most recent arrival, really only in the past decade or so, is the most controversial or contested, and is in the most marginal position. It is seldom taught, has much smaller networks of advocates or practitioners, and has reached far fewer books and journals. Yet, in the breadth of its challenge, the depth of its philosophical roots, and its important focus on language and meaning as the quintessential characteristics of human beings, it also offers the possibility of being the most radical and over-arching of the three perspectives: an alternative and post-modern metatheory.

Secondly, let us look at the three views in terms of the levels of analysis outlined at the start. Mainstream views are largely, but not entirely, limited to the first two levels. If all four levels are taken as a criterion (a standard of adequacy), they fall short. SIT clearly makes efforts to embrace all four levels, but is limited in that the heart of the theory still falls back on the problem of individual-social dualism. SC probably would not endorse the four levels of analysis, arguing that they are artificial and not useful constructions. However, SC has probably gone the furthest in efforts to bridge the individual-social divide in positing a thorough relational stance.

Subjectivity itself, as well as other phenomena, such as groups, categories and ideologies, are formed and cemented in and through sign systems between and among people. Thus, it could be said to cover the range covered by the four levels of analysis, but using different constructs.

There is no doubt that, at present, the field of social psychology is fragmented: it cannot claim to be unified in terms of assumptions, concepts, theories or methods. There is, and certainly has been, mutual antagonism. We could be asked to choose between them, asking which one is correct. We leave this choice to the readers. Alternatively, we could take a reading from constructionism, as boldly argued by Ken Gergen (1999, 2001): constructionism argues that there is no final arbiter, no foundationalism, no true method nor ultimate philosophy of science, no 'God's-eye view' to settle the question.

Each one has a position, and all are producing interesting and sharp research and contributing to understanding. Each one has an argument and, if Billig (1987) is correct, arguments are dialogical, two-sided: there is always a counter-argument. Arguments simply go away, or are superseded by other overarching arguments or new and more interesting ones. Gergen (2001) offers a pragmatic proposal: Which view is more useful in helping to solve the numerous problems and difficulties that we face as endlessly interacting human beings? It might be all three perspectives provided here, albeit in different forms.

Summary

This chapter gives an introduction to social psychology based on comparisons between three differing viewpoints:
- a 'mainstream' or individualistic approach;
- an approach from a SIT perspective; and
- a social constructionist perspective, or discursive psychology.

A general introductory framework sets out four different levels of analysis and locates the central problem as that of 'individual-societal' dualism. The topic of racism is taken as a key social problem and is looked at from the three differing perspectives. The issue of gender relations also takes a central place through the chapter.

The 'mainstream' viewpoint sets out key terms, processes and constructs such as self, identity, attitude, changing attitudes, social influence, conformity, obedience and minority influences. Famous studies are described.

Social identity theory, developed during the past 20 years, is outlined in terms of its key theoretical components and assumptions and is used to explain the dynamics of intergroup relations, stereotypes and conflicts.

Social constructionism, a recent viewpoint that places central emphasis upon language and discourse, is described in terms of the main propositions and assumptions. It is used to depict new ways of understanding the 'self' or human subjectivity. Examples are given of recent South African research using discursive approaches. The conclusion tries to compare and contrast the three main viewpoints in social psychology.

Further reading

Adorno, T., Frenkel-Brunswick, E., Levinson, D. & Sanford, R. (1950) *The Authoritarian Personality*. New York: Harper.

Allport, F. (1924) *Social Psychology*. Boston: Houghton Mifflin.

Allport, G. (1935) Attitudes. In G. Murchison (ed.), *A Handbook of Social Psychology*. Worchester: Clark University Press, pp. 798–844.

Allport, G. (1954) *The Nature of Prejudice*. Reading, Mass.: Addison-Wesley.

Alvesson, M. & Skoldberg, K. (2000) *Reflexive Methodology*. London: Sage.

Ajzen, I. (1988) *Attitudes, Personality and Behaviour*. Milton Keynes: Open University Press.

Asch, S. (1955) Opinions and social pressure. *Scientific American*, 193, pp. 31–5.

Bandawe, C. & Foster, D. (1996) Aids-related beliefs, attitudes and intentions among Malawian students. *AIDS Care*, 8, pp. 223–32.

Baron, R. & Byrne, D. (1981) *Social Psychology* (3rd edition). Boston: Allyn & Bacon.

Bartlett, F. (1932) *Remembering*. London: Cambridge University Press.

Baumeister, R. (1988) The self. In D. Gilbert, S. Fiske & G. Lindzey (eds), *The Handbook of Social Psychology* (4th edition), Vol. 1. Boston: McGraw-Hill, pp. 680–740.

Biko, S. (1978) *I Write What I Like*. London: Heinemann.

Billig, M. (1987) *Arguing and Thinking*. Cambridge: Cambridge University Press.

Campbell, C. (1995a) The social identity of township youth: An extension of social identity theory, Part 1. *South African Journal of Psychology*, 25(3), pp. 150–9.

Campbell, C. (1995b) The social identity of township youth: Social identity theory and gender, Part 2. *South African Journal of Psychology*, 25(3), pp. 160–7.

Deaux, K. & Lafrance, M. (1998) Gender. In G. Gilbert, S. Fiske & G. Lindsay (eds), *The Handbook of Social Psychology* (4th edition), Vol 1. Boston: McGraw-Hill, pp. 788–827.

Dixon, J., Reicher, S. & Foster, D. (1997) Ideology, geography, racial exclusion: The squatter camp as 'blot on the landscape'. *Text*, 17(3), pp. 317–8.

Doise, W. (1986) *Levels of Explanation in Social Psychology*. Cambridge: Cambridge University Press.

Duckitt, J. (1992) *The Social Psychology of Prejudice*. New York: Praeger.

Duncan, N. (1996) Discourses on public violence and the reproduction of racism. *South African Journal of Psychology*, 26(2), pp. 172–82.

Durrheim, K. (1997) Social constructionism, discourse and psychology. *South African Journal of Psychology*, 27(3), p. 175.

Durrheim, K. & Foster, D. (1997) Tolerance of ambiguity as a content specific construct. *Personality and Individual Differences*, 22(5), pp. 741–50.

Festinger, L. (1957) *A Theory of Cognitive Dissonance*. Stanford: Stanford University Press.

Finchilescu, G. & Dawes, A. (1999) *Adolescents' Socio-political Perspectives on South African Society*. Research Report for the Centre of Science Development, Pretoria.

Fishbein, M. & Ajzen, J. (1975) *Belief, Attitude, Intention and Behavior*. Reading, Mass.: Addison-Wesley.

Foster, D. (1993) The mark of oppression? In L. Nicholas (ed.), *Psychology and Oppression*. Johannesburg: Skotaville, pp. 128–41.

Foster, D. (1997) Perpetrators of gross violations of human rights. *Journal of Community and Health Sciences*, 4(2), pp. 1–35.

Foster, D. (1999) Racism, Marxism, psychology. *Theory & Psychology*, 9(3), pp. 331–52.

Foster, D. (2000) The Truth and Reconciliation Commission and understanding perpetrators. *South African Journal of Psychology*, 30(1), pp. 2–9.

Foster, D. & Finchilescu, G. (1986) Contact in a non-contact society. In M. Hewstone & R. Brown (eds), *Contact and Conflict in Intergroup Encounters*. Oxford: Blackwell, pp. 119–36.

Foster, D. & Louw-Potgieter, J. (eds) (1991) *Social Psychology in South Africa*. Johannesburg: Lexicon.

Foster, D. & Nel, E. (1991) Attitudes and related concepts. In D. Foster & D. Louw-Potgieter (eds), *Social Psychology in South Africa*, pp. 121–67.

Foster, D., Davis, D. & Sandler, D. (1987) *Detention and Torture in South Africa*. Cape Town: David Philip.

Foucault, M. (1972) *The Archaeology of Knowledge*. London: Tavistock.

Gergen, K. (1985) The social constructionist movement in modern psychology. *American Psychologist*, 40(3), pp. 266–75.

Gergen, K. (1991) *The Saturated Self*. New York: Basic Books.

Gergen, K. (1994) *Realities and Relationships*. Cambridge, Mass.: Harvard University Press.

Gergen, K. (1999) *An Invitation to Social Constructionism*. London: Sage.

Gergen, K. (2001) *Social Construction in Context*. London: Sage.

Harré, R. & Van Langenhove, L. (eds) (1991) *Positioning Theory*. Oxford: Blackwell.

Harris, E., Lea, S. & Foster, D. (1995) The construction of gender. *South African Journal of Psychology*, 25(3), pp. 175–83.

Hogg, M. & Abrams, D. (1988) *Social Identifications*. London: Routledge.

James, W. (1890) *The Principles of Psychology*. New York: Henry Holt.

Lea, S. (1996) Talking about race with young white South Africans. *South African Journal of Psychology*, 26(3), pp. 183–90.

Levett, A. (1988) Psychological trauma: Discourses of childhood sexual abuse. Unpublished doctoral thesis, University of Cape Town.

Levett, A., Kottler A., Burman, E. & Parker, I. (eds) (1997) *Culture, Power and Difference*. London: Zed Press.

Manganyi, N.C. (1973) *Being-black-in-the-world*. Johannesburg: Ravan.

MacCrone, I.D. (1937) *Race Attitudes in South Africa*. London: Oxford University Press.

MacCrone, I.D. (1949) Race attitudes. In E. Hellman (ed.), *Handbook on Race Relations in South Africa*. Cape Town: Oxford University Press, pp. 669–705.

McGuire, W. (1969) The nature of attitudes and attitude change. In G. Linzey & E. Aronson (eds), *Handbook of Social Psychology* (2nd edition), Vol. 3. Reading, Mass.: Addison-Wesley, pp. 136–314.

Milgram, S. (1974) *Obedience to Authority*. New York: Harper & Row.

Moscovici, S. (1976) *Social Influence and Social Change*. London: Academic Press.

Mugny, G. (1982) *The Power of Minorities*. New York: Academic Press.

Parker, I. (1992) *Discourse Dynamics*. London: Routledge.

Petty, R. & Cacioppo, J. (1986) The elaboration likelihood model of persuasion. In L. Berkowitz (ed.), *Advances in Experimental Social Psychology*,
Vol. 19. Orlando: Academic Press.

Potter, M. & Wetherell, M. (1987) *Discourse and Social Psychology*.
London: Sage.

Sampson, E.E. (1988) The debate on individualism. *American Psychologist*,
43, pp. 15–22.

Sampson, E.E. (1993) *Celebrating the Other*. New York: Harvester Wheatsheaf.

Sennett, J. & Foster, D. (1996) Social identity: Comparing South African
students in 1975 and 1994. *South African Journal of Psychology*, 26
(3), pp. 203–11.

Shefer, T. & Foster, D. (2001) Discourses on women's heterosexuality and
desire in a South African local context. *Culture, Health & Sexuality*,
3(4), pp. 375–90.

Sherif, M. (1936) *The Psychology of Social Norms*. New York: Harper & Row.

Shotter, J. (1993) *Conversational Realities*. London: Sage.

Stevens, G. (1998) 'Racialised' discourses: Understanding perceptions of
threat in post-apartheid South Africa. *South African Journal of
Psychology*, 28(4), pp. 204–14.

Tajfel, H. (1981) *Human Groups and Social Categories*. Cambridge:
Cambridge University Press.

Tajfel, H. & Turner, J. (1979) An integrative theory of intergroup conflict. In
W. Austin & S. Worchel (eds), *The Social Psychology of Intergroup
Relations*. Pacific Grove: Brooks/Cole, pp. 33–47.

Triplett, N. (1898) The dyamogenic factors in pacemaking and competition.
American Journal of Psychology, 9, pp. 507–83.

Truth and Reconciliation Commission (TRC) (1998) *Truth and Reconciliation
Commission of South Africa Report*, 5 Vols. Cape Town: TRC.

Wegner, D. & Bargh, J. (1998) Control and automaticity in social life. In D.
Gilbert, S. Fiske & G. Lindzey (eds) *The Handbook of Social
Psychology* (4th edition), Vol. 1. Boston: McGraw-Hill, pp. 446–96.

Wetherell, M. & Potter, J. (1992) *Mapping the Language of Racism*.
London: Harvester Wheatsheaf.

Wood, C. & Foster, D. (1995) Gender differentiated reasons for non-use of
condoms. *Psychology in Society*, 20, pp. 13–35.

Zajonc, R.B. (1998) Emotions. In D. Gilbert, S. Fiske & G. Lindzey (eds),
The Handbook of Social Psychology (4th edition), Vol. 1. Boston:
McGraw-Hill, pp. 591–632

9 Intelligence and Psychological Testing

M.C. Eaton, D.M. Luiz, I. Schwellnus and
D. de Klerk

Objectives

After studying this chapter you should:

- know how psychologists define intelligence
- know how intelligence is measured
- understand the relationship between IQ and intelligence
- understand the differences between EQ and IQ
- be able to identify the intelligence tests that draw the most critique
- understand how intelligence testing developed in South Africa
- understand what separates the mentally retarded from the intellectually gifted
- be able to assess whether intelligent people and creative people are similar or different
- understand what determines intelligence
- be able to identify whether intelligence is genetic or if the environment plays a role.

Introduction

> *For it is not enough to have a fine mind; the main thing is to learn how to apply it properly.*
>
> (DESCARTES)

In this chapter, we will describe theories and research that have been integral to the development of contemporary understanding and debate on the construct of intelligence. The theories propose various models of intelligence, some of which rely on psychological testing. As the theories evolved, so did the psychological tests measuring these constructs. This development has been unique in the South African context and much research has been dedicated to culture-fair testing.

It is clear that people have different interests, abilities and personality traits. People also differ in their levels of intellectual functioning and in their abilities to solve problems creatively. Take a few minutes to look at the following questions:

- If a certain number is multiplied by 2 and 3 is added, the answer is 63. What is the number?
- In what way are these two things the same or alike? An apple and an orange are both _____?
- Here's a more difficult one. In what way are these two things the same or alike? Salt and water both are _____?
- Identify what part is missing in this picture.

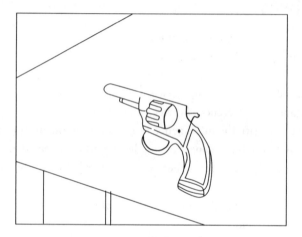

- On the left there is a pattern consisting of nine squares, one of which is empty; and on the right there are five squares. Which option on the right completes the pattern if it is placed in the open space?

A  B   C   D E

● Answer this one in a similar way as above. It is a little more difficult.

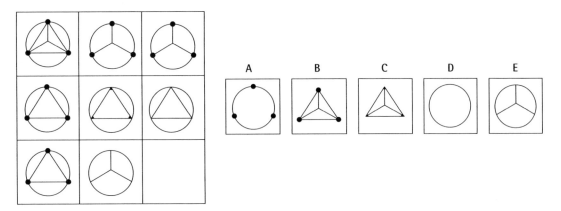

● Here is a pattern that would be presented to a child on a card. The child would be asked to assemble nine red and white coloured blocks according to the pattern below. It is more difficult than it looks!

These are sample items from various South African intelligence and scholastic aptitude tests. (The answers appear at the end of the chapter.) Do these questions adequately capture your understanding of the essence of intelligence? Do the items draw on general knowledge or specific knowledge in certain areas? Do the examples require a person to draw on previously learnt information or do they elicit current reasoning skills? These are important questions that intelligence test developers take into consideration when developing such tests. They are guided by the theories that define the elusive construct of intelligence.

So what is intelligence? You have probably used this word often in everyday speech, but when pressed for a comprehensive definition, you may find it difficult. This question has given rise to divergent answers from philosophers, psychologists and researchers alike; suffice to say that no consensus exists among professionals at present. However, most would agree that intelligence is a general term that refers to a person's intellectual ability in various tasks – for instance, problem-solving, use of language, or understanding picture puzzles. It also includes the capacity to learn new information, to profit from experience, and to adapt effectively to one's environment.

A fundamental question that theorists and researchers have attempted to answer is whether intelligence is a singular general ability or whether it is composed of multiple separate and distinct abilities.

Historical models of intelligence

The early theories and models developed by Spearman, Thurstone and Guilford contributed greatly to our understanding of intelligence. Each highlighted different conceptualisations of intelligence, and their definitions and models are outlined below.

Two-factor theory

Charles Spearman, a British psychologist, was one of the first theorists involved in the quest to define human intelligence. At the turn of the twentieth century, Spearman became aware of the fact that individuals who achieve high scores in one test of mental ability, also tend to display high scores in other tests of mental abilities. Based on these correlations, he concluded that mental ability is something that is general in nature. He developed the statistical procedure known as factor analysis, which led to his discovery of two kinds of abilities responsible for differences in individual intelligence scores. His two-factor theory (Spearman 1904) proposed the following factors of intelligence:

General intelligence (g)
This constitutes the first and most important aspect of intelligence, since it is vital in the performance of almost all tasks (Spearman 1904, 1923). It proposes that individuals who, for example, achieve high scores for mathematical ability, will achieve equally high scores for another mental ability, such as language competency. Spearman was not able to define g any further in his earlier work, but suggested in 1927 that it could be something one might call 'mental energy' (Spearman 1927).

Specific intelligence (S)
This factor refers to the specific abilities required to perform various tasks (Spearman 1904, 1923). The S factor varies from one act to

another, while g is available at the same level for all intellectual acts (Spearman 1927). However, the performance of any intellectual act requires a combination of g and S. The contribution of each would depend on the nature of the task.

An example that highlights the difference between g and S would be autistic savants (geniuses). Even though these individuals are mentally retarded (g), they may portray genius-like abilities within a specific field (S), of which the most common are numeric reasoning, memory feats, artistic ability and musical ability (Edelson 1995).

According to Spearman, though, intelligence tests should focus on the measurement of g and avoid any interference of S, since S is merely an indication of performance on individual subtests of intelligence. He considered g alone to be responsible for the meaningful interpretation of intelligence.

Group factors

After further research, Spearman noted that the specific abilities might overlap, since they are not necessarily independent of each other (Murphy & Davidshofer 2001). He named clusters of specific abilities that were related or overlapped group factors. Spearman, therefore, conceptualised intelligent behaviour in terms of g, S and group factors, but maintained his original assertion that intelligence tests should be designed to measure g.

Theory of primary mental abilities

Louis Thurstone, an American psychologist who started his career as an electrical engineer and worked as an assistant to Thomas Edison, the inventor, contested Spearman's theory that human mental performance consists of a general factor. Where Spearman was excited about the positive correlation of scores on different tests of mental abilities, Thurstone was more interested in the fact that the correlations were not quite perfect (Passer & Smith 2001). He maintained that the performance on any mental task is more influenced by specific abilities than a general ability. Thurstone argued that, if the statistical procedure of factor analysis was done in a different way, seven factors would appear. Based on his own research, Thurstone postulated the notion of primary mental abilities (or group factors), which he believed would collectively constitute general intelligence.

Seven primary factors were identified (Thurstone 1938) and are presented in Table 9.1, overleaf.

TABLE 9.1: Thurstone's seven primary factors

	Ability	Description
M	Rote memory	The ability to store and recall information
N	Number ability	The ability to work with figures (to add, subtract, divide, etc.)
P	Perceptual speed	The speed at which visual patterns are correctly perceived and compared
R	Reasoning	Dealing with novel problems in terms of rules, principles and experience
S	Spatial visualisation	Reasoning about visual forms and the relationship between parts, such as perceiving distance and managing rotation
V	Verbal comprehension	Comprehending verbal statements, ideas in word forms
W	Word fluency	Producing ideas fluently in word form

Thurstone believed that these abilities were independent, proposing that an individual might have exceptional word fluency, while simultaneously lacking the ability to reason. A general score of intelligence would, therefore, fail to convey specific strengths and weaknesses.

Structure of intellect model

Another American psychologist, J.P. Guilford, rejected the idea of a general intelligence factor and used the system of factor analysis in the development of his three-factor structure of intellect model (Guilford 1967, 1988a, 1988b). According to his theory, a distinction was made between operations, products and contents. He ascribed these as being the three separate dimensions of human intellectual functioning, each of which was divided into subordinate categories. The dimensions can be represented graphically by means of a cube (see Figure 9.1, on the next page), where the categories of one dimension always intersect with the categories of other dimensions (Guilford 1967, 1988a).

The three proposed dimensions are:

- **Operations:** The things an individual does that involve a mental operation.
- **Contents:** The things that an individual works with; the areas of information in which the operations are performed.

- **Products:** The ways in which information is organised; the results of the intellectual process.
(GUILFORD & HOEPFNER 1971)

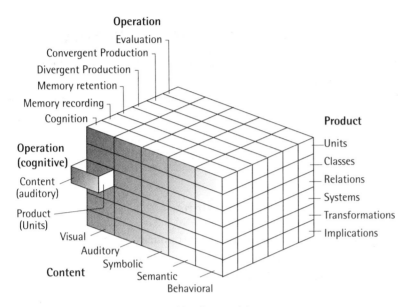

FIGURE 9.1: Guilford's structure of intellect model

Originally, four content, five operation and six product categories were identified, creating the possibility of 120 different components of intelligence or unique abilities (Guilford 1988b; Guilford & Hoepfner 1971). However, during 1977, Guilford revised this model based on the research and reports of Feldman (1969) and Horn (1973), and divided the figural category within the content dimension into auditory and visual categories. The structure of intellect model was further revised when Kamstra's (1971) research initiated the transformation of the memory category within the operation dimension into two separate categories of memory retention and memory recording.

Technically, in its current state, the structure of intellect model suggests the existence of 180 unique abilities (six operations × six products × five contents). Three examples would be the cognition of auditory units, memory for semantic relations, and the evaluation of behavioural systems. However, some combinations (represented per block of the cube) have been found to consist of two or more abilities, suggesting that the human mental capacity is not limited to 180 abilities.

Guilford's model has proved to have certain advantages, but has also been subject to criticism. Even though his model facilitates the expansion of the view of human intelligence (e.g. by introducing factors related to social judgement and creativity), it provides a problem in terms of complexity when having to predict or plan behaviours for real-life situations (McInerney & McInerney 1998; Woolfolk 1990).

Contemporary models of intelligence

The historical models of intelligence provided a platform for the development of more modern conceptualisations of this construct. Gardner and Sternberg describe models of intelligence that are complex and multidimensional in nature. The most recent developments in this field have expanded to include acknowledgement of the constructs of 'emotional intelligence' as well as 'spiritual intelligence'.

Theory of multiple intelligences

Howard Gardner is another avid proponent of multiple cognitive abilities (Gardner 1983, 1993, 1999). In 1983, Gardner presented his multiple intelligences theory in his book *Frames of Mind: The Theory of Multiple Intelligences*, and highlighted the fact that individuals exist within multiple contexts, each of which calls for a unique and different form of intelligence.

He suggested that humans possess at least nine different forms of intelligence (Gardner 1983, 1993). These forms of intelligence are related to different areas of learning (Walters & Gardner 1986; Gardner 1999).

The nine intelligences do not function in isolation, and each activity requires the interaction of several kinds and different levels of intelligence. All humans possess each of the different kinds of intelligence, listed on the next page though their levels of development and strength differ.

Gardner's theory has prompted critique from various psychologists. Some are concerned that it is not supported by adequate research and regard it as highly speculative. Furthermore, musical intelligence as a primary ability has been subject to question, since many are of the opinion that it is a talent (the same as the ability to play soccer) rather than a form of intelligence. In addition, many people regard interpersonal and intrapersonal intelligences as personality characteristics or traits, and believe that they cannot be classified as forms of intelligence.

Although widely criticised, Gardner's theory has made an important contribution towards the development of intelligence test items in which more than one answer can be considered correct and answers demonstrating creative thinking can be accommodated (Feldman 1993). It emphasises his philosophy that intelligence can be measured in more than one way.

Gardner's multiple intelligences

- **Bodily-kinaesthetic intelligence**
This involves the capacity to use the whole body or various parts of it to solve problems. People with a high degree of this type of intelligence are usually found, for example, among dancers, athletes and surgeons.

- **Interpersonal intelligence**
This involves the understanding and skills required for interaction with others. This ability should be the most developed in people who engage in careers such as teaching, marketing and politics.

- **Intrapersonal intelligence**
Having knowledge regarding oneself, including being aware of and in touch with one's own feelings and emotions, is characteristic of this form of intelligence. Ideally, psychologists and psychiatrists should rank high in this type of intelligence.

- **Linguistic intelligence**
This involves the production of language to express one's thoughts and understanding of others. People who 'specialise' in linguistic intelligence are lawyers, public speakers, and especially poets and authors.

- **Logical-mathematical intelligence**
Problem-solving skills and being able to think scientifically are associated with this type of intelligence. High levels of it are found among mathematicians and scientists.

- **Musical intelligence**
This requires the skill and ability to perform musical tasks, such as hearing, recognising and remembering pitches, tones, rhythm and melodic patterns, followed by its implementation during performance.

- **Spatial intelligence**
People with a high level of spatial intelligence can easily perceive and interpret three-dimensional shapes and images. It involves abstract visualisation, which is a characteristic found among sculptors, architects and navigators.

- **Naturalist intelligence**
This dimension was only added in 1996, and involves sensitivity toward living things and other aspects of the natural world, such as plants and clouds. Chefs, botanists and farmers should have a high level of naturalist intelligence.

- **Existentialist intelligence**
Although it still requires a great deal of research, this is Gardner's most recent addition to the list. He describes it as the capacity to pose questions regarding life and death, and considers it the foundation of art, religion and philosophy.

Triarchic theory of intelligence

As a child, Robert Sternberg suffered from intense anxiety, which worsened when he faced examinations. His performances on intelligence tests were generally not good. However, in spite of his childhood experiences, Sternberg obtained a doctorate in psychology and became renowned for his research in the field of intelligence.

Based on his background and his later achievements in life, Sternberg believed that intelligence is multidimensional, and that different kinds of intelligence are responsible for people being successful in various ways in specific areas of life. He developed a triarchic theory that suggests the existence of three different abilities: componential intelligence, experiential intelligence and contextual intelligence (Sternberg 1985, 1986, 1988, 1991).

Componential intelligence

This component resembles the traditional view of intelligence, which is known to include the acquisition of new information and abilities, and the development of problem-solving skills. These skills facilitate the successful execution of required tasks.

Componential intelligence is further divided into three specific categories: metacomponents, performance components and knowledge-acquisition components (Sternberg 1998).

- Metacomponents are the processes involved in the higher order, executive-type functioning tasks. They include problem-solving skills, such as the identification of problems, the formulation of hypotheses and strategies, and the logical testing of these hypotheses and strategies, followed by an evaluation of whether these would solve the problem adequately. These metacomponents, Sternberg believes, are crucial in directing the other two dimensions. Less intelligent people tend to bypass these processes and dive right into a situation, or neglect to spend sufficient time on the development of action strategies.
- Performance components are the cognitive processes involved in the actual execution of a task as mapped out by the metacomponents. Information retrieval and the generation of an appropriate response fall into this category.
- Knowledge-acquisition components do as the name suggests – they are responsible for storing the new experience or information, comparing it with already saved information, and then creating new insights based on this for future retrieval.

Experiential intelligence

Experiential intelligence suggests the use of adaptation skills, creativity and insight to formulate new ideas when faced with unfamiliar situations.

This type of intelligence is not only vitally important in order to master new tasks, but also for the automatic performance of difficult tasks such as reading and writing.

Contextual intelligence

On a daily basis, people find themselves in situations and surroundings that require them to cope with demands practically and successfully. Contextual intelligence assists in this process. It helps people to socialise, and to adhere to societal rules and principles. Sternberg believes that people with high levels of this kind of intelligence skilfully maximise their strengths and compensate for their weaknesses in order to suit their goals in a given context. It is a process of adaptation, shaping and selection (Sternberg 1985, 1988).

One would be using componential intelligence, for example, while studying for an exam that requires the restatement of facts. Experiential intelligence would be used to apply and integrate what one has learnt – for example, by analysing a case study according to a specific theory. Contextual intelligence would be used when one is, for example, provided with three questions in an exam and asked to select and answer one. By eliminating questions with which one struggles (e.g. an essay question requiring lots of theoretical comparisons) and selecting the question which with one is more confident (e.g. an essay question requiring explanations of more practical matters), one would be capitalising on strengths and compensating for weaknesses.

Sternberg's theory requires further research to substantiate his categories of intellectual ability. Until then, it remains an informative approach to understanding intelligence. It is also an acknowledgement that practical, everyday intelligent behaviour is considered an important component of intelligence.

Emotional intelligence

Emotional intelligence has been defined as 'the ability to perceive and constructively act on both one's own emotions and the feeling of others' (Ford-Martin 1995: p. 1). Also known as emotional quotient (EQ) and emotional literacy, the term emotional intelligence was originally introduced to the world by John Mayer and Peter Salovey in 1990 (Ford-Martin 1995). But it was Daniel Goleman, the *New York Times* journalist and professor from Harvard University, who turned emotional intelligence into a hot topic with his provocative book *Emotional Intelligence: Why It can Matter More than IQ for Character, Health and Lifelong Achievement (1995).*

According to Goleman (1995), the common characteristics found among persons high in emotional intelligence are impulse control, self-esteem, self-motivation, mood management and people skills. These individuals can identify, use, understand and manage emotions successfully. Goleman considers these qualities vital in one's success in life, and in personal relationships. Research has shown that there is a correlation between emotional skills and academic success, emphasising that both IQ and EQ are important, but in different ways (Goleman 1995).

Goleman blames today's problems of disrespect, conflict and loneliness among students on a lack of emotional intelligence. Fortunately, he is of the opinion that the skills involved in emotional intelligence can virtually all be learned and suggests that children should be trained in the development of emotional skills from a young age (O'Neil 1996).

Emotional intelligence has not only had an impact in the field of psychology, but different aspects of it have been incorporated into schools, communities and business, in order to enhance personal well-being and professional relations (Gibbs 1995).

Spiritual intelligence

Danah Zohar and Ian Marshall recently introduced the concept of spiritual intelligence or SQ in their latest co-authored book *Spiritual Intelligence: The Ultimate Intelligence* (2000). Although the study and practice of spirituality has a longstanding history, these authors situate spirituality within the domain of intelligence. In fact, they argue that without SQ, both IQ and EQ cannot function effectively. Spiritual intelligence, then, is the intelligence with which people address and solve problems of meaning and value. It allows us to place our lives in a wider, richer, more meaningful context, and helps us assess the degree to which our life-path is more or less meaningful than a potential myriad of others (Zohar & Marshall 2000).

SQ is inclusive of, but not limited, to religion. It is an 'internal, innate ability of the human brain and psyche' that allows us to 'find and use meaning in the solution of problems' (Zohar & Marshall 2000: p. 9).

People who have a highly developed SQ would have the capacity to be flexible, to be highly self-aware, and to be able to transcend suffering and pain. They would be holistic in their outlook on life, inclined to be inspired by vision and value, and be reluctant to cause unnecessary harm to others or to the universe (Zohar & Marshall 2000).

Critics of non-cognitive forms of intelligence argue that the concept of intelligence is becoming too far removed from its original focus on mental abilities (e.g. Cooper 1998). The proponents of these approaches respond that intelligence encompasses adaptive abilities, and argue that we should not resign ourselves to considering only cognitive realms of human ability. This debate is certain to continue well into the future.

Intelligence testing

Are some people more 'intelligent' than others? Well, everyday experience makes it apparent that certain people think and behave in more effective ways than their peers. An important question is whether it is possible to measure individual differences in intelligence and, further, whether it is desirable.

Psychological measurement involves assigning numbers to individuals so that the properties of the numbers are a faithful representation of the individuals' attributes under investigation. Intelligence testing allows us to give a numerical value to an individual's level of general mental functioning. Although arguments exist concerning the advantages and disadvantages of intelligence testing, it remains a convenient method of quantifying a person's level of functioning relative to others. The evolution and development of such psychometric assessment tools are described in the following sections.

Psycholgical measurement: The assigning of numbers to individuals so that the properties of the numbers are a faithful representation of the individuals' attributes under investigation.

Binet-Simon intelligence scale

Alfred Binet, a leading French psychologist, was commissioned in the late 1800s by the French Ministry of Public Education to devise an objective method of determining the educational aptitude of schoolchildren. The purpose was to identify, as early as possible, those children who would not benefit from normal public schooling, so that the ministry could provide specialised education for them.

Binet worked with a young physician, Théodore Simon, and they created an intelligence scale based on certain suppositions about the construct of intelligence. The first assumption was that mental competence develops with age. The second assumption was that the rate at which an individual develops his or her mental abilities is a characteristic of that particular individual and, therefore, fairly constant over time. For example, a child with delayed mental development at age six will also be delayed at age ten.

Binet and Simon drew samples of both intellectually 'normal' and 'deviant' children between the ages of three and 13, with the aim of describing what a child of a certain age should be capable of achieving. Once these competencies were clearly identified, they developed a standardised scale that measured a child's mental capacity, by assessing his or her performance on tasks of comprehension, judgement, reasoning and invention. According to Binet, these were all higher mental processes central to the assessment of intelligence.

The use of the scale was aimed at guiding the placement process with regard to regular classroom instruction or special educational needs satisfaction, and assessing whether a child was performing at the correct developmental level for his or her chronological age (actual age). The result was a score called the mental age. Comparing his or her score with the average scores of others within specific age groups derives the mental age of a person.

For example, a child of six may have the mental capacity to function at an eight-year-old level. This would make the child's mental age eight, although his or her chronological age would remain six. However, a six-year-old who experiences developmental deficiencies may lack the appropriate intellectual skills and be found to be functioning at the level of a four-year-old. This would make the child's mental age four, while his or her chronological age would remain six. In order to see if this six-year-old child is developmentally normal, it would make sense to contrast his or her intellectual development with that of other six-year-olds.

Stanford–Binet test

Lewis Terman, a psychologist at Stanford University in the USA, saw the need for the Americanisation of the Binet-Simon scale, noting that cultural factors were also a determinant of intelligence. In making the scale more culturally fair, a term discussed later in this chapter, and more appropriate in American culture, he subsequently rewrote and revised a great proportion of the items in the scale. This adapted measure was known as the Stanford-Binet scale. One of the major modifications that Terman made was the representation of the child's level of intelligence in the form of a score known as the intelligence quotient (IQ). Dividing the child's mental age by his or her chronological age and multiplying the dividend by 100 produced a score that allowed for the easier categorisation of intelligence.

$$\text{Intelligence Quotient (IQ)} = \left[\frac{\text{Mental Age (MA)}}{\text{Chronological Age (CA)}} \times 100 \right]$$

For example, if a child aged four had the mental capabilities of a child of aged five, his or her intelligence quotient (IQ) could be worked out as follows:

$$\left[\frac{\text{Mental Age (MA)}}{\text{Chronological Age (CA)}} \times 100 \right] \left[\frac{5}{4} \times 100 \right] = \left[1.25 \times 100 \right] = 125$$

This final score meant nothing in isolation and, therefore, a classification system was derived on which the child's score could be meaningfully interpreted (see Table 9.2).

TABLE 9.2: Classification of IQ scores

IQ score	Category
140+	Extremely gifted
130–139	Gifted
120–129	Superior
110–119	High average
90–109	Average
80–89	Low average
70–79	Borderline mental retardation
50–69	Mild mental retardation
35–49	Moderate mental retardation
20–34	Severe mental retardation
Below 20	Profound mental retardation

Bell-shaped curve

If the intelligence of every member of the population were to be assessed, the findings would show that the highest percentage of people would fall within the average score range, with smaller percentages of people falling both above and below average. If this data were to be represented in the form of a graph, known as a normal distribution of scores (see Figure 9.2. overleaf), it would look similar in shape to that of a bell, hence the name bell-shaped curve.

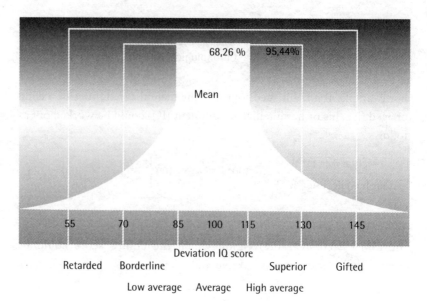

FIGURE 9.2: The bell-shaped curve and mental classification

The average IQ in the range of scores is 100. This average score is termed the mean score and you will notice that the graph is symmetrical on either side of the mean, representing equal percentages of the population scoring above and below this midpoint.

The deviation IQ

So far, our discussion about intelligence has been mainly concerned with the mental capacities of children. A problem arises if you think that most IQ tests measure intellectual processes rather than specific knowledge, and that a great proportion of our mental processes are generally learnt by the age of 16. Consequently, intelligence, measured by these tests, remains relatively static after the age of 16. The problem comes in when attempts are made to calculate the IQ of an adult.

Let us consider, for example, the case of a 16 year old with a mental age of 16. The IQ will equal 100:

$$\left[\frac{MA}{CA} \times 100 \right] = \left[\frac{16}{16} \times 100 \right] = \left[1 \times 100 \right] = 100$$

In four years time, this individual will have a chronological age of 20, although his or her mental age will remain a static 16 years as a result of the proportion of mental procedures already learnt. This will make this individual's IQ equal to 80, as shown in the following calculation:

$$\left[\frac{MA}{CA} \times 100 \right] = \left[\frac{16}{20} \times 100 \right] = \left[0.8 \times 100 \right] = 80$$

Therefore, although the individual is maturing mentally, his or her IQ appears to decrease.

In order to circumvent this incongruity, the concept of deviation IQ was introduced. This allowed the individual's test performance to be compared with performances of others in the same age group. Most IQ tests no longer provide a comparison IQ score, but rather an individual's performance is measured according to how much it deviates from the average for those age norms. For example, instead of saying that an individual has an IQ of 120, the individual's deviation IQ is qualified by stating that he or she performed better than 88% of his or her peers.

Development of intelligence testing in South Africa

For a detailed description of the development of modern psychological assessment in South Africa, refer to Claasen (1997), as well as Foxcroft and Roodt (2001). A summary of developments specific to intelligence testing in South Africa is outlined below.

Intelligence testing in South Africa began in the early twentieth century. As with the Binet-Simon scale, the South African counterpart was designed for investigating mental retardation of learners in schools in the Gauteng area. The other provinces soon followed, with Professor Eybers of the University of the Orange Free State adapting the Stanford-Binet scale for use in both English and Afrikaans, the official South African languages at the time.

The history of psychological testing is interwoven with, and has been adversely affected by, the advent of apartheid within South Africa since its very inception. As with political policies, tests were standardised for whites only, which ensured that placement programmes in schools were biased in favour of these learners. IQ tests with English norms were inappropriately used to reach conclusions about group differences, providing 'evidence' of the superiority of the English-speakers over the native-tongue inhabitants, who were not proficient in the language of administration, and thereby scored substantially lower than the population upon which the norms were standardised. Conclusions drawn from data such as this were strongly disputed by a proportion of the psychology fraternity (Foxcroft & Roodt 2001).

Biesheuvel, for instance, queried the cultural appropriateness of Western-type intelligence tests for blacks, highlighting the influence of different cultural, environmental and temperamental factors on intelligence test scores. This led him to conclude that 'under present circumstances, and by means of the usual techniques, the difference between intellectual capacity of Africans and Europeans cannot be scientifically determined' (Biesheuvel 1943: p. 191).

Although several other scales were designed in the interim, in 1926 M.L. Fick standardised an individual scale called the Fick scale, which was replaced by the New South African Individual Scale (NSAIS) in 1955. This scale was the most popular of children's intelligence measures at the time. The revised version of this scale was released in 1991, and is still in use. It is known as the Senior South African Intelligence Scale – Revised (SSAIS-R). A continuous focus on contemporary Westernised tests preceding 1980 allowed for the development of similar measures to be standardised for the various population and language groups in the country, albeit that few measures were being produced for blacks, coloureds and Indians. The Wechsler Adult Intelligence Scale (WAIS), although not designed in South Africa, was standardised for use with the white English- and Afrikaans-speaking population. This re-standardised measure was called the South African Wechsler Adult Intelligence Scale (SAWAIS).

Important advances in the field in the 1970s led to the formulation of legislation regarding the use, interpretation and control by psychologists of all tests, measures, questionnaires and instruments that 'tap psychological constructs' (Health Professions Act (Act 56 of 1974)). The aim of this legislation was to guide the assessment process and diminish the adverse consequences of misuse of psychological measures. Tests that were developed and standardised for the white population were still being used for other groups of individuals, although increased awareness initiated the interpretation of results with a certain amount of caution.

During the late 1980s, group intelligence testing in South Africa became more prevalent and offered certain advantages over individual assessment procedures. Group testing reduced tester bias and aided quick and objective scoring of the answer sheets. Because large numbers of people could now be tested, formulating norms became less of a complication. Two of the better-known group tests were the New South African Group Test (NSAGT) and the General Scholastic Aptitude Test (GSAT). The latter was constructed with norms for more than one racial group and is still in use throughout the country.

The Professional Board for Psychology is a professional body with the roles of protecting the public and guiding the profession of psychology. The Psychometrics Committee, formed under the Professional Board for Psychology, provides the board with a more direct way of controlling and regulating the use of psychological instruments in South Africa. The International Test Commission (ITC) is closely associated with the Psychometrics Committee in an attempt to develop internationally acceptable standards for testing. These committees, therefore, seek to protect the public from indiscriminate use and abuse of psychometric tests, and to improve the quality of current tests and testing practices.

Many of the measures of intelligence found in South Africa in the past were aimed at the assessment of white English- and Afrikaans-speaking individuals. If individuals from other cultures were tested, they were tested based on the white norms and were, therefore, at a distinct cultural disadvantage. Mistakes made in the past cannot be overlooked, but rather should be seen as learning experiences guiding the assessment process and sculpting the future of the profession.

The present ethical code of professional conduct strictly stipulates that:

> *Psychologists [should] attempt to identify situations in which particular assessment techniques or norms may not be applicable or may require adjustment in administration or interpretation because of factors such as the individual's gender, age, race, ethnicity, national origin, religion, sexual orientation, disability, language, or socio-economic status.*
> (PROFESSIONAL BOARD FOR PSYCHOLOGY, N.D.: p. 29)

South African researchers and test developers have a lot of work ahead of them. However, the socio-political changes that have happened in South Africa have created an infrastructure that will be supportive of future research and improvements in keeping with the policies of the Psychometrics Committee and ITC.

Characteristics of a good psychological measure

It is essential that a tester use a good assessment instrument that will provide an accurate reflection of a test-taker's ability. To obtain the best results from tests, including IQ tests, it is important to use not only the correct test, but also a good one. The tester is thus obliged to consider the following characteristics or checkpoints of good psychological tests before administering such an instrument.

Reliability

Reliability is defined as the extent to which a test measures a particular construct consistently. If a test is considered reliable, one would expect an individual to obtain similar or, ideally, the same test results on separate occasions. A number of methods to establish reliability exist and these are discussed below.

Test–re-test method

The test-re-test method is the most elementary procedure for examining reliability. This method involves:

- administering a test (for instance, an IQ test) to a group of people;
- re-administering the same test to the same group of people after a period of time; and
- correlating the scores to assess the extent to which the scores are similar.

The more similar the results, the more reliable the test is. Intelligence or IQ is a consistent construct that should not change dramatically over a period of weeks. Changes in people's scores across the two administrations of an IQ test would presumably reflect inconsistency in measurement and, therefore, decrease the reliability.

However, if the period between administrations of the test is too short, people may remember their previous responses; and if the time lapse is too long, the people may acquire or learn new information that could favour their performance during the second test administration. Such limitations led to the development of alternative methods of assessing reliability.

Parallel-forms method

The parallel-forms method of assessing reliability involves:

- administering one form of a test (e.g. form A) to a group of people;
- administering a parallel or equivalent form of the test (e.g. form B), which comprises related but not similar items, to the same group of people; and
- correlating the scores on forms A and B to assess the extent to which the scores are similar.

If an individual obtains similar results in both forms, then the test is considered reliable. This method also has limitations that hamper its effectiveness. There is great uncertainty about the possibility of developing a truly equivalent form of the first test. Learning or practising effects may also contribute to better performance on the second form.

Split-half method

The split-half method is a more cost-effective method of assessing reliability and involves:

- administering a test to a group of people;
- dividing the test into two halves (e.g. all even-numbered items form one half and all odd-numbered items form the second half of the test); and
- correlating the scores on the one half with the scores on the other half to assess the extent to which the scores are similar.

This method eliminates the time and expense involved in constructing a parallel form of the test and arranging two separate test administrations. The disadvantage, however, is that a test can be split in many ways, which results in different reliability estimates.

Internal consistency methods

Internal consistency methods of assessing reliability involve assessing consistency in performance across test items on a single test. This is done by:

- administering a test to a group of people;
- using statistical techniques to compute the correlations among all items as well as the average of those intercorrelations; and
- using a specific statistical formula to estimate the reliability of the test.

These methods allow one to assess the extent to which the items on the test consistently measure the same underlying characteristic or construct. The main criticism lodged against these procedures is that they constitute indirect methods of calculating reliability, whereas the test-re-test method provides a direct assessment. They are, however, very practical and cost-effective methods.

Validity

Validity is defined as the extent to which a test measures what it claims to measure. If an intelligence test is valid, one would expect it to measure the individual's level of intelligence. It would reflect the person's ability and not other constructs such as interests or personality. A number of methods to establish validity exist and these are discussed below.

Validity:
The extent to which a test measures what it claims to measure.

Content validity

Content validity:
The degree to which the test items on a test adequately represent aspects covered in a particular content domain.

Content validity refers to the degree to which the test items on a test adequately represent aspects covered in a particular content domain. For example, two tests claim to assess knowledge of famous musical composers over the centuries (i.e. the content domain); test A only asks questions about the bands of the sixties, and test B requires answers about composers from the Baroque period, the Romantic period and the Modern period. Clearly, test B would provide a better sample of questions tapping the particular content domain and would, therefore, have higher content validity. When it comes to intelligence tests, the test developers need to have clarity on what content they wish to sample.

Construct validity

Construct validity:
An abstract or theoretical label that summarises a group of related phenomena.

Construct:
The degree to which intelligence test items adequately sample the construct of intelligence as outlined by a theory.

Intelligence is a **construct**, which is an abstract or theoretical label that summarises a group of related phenomena (Murphy & Davishofer 2001). The first part of this chapter is dedicated to conveying how various psychologists describe the construct of intelligence. The greater degree to which intelligence test items adequately sample the construct of intelligence as outlined by a theory, the greater the construct validity. For instance, most theories state explicitly or implicitly that intelligence increases as a child's age increases. Should a test consistently measure older children to have lower IQ scores than younger children, this test would be lacking in construct validity.

Criterion-related validity

Criterion-related validity:
The term criterion-related validity refers to the validation procedure where an individual's tests scores are compared with ratings, classifications or other behavioural or mental measures.

Predictive validity:
The accuracy with which a test predicts future performance.

Concurrent validity:
The comparison of a newly developed test's results to that of a well established test of which the validity has already been proven.

The term **criterion-related validity** refers to the validation procedure where an individual's tests scores are compared with ratings, classifications or other behavioural or mental measures. Examples of criteria against which scores are related include school marks or supervisor's ratings.

There are two kinds of criterion-related validity: predictive validity and concurrent validity. **Predictive validity** refers to the accuracy with which a test predicts future performance. If a group of children excel on an intelligence test, and they achieve highly in their academic performance, as measured by class marks over the year, the test would have good predictive validity. Should there be consistent discrepancies between test results and future measures of the ability, the predictive validity would be suspect. **Concurrent validity** involves the comparison of a newly developed test's results to that of a well established test of which the validity has already been proven. If the results of a newly developed South African test correspond favourably with the SSAIS-R, for instance, the test developers could claim their test has concurrent validity.

The relationship between validity and reliability

A test can be reliable without being valid, but it cannot be valid without being reliable. It is important to note that the validity of a measure is dependent on its reliability. In other words, the reliability of a measure has a limiting influence on its validity. It is, therefore, pointless to validate an unreliable measure of intelligence because the starting point of what is being assessed is already uncertain and inconsistent.

Standardisation

Standardisation is another essential consideration of good psychological measurement. It refers to the presence of a systematic procedure for administering, scoring and interpreting a psychological test.

The following steps need to be taken during the administration of any psychometric test:

- Ensure that the test was designed for that specific population or age group.
- Ensure that the test takers are familiar with the language of administration.
- Avoid uncontrolled factors, such as noise and uncomfortable temperature, that may have a negative influence on the test takers' scores.
- Several intelligence measures, such as the SSAIS-R, entail standardised procedures outlined in the form of detailed instructions. You must adhere to these procedures during the testing process.

Standardisation: The presence of a systematic procedure for administering, scoring and interpreting a psychological test.

After a standardised administration of a psychological measure, the tester needs to take responsibility for scoring the completed test. The tester should;

- ensure that the correct value is allocated to an answer as stipulated in the test manual;
- ensure that the test is scored correctly by double-checking the scoring process; and
- request another psychologist to cross-check results as an additional validation measure.

The final stage of the administration process involves interpreting the test takers' results. The following steps should be taken when it comes to interpretation:

- Convert test scores into the appropriate scaled scores as stipulated in the test manual.
- Compare test takers' performance with the correct age-equivalent group.

- Use language that can be clearly understood by the test taker when reporting test results.

Norms

Another facet of standardisation involves the collection of norms. **Norms** are data collected from a representative sample of a particular age segment of the population. Norms allow one to assess an individual's test performance in relation to others. Comparing the individual's test scores to normative data not only puts the test taker's performance into perspective, but also enables testers to meaningfully classify the test taker's performance into various categories, such as high average, average, or low average. See Table 9.2 on page 295 for the category labels that correspond with specific IQ score ranges.

Culture-fair intelligence testing

Due to the diversity of South African society in terms of language and cultural groups, the construction of culture-fair tests poses tremendous difficulties for test developers. A **culture-fair test** is defined as a test that is supposed to be free of cultural biases, and is usually constructed so that language differences and other cultural effects are minimised.

Disagreements exist about what is considered fair and on what bases test items could be classified as being fair towards all cultural groups. Moreover, test developers' subjective judgements as to the selection of test items cannot be considered as reliable criteria for developing measures that are truly culture fair.

Based on these controversies surrounding the feasibility of developing a truly culture-fair test, the term 'culture-reduced test' has proved to be a more appropriate term to use in the diverse South African context. A **culture-reduced test** is defined as a test that contains universal objects, symbols and information that are equally familiar to test takers from different cultural backgrounds. In this test, all test takers have had an equal opportunity to be acquainted with and have experience of the test content. This reduces the chance that items would be unduly biased against certain groups, which would negatively affect this group's average scores.

Steps towards reaching this goal of developing culture-reduced tests have been made by developing language-free or non-verbal tests that would be equally difficult for members of any culture. The Raven progressive matrices test is an example of one of the most widely used culture-reduced tests.

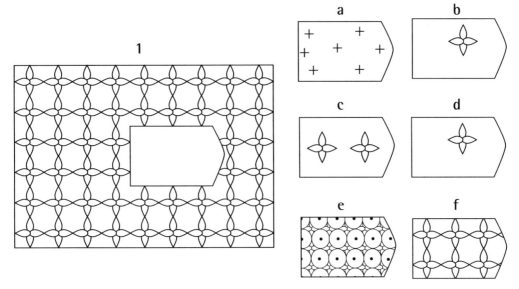

FIGURE 9.3: Raven progressive matrices sample item

These types of tests are advantageous because they require minimal verbal interaction. However, some cultures are more frequently exposed to the objects depicted in some test items than other cultural groups, which, in turn, benefits the former and disadvantages the latter. It is essential that test developers constantly strive to update and improve intelligence tests, especially by eliminating bias from test items.

Critique of intelligence testing

The content of many intelligence tests has proven to be a major concern for psychologists and test developers, due to the uncertainty of whether certain test results represent the test taker's true potential. Moreover, many psychological tests that claim to measure intelligence fall short of achieving that goal because they have less than adequate construct validity.

Many critics argue that intelligence tests only assess a very narrow set of skills, which include passive verbal understanding, the ability to follow instructions, common sense, and especially scholastic aptitude. Blum comments:

> Intelligence tests measure how quickly people can solve relatively unimportant problems, making as few errors as possible, rather than measuring how people grapple with relatively important problems, making as many productive errors as necessary with no time factor.
>
> (BLUM 1979: p. 83)

Other concerns associated with IQ tests relate to the language content and the test administration procedures that might discriminate against minority groups. The reason for this is that the language usage that forms part of the IQ battery and test instructions biases the test in favour of middle- and upper-class white participants. Furthermore, white middle-class instructors might not be familiar with the speech patterns of lower-income groups, minority participants, or those whose home language might not be primarily English. A question may also have a different meaning in different social classes, which leads to further complications that may hamper good test performance.

Critics also argue that, although a great deal of discussion exists regarding the nature of the processes underlying intellectual behaviour, theoretical specification about it remains vague. This once again highlights the difficulty in defining the specific meaning and nature of the construct of intelligence. These theoretical discrepancies and ambiguous definitions of intelligent behaviour largely invalidate interpretations made concerning the degree of difference in performance between different groups.

Any test is merely a sample of selected behaviour at a certain point in time. The IQ score, in part, reflects the relationship between the kind of questions asked in the test and the experiential background of the test taker. Since different questions are asked in different intelligence tests, an individual's score often varies from one test to another. Intelligence scores are also affected by the person's attitude and general mood on the day of testing. It is through highlighting and being aware of the critiques and limitations of intelligence testing that we can empower ourselves to use and interpret such measures both ethically and responsibly.

Range of intelligence

The earlier discussion of the bell-shaped distribution of cognitive performance across the population highlights that IQ scores fall on a continuum. The lower spectrum constitutes the mentally retarded population and the upper range of scores constitutes the intellectually gifted.

Mental retardation

Mental retardation, in its most narrow description, is the label given to anyone who has been assessed to have an IQ score of 70 or less on a psychological test of intelligence. However, mental retardation not only affects performance on tests of general mental functioning, but places limitations on one's capacity for self-care, language and speech ability, social educability and vocational proficiency. **Mental retardation is** defined by the American Psychiatric Association (1994 p. 39) as 'signif-icantly sub-average general intellectual functioning ... that is accompanied by significant limitations in adaptive functioning'.

This highlights that the IQ score is only one of a number of criteria used to achieve a comprehensive assessment of a person's functioning. Table 9.3 lists the degrees of severity of mental retardation with their corresponding level of functioning.

Mental retardation: Significantly sub-average general intellectual functioning that is accompanied by significant limitations in adaptive functioning

TABLE 9.3: Mental retardation categories

Category	IQ range	Level of functioning	% of mentally retarded population
Mild	50–70	These individuals are 'educable', being able to perform academic activities comparable to a child in grade six. They can be minimally self-supporting, being able to acquire basic social and vocational skills. They may require supervision andspecial guidance in times of unusual stress.	85%
Moderate	35–49	These individuals are 'trainable', being able to perform academic activities comparable to a child in grade two. If provided with supervision and guidance in a sheltered workshop, they are able to perform unskilled or semi-skilled work.	10%
Severe	20–34	These individuals are seriously impaired in their motor and speech development, and only learn basic language and practice basic hygiene after age six. As adults, they are able to complete simple tasks under direct supervision. They are usually permanently dependent on others and therefore spend their lives with family, in community homes, or in institutions.	3–4%

Category	IQ range	Level of functioning	% of mentally retarded population
Profound	< 20	These individuals are fully reliant on caregivers. They are often diagnosed with a neurological disorder and epilepsy, spasticity and mutism are common. Their locomotive, speech and self-care skills are impaired to the point that makes institutionalisation inevitable.	1–2%

(BASED ON APA 1994)

Causes of mental retardation

Causative factors in mental retardation include genetic, biological and environmental factors. The more severe forms of retardation often result from genetic or biological disorders. In most cases, however, the causes are unknown (Beirne-Smith *et al.* 1994; Hallahan *et al.* 1985). This is particularly true of mildly mentally retarded individuals who constitute approximately 85% of the total mentally retarded population. Preventative strategies at each of the three levels (genetic, biological and environmental) can work to curb the incidence of mental retardation, and so these are included in the following discussion.

Genetic factors

More than a hundred genetic causes of mental retardation have been identified (Plomin 1997a, 1997b; Shaffer 1989). For instance, Down's syndrome, fragile X syndrome and phenylketonuria (PKU) are genetic disorders usually characterised by moderate to severe mental retardation. People with Down's syndrome have characteristic physical deformities, in addition to cognitive deficits. This disorder is characterised by an abnormality of the 21st chromosomal pair (Brooks 2001; Hastings 2001). Fragile X syndrome results from a mutation at a 'fragile' site on the X chromosome (Boxer & Hastings 2001), whereas PKU is a result of a metabolic defect involving phenylalanine, an essential amino acid (Kaplan & Sadock 1998). There is much variability in terms of physical and cognitive characteristics of people with the latter two disorders. The degree of mental retardation for people with fragile X syndrome ranges from mild to severe, whereas deficits fall mostly in the severe category for those with PKU.

TABLE 9.4: Maternal risk for Down's syndrome

Age	Risk
25–29	1 in 1 400
30–34	1 in 800
35–37	1 in 380
38–39	1 in 190
40–45	1 in 110
45+	1 in 30

(BROOKS 2001: p. 51).

An older than average age mother and exposure to X-ray radiation are predisposing factors causing increased incidence of chromosomal disorders (Kaplan & Sadock 1998). Prevention at this level focuses primarily on the genetic counselling and education of prospective parents. In South Africa, legislation exists that allows pregnant females to consider termination of pregnancy (Choice of Termination of Pregnancy Act (Act 92 of 1996)). Although this option remains controversial, the Act provides prospective parents with a choice to terminate the pregnancy if early identification of genetic abnormalities occurs.

Biological factors

Many biological factors can affect a child's cognitive development. Mental retardation can result from in-utero exposure of the foetus to diseases such as rubella (German measles), syphilis (a venereal disease), and acquired immune deficiency syndrome (AIDS). Excessive consumption of alcohol by the pregnant mother may also result in foetal alcohol syndrome in the child, which has concomitant cognitive handicaps. Birth trauma and injury resulting in severe lack of oxygen to the brain, called anoxia, can result in neural cell death, causing permanent brain damage.

Prevention at this level focuses primarily on the education of prospective parents regarding the mother's physical, psychological and nutritional health during pregnancy. Immunisation is important to prevent maternal rubella. A healthy diet and recommended supplements (e.g. folic acid) can reduce the percentage chance of abnormalities in neurological development in the foetus (Kaplan & Sadock 1998). Education about the dangers of excessive alcohol, drug and nicotine consumption also constitutes important primary prevention.

Environmental factors

Deprivation of stimulation is the primary environmental precursor of delayed development, which can lead to cognitive disabilities. Mild mental retardation is significantly prevalent in low socio-economic groups, where cognitive stimulation is limited. Such environments are often characterised by exposure to poor medical and nutritional care, family instability and inadequate caregivers. Prevention at this level needs to occur in various areas, e.g. socio-political petitioning for government to alleviate poverty and lack of basic necessities, provision of basic nutrition and health care for newborns, community education of parents, and provision of adequate schooling facilities.

The South African education system has recently adopted mainstreaming or inclusion policies that have been in place in the United States for some time (Conroy 1996; Landesman & Butterfield 1987; Lemmer 1998; Maisto & Hughes 1995; Stancliffe 1997). This legislation encourages many cognitively challenged and learning disabled children to attend school in regular classrooms, which allows them the opportunity to experience more normal peer environments and reduces unnecessary stigmatisation (Gaylord-Ross 1990; Lemmer 1998). The legislation does not imply that special schools need to be abolished. Such special schools function as valuable resource centres in their communities. However, where possible, learners with disabilities are being accommodated in mainstream education classes.

Intellectual giftedness

From a psychometric perspective, a small percentage of people can be considered as being intellectually gifted relative to others. Some regard an IQ score of 130 and higher as the criterion for giftedness (Eysenck et al. 1975; Morgan et al. 1984). Gifted people are those, for example, who win academic awards and honours, have patents on many brilliant scientific inventions, or have discovered cures for certain tropical or infectious diseases.

Lewis Terman identified 1 500 American children who had an average IQ of 150. These children were studied over a 70-year period. It was found that they grew up to be highly functioning adolescents and adults who had adjusted extremely well in various areas of their lives. By midlife, they had collectively authored 92 books 2 200 scientific research articles, and obtained 235 patents. Their social and emotional lives were characterised as happy and healthy, with evidence of good psychological adjustment (Sears 1977). From this study, therefore, high

IQ seems to be predictive of high and adaptive functioning in many areas and domains of life, and this appears to extend over the course of a person's lifespan.

High intelligence alone, however, cannot be equated with the kind of eminence termed 'genius' (Passer & Smith 2001). Many people have brilliant ideas and goals, but many of them never persevere to convert such intentions into real products. The term 'genius' would involve people using creative problem-solving skills, having the motivation and perseverance to develop their gifts and to generate work and products at an extraordinary level (Renzulli 1986). This is an example of how emotional intelligence, together with cognitive intelligence, may be more predictive of success and genius than cognitive intelligence alone.

Creativity

Creativity is the ability to create original, novel, personally or socially valued ideas or objects (Jackson & Messick 1968; Jones 1972; Mumford & Gustafson 1988). Such ideas or objects may take the form of a sculpture, a poem, a new economic strategy, or an interesting alcoholic drink. Attempts at exploring the relationship between creativity and intelligence have led to a greater understanding of the construct of creativity.

IQ tests are poor predictors of creative ability. It has been found that individuals with very similar IQs can differ considerably in their creativity (Torrance & Wu 1981). The discrepancies found between measured intelligence in the form of IQ and that evident in creativity allowed theorists to identify two different processes at work: convergent production and divergent production (Guilford 1983). **Convergent production** relates to the ability to draw from one's acquired knowledge, and to identify a practical solution to a presenting problem. Most IQ tests rely heavily on this skill. **Divergent production**, however, involves an ability to escape the confines of rational logic and find many alternative, novel or unexpected ideas as solutions to problems. The latter is characteristic of a creative thought process.

So, are intelligent people and creative people a similar or different group of individuals? Research has found that intelligence and creativity are correlated up to an IQ of 110, but above this threshold there is little or no relationship between these constructs (Bachtold & Werner 1973; Barron 1963). This means that those people who have below average or average intelligence are likely to have below average or average levels of creativity, respectively. For people of above-average intelligence, there is

Creativity:
The ability to create original, novel, personally or socially valued ideas or objects.

Convergent production:
The ability to draw from one's acquired knowledge, and to identify a practical solution to a presenting problem.

Divergent production:
The ability to escape the confines of rational logic and find many alternative, novel or unexpected ideas as solutions to problems.

no direct relationship that would allow one to predict how creative they may be. Therefore, a certain level of intelligence seems to be a necessary, but not sufficient, condition for creative work (Amabile 1983). Interestingly, creative people are often perceived to be more intelligent than less creative people who have equivalent IQ scores (Barron & Harrington 1981).

Determinants of intelligence

The nature-nurture controversy is a longstanding debate about whether intelligence is primarily determined by heredity (one's biological make-up), or the environment (one's personal experiences). In fact, both heredity and environmental influences make significant contributions to an individual's cognitive abilities.

Heredity, environment and intelligence

Evidence for the heritability of intellectual functioning has been support-ed by much research. The groundwork for such research began with Robert C. Tryon's (1942) experiments on rats. Tryon, a pioneering behaviour geneticist at the University of California, Berkeley, undertook to selectively breed rats to see if skill in maze-solving ability could be passed on to offspring. He identified those rats that were 'bright' and those that were 'dull' in running mazes, separated them into two groups, and allowed them to breed. He continued this procedure for each succeeding generation, making sure to selectively breed the 'bright' rats with one another and the 'dull' rats with one another. Tryon observed that the differences in maze-running ability between these two groups of rats were astounding. The 'dull' rats consistently made many more errors learning a maze than their 'bright' counterparts (Tryon 1942).

It was proposed by some that his findings were conclusive evidence that genetics played a dominant role in determining human intelligence. Critics, however, highlighted that research findings from animal studies cannot pertain directly to humans without qualification. In Tryon's study, rats were required to master a maze, a narrowly defined skill, which certainly cannot compare to the versatile and complex nature of human intelligence.

Because it is unethical to selectively breed humans in a laboratory, researchers needed to be creative in testing out the hypothesis that human intelligence is primarily genetically determined. Twin studies have contributed greatly to genetic heritability research. They classically involve comparing the observed phenotypic correlations of monozygotic (MZTs) and same-sexed dizygotic twins (DZTs) who have been raised together. **Phenotype** refers to the observable characteristics of people, whereas the **genotype** refers to their underlying genetic composition. When the phenotypic characteristics of MZTs are more similar than those of the DZTs, the difference is attributed to the excess genotypic similarity of the MZTs.

MZTs have exactly the same genetic make-up. DZTs, as well as other non-identical brothers and sisters, share only half their genes. Many studies have researched the correlations in IQ test scores between identical twins, fraternal twins, and other relatives and non-relatives. The results of such studies are represented in Table 9.5, below.

These results indicate that the correlations between the IQ scores of identical twins are higher than any other correlations. In fact, the correlations found for identical twins raised together is almost as high as when the same people are tested on two separate occasions (Passer & Smith 2001). The IQ scores of identical twins who grew up together are more similar than those reared apart. The reason for this is that the environment is very similar for identical twins raised together. They would have had the same parents, teachers, babysitters, friends, home life, social experiences, access to health care, and nutritional intake – environmental factors that influence intelligence.

Phenotype:
Observable characteristics of people.

Genotype:
Underlying genetic composition.

TABLE 9.5: Correlations in intelligence among people differing in genetic similarity who live together or apart

Identical twins, reared together	Identical twins, reared apart
Fraternal twins, reared together	Fraternal twins reared apart
Siblings, reared together	Siblings, reared apart
Parent-offspring, reared by parent	Parent-offspring, not reared by parent
Adopting parent-offspring	Adopted children, reared together

(DATA FROM BOUCHARD & MCGUE 1981; BOUCHARD ET AL. 1990; SCARR 1992.)

The correlation for identical twins reared apart is higher than for non-identical twins reared together, and nearly as high as that for identical twins raised together (Bouchard *et al.* 1990; Plomin 1997b). As the degree of similarity in genes decreases, so does the correlation of IQ scores. These findings are supportive of the hypothesis that genetic factors play an important role in intelligence in humans.

However, there is a pattern in the results showing higher correlations of IQ scores for identical and other types of siblings raised together than for those raised apart. This trend supports the hypothesis that environmental factors do mediate the effects of genetics on intelligence.

Longitudinal studies:
Studies taking place over a period of time.

Research close-up

A recent review of two major ongoing research projects that employ twin samples in behavioural research proposes a sceptical view on reported heritability correlations for various variables, including intelligence. (KAMIN & GOLDBERGER 2002).

The Minnesota Study of Twins Reared Apart (MISTRA)

The copious research findings that this study has produced have had popular impact worldwide through coverage in printed and television news. The studies employ monozygotic twins reared apart (MZAs) and a control group of dizygotic twins reared apart (DZAs).

The design is based on two premises. Firstly, identical twins that are separated early in life are assumed to have had uncorrelated environments, in which case any behavioural and psychological similarities in adulthood can be assumed to be indicative of their identical genotype. Secondly, the twins are assumed to represent the range of genetic and environmental variation in the general population that, the researchers propose, allows for the correlation of MZAs for any trait to be taken as an estimate of the heritability of that trait in the general population.

The Swedish Adoption/Twin Study of Ageing (SATSA)

Despite SATSA's advantages both in design and procedure, it has not received the media attention of MISTRA. This study drew its subjects from a national Twin Registry. Firstly, a mailed questionnaire was used to assess which twin respondents had been separated before the age of 11. After these respondents were recruited, a control sample of reared-together twins was drawn and matched to the separated twins for the variables of age, sex and presumed zygosity. Simply, SATSA's research attempts to estimate shared and non-shared components of environmental variance in addition to the effect of genetics on heritability.

The two broad studies are **longitudinal** in nature, meaning that the twins are assessed on multiple occasions. They are assessed on various cognitive and personality variables.

The studies both reach similar conclusions. Each finds substantial heritability for all traits assessed, with heritability higher for cognitive than for personality measures. Environmental effects on a trait, even when detected, were interpreted as being indicative of unique experiences not shared by family members.

Critique

Kamin and Goldberger (2002) draw attention to serious problems in the sample selection and design of these studies, and highlight inconsistencies in the analyses and reporting of findings by the psychologists engaged in the MISTRA and SATSA projects. Some examples of methodological and interpretative problems are described below.

MISTRA researchers have been slow to publish DZA correlations on cognitive measures, despite their emphasis on the importance of DZAs as a control group. For the Wechsler IQ test, researchers reported an MZA correlation of 0,69 for 48 pairs, suggesting a heritability of approximately 70% (Bouchard *et al*.1986). They gave no DZA figure, reportedly because of the small size of the DZA sample (30 pairs) at that time.

According to Kamin and Goldberger (2002), the first and only study to date that reports DZA correlations for cognitive measures was a study by Newman *et al*. (1998). Correlations on the Wechsler IQ scale for this study were 0,75 for 35 MZA pairs and 0,47 for 26 DZA pairs. For a measure of 'verbal reasoning', in the same study, the MZA and DZA correlations were 0,46 and 0,53 respectively. Newman (1998) used an estimator that calculated from this data that the heritability of IQ was 76% and that of verbal reasoning 65%.

Kamin and Goldberger (2002: p. 5) comment: 'It may seem surprising to see heritability of 65% reported for a measure on which the fraternal twin correlation ... is larger than the identical twin correlation'. An alternative and more logical estimator, considering the research design, would have given heritabilities of 56% for IQ and -14% (*sic*) for verbal reasoning. This highlights disagreement in the results dependent on estimators used, and shows by how much heritability indexes can vary when different estimators are utilised.

The SATSA studies employ four twin sample groups: monozygotic twins and dizygotic twins reared together (MZTs and DZTs), and monozygotic twins and dizygotic twins reared apart (MZAs and DZAs).

The major SATSA article published on general cognitive ability was based on a sample of 67 MZT, 89 DZT, 46 MZA and 100 DZA pairs, with an average age of 65,6 years, who completed a battery of 13 brief subtests of various cognitive abilities (Pedersen *et al*. 1992). Longitudinal research commenced three years later, when the same test battery was administered to many of the twins in the original sample. These results appear in Table 9.6.

TABLE 9.6: Correlations for general cognitive ability reported by SATSA

Date set	Full original sample	Longitudinal sample, first testing	Longitudinal sample, second testing
MZT	0,80	0,84	0,88
DZT	0,22	0,06	0,03
MZA	0,78	0,84	0,70
DZA	0,32	0,50	0,48

(KAMIN & GOLDBERGER 2002)

In the full sample, the correlations of twins reared together are no higher than those for twins reared apart, which suggests no effect whatever of shared environment.

The dizygotic twin correlations are considerably less than half the monozygotic correlations, which suggest non-additive genetic variance. After the longitudinal study results, SATSA's modelling ruled out non-additivity and produced heritability estimates of 82 and 80% for the two testing occasions.

Much inconsistency in SATSA's publications about whether these results suggest additive or non-additive gene action is unsatisfactorily explained in their statement 'twin analyses have little power to distinguish between the two components of genetic variance' (Pedersen et al. 1992).

Kamin and Goldberger (2002) convey that much scepticism should be employed with regard to reported heritability correlations for various cognitive and personality variables.

An interactionist perspective

Most psychologists recognise the complementary contributions made by heredity and environment in determining intellectual ability. Specifically, genetic and biological factors prescribe the upper and lower limits of intelligence. The environment either facilitates or hinders the full actualisation of an individual's intellectual ability. The more educational resources and stimulation children are exposed to, the closer they will be to their upper limits determined by their genetic potentials. For example, if a child is genetically predetermined to fall within the mild mentally retarded category, lots of attention and stimulation will help him or her to function as well as possible, but will not likely lead to him or her surpassing their upper limits of adaptive functioning.

The interactionist model is a useful way of conceptualising the resultant intellectual ability of an individual. However, it is important to note that the relative contributions of genetic and environmental factors may vary from person to person. Sometimes heredity may have a more dominant contribution than environmental factors, and vice versa. What is essential to realise, though, is that improved environmental conditions can lead to a marked improvement in intellectual functioning of most people, up to a possible 15 or 20 IQ points (Dunn & Plomin 1990; Weinberg 1989). South Africa is seeking to upgrade the environmental and educational resources available to its previously disadvantaged populations. Educational enrichment programmes for environmentally deprived children are recommended to maximise their intellectual potential.

Gender and cultural differences in intelligence

Important contextual variables of gender and culture cannot be omitted in a discussion of intelligence. Investigations into the similarities and differences in intellectual ability between groups have fuelled much debate and controversy over the years.

Gender differences in intelligence

Much research has been published that has focused on eliciting and documenting gender differences in multitudes of tasks and characteristics. In 1974, Maccoby and Jacklin published a review of psychological research on gender differences. Most of the studies they examined showed no significant differences between males and females. However, when it came to cognitive abilities, they reported that females tended to exhibit greater verbal ability and males tended to display stronger spatial and mathematical abilities. Subsequent reviews and research indicate that gender differences in mathematical and verbal ability may be virtually non-existent (Hyde & Linn 1988).

Current research indicates that, in general, men and women do not differ significantly in general intelligence as measured by scores on standardised tests (Halpern 1992; Hyde & Linn 1988). Cognitive differences between males and females appear to be restricted to specific cognitive skills (Stumpf & Stanley 1998). For instance, slight gender differences have been found for mathematical computational skills and spatial ability. While no gender differences are evident in the understanding of mathematical concepts, females perform significantly better than males in mathematical computation (Hyde *et al.* 1990). Males do perform on average slightly better than females when it comes to spatial ability (Halpern 1992, 1997). **Spatial ability** refers to skills involving mental rotation of objects in two and three dimensions; useful in solving certain architectural, engineering and geometrical problems. Mostly, gender differences are slight and in some cases appear to be diminishing over time (Skaalvik & Rankin 1994). There is also a trend of moving away from assessing between-group gender differences (i.e. differences between males and females on tasks) towards understanding within-group gender differences (i.e. why some females perform better than other females on cognitive tasks, and the same for males).

Spatial ability:
Skills involving mental rotation of objects in two and three dimensions.

Cultural differences in intelligence

Some of the most controversial debates in psychology have arisen from studies describing the existence and meaning of cultural and racial differences in intelligence. International and South African research has shown that average IQ levels of various cultural and racial groups differ significantly.

National comparisons indicate that Japanese children have the highest average IQ in the world (Hunt 1997). Within the USA, Asian-Americans test somewhat above the Caucasian norms, Hispanics score at approximately the same level as Caucasian Americans, with African-Americans scoring on average about 12 to 15 IQ points below the Caucasian American average (Humphreys 1988; Murphy & Davishofer 2001). South African authors (e.g. Biesheuwel 1943; Fourie 1967; Groenewald 1976; Swanepoel 1975) state that the situation in South Africa is similar to international findings, with average IQ scores of black samples usually being lower than those of whites.

While it is clear that measured average IQ differences exist, the question remains, 'To what do we attribute these differences?' Some authors propose that differences are real, and others deny this, claiming that the measured differences are a result of culturally biased tests, under-representation of minorities in the test development and standardisation samples, and/or are a function of differential psychosocial dynamics during test administration procedures.

Of those believing that the differences are real, some attribute the observed differences between racial and cultural groups to genetic factors (e.g. Jensen 1969, 1980, 1998), while others contend that environmental factors play a predominant role (e.g. Kamin 1976; Nisbett 1998).

The pattern of uncertainty revolves around the dynamic interplay of factors that make it difficult, if not impossible, to conclusively separate the effects of genetic variability, environmental variability and cultural-bias in measures of intelligence.

Recent research indicates how stereotype-based aspects of the self-concept can affect cognitive performance. Steele (1997) reported on two experimental studies with university students. In the first study, men and women who generally performed well in mathematics were randomly assigned to two groups. Participants in the 'stereotype-relevant' condition were told that the test of mathematic ability they were going to complete generally showed gender differences. This was expected to activate the stereotype of women being inferior to men in mathematics tasks. The group in the other condition were informed that scores on the test showed no gender differences.

In the second study, African-American and Caucasian-American students were tested on a difficult test of verbal ability. Random assignment to two groups occurred. One group was informed that the test they were about to complete was a measure of intelligence. This was expected to activate the stereotype of African-Americans as being less intelligent. The group in the other condition were informed that the items were unrelated to general intellectual ability.

Results for the first study showed no significant differences between men and women on mathematics problems when they were informed that there were no gender differences on the test (Steele 1997). When the task was made relevant to gender stereotype, the women's performance dropped and the men's performance increased, which, therefore, produced marked gender differences on the mathematics task. A similar pattern of results was found when racial stereotypes were made relevant to the task. African-American students performed more poorly than Caucasian students in the group informed that test performance was related to intellectual level, as opposed to no racial differences in performance in the other condition (Steele 1997). Steele believes that personally held and/or societal stereotypes about the intellectual abilities of women and racial minorities may function as important environmental determinants of their performance on tests of general mental ability.

There are greater differences within groups than between groups on a variety of psychological characteristics (Rowe 1999; Zuckerman 1990). The implication is that studying differences within a race, culture or gender is of greater explanatory importance than focusing on differences between groups.

Summary

Although a comprehensive definition of intelligence remains elusive, researchers continue to explore and refine the fundamental nature of this construct. The models of intelligence discussed in this chapter show that conceptualisations of intelligence have moved from more singular understandings to more multifaceted explanations. Recent developments have led to the introduction of emotional and spiritual intelligence, which also offer meaningful expansions in the theory and research on why certain people achieve and adapt better than others.

As understandings of intelligence evolve, so should the assessment tools designed to measure it. Herein lies a paradox. Many critics comment that intelligence is only what intelligence tests measure. It is essential, therefore, that such tests need to be continually researched and updated to ensure that they are reliably and validly measuring the construct of intelligence, and that they are underpinned by a comprehensive model of intelligence.

In South Africa, we are faced with a unique opportunity to research and develop culturally reduced tests of general mental ability for a diverse population from various cultural and socio-economic environments. Some of the challenges in testing that need to be overcome include the existence of 11 official South African languages, as well as there being vast differences within and between urban and rural communities in terms of their exposure to tests and testing materials.

South African researchers have an important role to play in furthering our understanding of intelligence, especially guidelines for how to assess it psychometrically. In addition to IQ, EQ and SQ, could there be a 'cultural intelligence' or CQ? Such developments could extend our understanding about what determines intelligence.

The nature-nurture debate revolves around whether intelligence is primarily determined by genetic or environmental factors. Research suggests that these two factors work additively in determining the degree of intelligence, which can range from profound mental retardation to intellectual giftedness.

Further research and critical inquiry into intelligence and its measurement will assist psychology's general goals of describing, explaining, predicting and controlling the behaviour of individuals.

Answers to IQ test items at the beginning of the chapter

30

Fruit

Chemical compounds or chemical substances

The trigger

C

A

(This is a performance task and so the answer must be demonstrated.)

Further reading

American Psychiatric Association (APA) (1994) *Diagnostic and Statistical Manual of Mental Disorders* (4th edition). Washington, DC: American Psychiatric Association.

Bachtold, L.M. & Werner, E.E. (1973) Personality characteristics of creative women. *Perceptual and Motor Skills*, 36, pp. 311–19.

Barron, F. (1963) *Creativity and Psychological Health*. Princeton: Van Nostrand.

Barron, F. & Harrington, D.M. (1981) Creativity, intelligence, and personality. *Annual Review of Psychology*, 32, pp. 439–76.

Beirne-Smith, M., Patton, J. & Ittenbach, R. (1994) *Mental Retardation* (4th edition). New York: MacMillan.

Biesheuwel, S. (1943) *African Intelligence*. Johannesburg: South African Institute for Race Relations.

Blum, J.M. (1979) *Pseudoscience and Mental Ability: The Origins and Fallacies of the IQ Controversy.* New York: Monthly Review Press.

Bouchard, T.J., & McGue, M. (1981) Familial studies of intelligence: A review. *Science*, 212, pp. 1055–9.

Bouchard, T.J. Lykken, D.T., McGue, M., Segal, N.L. & Tellegen, A. (1990) Sources of human psychological differences: The Minnesota study of twins reared apart. *Science*, 250, pp. 223–8.

Boxer, M. & Hastings, R. (2001) Fragile X syndrome. *Inside the Human Body*, 27, p. 4.

Brooks, D. (2001) Down's syndrome. *Inside the Human Body*, 99, p. 51.

Claasen, N.C.W. (1997) Cultural differences, politics and test bias in South Africa. *European Review of Applied Psychology*, 47(4) pp. 297–307.

Conroy, J.W. (1996) The small ICF/MR program: Dimensions of quality and cost. *Mental Retardation*, 34, pp. 13–26.

Cooper, J. (1998) Unlearning cognitive dissonance: Toward an understanding of the development of dissonance. *Journal of Experimental Social Psychology*, 34, pp. 562–75.

Descartes, R. (1960) *Discourse on Method.* Translated by Arthur Wollaston. London: Whitefriars Press.

Dunn, J. & Plomin, R. (1990) *Separate Lives: Why Siblings are so Different.* New York: Basic Books.

Edelson, S.M. (1995) Autistic savant. Centre for the Study of Autism. www.autism.org.

Eysenck, H.J., Arnold, W.J. & Meili, R. (1975) *Encyclopedia of Psychology.* London: Fontana/Collins.

Feldman, B. (1969) Prediction of first-grade reading achievement from selected structure-of-intellect tests. Unpublished doctoral dissertation, University of California.

Feldman, R.S. (1993) *Understanding Psychology* (3rd edition). New York: McGraw-Hill.

Ford-Martin, P. (1995) Emotional intelligence. *Gale Encyclopedia of Psychology.* www.findarticles.com.

Fourie, A.B. (1967) Ondersoek na die implikasies van gestandaardiseerde toetse vir st. VI-Bantoeleerlinge. Unpublished dissertation, University of Pretoria.

Foxcroft, C.D., & Roodt, G. (2001) Psychological assessment: A brief retrospective overview. In C.D. Foxcroft & G. Roodt (eds), *An Introduction to Psychological Assessment in the South African Context.* Cape Town: Oxford University Press.

Gardner, H. (1983) *Frames of Mind: The Theory of Multiple Intelligences.* New York: Basic Books.

Gardner, H. (1993) *Multiple Intelligences: The Theory in Practice.* New York: Basic Books.

Gardner, H. (1999) *Intelligence Reframed: Multiple Intelligences for the 21st Century.* New York: Basic Books.

Gaylord-Ross, R. (1990) *Issues and Research in Special Education.* New York: Teachers College Press.

Gibbs, N. (1995) The EQ factor. *Time Magazine,* 146, 14, pp. 60–9.

Goleman, D. (1995) *Emotional Intelligence.* New York: Bantam Books.

Groenewald, F.P. (1976) *Aspekte in die Tradisionele Kultuurwêreld van die Bantoekind wat die Verwerkliking van sy Intelligensie Strem: 'N Kultureel-opvoedkundige Oriënteringstudie.* Pretoria: HSRC.

Guilford, J.P. (1967) *The Nature of Human Intelligence.* New York: McGraw-Hill.

Guilford, J.P. (1983) Transformation abilities or functions. *Journal of Creative Behavior,* 17, pp. 75–83.

Guilford, J.P. (1988a) Fluid and crystallized intelligences: Two fanciful concepts. *Psychological Bulletin,* 88, pp. 406–12.

Guilford, J.P. (1988b) Some changes in the Structure-of-Intellect model. *Educational and Psychological Measurement,* 48, pp. 1–4.

Guilford, J.P. & Hoepfner, R. (1971) *The Analysis of Human Intelligence.* New York: McGraw-Hill.

Hallahan, D., Kauffman, J. & Lloyd, J. (1985) *Introduction to Learning Disabilities* (2nd edition). Englewood Cliffs: Prentice-Hall.

Halpern, D.F. (1992) *Sex Differences in Cognitive Abilities* (2nd edition). Hillsdale: Erlbaum.

Halpern, D.F. (1997) Sex differences in intelligence: Implications for education. *American Psychologist,* 52, pp. 1091–102.

Hastings, R. (2001) Down's syndrome. *Inside the Human Body,* 36, p. 5.

Horn, J.L. (1973) Theory of functions represented among auditory and visual test performances. In J.R. Royce (ed.), *Multivariate Analysis and Psychological Theory.* London: Academic Press.

Humphreys, L.G. (1988) Trends in levels of academic achievement of blacks and other minorities. *Intelligence,* 12, pp. 231–60.

Hunt, E. (1997) The status of the concept of intelligence. *Japanese Psychological Research,* 39, pp. 1–11.

Hyde, J.S. & Linn, M.C. (1988) Gender differences in verbal ability: A meta-analysis. *Psychological Bulletin*, 104, pp. 53–69.

Hyde, J.S., Fennema, E. & Lamon, S.J. (1990) Gender differences in mathematics performance: A meta-analysis. *Psychological Bulletin*, 107, pp. 139–55.

Jackson, P.W. & Messick, D. (1968) Creativity. In P. London & D. Rosenhan (eds), *Foundations of Abnormal Psychology*. New York: Holt.

Jensen, A.R. (1969) How much can we boost IQ and scholastic achievement? *Harvard Educational Review*, 39, pp. 1–123.

Jensen, A.R. (1980) *Bias in Mental Testing*. New York: Free Press.

Jensen, A.R. (1998) The g factor and the design of education. In R.J. Sternberg & W.M. Williams (eds), *Intelligence, Instruction, and Assessment: Theory into Practice*. Mahwah: Erlbaum.

Jones, T.P. (1972) *Creative Learning in Perspective*. London: University of London Press.

Joseph, J. (1998) The equal environment assumption of the classical twin method: A critical analysis. *Journal of Mind Behavior*, 19, 325–58.

Kamin, L.J. (1976) Heredity, intelligence, politics and psychology. In N. Block & G. Dwarkin (eds), *The IQ Controversy*. London: Quartet Books.

Kamin, L.J. & Goldberger, A.S. (2002) Twin studies in behavioural research: A skeptical view. *Theoretical Population Biology*, 1555, 1–13. http://www.idealibrary.com http://www.idealibrary.com.

Kamstra, O.W.M. (1971) *De Dimensionaliteit van het Geheugen: Ein Faktoranalytisch Onderzook*. Amsterdam: Drukherin van Soet.

Kaplan, H.I. & Sadock, B.J. (1998) *Synopsis of Psychiatry: Behavioral Sciences/Clinical Psychiatry* (8th edition). Baltimore: Williams & Wilkins.

Kendler, K.S., Thornton, L.M. & Pedersen, N.L. (2000) Tobacco consumption in Swedish twins reared apart and reared together. *Archive of General Psychiatry*, 57, pp. 886–92.

Landesman, S. & Butterfield, E.C. (1987) Normalization and deinstitution of mentally retarded individuals: Controversy and facts. *American Psychologist*, 42, pp. 809–16.

Lemmer, E.M. (1998) The teacher and the learner. In F. Pretorius & E.M. Lemmer (eds), *South African Education and Training: Transition in a Democratic Era*. Johannesburg: Hodder & Stoughton.

Maisto, A.A. & Hughes, E. (1995) Adaptation to group home living for adults with mental retardation as a function of previous residential placement. *Journal of Intellectual Disability Research,* 39, pp. 15–18.

McInerney, D.M. & McInerney, V. (1998) *Educational Psychology: Constructed Learning* (2nd edition). Sydney: Prentice-Hall.

Morgan, C.T., King, P.A. & Robinson, N.M. (1984) *Introduction to Psychology.* New York: McGraw-Hill.

Mumford, M.D. & Gustafson, S.B. (1988) Creativity syndrome: Integration, application, and innovation. *Psychological Bulletin,* 103, pp. 27–43.

Murphy, K.R. & Davishofer, C.O. (2001) *Psychological Testing: Principles and Applications* (5th edition). Upper Saddle River: Prentice-Hall.

Newman, D.L., Tellegen, A. & Bouchard, T.J. (1998) Individual differences in adult ego development: Sources of influence in twins reared apart. *Journal of Personality and Social Psychology,* 74, pp. 985–95.

Nisbett, R.E. (1998) Race, genetics, and IQ. In C. Jencks & M. Phillips *et al.* (eds), *The Black-White Test Score Gap.* Washington, DC: Brookings Institute.

O'Neil, J. (1996) On emotional intelligence: A conversation with Daniel Goleman. *Educational Leadership* 54(1) pp. 6–11.

Passer, M.W. & Smith, R.E. (2001) *Psychology: Frontiers and Applications.* Boston: McGraw-Hill.

Pedersen, N.L., Plomin, R., Nesselroade, J.T. & McClearn, G.E. (1992) A quantitative genetic analysis of cognitive abilities during the second half of the life span. *Psychological Science,* 3, pp. 346–53.

Plomin, R. (1997a) *Behavioral Genetics.* New York: St Martins Press.

Plomin, R. (1997b) Identifying genes for cognitive abilities and disabilities. in R.J. Sternberg & E. Grigorenko (eds), *Intelligence: Heredity and Environment.* New York: Cambridge University Press.

Professional Board for Psychology (n.d.) *Ethical Code of Professional Conduct.* Pretoria: Health Professions Council of South Africa.

Republic of South Africa (1996) Choice of Termination of Pregnancy Act: Act 92 of 1996: Pretoria: Government Printers.

Renzulli, J.S. (1986) The three-ring conception of intelligence: A developmental model for creative productivity. In R.J. Sternberg & J.E. Davidson (eds), *Conceptions of Giftedness.* Cambridge: Cambridge University Press.

Rowe, D.C. (1999) Heredity. In V.J. Derlega, B.A. Winstead & W.H. Jones (eds), *Personality: Contemporary Theory and Research.* Chicago: Nelson-Hall.

Scarr, S. (1992) Developmental theories for the 1990s: Development and individual differences. *Child Development*, 63, pp. 1–19.

Sears, R.R. (1977) Sources of life satisfaction of the Terman gifted men. *American Psychologist*, 32, pp. 119–28.

Shaffer, D.R. (1989) *Developmental Psychology: Childhood and Adolescence* (2nd edition). Pacific Grove: Brooks/Cole.

Skaalvik, E.M. & Rankin, R.J. (1994) Gender differences in mathematics and verbal achievement, self-perception and motivation. *British Journal of Education Psychology*, 64, pp. 419–28.

Spearman, C. (1904) 'General intelligence' objectively determined and measured. *American Journal of Psychology*, 25, pp. 210–12.

Spearman, C. (1923) *The Nature of 'Intelligence' and Principles of Cognition*. London: Macmillan.

Spearman, C. (1927) *The Abilities of Man*. New York: Macmillan.

Stancliffe, R.J. (1997) Community residence size, staff presence and choice. *Mental Retardation*, 35, pp. 1–9.

Steele, C.M. (1997) A threat in the air: How stereotypes shape intellectual identity and performance. *American Psychologist*, 52, pp. 613–29.

Sternberg, R.J. (1985) Implicit theories of intelligence, creativity, wisdom. *Journal of Personality and Social Psychology*, 49, pp. 607–27.

Sternberg, R.J. (1986) *Intelligence Applied*. Orlando: Harcourt Brace Jovanovich.

Sternberg, R.J. (1988) *The Triarchic Mind: A New Theory of Human Intelligence*. New York: Viking Press.

Sternberg, R.J. (1991) Theory-based testing of intellectual abilities: Rationale for the triarchic abilities test. In H.A.H. Rowe (ed.), *Intelligence: Reconceptualization and Measurement*. Hillsdale: Erlbaum.

Sternberg, R.J. (1998) *Successful Intelligence: How Practical and Creative Intelligence Determine Success in Life*. New York: Plume.

Stumpf, H. & Stanley, J.C. (1998) Stability and change in gender-related differences on the college board advanced placement and achievement tests. *Current Directions in Psychological Research*, 7, pp. 192–6.

Swanepoel, H.F. (1975) 'n Psigometriese ondersoek na die geldigheid en gebruik van die voorligtingstoets vir junior sekondêre Bantoeleerlinge in Vorm III. Unpublished dissertation, PU for CHE.

Thurstone, L.L. (1938) *Primary Mental Abilities*. Chicago: University of Chicago Press.

Torrance, E.P. & Wu, T. (1981) A comparative longitudinal study of the adult creative achievements of elementary school children identified as high intelligent and as highly creative. *Creative Child and Adult Quarterly*, 6, pp. 71–6.

Tryon, R.C. (1942) Individual differences. In F.A. Moss (ed.), *Comparative Psychology*. New York: Prentice-Hall.

Walters, J.M. & Gardner, H. (1986) The theory of multiple intelligences: Some issues and answers. In R.J. Sternberg & R.K. Wagner (Eds.), *Practical Intelligence*. Cambridge: Cambridge University Press.

Weinberg, R.A. (1989) Intelligence and IQ: Landmark issues and great debates. *American Psychologist*, 44, pp. 98–104.

Woolfolk, A. (1990) *Educational Psychology* (4th edition). New York: Prentice-Hall.

Zohar, D. & Marshall, I. (2000) *Spiritual Intelligence: The Ultimate Intelligence*. London: Bloomsbury.

Zuckerman, M. (1990) Some dubious premises in research and theory on racial differences. *American Psychologist*, 45, pp. 1297–303.

10 Biological Bases of Behaviour

J. Singh

Objectives

After studying this chapter you should:

- be able to describe the cells that make up the nervous system
- be able to distinguish between neurons and glia cells
- be able to explain resting potential and describe the events leading to an action potential
- be able to list the various types of neurotransmitters and their effects on behaviour
- be able to describe the endocrine glands and the effects of the hormones they release
- be able to describe the divisions of the nervous system
- be able to describe the structure and function of the spinal cord and the components of the hindbrain, mibrain and forebrain
- be able to distinguish between the sympathetic nervous system and the parasympathetic nervous system activities
- be able to describe the lobes of the cerebral cortex and the effects of damage
- be able to explain cerebral laterisation and specialisation of the hemispheres
- be able to describe the methods used to investigate the brain.

Introduction

According to James Watson, one of the discoverers of the double helix model of DNA, the brain is the last and greatest biological frontier, and the most complex and remarkable structure we have ever discovered in the universe (Halonen & Santrock 1996). The co-discoverer, Francis Crick (1994), asserts, 'you, your joys and your sorrows, your memories and your ambition, your sense of personal identity and free will are, in fact, no more than the behaviour of a vast assembly of nerve cells and their associated molecules'. One might disagree with Crick by saying that we cannot reduce mental activities to the physical activities of the brain. But, because of the importance of the nervous system in controlling behaviour and because human beings, at their most basic level, are biological entities, psychologists and researchers from other fields – called neuroscientists – have paid special attention to the biological underpinnings of behaviour (Cacioppo & Tassinary in Feldman 1993). Biopyschologists, sometimes called physiological psychologists, are psychologists who study the ways biological structures and body functions affect behaviour (Feldman 1993).

Behaviour depends on complex information processing in the nervous system. The nervous system is the interacting network of nerve cells that underlies all psychological activity (Westen 1999). Our thoughts, feelings and behaviours reflect the interactions of millions of nerve cells. The ability to smile, which most of us view as a simple action, is actually quite a complex process. In the case of Thando (see below), she was unable to smile, but after doctors implanted nerves, arteries and muscles in her cheeks, she could smile for the first time. All our movements, such as smiling, talking, running and dancing, are controlled by the nervous system. The movement of your eyes while you

Moebius syndrome

'Your daughter has a smile just like yours', a smiling Thabile Manyathi was told, minutes before she was reunited with her daughter, Thando, eight, after an operation to enable the child to express facial emotion for the first time.

The mother smiled and tears ran down her cheeks as a team of doctors and nurses brought her sleeping daughter to her after the marathon $11^1/_2$-hour operation. Thando was born with moebius syndrome, a rare genetic disorder characterised by facial paralysis that had left her unable to frown or smile. The disease strikes one in every million people. 'As a mother, I never knew whether she was happy or sad', said Thabile. Thabile, from the East Rand in Gauteng, had approached former president Nelson Mandela, who had then promised to do his best for her. Marc Lubner, who had been asked by Mandela to see the promise fulfilled, worked on the project for seven months to ensure that the funds and medical resources were brought together. The Manyathi family's dream came true when a team of doctors – headed by Canadian plastic surgeon Ronald Zucker, the world leader in such procedures – met at a Johannesburg hospital. The team also included South African specialist George Psaras and American paediatrician Craig van der Kolk. The operation involved taking a section of muscles, nerves and arteries from Thando's thigh and implanting them into her cheeks, where, after two months of healing, they are expected to begin working of their own accord. Zucker explained, 'The muscle will take about eight weeks to begin working. The nerves will grow into the muscle and stimulate it to contract.' He had stimulated the newly transplanted tissue electronically shortly before the operation had ended, enabling those in theatre to see Thando's first smile.

(FERIS 2000; GILFORD 2000)

read this paragraph and the movement of your fingers when you turn the page both depend on the complex interactions of thousands of neurons. Movement is not the only function in which the nervous system plays a role: your emotions, thoughts and all your sensory experiences and behaviour depend on the firing of billions of nerve cells.

In this chapter, we will explore the workings of the nervous system. We start by looking at the cells that make up the system; we then take a closer look at the neurons and how they fire in order to communicate with one another. Events that occur at this point of communication (the synapse) will be examined, followed by a discussion of the chemicals (neurotransmitters and hormones) that affect our behaviour. Thereafter we investigate the broad divisions of the nervous system, focusing on the structure and functions of significant areas. A brief description of the specialisation of the hemispheres follows and, finally, we look at the techniques employed in studying the brain.

Cells of the nervous system

Within the brain there are two types of cells: glial cells and neurons. The neurons are the elite class, the 'kings and queens' of the brain, and they are responsible for various functions, such as thinking, feeling, hearing, seeing, moving, loving and hating. The glial cells are the 'attendant' class, but their role is so important to the survival of the neurons that they are the unsung heroes of the brain. It is the role of the glial cells to meet the needs of the neurons, creating an ideal environment for neurons to live, grow and work comfortably (Drubach 2000).

Glial cells

These cells are more abundant than neurons, and an estimate of the number of glial cells would be 900 billion (Plotnik 1999). Glial means 'glue' and this word describes one of the functions glial cells serve: they hold the neurons in place (Loftus & Wortman 1992). In addition to providing support to the neurons, they regulate the environment in which the neuron lives and get rid of dead cells (debris). Another very significant role of glial cells is that they wrap themselves around neurons to form myelin, thereby preventing short-circuiting of the neurons (Drubach 2000; Kalat 2001). Glial cells grow throughout one's lifetime (Plotnik 1999).

Neurons

The basic element of the nervous system is the nerve cell or neuron. These cells receive, integrate and transmit information. Neurons communicate with one another electrochemically. The communication of messages between neurons brings about the activities we know as human behaviour. These activities include ones that we can easily observe, such as talking, eating and swimming, and experiences that are not so clearly observable, such as remembering a past event or feeling sad. More than 100 billion nerve cells are generated in the nine months before a baby is born – an average of a quarter of a million every minute (Loftus & Wortman 1992). Neurons are the oldest and longest cells in the body. An example of a neuron with a long axon would be one that runs from your foot to your spine, measuring about one metre. You have many of the same neurons for your whole life. Although other cells die and are replaced, many neurons are never replaced when they die. In fact, you have fewer neurons when you are old compared to when you are young. Recent studies have, however, reported that in at least one area of the brain, the hippocampus, new neurons can grow in adult humans.

The structure of a neuron

Although neurons occur in various shapes and sizes, most of them typically comprise four parts: dendrites, cell body (soma), axon and terminal buttons.

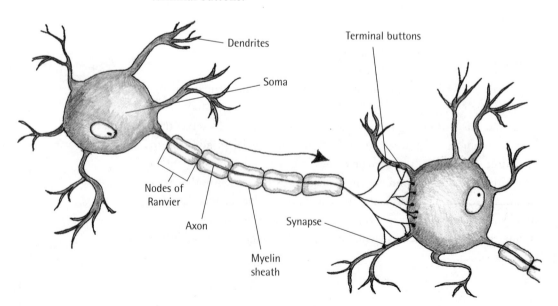

Dendrites

Soma

Terminal buttons

Nodes of Ranvier

Axon

Synapse

Myelin sheath

FIGURE 10.1: The Structure of a neuron

Dendrites

'Dendrite' is the Greek word for 'tree'. The dendrites of a neuron are similar to trees, since they have branch-like extensions from the cell body. They are specialised to receive information (in the form of impulses) from other neurons.

Cell body (soma)

This part contains the nucleus that carries genetic information. It also contains other structures, such as ribosomes, which are involved in protein synthesis, and mitochondria, which provide energy to the cell.

Axon

The term 'axon' refers to the slender fibre that conveys information from the cell body towards the neurons of a muscle or gland. Most vertebrate axons are covered by a myelin sheath, which is a fatty substance called lipid. It acts as insulating material and speeds up the rate of conduction of the electric impulse. If an axon's myelin sheath deteriorates, its signals may not be transmitted effectively. Multiple sclerosis is a condition characterised by loss of muscle control and is due to myelin sheath degeneration (Weiten 2001). In the diagram of the structure of the neuron, you can see that some areas of the axon are exposed and not myelinated. These naked portions we call the Nodes of Ranvier. They make the axon look like a string of sausages.

Terminal buttons

These swellings, which look like bulbs, are located at the end of the axon. The terminal buttons contain packages called synaptic vesicles. These packages contain chemicals called neurotransmitters that facilitate the transmission of information to other cells.

Types of neurons

Three types of neurons have been identified: sensory neurons, motor neurons and interneurons.

- **Sensory neurons** are also known as afferent neurons. These neurons convey information from sensory cells or receptors (of tissue and organs of the body) to the brain, either directly or via the spinal cord (Vander *et al.* 1998; Westen 1999).

- **Motor neurons** are also referred to as efferent neurons. These neurons transmit information from the brain to the effector organs, which are the muscles and glands.
- **Interneurons** connect neurons to each other in the central nervous system (the brain and spinal cord).

The neural impulse

Neurons send information down the axon as brief impulses, or waves, of electricity. Telegraph operators send a series of single clicks down a telegraph wire to the next station. Neurons work in a similar fashion. To send messages to other neurons, they send a series of single electrical clicks down their axons. By changing the timing and rate of the clicks, the neuron can vary the nature of the message it sends. As you reach to turn this page, hundreds of clicks will stream down the axons in your arm to tell your muscles just when to flex and how vigorously (Halonen & Santrock 1996).

The resting potential

This refers to the state when the neuron is not firing – in other words, when it has not been stimulated. When a neuron is at rest, it is polarised, which means that it has a negative side and a positive side. It can be compared to a battery, which has a positive pole and a negative pole.

How does the neuron achieve this state? The axon is similar to a tube filled with fluid and is surrounded by fluid. Its membrane is selectively permeable. This means that it allows only certain substances to enter. This is possible because it has chemical gates that open and close, allowing only certain electrically charged particles to enter. The particles that carry electrical charges are referred to as ions. They are found both inside and outside the cell. Ions are chemical and carry either a positive charge, such as sodium ($Na+$) and potassium ($K+$), or a negative charge, such as chloride ($Cl-$).

The outer membrane of the axon selectively regulates the flow of these ions into and out of the neuron. The larger ions, such as the organic negative ions, are trapped inside the neuron, while the smaller ions ($Cl-$, $K+$ and $Na+$) pass through the membrane. When the membrane is at rest, which is when it is not stimulated, K ions move outward more easily than Na ions can move inwards. This creates a state where the inside of the axon is more negatively charged relative to the outside. We say that the cell membrane is polarized, since the inside surface is more negatively charged and the outside surface is more positively charged. This electrical imbalance is called the resting potential. The resting potential is measured in volts (V), because there is a difference in voltage (potential) between the inside and the outside. The actual potential differs from one neuron to another, but a typical level is −70 millivolts (mV). Another factor that contributes to maintaining this resting potential is the sodium potassium pump. In sum, resting potential describes the stable, negative charge of an inactive neuron.

Action potentials

The resting potential is not permanent. If the neuron is stimulated, the potential changes. One of two things can happen:

- **Depolarisation**: This is a decrease in negativity, which means that the inside of the neuron gets less negative and the voltage starts moving towards zero. For example, if the resting potential is −70 mV, and positive ions enter the cell, the voltage would start to get less negative and might move to −60 mV, or to −50 mV, in a positive direction.
- **Hyper polarisation**: This is an increase in negativity, which means that the inside of the neuron would become more negative and the voltage would change from −70 mV to −80 mV, and so on.

When a neuron is stimulated, a few of its Na gates open, which allows Na ions to start entering the cell. As more Na starts to flow in, the potential across the membrane starts to decrease. This means that the inside of the cell is becoming more positive (we can see that depolarisation is taking place because Na carries positive charge into the cell). When it reaches a certain voltage, called the threshold, Na gates suddenly open and there is a massive influx of Na. For a very brief period, the inside of the cell is now positive (reversed polarity). The K ions, which carry positive charge, then move out of the cell to restore the resting potential (making the inside of the cell negative again). The excess Na that is inside the cell is pumped out by the sodium potassium (Na-K pump), which pushes in two K ions and pushes out three Na ions. This exchange mechanism, which keeps Na out and K in, together with the selective permeability of the membrane, helps maintain the resting potential of the neuron.

The all-or-nothing law

According to this principle, an axon either produces an action potential or it does not. This means that a neuron will react fully to a stimulus or it will not react at all. For an action potential to occur, the threshold must be reached. If the stimulus does not reach the threshold, the neuron will not fire, but if the stimulus reaches or exceeds the threshold, an action potential will occur. The all-or-nothing law can be illustrated using the metaphor of firing a gun. If you press the trigger below a certain point, the gun will not fire. If, however, you press hard enough on the trigger, there will be a point at which the gun will fire. Pressing the trigger harder (past the point of the threshold) does not make the bullet go any faster or further. Similarly, an action potential will travel along the axon of the neuron at a constant strength, showing that the strength of the stimulus that started the impulse does not affect the strength of the impulse.

Refractory period

Immediately after firing, the neuron's membrane enters a state where it cannot fire. This period of one to a few milliseconds is called the absolute refractory period, where the neuron cannot be stimulated again no matter how strong the stimulus. The neuron in this stage can be compared to a runner who has just completed a 400 m sprint and needs a brief moment to restore his or her resources (Smith 1998).

After this period, the membrane enters a state called a relative refractory period, where the neuron will be stimulated to fire if the stimulus is very strong.

The synapse

The gap between the pre-synaptic and post-synaptic neuron is called the synaptic cleft. The neuron that sends the impulse and is before the synapse is called the pre-synaptic neuron, while the neuron that receives the impulse is called the post-synaptic neuron. We know that neurons do not physically touch one another, but instead release chemicals to facilitate the communication of a message. When the action potential reaches the terminal buttons (of the pre-synaptic neuron), this results in the opening of calcium channels. Thereafter, the synaptic vesicles move to the edge of the terminal buttons and release their neurotransmitters.

The neurotransmitters then diffuse across the synaptic cleft and attach on to receptor sites of the post-synaptic membrane. This could result in a depolarisation or hyper-polarisation of the post-synaptic cell. Depolarisation is needed to excite the neuron and an action potential will occur if the threshold is reached. If the neurotransmitter hyper-polarises the post-synaptic neuron, this causes inhibition.

An impulse from a single neuron causes activation in the synapses it forms with others. Even the simplest mental or physical process involves hundreds of neurons receiving and transmitting impulses in complex cascading waves of communication and cooperation. Everything we do and experience, therefore, involves this intricate bioelectrical process (Buzan & Dixon n.d.)

Neurotransmitters and behaviour

A transmitter is a chemical messenger that transmits information between nerves and the body organs such as the muscles and heart. You may have experienced a pounding heart when you were scared, angry or stressed. The reason for this has to do with transmitters. Transmitters play a role in everything you do, such as thinking, feeling, making decisions and getting angry (Plotnik 1999).

Neurotransmitters are chemicals that are made by neurons and then used for communication between neurons during the performance of mental or physical activities. You might wonder how the neurons make these neurotransmitters. Well, neurons get the raw materials for manufacturing neurotransmitters from the foods we eat. An example is the neurotransmitter acetylcholine, which can be produced from foods such as cauliflower, milk, soybeans, liver and peanuts (Drubach 2000).

The cell body of the neuron is the site of production of smaller neurotransmitters. From there, the neurotransmitters are transported to the terminal buttons. Larger neurotransmitters are produced in the terminal buttons themselves, including acetylcholine.

When an action potential travels down the axon and finally hits the terminal buttons, a small explosion occurs that results in the neurotransmitters being rocketed out of the vesicles and into the synaptic gap. The parts of the neuron that receives information are the dendrites. Thus, on the dendrites of the post-synaptic membrane, we find receptor sites for neurotransmitters. These, in turn, attach to the receptors of the post-synaptic neuron. This system works like a lock and key mechanism, which means that a specific neurotransmitter will only fit into a specific receptor. This attachment of the neurotransmitter to the receptor results in the opening of the lock, i.e. the exciting of the post-synaptic neuron (depolarisation), or it could close the lock, inhibiting the post-synaptic neuron (hyperpolarisation).

Early researchers believed that each neuron released a single neurotransmitter. Later studies indicated that one neuron might release two, three or more neurotransmitters (Hâkfelt, Johansson & Goldstein in Kalat 2001). A neurotransmitter can activate many receptors and different receptors will produce different effects from the same neuro-transmitter. The same neurotransmitter can excite or inhibit different neurons, depending on which part of the brain it is produced in (Westen 1999). An excess or deficiency of neurotransmitters can lead to brain and behaviour disorders. We will now look at some of these neurotransmitters and how they are related to our behaviour.

Endorphins

These neurotransmitters elevate mood and reduce pain. They are the body's natural painkillers, as they work by blocking the transmission of pain. One example of its effects on mood can be seen in the 'runners' high' that athletes experience after a long period of exercise (Hoffman in Westen 1999). Endorphins are most often released after injury or physical stress.

Dopamine

Pathways that use dopamine are involved in the experience of pleasure and in the learning of behaviours associated with reward. Dopamine is also needed for voluntary movement, attention and decision making, and other cognitive processes. One disorder associated with dopamine is Parkinson's disease, which is characterised by uncontrollable tremors, rigidity, difficulty initiating movement and speech, and other severe problems (Van de Graaff & Fox 1995). Medical research indicates that the neurons of the substantia nigra, an area connected to the basal ganglia, release dopamine. In patients with Parkinson's, there is degeneration of these dopamine-secreting neurons of the substantia nigra. Since the basal ganglia play a role in movement, a dopamine shortage will affect movement. Abnormalities in the activity at dopamine synapses have been implicated in the development of schizophrenia. Studies suggest that overactivity at dopamine synapses is the neuro-chemical basis for schizophrenia (Weiten 2001).

Serotonin

Serotonin regulates mood, eating, sleeping, pain and arousal. Low serotonin levels have been associated with severe depression, trouble eat-ing and sleeping, anti-social behaviour in adults and delinquency in children. Low serotonin levels have also been associated with increased aggression. Serotonin is mostly an inhibitory neurotransmitter. It is derived from a substance called tryptophan, which is found in warm milk. This is why it makes sense to have a glass of warm milk if you are having trouble sleeping.

Acetylcholine

This neurotransmitter facilitates muscle contraction and plays a role in memory and learning. A deficiency of acetylcholine has been implicated in Alzheimer's disease, which is characterised by memory problems. In experiments with rats, tissue rich in acetylcholine was transplanted into the brains of rats with learning impairments. The results showed that there was significant improvement in learning. Whether the same applies to humans has not yet been proven (Bjorkland & Gage in Westen 1999).

Norepinephrine

This chemical plays a role in regulating mood, especially in controlling anxiety and stress. Both norepinephrine and epinephrine are involved in emotional arousal, particularly fear and anxiety.

Glutamate

Glutamate is widespread and can excite almost one-third of all neurons in the nervous system (Van de Graaff & Fox 1995). Thus, it is an excitatory neurotransmitter and is involved in learning.

GABA

Like glutamate, GABA affects several neurons. However, unlike glutamate, GABA is an inhibitory neurotransmitter. GABA regulates anxiety and plays a role in motor control by inhibiting the activity of the spinal motor neurons. Low GABA levels have been associated with depression and mania.

The endocrine system: Hormones and behaviour

The endocrine system is made up of a set of glands that manufacture and secrete hormones directly into the bloodstream. Hormones are chemicals that affect physiological and emotional functioning. They are similar to neurotransmitters in that they affect the nervous system (Kalat 1999). Hormones affect organs, muscles and other glands of the body. Whereas the action of neurotransmitters is short and quick, hormonal effects are longer lasting, ranging from minutes to months. Hormones act over wider areas; their effects are more diffuse than those of neuro-transmitters. The functioning of the endocrine system is intimately connected with that of the autonomic nervous system (Smith 1998).

The pituitary gland

The hypothalamus controls most of the endocrine system by regulating the pituitary gland. A stalk links the hypothalamus and the pituitary gland. The pituitary gland is often called the chief (master) gland of the endocrine system. It is divided into anterior and posterior portions. The posterior pituitary, at the back, is responsible for regulating water and salt balance. The anterior part regulates growth by secreting growth hormone. It also manufactures hormones that control the adrenal cortex, pancreas, thyroid gland and the gonads.

Problems with the pituitary gland will create problems in the glands that it controls. For example, if there is too little growth hormone, the result would be dwarfism, whereas excess causes gigantism.

The pancreas

The pancreas regulates blood sugar levels by secreting insulin. Insulin deficiency results in diabetes, while an excess of insulin results in hypoglycaemia (low blood sugar).

The thyroid gland

This gland, which is found in the neck, controls metabolism by secreting the hormone thyroxin. Iodine is used to produce thyroxin. Too little thyroxin results in the enlargement of the thyroid gland, a condition called goitre. Hypothyroidism (too little thyroxin) results in cretinism in children (dwarf-like appearance) and adults experience fatigue, an increase in body mass, a decrease in metabolism and a decrease in body temperature. Hypothyroidism also leads to psychological impairments and reduced motivation. Over-secretion of thyroxin (hyperthyroidism) results in higher metabolism, weight loss, increased heart rate and enlargement of the thyroid gland (Van de Graaff & Fox 1995; Louw & Edwards 1997).

The adrenal glands

The cortex of the adrenal gland releases hormones that regulate salt and sugar balances, and helps the body resist stress. These hormones are also responsible for the growth of pubic hair. The adrenal medulla releases two hormones: adrenalin (epinephrine) and noradrenalin (norepinephrine), which arouse the body so that it can handle stress. A deficiency of cortical hormones will result in the body being unable to cope with stress.

The gonads

The gonads produce hormones that affect bodily development and maintain reproductive organs in adults. Dysfunction occurs when there is a lack of sex hormones during puberty, which results in problems in the development of secondary sexual characteristics (facial and body hair, muscles in males and breasts in females).

Divisions of the nervous system

The nervous system can be divided into two broad sectors: the central nervous system (CNS) and the peripheral nervous system (PNS). The brain and spinal cord together make up the central nervous system. The peripheral nervous system is made up of all the other parts (neural structures) of the nervous system, excluding the brain and spinal cord. The central nervous system communicates with the rest of the body through the PNS. Thus, the PNS is directly involved in the functioning of both the muscles and the internal organs (Smith 1998).

The PNS can be divided into two further systems: the somatic nervous system and the autonomic nervous system.

The somatic nervous system

This component of the PNS is responsible for the control of voluntary movements and the communication of information to and from the sense organs. The somatic nervous system has nerves that communicate with the skin and muscles. If you want to turn the page of a book, this voluntary action involves the somatic nervous system.

The autonomic nervous system

'Autonomic' means 'involuntary' or 'automatic'. The autonomic nervous system (ANS) is made up of the peripheral nerves responsible for controlling involuntary movements of internal organs, such as those that control the heart, the lungs, the stomach, the kidneys and the rest of the organs that keep us alive. The ANS carries information both ways, from the organs to the brain and from the brain to the organs. The ANS has two divisions: the sympathetic nervous system and the parasympathetic nervous system.

The sympathetic nervous system comes into play in emergencies. This response is commonly called the 'fight-or-flight' response. When one is faced with a threatening situation, the sympathetic nervous system activation prepares the body to fight or to flee from danger. The basic purpose of the stress response is to enable us to cope swiftly and effectively with life-threatening challenges. Whether you have to run away or stand and fight, your body needs extra energy – and fast. It is the brain and your muscles that need this energy most (Martin 1997).

Why does your heart start pounding so rapidly? The activation of the sympathetic nervous system leads to the release of adrenalin, which increases your pulse, your blood pressure and your breathing. Also, more glucose is made available to provide energy to the brain and muscles. Other effects of the stress response are the dilation (widening) of the air passages for extra air. The blood vessels that supply the muscles expand. The palms and the soles of the feet become moist, because a moist surface provides a better grip (the stress response evolved to cope in a world without shoes). Pupils dilate to let in more light, thereby improving vision. Mental alertness also improves. Digestive responses are decreased, since they use up too much energy, which explains why you experience a dry mouth, loss of appetite and a churning gut feeling. In ancient China, police interrogators exploited the dry-mouth effect of stress to identify lawbreakers. They filled the mouths of suspects with dry cooked rice, and assumed that those who were guilty would be dry-mouthed from stress and therefore unable to swallow the rice – an early version of the lie detector! (Martin 1997).

The parasympathetic nervous system supports activities that regulate the body's energy stores. Once the emergency is over, the parasympathetic nervous system takes control to calm the body. We can say that the actions of the parasympathetic nervous system are opposite to those of the sympathetic nervous system, which implies that it regulates the heart rate and pupil size, increases secretion of saliva for digestion and regulates the blood sugar levels.

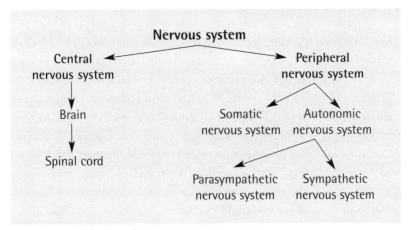

FIGURE 10.2: Divisions of the nervous system

The central nervous system

The central nervous system is composed of the brain and the spinal cord. More than 99% of all neurons are located in the central nervous system. These neurons are connected in precise ways, making the central nervous system highly ordered and organised (Halonen & Santrock 1996). We will now take a brief look at the anatomy and functions of the components of the central nervous system.

Embryological development

As the human embryo develops inside the uterus, the central nervous system begins as a long, hollow tube on the embryo's back. Three weeks after conception, the brain forms into a large mass of neurons and loses its tubular appearance. The elongated tube changes shape and develops into three major divisions: the hindbrain, which is above the spinal cord; the midbrain, which is above the hindbrain; and the last region called the forebrain. We will discuss the structure and functions of all these components, beginning at the level of the spinal cord and progressing to the forebrain region.

The spinal cord

The spinal cord is a long, thick, neural tube that connects the brain to the areas of the body below the neck. The spinal cord, as thick as a little finger, is protected by the vertebral column, which has 24 vertebrae (Carlson 1999). The inside of the spinal cord contains a central canal containing fluid called cerebrospinal fluid. There are two types of nerve fibres in the spinal column: sensory nerves and motor nerves. The sensory neurons enter the spinal cord on the dorsal side, the back of the cord, and the motor nerves exit through the ventral (front) side of the spinal cord. In essence, the spinal cord functions to relay information from the brain to the rest of the body and vice versa. Another crucial function of the spinal cord is the processing of reflex actions. A reflex is a rapid, automatic response to a stimulus (Kalat 1999). If you touch a very hot iron, this stimulates the pain receptors in your fingers, exciting the sensory neurons. In the spinal cord, these make contact with interneurons that send the message to the motor neurons, which transmit the impulse to the muscles of your hand to pull your hand away from the hot iron. The spinal cord is also needed for voluntary movement. Therefore, damage to the spinal cord will result in loss of feeling and paralysis at all levels below the injury that can no longer communicate with the brain (Westen 1999).

The brain

The brain is soft and jelly-like, about the size of half a loaf of bread, and weighs about 1,4 kg (Carlson 1999; Feldman 1993). Many writers have described the brain as an oversized walnut, others say its looks like a cauliflower, and some have even compared it to a dried prune. The common feature of these descriptions is the folds that we see on the surface of the brain (the cortex). The cerebrum is the largest and most complex part of the human brain. It includes brain areas that are responsible for the most complex mental activities, such as learning, remembering, thinking and consciousness. The cerebral cortex is the convoluted outer layer of the cerebrum (Weiten 2001). These convolutions increase the surface area of the brain. Over several million years, the human brain has evolved considerably, forcing it to fold in on itself so that it can fit into its small casing – the skull.

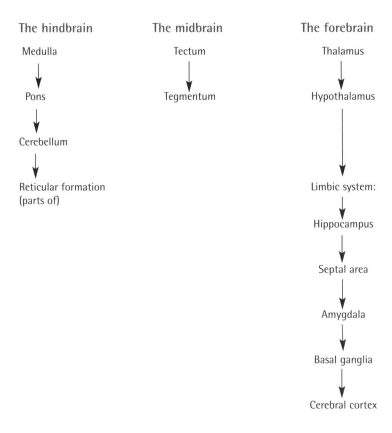

The hindbrain	The midbrain	The forebrain
Medulla	Tectum	Thalamus
↓	↓	↓
Pons	Tegmentum	Hypothalamus
↓		↓
Cerebellum		Limbic system:
↓		↓
Reticular formation (parts of)		Hippocampus
		↓
		Septal area
		↓
		Amygdala
		↓
		Basal ganglia
		↓
		Cerebral cortex

FIGURE 10.3: The structure of the brain

The hindbrain

This is made up of the medulla oblongata, the cerebellum, the pons, and the reticular formation. The hindbrain forms the link between the spinal cord and the brain.

The medulla oblongata

This structure is found just above the spinal cord (where it enters the brain) and appears as an extension of the spinal cord. It plays a role in controlling and regulating vital processes such as breathing and heart rate. Large amounts of alcohol, heroin or other depressant drugs suppress the function of the medulla and cause death by stopping breathing (Plotnik 1999).

The pons

'Pons' means 'bridge' and, although it does not actually look like a bridge, it does function as a link connecting the two halves of the cerebellum. The pons is involved in sleep and arousal.

The cerebellum

Its name means 'little brain', as it looks like a miniature version of the forebrain (Loftus & Wortman 1992). This two-hemisphere structure also has several deep folds. The functions of the cerebellum range from coordinating movement to maintaining balance and coordination (Carlson 1999). Thus, damage to the cerebellum results in uncoordinated movement and lack of balance – a condition called ataxia (Loftus & Wortman 1992). Some researchers propose that the staggering and slurred speech evident after one too many drinks is evidence of the effects of alcohol on the cerebellum (Westen 1999). Even small volumes of alcohol affect a person's ability to perform smooth and accurate movements, and larger volumes seriously affect coordination and balance, a fact well known to police officers assessing people for drunk driving (Drubach 2000). The cerebellum also plays a role in the learning and remembering of motor tasks (Thompson in Loftus & Wortman 1992).

The reticular formation

The reticular formation is a loose network of neurons that extends from the medulla to the upper end of the midbrain. It sends its neurons to the brain and spinal cord. The basic functions of the reticular formation are to maintain consciousness and to regulate arousal levels (Westen 1999). The reticular formation alerts and arouses the forebrain so that it is ready to process incoming information from the senses. Damage to the reticular formation – for example, from a blow to the head – will result in the person becoming unconscious or possibly going into a coma because the forebrain could not be aroused (Steriade in Plotnik 1999).

The midbrain

The midbrain, located between the forebrain and the hindbrain, consists of two structures: the tectum and the tegmentum. The roof of the midbrain is called the tectum and forms part of the route for sensory information, mostly visual and auditory (Kalat 2001). Beneath the tectum is the tegmentum, which is involved in movement and arousal (Westen 1999). The midbrain plays a role in visual and auditory reflexes, such as automatically turning your head towards a noise (Plotnik 1999).

The forebrain

The forebrain is the largest of the three divisions and is made up of the hypothalamus, the thalamus and the cerebrum. The cerebral hemispheres (also known as the forebrain) are considered the most recent development in the brain's long evolutionary history (Loftus & Wortman 1992).

The hypothalamus

This is a small structure found just below the thalamus. The hypothalamus controls the autonomic nervous system and the endocrine system, and also organises behaviour related to survival, such as fighting, fleeing, eating and mating (Carlson 1999). Damage to the hypothalamus would result in abnormalities of one or more motivated behaviours, such as feeding, drinking, temperature regulation, sexual behaviour, fighting or the activity level (Kalat 2001).

The thalamus

The thalamus looks like a pair of avocados (the size of the tip of your index finger), joined side by side and located above the hypothalamus. Its function is to relay messages. Most sensory information goes through the thalamus, which processes this neural input and then relays it to the cerebral cortex. The thalamus also receives information from the cerebral cortex (Kalat 2001).

The limbic system

The limbic system comprises the septal area, the amygdala and the hippocampus. The word 'limbic' is derived from the Latin word *limbus*, which means 'border'. These structures form a border around the brain stem and regulate behaviours related to motivation and emotion.

The word 'hippocampus' comes from the Latin word for 'seahorse' (Kalat 2001). This large structure is situated between the thalamus and the cerebral cortex. Of the many roles played by the hippocampus, its most important is storing certain kinds of memories. Researchers have observed that damage to the hippocampus leads to problems forming new memories.

The septal area plays a role in emotions. Research indicates that stimulation of this area is associated with the experience of pleasure.

The Latin word *amygdala* means 'almond', hence this structure received its name from its almond shape. The role of the amygdala is linked to learning and memory. It is also involved in linking feelings with other experiences, and plays a role in expressing emotions. Researchers have found that the amygdala is important in fear responses and in recognising fear in other people (Westen 1999).

The basal ganglia

These structures are found close to the thalamus and the hypothalamus. They play a major role in movement and a minor role in mood and memory. The basal ganglia receive signals from a dopamine-rich structure called the substantia nigra, which is in the midbrain. When the neurons of the substantia nigra die, no signals can be sent to the basal ganglia. This creates problems with movement, such as those evident in people with Parkinson's disease, which is characterised by tremors and jerky, uncoordinated movements. Former boxing champion Muhammed Ali developed Parkinson's disease, presumably because of the repeated blows he received to his head (Kalat 1999).

The cerebral cortex

The cortex is a 3 mm-thick layer of tightly packed interneurons that is greyish in colour and highly convoluted. The cerebral cortex allows the flexible construction of sequences of voluntary movements, enables people to discriminate complex sensory patterns, and permits symbolic thinking (Westen 1999).

The basic function of the primary areas is to receive direct sensory information or to initiate motor movements. The association areas, however, are responsible for creating perceptions, ideas and plans.

The lobes of the cerebral cortex

The cerebrum can be divided into two hemispheres – the left cerebral hemisphere and the right cerebral hemisphere. These two hemispheres are connected to each other by a band of nerve fibres called the corpus callosum. The right and left hemispheres communicate with each other through the axons of the cerebral hemispheres. An interesting feature is that the left hemisphere controls the right side of the body and the right hemisphere controls the left side of the body. The right and left hemispheres both have four lobes: the frontal lobe, the parietal lobe, the occipital lobe and the temporal lobe. We will look at the importance of and the consequences of damage to each lobe.

Frontal lobe

This lobe makes up about half the surface of the cerebral cortex and is found in front of a large groove called the central fissure. Within the frontal lobe, there is the motor strip (the primary motor cortex), which plays a role in voluntary movement. The left hemisphere mostly controls muscles on the right side of the body and the right hemisphere mostly controls muscles on the left side of the body. The primary motor cortex is important in fine movement control. Each area of the primary motor cortex controls a different part of the body. Larger areas (as seen from the motor homunculus) are dedicated to movements that need to be precision-controlled, such as the fingers and the eyeballs, rather than to areas such as the back. Damage to neurons of the motor strip can lead to paralysis. Also located in the frontal lobe's left hemisphere is the area responsible for speech. This was discovered by Paul Broca and is named Broca's area. This region is specialised for movements of the mouth and tongue needed for speaking. If there is damage to this area, it would result in a condition called Broca's aphasia, which is the inability to communicate effectively.

The frontal regions are often viewed as the source of some uniquely human abilities. They are generally associated with the planning and guidance of behaviour, and therefore considered the 'executive' of the brain. They organise behaviour coherently and give us the ability to realise the future consequences of our current behaviour (Banich 1997). The case of Phineas Gage, which is describedon the next page, gives us an idea of the effects of damage to the prefrontal cortex.

The most anterior portion of the frontal lobe (the prefrontal cortex) receives information from sensory systems and is involved in planning movements, regulating emotional expressions and contributing to memories of current and recent stimuli (Kalat 2001). The association areas of the frontal lobe play a role in thought processes required for reasoning, problem-solving, planning and purposeful behaviour, and are involved in the general organisation of behaviour (Louw & Edwards 1997).

Damage to the frontal lobe:
- affects the ability to organise and sequence behaviour;
- affects the ability to modulate behaviour, especially initiation and cessation;
- affects the ability to generate appropriate social responses;
- affects the ability to use strategies for retrieving memories (Banich 1997);
- causes lack of insight and judgement;
- causes concentration problems;
- causes mood changes and unpredictable emotions;
- reduces social inhibition;
- creates apathy and a general lack of interest in life; and
- causes speech problems.

The effects of frontal lobe damage are illustrated by the case of Phineas Gage.

Phineas Gage

In 1848, in Vermont, USA, Phineas Gage was involved in a tragic accident, which subsequently has helped us to understand more about the brain. Phineas Gage was a foreman on a railway site that was undergoing expansion. One of his duties was to use dynamite to blow up any obstacles in the path where the new tracks would be built. The tool used to push the dynamite down the hole in which it was positioned was called a tamping iron. This was an iron rod, about 1m in length and weighing 3kg. One explosion resulted in the tamping iron shooting into Phineas Gage's left cheek, piercing his frontal lobes and damaging his prefrontal cortex. He was taken to a doctor and survived this event. Phineas Gage's senses and movements were unaffected, but those that knew him well observed changes in his personality. Before the accident he was a friendly cooperative, balanced and responsible person. Afterwards, he became uncaring towards people, arrogant, stubborn, overbearing, indecisive, moody, impatient and childish. He could not keep his job as foreman and became a fairground freak. He died about 13 years later.

Parietal lobe

This lobe extends from behind the central fissure to the area in front of the occipital lobe. Thus, the central fissure forms the boundary between the frontal lobe and the parietal lobe. The strip just behind the central fissure in the parietal lobe is the somatosensory cortex. This somatosensory strip receives information about touch from different parts of the body. Larger areas receive impulses from more sensitive body parts, such as the lips, rather than less sensitive areas, such as the back. (This is evident in the somatosensory mappings on the homunculus.)

The functions of the parietal lobe include:

- touch sensation and perception;
- detecting movement in the environment;
- locating objects in space (spatial orientation);
- the experience of one's own body as it moves through space; and
- performing sensory motor tasks.

Occipital lobe

These lobes are found at the back of the cortex. Since the primary area of the occipital lobe receives visual input from the thalamus, the main function of this lobe is to analyse and process visual information (Westen 1999; Louw & Edwards 1997). If we hear that someone has damaged part of their occipital lobe, we can predict visual problems such as partial blindness or tunnel vision.

Temporal lobe

This lobe plays an important role in hearing and language. The left hemisphere of the temporal lobe is specialised for language. Wernicke discovered a region in the temporal lobe that is involved in language comprehension. This area became known as Wernicke's area. Anyone who has experienced damage to this area would be diagnosed with a condition called Wernicke's aphasia, characterised by a difficulty understanding the meaning of words and sentences.

Split brain studies

William van Wagenen, a neurosurgeon, discovered in 1940 that by severing the corpus callosum he could decrease the incidence of seizures in patients with epilepsy (Smith 1998). In 1964, Roger Sperry investigated this split-brain technique further. Sperry found that the operation had little effect on general intelligence, personality, temperament and memory (Clarke & Geffen in Smith 1998).

Unconvinced that this operation could leave a patient with such minimal effects, Sperry designed techniques such as the visual half-field experiment to detect differences between split-brain and 'whole brain' people. An example of this method would be to flash a picture to the left or to the right of the visual field. You will learn in the chapter on sensation and perception that the nerve fibres from the eye cross at a point called the optic chiasm, which implies that what you see in the left visual field will go to the right side of the brain for processing and vice versa. When split-brain patients were asked to report what they saw when a picture was flashed in the right visual field, they could easily identify and report verbally the picture they had seen. However, they experienced problems when pictures were flashed in the left visual field. Remember that Broca's area is responsible for speech production, and is found in the left frontal lobe. If a picture is flashed in the left visual field, it would be projected to the right hemisphere, which is not dominant for speech, and we would expect the problem of patients not being able to name what they see.

Sperry and Gazzaniga, another neuroscientist, gave a split-brain patient a set of four blocks with surfaces that had different colours and patterns. They asked the patient to arrange the blocks to match the patterns on the cards. They observed that the patient could complete the task easily with the left hand, but not with the right, which indicates the right hemisphere's superior spatial ability.

Lateralisation: Specialisation of the hemispheres

In spite of the two hemispheres of the brain being almost mirror images, we find that there are significant differences in the functions of each hemisphere. In all right-handed and most left-handed people, we find that the left hemisphere is responsible for both producing and understanding speech.

The right hemisphere plays a role in interpreting and expressing emotions. We would expect a person with right hemisphere damage to have problems identifying the facial expressions of others – such as whether they are happy, sad, angry or scared. The right hemisphere is also responsible for displaying emotions. For example, if you are happy and want to display the emotion, you will smile. Right hemisphere damage would lead to an inability to express emotions. Another function of the right hemisphere is to identify and express emotional tone in everyday language. When somebody speaks to you, the right hemisphere will decide from the tone whether the person is happy, angry, sad, etc. Recognising complex non-verbal images, such as faces and three-dimensional figures, is also the job of the right hemisphere. Processing music and emotional and intuitive thinking have also been linked to the duties of the right hemisphere (Drubach 2000). Remember that, although certain tasks activate one hemisphere more than the other, no task relies on just one hemisphere (Kalat 1999).

Techniques for studying the brain

How is it possible for scientists to investigate the brain when it is sealed in a hard, thick skull? An early study conducted by Samuel Morton to measure brain size by pouring lead pellets into skulls of members of various race groups illustrated the importance of having rigorous methods of investigation and, more importantly, highlights the damaging effects of the prejudices of the researcher.

Cultural diversity: Brain size and racial myths

In 1839, a scientist, Samuel George Morton, collected skulls of different races to determine which had the biggest brain. At that time, it was believed that a bigger brain implied greater intelligence and innate mental ability. To measure the size of the brain, Morton poured tiny lead pellets into each skull and then counted the number of pellets used. Through this method, Morton concluded that whites had the largest brains, followed by Mongolians, American Indians and, lastly, Negroes. Some 130 years later, an evolutionary biologist, Stephen J. Gould, reanalysed Morton's investigation of brain size and found that there was no significant difference in brain size among the four races. Gould also concluded that Morton's strong biases about which race should have the biggest brains had swayed his scientific judgement to fit the discriminatory racial notions of the time. Morton had included skulls that matched his personal expectations and omitted skulls that did not support his beliefs.

(ADAPTED FROM PLOTNIK 1999)

Techniques that have recently been developed offer us the opportunity to observe the brain through the thick skull without harming the extremely fragile neurons. New methods of investigation include high-powered microscopes, electroencephalographs, single-unit recordings, CAT scans, PET scans and MRI scans (Halonen & Santrock 1996; Plotnik 1999).

High-powered microscopes allow neuroscientists to view and study every part of a stained neuron in microscopic detail.

Electroencephalographs record the electrical activity of the brain. Brain wave activity is recorded by placing electrodes on a person's scalp. The chart showing the brain wave activity is called an electroencephalogram (EEG). This method allows doctors to detect brain damage, epilepsy and other problems.

Single-unit recordings is a technique used to observe a single neuron's electrical activity.

A computer-assisted axial tomography (CAT) scan is a three-dimensional imaging technique achieved by passing X-rays through the head. A computer then arranges the individual pictures into a composite image. CAT scans offer information about the location of damage due to a stroke, language disorders and memory loss.

A positron-emission tomography (PET) scan measures the amount of specially treated (radioactive) glucose in various areas of the brain, and then sends this information to the computer. Since glucose levels vary with the levels of activity throughout the brain, tracing amounts of glucose generates a picture of activity level in the brain.

Magnetic-resonance imaging (MRI) involves passing non-harmful radio frequencies through the brain. It creates a magnetic field around a person's body and uses the radio waves to construct images of brain tissue and biochemical activity.

These spectacular advances in technology help researchers to more effectively investigate brain-behaviour relations and to detect pathologies. Researchers have found that the brains of schizophrenics have enlarged ventricles (cavities in the brain through which cerebrospinal fluid circulates) (Weiten 2001).

Conclusion

The human nervous system makes possible all that we can do, all that we can know and all that we can experience. Its complexity is immense and the task of studying and understanding it dwarfs all previous explorations our species has undertaken (Carlson 1999). Most physiological psychologists believe that, by understanding how the nervous system works, we will understand how we think, remember and behave, and may even understand the nature of our own self-awareness.

Summary

- The nervous system is the interacting network of nerves that underlies all psychological activity.
- The building blocks of the nervous system are the neurons and the glia. The neurons carry information by electrical and chemical means, while glia provide support to the neurons.
- Neurons typically have dendrites that receive impulses, a cell body that contains the genetic information and an insulated axon that ends at the terminal buttons that contain the neurotransmitter substances.
- Neurons communicate with each at the point called the synapse. The pre-synaptic neuron releases neurotransmitters into the synapse which attach onto the post-synaptic cell causing excitation or inhibition.
- When the neuron is not stimulated, it has a resting potential that is negative. If it is depolarised and reaches the threshold, sodium gates open, further depolarising the neuron. This then leads to an action potential. Potassium ions have to leave the neuron for it to reach resting state again.
- The action potential will occur if it reaches the threshold or it will not occur at all. It follows the all-or-nothing principle.

- Neurotransmitters and hormones are chemicals that alter behaviour. Hormones are released by endocrine glands.
- The nervous system can be divided into the central nervous system (the brain and spinal cord) and the peripheral nervous system, which consists of the nerves that communicate between the CNS and the rest of the body.
- The spinal cord functions in reflex actions and voluntary actions.
- The brain can be divided into the hindbrain, the midbrain and the forebrain.
- Hindbrain structures include the medulla, the pons, the cerebellum and the reticular formation.
- Midbrain structures include the tectum and the tegmentum.
- The forebrain contains the hypothalamus, the thalamus, the limbic system, the hippocampus, the septal area, the amygdala, the basal ganglia and the cerebral cortex.
- The cerebral cortex has two hemispheres that have contralateral control. It contains several folds. The two hemispheres are connected by a band of fibres called the corpus callosum. These fibres are cut in patients with split brains.
- The cerebral cortex has four lobes: frontal, parietal, temporal and occipital.
- Techniques for studying the brain include high-powered microscopes, electroencephalographs, single-unit recordings, computer-assisted axial tomography (CAT) scans, PET scans and magnetic resonance imaging (MRI).

Further reading

Banich, M.T. (1997) *Neuropsychology*. New York: Houghton Mifflin.

Buzan, T. & Dixon, T. (n.d.) *The Evolving Brain*. London: David & Charles.

Carlson, N.R. (1999) *Foundations of Physiological Psychology*. Boston: Allyn & Bacon.

Drubach, D. (2000) *The Brain Explained*. Upper Saddle River: Prentice-Hall

Feldman, R.S. (1993) *Understanding Psychology*. New York: McGraw-Hill.

Feris, M. (2000, 8 February) Mandela steps in to help child smile. *The Star*.

Gilford, G. (2000, 15 February) Operation smile a 'miracle' for Thando. *The Star*.

Greenfield, S. (1997) *The Human Brain: A Guided Tour*. London: Orion.

Halonen, J.S. & Santrock, J.W. (1996) *Psychology Contexts of Behavior.* Boston: McGraw-Hill.

Kalat, J.W. (1999) *Introduction to Psychology.* Pacific Grove: Wadsworth.

Kalat, J.W. (2001) *Biological Psychology.* Belmont: Wadsworth/Thompson Learning.

Loftus, E.F. & Wortman, C.B. (1992) *Psychology.* New York: McGraw-Hill.

Louw, D.L. & Edwards, D. (1997) *Psychology: An Introduction for Students in Southern Africa* (2nd edition). Johannesburg: Heinemann.

Martin, P. (1997) *The Sickening Mind.* London: Flamingo/Harper Collins.

Plotnik, R. (1999) *Introduction to Psychology.* Belmont: Wadsworth.

Smith, B.D. (1998) *Psychology: Science and Understanding.* Boston: McGraw-Hill.

Vander, A., Sherman, J. & Luciano, D. (1998) *Human Physiology: The Mechanisms of Body Function* (7th edition). Boston: McGraw-Hill.

Van de Graaff, K.M. & Fox, S. I. (1995) *Concepts of Human Anatomy and Physiology* (4th edition). Dubuque: Brown.

Weiten, W. (2001) *Psychology: Themes and Variations* (3rd edition). Sydney: Wadsworth.

Westen, D. (1999) *Psychology: Mind, Brain and Culture.* New York: John Wiley.

11 Cognitive Processes: Memory, thinking and language

A.D. Watts and T. Lazarus

Objectives

After studying this chapter you should:

- understand contemporary models of memory as memory systems
- be able to appreciate the role of the information processing model in understanding memory
- be able to critically evaluate the different processes underlying the organisation of memory
- understand the concepts of short-term, working and long-term memory
- be able to delineate the micro processes involved in the acquisition of information through the various memory processes
- understand the concepts of implicit, explicit, episodic and semantic memory
- have a biopsychosocial view of the dynamic organisation of the memory processes
- understand thinking and delineate its different aspects
- be able to describe the steps involved, and methods used, in problem-solving
- be able to explain how concepts are formed
- be able to differentiate between forms of reasoning
- be able to discuss creativity
- be able to critically discuss the relationship between thinking and language
- be able to describe the structures underlying language and communication and the role they play in these activities
- be able to identify the main stages of language development
- be able to critically evaluate theories of language development
- be able to discuss the effects of culture and education on cognitive development.

Introduction

Cognition refers to the information-handling aspects of behaviour. This chapter deals with the interdependent, yet different processes of memory, thinking and language. Memory enables us to store and retrieve information, while thinking involves the organisation and reorganisation of information. Language is the means by which we communicate information. All are important for dealing effectively with our environment.

This chapter is divided into three parts. The first part deals with memory, the second with thought and the third with language. In the sections, these cognitive processes are defined, the fundamental percepts delineated, and the main issues and fields of endeavour discussed.

Memory

This section begins by briefly laying out the basic cognitive model that has guided memory research for the last three decades. Then, the various memory systems are explored and the information-processing model is outlined from the initial brief stores that hold sensations for a flicker of an instant, through to long-term systems that can retain information for a lifetime. The implications of memory research for questions such as the accuracy of eyewitness testimony in court and the existence of repressed memories in victims of childhood sexual abuse are considered. In the concluding section, a discussion of the limits of the information-processing model and some thoughts on the evolution of memory are presented.

Memory and information processing

The cognitive perspective focuses on information processing and is predicated on an analogy between the mind and the input, processing, storage and output functions of computers.

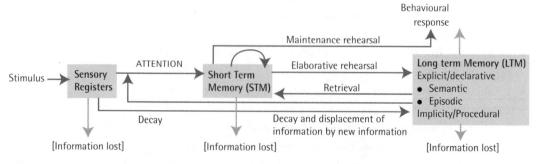

FIGURE 11.1: An information-processing model of memory. Stimulus information enters the sensory registers and may receive attention or exit the system. Some information enters the STM or activates information in LTM. Other information is lost from STM and presumably never encoded in LTM.

Figure 11.1 presents an information-processing model of memory. The first stage is the presentation of a stimulus, such as an unfamiliar road sign. When a stimulus like a road sign is viewed, the image that is first formed on the retina of the eye is held momentarily in the visual sensory register. **Sensory registers** hold information about a perceived stimulus for a split second after the stimulus disappears, allowing a mental model or representation of that stimulus to remain in memory briefly for further processing. A sensory register probably exists for each sensory modality (for vision, audition or hearing, etc.).

Sensory register:
Brief mental representation of a perceived stimulus.

Many of the stimuli people perceive in the course of a day register so briefly that they drop out of the memory system without further processing or storage. Others, however, depending on their importance to the person, make a greater impression. The road sign may depict what looks like falling rocks on a mountain road. Information about these objects is passed along to **short-term memory** (STM), which stores information for roughly 20–30 seconds. Short-term memory is also called working memory, because it functions like a mental sketch-pad on which people make mental notes, solve problems and hold relevant information in consciousness for a brief period (Goldman-Rakic 1995).

Some of the information that enters STM goes on to be processed in **long-term memory** (LTM), where memories for facts, images, thoughts, feelings, skills and experiences may reside for a lifetime. Recovering information from long-term memory, known as **retrieval**, involves bringing it back into short-term memory (which is often used in information-processing models as a synonym for consciousness).

Three major modifications have been introduced into this basic information-processing model. Firstly, memory is not viewed as a single function, but as a set of memory systems that are discrete, but interdependent processing units responsible for different kinds of remembering. Secondly, other forms of remembering that do not involve retrieval into consciousness are recognised. Thirdly, not all information in the model follows the path described above. Some information from the sensory registers may be transferred directly to long-term memory, bypassing short-term memory or consciousness altogether. This phenomenon accounts for the familiar experience of finding oneself humming a tune that was playing in the background at a food store without even noticing that it was playing. Furthermore, the model proposed is not unidirectional (i.e in one direction only) , and it is now recognised that the sensory information processed in short-term memory is actually influenced by the long-term memory.

This information-processing model provides a useful road map and will be used as a framework to organise this section. We consider each stage of the model, from sensory registration to short-term memory and long-term memory. In the process, we examine the way information is represented in memory.

Sensory registration

Each sense modality offers an opportunity to **register** information in various distinct ways. However, to date, most research has focused on visual (**iconic**) and auditory (**echoic**) registration.

Iconic storage:
Visual registration of a stimulus.

The term **iconic storage** is used to describe visual sensory registration. For a brief period after the image disappears from vision, a mental image (or icon) of what is seen is retained. This visual trace is remarkably accurate and contains more information than people can report, since it fades from memory long before they can verbalise what they have seen.

The duration of icons varies from approximately half a second to two seconds, depending on the individual, the content of the image and circumstances. Presenting another image, or even a flash of light directly after the first image disappears, erases the original icon, like a new movie recorded on old videotape erases previous material.

Echoic storage:
Auditory registration of a stimulus.

The auditory counterpart of iconic storage is called **echoic storage**. It is likely that you have had the experience of hearing a voice or a sound 'echo' in your mind after the actual sound has stopped. Some researcher have suggested that humans might have two types of echoic memory systems: one for nonspeech sounds and the other for speech sounds, lateralised to the right and left hemispheres of the brain respectively. As with iconic storage, echoic storage is apparently relatively brief and quickly erased if another auditory stimulus is represented.

Representation

Mental representation:
An internal model of a stimulus or category of stimuli.

When information passes through the sensory registers to be processed and stored, this happens in the form of **mental representation**, i.e a mental model of a stimulus or category of stimuli. Information therefore can be represented in various ways, though most representations are sensory or verbal.

Sensory representation

Sensory representations store information in a sensory mode, such as the sound of a dog barking or the image of a city skyline. People rely on visual representation to recall where they put their keys the previous night or what information was on a page of notes that is relevant to answering an examination question. If asked, 'How many light fixtures are in your home?' most people could offer an answer, despite never having counted, by forming a mental image of the rooms in the house and simply counting the fixtures as they travel mentally from room to room.

An extreme example of visual representation is eidetic imagery, or photographic memory. An individual with eidetic imagery might look at a painting and hold it so clearly in memory as to later describe each person in it. Only a small fraction of the population possesses eidetic memory, and this ability is far less common among adolescents than among pre-adolescent children (Giray 1985).

Auditory modes of representation are also important for encoding information, particularly language. Some forms of auditory information would be difficult to represent in other modes. For instance, most readers would be able to retrieve pieces of Michael Jackson's 'Beat It' quite easily. In this case, the representation that is retrieved is a series of patterned segments of sound.

Although visual and auditory are not the only sensory representations, other modalities have rarely been studied. Emotions must also be stored and represented in memory, as this becomes apparent when recalling the loss of a significant other or the feeling of being surrounded by family at Christmas.

Verbal representations

Although many representations are stored in sensory modes, much of the time people think with words using verbal representations, either in lieu of or along with other modes. For example, try to think what 'liberty' means without thinking in words. Other experiences, in contrast, are virtually impossible to describe or remember verbally, such as the smell of frying bacon.

Thus, representational modes are like languages that permit discourse within our own minds. The content of our thoughts and memories – a bird, an angry friend – can best be described or translated into many languages, but some languages simply cannot capture certain experiences the way others can.

Short-term memory

Short-term memory refers to a set of brief memory stores that holds information in consciousness for roughly 20 to 30 seconds (unless the person makes a conscious effort to maintain it longer). After a time, the information is either stored for longer-term use, or it disappears from consciousness.

Short-term memory: Type of memory that stores information for a brief time only.

Characteristics of short-term memory

Short-term memory is distinguished by four characteristics (Bower 1975). Firstly, short-term memory is **active**. Information remains in STM only as long as the person is consciously processing, examining or manipulating it. People use short-term memory as a 'workspace' to process new information and to call up relevant information from long-term memory. Taking away a person's conscious workspace apparently makes the job of remembering much more difficult.

Secondly, short-term memory is **rapidly accessed**. This may be demonstrated by the fact that you are able to repeat the last sentence you read without looking back, but would likely take longer to recall the first sentence in this section, which is no longer immediately available to consciousness and has to be accessed from long-term memory. In this respect, the difference between STM and LTM is the difference between pulling a file from the top of the desk versus searching for it in a file drawer.

Thirdly, STM **preserves the temporal sequence of information**. The order in which information is temporarily 'stored' in STM is retained when recalling this information, such as a list of words. Fourth, short-term memory has **limited capacity**. On average, people can hold about seven pieces of information in STM at a time, with a normal range of five to nine items. The limits of STM seem to be neurologically based, as they are similar in other cultures, including those with very different languages (Yu *et al.* 1985).

Controlling information in short-term memory

Because STM's capacity is limited, using the conscious workspace requires controlling the information in it. Two conscious processes allow more efficient use of STM: rehearsal and chunking (Atkinson & Schifrin 1968).

Rehearsal:
Repeating information over and over again.

Rehearsal involves repeating the information over and over again to prevent it from fading. This kind of rehearsal is called maintenance rehearsal, since its purpose is to maintain information in STM. Rehearsal is also important in transferring information to LTM – which will not surprise anyone who has ever memorised a poem, lines from a play or a maths formula.

Chunking:
The grouping of information into larger units or chunks.

Chunking is one method used to increase the workspace of STM, since its capacity is limited to seven pieces of information. Thus, one way to increase the capacity of STM is to increase the size of the unit or chunk. Chunking is essential in everyday life, particularly in cultures that rely upon literacy – for example, requiring momentary memory for telephone numbers.

Long-term memory

We now explore the nature of **long-term memory**, starting with a phenomenon called the serial position effect, in which STM and LTM operate in tandem.

Long-term memory:
Type of memory that stores memory for long periods.

Serial position effect

One way to test long-term memory is through free recall tasks, in which the experimenter presents subjects with a list of words, one at a time, and later asks them to recall as many as possible. Researchers who first employed this technique noticed a curious pattern to the responses: Subjects were more likely to remember the earlier and later items on the list than the words in the middle. This phenomenon, known as the **serial position effect**, can be graphed in a curve showing probability of recall.

Serial position effect:
Effect in which the retention of information is effected by its position in a sequence.

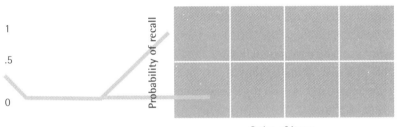

FIGURE 11.2: Primacy and recency effects. Items earlier in a list and those at the end show a heightened probability of recall in comparison to those in the middle. A likely explanation is that the primacy effect results from rehearsal, which transfers early information into LTM, whereas the recency event reflects the storage of the most recent information in STM.

Psychologists have offered various explanations for the serial position effect, but most agree that both STM and LTM are implicated. When subjects learn a list of words (or other items) presented one at a time, they use rehearsal strategies to remember them. The first words on the list receive considerable rehearsal, but as the number of words steadily increases, the subject has less opportunity to rehearse each one. This phenomenon, in which words at the beginning of the list are more likely to be committed to long-term memory than those that appear later, is known as the **primacy effect**.

Primary effect:
Effect in which information that appears first in a sequence is remembered better.

Items at the end of the list are also remembered better than those in the middle – a phenomenon known as the **recency effect**. Since STM has a limited capacity, each successive word in the list bumps a previously presented word from STM. Because the last words on the list are not displaced by new words, however, they are remembered.

Recency effect:
Effect in which information that appears last in a sequence is remembered better.

Long-term memory systems

Long-term memory appears to be comprised of multiple systems. Two types of LTM are distinguished – explicit and implicit memory (Schacter 1992).

Explicit memory, also known as declaratory memory, refers to knowledge that can be consciously brought to mind and 'declared'. Explicit memory is conscious memory for facts and events. Explicit memory may be semantic or episodic (Tulving 1972, 1987). **Semantic memory** refers to general world knowledge or facts, such as the knowledge that summers are hot in Durban or that NaCl is the chemical formula for table salt. **Episodic memory** consists of memories of particular episodes or events from personal experience. Episodic memories are connected with a time or date and typically include much more personal or autobiographical elements than semantic memories. When people remember what they did on their sixteenth birthday or what they did yesterday, they are retrieving episodic memories. The way people recall events depends on the way they organise these events in their minds. A person who is sensitive to potential abuse in relationships – whether or not he or she was ever actually abused – is likely to recall unhappy childhood experiences and expects to be treated unfairly or malevolently as an adult (Higgins 1990).

Implicit memory cannot be brought to mind consciously, but is expressed in behaviour (Roediger 1990). One of the most important kinds of implicit memory is procedural memory: 'how to' knowledge of procedures or skills. People are often astonished to find that, even though they have not skated for 20 years, or have not ridden a bicycle for a similar period, the skills are easily reactivated – almost as if their use had never been interrupted.

Although procedural memories require no consciousness, they are frequently acquired consciously. A beginner guitar player must often 'think out' a piece and consciously use a particular fingering, but gradually his or her conscious efforts become unconscious and effortless. A more advanced guitarist may not even be able to describe the chord structure of a complicated piece played from memory, and the performance may be inhibited if he or she thinks consciously about what he or she is doing.

Encoding and long-term memory

Most people have had the embarrassing experience of meeting someone at a party, repeating the individual's name in greeting, conversing for a few minutes, and then having no recollection of the person's name. Why

Explicit memory:
Memory containing knowledge that can be consciously brought to mind.

Semantic memory:
Explicit memory of facts.

Episodic memory:
Explicit memory of episodes.

Implicit memory:
Memory containing knowledge that cannot be consiously brought to mind.

do we retain some information for years and lose other information within seconds? If information is to be stored for long-term use, it must be encoded or cast into a representation form or 'code' that can be readily accessed from memory. As with STM, the way people rehearse and mentally represent information plays an important role in retention.

Rehearsal and levels of processing

One factor that influences the storage and retrieval of long-term memories is the extent and manner of **rehearsal** – how much and at what intervals the person rehearses. Any student who has ever crammed for a test knows that rehearsal is important for storing information in LTM. As noted earlier, the simple repetitive rehearsal that maintains information momentarily in STM is not optimal for storage in LTM. Effective LTM rehearsal requires forming associative links to previously stored information. The degree to which information is elaborated, reflected upon or processed in a meaningful way during memory storage is referred to as the level or depth of processing (Jelicic & Bonke 1991).

The durability of new information in memory is a function of the depth to which it is processed. Information may be processed at a shallow, structural level (focusing on physical characteristics of the stimulus), a somewhat deeper, phonemic level (focusing on simple characteristics of the language used to describe it), or at the deepest, semantic level (focusing on the meaning of the stimulus). At a shallow structural level, for instance, people may walk into a restaurant and notice the typeface and colours of its sign. At a phonemic level, they may read the sign to themselves and notice that it sounds, say, African. Processing material deeply, in contrast, means paying attention to its meaning or significance – noticing, for instance, that this is a restaurant a friend has been recommending for months.

While deeper processing is necessary for storage and retrieval from LTM, recent research suggests that the best encoding strategy depends on what the person needs to retrieve later (Anderson 1995). The way a person rehearses information, then, influences retention and retrieval. Another variable related to rehearsal is of practical significance from an educational point of view: the spacing of rehearsals (the interval between rehearsal sessions). While students intuitively know that, if they cram the night before a test, the information is likely to be available to them when they need it the next day, this process is not optimal for long-term information retention.

Memory as a constructive and reconstructive process

Most people think of memories as analogous to mental photographs than can be examined like pictures in an album. A class of episodic memories that typically exemplifies this intuitive view is **flashbulb memories**: vivid memories of exciting or highly consequential memories (Weaver 1993). For example, most people living in New York City in the USA will probably recall precisely where they were when the World Trade Centre collapsed on 11 September 2001. Flashbulb memories are so clear and vivid that we tend to think of them as totally accurate. However, considerable evidence suggests that most memories, including flashbulb memories, are not of snapshot clarity or accuracy and, in fact, can be entirely incorrect (Neisser 1991). Memory is not a matter of opening a mental scrapbook. Rather, we build or rebuild a mental representation of an event by combining our general store of information with specific recollections of an event in a constructive or reconstructive process.

Flashbulb memories:
Vivid memories of highly significant events.

Schemas and the construction of memory

When students walk into a classroom on the first day of lectures and a person resembling a lecturer begins to lecture, they generally find this rather unremarkable. Instead, they listen and take notes in routine fashion. The reason they are not surprised that one person has assumed control of the situation and begun talking is that they have a **schema** for events that normally transpire in a classroom. Schemas are patterns of thought that render the environment relatively predictable. In other words, schemas represent general knowledge about particular situations or domains (Wilcox & Williams 1990).

Schema:
Patterns of thought that make the environment predictable.

Just as schemas provide frameworks for understanding new information, they are also involved in the formation and retrieval of memories. Schemas affect the way people remember in two ways: by influencing the information they encode and by shaping the way they reconstruct data already stored.

Schemas influence the way people initially construe an event and, thus, the way they encode it in LTM. Schemas not only provide hooks on which to hang information during encoding, but also provide hooks for fishing information out of LTM. Without schemas, life would seem like one random event after another and efficient memory would be impossible. Yet, schemas can lead people to misclassify information, to believe they have seen something they really have not seen, and to fail to notice things that might be important. When perceiving a sunset, remembering an elementary school experience or studying astrophysics, we are constantly and actively ordering our experience. In this lies both our knowledge and our ignorance, and separating the two is not an easy task.

Thus, understanding the role of schemas in the reconstruction of memories has an important legal application. How accurate is eyewitness testimony? Numerous studies have explored this question experimentally, usually by showing subjects a short film or slides of an event such as a car accident (Wells & Turtle 1987). The experimenter then asks subjects specific questions about a scene, sometimes introducing information that was not present in the actual scene or contradicting what the subjects saw. Even seemingly minor variations in the wording of a question can determine what subjects 'remember' from a scene. One study simply substituted the definite article 'the' for the indefinite article 'a' in the question, 'Did you see the/a broken headlight?' Using the definite article increased the likelihood that subjects would recall seeing a broken headlight and their certainty that they had, even if they never actually observed one (Loftus & Zanni 1975). In another study, subjects gave higher estimates of the speed at which vehicles were travelling at the time of a collision if they were asked 'About how fast were the cars going when they smashed into each other?' than if the word 'hit' was substituted for 'smashed into'. Using the phrase 'smashed into' also increased the likelihood that they would remember seeing broken glass when questioned a week later, even when no broken glass was at the scene. Clearly, new information presented after an event has occurred can influence memory of the event.

Thinking

Thinking involves the mental manipulation of words and images, as when one forms concepts, solves problems, makes decisions or is creative. Each of these aspects of thinking will be dealt with in this section.

Problem solving

All of us are constantly beset by problems for which we have to find solutions: the car won't start, the video recorder won't record, the washing machine is leaking water, and your relationship with your girlfriend or boyfriend is not working. To solve each of the problems, we have to work out a series of steps to follow. The steps in Figure 11.3 are generally followed when we solve problems.

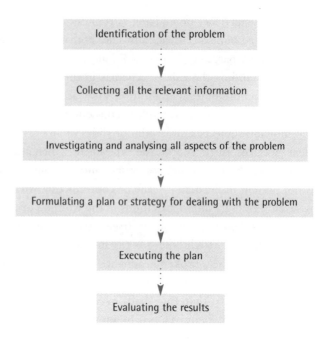

FIGURE 11.3: Stages of problem solving (Luria 1973)

Let us imagine that your washing machine is leaking water. First, you **identify the problem**, which is that your washing machine is leaking. Then you **gather all the relevant information**, and **integrate** and **analyse** all the relevant aspects of the problem. (Is there a leak in the inlet pipe or the outlet pipe? Has something like a sock caused the blockage in the machine?) Then you **formulate a plan** or strategy for dealing with the problem. (First check for a blockage, then check the inlet and outlet pipes.) You thereafter try a solution or execute the plan. (There is nothing causing a blockage so I should check the outlet pipe for leaks.) Finally, you **evaluate the results**. (There is a hole in the outlet pipe, so that is the cause of the leak.) If, however, your first plan does not work, you try a different one. (There is no leak in the outlet pipe, so I'll check the inlet pipe.) In order to solve such problems, various strategies are often used. These include trial and error, insight, algorithms and heuristics. Each of these strategies will be briefly considered.

Trial and error:
Problem solving by trying different possible solutions.

When attempting to solve a problem, a frequent strategy is **trial and error**. This involves trying one solution after another until one works. Although this method of problem solving is often successful, it is usually not time-efficient. For example, if you are staying at a friend's house and he or she has given you a large bunch of keys, one of which will open the front door, you will need to try one key after another until you find the key that fits. This may prove to be a time-consuming task and it may be quicker to phone your friend and ask him or her to identify the correct key.

If we attempt to solve a problem without success, a period of 'doing nothing' (the **incubation period**) often follows. This frequently leads to the sudden realisation of how to solve the problem. This is called **insight** (i.e. the mental manipulation of information, rather than trial and error). The sudden recognition of how to solve a problem is known as the **'Aha' phenomenon**. Many of you may have experienced this when writing a difficult essay. You research the topic and start writing the essay, but realise that your organisation of the material and integration of the issues is not clear. Provided you are not attempting to write the essay the night before it is due, you may, in frustration, decide to leave it for a while (the incubation period). You may find that while sitting on the beach the following weekend, you have a sudden insight or 'Aha' experience of how to tackle it.

Another method that may be used to solve problems is an **algorithm**. This is a rule that if followed systematically, ensures that a solution will be found to a problem. A simple example of an algorithm is the use of a mathematical formula, such as 'length x breadth' to work out the floor area of your bedroom. The concept of an algorithm has its origins in computer science research by cognitive psychologists Allen Newell and Herbert Simon (1972). **Heuristics** are 'rules of thumb' or general principles that guide our problem solving. They do not, however, guarantee a solution. An example would be to use this strategy when completing a large jigsaw puzzle, rather than that of trial and error. One heuristic may be to sort the pieces into groups of similar colours.

We often find that we cannot reach a solution to a problem. This sometimes occurs when we continue to use a solution that worked in the past, but which is ineffective or inefficient in the current situation. This is called **response set**. The problem presented in Table 11.1 illustrates this.

Incubation period: Period allowing the brain to manipulate information without.

Algorithm: Rule that ensures finding the solution to a problem.

Heuristics: General principles that guide problem solving.

Response set: Solution to a problem that worked in the past but no longer applies.

Subjects were asked to use jugs A, B and C to measure the goal amount of water indicated in the right hand column.

Problem	Jug A	Jug B	Jug C	Goal amount
1	21	127	3	100
2	14	46	5	22
3	18	43	10	5
4	7	42	6	23
5	20	57	4	29
6	23	49	3	20
7	15	39	3	18

TABLE 11.1: An example of a water-jug experiment used to investigate response set (Luchins 1942)

The best way to solve the first five problems is to fill jug B; then fill jug A from jug B and discard; then fill jug C from jug B twice and discard. The water left in jug B is the required amount. People generally use this solution for all the problems, even though problems 6 and 7 are best solved using only jugs A and C.

People are sometimes unable to solve problems due to a tendency to perceive a problem from only one perspective. This is known as **functional fixedness**. The 'box and candle' problem developed by Duncker (1945) provides a good example of this. The subject is presented with a candle in a box, a box containing thumbtacks, and a box of matches. The problem is to attach the candle to a wooden door so that, once lit, it will act like a lamp. The solution is to tack one of the boxes to the door, and to use it as a platform for the candle, which is then lit. However, as the boxes all contain objects, the subjects often fail to see them as having other potential uses. Control subjects who were given the candle, tacks, matches and boxes separately, generally solved the problem more easily.

Functional Fixedness: Tendancy to view a problem from only one perspective.

Concept formation

What do Nelson Mandela, Bill Clinton and Margaret Thatcher have in common? The correct answer is that they are all past leaders of their respective countries. To answer this question correctly, you need to identify the common feature or concept they share – in this case, leader status. A **concept** is, therefore, a category of objects, events, qualities or relations that share certain features. During our lifetime, we form thousands of concepts that are important for thinking, in that they enable us to store information in an organised manner and respond to events in an appropriate way (see Figure 11.4).

Concept: A category of objects, events, qualities or relations that share certain features.

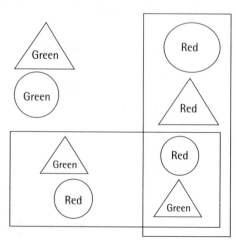

FIGURE 11.4: An example of the type of stimuli presented to subjects in laboratory studies of concept formation. Stimuli may differ in terms of size (small or large), colour (red or blue) and shape (circle or triangle). The subject is then required to sort the stimuli according to a specific feature that forms the concept. In the example above, concepts are small and red (Lerner *et al.* 1986).

How do we form concepts? A **logical concept** is formed by identifying the specific features held by everything that it applies to. Whereas we form strictly logical concepts when we need to, such as in logical reasoning tasks or in mathematics, in everyday life we form 'fuzzy concepts', which do not have clearly definable boundaries. These are usually formed through our everyday experience and are often referred to as **natural concepts**. Such concepts include those of 'emotions' and 'love'. Because of the difficulty frequently experienced in defining natural concepts, Eleanor Rosch (1975) proposed that people conceptualise the world in terms of discrete **prototypes**. Rosch regarded a prototype as an 'ideal instance' of a concept that incorporates the features shared, in different degrees, by most instances of the concept. Thus, the concept of a bird allows one to include unbird-like birds, such as ostriches, penguins and chickens. These do not share the most common property of birds – that they fly – but they do possess certain properties of birds, though not all of the same ones as each other. According to Rosch, the greater the similarity between an instance and a prototype, the more likely we are to consider the instance as a member of a concept that the prototype represents. Thus, a robin should be perceived of as a more typical bird (i.e. prototype) than a penguin, as whereas both have feathers and wings, the robin can fly. Rosch's ideas about the nature of human concepts revolutionised the experimental study of concept formation. Although there are certain difficulties with her theories, which are mentioned here, her work and that of her collaborators have contributed to the realisation that our thinking is not synonymous with purely logical processing. Her theory has also helped us to understand differences in thought processes that are observed between individuals, groups and cultures.

Logical concept: Concept formed by identifying the specific features held by everything that it applies to.

Natural concept: Concept formed by our everyday experience.

Prototype: An ideal example of a concept.

Reasoning

In general, reasoning involves evaluating information and generating logical arguments. To do this, physical, pictorial or linguistic symbols have to be manipulated cognitively. Two main forms of reasoning may be identified: inductive reasoning and deductive reasoning. **Inductive reasoning** involves people working out what hypothesis may be abstracted from a particular set of observations. It therefore proceeds from the specific to the more general. One of the hallmarks of inductive reasoning is that it occurs in an open system, in the absence of full information. Inductive reasoning has two aspects: hypothesis formulation and hypothesis evaluation. An example of the kind of work that has been done on inductive reasoning is a study by Kotovsky and Simon (1973) that looked at our ability to discover patterns in sequences of letters or numbers. For

Inductive reasoning: Reasoning that works from the particular to the general.

example, consider the letter sequences ABBA, CDDC, E - - -. What letters are needed to complete the sequence? The answer here is FFE. Similarly, consider the number sequences 1221, 3443, 5 - - -. The numbers that will complete the sequence are 665. In both examples, inductive reasoning was needed to formulate the correct answer. In addition, one can induce that, in both instances, the same formal rule – initial item (letter or number), next item in the logical sequence, repetition of this item, return to the original item – can be used to form the correct solution. **Deductive reasoning** refers to reasoning in which one moves cognitively from the general to the specific. In other words, one begins with the general idea or rule and then deduces instances of this. Syllogisms use deductive reasoning, and typically comprise three components:

Deductive reasoning: Reasoning that works from the general to the particular.

- a general premise is made;
- a statement of fact is presented that relates to the first premise; and
- a statement or assertion is made that represents a conclusion deduced from the prior premise and fact.

The issue in a syllogism is whether the final statement is true or not. For example, consider the following syllogism, which is attributed to Woody Allen, the American comedian:

Premise:	Aristotle is a man. A.
Fact:	I am a man. B.
Conclusion:	Therefore, I am Aristotle! C.

Given the premise A, and the fact B, can we deduce that C is correct? No. Human beings other than Aristotle fall into the category 'man'. The fact that B is true does not enable us to logically deduce that the person referred to in C 'is Aristotle'. This is an example of an invalid syllogism. In a valid syllogism, the conclusion follows logically from the premise, for example:

Premise:	Boats and only boats float on water. A.
Fact:	X is floating on water. B.
Conclusion:	Therefore, X is a boat. C.

Research has shown that people perform better on valid rather than invalid syllogisms (Dickstein 1976).

Creativity

Creativity: A form of problem solving involving finding novel, useful and socially valued solutions to problems.

Creativity is difficult to define (Barron & Harrington 1981; Guilford 1950). However, psychologists have generally defined **creativity** as a form of problem solving that is characterised by finding solutions that are novel, useful and socially valued, whether they are practical, artistic or scientific (Sdorow 1998). Creative people have generally been found to have a number of characteristics. Firstly, they tend to be of above-average intelligence. They also tend to prefer novelty, complexity and making independent judgements (Barron & Harrington 1981). In addition, they are adept at combining different kinds of thinking (such as verbal and visual) (Kershner & Ledger 1985), and tend to be more creative when engaged in creative behaviour for its own sake rather than to obtain some kind of reward (Amabile 1989). Guilford (1984) argued that one of the hallmarks of creativity in thinking is the ability to think **divergently** – to think in an unusual or atypical way about a topic. An instance that illustrates divergent thinking involves brainstorming, where one is encouraged to think of as many solutions to a problem as possible. For example, although we may think that a brick can only be used for building or construction purposes, a divergent thinker might be able to generate numerous other uses for it (e.g. as a paperweight, as a weapon, as a bed warmer if heated, as a footrest, as a bookend). Divergent thinking can be contrasted with **convergent thinking**, which is involved in finding conventional solutions to problems (Guilford 1984).

Divergent thinking:
Thinking in an unusual or atypical way.

Convergent thinking:
Thinking in a conventional way.

Intelligence

In the previous sections, thinking has been discussed as a general cognitive process common to all people. Thus, the ways in which people generally go about thinking have been outlined by describing the way they make decisions, solve problems and formulate concepts. However, people differ in terms of the effectiveness with which they can think. Some are just better at it than others. Another approach to thinking has therefore been to look at differences in people's thinking ability. This work has been the focus of the study of intelligence and is discussed in Chapter 9.

Language

Language may be defined as an organised system of combining symbols (spoken, written or gestural) in order to communicate (Sternberg 1994). We use spoken symbols to communicate through speech, written symbols to communicate in writing, and gestural symbols to communicate in sign language. (See Figure 11.5 for a description of a uniquely South African form of taxi sign language that has evolved in response to the specific needs of minibus taxi users.)

Language:
An organisational system of combining symbols in order to communicate.

FIGURE 11.5
Taxi signaling (a form of sign language developed by the uses of minibus taxis in the Durban area, South Africa).

This U-shaped hand signal will get you a ride to Umlazi's U Section.

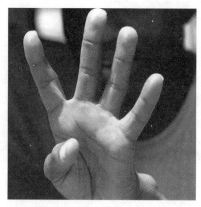

Four fingers in the air indicate a trip to Umlazi's AA and BB sections.

An index finger pointing downwards indicates a trip to Chatsworth's Unit 1.

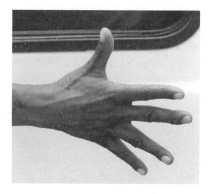

Five fingers pointing parallel to the ground mean a trip to Chatsworth's Unit 5.

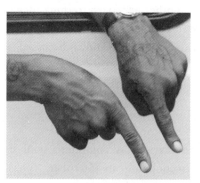

These two downward pointing fingers will take you to Chatsworth's Unit 11.

This is the most commonly used sign to get to Durban.

A question often asked by psychologists is whether language is unique to humans. Some of the original work in this field is described below.

Can animals use language?

Every human society has a language. However, the question psychologists have asked is whether it is confined to humans. In other words, do animals use language? Many animals have communication systems. For instance, bees communicate with one another about the distance and direction of pollen and nectar by means of a series of movements, which has been likened to a dance. However, the bees' system of communication is closed in that no new information can be added. Communication systems used by various species of birds and animals are also stereotypical in nature.

Psychologists have questioned whether animals are incapable of learning language or whether they do not develop it spontaneously in their natural environments. In an attempt to answer this question, they have tried to teach animals, in particular the great apes, language. Early attempts to do so failed (e.g. Hayes 1951; Kellog & Kellog 1933). For example, Hayes reared a chimp, Vicki, at home as a child. Vicki learned to follow numerous directions, but after extensive training, only learned to say 'mama', 'papa' and 'cup'.

Such attempts failed, as an ape's vocal apparatus is not designed to produce speech.

Therefore, subsequent investigators have attempted to teach apes non-verbal languages. For instance, Gardner and Gardner (1969, 1975) attempted to teach American Sign Language (ASL) to a chimp, Washoe. Washoe learned about 130 signs and was also able to string signs together to make primitive sentences (e.g. 'Greg tickle'). However, these were often irregular and repetitive. Patterson (1978) taught ASL to a gorilla, Koko. According to Patterson, by about four years of age, Koko was able to produce over 150 signs a day. She also used signs in consistent word order in combinations such as 'tickle me'. In addition, Koko at times produced novel contributions such as 'cookie rock' when she was given a stale sweet roll.

Psychologists argue that these studies do not indicate that apes can be taught language. Although they can learn words and primitive sentences, this does not constitute language. The apes have, to date, not shown the ability to develop a hierarchical language structure that will allow them to generate complex sentences. Research in this area continues and may provide further insights into this fascinating question.

The relationship between thinking and language

Although language and thought are viewed as related events, one of the most interesting and vexing questions in the field of language is the nature of this relationship. Most of us know that language can, to some extent at least, be used to influence our thoughts and how we think about things. This is a tactic widely used by, for example, the so-called 'spin doctors' in government and people in the business and advertising fields. Thus, a second-hand car dealer may refer to vehicles as 'previously owned' rather than 'used' or 'second hand', and a copywriter in an advertising agency may refer to a cosmetic product as being suitable for 'mature' skin rather than for 'ageing' or 'old' skin.

This relationship between thought and language has been studied in a number of ways. For instance, cognitive psychologists and psycholinguists have compared users of different languages and dialects. Others have explored the influence of language on people's perceptions of colour. This has led to the formulation of two main views on the relationship between thought and language: linguistic relativity and linguistic determinism.

Linguistic determinism: The hypothesis that language determines thought.

The hypothesis that language determines thought (**linguistic determinism**), and that individuals speaking different languages will have different cognitive systems that will influence the way they think about the world (**linguistic relativity**) is primarily associated with Benjamin Whorf (1956). The extreme version of the linguistic determinism hypothesis is that not just language, but specifically speech, determines thought. This was exemplified in the work of behaviourists such as Watson (1924) and Skinner (1957). Behaviourists argued that psychologists can only theorise about observable behaviour, and believed that intangibles such as 'thought' and 'mind' are not the domain of psychological research. They therefore argued that the overt behaviour of speech is the origin and controller of the covert behaviour we experience as thought. There are, however, a number of clear objections to the so-called 'strong' versions of the hypothesis. There is developmental evidence indicating that children understand language well before they can produce it. There are also cases of children who have serious language handicaps who can still think and behave intelligently.

The 'weak' version of Whorf's hypothesis is that, while language may not determine thought, it does influence it. The most frequently cited example for linguistic relativity is the word 'snow'. The Eskimos have perhaps a dozen different words for snow (Pullum 1991). In contrast, English speakers have only one word for this concept. According to Whorf, the variety of words Eskimos have for snow will result in them perceiving differences in this medium that English speakers, with only one word for the concept, do not. Critics have pointed out that the number of words that Eskimo languages have for snow may have been exaggerated. Furthermore, perhaps because snow and its different forms (e.g. falling versus fallen snow) are important to Eskimo cultures, they develop different words to describe these states. In addition, English speakers to whom snow is important, such as ski instructors, use various adjectives to describe different types of snow (e.g. powdery, crusty), which implies that they can perceive differences in the state of snow.

Empirical research into linguistic determinism and relativity has generally suggested that language can influence thought in some ways and in some circumstances. However, the concept of linguistic determinism (i.e.

the idea that language determines differences in thought among members of different cultures) is inconsistent with the available evidence. The following two studies are widely cited to illustrate this point.

In an early study by Carmichael *et al.* (1932), two groups of subjects were shown a set of ambiguous line drawings. Each group heard different labels for the drawings. When asked to draw what they had seen, the drawings were influenced by the labels they had heard (see Figure 11.6). This was supportive of Whorf's linguistic relativity hypothesis, as it indicated that language influenced the subjects' recall of the objects.

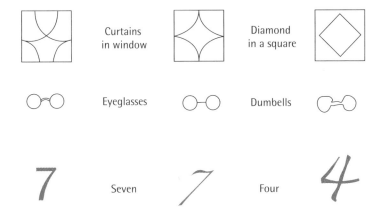

FIGURE 11.6: Some of the stimulus figures, labels and results from the experiment conducted by Carmichael *et al.* (1932)

Another area of research that has been used to investigate the influence of language on thought is colour perception. For example, Rosch (1973, 1975) hypothesised that, if the linguistic relativity hypothesis was correct, people who speak a language that has many colour names will perceive colours differently from people who speak a language that has few colour names. To do this she compared the ability of the Dani people of New Guinea to distinguish and recognise colours to that of English people. The Dani people have only two colour words in their vocabulary: '*mili*' for dark and '*mola*' for light colours. In contrast, English has 11 basic or focal colour words: black, white, red, green, yellow, blue, brown, purple, pink, orange and grey. The Dani and the American subjects were given a series of trials in which they were shown a colour chip for five seconds. Thirty seconds later, they had to choose the chip from among 160 colour chips. Rosch found that the Dani and the English speakers were equally proficient in distinguishing between focal colours, despite the fact that the Dani people use only two colour names.

This study, and other similar work on colour naming and linguistic relativity (Curran 1980; Kay & Kempton 1984), pointed to some universal cognitive functions that are not constrained or limited by a particular language. Furthermore, research has also suggested that, while language can influence thought in certain instances, linguistic determinism (i.e. the notion that language determines differences in thinking between different cultures) has, to date, not been supported.

Structures underlying language and communication

Language needs to be viewed from two perspectives. The first involves establishing so-called **competence rules** for language – describing what language is and what it does. The second aspect involves establishing **performance rules** for how language, as a mechanism, works or is used in practice. This has been labelled a distinction between competence and performance.

All spoken languages are made up of **phonemes**, which are the basic sounds of a language. Each phoneme represents a letter, such as the 'o' sound in 'go', or a combination of letters such as the 'sh' sound in 'shell'. Each language has a limited number of phonemes. English uses about 40, whereas some use as few as 11 (Hawaiian) or as many as 70 (Abkhaz). Different languages therefore have different phonemes, which is one of the reasons why it is difficult to learn a foreign language. For example, in English 'r' and 'l' are different phonemes, so 'break' is perceived as different from 'bleak'. In contrast, in Japanese, 'l' and 'r' belong to the same phoneme and may be substituted for each other without changing the meaning of the word. Each language has its own rules for combining phonemes.

Individual phonemes and combinations of phonemes form **morphemes**, which are the smallest meaningful units of a language. Words are made up of one or more morphemes. Words such as 'dog' and 'hat' are made up of only one morpheme, while other words require that at least one or more morphemes be combined. These include prefixes (e.g. unhappy) and suffixes (e.g. eating, beaten). Finally, morphemes and words are combined into **phrases** and **sentences**. The rules that govern acceptable combinations of sounds in words are referred to as the **syntax** of the language. Syntax varies from language to language. For instance, in English, verbs usually follow nouns, whereas in Japanese the order is the opposite. The English sentence 'John hit Peter' would translate into Japanese as 'John Peter hit'.

In English, the 40 or so phonemes build more than a 100 000 morphemes, which, in turn, build almost 500 000 words. Using these words, we can create an infinite number of words and sentences. This reflects one of a language's distinctive properties: its **productive** nature.

Words must not only be arranged correctly in phrases and sentences, but also have meaning. The study of how language conveys meaning is called **semantics**. An area that has intrigued psycholinguists such as the

---

Competence rules:
Rules describing what language is and what it does.

Performance rules:
Rules defining how language works in practice.

Phonemes:
The basic sounds of a language.

Morphemes:
The smallest meaningful units of a language.

Syntax:
The rules that govern acceptable combinations of sounds in words.

Semantis:
The study of how language conveys meaning.

famous Noam Chomsky (1957) is that the same meaning can be conveyed using different phrases and sentences. For instance, the sentence 'The girl fed the dog' and 'The dog was fed by the girl' have the same meaning, although the syntax (grammatical structure) is different. To explain this, Chomsky distinguished between the surface and deep structure of the sentence. The **deep structure** refers to the underlying meaning of the sentence, while the **surface structure** refers to the arrangement of words in a sentence. Chomsky proposed that there are **transformational rules** that convert different deep structures into the same surface structures, or the same deep structures into different surface structures. According to this view, we understand language by transforming the surface structure (or verbal message) into a deep structure, which is its meaning. Thus, the sentences 'The girl fed the dog' and 'The dog was fed by the girl' are transformed into the same deep structure or meaning (Chomsky 1968).

The meaning of a statement depends not only on its words and their arrangement, but also on the social context in which the statement is made. The area of semantics that deals with the relationship between language and its social context is called **pragmatics**. To illustrate this, consider the following statement made by a student about a dinner in the dining room at her residence: 'I can't wait for dinner tonight.' If spoken enthusiastically, the statement may mean that she is looking forward to a tasty meal, but if spoken in a sarcastic voice, the same statement may mean that the student is anticipating the usual unappetising fare generally associated with such establishments. Cultural knowledge also forms a basis for language pragmatics. For instance, the term 'kitchen tea' to certain groups of people refers to a tea held for a bride-to-be, for whom people bring gifts for her new kitchen. To a person who is unfamiliar with this term, it may be literally interpreted as having tea in the kitchen, or as a brand of tea called 'kitchen tea'!

To use language, two distinct processes must be coordinated: production and comprehension. **Production** involves the generation of language (words, sentences, paragraphs, etc.). In contrast, **comprehension** refers to the understanding of language.

Deep Structure:
The underlying meaning of a sentence.

Surface structure:
The arrangement of words in sentences.

Transformational rules:
Rules that convert deep structures into the same surface structures.

Pragmatics:
The area of semantics that deals with the relationship between language and its social context.

Production:
The generation (production) of language.

Comprehension:
The understanding of language.

Language acquisition

All individuals seem to acquire language in the same sequence, in similar ways and at about the same time. The stages of language acquisition are:

- **Cooing:** During the first few months after birth.
- **Babbling:** Starts at age four to six months and comprises the repetition of sequences of phonemes (e.g. ba-ba-ba).
- **Holophrastic speech:** Comprises one-word utterances and starts at

about age one. The single words are used to convey wants and indicate intentions. During this phase, children use overextension when they apply words too broadly (e.g. an infant who refers to his or her father, and all other men, as 'Dada').

- **Telegraphic speech:** Occurs between age 18 and 24 months and involves the use of two- and, at times, three-word phrases, which comprise only nouns and verbs.
- **Basic adult sentence structure:** Present by age four.

Theories of language acquisition have explored the extent to which language is based on learning rather than the maturation of an inherited predisposition to develop language. Proponents of the learning view have argued that language is acquired either by conditioning or by imitation. Perhaps the best-known proponent of the conditioning view is B.F. Skinner (1957), who argued that children primarily acquire language through the positive reinforcement of correct speech. According to this view, a one-year-old child may learn to say 'milk' because, when her parents give her milk, they praise her for saying the word. Although research has shown that positive reinforcement can affect language acquisition (e.g. Routh 1969), it has also shown that the explanation is too simplistic to account, for instance, for the fact that children constantly use novel utterances that they have never heard before and certainly never received any reinforcement for using. Albert Bandura (1977) argued that language acquisition occurs through children imitating the vocabulary and grammar used by their parents and others with whom they have daily contact. However, imitation does not explain many aspects of language acquisition. For example, it does not explain why all children go through the same stages of development described at the beginning of this section, as imitation would suggest that they would start by using complete sentences. A further explanation is required. Noam Chomsky (1965, 1972) challenged the idea that language is acquired solely through imitation and proposed that humans inherit a language-acquisition device, which implies that humans are mentally and biologically pre-wired to acquire language. Evidence to support Chomsky's view has come from the universality of both the basic features of language and the stages of language acquisition that, it has been argued, indicate that the tendency to develop language is inborn. Current views seems to support the idea that, while we are born with the potential to develop language, we might learn our specific language, including its grammatical structure, primarily through imitation and operant conditioning.

As noted above, most children acquire language in roughly the same sequence and at about the same time. However, the linguistic environment in which they are reared also plays a role in the process of language acquisition. Researchers have pointed to a **critical period for language acquisition** that extends from infancy to adolescence, during which time language learning is optimal. A well-documented case illustrating this is that of a girl, Genie, who was raised in isolation. She was discovered by welfare workers at the age of 13 in a room where she had been kept restrained in a harness by her father and isolated from all social contact, including language, since infancy. Over a decade after returning to society and receiving intensive language therapy, although Genie had acquired a large vocabulary, she was only able to speak telegraphically and unable to use proper syntax. This suggested that she might have passed her critical period for language acquisition before the time that she joined society (Pines 1981). Another critical period is that concerning adults who acquire second languages. With age, these become increasingly more difficult to learn (e.g. Johnson & Newport 1989). However, work is still needed to explore other factors that may account for differences in the ease with which younger and older individuals learn second languages.

Critical period for language acquisition: Time during which language learning is optimal.

Cultural and educational factors

The effect of culture on cognitive development has been explored by a number of psychologists. Interestingly, it has not been a feature of mainstream Piagetian theory (e.g. Piaget 1977). In contrast, an American psychologist, Jerome Bruner, and the Russian school of psychologists, which included Vygotsky, Luria, Leontiev and Zaporozhets (Cole 1978; Luria 1979), emphasised the role of culture or society in the development of thinking in children. Both Bruner and the Russian group highlighted the importance of parents, teachers and other adults in transmitting a culturally appropriate conceptual framework. All see language as an important tool in this regard. (This emphasis on language is reminiscent of the linguistic relativity hypothesis discussed earlier.) They argued that parents, teachers and other adults shape children's behaviour and, ultimately, their mental constructs, by instruction and comments. Vygotsky viewed the internalisation of speech as a major process in the mental development of the child. Bruner's (1983) ideas about the social moulding of a child's thinking are similar. He also placed strong emphasis on the importance of schooling and literacy.

Vygotsky's conceptualisation of the mental development of the child made an important contribution to our knowledge in this area, and has educational applications that have been developed in South Africa by researchers such as Miller and Craig (1985). More specifically, Vygotsky (1962, 1978) argued that, during the development of mental processes, external or outer regulation (e.g. instruction by a teacher or a parent) is internalised by the child so that the regulation becomes inner directed or 'voluntary'. Thus, an activity that was initially divided between two people later becomes an internal mental activity (Luria 1959). In other words, during development, an interpersonal (societal/cultural) activity is converted into an intrapersonal process (Vygotsky 1978). Vygotsky (1978: p. 85) described a 'zone of proximal development' according to which the child initially only completes activities with the aid of an experienced learner, but later accomplishes these alone.

Vygotsky (1978: pp. 85–90) described the 'zone of proximal development' as the distance between a child's actual level of development (indicated by his or her ability to solve certain problems independently) and the level of potential development (determined by the child's ability to solve other, more complex problems with either adult assistance or the help of a more capable peer). Vygotsky thus argued that the process of development lags behind learning, and that this sequence creates a zone of proximal development.

Summary

Memory

Contemporary cognitive models regard memory as a series of memory systems; sets of discrete but interdependent processing units responsible for different kinds of processing. This fits well with the modular conception of the nervous system. In the information-processing model, the sensory register refers to the split-second mental representation of a perceived stimulus that remains very briefly after the stimulus disappears. Information that passes through the sensory registers to be processed and stored is put into the form of a mental representation. Short-term memory (STM) stores information for roughly 20 to 30 seconds, unless the information is maintained through rehearsal of some kind. Memory can then be encoded to be stored into long-term memory (LTM) and may last a lifetime.

Thinking

Thinking involves the mental manipulation of words and images, as when one solves problems, forms concepts or makes decisions. Problem solving involves working out the series of steps we need to follow in order to solve a problem. This can involve such tactics as trial and error, allowing an incubation period, and using algorithms and heuristics.

Phenomena like response sets and functional fixedness limit problem solving. Concepts help us to understand our environment, while reasoning involves evaluating information and generating logical arguments. Creativity is generally defined as a form of problem solving, which involves finding solutions that are novel, useful and socially valued.

Language

Language may be defined as an organised system of combining symbols (spoken, written or gestural) in order to communicate. Some people argue that language determines thought. Certain structures underlie language and communication. Competence rules for language describe what language is and what it does, while performance rules govern how language is used in practice. Syntax refers to the rules that govern the combination of sounds in words. Semantics is the study of how language conveys meaning. Production refers to the generation of language, while comprehension refers to the understanding of language. When using language these two processes are coordinated. All individuals acquire language in the same sequence and at about the same stage. Some believe that language is acquired by means of imitation, while Noam Chomsky argued that we have an innate language acquisition device or predisposition to develop language. Others emphasise the role of culture and society in the development of thinking in children, and highlight the importance of language as a tool in this regard. Vygotsky described a zone of proximal development according to which the activities a child can initially only complete with aid of an experienced learner, he or she later accomplishes alone.

Further reading

Amabile, T.M. (1989) *Growing up Creative*. New York: Random House.

Anderson, J.R. (1995) *Learning and Memory: An Integrated Approach*. New York: John Wiley.

Atkinson, R.C. & Shifrin, R.N. (1968) Human memory: A proposed system and its control processes. In K.W. Spence and J.T. Spense (eds), *The Psychology of Learning and Motivation*, Volume 2. New York: Academic Press, pp. 32–65.

Bandura, A. (1977) *Social Learning Theory*. Engelwood Cliffs: Prentice-Hall.

Barron, F. & Harrington, D.M. (1981) Creativity, intelligence, and personality. *Annual Review of Psychology*, 32, pp. 439–76.

Bower, G. (1975) Cognitive psychology: An introduction. In W.K. Estes (ed.), *Handbook of Learning and Cognitive Processes: Volume 1, Introduction to Concepts and Issues*. Hillside: Erlbaum, pp. 25–80.

Bruner, J.S. (1983) *Children's Talk: Learning to Use Language*. Oxford: Oxford University Press.

Carmichael, L., Hogan, H.P. & Walter, A.A. (1932) An experimental study of the effect of language on the reproduction of visually perceived forms. *Journal of Experimental Psychology*, 15, pp. 73–86.

Chomsky, N. (1957) *Syntactic Structures*. The Hague: Mouton.

Chomsky, N. (1965) *Aspects of the Theory of Syntax*. Cambridge, Mass: MIT Press.

Chomsky, N. (1968) *Language and Mind*. New York: Harcourt Brace & World.

Chomsky, N. (1972) *Language and Mind*. New York: Harcourt Brace Jovanovich.

Cole, M. (1978) *The Selected Writings of A.R. Luria*. White Plains: M.E. Sharpe.

Curran, H.V. (1980) Cross-cultural perspectives on cognition. In G. Claxton (ed.), *Cognitive Psychology: New Directions*. London: Routledge & Kegan Paul, pp. 304–34.

Dickstein, L.S. (1976) Differential difficulty of categorical syllogisms. *Bulletin of the Psychonomic Society*, 8, pp. 330–2.

Duncker, K. (1945) On problem solving. *Psychological Monographs*, 58 (270), pp. 1–113.

Gardner, R.A. & Gardner, B.T. (1969) Teaching sign language to a chimpanzee. *Science*, 165, pp. 664–72.

Gardner, R.A. & Gardner, B.T. (1975) Forty signs of language in child and chimpanzee. *Science*, 187, pp. 752–54.

Giray, E.F. (1985) A life span approach to the study of eidetic imagery. *Journal of Mental Imagery*, 9, pp. 21–32.

Goldman-Rakic, P. (1995) Cellular basis of working memory. *Neuron*, 14, pp. 477–85.

Guilford, J.P. (1950) Creativity. *American Psychologist*, 14, pp. 469–79.

Guilford, J.P. (1984) Varieties of divergent production. *Journal of Creative Behaviour*, 18, pp. 1–10.

Hayes, C. (1951) *The Ape in Our House*. New York: Harper & Row.

Higgins, E.T. (1990) Lay epistemic theory and the relation between motivation and cognition. *Psychological Inquiry*, 1, pp. 209–10.

Jelicic, M. & Bonke, B. (1991) Level of processing affects performance on explicit and implicit memory tasks. *Perceptual and Motor Skills*, 72(3), pp. 1263–6.

Johnson, J.S. & Newport, E.L. (1989) Critical period effects in second language learning: The influence of maturational state on the acquisition of English as a second language. *Cognitive Psychology,* 21, pp. 60–99.

Kay, P. & Kempton, W. (1984) What is the Sapir-Whorf hypothesis? *American Anthropologist,* 86(1), pp.65–79.

Kellog, W.N. & Kellog, L.A. (1933) *The Ape and the Child.* New York: McGraw-Hill.

Kershner, J.R. & Ledger, G. (1985) Effect of sex, intelligence, and style of thinking on creativity: A comparison of gifted and average IQ children. *Journal of Personality and Social Psychology,* 48, pp. 1033–40.

Lerner, R.M., Kendall, P.C., Miller, D.T., Hultsch, D.F. and Jensen, R.A. (1986) *Psychology.* New York: Macmillan.

Kotovsky, K. & Simon, H.A. (1973) Empirical tests of a theory of human acquisition of concepts of sequential patterns. *Cognitive Psychology,* 3, pp. 399–424.

Loftus, E.F. & Zanni, G. (1975) Eyewitness testimony: The influence of the wording of a question. *Bulletin of the Psychonomic Society,* 5, pp. 86–8.

Luchins, A.S. (1942) Mechanization in problem solving. *Psychological Monographs,* 54, p. 248.

Luria, A.R. (1959) The directive role of speech in development and dissolution. Part 1. *Word,* 15, pp. 341–52.

Luria, A.R. (1973) *The Working Brain.* New York: Penguin Books.

Luria, A.R. (1979) *The Making of Mind: A Personal Account of Soviet Psychology.* Cambridge, Mass.: Harvard University Press.

Miller, R. & Craig, A. (1985) Exploring the zone of proximal development: The Necker cube effect. Paper presented at the Third National Congress of the Psychological Association. October.

Neisser, U. (1991) A case of misplaced nostalgia. *American Psychologist,* 46, pp. 34–6.

Newell, A. & Simon, H. (1972) *Human Problem Solving.* Englewood Cliffs: Prentice-Hall.

Patterson, F.G. (1978) The gestures of a gorilla: Language acquisition in another pongid. *Brain and Language,* 5, pp. 72–97.

Piaget, J. (1977) *The Development of Thought.* Oxford: Basil Blackwell.

Pines, M. (1981) The civilizing of Genie. *Psychology Today,* September, pp. 28–34.

Pullum, G.K. (1991) *The Great Eskimo Hoax and Other Irreverent Essays on the Study of Language*. Chicago: University of Chicago Press.

Roediger, H.L. (1990) Implicit memory: Retention without remembering. *American Psychologist*, 45(9), pp. 1043–56.

Rosch, E. (1973) On the internal structure of perceptual and semantic categories. In T.E. Moore (ed.), *Cognitive Development and the Acquisition of Language*. New York: Academic Press. pp. 111–44.

Rosch, E. (1975) Cognitive representations of semantic categories. *Journal of Experimental Psychology*, 104, pp. 192–223.

Routh, D.K. (1969) Conditioning of vocal response differentiation in infants. *Developmental Psychology*, 1, pp. 219–26.

Schacter, D.L. (1992) Understanding implicit memory: A cognitive neuroscience approach. *American Psychologist*, 47, pp. 559–69.

Sdorow, L.M. (1998) *Psychology* (4th edition). New York: McGraw-Hill.

Skinner, B.F. (1957) *Verbal Behavior*. New York: Appleton-Century-Crofts.

Sternberg, R.J. (1994) *In Search of the Human Mind*. New York: Harcourt Brace.

Tulving, E. (1972) Episodic and semantic memory. In E. Tulving and W. Donaldson (eds), *Organization of Memory*. New York: Academic Press, pp. 381–403.

Tulving, E. (1987) Multiple memory systems and consciousness. *Human Neurobiology*, 6(2), pp. 67–80.

Vygotsky, L.S. (1962) *Thought and Language*. Cambridge, Mass.: MIT Press.

Vygotsky, L.S. (1978) *Mind in Society*. Cambridge, Mass.: Harvard University Press.

Watson, J.B. (1924) *Behaviorism*. New York: Morton.

Weaver, C.A. (1993) Do you need a flash to form a flashbulb memory? *Journal of Experimental Psychology*, 122, pp. 39–46.

Wells, G.I. & Turtle, J.W. (1987) Eyewitness testimony: Current knowledge and emerging controversies. *Canadian Journal of Behavioral Science*, 19(4), pp. 363–88.

Whorf, B.L. (1956) Science and linguistics. In J.B. Caroll (ed.), *Language, Thought and Reality: Selected Writings of Benjamin Lee Whorf*. Cambridge, Mass.: MIT Press, pp. 202–19.

Wilcox, C. & Williams, L. (1990) Taking stock of schema theory. *Social Science Journal*, 27(4), pp. 373–93.

Yu, B., Zhang, W., Jing, Q., Peng, R., Zhang, G. & Simon, H.A. (1985) STM capacity for Chinese and English language materials. *Memory and Cognition*, 13, pp. 202–7.

12 Sexuality

L.J. Nicholas

Objectives

After studying this chapter you should:

- be familiar with the key figures in the development of sexology and its history
- understand the main theories of sexuality and have an overview of male and female sexual problems
- understand why HIV/AIDS has implications for safer sexuality, with a particular emphasis on first sexual intercourse.

Introduction

The establishment of sexology as a distinct discipline is credited to three German physicians: Ivan Bloch, Albert Moll and Magnus Hirschfield. Bloch coined the term 'sexology' and encouraged a multidisciplinary approach to the study of sexuality. Moll founded the International Society for Sex Research in 1913. His research interests were homosexuality, libido and infantile sexuality, and he published a volume on the sexual life of the child in 1909. Hirschfield's primary interest was in homosexuality and he did a great deal of research on the problems experienced by homosexuals. He coined the term 'transvestism', edited the first *Journal of Sexology* and founded the first Institute of Sexology. Most sex research was stifled by the rise of Nazism, and the contents of the institute were publicly burned in 1933.

H.A. Ellis was a contemporary of the German sexologists and published a six-volume series, *Studies in the Psychology of Sex* (1897–1910), which anticipated much of what Freud later wrote about childhood sexuality and contributed to a more open discussion of sexuality. Ellis contended that sexual customs were relative to a particular society; that sexual response was equally strong in women and men; that homosexuality was not pathological; and that masturbation was harmless. He coined the term 'auto-erotism'.

Ellis' views on the varied nature of human sexual behaviour gave a more balanced perspective than R. von Krafft-Ebbing's disease-oriented perspective. Krafft-Ebbing had published a detailed classification of sexual disorders in 1886, which had widespread impact and led to his being often considered the founder of modern sexology.

John B. Watson was one of the earliest converts and casualties of sex research advocates. The anti-VD (venereal disease) films shown to soldiers during World War I stimulated his interest in research. Watson decided to show these films to civilian audiences after the war and, with the help of Karl Lashley, showed them to about 5 000 people. Questionnaires were issued to all respondents and follow-up interviews were done of selected samples. This research convinced Watson of psychology's usefulness in studying sexuality and he devised a lengthier questionnaire, with which he proposed to study the attitudes of medical doctors to sexuality and specifically to sex education as a means of preventing venereal disease. He found that medical doctors seemed to view sex itself as a disease and became convinced that psychologists should study sexual behaviour.

Watson constructed a set of instruments to measure female physiological responses during sexual arousal. Watson's wife refused to participate, but his laboratory assistant, Rosalie Rayner, consented and he acquired several boxes of scientific data. Watson's wife discovered why he was spending so much time in the laboratory and sued him for divorce. She also confiscated the scientific records. He was forced to resign his professorship at Johns Hopkins University, and most of his friends and colleagues deserted him. Even after his divorce and subsequent marriage to Rosalie Rayner, Watson was unable to find a job at a university, but found work in an advertising agency.

The Kinsey studies

In 1938, the Association for Women Students at Indiana University, under instructions from A.C. Kinsey, requested a course in human sexuality for students who were engaged, married or considering marriage (Gathorne-Hardy 1998). At this time, it was illegal to import sex information and even contraceptive information into the USA or to send it through the postal system, although a booming underground system for the distribution of erotic material existed. Kinsey consequently presented the sexuality course and, finding few scientific data available, set about collecting data relevant to his course, culminating in his 1948 book *Sexual Behavior in the Human Male* and, in 1953, *Sexual Behavior in the Human Female*. The books elicited much controversy and criticism. Kinsey used his experience as an entomologist with wide acclaim for his gall wasp studies as a model for collecting the sex histories that form the basis of the two books. The variety and extent of sexual practices uncovered by Kinsey *et al.* (1948), and Kinsey *et al.* (1953), were greeted with disbelief and shock (Jones 1997; Gathorne-Hardy 1998).

Laumann *et al.* (1994) outline three main reasons for the controversial nature of scientifically investigating sexual behaviour:

- Political opposition from the right and the left wings is a major factor. Right-wing opposition usually resides in their opposition to particular sexual practices that they believe, if investigated, might encourage or legitimate such practices. Left-wing opposition usually resides in their approval of particular sexual practices that they believe, if investigated, would indicate negligible endorsement of such practices that might subject those engaged in these practices to greater ostracism and possibly encourage prevention of the practices. Such was the case in the Laumann *et al.* (1994) study.
- There are those who believe sex should be private and that public funding should not be used for sex research.
- There are those who believe that it is not possible to randomly sample sexual behaviour and achieve accurate and honest reporting in this area of study.

Senator Jesse Helms blocked federal funding in the USA for national surveys of sexual research because he believed they would help legitimate homosexuality by showing an increased incidence of it. Kinsey's research found out the following about homosexuality:

- Some 37% of the total male population has at least some overt homosexual experience to the point of orgasm between adolescence and old age. This accounts for nearly two males out of every five.
- Some 50% of all males (approximately) have neither overt nor psychic experience of homosexuality after the onset of adolescence.
- Some 25% of the male population has more than incidental homosexual experience or reactions for at least three years between the ages of 16 and 55. In terms of averages, one male out of approximately every four has had or will have such distinct and continued homosexual experience.
- Some 10% of males are more or less exclusively homosexual for at least three years between the ages of 16 and 55. This is one male in ten in the white male population, and would rate 5 or 6 on the scale in Figure 12.1, overleaf.
- Some 4% of white males are exclusively homosexual throughout their lives, after the onset of adolescence

(KINSEY *et al.* 1948: p. 650–1)

Kinsey's figures are much higher than recent population surveys. The differences are often attributed to the purposefully recruited research participants and institutionalised participants who characterised Kinsey's studies and who may have increased these figures compared to probability samples. The sexual landscape was also very different in the years 1938–1947 when Kinsey interviewed his samples. Laumann *et al* . (1994) contended that the increasing visibility and labelling of homo-sexuality might have inhibited the amount of adolescent sexual experimentation and brought about changes in the structure of adoles-cence. Another factor may be the greater opportunities for heterosexual experimentation that accompanied the liberalisation of sexual values.

Kinsey proposed a continuum from homo- to heterosexuality rather than focusing on discrete subtypes.

Scale	Point description
0	Exclusively heterosexual behaviour
1	Incidental homosexual behaviour
2	More than incidental homosexual behaviour
3	Equal amount of homosexual and heterosexual behaviour
4	More than incidental heterosexual behaviour
5	Incidental heterosexual behaviour
6	Exclusively homosexual behaviour

FIGURE 12.1: KINSEY'S SUBTYPES

Laumann *et al.* (1994) found that 0,6% of men have had sex only with boys or men and never with a female partner, and 0,2% of women have only had sex with women. Their data also indicated that about 9% of 18- to 59-year-old men living in the largest central cities in the USA identify as homosexual or bisexual, 14% had male partners in the past five years, and a further 2% had some level of sexual attraction to other men. These figures illustrate the disparities in sexual profiles of different communities. Coleman (in Mackay 2001) contended that between 3 and 4% of the world's adult male population live exclusively as homo-sexuals, as do 1,5% to 2% of women. Homosexuality is illegal in at least 50 countries and there are several countries that impose the death penalty for homosexuality (Mackay 2001).

Sex therapy: The early years

William Masters and Virginia Johnson's contributions to sex research
and therapy were their development of a brief treatment of sexual
dysfunctions and their physiological studies of sexual response. They
provided laboratory evidence of the origins of vaginal lubrication,
documented typical vaginal and uterine changes occurring during sexual
arousal and orgasm, and documented the evidence of multiple orgasms
in women (at a time when this was disputed by medical authorities)
(Kolodny 2001). Kinsey and his colleagues had also observed male and
female bodily responses during masturbation and coitus, but did not
publish their findings. Robert Latou Dickenson also studied female
sexual responses during masturbation before Masters and Johnson, and
introduced the electrical vibrator into gynaecological practice. Masters
and Johnson were, however, the first to couple visual observation of
sexual intercourse and masturbation with physiological recording
instruments.

Masters displayed an early interest in problems of human sexuality
as a student under the supervision of George Washington Corner, an
authority on the biology of sex. He was intrigued by the use of hormone
replacement therapy for aged and aging women, and published widely
in this area. He launched his studies on sexual physiology, partly because
of the favourable public response to Kinsey's work and partly because of
his commitment to the importance of research on human sexual functioning. Masters and Johnson's research was curtailed by political
pressure, which prevented governmental support. Many medical journals would not publish their findings and they delayed their presentation
of these until 1962, at a meeting of the American Psychological
Association (APA). In the 1990s, governmental obstruction of sex
research limited a major sex survey in the USA (Laumann et al. 1994).

In the 1930s, a variety of surgical procedures for impotence were
used, such as cautery, tightening of the perineal musculature, and the
application of testicular diathermy. An operation for vaginismus was the
main surgical procedure for female sexual dysfunction. During the
1940s, the first attempts to insert penile splints for erectile failure were
made. A range of sophisticated surgical methods has developed in the
last decade. These interventions are likely to diminish with the discovery
of Viagra® (sildenafil citrate).

Viagra® is the first oral pill to treat erection dysfunction and enhances the smooth muscle relaxant effects of nitric oxide, which is normally released in response to sexual stimulation. The smooth muscle relaxation allows increased blood flow into certain areas of the penis, leading to erection. Progressive relaxation and stop-start methods for controlling premature ejaculation were developed in the 1950s, and a graded series of dilators was used for vaginismus in the 1960s, although no particular theoretical assumptions guided these interventions.

Modern behaviour therapy applied to the modification of undesirable sexual behaviour was based on theoretical principles of learning derived from laboratory experiments. Because of early theoretical constraints, and partly as an ideological reaction to psychoanalysis, treatment of sexual problems was restricted to those problems that would fit an experimental learning model. The early emphasis was on aversive procedures, such as changing sexual preference from homosexual to heterosexual, whereas now more emphasis is placed on learning new behaviour. In 1958, H. Wolpe suggested systematic desensitisation for erectile dysfunction and other difficulties, which started a shift from psychoanalytic approaches.

Until the late 1960s, sexual dysfunction – and most psychological problems – were typically treated psychoanalytically. Only a few clinicians, such as A. Lazarus (a South African psychologist), H. Wolpe (a South African psychiatrist) and M. Obler explicitly used behavioural principles in treating sexual dysfunction (Weiderman 1998). In 1970, Masters and Johnson published *Human Sexual Inadequacy*, claiming effective treatment in a short two-week intensive treatment period. They led the shift of sex therapy from individual to couple therapy. Eclecticism has grown in modern sex therapy. Helen Kaplan has, for example, attempted to combine behavioural and psychoanalytic principles in treating sexual disorders.

Theories of sexuality

Gagnon *et al.* (1994) contended that little progress had been made in the social sciences towards developing systematic theories about the social processes involved in sexuality. We will explore psychoanalytic theory, learning theory, scripting theory and evolutionary psychology theories such as sexual strategies theory.

Psychoanalysis

In a letter to W. Fliess on 28 January 1900, Sigmund Freud wrote: 'I am putting together material for the theory of sexuality and waiting till some spark can set what I have collected ablaze' (Strachey 1962). Freud made many modifications and additions to his theory of sexuality over the next 20 years.

Freud's general investigation into the nature of sexuality was stimulated by clinical observations of the importance of sexuality in the causation of anxiety neurosis. His first approaches, during the early 1890s, emphasised chemistry and physiology. By 1895, Freud had developed a complete explanation of hysteria based on the traumatic effects of seduction during early childhood. In the summer of 1897, Freud abandoned his seduction theory, in which infantile sexuality was regarded as dormant and only brought into the open by the disastrous intervention of adults, and adopted the position that sexual impulses operated normally in the youngest of children, without external intervention.

According to Erickson women fear their reproductive inner space being left unfulfilled

Freud proposed that early sexual feelings pass through five developmental stages: oral, anal, phallic, latency and genital. In the oral stage, during the first year of life, the mouth is the primary focus of sensual gratification. In the anal stage (one to three years), sensual pleasure shifts to the anal region. During toilet training, the child asserts independence by holding back or letting go bowel movements, which produce physical and psychological pleasure, but gradually learns socially acceptable behaviour in this regard. In the phallic stage (three to five years), the child's erotic interest shifts to the genitals.

Freud suggests different pathways for boys and girls. A boy's attachment to his mother becomes genitally centred and he comes to see his father as his rival for his mother's love. Wishing to replace his father, he has fantasies of killing him, but also fears retaliation in the form of castration by his father. He therefore gives up on his attachment to his mother, repressing his sexual feelings toward her, and identifies with the aggressor, his father, hoping that in this way he will ultimately exclusively possess his mother. The boy moves forward in his development through identification with the father in latency, with further repression of his sexual wishes.

When a girl becomes aware of the anatomical differences between her and a boy, and discovers that she does not have a penis, she feels envious and cheated, resulting in the girl wanting to possess her father and replace her mother, whom she blames for the dilemma. The girl feels competitive towards her mother and longs for her father to give her the penis that she has lost. She then longs for a baby from her father to substitute for the penis. She ultimately abandons this wish, as it becomes clear that her father will not give her a baby. Only through identifying with her mother will she eventually possess her father and get a baby. Girls enter latency more gradually, but cease all masturbation and repress their sexuality.

During the latency stage, the sexual impulses recede in importance. The stage ends at the time of puberty, when the genital stage is activated by internal biological forces, eventually expressing mature adult genital sexuality (Striver 1986).

Psychoanalytic theory has not produced many empirically verifiable theories and the empirical support it does have was drawn mainly from small samples of clinical populations. Psychoanalytic ideas about sexuality have also been attacked by feminists because of their phallocentric bias, which assumes implicitly that the male is the model human being and that the white European is the model for all humanity. However, Williams (1977) contended that the followers and critics of Freud have ignored his assertions of the tentative nature of his ideas on feminine psychology. Mead (1979) also cautioned against ignoring Freud because of his culture-boundedness in relation to the psychology of woman, asserting that he opened up a whole new way of understanding ourselves, even though he understood very little about women. Richards (1979) pointed out that Freud made frequent complaints about the obscurity of the sexual life of females:

> The significance of the factor of sexual over evaluation can be best studied in men, for their erotic life alone has become accessible to research. That of women – partly owing to the stunting effect of civilised

conditions and partly owing to their conventional secretiveness and
insincerity, is still veiled in an impenetrable obscurity.
(FREUD IN RICHARDS 1979: p. 63)

Freud justified publishing new, unconfirmed observations based on a
handful of studies for two reasons:

- He felt that the time he had available for work was becoming increasingly limited and an eager crowd of fellow workers was available to
  make use of what was unfinished or doubtful.
- He concluded that if his findings were found not to have general
  validity, it: 'would remain no more than a contribution to our knowledge of the different paths along which sexual life develops'.
(RICHARDS 1979: p. 343)

Williams (1977) argued that biology, as an innate determinant of
personality, is not inherent in psychoanalytic theory, because psychoanalysis deals with the transformation of biological facts, such as gender
differences, to mental representations. Psychoanalysis therefore deals
with the inheritance of a social order of patriarchy within which the girl
and boy learn their respective places. The way that this happens is asym-
metrically consistent with the asymmetry of their places in society.
Williams (1977) contended that the little girl's renunciation of her
pre-oedipal sexuality and desire for the mother are a prerequisite to the
assumption of her place in the real society of ubiquitous patriarchy, just
as the destruction of the boy's Oedipal attachment and identification
with the father prepares him to assume the role. Williams (1977) therefore contended that the feminist criticism of Freud erred in placing
his statements outside of psychoanalysis, within a patriarchal society.
Within this context, she believed Freud's statements of female psychology to be accurate.

Helen Deutsch was analysed by Freud and worked within the
Freudian framework. She refuted two key Freudian concepts, penis envy
and Oedipal conflict. Deutsch believed that penis envy is a secondary
development, which grows out of a general tendency to envy in all
children, when they observe others being given attention, and is not
peculiar to women. She also challenged Freud's contention of the girl's
abandonment of her mother as a love object in favour of the father,
believing that this detachment is never fully achieved and that the girl-
mother bond is of crucial importance to her personality development.
She, however, believed that the sexuality of woman was less important
within the overall context of their lives than that of men.

Erik Erikson studied with Helene Deutsch and was analysed by Anna Freud. His model of psychosocial development assumed the male as the prototype of reality. He thought of the concept of penis envy as less important than the 'productive inner space that all women know'. Feelings of deprivation experienced by women should not be interpreted as evidence of resentment at not being a boy, but rather the fear of this productive inner space being left empty and unfulfilled (Williams 1977). Women's nature, therefore, is still determined by her anatomy (Rohrbaugh 1981). In psychoanalytic theories it is implicit that the model is male and that females are brought into theory through conceptual spin-offs.

The girl wants to possess her father and replace her mother.

Karen Horney challenged the concept of penis envy, cautioning against extending the applicability of the concept derived from neurotic females to all females. She argued against the importance that Freud ascribed to penis envy, masculinity complex and basic feelings of inferiority in women, and felt that they should also apply to men. She did not, however, reject the use of the concepts.

Learning theory

Learning theory has gained more research support in its explanation of various aspects of human sexuality than other theories. According to learning theory, sexual responses are natural, unconditioned reactions, and dysfunctional symptoms are learned inhibitions, acquired through conditioning and reinforcement. These processes can occur outside of the person's awareness and, once the conditioned response is established, it may be beyond the individual's control. Learning theory therefore does not specify particular causal factors, but focuses on mechanisms and events that precipitate sexual problems. Classical conditioning explains how a previously neutral stimulus with repeated pairing with a stimulus known to elicit a particular response becomes capable of eliciting a similar response. For example, if one is repeatedly admonished to inhibit sexual feelings, this may influence one's future enjoyment of sexual intercourse.

Through this form of learning, people come to be sexually aroused by, for example, leather, pain, rubber or urination. When one of these objects or events is paired with sexual arousal, the person may develop a sexual response to the object or event through the process of classical conditioning. Through stimulus generalisation, the person may present a learned sexual response to all stimuli with a certain common characteristic. The number of learning trials and the intensity of the experience influence these learning processes. It is unlikely that much learning will take place with one learning trial and/or when the intensity of the experience is that of a passing observation.

Operant conditioning holds that a behaviour has a greater likelihood of occurring if it is immediately followed by a reinforcer than if it is punished or ignored. It explains how particular sexual behaviours are acquired, such as dysfunctional sexual responses, which, while being a source of distress, may persist because of being covertly rewarded. A women's anorgasmia may, for example, be her only way of expressing her power should her partner want her to be orgasmic.

Social learning theory acknowledges the influence of classical and operant conditioning, but contends that much more important learning occurs by observing and imitating others. Social learning theory does not place sex-typed behaviour and sexuality as central. The same principle governs all social learning, regardless of gender. Sex-typed behaviour is not examined in relation to sexuality, but rather as a prototype of certain social conduct.

Masters and Johnson (1970) conceptualised sex as a natural phenomenon rather than a learned one. They believed that sexual dysfunctions might be separated from neurotic and characterological disorders, and treated directly. Sexual problems stemmed primarily from anxiety, specifically fears of performance, which may be eliminated through specific re-education procedures.

The importance of learning and conditioning in creating and maintaining adaptive and maladaptive sexual behaviour had been acknowledged since the inception of behaviour therapy. However, behaviour therapy in the late 1950s and early 1960s focused mainly on the treatment of deviant sexual behaviour.

The publication of *Human Sexual Inadequacy* in 1970 stimulated more behaviour therapists to apply behaviour therapy techniques to individuals and couples with sexual difficulties. Leiblum and Pervin (1980: p. 16) contended that:

> *Although not self-described behaviour therapists, Masters and Johnson had provided a clinical approach that was uniquely appealing to behavioural clinicians, an approach that incorporated many explicitly behavioural strategies and principles: the identification of anxiety as the primary cause of dysfunctional behaviour; viewing overt symptomatic behaviour as the target of change, rather than hypothetical underlying intrapsychic conflicts; changing undesired behaviours through step-by-step successive approximations to the desired end goal; and using active, directed behavioural assignments for promoting behavioural change, rather than insight and interpretation.*

Masters and Johnson heralded the first substantial challenge to the dominance of the psychoanalytic approach to sexual dysfunction. Before their pioneering work, sexual dysfunctions were viewed as symptoms of a more pervasive deep-seated developmental problem, or the result of unconscious conflicts. Sexual inhibitions were assumed to be acquired through negative contingencies that result from parent-child interactions during the Oedipal phase. They were thought to persist because repression and avoidance of incestuous impulses reduce castration anxiety.

Their approach, even with its limitations, proved to be much more effective than the psychoanalytic approaches. Their innovations were, however, not derived from formal psychological theories, but contained elements that could be explained by a number of psychological theories. Integrated approaches have increasingly been employed in sex therapy, particularly combining psychodynamic and learning theory.

Practicing the tactics of attraction.

Mating strategies
take many forms.

Scripting theory

This theory assumes that patterns of sexual behaviour are culture-
specific, that biological instincts do not affect sexual behaviour or that
such effects are minor in comparison to socially determined scripts of sexual conduct. Patterns of sexual behaviour are acquired through a process
of acculturation lasting from birth to death. Minor adaptations to cultural scripts are made to suit individual needs (Laumann *et al.* 1994).

Sexual strategies theory

According to this theory, desire lies at the foundation of sexuality and
mating. The desires of one sex therefore determine which tactics of
attraction are effective when used by the opposite sex. The theory differs
from other evolutionary theories in that it proposes that humans have a
complex repertoire of short- and long-term mating strategies, which are
activated differently depending on the context. Other evolutionary theorists have argued that humans are inherently promiscuous and
that humans evolved primarily for long-term monogamous mating
(Buss 1998).

Evolutionary psychology

Evolutionary psychology has become increasingly influential in the last
decade and examines behavioural processes in terms of their adaptive
value for species over the course of many generations (Weiten 1998).

Charles Darwin's (1859) theory of evolution by natural selection is often confused with survival selection, whereas survival only becomes important to the extent that it contributes to reproduction. Differential reproductive success linked with differences in heritable design is the core of natural selection. Darwin's (1871) proposal of a second evolutionary process is more germane to sexual strategies theory – that is, characteristics that give organisms an advantage in competing for mates can evolve through intrasexual competition and intersexual selection (see Buss 1998).

Intrasexual competition
Members of one sex compete for preferential sexual access to mates, and the qualities that lead to success will be selected and evolve over time. Reproductive advantage therefore accrues to the winner through increasing sexual access.

Intersexual selection
Consensus exists among members of one sex about the qualities desired in mates, and those who possess the desired qualities have a mating advantage. Those without the desired qualities get excluded. The progeny are also more likely to carry both the preferences and the preferred characteristics (Buss 1998; Ridley 1993).

Fisher (1930) cited in Buss (1998) provided a theory to explain the origins of mate choice that Darwin's theory of sexual selection left unexplained. Fisher's theory of 'runaway selection' proposed the following: Assume that there is genetic variation in a trait – for example tail length – and males with slightly longer tails survive longer than those with slightly shorter tails. Suppose further that there is a genetic variation among females in choosing males of differing tail lengths. Females who prefer mating with the longer-tailed males will bear sons with longer tails who will survive better than short-tailed males. Over generations, genes for long tails and for female preferences for long tails will spread. This feedback loop produces a 'runaway process' until halted by the process of natural selection (Buss 1998; Ridley 1993).

Trivers (1972) cited in Buss (1998) reasoned that males of many species engaged in intrasexual combat, but not females, because the sex that invests more in offspring should be expected to be more selective in choice of mates. The sex with lower investment would be expected to be

Alcohol is often used to lubricate mating strategies.

more competitive with members of their sex for sexual access to the higher-investing sex. Female desire can therefore determine the areas of competition men would engage in by granting greater access to those males with particular resources valued by females and excluding those who fail to accrue such resources.

Buss (1998) contended that, more than any other theory of human sexuality, sexual strategies theory explains why men and women have evolved a complex repertoire of short- and long-term sexual strategies.

Acquired Immune Deficiency Syndrome (AIDS)

AIDS is a disease characterised by progressive damage to the body's immune system, which results in the development of so-called opportunistic infections, which are eventually fatal. It results from infection by the human immune deficiency virus (HIV) and was first described in 1981 as a distinct clinical entity. It was initially named 'gay compromise' disease or 'gay-related immune deficiency', because the first patients were predominantly homosexual. Recipients of contaminated blood, intravenous drug users, sexual contacts of infected persons and babies born to mothers in these groups were also found to be HIV-positive.

In June 1981, five gay men presented with rare symptoms suggestive of immunological problems and five women from the Ugandan border region presented with untreatable anaerobic ulcers of the groin and anus. By 1983, this condition of immune collapse had devastated gay communities in the West and was named AIDS. In Tanzania, it was known as 'Juliana' and in Uganda as 'slim' (Hooper 2000).

The incidence of HIV/AIDS in South Africa

The first antenatal survey in 1990 provided a baseline from which HIV trends have been assessed annually. Anonymous, unlinked, cross-sectional surveys were conducted among first-time pregnant women attending public antenatal clinics during October. October was selected because surveys undertaken by Statistics South Africa indicated that during this period the population tends toward more stability and is less mobile. A weighted systematic cluster random sample was used that, in 2000, surveyed 16 607 women from 400 sites. Public antenatal clinics are attended by 80% of pregnant women in South Africa, of whom 85,2% are African (Department of Health 2000). In the Western Cape, 4% of attendees refused to be tested (Shaik & Adendorff 2000). Of the 16 607 women, 24,5% were infected with HIV, an increase on 22,8% in 1998 and 22,4% in 1999. Blood specimens were tested with one ELISA (enzyme-linked immunosorbent assay), except in the Western Cape, where two ELISAs were used because of the low HIV prevalence rate. Given these results, it is estimated that approximately one in nine South Africans is infected with HIV (Department of Health 2000)

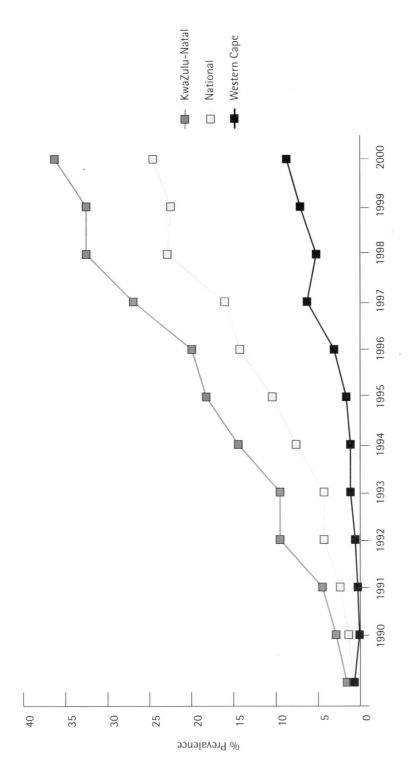

FIGURE 12.2: National, Western Cape (lowest) and KwaZulu-Natal (highest) HIV trends, 1990 to 2000

(SOURCE: DEPARTMENT OF HEALTH 2000)

Risk of HIV infection

Receptive anal intercourse has shown the strongest association with HIV transmission in homosexual men, whereas insertive anal intercourse posed a lesser risk. Various studies cited in Glasner and Kaslow (1990), and Masters *et al.* (1988) found no evidence of an increased risk of HIV infection linked to oral sex. However, Masters *et al.* (1988: p. 24) asserted that:

> *Though there is as yet no research conclusively proving that the AIDS virus can be transmitted by oral sex, we want to stress that it is a virtual certainty that this mode of spreading the infection is real. For one thing, there is no known viral or bacterial STD that is not spread, at least at times, by oro-genital contact.*

Master *et al.* (1988) also expressed scepticism about the AIDS virus not being transmitted by deep kissing, asserting that other sexually transmitted diseases (STDs) can be spread in this manner, especially where cuts and abrasions are present on the lips or in the mouth. They advocate adopting precautions against the worst-case possibility, rather than making the most optimistic assumption, given the fatal nature of the disease.

In a study of monogamous partners of individuals with transfusion-associated infections, most partners did not acquire the infection, despite repeated sexual contacts, but in certain couples, transmission occurred after only a few contacts. For female-to-male transmission, the rate of infection for husbands was 8% (Glasner & Kaslow 1990).

The estimate that the risk of an infected man transmitting HIV to a woman through a single act of unprotected vaginal intercourse is approximately 1 in a 1 000, and the risk of an infected woman transmitting HIV to a man through a single act of unprotected vaginal intercourse is approximately 1 in 2 000, has been disputed by Masters *et al.* (1988). Indicated by their research, they cited the risk as 1 in 400 for women and 1 in 600 for men (Glasner & Kaslow 1990). Raymond (1991) reported that a survey of 200 research reports found that North American women are 12 times as likely as men to become infected during heterosexual intercourse. The reasons were that a higher proportion of men were already infected and semen infected with HIV can reside for days within the vaginal canal, increasing the length of time a woman is exposed to the virus. Among younger age groups, the proportion of women infected with HIV is approaching that of men. Women live an average of 298 days after the first appearance of symptoms of AIDS, which is about 20% less than the 374-day average for men.

In South Africa, the rate of infection among males and females at 15 years of age is close to zero, but rises to a peak at about 26 years for women and about 32 years for men. The peak prevalence for men is consistently about 25% lower than for women (Williams *et al.* 2000). Lachenicht (1993) made the point that frequently recurring temptation, such as opportunities for sexual intercourse, are hard to resist, even if the risks associated with the temptation are well known. He suggested more emphasis should be placed on structural interventions, such as legalising and regulating sex workers. Better research on HIV/AIDS incidence is also crucial, so that those at highest risk can be offered access to more resources rather than according limited resources based on estimates and conjecture.

Transmission of the virus

Initially epidemiological investigation showed that HIV transmission was associated with homosexual and bisexual men, intravenous drug users, haemophiliacs, transfusion recipients, children of infected mothers and sexually active heterosexuals with multiple partners. HIV transmission is now known to occur from person to person during sexual contact, from mother to child during pregnancy in the perinatal blood, or through parenteral exposure to blood or blood products. Evidence exists for HIV transmission through breast milk, after organ transplantations and through artificial insemination. Although HIV has been isolated from body fluids such as saliva, urine and tears, there is no epidemiological evidence that HIV transmission has occurred from contact with these fluids.

There is, however, no evidence that casual social contact with HIV seropositive individuals poses a risk of infection, nor can HIV be transmitted through sneezing or coughing airborne droplets, or the sharing of eating, drinking or washing utensils, or toilet facilities. Transmission via vectors such as ticks, fleas and mosquitoes has not been found.

Sexuality-related practices in South Africa

In a survey of 12 247 households including 11 735 women, only 8% reported that their partner had used a condom during their last intercourse. This figure doubled for those whose last intercourse was with a casual acquaintance or a boyfriend, but this is still very low. Overall condom use is highest among African women and lowest among Asian women, who are, however, more likely than Coloured or white women to use condoms with their husbands. Some 12% of adult men reported having recently had symptoms associated with sexually transmitted diseases (STDs). National syphilis trends show a decrease among pregnant women in all age groups, from 10,8% in 1998 to 4,9% in 2000. In the Western Cape, the prevalence rate of syphilis infection increased by 16% between 1998 and 1999 and between 1999 and 2000 (Shaikh & Adendorff 2000).

Half of the women surveyed are currently using a contraceptive method and almost all women who have ever used contraception have used a modern contraceptive. The most widely used method is the injection (27%), followed by the pill (9%) and female sterilisation (9%). Asian women are most likely to use contraception, followed by whites, Coloureds and Africans. Asian and white women tend to use the pill and female sterilisation, while African and Coloured women tend to use injections. Male sterilisation is commonly used by white couples (Department of Health 1998).

Some 4% of women who had ever been pregnant reported that they had been physically abused during pregnancy. One in eight women reported having been beaten by a partner, 6% reported abuse in the last year, and of these, 43% reported needing medical attention. Some 4% of all women reported having been raped (Department of Health 1998).

Only 3% of teenagers in the sample were married. More than half of the respondents indicated never having had sexual intercourse and 60% indicated having no sexual partner in the year prior to the interview. About one in five teenagers had sex in the month preceding the survey. Age at first intercourse was reported as 18 years, and age at menarche for most teenagers was below 15 years. By age 19, 35% of all teenagers have been pregnant or have had a child. One in eight teenage deliveries is by Caesarean section.

Among sexually active teenagers, almost two-thirds are currently using modern contraception, of which the injection is the most popular (50%). One in every five teenage women reported using a condom in their last sexual intercourse. Only 13% of teenage women reported knowing someone with HIV/AIDS (Department of Health 1998).

First sexual intercourse

The risks associated with unprotected sex are particularly pertinent to first intercourse, which is usually unplanned and may expose individuals to unwanted pregnancy, STDs or AIDS. Many students only become sexually active in college and are, therefore, an important target group for safer sex programmes (Thornton 1990; Darling *et al.* 1992).

Apart from the vulnerabilities of the transition to non-virginity, there are many highly valued benefits that adolescents believe they will derive from their first sexual intercourse. This sexual act is often seen as a marker of independent decision making and, consequently, as challenging parental values. Admiration from peers for being sexually experienced is often held to the extent of having students ignore the possible risks of unplanned first intercourse. Peers rarely escape the parental values they are trying to oppose and often are caught in new dilemmas of double standards within the peer-pressure context. Males are, for example, still seen as the initiators of sexual intercourse (Masters & Johnson 1986).

Kaats & Davis (1970) found a premarital coital rate of 40% for women and 60% for men. Women received little support for liberal sexual behaviour, whereas men felt their friends approved of their premarital sexual intercourse. Double standards for males and females continue, with some influence of its maintenance exerted by parents.

Bowers and Christopherson's (1977) cohabitation study of 1 191 students at 14 state universities found approximately one-quarter of all students having cohabited at some time, with females expecting greater disapproval from parents than males. Similar findings were reported by Catlin *et al.* (1976) in their survey of 89 cohabiting college couples. Daughterty and Burger's (1984) survey of 200 undergraduates also found parental influence applied inconsistently to male and female students' sexual behaviour and attitudes.

Abler and Sedlacek (1989), in a 15-year random sampling of first-year students, measured at five-year intervals, found that students had become more liberal in their sexual behaviour and attitudes. Students also indicated increasingly liberal personal codes of sexuality and fewer gender differences for sexual attitudes, behaviours and standards for men and women. In Robinson and Jedlicka's (1982) study of sexual attitudes and behaviour, premarital intercourse was found to have increased consistently, with fewer differences in attitudes and behaviour of male and female students. However, they found increased disapproval for premarital sexual behaviour for both the male and the female students in the sample, in comparison with their previous research on student sexuality. They sampled students from social science classes who completed questionnaires in 1970, 1975 and 1980.

Darling and Davidson (1986) contend that the last 15 years saw a major increase in heterosexual intercourse for adolescents and young adults. Age-adjusted rates of pre-marital sexual intercourse for young females have caught up with males. However, males' earliest experience of sexuality is through solitary masturbation, whereas females experience sexuality through relational activities.

They found that males were more likely to experience first coitus with feelings of excitement, happiness and joy, whereas a significant percentage of females experience first coitus as a negative event. Females were more likely to have a greater emotional attachment to their first coital partner than males. New sexual scripts of increased performance in speed and number of orgasms expected during sexual intercourse have heightened the anxieties of both men and women in negotiating sexual intercourse. Female students expressed feelings of guilt and fear, lack of orgasm during sexual intercourse, painful intercourse and lack of stimulation to breasts. Males were concerned about infrequent opportunities for sexual intercourse, insufficient oral-genital contact and lack of variety in sex partners.

Knox and Wilson (1981), in their study of dating, found as expected that men want to kiss, pet and have intercourse in a shorter number of dates than women. Similarly, Houston (1981) found that males were more inclined toward eroticism and females to romanticism, and that the discrepancy for blacks is greater than for whites.

A local study (Nicholas 1994) found the following in a sample of 1 737 students. On average, females experienced first intercourse with a partner who was 2,5 years older, whereas males experienced intercourse with a partner who was 0,1 years younger. Male respondents' mean age at first intercourse was 15,5 years and their partners' age was 14,5 years. Female respondents' mean age was 17,8 years and their partners' mean age was 20,3 years. Most respondents indicated that they experienced their first intercourse with a steady friend. Males were, however, much more likely than females to have their first intercourse experience with an unknown partner or casual acquaintance. It is cause for concern that 4,1% of the sample indicated that first intercourse was experienced with a close relative.

Males were more likely to have sexual intercourse again with their first partner compared to females. While most respondents had further sexual intercourse with their first partner, 35,5% of females reported no further intercourse with their first partner, compared to only 20,6% of the male respondents. Almost 70% of respondents had sexual inter- course between one and five times with the first partner, which points to the short-lived nature of the sexual relationship with the first sexual partner for most respondents. First intercourse may, therefore, influence the relationships of the 60,6% of respondents who indicated a 'steady friend' as their first intercourse partner because, for at least half of this group, sexual intercourse occurred only one in five times during the 'steady' relationship.

Twice as many males as females indicated that they greatly enjoyed their first sexual intercourse experience. A third of respondents disliked or greatly disliked their experience of first sexual intercourse (14,4% of males and 56,9% of females).

Of respondents, 46,3% had one sexual partner in high school and 20,8% had their first intercourse experience after leaving high school, but before entering university. Males reported significantly higher numbers of high-school partners than females.

Peers were reported as the overall primary first source of learning about sexual intercourse. Male and female respondents received information more from opposite-sex friends (35% and 25,2% respectively), than from same-sex friends (18,2% and 19% respectively). Together with reading, this accounted for 73% of the sources of learning for this topic. Although peers were still ranked as the preferred source of information about sexual intercourse, only half of the respondents who indicated peers as their first source of knowledge also included them as their preferred source. The respondents indicated a much greater role for the school or guidance teacher (18,3%), mothers (18,2%) and fathers (5,1%). Peers were the preferred source of sex information for only a quarter of respondents.

Peers were also supplanted by reading as the most important source of sexuality information. The father's role in imparting important sexuality information was negligible, but he was the preferred source for 8,1% of males, rivalling the same-sex peer, which was the preferred source for 8,3% of male respondents.

First intercourse comments

What a surprise it was, when making love was a unique experience. Not anything like I expected. It was thrilling, exciting and, yes, it felt as if the Earth was shattering, but it also met with certain anxieties: 'Am I doing the right thing?', 'Am I as good as the other women he's had?' and 'Is he enjoying it?'
(RESPONDENT NO. 1)

It was painful, very painful, at least this is what I suspected would happen, but to be honest, I didn't really enjoy it. Afterwards I was scared, very shy to look into his eyes and guilty, of course.
(RESPONDENT NO. 2)

Penetration itself was painful, although we used a lubricant to make it easier.
(RESPONDENT NO. 3)

It was very painful, but he was supportive, there was really nothing to enjoy.
(RESPONDENT NO. 7)

Sometimes it starts with the kissing, caressing and then ends up with mutual satisfaction of the genitals through masturbation. We once had oral genital contact but for me I must still get used to the idea.
(RESPONDENT NO. 9)

The process was a very painful one, especially the penetration itself. He was always assuring me of the pain vanishing at some time and was very gentle as he entered, but I was feeling the pain. He was very patient and understanding of the whole process and always stopped when the pain was high.
(RESPONDENT NO. 10)

We became involved so quickly and so intensely. Physically we came extremely close to the point of oral sex, to initiating a transition, but emotionally he was not ready to commit himself to another serious relationship.
(RESPONDENT NO. 11)

The penetration was a little bit painful though as it will always be like wearing new shoes for the first time, that will pinch you and pinch you. So it was a little painful since I have cracked up. So since it was still painful the following morning I went to a doctor. He explained to me that it was just a minor crack and that if I could keep on using Savlon it will heal up with time.
(RESPONDENT NO. 15)

I was shy and one of my anxieties was the tension of the vaginal muscles as I once heard from my peer group. I first tensed, felt that sharp pain when he penetrated me. This was a burning pain but I was carried at the same time, trying to pretend that I am passive and that I do not need him. After the encounter, I felt different. My vaginal lips were painful and a little swollen. I was shocked by the bloody mess on the sheet, not heavy blood.
(RESPONDENT NO. 16)

I felt that I was ready for sexual intercourse, although my partner was very careful and gentle it was painful for me. The blood was a sign (important) that I lost my virginity because I had a minor accident when I was young and I used to think that my hymen was broken. We made

love in the veld and I did not reach an orgasm.
(RESPONDENT NO. 18)

I had a picture of what was going to happen, but it was difficult for me to practise what I used to watch in videos. That was caused by my inexperience. When he touched me I couldn't respond the way I was supposed to respond, although I was not passive. I couldn't stop him because I was there already, so I had to let him continue. My body couldn't respond; i.e. I was not aroused, so I felt too much pain when he penetrated me. I tried to do the act, but being uncomfortable and anxiety caused by lack of experience spoiled the whole thing. I was so embarrassed when I saw the blood, especially when he saw it, but he didn't comment on that. The other thing was the lack of verbal communication, maybe that could have relieved or made me comfortable. About standing in front of him, naked that I avoid by putting on the towel, I was shy to stay nude.
(RESPONDENT NO. 19)

Penetration was painful, though not as much as I envisaged, afterwards feeling something like a burning infection. My first sexual encounter was OK if I should rate it but the ones thereafter much more satisfying. I think it's due to the fact I felt more relaxed and even more loved, a form of recognition important for every human being.
(RESPONDENT NO. 24)

My first sexual encounter was more than I bargained for. My wedding night, a luxury hotel and a sexually starved husband! Immediately my role was shifted. I was no longer the manipulative (X). I became silent, very much like a lamb. I wasn't scared, maybe nervous. I wasn't anxious, I don't quite know now. My husband (as patient as Job) was accommodating in every respect and soon we were engaged in foreplay. This helped very much and for the moment sex was in the distant future. I felt, however, this dying need to always be covered and the lights should be out. I was really foolish, my requests were all granted and the next moment the most beautiful thing happened. A miracle of nature. This act was a manifestation of our mutual understanding and shared dreams and future plans. The ultimate form of communication.
(RESPONDENT NO. 25)

However, when this actually happened there was no persuasion from both of us, and the act came upon us very unexpected and unintentional. I however accepted this encounter to be very joyful. But it however was not. My thoughts at this time were that I was going to get pregnant and that I brought this situation upon myself. Ignorant about matters of the heart in injuring this experience I found myself becoming very realistic about this situation, wondering what is he doing now, or would he be able to pull out in time, or am I going to get a baby. I therefore was unable to enjoy such a precious experience due to my morality 'bugging' my subconscious of the fact of having a child at a young age. The pain endured was not very intense as his sensitivity towards me, more than enough made up for this act.

(RESPONDENT NO. 27)

Overview of sexual problems

Sexual dysfunction:
The persistent impairment of the normal pattern of sexual interest or response.

Primary dysfunction:
Dysfunction that has always been present.

Secondary dysfunction:
Dysfunction that arises after a period of satisfactory sexual functioning.

Broadly, the sexual problems of men can be classified into impotence, premature ejaculation, ejaculatory incompetence and dyspareunia. The problems of women can be classified into orgasmic dysfunction, vaginismus and dyspareunia. **Sexual dysfunction** is the persistent impairment of the normal pattern of sexual interest or response. A further dimension recognised by Masters and Johnson (1970) is the time of the onset of the problem and the situations in which it occurs. A **primary dysfunction** is one that has always been present, and a **secondary dysfunction** arises after a period of satisfactory sexual functioning. Masters and Johnson (1970) also distinguish **situational problems** that may occur in one setting and not in another and **total dysfunction** for problems that occur in all settings.

Premature ejaculation

Situational problems:
Problems that may recur in one setting and not in another.

Total dysfunction:
Problems that occur in all settings.

Before 1970, premature ejaculation was often classified as a form of impotence (Masters *et al.* 1985). Some definitions emphasise duration, others a specific number of penile thrusts. More recent definitions focused on the interaction between the sexual partners. Premature ejaculation was said to occur if the man's partner was not orgasmic in at least 50% of the coital episodes. Helen Kaplan emphasised the male's voluntary control over ejaculation. The American Psychiatric Association cited reasonable control of ejaculation as a criterion. Lo Piccolo suggested that premature ejaculation does not exist if both partners agree that the quality of sexual intercourse is not influenced by attempts to delay ejaculation.

Premature or rapid ejaculation is considered the most common male sexual dysfunction. Sarrel and Sarrel (1979) found that 90% of male students experience premature ejaculation at least some of the time. Kinsey *et al.* (1948) found that 75% of men ejaculate within two minutes of vaginal entry. Masters *et al.* (1985) questioned the accuracy of Kinsey's data, estimating this percentage to be much lower, in the region of 15 to 20%.

Masters *et al.* (1985) attributed what they consider Kinsey's overestimation of incidence of premature ejaculation to Kinsey's belief that:

> ... *in many species of mammals the male ejaculates almost instantly upon intromission, and that this is true of man's closest relatives among the primates* ... . *Far from being abnormal, the human male who is quick in his sexual response is quite normal among the mammals, and usual in his own species. It is curious that the term 'impotence' should have ever been applied to such rapid response. It would be difficult to find another situation in which an individual who was quick and intense in his responses was labelled anything but superior, and that in most instances is exactly what the rapidly ejaculating male probably is.*
> (KINSEY *et al.* 1948: p. 580)

Viewing sex as primarily for the man's pleasure was once more widespread than predominant current perspectives, and the endorsement of quick ejaculation as superior should take into account that female sexual partners may desire a male sexual response that would facilitate female orgasm. However, Kinsey's idea that rapid ejaculation should not automatically be considered as pathological deserves scrutiny. When one considers that exploring one's sexuality during adolescence is often accompanied by guilt or fear of being caught, it is not surprising that young men learn to reach orgasm as quickly as possible. Also, given a period of abstinence, most men will ejaculate faster than they normally do.

An effective technique to prevent premature ejaculation is Seman's technique, where the man masturbates until he is about to ejaculate, stops, then resumes stimulation, repeating the procedure until he can experience intense arousal without ejaculating. This was modified by Masters *et al.* (1985) to include a female partner, who stimulates her partner and, whenever he feels the urge to ejaculate, she squeezes firmly around the fraenulum of the penis. This is known as the 'squeeze technique'.

Erectile dysfunction

Erectile dysfunction is the inability to have or to maintain a firm enough erection for sexual intercourse. It is considered to either have psychogenic or organic causes, and in some cases the dysfunction has strong components of both (Rosen & Hall 1984). Erectile dysfunctions can result from many medical conditions, such as diabetes, alcoholism

Erectile dysfunction:
The inability to have or maintain a firm enough erection for sexual intercourse.

and neurologic, vascular and hormonal abnormalities. A useful guide to the causes of erectile dysfunction was developed by Cole and Dryden (1989). Diabetes and alcoholism are the two most prominent organic causes of erectile dysfunction.

Most erectile failures are due to psychogenic factors. The immediate causes are: demands of a sexual partner, performance anxiety, disagreements with a sexual partner, an inability to relax, and emotional stress from non-sexual activities. Among the remote causes of erectile failure are the early learning of negative attitudes toward sex, religious indoctrination, and the effects of parental dominance on feelings of masculinity.

Dyspareunia

Dyspareunia:
Painful intercourse.

Dyspareunia in males is caused at least half the time by psychosocial factors and by several organic problems. Inflammations of the penis, foreskin, testes, urethra or prostate are the most likely organic causes. Dyspareunia is psychogenic when it can be linked to unconscious sexual conflicts that are experienced as painful. Painful sexual intercourse can also be associated with depression or overreactions to normal physical sensation. Hypersensitivity of the glans penis after orgasm and ejaculation is common, and may be so extreme that a man fears ejaculation. Other factors are inadequate sexual information about foreplay and arousal techniques, anxiety and/or guilt about sex that block the physical process of arousal, and relationship problems.

Psychosocial factors may be as frequent as organic ones in causing female dyspareunia. Conditions that result in poor vaginal lubrication, chiefly drugs that have a drying effect, can cause discomfort during sexual intercourse. Other causes are skin problems around the vaginal opening or affecting the vulva, irritation or infection of the clitoris, scarring of the vaginal opening, surgical scarring, thinning of the walls of the vagina, chemicals found in contraceptive materials or douches, and pelvic disorders such as infection, tumours, abnormalities of the cervix or uterus, or torn ligaments of the uterus. Psychosocial causes of dyspareunia may include fear of sex-related activity, pain or intimacy, a traumatic sexual experience, and strong traditional attitudes.

Orgasmic dysfunction

Orgasmic dysfunction:
Problems with achieving orgasm.

Masters and Johnson (1985) distinguished among primary orgasmia (never having had an orgasm), secondary orgasmia (referring to once having been regularly orgasmic but no longer), situational orgasmia (the ability to have orgasms only under certain circumstances), random anorgasmia (the experience of different types of orgasm, though infrequently) and rapid orgasmia (reaching orgasm too quickly and finding continued sexual activity uncomfortable).

Orgasm and ejaculation are viewed as the same event for men, therefore orgasmic difficulties are equated with ejaculatory difficulties. It has been suggested that some women experience a form of ejaculation at orgasm. Masters and Johnson (1986) agreed that some women experience an ejaculation-like response, but contended that a number of these cases result from urinary stress incontinence. In Davidson *et al.*'s (1989) study of 1 289 women, which represented a 55% questionnaire return rate, 463 women reported having experienced ejaculation at the moment of orgasm and 84% believed that a sensitive area exists in the vagina which, if stimulated, produces pleasurable feelings. The confusion about the nature of ejaculatory response in women has yet to be resolved. Ejaculation in males generally accompanies orgasm, though some males experience orgasm without ejaculation. **Orgasm** is a neuromuscular release of built-up sexual tension, whereas **ejaculation** is the muscular contraction of tissues in the body that transport ejaculate.

Freud argued for the existence of two types of orgasm: a 'mature' vaginal orgasm and an 'immature' clitoral orgasm. Masters & Johnson (1966) reported that, physiologically, there is only one type of female orgasm, regardless of where stimulation takes place on the body. The clitoris remains the centre of sexual sensation and the most effective stimulation to orgasm would therefore be direct stimulation of the clitoris. Further assumptions were that the penis moving in and out of the vagina during sexual intercourse would result in ineffective stimulation of the clitoris. The reasons offered were that very little contact takes place between the clitoris and the penis, and that vaginal walls contained too few nerve endings to be highly sensitive to the penis.

Fisher, cited in Mahoney (1983), found that a number of women reported different types of orgasm depending on the kind of stimulation they experienced. However, his report was seen as an attempt to revitalise the generally discredited Freudian notion of mature and immature vaginal and clitoral orgasms. Mahoney (1983) contended that a physiological basis for women experiencing two types of orgasm does exist as there are two nerve pathways to the genitals: the pudendal nerve leads to the outer third of the vagina and clitoris, and the pelvic nerve allows sensitivity to deeper vaginal penetration.

Orgasm is also related to differences in muscle strength, with primary anorgasmia characterised by lower vaginal and uterine muscle strength and the reverse. Clitoral orgasms are associated with lower vaginal and uterine strength and dominance of the pudendal nerve path-

Orgasm:
The neuromuscular release of sexual tension.

Ejaculation:
The muscular contraction of tissues in the body that transport ejaculate.

way, and vaginal orgasms are associated with greater muscle strengths and dominance of the pelvic nerve pathway.

Mahoney (1983) attributed some of the difficulties he has with Masters and Johnson's (1966) landmark study to their equating orgasm and ejaculation. Masters *et al.* (1985) acknowledged not making a clear distinction between orgasm and ejaculation, but remain sceptical about vaginal and clitoral orgasms.

Anorgasmia

Anorgasmia:
Inability to achieve orgasm.

Orgasmic dysfunction is the most frequent sexual complaint of women. Physical causes include alcohol, drugs, neurological degenerative diseases or tumours that damage spinal centres and nerves that mediate the orgasmic reflex, and damage to the genital organs. Other causes may be lack of information or misinformation, inadequate stimulation, belief in a standard orgasmic response, females being role-scripted not to have orgasms and fear of loss of control.

Psychological factors can inhibit the woman's reaching the level of sexual arousal where vaso-congestion creates sufficient muscle tension for the orgasmic reaction to take place (Mahoney 1983). Lo Piccolo and Stock (1986) contended that the most effective treatment of lifelong lack of orgasm in women is a programme of directed masturbation based on a sexual skills learning model and as adjunct to a behavioural, time-limited treatment programme involving both partners. Barbach (1980) has also developed a successful group method for anorgasmic women.

Vaginismus

Vagginismus:
Involuntary contraction of the vagina that makes penile insertion painful or impossible.

Vaginismus is the condition where the muscles in the outer one-third of the vagina contract involuntarily so that penile insertion is not possible or difficult and painful. Therapy for vaginismus always includes teaching a woman to learn to relax in the presence of sexual stimulation. The following steps may be followed, but several repetitions of each step may be necessary before the woman is relaxed enough to continue.

- Explain the nature of the involuntary reflex spasm.
- Demonstrate the reflex in a pelvic examination (the male partner is present if the client is partnered).
- Teach techniques for relaxing muscles around the vagina (e.g. tightening and then relaxing muscles).
- Provide a set of various-sized dilators.

- The physician inserts the smallest dilator, indicating how to practice, using a sterile lubricating jelly.
- The client is asked to practice at home, keeping the dilator in place for 10 to 15 minutes.
- Finally, change to inserting the penis into the vagina, with the woman remaining in control.

Paraphilias

Paraphilias are recurrent, intense, sexually arousing fantasies, sexual urges or behaviours generally involving non-human objects, suffering, or humiliation of oneself or a partner or children or other non-consenting persons, that occur over a period of at least six months (DSM-IV-TR 2000). Diagnosis of the behaviour, urges or fantasies causes clinically significant distress or impairment in social, occupational or other important areas of functioning. Sexual deviance is largely a male predisposition and the majority of recipients are females (Laws & O'Donohue 1997).

Paraphilias: Recurrent, intense, sexually arousing fantasies, sexual urges or behaviours generally involving non-human objects, suffering, or humiliation of oneself or a partner or children or other non-consenting persons, that occur over a period of at least six months.

Exhibitionism	Exposure of one's genitals to a stranger.
Fetishism	Relying on non-human objects as a stimulus for sexual arousal and gratification.
Frotteurism	Touching and rubbing against a non-consenting person.
Paedophilia	Sexual activity with a pre-pubescent child, usually 13 years or younger. The perpetrator must be at least 16 years old and older than the child.
Sexual masochism	The act of being humiliated, beaten, bound or made to suffer in other ways.
Sexual sadism	Deriving sexual excitement from the psychological or physical suffering of the victim.
Voyeurism	Observing unsuspecting individuals who are naked, in the process of disrobing or engaging in sexual activity.
Other paraphilias	Telephone scatologia (obscene phone calls), necrophilia (corpses), partialism (exclusive focus on a part of a body), zoophilia (animals), coprophilia (faeces), klismaphilia (enemas), urophilia (urine), asphyxophilia (oxygen deprivation).

Gender identity disorder

Gender identity disorder:
Condition involving strong, persistent desire/insistance that one is of the other sex and evidence of persistent discomfort about one's assigned sex.

There must be strong and persistent desire and/or insistence that one is of the other sex and evidence of persistent discomfort about one's assigned sex.

South African case studies

Respondent One

Would you allow me to beg to be used as your human chair? And, while I lie on my back, sit on my face for at least one hour, or for as long as you desire, even while wearing your most well-worn panties? Allowing me to occasionally breathe through your panties. I would not even dream of using my tongue, although I would really be tempted to, but knowing full well that you would probably make me pass out by totally asphyxiating me if I tried.

At regular intervals you could balance your whole weight on me, just to remind me of your entire authority and power. And shuffle yourself to make sure that you are at all times comfortable and ensure exactly where you want my nose and mouth to be positioned. If you didn't require me fully restrained, I can use my arms as your back rest to support you. After seeing your pictures, I would be most honoured to carry your exquisitely beautiful hypnotic body above me.

So that I can prepare for my ordeal, please let me know how long you think it is necessary to sit on me for, taking into consideration your weight, how cruel you can be and how intense your panty musk can get.

I am very clean, fit, athletic, single and in my thirties. And needless to say, accustomed to being mercilessly smothered.
Awaiting your every command
  Slave guy.

Respondent Two

I am a 20-year-old Indian virgin male. I don't like pain, but I have this tendency of liking to wear woman's clothes. This is something that I have grown up with. To begin with, when I was 14 years old, I used to like to wear pantyhose that was kept in the spare room. Then it got more courageous, I used to try on my mom's or sister's sari (traditional Indian clothing). I was caught once, and to avoid embarrassment I stopped, but every now and again, I take my sister's used panties from the laundry and keep them with me for the night.

About 2 years ago, I moved to Johannesburg, and then last year my sister moved in with me. Last month, while she was on vacation, I went and bought myself a dress and high heel sandals. I used to wear it every night she was gone. When she came back, I felt guilty and threw everything away.

I'm a very timid and shy person. My sister often takes advantage of this; this can be seen in that she never washed the bathroom or toilet once since she moved in. She often gets me to do the laundry and the dishes. To be honest with you, I don't really mind.

I have also done some more things ... like coming to work, wearing my sister's undies and pantyhose, and smelling/sniffing her panties from the laundry. I'm also interested in maybe some role-playing, something like mother/baby, etc.

After browsing your web site, I have some questions to ask you ... I've never done anything like this before, like making these feelings known, so here goes ...

1. *Do you think I'm crazy? I often feel guilty.*
2. *How can you help me?*
3. *Do you think a session, where I dress up as a lady will help me? I often get turned on by ladies' clothing and would love to dress up and act as a proper lady.*
4. *How does your domestication service work?*
5. *The most important ... what are your rates?*

Respondent Three

I would like to make an appointment to bring my slave to you for a very severe punishment. I would like to watch and learn about his limits. I am happy to just watch, but if you need an assistant, that would be even better. On arrival, it would be ideal if he could be dressed for humiliation and pain, and then left to ponder his fate while I go and change, and you and I have a chat.

If possible, I would like the victim to be dressed as follows:
Rubber leggings (thigh high)
Very high-heeled, tight ladies shoes/boots
Arm length mittens (I have some)
Tight black corset
Hood
Gag
Collar
Anklets and wristlets

When we return, I would like him to kneel in front of me and light a cigarette for me with matches (obviously with his mittens on, which makes it very difficult for him). I will inspect his attempt at lighting my cigarette and then request you to cane him. You then take over.

Note: About our BDSM background:
We used to have very good sessions in our sessions ±3 years ago, usually using stimulants. Since we stopped using these stimulants, we cannot seem to get together properly, which is why we are seeing you for help. On a typical evening, a session would last about four hours and my slave would receive 100 to 150 cuts. Most of the time was taken up by oral sex (which we obviously don't want for this session).

For our planned session it will hopefully be all PAIN and NO pleasure for the victim.

I was thinking of splitting the session into three parts of 20 minutes each (or half hours if you prefer).

Part one: Starts after my cigarette has been lit and I have requested you to cane him. I would like you to sentence him to between 48 and 72 cuts. If you don't think it is too severe, I think very hard judicial-type caning would be ideal. I would love to see him tied to a flogging horse/bench and shrieking into his gag after 24 or so cuts, knowing that dozens more are coming. Ideally he will have a very punitive butt plug fitted into his slave hole, while you slowly (±4 strokes a minute) cane him with a selection of four heavy, bruising canes.

Part two: I would love to see proper torture administered to my slave. I see on your web site that you have a stretch couch. Perhaps stretched on his back while you work on him. Here I am in your hands regarding genital and nipple torture. Perhaps clamps, wax/cigarette burning, whipping?

Part three: Perhaps severe caning again? Here we could really make him scream with thinner cutting-type canes and push him to his limits. Maybe some dildoing every 12 cuts or so?

Please understand that, although we would really like to get into the scene again, I love my husband very much and do not want to cause any type of permanent damage.

P.S. He has high blood pressure but is under strict medication.

When I emailed you before, you quoted a price of R400 for the one-hour session. Please let me know if that is still OK. I would like to make an appointment for 14 June, ideally your last appointment of the day. If this is not convenient, anytime on Friday will do.

Looking forward to hearing from you.
   Yours in anticipation

Summary

- Block, Moll, Hirschfield, Ellis and Von Krafft-Ebbing were the early pioneers of sexology.
- Watson and Kinsey brought a research perspective to bear on the discipline and Masters and Johnson heralded the move away from psychoanalytic treatment of sexual problems.
- High-risk sexual practices are an everyday reality with serious implications for South Africa, given its HIV/AIDS figures.
- The risks associated with first sexual intercourse are of particular concern, especially in relation to university students.
- Sexual problems, such as impotence, paraphilias, premature ejaculation, dyspareunia, orgasmic dysfunction and vaginusmus are central to the work of sexologists.
- Orgasmic dysfunction is the most common female sexual problem and premature ejaculation is the most common male sexual dysfunction.

Further reading

Abler, R.M. & Sedlacek, W.E. (1989) Freshman sexual attitudes and behaviors over a 15-year period. *Journal of College Student Development*, 30, pp. 201–9.

American Psychiatric Association (APA) (2000) *Diagnostic and Statistical Manual of Mental Disorders: Text Revised* (4th edition). Washington, DC: American Psychiatric Association.

Bowers, D.W. & Christophersen, V.A. (1977) University student cohabitation: A regional comparison of selected attitudes and behaviour. *Journal of Marriage and the Family*, 39, pp. 447–52.

Buss, D.M. (1998) Sexual strategies theory: Historical origins and current status. *Journal of Sex Research*, 35(1), pp. 19–31.

Darling, C.A., Davidson, J.K. & Passarello, L.C. (1992) The mystique of first intercourse among college youth: The role of partners, contraceptive practices and psychological reactions. *Journal of Youth and Adolescence*, 21, pp. 97–117.

Department of Health (1998) *South African Demographic and Health Survey*. Pretoria: Department of Health.

Department of Health (2000) *National HIV and Syphilis Sero-prevalence Survey of Women Attending Public Antenatal Clinics in South Africa*. Pretoria: Department of Health.

Gathorne-Hardy, J. (1998) *Alfred C. Kinsey: A Biography: Sex the Measure of All Things*. London: Chatto & Windus.

Hooper, E. (2000) How did AIDS get started? *South African Journal of Science*, 96(6), pp. 265–7.

Jones, J. (1997) *Alfred C. Kinsey: A Public/Private Life*. New York: Norton.

Kaats, G.R. & Davis, K.E. (1970) The dynamics of sexual behaviour of college students. *Journal of Marriage and the Family*, 32, pp. 390–9.

Kinsey, A.C., Pomeroy, W.B. & Martin, C.E. (1948) *Sexual Behavior in the Human Male*. Philadelphia: W.B. Saunders.

Kinsey, A.C., Pomeroy, W.B., Martin, C.E. & Gebhard, P.H. (1953) *Sexual Behavior in the Human Female*. Philadelphia: W.B. Saunders.

Kolodny, R.C. (2001) In memory of William H. Masters. *The Journal of Sex Research*, 38(3), pp. 274–6.

Knox, D. & Wilson, K. (1981) Dating behaviours of university students. *Family Relations*, 30, pp. 255–8.

Lachenicht, L.G. (1993) A sceptical argument concerning the value of a behavioural solution for AIDS. *South African Journal of Psychology*, 23(1), pp. 15–19.

Laumann, E., Gagnon, J., Michael, R. & Michaels, S. (1994) *The Social Organisation of Sexuality: Sexual Practices in the United States*. Chicago: University of Chicago Press.

Laws, D.R. & O'Donohue, W. (1997) *Sexual Deviance: Theory, Assessment, and Treatment*. New York: Guilford Press.

Mackay, J. (2001) Global sex: Sexuality and sexual practices around the world. *Sexual and Relationship Therapy*, 16(1), pp. 71–82.

Masters, W.H. & Johnson, V.E. (1986) *Human Sexual Response*. Toronto: Bantam.

Masters W.H., Johnson, V.E. & Kolodney, R.C. (1985) *Human Sexuality*. Boston: Little, Brown.

Masters, W.A., Johnson, V.E. & Kolodny, R.C. (1988) *Crisis: Heterosexual Behavior in the Age of AIDS*. London: Graffon.

Nicholas, L.J. (1994) *Sex Counselling in Educational Settings*. Johannesburg: Skotaville.

Nicholas, L.J. (1995). Black South African freshmen's experience of first coitus and contraception. *International Journal for the Advancement of Counselling*, 17, pp. 275–82.

Papalia, D.E. & Olds, S.W. (1985) *Psychology*. New York: McGraw-Hill.

Ridley, M. (1993) *The Red Queen: Sex and the Evolution of Human Nature.* London: Penguin Books.

Shaikh, N. & Adendorff, T. (2000) *The Provincial and District HIV Antenatal Survey Report.* Cape Town: Western Cape Department of Health.

Strachey, J. (1962) *Sigmund Freud: Three Essays on the Theory of Sexuality.* New York: Basic Books.

Thornton, A. (1990) The courtship process and adolescent sexuality. *Journal of Family Issues,* 11, pp. 239–73.

Williams, B., Gouws, E. and Abdool Karim, S. (2000) Where are we now? Where are we going? The demographic impact of HIV/AIDS in South Africa. *South African Journal of Science,* 96(6), pp. 297–305.

13 Community Psychology

A.V. Naidoo, N.J. Shabalala and U. Bawa

Objectives

After studying this chapter you should:

- be able to define community psychology as a branch of psychology
- understand the historical forces that have shaped its development
- understand the core values, principles and goals of community psychology
- comprehend why the need for a contextual understanding is central for the community psychologist
- be able to describe various roles in which community psychologists work
- identify the different levels and models of interventions used in community psychology.

Introduction

Community psychology, as an emerging branch of applied psychology, is likely to be relatively unfamiliar to many students. Most South African universities offer specialised training in counselling, clinical or educational psychology. Some may offer modules or courses in community psychology, but few offer post-graduate programmes in community psychology (Wingenfield & Newbrough 2000). This reflects traditional psychology's preoccupation with individual-oriented, **Eurocentric models** of conceptualising and understanding human behaviour, and as a basis for developing interventions. However, the introduction of undergraduate training specialising in psychology (generically under the label of B.Psych) leading to the qualification of registered counsellor will require academic departments to bring community psychology into the mainstream.

Community psychology evolved during a period of social reform in the early 1960s in the USA, in response to the concern that the remediation and prevention of social problems and improving the

Community psychology:
An emerging branch of psychology that uses a variety of interventions (including prevention and health promotion) to facilitate change and improved mental-health and social conditions for groups, organisations or communities.

Eurocentric models:
Models based on or derived from essentially European or Western values, norms and behaviours.

quality of life require more than simply changing the behaviour of individuals. The following story illustrates this shift in perspective from traditional psychology.

> A young woman was taking a stroll by a river swollen by recent rains. As she was walking, her attention was drawn to an elderly man in the middle of the river who was in obvious difficulty. She jumped into the water without hesitation, swam out, grabbed him, and pulled him to safety on the bank. As she was recovering, a girl floated past, flailing her arms and yelling for help. Again, the young woman dived into the river and rescued the girl in the same brave way she had the old man. To the young woman's chagrin, and to the amazement of a small crowd gathering on the banks of the river, a third person, a middle-aged woman, came floundering by in the water, also in dire straits. For the third time, the young woman was the rescuer, bringing the grateful victim to safety.
>
> Exhausted, she then started walking upstream. As she passed, one of the bystanders asked her, 'Aren't you going to wait to rescue others who may fall in the river and need you?'
>
> 'No,' replied the young woman, 'I'm going further up the river to find out why these people are falling in and to see if I can prevent this from happening.'
> (SOURCE: GLADDING 1997: p. 3)

The heroine's response reflects the paradigm shift that characterises community psychology. Community psychology moves beyond individual psychological difficulties, not only in thinking about higher levels of causation and influence, but also in trying to bring about changes at these levels (Orford 1992). Rappaport (1977, 1981), one of the pioneers in the development of community psychology, cautioned that, when we intervene at an inappropriate level, we run the risk of neglecting the most important causes of a problem. A contextual analysis of the problem may lead to a different understanding of it, and a different, more effective, level of intervention. The story illustrates several tenets central to community psychology: that it is important to focus on people's environment rather than merely on their symptoms, that a multilevel approach to understanding the problem is beneficial, that multifaceted intervention is better than one based on a single-service plan, and that prevention is more efficient and effective than remediation. This resonates with the popular Chinese dictum often invoked to illustrate the empowerment motive of community psychology interventions: Give a person a fish, and you feed him or her for a day; teach that person how to fish, and he or she will able to feed him- or herself for a lifetime.

Interventions at the individual level run the risk of appearing to blame the individual, who might be more appropriately seen as the victim of external forces operating at a higher level. Moreover, with escalating mental-health concerns and dwindling resources, the efforts of psychologists could also be more meaningfully directed at preventive and developmental interventions, aimed at broader macro levels of society.

This chapter provides an exposition of community psychology as a branch of psychology. Firstly, we trace some of the historical forces that have shaped community psychology development. Secondly, we define the field of community psychology. Thirdly, we discuss the seminal values, principles and goals of community psychology. Fourthly, we discuss some of the contextual issues central to community psychology. Fifthly, we describe the roles that community psychologists can perform. Sixthly, levels of analysis are articulated, together with different models of intervention. To conclude the chapter, some directions for the future are intimated, followed by a case study illustrating the application of theory and **praxis** from a community psychology perspective.

Praxis:
The practical application of theory by translating theory into interventions that suit the particular context and circumstances.

History and development

Community psychology can be defined and articulated in a variety of ways. However, its major concerns, emphases and objectives are more clearly discerned in relation to its historical roots. The emergence of community psychology in South Africa and its genesis in the USA follow a similar pattern. In the wake of the social upheaval in both countries (the 1960s civil rights era in the USA and the socio-political conflict and resistance to apartheid during the 1960–1990 period in South Africa), a growing reaction was expressed about how existing psychological service delivery was elitist, unavailable to those who could not afford it, and maintained the status quo. There was concern that applied psychology was not addressing the social issues that were playing a manifest role in creating and compounding mental-health problems (Lazarus 1988; Lazarus & Seedat 1995; Rappaport 1977).

The motivation for forming a community psychology specialty in the USA was mainly a desire to reduce social inequality and to right social wrongs. There was great concern with issues such as poverty, educational deprivation and racial tension, and a sense of dissatisfaction with the apparent irrelevance of individual therapy as a way of relieving such problems (Orford 1992). There was also an increasing awareness of the inherent limitations of applied psychology in cross-cultural contexts. Historically, the psychology profession has adhered to an individual-oriented helping paradigm, emphasising one-to-one inter-vention focusing on clients' intrapsychic experiences and based on implicit Eurocentric values (Katz 1985; Naidoo 1996). This traditional paradigm, which is typically time-bound, office-bound and remedial in nature (Lewis *et al.* 1998), locates the locus for change in the individual clients rather than in their environments. While this paradigm has dominated the profession for several decades, researchers and 'converted clinicians' increasingly advocated a change in orientation (Bennett *et al.* 1966). At a conference at Swampscott, Massachusetts, in 1965, described as the event that gave birth to community psychology, partici-pants were urged to change their focus from treatment to prevention, and to focus beyond individual behaviour to broader ecological levels. At the second major conference on community psychology convened at Austin, Texas, in 1975, there was a call for psychologists to give up their encapsulated focus on the individual, learn more about processes of community change, and consequently to shift the focus from pathology to an emphasis on psychological strengths and competencies (Heller *et al.* 1984). Community psychology thus emerged in response to the growing critique of **mainstream psychology**. This approach may be construed as part of the fourth force in psychology (a multicultural perspective) suggested by Pedersen (1991), following the psychoanalytic, behaviourist and humanistic-existentialist periods of influence.

Mainstream psychology: The predominating and prevailing way psychology is defined and practised in a society. The underlying values and philosophy determine how the theory and praxis of the discipline and profession are translated into teaching and training emphases and objectives.

Parallel to the social reforms happening in the USA, there emerged in South Africa during the 1970s and 1980s a growing disquiet and discontent about the role of psychology in an oppressed society (Naidoo 2000a). Psychologists were challenged to radically rethink their role amidst the burgeoning political struggles at a time when apartheid was at its most repressive (Swartz & Gibson 2001). Communities were under siege, their organisations harrassed, students and community leaders detained, campuses occupied by riot police, and the like. An article in a local progressive journal criticised psychology for being a middle-class enterprise and argued for a relevant psychology that would discover the socio-political context of oppressed groups (Anonymous 1986). Concern was expressed at the silence of organised psychology in response or reaction to the state's oppression on the one hand, and its apathy towards the needs of the oppressed communities on the other. A myriad of research reviews and reports (Dommisse 1987; Foster *et al.* 1997; Holdstock 1981; Lambley 1980; Nzimande 1986; Swartz 1987; Van der Spuy & Shamley 1978) exposed the horrendous social and psychological harm and damage that apartheid was inflicting upon individuals, communities and society at large.

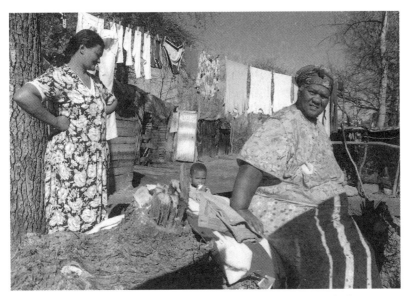

FIGURE 13.1: Intergenerational poverty: Bad genes, oppression or lack of development?

Existing mental-health provision was considered inadequate, in-accessible (particularly for rural communities), inappropriate and discriminatory (Lazarus 1988), reflecting broader class, race, gender and urban-rural inequalities. While the white patient-to-caregiver ratio was relatively on par with Western countries, black South Africans did not have access to adequate, appropriate mental-health services (Centre for the Study of Health Policy 1990). This imbalance was further evident in that the majority of psychologists in South Africa were predominantly white, middle class, male and Afrikaans/English speaking, serving predominantly white, middle-class clients (Swartz *et al.* 1986). Hence, the mental-health needs of black South Africans and disadvantaged communities were largely neglected (Naidoo 2000a). The preoccupation with the individual at the expense of social determinants of human behaviour, without examining and confronting the underlying structur-al societal conditions, resulted in psychology being branded as maintaining and perpetuating an oppressive racist, economic-political system (Bulhan 1985; Dawes 1985; Lazarus 1988). Psychologists were labelled as the servants of power and, more specifically, as 'servants of apartheid' (Webster 1986).

This burgeoning discontent with mainstream psychology in South Africa fomented the call for a relevant psychology (Anonymous 1986; Dawes 1986). Various responses emerged under the umbrella of 'community psychology'.

Indigenous psychology:
Psychology that focuses
on understanding
behaviour in the local
context, including
understanding local
cultural norms, values,
traditions and beliefs.
Interventions would
thus be informed by
understanding this
context.

Some initiatives evolved under other labels or groupings, such as contextual psychology, critical psychology, **indigenous psychology**, progressive psychology and social psychology. Other initiatives have developed under no particular label, but have reflected the values, philosophy and aims that underpin community psychology (Lazarus 1988). See Foster (1986), Vogelman (1987), Lazarus (1988), Cooper *et al.* (1990), Nell (1990), Nicholas (1990), Wouters (1993), Naidoo (2000a) and Swartz and Gibson (2001) for further analysis of this crucial period in the emergence of community psychology in South Africa. It has been posited that relevance is the most divisive issue for the profession (Kriegler 1989), the most predominant concern of South African psychologists, and the most significant value influencing psychological research (Retief 1989).

The groundswell of the political transformation in the decade leading up to the 1994 elections served as a catalyst to foment changes within the formal organisation of the psychology profession. Three organisations emerged in which progressive psychologists sought to give action to the call for relevance in community settings. These were the Organisation for Alternative Social Services in South Africa (OASSA), a grouping of largely white psychologists; the Psychology and Apartheid Group, consisting of black psychologists; and the South African Health and Social Services Organisation (SAHSSO), a grouping for interdisciplinary health workers (Hamber *et al.* 2001). Despite underlying racial divisions and serious differences between them, these organisations were engaged in challenging the apartheid system, locating mental health within a political context, and involved in pioneering community psychology initiatives. The recently published text *Community Psychology: Theory, Method and Practice* (Seedat *et al.* 2001) represents an important milestone in the history of community psychology in South Africa, being the first indigenous volume devoted in part explicitly to community psychology debate in the local context.

Community psychology defined

As the paradigm of community psychology is still evolving, a formal definition might be premature and somewhat limiting. However, we can begin to construct a definition of community psychology as being a branch of applied psychology that is concerned with:

- 'the reciprocal relationships between individuals and the social systems with which they interact' (Bennett *et al.* 1966, p. 7);
- transforming the way in which the genesis, nature and development of psychosocial problems are conceptualised and understood;
- seeking a **contextual analysis** that takes cognisance of social issues and addresses environmental stressors;
- being culturally relative rather than absolutist, respecting diversity between, for example, men and women and different ethnic groups, rather than imposing one dominant set of norms (Rappaport 1977);
- addressing the expressed needs of communities, while being sensitive to local cultural norms and traditions, and developing programmes in consultation (in planning, implementing and managing) with community residents and organisations (Scileppi *et al.* 2000);
- developing programmes that empower communities to remedy difficulties of living linked to lack of resources and to political inequity;
- extending mental-health services to all citizens, in particular the historically neglected, underserved and oppressed (Lazarus & Seedat 1995);
- broadening the focus of psychological service delivery to include prevention and development initiatives; and
- redefining the role of psychologists towards a broader public-health portfolio that embraces the functions of advocacy, lobbying, community mobilisation, community networking and policy formulation (Lazarus & Seedat 1995).

Contextual analysis: Analysis that takes into account all the prevailing conditions at multiple levels (historical, social, economic, political and cultural, among others) to inform an understanding of a society, community, group or individual as the focus of study.

Core values

Every field of study requires a map for itself – a vision of its possibilities, a script that explains why it studies what it deems to be important, a picture that shows the lie of the land, interesting destinations, and the ways to get there from here (Rappaport & Seidman 2000). Choosing problems considered legitimate for study, and adopting certain intervention strategies to solve these problems, reflect social values. Community psychology is overtly value-based. A brief overview of some of the seminal values and principles that characterise the map of community psychology is presented here.

An ecological perspective

Ecological perspective:
Looking at the person-and-environment fit, with a view to understanding the relationship between individuals (or groups, or community) and their social settings.

Community psychology views human behaviour from an **ecological perspective**. This perspective acknowledges that all behaviour occurs in a context or setting, and that, to understand why a particular behaviour occurs, it is necessary to investigate the person and his or her environment, and the fit of the person-and-environment. The person and the systems in which he or she functions and adapts become understandable when they are examined as part of a multilevel, multistructured, multidetermined social context (Bronfenbrenner 1979; Rappaport 1977). For example, Reiff (1968) proposed six levels of analysis to include individual, family, group, organisation, community and society.

In adopting an ecological approach, the community psychologist seeks to do the following:

The microsystem:
The smallest unit of analysis in ecological theory. Depending on the focus of study, it could be an individual (a specific child) or group (pre-schoolers at a specific crèche) and would include all the people with whom the child(ren) would interact with on a regular and frequent basis.

- distinguish among the different systems that compose the broad ecological environment of the target population (such as AIDS patients, unemployed youth) or a specific individual;
- understand how transactions between the individual or specific community and their social environments impact on their development (for instance, are AIDS sufferers supported or marginalised in their neighbourhoods?);
- recognise how individuals or communities are currently impacting on their social environment (what social support mechanisms are AIDS sufferers and their families creating to cope with their situation?); and

The mesosystem:
The second level in Bronfenbrenner's theory, consisting of the links between two (or more) microsystems. For instance, the link between a pre-schooler and teachers, peers, family and neighbours would be examples of this level of analysis.

- consider how individuals could impact on various ecological systems in which they function (their families, schools, neighbourhoods, work settings and communities) in the future.

(Orford 1992: p. 222)

In his theory of the ecology of human development, Bronfenbrenner (1979) describes the following components of the ecological system: the **microsystem**, the **mesosystem**, the **exosystem** and the **macrosystem**. These systems are nested in each other, mutually influence one another, influence the individual's behaviour and development, and are reciprocally impacted upon by the individual.

TABLE 13.1: ECOLOGICAL LEVELS

Level	Description	Example
Microlevel	Includes all people with whom the person interacts on a regular basis over time.	Family, nuclear and extended; classroom and school; friends and neighbourhood; church, club.
Mesolevel	Consists of links between two or more microsystems.	Home-school; father's work-home; hospital-patient's home; home-extended family; mother's family-father's family after separation.
Exolevel	Systems that influence the person and the person's micro- and mesolevel system, but of which the person has no direct experience.	The school's governing body; parents' place of employment; local government.
Macrolevel	Includes large-scale societal factors that have an impact on the individual, not only through policies and governmental decisions, but also through ideologies and belief systems.	Ideology (e.g. apartheid, individualism, democracy, capitalism); culture; religion; economic conditions; political conditions; affirmative action.

(BASED ON BRONFENBRENNER 1979; ORFORD 1992)

Following Kurt Lewin's equation B = f(P,E) – i.e. that behaviour is a function of the person and the environment – community psychologists contend that, to change behaviour, it is necessary to alter both the perception and the abilities of individuals and the characteristics of the environment. For example, if we want to reintegrate AIDS patients into the community, three types of concerns must be addressed. Firstly, it is necessary to teach the patients more effective coping skills (basic health care, personal hygiene, coping with prejudice, information about support services, etc.). Secondly, it is essential to change the patients' perceptions, enabling them to believe they can cope and survive in the community. Self-esteem, personal empowerment, assertiveness and contending with negative reactions of others must be addressed. Thirdly, environmental factors, such as adequate accommodation, facilities and support services, must be ensured and that patients have access to them. In addition, educational programmes need to be devised and presented to ensure that the community residents are better informed about HIV/AIDS and are supportive of the patients (Scileppi et al. 2000). When interventions at different levels in the system are aligned, synergy results and enhances the desired outcome.

The exosystem:
The third level of analysis, which focuses on the interconnection of the microsystem and settings that can influence the unit of study but are rarely experienced directly. For instance, for the pre-schooler, relevant exo-systems could include the pre-school's management body, the parents' place of employment, the local primary health clinic, and the crime level in the community.

The macrosystem:
This includes broader societal factors, such as cultural, economic and political conditions, in which any particularly rapid change would invariably affect the lives of each person in the society.

Person-in-context:
This refers to the need to adopt a contextual or ecological understanding of the person as a unique individual whose behaviour is shaped by internal factors (inherited dispositions) and external forces (socio-economic and political circumstances).

Viewing the **person-in-context** permits a more holistic approach to behaviour, and enables us to understand normal activity and explain abnormal or pathological behaviour by focusing on the setting. This reduces the need to apply stigmatising, deviant labels to people. Furthermore, the ecological perspective enables us to generate multiple interventions at all levels to reduce problems in living and to create a better person-environment fit (Scileppi *et al.* 2000).

Prevention

Prevention:
As a goal of psychology, prevention focuses intentionally on changing those processes and structures that lead to the emergence of mal-adaptation, to reduce the onset of the target problem(s). Prevention may take a variety of forms, ranging from effecting direct changes in community services and facilities, education and early treatment, to controlling the spread of the problem or disease.

One of the realisations leading to the founding of community psychology was the recognition that clinical treatment of mental-health problems would never meet all the mental-health needs of a society (Dalton *et al.* 2001). **Curative or rehabilitative approaches** have also proven to be inadequate to the task of reducing the escalating levels of social and health problems facing society. There will never be adequate levels of economic or human resources to address the epidemic levels of need if there is sole reliance on reconstructive and/or individually focused models of intervention. To have a realistic hope of combating these problems, psychological intervention must include efforts to reduce the incidence of new cases of the social problem or dysfunction (Albee 1982; Felner *et al.* 2000). Prevention interventions have shown their potential to be far more effective and cost efficient than curative ones (Cowen 1996).

Curative or rehabilitative approaches:
These focus on understanding the nature of problems and diseases and their causation, with a view to developing an appropriate treatment, cure or rehabilitation of the condition.

FIGURE 13.2: Young boy playing marbles oblivious to his circumstances.

Moreover, prevention initiatives are consistent with the ecological orientation of community psychology. If social problems and difficulties in living are the result of a poor fit between a person's needs and environmental resources, these can be prevented by either bolstering the individual's competence or improving the services available in the community (Scileppi *et al.* 2000). Three targets of prevention strategies can be identified here. The first strategy focuses on the person and involves empowering the person (discussed in the next section) or enhancing the person's skills. Providing training in social skills, problem solving, anger management and stress reduction are examples typifying this approach. The second strategy is directed at the social milieu. Intervening to enhance community-based programmes on AIDS awareness, to provide life-skills programmes at schools, to develop better social support systems, and to provide better access to resources are examples of this approach. The third strategy targets proximal agents in the community (Berman & Jobes 1995). **Proximal agents** are people in the community who, because of their role in the community, have close and regular contact with residents likely to face specific challenges in life. Parents, teachers, community health workers, primary health nurses and police personnel are typical proximal agents who can be educated and trained to be alert for the warning signs of potential problems (such as domestic violence or child abuse) and how to take action when these signs are observed. All three strategies can be combined to enhance the person-environment fit, and prevent the occurrence of social problems and mental illness (Scileppi *et al.* 2000).

Proximal agents: People in the community who have regular contact with residents likely to face specific challenges in life.

In 1964, Caplan proposed a three-level typology of prevention that has subsequently served as the basis for much of the research in the field. While his model has evoked debate about the boundary points between levels and whether particular interventions fall into one category or another, it provides a useful way of viewing a variety of possible interventions to help people at different levels of health or illness (Orford 1992). Caplan (1964) differentiates between primary, secondary and tertiary levels of prevention.

- **Primary prevention** seeks to keep healthy people healthy and involves steps taken to prevent the occurrence of a mental illness or other forms of psychosocial dysfunction. The key strategy is to counteract or reduce potentially harmful circumstances before they get a chance to produce illness or dysfunction (Dalton *et al.* 2001). Therefore, primary prevention is often directed at a designated population rather than at individuals. Examples of primary prevention from the health field include such strategies as vaccinations and fluoridating water. Similarly, in the mental-health field, primary intervention can be

Primary prevention: Intervention that seeks to reduce potentially harmful circumstances before they have a chance to create difficulty. These interventions often target entire populations.

thought of as being applied to all persons in a given setting, regardless of risk or potential need (e.g. sexuality awareness programmes for all learners at a high school, or career guidance for all first-year university students).

Secondary prevention:
Sometimes called early intervention, this focuses on identified groups showing early signs of difficulty, with the goals of reducing the intensity, the severity and the duration of the condition.

- **Secondary prevention**, also known as early intervention, is directed at detecting early signs of psychological dysfunction or difficulty. By effective treatment at an early stage in the development of the condition, secondary prevention strategies attempt to nip the problem in the bud and, as a result, reduce the severity and duration of the illness (Dalton *et al.* 2001). Examples of secondary prevention are interventions targeted at children who are bed-wetting, learners who are beginning to have academic difficult, or prisoners who are getting into conflict with their peers.

Tertiary prevention:
Intervention that focuses on individuals already displaying maladaptation or dysfunction, with the intention of limiting the disability caused by the condition both for the individual and his or her family, and to prevent recurrence or additional complications.

- The focus of **tertiary prevention** is to alleviate the harmful consequences of long-term illness. Individuals already suffering from chronic disorders are targeted with the intention of limiting the disability caused by the disorder, reducing its intensity and duration, and thereby preventing recurrence or additional complications. Although similar to clinical treatment, the goal of tertiary strategies is to help individuals cope with the illness and to return to a normalised lifestyle in spite of the disorder.

Caplan's framework enables us to see the continuity that exists between what is commonly thought of as 'prevention' and what is normally termed 'treatment'. This underscores the perspective that a community emphasis in psychology is complementary and not contradictory to prevailing approaches that have emphasised individual treatment (Orford 1992). Due to the efforts of Caplan, a preventive way of thinking began to permeate the traditional treatment-oriented medical, psychiatric, mental-health and social service fields. Prevention has become a central tenet of community psychology (Dalton *et al.* 2001).

Empowerment

Empowerment:
An intentional community-based process involving mutual respect, critical reflection, caring, collaboration and participation, through which people gain greater access to and control over valued resources that impact on the quality of their lives and communities.

Empowerment is another central value orientation of community psychology (Rappaport 1981). Empowerment is defined as an intentional, ongoing process centred in the local community, involving mutual respect, critical reflection, caring and group participation, through which people lacking an equal share of valued resources gain access to and control over these resources (Cornell Empowerment Group 1989). This definition explicitly incorporates person-environment interaction, and provides a distinct approach for developing interventions and creating social change. The value of empowerment directs attention toward health, adaptation, competence and indigenous helping systems. It links with the perspective that many social problems exist due to unequal distribution of, and access to, resources (Zimmerman 2000). Cowen (2000: p. 88) confirms 'the compelling associations between disempowerment, injustice, and lack of opportunity and problems of living'.

An empowerment approach goes beyond ameliorating the negative aspects of a situation by searching for the positive aspects. Enhancing wellness instead of fixing problems (Cowen 2000), identifying strengths and competencies instead of listing risk factors, and searching for environmental influences instead of blaming victims (Rappaport 1981) characterise such an empowerment approach (Zimmerman 2000). As an alternative to the deficit or pathology emphasis of traditional psychology, community psychology focuses more directly on psychological strengths, resilience and competencies (Heller *et al.* 1984). This is more than a semantic shift, having implications for how behaviour is conceptualised, and for how interventions are planned and designed. Moreover, traditional psychological language used to describe the helping process unwittingly tends to encourage dependence on professionals, creates the view that people are clients in need of help, and maintains the idea that the professional is the expert, reducing the likelihood of people helping each other (Rappaport 1985), and discovering and harnessing indigenous resources.

An empowerment approach replaces terms such as 'client' and 'expert' with 'participant' and 'facilitator' (Zimmerman 2000), and redefines our roles as professional helpers (Rappaport 1985). As a collaborator, the professional learns about the participants in their settings; learns from the participants; works with the participants instead of advocating for them; and does not impose his or her skills, interests or plans on the community, but rather becomes a resource for the community. There are some individuals and communities that are best served by mutual help, helping others, or working for their rights, rather than by having their needs fulfilled by a benevolent professional (Gallant *et al.* 1985).

A psychological sense of community

Community psychology also espouses the value of promoting a psychological sense of community (Sarason 1974) through citizen participation and empowerment. Sense of community refers to a feeling of belongingness and mutual commitment that links individuals in a collective unity (McMillan & Chavis 1986). Irrespective of whether a community

A psychological sense of community: A feeling of belonging, a feeling that members matter to one another and the group, and a shared faith that members' needs will be met by their commitment to be together.

defines itself according to territorial localities or relational terms, community psychologists are interested in the strength of this bonding among its members. McMillan and Chavis (1986) identified four major elements of this bonding or sense of community: membership, influence, integration and fulfilment of needs. Membership refers to the sense of investment of the person in the community and the degree of his or her sense of belonging to it or identifying with it. Influence refers to the power that members exercise over the community, and the reciprocal power that the group dynamics exert on members. Bonding is also enhanced by the shared values among members, as well as the exchange of resources and satisfaction of individual needs among community members. The shared emotional connection represents a 'spiritual bond' based on a shared history among members of the community. This represents, according to McMillan and Chavis (1986), the definitive element for true community. Several processes, particularly events that emphasise shared values and history, strengthen this.

Defining community as 'a readily available, mutually supportive network of relationships on which one can depend', Sarason (1974: p. 1) argued that the 'absence or dilution of the psychological sense of community is the most destructive dynamic in the lives of people in our society'. Hence, the development and maintenance of this psychological sense of community has emerged as a keystone value for community psychology (Dalton et al. 2001). Community psychologists apply this value by conducting action research, and applying various interventions to strengthen communities and promote participation of residents or members in collective initiatives that will enhance both individual and community wellness. These collaborative relationships with community groups must be grounded in processes and values espousing equality, empowerment and respect for diversity.

Contextual issues in community

It is imperative to have a critical understanding of contextual issues when planning any intervention programmes in community settings. This understanding should be informed by the history and cultural heritage of the community, its present composition and its prevailing psychosocial and economic circumstances.

Socio-economic disparities

The major contribution of a contextual understanding to community psychology is the awareness that social systems influence development at local, national and international levels. Whether the prevailing system is capitalist, socialist or Marxist, an understanding of the political economy of the social order is essential for the community psychologist to address social problems occurring in society and the symptomatic discrepancy between the wealthy and the poor.

Ahmed and Pretorius-Heuchert (2001) proposed that it is impossible to adequately understand the process of political and social change without examining the economic structures that foster social inequity and 'under-development' in a global economy. 'What happens in the world outside, affects us at home' is the common adage. The imbalance between resource distribution and ownership, and its impact on the poor has been explored by Marxist theorists, who suggest that these imbalances are linked to economic exploitation and global economic trends.

These trends, on a local community level, manifest as social problems of poverty, anomie and self-destructive behaviour. Even though these problems may seem to be rooted in individual culpability, their **etiology** (cause) is largely systemic. In situations of social and economic disparity, much of an individual's time and energy is spent in addressing the problems of daily living. These range from looking for a job and earning enough to feed one's family to protecting him- or herself from diseases and violence and keeping hope alive. The frustration that is often experienced in these struggles of daily life for the poor is sometimes expressed in excessive alcohol use, family violence, sexual abuse and assault. These behaviours can be construed as forms of internalised oppression – the high levels of rape, child abuse and battery in South Africa currently emphasise the importance of the community psychologist having a critical understanding of these contextual issues when planning any intervention programmes.

Etiology:
The causative factors giving rise to a problem, condition, disease or maladaptation.

Our African context

Earlier in the chapter, we contended that the development of community psychology derived largely from dissatisfaction with mainstream Eurocentric theories of psychology. These tend to take an individualistic approach to the understanding of human beings, so that both mental health and mental illness are explained according to intrapsychic processes. Community psychology argues that people have to be understood in their social context. The values of community psychology articulate well with how African and other 'traditional' societies view humankind. While the views that we put forward in this section may not necessarily be unique to African people, we have chosen to present an

African perspective because of our socio-historical positioning as part of the African continent, the demographic make-up of the country and the collective unconscious that feeds into our context.

Africa is a huge continent with diverse geographic, cultural, linguistic and religious groupings. It would be impossible to cover in depth all the viewpoints about human nature that are espoused by all the African-language groups in South Africa, let alone the rest of Africa. It is equally problematic to talk about a unified African perspective, as there are cultural variations in belief systems, such as in rules governing courtship and marriage preferences. There are, however, sufficient commonalities among the different groupings to allow one to talk about what Meyer *et al.* (1997) refer to as an overarching African perspective, characterised by a unity among the cultures that can be seen in the realms of spirituality, symbols, myths and rituals.

For this section, we have selected to synthesise the belief systems that are reflective of the South African aBantu groups. These groups were at the forefront of the southerly migration of a larger grouping of Bantu-speaking peoples from central Africa. During the southward migration, a division occurred, with one group moving west towards the Namibian region and another into the southern region. The southern group consisted of two main groups: the Sotho, who moved into the highveld plateau, and the Nguni tribes, who moved along the east coast. Two other groups from Mozambique and Zimbabwe moved into the northern part much later. (See Gumede 1990; Levitas 1983; and Hammond-Tooke 1974 for a detailed history of southern African groupings.)

We recognise that the socio-cultural map of South Africa is changing at a rapid rate, with a growth in the population of Africans from outside the borders of South Africa. Furthermore, even with the indigenous population of South Africa, there is no homogeneity. There is always some danger of assuming that every African person subscribes, wholly or in part, to the traditional perspective. Contact with Western and other cultural groups is likely to have resulted in huge modifications to people's traditional beliefs. Hence, there is a need to guard against stereotyping and making assumptions about people on the basis of their belonging to a particular cultural and/or language group (Gobodo 1990). Nevertheless, traditional beliefs remain an integral part of the lives of many South Africans, with research in many areas of health indicating that a large section of the population will first consult traditional healers when they have health problems (Faxelid *et al.* 1998; Freeman & Motsei 1992), or use a combination of Western and traditional, indigenous methods of healing (Swartz 1986).

We believe that, if community psychology is serious about understanding people in their context and rendering a service relevant to the people of this country, that it is important to have an idea of their world and **world view**. While much has changed in the social and political structuring of the country, many traditional ways of being-in-the-world have survived in the way people live their lives and in the collective unconscious of people.

World view:
The way an individual, group, community or society construes its own identity and how it views the external world.

African belief systems and world view

The African world view is underpinned by a holistic view of humankind and the world, characterised by continuity and unity between the person, the community and the cosmos. A meaningful schema is provided by Meyer *et al.* (1997: p. 617), who describe this cosmic whole under the three cosmic orders or realities as: the **macrocosmos**, the realm of God and ancestors; the **mesocosmos**, which is the spirit realm; and the **microcosmos**, the social world over which the first two have a great influence. Humans are positioned as 'the point of departure and the centre of the universe, from which everything is understood and explained'. Although these three realities are presented separately, it is an artificial separation because they are interrelated and interact in various ways to form the fabric of the traditional day-to-day life. (See Meyer *et al.* (1997) for a full explanation of these cosmic systems.)

Macrocosmos:
The dimension or realm in African tradition dominated by God and ancestors (deceased family members), with ancestors serving as mediators between God and people.

Mesocosmos:
The realm in African tradition in which evil spirits, sorcerers and witches interact with individuals to produce malevolent outcomes (hate, envy, revenge or malice). The protective powers of ancestors are evoked to ward off the evil intentions of witch-craft and malignant spirits.

The world of God and ancestors

The macrocosmos is the realm dominated by God and ancestors, where God is the supreme being and ancestors serve as mediators between God and people's day-to-day functioning. God is the creator of the universe, and is called by various names (*uNkulunkulu* in isiZulu, *Modimo* in seSotho, *Qamatha* in isiXhosa). Although God is the supreme being, the first ancestor, God is far removed from the daily life of people and is concerned more with natural phenomena such as lightning and rain. Ancestors are the ones involved in life and act as intermediaries between God and the living. Because of their mediatory role, religious beliefs and practices tend to be concentrated on ancestors. Ancestors consist of generations of deceased relatives, particularly the more significant and influential members of the family. An ancestor's status and role in the spirit world is similar to the one he or she had while still alive (Levitas 1983). The structure of this world mimics that of the social world of the living so that one's **patrilineal** ancestors supersede the **matrilineal** ones, though there may be circumstances that specifically require the involvement of the latter. The transition to status of ancestor is not automatic, requiring the performance of certain rituals during and after the burial, as rites of passage, for incorporation into the ancestor realm.

Microcosmos:
The realm in which an individual lives out his or her existence within the community, with particular emphasis on his or her interaction with others in the family, clan and broader community.

Patrilineal:
The father's family line of descent or ancestry.

Matrilineal:
The mother's family line of descent or ancestry.

Interactions between the living and the dead occur in various ways. Ancestors communicate with the living through dreams, spirit mediums and other symbols (e.g. snakes). Although individuals often acknowledge their ancestors in informal ways, such as using the family praise name to greet someone or express gratitude, more formal interactions are officiated by the male head of the family during the performance of family rituals and ceremonies. In cases where a community or individual has incurred the displeasure of the ancestors by neglecting some religious or kinship duty, the latter may withdraw their protection, thus making the community or individual vulnerable to the evil effects of sorcery or malignant spirits. When cleansing, healing and/or appeasement of ancestors is needed on issues that affect the broader social group, only the head of the group can make intercession with 'chief' ancestors on behalf of the community (Levitas 1983).

The spirit world

The mesocosmos is the realm of evil spirits, sorcerers and witches, and 'represents the dark, malevolent urgings that lie at the heart of man – the product of hate, envy, revenge or malice – It threatens the very basis of social life' (Hammond-Tooke 1974: p. 336). The term 'witches' is sometimes used to denote people who can cause harm through psychic means, often without being conscious of the fact and therefore not acting in bad faith. Sorcerers, however, act consciously in using magic to harm others. Interestingly, the less active power of witches tends to be attributed to elderly, often widowed and self-sufficient women, while men are more likely to be labelled as sorcerers. Despite the semantic differences, both types (referred to as *abathakathi* in isiZulu, *baloi* in seSotho and *amagqwira* in isiXhosa) use familiars as agents of harm. Familiars are usually animals or animal-like mystical beings with a strong sexual element. Hammond-Tooke (1974) discusses the implications of the sexual elements of familiars and the gendered divisions between witches and sorcerers in greater depth.

The mesocosmos is also the space where battles between forces of good and evil take place. The protective powers of ancestors are brought to bear to ward off the evil influences of witchcraft and malignant spirits. It has been argued that the location of evil and the responsibility for protective action in the spirit world (Hammond-Tooke 1974; Meyer *et al.* 1997) may provide an understanding for the seemingly external locus of control orientation some Africans may adopt.

The social world

The microcosmos consists of the individual and his or her existence as lived within the community. Contrary to the individualistic Western model, the African way of being is premised on the collective and loyalty to the group. Emphasis and value are placed on family, clan and community-oriented functions and customs, such as cooperation and collective decision making (Meyer *et al.* 1997). The importance of the collective to the individual identity is captured rather succinctly in an isiZulu saying, '*umuntu ngumuntu ngabantu*', which means that one's humanity is defined through the quality of one's interactions with others.

The structure of the social world

Traditional African societies are made up of interrelated and connected parts. While we talk about clan groups and tribes, we are conscious that the use of these terms is problematic. Firstly, the terms have acquired negative political connotations through their use by past oppressive governments, who used them to justify and perpetuate separatist and oppressive policies. In addition, the fragmentation of traditional 'tribal groups' due to these policies, and their own dynamic processes, makes it difficult to talk about or to construe them as separate entities. In addition, tribes have always been open systems that influenced and were influenced by other social groupings and their customs and beliefs. Nevertheless, we will use the terms to describe traditional social formations because they continue to influence, to a greater or lesser extent, the way of life among African people, such as the value placed on extended family members with whom a common ancestry is shared.

Clan groups consist of members who are defined by their relatedness to a common ancestor, often manifest through a common surname or name (*isibongo*) among the Nguni, or a totem (often an animal) among the Sotho. Clan members may not know how they are related but a common clan name is sufficient proof of being related. A tribe is made up of a number of clans and often gets its name from the dominant clan. The term itself is problematic, having been defined in different ways by anthropologists, politicians and lay people. For our purposes, we combined elements of Gluckman and Evans-Pritchard's (both cited in Hammond-Tooke 1974) definitions to refer to a **clan** as a large group of people who recognise themselves as a distinct local community dominated by kinship-based status. The dominant clan is of aristocratic descent, with a status of chief that gets transmitted from generation to generation.

Clan:
Large group of people who recognise themselves as a distinctive local community dominated by kinship-based status.

Within the clan can be found lineages consisting of the descendants from one line of a particular person, usually through not more than six generations (Levitas 1983), and it is here where extended family members are located. The most important grouping within lineages is that of the family, either nuclear or compounded in polygamous marriages.

While the predominant form of marriage is between a man and his wife or wives, marriages between two women are sometimes found among baVenda and baLobedu (Levitas 1983). In all cases of marriage, a bride-price (*lobola* in Nguni, *munyalo* in Lobedu or *bogadi* in Sesotho) is given by the groom to the bride's family, to compensate them for the loss of her labour and to legitimise children born from the union. It also symbolises the uniting of the two families.

The society is highly structured and hierarchical, with age and sex being the main determinants of one's status within society. The male, as head of the family, is morally and ritually bound to look after those who fall under his care. Should he die, the eldest male child assumes this authority and responsibility. One's status and roles within the group are defined from birth, with a strong emphasis on one's sex, parents' position and rank, and one's position within the family structure. The socialisation process is then geared towards the expected roles and all institutions involved in the process work together within a homogenous framework to ensure the individual becomes a productive member of the group.

From an early age, children are divided into age and sex groupings, with each peer group having set functions and exercising social control over its members (Levitas 1983). Children are taught absolute obedience to parents. All elders in the group are addressed as mother or father and accorded the same kind of respect and obedience as one's parents. The birth of a child is an important event that affects the mother's position within the family – it ratifies the bride price, strengthens relations between the families and legitimates her role as a wife.

Puberty marks the transition from childhood to adulthood. Peer groups of both sexes undergo initiation and, although the process may differ for the two sexes, initiation schools teach adolescents about sexuality, as well as the duties, responsibilities and obligations of adulthood. The process of initiation is marked by extreme hardships and painful lessons under the guidance of designated elders in the community. Apart from lessons on sexuality and expected role functioning, initiates have to learn to endure hardship as a rite of passage. The process itself is marked by secrecy, and divulging the activities of the 'forest or mountain', as initiation schools are called by some groups, is punishable by exclusion from the society and even death. In most cultural groupings, circumcision is a significant part of the process, with female circumcision being less common than in other parts of Africa. Going through the initiation process confers the status of adulthood, with some cultural groups giving the returnees new names to signify their right to participate fully as adults in the community.

There are obvious advantages in the group-oriented organisation of the social world, since membership assures individuals of the group's support and protection when needed. While traditional ties have been disrupted through urbanisation, previous government policies (such as the Group Areas Act and the migrant labour system), and modernisation, much of this communalism has survived and is integrated into the new and emerging ways of life. This can be seen in the value placed on belonging to a group and the way communities unite in times of crisis, despite language, tribal and other differences. However, problems may arise when the supremacy of group needs leads to the suppression of individual goals and needs, especially as modern-day Africans have, through interactions with Western culture, adopted some of the individualist values of the latter.

The next section provides a brief overview of how health and legal problems are dealt with in traditional society. There is always differentiation between the private and the public realm when it comes to problem definition and solving. For personal and/or family problems, the individual or family takes primary responsibility for solving the problem.

Health, illness and healing

Like people everywhere, when things go wrong and illness strikes, Africans seek a causal explanation and treatment. Contrary to Western theories about germs, viruses and such causative organisms, Africans find explanations based on customs, traditions and their usage more plausible.

While most forms of ill health are considered unnatural, phenomena such as injuries and old age, as well as illnesses like the common cold, measles and whooping cough among others are accepted as natural. Such natural illnesses require no interventions either from doctors or traditional healers, with families relying on a variety of herbs and home remedies. Aside from these, illness is understood to develop as a result of bewitchment or displeasure of the ancestors. Illness is visited upon the living as direct punishment or reminder of one's obligations to the ancestors (Gumede 1990). Alternatively, it may be the result of ancestors withholding their protection and rendering one susceptible to the evil doings of witches and their familiars. Other illnesses, especially those that may be categorised as mental illness within mainstream psychology and psychiatry, may be a call for one to train as a traditional healer. (See Swartz (1998) for a comprehensive discussion of mental health and illness.)

The realm of traditional healing is structured, with clear divisions among the roles of each grouping. Destructive and evil forces (the witches) cause illness, diviners perform the diagnosis, and herbalists and medicine men or women provide the therapy. There may also be specialists, such as rainmakers and military doctors (who fortify armies before they go into battle). Gumede (1990) gave a detailed description of the types and structure of traditional healers among the Zulu.

Legal and political organisation/issues

Legal systems in traditional societies are not codified law, deriving instead their power and legitimacy from group values and traditions. Existing rules are inspired and informed by the cumulative experience and wisdom of the group's history. Because of its foundation in common values and tradition, all adults are expected to know and comply with the law and, according to Levitas (1983), ignorance of the law is no excuse for dereliction of duty. Some laws are derived from decrees by rulers, chiefs acting in consultation with their counsellors, or mandates from a general assembly of the group (Myburgh in Hammond-Tooke 1974).

Private or civil offences indirectly affecting the broader community are generally dealt with by the parties (individuals or family groups) involved in the dispute. In cases of marital discord, for example, if the couple fail to resolve their problems, either party can invite their family of origin into the conflict. It is only when settlement cannot be reached that public authorities are involved in private matters.

Public offences, including crimes like murder, assault, offences against the chief or treason, are tried by a tribal court consisting of the chief, counsellors, and influential individuals with ability, and other interested male members of the community. The chief, as a representative of the ruling clan, is the legislative, executive and judicial head of the group. While all the court participants have the right to engage in discussions about the case, and to voice their opinions on issues raised during the proceedings, the chief retains sole power for imposing sentences ranging from fines to banishment and death.

The last two sections looked briefly at the resolution of health and legal matters, and delineate that although there is respect for private space, the broader social group has a role to play in issues affecting the whole group. In addition, the group has responsibility towards helping individuals where they are unable to deal with private matters on their own. When private parties are unable to resolve a problem, the wisdom of the collective is brought to bear.

It is this cultural and contextual understanding and collective wisdom that is harnessed by the community psychologist in understanding and addressing the issues of concern in the community. By empowering communities to exercise their collective wills through focused action, the community psychologist plays important roles in encouraging change and development. These roles are manifold, as will be further discussed in the next section.

The roles of community psychologists

The roles and activities that community psychologists engage in are diverse and wide-ranging, and not easily enumerated. In a recent chapter devoted to practitioners' perspectives, Wolff (2000) indicated that there are no clear settings that can be declared the province of applied community psychology. The advantage of this lack of clear settings is that community psychologists end up working directly in communities through NGOs, state education, health and welfare departments and agencies, community action groups, community organisations (e.g. Life Line), and university training and outreach programmes at schools, clinics and community centres. Typically, community psychologists have been pioneers creating or shaping settings that would be amenable to their ideals and practice, or by filling a position where they will be able to use their community psychology skills (Wolff 2000).

One practitioner described this pioneering spirit as follows:

The field of community psychology is an emerging one – its mission, methodology and principles continue to be debated. To translate its mission into action is to work at the edge of an ecological frontier. And with that work comes all the excitement of the frontier – the adventure, the risk, the boom and the bust outcomes that reflect the convergence of ideology, technology, and setting.

(SWIFT IN WOLFF 2000: p. 757)

In tackling the needs of communities, community psychologists also engage in conducting research and in developing social policy. Community research is a collaborative process that seeks to study and understand needs, issues, concerns and problems affecting the health and wellness of a defined community. Community research also seeks to evaluate the outcome and effectiveness of programmes, interventions and processes designed to ameliorate conditions in the community. Dalton and his colleagues (2001) delineate five questions that guide community research (Table 13.2, overleaf). These questions will shape the collaborative, participative partnership between the community psychologist as researcher and the community as the research subject and empowered participant. The community psychologist/researcher must be guided by a commitment to identifying, facilitating or creating contexts in which hitherto silent and marginalised people – those who are the outsiders in various settings, organisations and communities – gain understanding, a voice and influence over decisions that affect their lives (Rappaport in Bhana & Khangee 2001).

TABLE 13.2: QUESTIONS GUIDING COMMUNITY RESEARCHERS

1 What phenomenon (need, issue, concern, process, intervention) will be studied?

2 From what perspective of theory and values will it be studied?

3 At what level of analysis will this research be conducted?

4 Within which cultural context will this research be conducted, and how will that context be understood?

5 Within what relationship with the community will this research take place?

Regarding social policy, Lazarus (2001) described a number of activities related to social policy that fall within the ambit of the community psychologist's role. These include:

• policy analysis;
• evaluation of policy outcomes/implementation;
• dissemination of information regarding the nuts and bolts of the policy, the legislative process, and policy implications for the community;
• conducting research to impact directly on policy; and
• facilitating citizen participation in the policy-making process.

Solarz, in Lazarus (2001), highlights several reasons why psychologists should become involved in policy-related activities:

• political decisions regarding funding on mental health affect the lives (and livelihood) of psychologists whether they like it or not;
• psychologists have substantive expertise to contribute to the process and products of social policy; and
• if psychologists do not address these pertinent issues, others, who are perhaps not as well equipped, will.

Community psychologists can also play an important advocacy role by addressing public-interest issues, formulating policies that address the needs of those who are disadvantaged, who are subject to discrimination, or who have special needs related to developmental factors (including women, children, the aged, racial and ethnic minorities, people living in poverty, and people with disabilities), and all people in need of health and mental-health services (Lazarus 2001).

Models of intervention

Community psychologists have identified several models of intervention: a mental-health model, a social-action model, a public-health model and a social-community approach.

The mental-health model

With its root in the community mental-health movement, the mental-health model aims to offer mental-health services primarily within a geographical area located as near as possible to where communities live (Van Wyk 2002). While this community-based approach seeks to strengthen, conserve and develop human resources, primary prevention is the underlying paradigm, focusing on greater access, early detection, reduction of the incidence and prevalence of mental-health problems and large-scale health-promotive interventions (Ahmed & Pretorius-Heuchert 2001). Examples of psychological practices within this approach include crisis intervention, consultation, training, psycho-education and the development of community mental-health centres (Lazarus 1988).

The model has been criticised for entrenching the medical discourse and associated power hierarchies. The mental-health worker is still regarded as the expert, even though cognisance is taken of the impact of the broader social context. The focus is still on pathology, with heavy reliance on medication. Though attempts are made to make mental-health services accessible, the model is essentially individualistic in focus. Despite the emphasis having shifted from treatment to prevention, any change that occurs is incidental and not transformative in terms of community psychology's goal for broad social change on a macrolevel (Ahmed & Pretorius-Heuchert 2001; Van Wyk 2002).

The social-action model

This model is regarded as one of the most revolutionary theories in community psychology and defines communities both politically and geographically. It emphasises the causal link between behaviour and social systems in the manifestation of mental-health difficulties. According to social action theory, there is a direct link between mental ill-health and psychological difficulties, and the unequal distribution of power and resources within a society (Van Wyk 2002). These structural inequalities in society (differences in the extent and quality of resources, facilities, funding, access to political power and decision-making

The mental-health model: Model that seeks to strengthen, conserve and develop human resources in order to prevent mental dysfunction and promote mental health, and seeks to mobilise community structures to promote prevention, greater access, and the reduction of the incidence and prevalence of mental-health problems.

The social-action model: Model that strives for social change by focusing on the connection between behaviour and social systems in the manifestation of mental-health difficulties, emphasising the structural inequalities in society and their impact on individuals and their communities, and putting pressure on relevant authorities.

processes), impact negatively on the ability of individuals and communities to address emerging needs and concerns.

The primary goal of this model is to facilitate social change. It would be more meaningful and lasting to change the social conditions of the poor than to temporarily address their problems. A social-action approach seeks to exert pressure on those in power to make the necessary changes that would benefit the lives of community residents. Citizen participation and empowerment are key processes in this model as they encourage the transformation of existing social conditions through individual and collective action. Social action therefore aims to organise communities to realise their inherent power as a collective and raise their awareness of the effects of the structural inequalities in their lives (Ahmed & Pretorius-Heuchert 2001; Dalton *et al.* 2001; Seedat *et al.* 2001; Van Wyk 2002). To achieve these goals, the psychologist is not a neutral agent, but actively organises, mobilises and conscientises oppressed groups to gain more equitable access to resources and services, compelling social institutions to be more responsive to community needs. Psychological practice in this model would include community organisation, political activism, public education, action research and advocacy (Lazarus 1988).

The public-health model

The public-health model:
Model that is based on the provision of primary health care or front-line care in community settings. While the traditional focus has been on physical health problems, this approach can be extended to provide basic mental-health services in under-resourced communities, and can be utilised for health education and primary prevention.

The public-health model refers to the provision of primary health care or front-line care for all members of the public. In declaring that health is a fundamental human right and that governments are responsible for providing the appropriate health infrastructure to meet this goal, the World Health Organisation (1978) has set certain parameters that primary health care (PHC) should be based on accessible, affordable, practically sound and socially acceptable health services to individuals and communities (Van Wyk 2002). Within the South African context, health delivery is rendered at three levels of intervention: primary, secondary and tertiary levels.

The first point of contact with the health system for individuals, families and communities is PHC. This front-line level of dealing with health issues includes primary health clinics, district hospitals, general medical practitioners and traditional healers (Pillay & Lockhat 2001). Patients needing more specialised treatment are referred to secondary level institutions, such as regional hospitals, larger day-hospitals and specialised mental-health settings. Tertiary level intervention is typically highly specialised, short-term in-patient treatment located at academic hospitals at provincial level. Patients are referred back to the secondary

and primary health sectors for recuperation, follow-up and maintenance. Given the inequities and neglect of the past, and the barriers to
health services, the Department of Health (2002) has declared primary
and community-based health care as its primary objective. In proposing
to incorporate appropriate mental-health services, community care and
psychosocial rehabilitation within the primary health-care framework,
the department's strategic plan will give special focus to: children,
adolescent and women's health; prevention of teenage pregnancies;
HIV/AIDS treatment and prevention; violence against women; and the
prevention of smoking and substance abuse (Van Wyk 2002).

The public-health model offers many advantages to the community
psychologist aiming to address the mental-health needs of disempow-
ered or disadvantaged communities. The holistic nature of this approach
to health, when coupled with the diminished stigmatisation of receiving
mental-health services in a medical setting, is a major advantage in
health education and primary prevention, and will require creative partnerships across service sectors. The cost of treatment is reduced
when the health intervention combines both medical treatments with
out-patient psychiatric services. The community psychiatric nurse
trained in basic psychiatry and primary health care is also an invaluable
asset in this model. Mental-health services in under-resourced communities may benefit from using this model, as front-line health workers may
be trained to detect, screen and treat less severe mental-health problems.
While the disadvantages of the mental-health model also apply here,
additional concerns include the secondary status of mental-health
services in the heavily medicalised health-care system that may compromise genuine holistic care, and the additional burden of growing
patient numbers and inadequate training, coupled with over-burdened
PHC staff, may affect staff morale and service delivery. That mental-
health services are to be included in PHC and form part of an
integrated, holistic approach to health augers well for community psychology to mobilise active community involvement and partnerships in
the assessment of needs and the establishment of relevant services (Van
Wyk 2002).

The social–community model

This model, sometimes referred to as the ecological model, integrates
various frameworks, with its primary goal being to 'promote
social change to alter unjust and oppressive situations by generating
knowledge, carrying out research and developing interventions'
(Serrano-Garcia in Ahmed & Pretorius-Heuchert 2001). This approach

The social–community model:
Model that is similar to the social-action model, but uses a Marxist framework to facilitate social action to mobilise individuals and communities to change their consciousness and to engage and shape their social reality.

recognises the role that social systems play in determining social processes in any given context. The psychologist is the agent of social change, either encouraging short-term adaptation to societal values, or medium-term accommodation by changing societal structures, or the longer-term goal of transforming attitudes and institutional values in society. Central to an understanding of this model is the notion that humans can bring about social change, and that awareness and collective social action can bring about empowerment, transformation and change at a community level. Multilevel analysis and intervention is emphasised. Psychological practice would include needs analysis, systems analysis, programme planning and programme evaluation (Lazarus 1988).

Case study [1]

Setting up a community project in a peri-urban community

This case study presents a glimpse into processes, structures and dynamics in setting up a psychological intervention in the community of Jamestown, based on principles, values and methods consonant with that of community psychology. Jamestown is a small peri-urban community of approximately 5 000 residents located on the outskirts of Stellenbosch. Its tranquil and panaromic setting against the Simonsberg mountain, its strawberry fields and its working-class and middle-class appearance, obscure the characteristic endemic psychosocial problems, difficulties and needs confronting this and other rural communities. Hidden from the public view, Jamestown has a second community tier consisting of pockets of informal settlements that arose when workers were displaced from farms they had been living on for generations. Many of these residents get by on seasonal and casual work. A third tier to the community is composed of workers and their families living on surrounding farms and small-holdings who use the facilities and resources in Jamestown. Approximately 60 to 70% of the learners at the primary and high schools are bussed in from farms in the district. The high level of need for psychological services at the recently opened primary health clinic in the community in 1999 prompted the staff to approach the Department of Psychology at Stellenbosch University for assistance.

Setting up the project

Resisting the inclination to jump in and set up psychological services at the primary health clinic, a series of consultative meetings was first set up between staff of the department and the relevant community role players and organisations, including the staff of the clinic, the primary and high school principals, clergy, the Jamestown Area Executive Forum (the local governance structure) and Stellenbosch Municipality. These consultation processes served several purposes: to establish formal links and personal relationships among the proposed project team and community role players; to provide an informed understanding of the context of this community (its history, socio-economic conditions, psycho-social

---

[1] In a **case study**, research is focused on describing and understanding the context of a particular unit of study, whether it is an individual, a group, an organisation or a community

needs, and risk and resilience factors among others); to establish the bona fides of the project team; to help identify potential partners and resources, and to increase community participation in the process. At a community meeting at the clinic, set up between community role players and the students and staff from the Counselling Psychology masters programme, the profile and contextual factors of the Jamestown community were presented by the community leaders and the goals of the project discussed, after which the community elders formally invited the students into their community.

Given the inherent racial and power imbalances in collaborative community projects, and universities' predilection to use community settings for their own purposes, the project team proposed a community partnership model to guide the development of the project (Naidoo 2000b) and ensure that the interests and accountabilities of all three parties (the community, the university and the local municipality) would be addressed. For the community, relevant psychological services addressing local needs would be provided, while the municipality's responsibility to provide mental-health facilities and services would be addressed, and community development objectives furthered. For the university, the model provided an opportunity to fulfil its community service mandate, but, moreover, establish an academically sound and professionally accountable model for training psychology students in a community context.

Out of this process involving role players from macro- to microlevels, the following broad goals of the Jamestown Community Project were established:

- provision of counselling and psychological services at the primary health clinic to the residents of the community, workers from surrounding farms, and learners from the primary and high schools;

- preventive programmes at the primary and high schools to deal proactively with specified needs in these settings; and
- development of the potential of the youth in the community by establishing relevant development programmes, such as leadership training, mentoring and the like.

In terms of the partnership, the community gave its endorsement and support for the project; the municipality gave permission for the project to be located at the clinic; and the university undertook to provide the personnel (students and staff) to render the counselling and psychological services and interventions.

Levels of intervention

In 2000, the masters students began rendering counselling and psychological services at the clinic two days per week. (This was one of four practicum rotations in the masters programme that included the traditional student counselling setting at the university, a prison placement and a hospital placement.) Initially most of the referrals came via the nursing staff and the school principals. To broaden the intervention beyond the remedial-curative focus, preventive and promotive interventions were also set up at the schools. In one project, the team of eight students was given a consultation assignment at the primary school, in response to a request for an intervention on motivation for the learners. After an initial briefing with the principal and teachers concerned, each student was assigned to work with a group of learners over four sessions. In addition to incorporating relevant life-skills activities into their intervention, students were asked to explore the factors affecting the learners' level of motivation. At the end of the group activities, the consultation team compiled a joint report and engaged with the principal and teachers concerned to not only share their observations and findings, but also to develop ways of addressing the systemic issues identified for the staff to take back into their school structures and processes (Naidoo *et al.* 2001). Some of the recommendations readily implemented by the school included selecting and training class leaders in each grade who could play a role in school activities, establishing a vegetable garden for learners to take pride in their environment and their school, and in training the Grade 7 learners for an active leadership role in the school. In addition, the masters students conducted assessment sessions and ran several groups at the school.

A **life-skills programme** [2] was also implemented at the high school, with volunteers recruited from the department's honours class. Groups based on particular themes were set up to run one-hour sessions per week for the duration of the semester. Teachers were involved in identifying learners for these groups.

With the increasing caseload at the clinic and emerging needs at the schools, a full-time counselling internship was set up at the clinic for 2001 through external funding, after a proposal submitted to the municipality for this purpose had been unsuccessful. With a full-time intern located at the clinic, psychological and counselling referrals from clinics in neighbouring communities could also be accommodated, and more focused interventions could be undertaken in the schools. In addition, the intern provided multilevel support to a diversion project that was being set up at the high school.

The diversion project was developed in response to the community role players' concern that the youth in the community were becoming increasingly susceptible to gang influence, and to substance and alcohol abuse. In partnership with an organisation called *Usiko*, an intervention programme for 'at risk' youth in the community was conceptualised, based on the following corner-stones:

- The project, to run over a nine-month period, would be a **diversion programme** [3] with a strong preventive and promotive focus (developing the skills, potential and vision of young men).
- The project would be based on a rites of passage philosophy to offer the participants sequential guidance in their transition from boys to men.
- The participants would undergo wilderness experiences at the beginning and at the end of the programme, as important threshold milestones.
- A team of mentors would be recruited from the community to guide the participants through the process and to shape the nature of the project.
- The participants (mentees) would engage in a community project of their own choice to acknowledge their role in their community.
- And, because it was being piloted, the project would be subjected to **formative** [4] and **summative evaluation** [5].

[2] **Life-skills programmes** are typically psycho-educational, preventive and promotive in nature, seeking to provide specific knowledge and skills to a target audience, to improve their understanding of the behaviour under focus and their ability to use the skills acquired. Examples include assertiveness training, handling peer pressure, sexuality awareness, handling conflict, improving communication, job hunting skills and the like.

[3] **Diversion programmes** are specialised life-skills programmes designed to provide participants with alternative ways (attitudes, behaviours, resources, vision) of dealing with adverse social circumstances that may lead to negative behaviours such as delinquency, crime and ganging.

FIGURE 13.3: Mentors preparing for their role in the programme.

After a community meeting to discuss the goals of the project, learners at the high school were invited to apply and motivate their personal reasons for wanting to be part of the programme. Teachers at the school assisted in making the final selection of 20 participants. A team of 13 mentors was eventually recruited by means of a letter to community organisations, a media article about the project, an invitation delivered to all the houses in the community and by personal invitation. Dual processes then unfolded. The mentors began their training programme for their role in the project, while the mentees were first individually assessed (home circumstances, scholastic record, psychological profile) before they were prepared for the first wilderness experience.

After the mentees returned from their nine-day wilderness experience, they were assigned individual mentors. In addition to a weekly meeting between the mentor and the mentee, mentors met weekly to discuss issues arising from their contact with mentees.

Several joint activities were also convened to bring mentors and mentees together. Two of these activities of particular significance included a visit to Robben Island, in which the mentees were encouraged by an ex-prisoner tour guide to rise above the adversities that might currently imprison them (poverty, adverse family circumstances, being stigmatised as farm children), and become willing to set their own vision for their future. The second activity had the mentor and mentees join other youth in the International AIDS Day all-night vigil at St George's Cathedral, where the group played a role in organising the venue and in the catering arrangements. The following evening, the mentees were challenged to sleep out on the street in the city (under supervision of the mentors), to gain insight into the realities of street life. Both activities provided a wealth of opportunity for mentees to reflect on their own contexts. These experiences were thoroughly debriefed in the regular life-skills sessions at the school. After a series of life-skills workshops, the mentees undertook their second wilderness experience, in which many of the young men crossed the threshold to make personal commitments about themselves and their vision for the future. Soon after their return, in April 2002, a community ceremony was held to celebrate their journey and their achievements.

While the evaluation of the *Usiko* project is still in progress, indications are that the project created a strong psychological sense of community for all involved, with many positive outcomes for the individual mentees, mentors, the school and the community (Naidoo 2002). A strong recommendation has emerged for a

---

[4] **Formative evaluation** occurs while a programme is in process to assess whether the short-term goals are being reached and to inform planning for the next phase of the programme.

[5] **Summative evaluation** is done at the end of a programme to assess the overall outcome of the programme against its predetermined objectives.

similar programme to be developed for the girls in the community, with community women to take the lead. Plans for the second phase include the continuation of support to the mentees who graduated from the first programme and for a new programme to be conducted concurrently in another community.

Behind the scenes, the intern psychologist based at the clinic assisted at multiple levels in the project. At a macrolevel, she was part of the advisory committee that planned some of the project activities, including the assessment protocol for the mentees and the evaluation processes. She also served as consultant for the project coordinator and the school principal. At a mesolevel, she ran the life-skills sessions for the mentees at the school, conducted workshops with the mentors on developmental tasks of adolescence, and facilitated some of the evaluation processes separately with the mentors and mentees. At a microlevel, she rendered counselling and crisis intervention services to some of the mentees and their family members. See Van Wyk (2002) for a detailed evaluation of this community-based internship, straddling the community mental-health and social-community models. The work in this community continues.

Future directions

In a recent international review of the status of community psychology, Wingenfield and Newbrough (2000) concluded that community psychology will expand and gain in significance as the new century unfolds. The success and direction will differ from country to country because of the variability in political, economic, social and cultural contexts, but more so whether the discipline positions itself on the progressive or conservative side of the political spectrum.

In the South African context, the following markers point the way for the future direction of community psychology.

- The burgeoning psychosocial needs of the country will necessitate that mainstream specialties of clinical, counselling and educational psychology increasingly incorporate community psychology theory and praxis into their respective frames of reference and training objectives.
- Universities will need to give more attention to establishing community psychology programmes at post-graduate level. This will lead to an improved status for community psychology as a specialty in its own right.
- The new B.Psych programmes will produce registered counsellors who will move into mental-health positions in community settings. The onus will be on the profession to engage national and local government to create employment opportunities for this new cadre of professionals, who will directly interface with communities.

- The establishment of community service for all categories of psych-ologists will stimulate a new discourse and debate in psychology as reality demands challenge the inadequacies and limitations of mainstream training.
- The problems attendant to socio-political transformation and changing economic circumstances will require a greater emphasis on the part of community psychologists to conduct research and to establish practice based on local needs, to influence policy develop-ment by lobbying government, and to engage in advocacy and specific social intervention activities.
- As agents of social change, community psychologists can play a vital role in the political and social challenges ahead, helping to inform appropriate social services and interventions, facilitating greater citizen participation in community issues, and helping a society fragmented by the machinations of apartheid and other ideologies to develop a sense of community.

Conclusion

There is much debate whether community psychology should be construed as a different lens (with its own philosophy, **epistemology**, methods and practice) for looking at psychology, or whether it is a branch of applied psychology using a variety of interventions (including prevention and health promotion) to facilitate change and improve mental-health and social conditions for groups, organisations and communities. The socio-political conditions in South Africa in the two decades preceding 1994 have imbued community psychology with a radical underlying philosophy challenging the discriminatory found-ation, theory, method and practice of psychology (Seedat *et al.* 2001). While it encourages a critical examination of the assumptions of the discipline, and fosters new ideas and ways of intervening, community psychology still falls short of adequately addressing the agendas of the unemployed, the working class, children, rural communities, feminists, and many other oppressed and marginalised groups.

Epistemology:
Theory of the methods or grounds of knowledge.

Community psychology does, however, extend the agenda of psychology beyond the mainstream gaze of treatment and the individ-ual. In emphasising the need for an ecological perspective in understanding the socio-historical context of social issues, community psychology broadens its gaze to embrace intervention goals of preven-tion, health promotion, development, and empowerment of individuals, groups and other social units and communities, as active participants in the intervention process.

Returning to the river analogy at the beginning of the chapter, it is in understanding the context of why people are drowning, and simultaneously recognising that drowning people need to be rescued, that community psychology, with its values, models, methods and practice can make a concerted contribution to the discipline of psychology. For the students of psychology, the challenge is to open their lenses to the full potential of the role that community psychology can play in responding to the needs and development opportunities in society.

Summary

In this chapter, we have presented an overview of community psychology as a branch of applied psychology. Tracing its historical roots, the evolving character of community psychology was described by way of its seminal values, principles and goals. In addition, ways of analysing communities and models of intervening in communities were delineated. The work activities that occupy community psychologists were also described, presenting a range of interesting possibilities for students wanting to become active in their communities. The chapter also presents a focus on understanding aspects of the African world view, with the goal of broadening cultural understanding and shifting psychology's traditional focus beyond individualistic notions of behaviour.

Activities

1 Think of a need or problem in your community. Brainstorm how this need or problem arose (the factors contributing to its manifestation).
2 Deepen your understanding of the context of the need or problem by using Bronfenbrenner's levels of analysis to see how broader macro factors have contributed to the problem.
3 Plan an intervention strategy to address the problem. Identify local resources (people, organisations, facilities) that would need to be included. What model or combinations of models would be important to adopt to address the need? Motivate your answer.
4 Project yourself into all of the roles of the community psychologist. Discuss with your class which role would be meaningful for you.
5 Contrast the role of the community psychologist with the traditional role of psychologists.

Further reading

Ahmed, R. & Pretorius-Heuchert, J.W. (2001) Community psychology: Past, present and future. In M. Seedat, N. Duncan & S. Lazarus (eds), *Community Psychology: Theory, Method and Practice.*

Albee, G.W. (1982) Preventing psychopathology and promoting human potential. *American Psychologist*, 37, pp. 1043–50.

Anonymous (1986) Some thoughts on a more relevant or indigenous counselling psychology in South Africa: Discovering the socio-political context of the oppressed. *Psychology in Society*, 5, pp. 81–9.

Bennett, C., Anderson, L., Cooper, S., Hassol, L., Klein, D. & Rosenblum, G. (1966) *Community Psychology: A Report of the Boston Conference on the Education of Psychologists for Community Mental Health.* Boston: Boston University Press.

Berman, A.J. & Jobes, D.A. (1995) Suicide prevention in adolescents. *Suicide and Life Threatening Behavior*, 25, pp. 143–5.

Bhana, A. & Kanjee, A. (2001) Epistemological and methodological issues in community psychology. In M. Seedat, N. Duncan & S. Lazarus (eds), *Community Psychology: Theory, Method and Practice.*

Bronfenbrenner, U. (1979) *The Ecology of Human Development: Experiments by Nature and Design.* Cambridge, Mass.: Harvard University Press.

Bulhan, H.A. (1985) *Frantz Fanon and the Psychology of Oppression.* New York: Plenum Press.

Caplan, G. (1964) *Principles of Preventive Psychiatry.* New York: Basic Books.

Centre for the Study of Health Policy (1990) *The Need for Improved Mental Health Care in South Africa.* Briefing document. Johannesburg: Centre for the Study of Health Policy, University of the Witwatersrand.

Cooper, S., Nicholas, L.J., Seedat, M. & Statman, J.M. (1990) Psychology and apartheid: The struggle for psychology in South Africa. In L.J. Nicholas & S. Cooper (eds), *Psychology and Apartheid: Essays on the Struggle for Psychology and the Mind in South Africa.* Johannesburg: Vision/Madiba.

Cornell Empowerment Group (1989) Empowerment and family support. *Network Bulletin*, 1, pp. 1–3.

Cowen, E.L. (1996) The ontogenesis of primary prevention: Lengthy strides and stubby toes. *American Journal of Community Psychology*, 22, pp. 149–79.

Cowen, E.L. (2000) Community psychology and routes to psychological wellness. In J. Rappaport & E. Seidman (eds), *Handbook of Community Psychology.*

Dalton, J.H., Elias, M.J. & Wandersman, A. (2001) *Community Psychology: Linking Individuals and Communities.* Belmont: Wadsworth/Thomson Learning.

Dawes, A. (1985) Politics and mental health: The position of clinical psychology in South Africa. *South African Journal of Psychology,* 15, pp. 55–61.

Dawes, A. (1986) The notion of relevant psychology with particular reference to Africanist pragmatic initiatives. *Psychology in Society,* 5, pp. 28–48.

Dommisse, J. (1987) The state of psychiatry in South Africa today. *Social Science Medicine,* 24, pp. 749–61.

Faxelid, E., Ahlberg, J., Ndulo, J. & Krantz, I. (1998) Health-seeking behaviour of patients with sexually transmitted diseases in Zambia. *East African Medical Journal,* 74(4), pp. 273–303.

Felner, R.D., Felner, T.Y. & Silverman, M.M. (2000) Prevention in mental health and social intervention: Conceptual and methodological issues in the evolution of the science and practice of intervention. In J. Rappaport & E. Seidman (eds), *Handbook of Community Psychology.*

Foster, D. (1986) The South African crisis of 1985. *Psychology in Society,* 5, pp. 49–65.

Foster, D., Freeman, M. & Pillay, Y. (1997) *Mental Health Policy Issues for South Africa.* Pinelands: Medical Association of South Africa.

Freeman, M. & Motsei, M. (1992) Planning health care in South Africa – is there a role for traditional healers? *Social Science and Medicine,* 34(11), pp. 1183–90.

Gallant, R.V., Cohen, C. & Wolff, T. (1985) Change of older persons' image, impact, on public policy results from Highland Valley Empowerment Plan. *Perspective on Aging,* 14, pp. 9–13.

Gladding, S.T. (1997) *Community and Agency Counseling.* Upper Saddle River: Prentice-Hall.

Gobodo, P. (1990) Notions about culture in understanding black psychopathology: Are we trying to raise the dead? *South African Journal of Psychology,* 20(2), pp. 93–7.

Gumede, M.V. (1990) *Traditional Healers: A Medical Doctor's Perspective.* Johannesburg: Skotaville.

Hamber, B., Masilela, T.C. & Terre Blanche, M. (2001) Towards a Marxist community psychology: Radical tools for the community psychological analysis and practice. In M. Seedat, N. Duncan & S. Lazarus (eds), *Community Psychology: Theory, Method and Practice.*

Hammond-Tooke, W.D. (ed.) (1974) *The Bantu-speaking Peoples of Southern Africa.* Boston: Routledge & Kegan Paul.

Heller, K., Price, K.H., Reinharz, S., Riger, S., Wandersman, A. & D'Aunno, T.A. (1984) *Psychology and Community Change.* Homewood: Dorsey.

Holdstock, T.L. (1981) Psychology in South Africa belongs to the colonial era: Arrogance or ignorance? *South African Journal of Psychology,* 11, pp. 123–9.

Katz, J. (1985) The sociopolitical nature of counselling. *Counselling Psychologist,* 13, pp. 615–24.

Kriegler, S. (1989) Educational psychology in South Africa. *School Psychology International,* 10, pp. 217–24.

Lambley, P. (1980) *The Psychology of Apartheid.* London: Secker & Warburg.

Lazarus, S. (1988) The role of the psychologist in South African society: In search of an appropriate community psychology. Unpublished doctoral dissertation, University of Cape Town.

Lazarus, S. (2001) Social policy and community psychology in South Africa. In M. Seedat, N. Duncan & S. Lazarus (eds) *Community Psychology: Theory, Method and Practice.*

Lazarus, S. & Seedat, M. (1995) Community psychology in South Africa. Paper presented at the Fifth Biennial Conference of the Society for Community Research and Action, University of Illinois, Chicago.

Levitas, B. (1983) *Ethnology: An Introduction to the Peoples and Cultures of Southern Africa.* Cape Town: Oxford University Press.

Lewis, J.A., Lewis, M.D., Daniels, J.A. & D'Andrea, M.J. (1998) *Community Counseling: Empowering Strategies for a Diverse Society.* Pacific Grove: Brooks/Cole.

McMillan, D.W. & Chavis, D.M. (1986) Sense of community: Definition and theory. *Journal of Community Psychology,* 14, pp. 6–23.

Meyer, W.F., Moore, C. & Viljoen, H.G. (1997) *Personology: From Individual to Ecosystem.* Johannesburg: Heinemann.

Myburgh, A.C. (1974) Law and justice. In W.D. Hammond-Tooke (ed.), *The Bantu-speaking Peoples of Southern Africa.*

Naidoo, A.V. (1996) Challenging the hegemony of Eurocentric psychology. *Journal of Community and Health Sciences*, 2(2), pp. 9–16.

Naidoo, A.V. (2000a) Community psychology: Constructing community, reconstructing psychology in South Africa. Inaugural lecture, University of Stellenbosch.

Naidoo, A.V. (2000b) *The Jamestown Community Project: Annual Report 2000*. Stellenbosch: Department of Psychology, University of Stellenbosch.

Naidoo, A.V. (2002) *The Jamestown Community Project: Evaluation Report 2000–2002*. Stellenbosch: Department of Psychology, University of Stellenbosch.

Nell, V. (1990) One world, one psychology: Relevance and ethnopsychology. *South African Journal of Psychology*, 20, pp. 129–40.

Nicholas, L.J. (1990) Psychology in South Africa: The need for an openly politically contextualised discipline. In L.J. Nicholas & S. Cooper (eds), *Psychology and Oppression: Critiques and Proposals*. Johannesburg: Skotaville.

Nzimande, B. (1986) Industrial psychology and the study of black workers in South Africa: A review and critique. *Psychology in Society*, 2, pp. 54–91.

Orford, J. (1992) *Community Psychology: Theory and Practice*. Chichester: John Wiley.

Pedersen, P. (1991) Multiculturalism as a generic approach to counseling. *Journal of Counseling and Development*, 70(1), pp. 6–12.

Pillay, A. & Lockhat, R. (2001) Models of community mental health services for children. In M. Seedat, N. Duncan & S. Lazarus (eds), *Community Psychology: Theory, Method and Practice*.

Rappaport, J. (1977) *Community Psychology: Values, Research and Action*. New York: Holt, Rinehart & Winston.

Rappaport, J. (1981) In praise of paradox: A social policy of empowerment over prevention. *American Journal of Community Psychology*, 9, pp. 1–25.

Rappaport, J. (1985) The power of empowerment language. *Social Policy*, 16, pp. 15–21.

Rappaport, J. (1990) Research methods and empowerment social agenda. In P. Tolan, C. Keys, F. Chertok & L. Jason (eds), *Researching Community Psychology*. Washington, DC: American Psychological Association.

Rappaport, J. & Seidman, E. (eds) (2000) *Handbook of Community Psychology*. New York: Kluwer Academic/Plenum.

Reiff, R. (1968) Social interventions and the problem of psychological analysis. *American Psychologist*, 23, pp. 524–31.

Retief, A. (1989) The debate about the relevance of South African psychology – a metatheoretical perspective. *South African Journal of Psychology*, 19, pp. 75–83.

Sarason, S. (1974) *The Psychological Sense of Community: Perspectives for Community Psychology*. San Francisco: Jossey-Bass.

Scileppi, J.A., Teed, E.L. & Torres, R.D. (2000) *Community Psychology: A Common Sense Approach to Mental Health*. Upper Saddle River: Prentice-Hall.

Seedat, M., Duncan, N. & Lazarus, S. (eds) (2001) *Community Psychology: Theory, Method and Practice*. Cape Town: Oxford University Press.

Swartz, L. (1986) Transcultural psychiatry in South Africa, Part I: Cross-cultural issues in mental health practice. *Transcultural Psychiatric Research Review*, 23, pp. 273–303.

Swartz, L. (1987) Transcultural psychiatry in South Africa, Part II: Cross-cultural issues in mental health practice. *Transcultural Psychiatric Research Review*, 24, pp. 5–25.

Swartz, L. (1998) *Culture and Mental Health: A Southern African View*. Cape Town: Oxford University Press

Swartz, S., Dowdall, T. & Swartz, L. (1986) Clinical psychology and the 1985 crisis in Cape Town. *Psychology in Society*, 5, pp. 131–38.

Swartz, L. & Gibson, K. (2001) The 'old' versus the 'new' in South African community psychology: The quest for appropriate change. In M. Seedat, N. Duncan & S. Lazarus (eds), *Community Psychology: Theory, Method and Practice*.

Van der Spuy, H.I.J. & Shamley, D.A.F. (eds) (1978) *The Psychology of Apartheid*. Lanham: University Press of America.

Van Wyk, S. (2002) Locating a counselling internship in a community setting. Unpublished masters thesis, University of Stellenbosch.

Vogelman, L. (1987) The development of an appropriate psychology: The work of the organisation of appropriate social services in South Africa. *Psychology in Society*, 7, pp. 24–35.

Webster, E. (1986) Excerpt from *Servants of Apartheid*. *Psychology in Society*, 6, pp. 6–28.

Wingenfeld, S. & Newbrough, J. R. (2000) Community psychology in international perspective. In J. Rappaport & E. Seidman (eds), *Handbook of Community Psychology*.

Wolff, T. (2000) Practitioners' perspectives. In J. Rappaport & E. Seidman (eds), *Handbook of Community Psychology*.

World Health Organisation (WHO) (1978) WHO Declaration of Alma-Ata, International Conference on Primary Health Care, 6–12 September. http:www.who.int/hpr/archive/docs/almaata.html on 2 Feb. 2002.

Wouters, A.R. (1993) Relevant psychological help in the South African context: A personal empowerment model. Unpublished doctoral dissertation, Vista University.

Zimmerman, M.A. (2000) Empowerment theory: Psychological, organizational, and community levels of analysis. In J. Rappaport & E. Seidman (eds), *Handbook of Community Psychology*.

14 Industrial Psychology: Selected topics

F. Abrahams and R.R. Ruiters

Part 1: Industrial psychology

Objectives

After studying this section you should:
- be able to define the term 'industrial psychology'
- understand the importance of industrial psychology in the world of work
- be able to identify the major fields of industrial psychology
- understand how industrial psychology evolved
- understand what is meant by 'professionalistion of industrial psychology'
- know the requirements to register as an industrial psychologist
- understand a few key issues related to strategic industrial psychology
- have an understanding of the legislative framework that governs industrial relations in South Africa.

Introduction

Whether we like it or not, we spend most of our waking lives at work. Work plays a major influence in our lives, as it governs where we are going to live, how we are going to live, and who our friends are going to be. Therefore, it makes sense to find out more about our own attitude and work behaviour, and the world of work in general (Riggio 2000).

For some people, work is so important that they continue to go to work each day, even if they do not need to because they are financially secure. A study conducted by Quintanilla (1990) in Schultz and Schultz (1998), showed that 84% of Japanese, American and German employees stated that they would continue to work even though they would not need the income. So, why do people work?

Clearly people get much more from their jobs than just a pay cheque. Those who are fortunate to find a job most suited to their skills, abilities and education experience a sense of accomplishment and personal satisfaction that provides its own reward. A career can offer a sense of identity and status, a chance to learn new skills and master new challenges, provide financial and social reward, and create opportunities to make friends and meet people from diverse backgrounds.

However, work can also be dangerous to your health. In addition to physical dangers in some work environments, a job that does not match your skills, abilities and education can lead to frustration and anxiety. This kind of work stress can lead to emotional and physical health problems. Long-term research has shown that employees who are satisfied with their jobs tend to live longer than those who are not.

Therefore, selecting a job that is right for your skills, abilities, education and interests is of vital importance, and that is where industrial psychology can help. In fact, in addition to matching people with jobs, the findings and practices of industrial psychologists will impact on your life from your first interview to your last retirement function (Schultz & Schultz 1998). So, what is industrial psychology?

What is industrial psychology?

Industrial psychology:
One of the applied areas within the broad field of psychology that studies behaviour within the work context.

Industrial psychology is one of the applied areas within the broad field of psychology that studies behaviour within the work context (Berry & Houston 1993; Muchinsky 1997). It is interesting to note that different countries use different terminology to describe the field of industrial psychology. The term 'industrial psychology' was replaced by the term 'industrial/organisational psychology' (I/O psychology) about 20 years ago in the USA. In the United Kingdom it is referred to as 'occupational psychology', and some countries in Europe refer to it as 'work and organisational psychology'. In South Africa, 'industrial psychology' is still used to describe the broad fields of industrial and organisational psychology, although there is debate among academics and industrial psychologists in commerce and industry as to the appropriateness of the term within the current environment (Berry & Houston 1993; Muchinsky et al. 1998). As it is current terminology widely used in South Africa, we will continue to refer to the field as industrial psychology.

Because industrial psychology has two sides (science and practice), it is not only concerned about understanding behaviour at work through verifiable observation, experience and experimentation (not hunches or guessing), but also applies this knowledge to solve real problems in the world of work. The findings of industrial psychologists can be used to hire better employers, increase job satisfaction, improve communication and resolve countless other problems (Schultz & Schultz 1998; Muchinsky 1997).

Fields of industrial psychology

Just like psychology in general, industrial psychology is made up of a number of speciality areas. Although personnel management and organisational behaviour comprise a major part of the field, other areas are also important.

Personnel psychology

The word 'personnel' means 'people'. So, personnel psychology is concerned with individual differences and predicting a fit between the employee and the employer. Among other things, it is concerned with the recruitment, selection, placement and training of employees. It is also referred to as human resource management.

Personnel psychology: Branch of psychology concerned with individual difference and predicting a fit between the employee and the employer.

Organisational psychology

Work in this area focuses on role-related behaviour, group pressure, commitment to the organisation and patterns of communication. The basic aim is to foster worker adjustment, satisfaction and productivity. Organisational psychology is more concerned with social and group influences, whereas personnel psychology is more concerned with individual level issues, such as recruitment and selection.

Organisational psychology: Branch of psychology that focuses on role-related behaviour, group pressure, commitment to the organisation and patterns of communication.

Ergonomics

This area is concerned with the design of tools, equipment and workspaces to make it more compatible with the abilities of employees. The limitations and abilities of employees, and the characteristics of the equipment, are considered to produce an efficient person-machine system. It is also referred to as human factors psychology and engineering psychology.

Ergonomics: Area concerned with the design of tools, equipment and workspace to make them more compatible with the abilities of employees.

Career psychology

This field is a cross between counselling psychology and industrial psychology. It is concerned with career and organisational choice, career issues that affect individuals, and changes in organisations that affect careers. Topics such as career counselling, career planning and development are included.

Career psychology: Branch of psychology concerned with career and organisational choice, career issues that affect individuals, and changes in organisations that affect careers.

Labour relations

This field deals with the relationship and problems between employers and employees, where a union usually represents employees. The focus is on issues such as conflict and cooperation between workers, resolution of disputes, and bargaining or negotiation of agreements. These issues are governed by legislation and it is important to have knowledge of this if you are working in this area.

Consumer psychology

Industrial psychologists in this field devote their attention to understanding the actions of individuals who are purchasing, using and disposing of consumer goods. Consequently, decision-making processes before and after purchasing are important.

Cross-cultural industrial psychology

This is also referred to as diversity management and, even though it is not a recognised field of industrial psychology, several South African universities have introduced it as part of their programmes. Industrial psychology has become compelled to examine cross-cultural factors in work behaviour as significant changes in the work environment affect our lives. These changes include increased cultural diversity of the workforce, mergers and acquisitions, and the impact of technology and telecommunication systems.

Occupational mental health

This field is concerned with the psychological well being of the worker, involving adjustment and maladjustment in the work context. The focus is on the mental health of employees (Bergh & Theron 1999; Muchinsky 1997; Schultz & Schultz 1998).

Evolution of industrial psychology

When the field of psychology was still in its infancy, a few psychologists and others (largely from the United States) started conducting basic research in work behaviour. Hugo Munsterberg, a German who taught at Harvard University in the USA, was an experimental psychologist who became interested in the design of work and the selection of workers for jobs such as streetcar operators. Another pioneer of industrial psychology, who is often referred to as the 'father' of industrial psychology (although the term only really became popular in the 1970s), was Walter Dill Scott. He focused his research on the work behaviour of salespersons and the psychology of advertising (Riggio 2000).

Labour relations: Process that deals with the relationship and problems between employers and employees where employees are usually represented by a union.

Consumer psychology: Branch of psychology that attempts to understand the actions of individuals who are purchasing, using and disposing of consumer goods.

Cross-cultural industrial psychology: Branch of psychology that examines cross-cultural factors in work behaviour as significant changes in the work environment affect our lives.

Occupational mental health: Branch of psychology concerned with the psychological well being of the worker, involving adjustment and maladjustment in the work context.

Culture: The set of values, customs, and beliefs common to members of a social unit, e.g. a nation.

Another early contributor, Frederick W. Taylor, an engineer, believed
that scientific principles could be applied to the study of work behaviour
to increase the efficiency and effectiveness of workers. He wrote the
book *Principles of Scientific Management* in 1911, where he outlined
his method of breaking down the job scientifically into parts that are
measurable and then recording the time needed for each component.
This became known as **time and motion studies**, and often doubled or
quadrupled employee output. Taylor and his followers, including
husband-and-wife team Frank and Lillian Gilbreth (the latter being one
of the earliest women industrial psychologists), implemented the system
that became known as scientific management, and changed several physical labour jobs by making them more efficient and productive.
Unfortunately, Taylor's philosophy had its limitations, as it focused on
manual labour that was easily broken down. Today, jobs are more complex and cannot always be broken down into small parts. Its philosophy
was also viewed as inhumanly exploiting workers for a higher wage,
which resulted in greater numbers of workers becoming unemployed
(Bergh & Theron 1999; Riggio 2000; Muchinsky 1997).

Time and motion studies:
These break down the job
scientifically into parts
that are measurable
and then record the
time needed for each
component.

It was during World War I that industrial psychology gained in
popularity and interest. Psychologists presented a number of proposals
to the military that included screening recruits for mental deficiency,
assigning selected recruits to specific jobs, and assisting with morale,
and psychological and discipline problems. However, the military
viewed the psychologists with scepticism and, eventually, only approved
a small number of proposals, mostly related to the assessment of
recruits. The Army Alpha and the Army Beta Tests (for illiterates) were
developed to assess recruits. At the end of the war, over one million
recruits had been assessed. Unfortunately, the actual use of the results
was minimal, due to the delay in the implementation of the testing programme. Nonetheless, due to the recognition given to psychologists,
there was a boom in the number of psychological consulting firms operating in the USA after the war (Muchinsky *et al.* 1998).

In 1924, Mayo conducted the now-famous Hawthone studies at the
Hawthorne works of the Western Electrical Company in the USA.
The objective was to determine the influence of environmental working
conditions, such as different levels of illumination (light) and different
lengths of rest periods on productivity. The research revealed that other
factors, such as the interest displayed by the researchers, influenced
productivity (Riggio 2000).

During World War II, industrial psychologists were called upon to
assist with the selection and placement of army and civilian recruits.
After the war, the field of industrial psychology mushroomed and

speciality areas, rather than just the focus on psychological tests, emerged (Riggio 2000). From 1960 to the early 1990s, research and practice blossomed in these speciality areas. It was also during this period that criticism mounted against the use of psychological tests, as they were deemed culturally biased, and many court actions resulted (Kamin 1974). Nonetheless, psychological tests remain an important part of the industrial psychologist's work, but greater emphasis and research is placed on the use of tests in a cross-cultural environment.

In South Africa, industrial psychology had its origins as an experimental science in 1946, when the National Institute for Personnel Research (NIPR) was established (later incorporated into the Human Sciences Research Council). It focused on the development, selection and classification of tests for black mineworkers. These tests measured trainability and leadership among a predominately pre-literate black population speaking a number of dialects and languages. The NIPR's activities generated vast amounts of research, and findings were published both locally and internationally (Biesheuvel 1987). Psychology in general and the activities of the NIPR have been critiqued because its research focus appeared to be influenced by the apartheid ideology of the Nationalist government (1948–1994) and was therefore not in the interests of all South Africans (Cloete et al. 1986; Dubow 1981).

Nonetheless, the field of industrial psychology has experienced tremendous growth over the last three decades in South Africa. Almost all universities have industrial psychology departments in addition to psychology departments (established in the 1960s or 1970s), and student numbers at these universities continue to rise. More recently, the practices of industrial psychology have been largely influenced by legislation passed by the post-1994 democratically elected government. According to the Constitution, the Labour Relations Act and the Employment Equity Act, the onus is on industrial psychologists to establish and implement fair employment standards.

Professionalisation of industrial psychology

Whatever their focus, industrial psychologists must keep abreast of developments in the field. One way to do this is to participate in the activities of professional organisations. In South Africa, these include the Society for Industrial Psychology, a division of the Psychological Society of South Africa (PsySSA); the Institute for Personnel Management (IPM), and the Psychological Assessment Initiative (PAI). These organisations offer research journals (e.g. *The South African Journal of Psychology* and the *Journal of Industrial Psychology*), and other kinds of publications, organise conferences and meetings where new research and other issues of importance are discussed, represent the interests of industrial psychologists in public affairs and provide ethical standards for their professional activities.

Industrial psychologists, like other psychologists, are committed to certain values. Like the American Psychological Society, PsySSA also enforces a code of professional ethics. This states that psychologists must be responsible and competent, personally moral and sensitive, respectful of the rights to privacy and concerned with the welfare of clients and research subjects. In addition, the Society for Industrial psychology has also published *Guidelines for the Validation and Use of Personnel Selection Procedures* in 1992 that specifically relates to the use of psychological test results. In 1998, the PAI also published the *Code of Practice for Psychological Assessment in the Work Place* (Foxcroft *et al.* 2001a; Muchinsky *et al.* 1998; Berry & Houston 1993).

To practice as an industrial psychologist, you need to register with the Professional Board for Psychology, in terms of the Health Profession Act No. 56 of 1974. The main function of the board is to protect the public and set standards for professional training and conduct. To register with the Professional Board, a masters degree in industrial psychology and a formal 12-month internship in an organisation were requirements. However, in 1999, the training of psychologists underwent a major change, as the Professional Board adopted a new practice framework. From 2004 onwards, a DPsych (doctoral) degree and a 12-month internship will be required for registration as an industrial psychologist. The final details to the changes are still be made (Foxcroft *et al.* 2001).

Many industrial psychologists also register as personnel practitioners with the South African Board for Personnel Practice (SABPP). Although this is not a statutory body, and not regulated by legislation, it also aims to establish and maintain a high level of professionalism and ethical behaviour in personnel practice. Individuals can be registered as personnel practitioners or associate personnel practitioners. An honours degree or technikon diploma with a two-year internship is required for registration as a personnel practitioner, but a bachelors degree or diploma (with Industrial Psychology or Human Resource Management as a major) is required for registration as an associate personnel practitioner (Muchinsky *et al.* 1998).

In the last three sections the focus was largely on defining the field of industrial psychology, and placing it in a professional context. In the next section we will briefly focus on strategic industrial psychology, the role it plays in shaping the strategic direction of organisations, and factors that influence it.

Strategic industrial psychology

Organisations operate in a dynamic environment, which means that external and internal forces are continually changing. As often referred to in sports, both the playing field and the rules of the game are constantly being revised for the organisation. To survive in a dynamic environment, organisations must be prepared to diagnose their opportunities and revise their strategies. Choosing the right strategy often makes the difference between success and failure (Leonard 1992). Organisational strategies must be aligned with other functional strategies, including human resource strategies. A typical representation of such strategies can be seen in Figure 14.1.

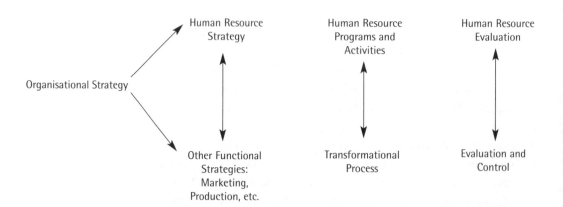

FIGURE 14.1: Strategic human resource management model

(SOURCE: ADAPTED FROM CHERRINGTON (1995))

Human resource activities that are excellent and unique can be a source of competitive advantage for an organisation. Research has demonstrated that if organisations expect to survive in a dynamic environment, they must have carefully developed organisational strategies to guide them and be supported by consistent human resource strategies (Gupta & Singhal 1993).

Human resource planning (HRP)

This refers to the process of systematically reviewing human resources requirements to ensure that the required number of employees with the required skills are available when needed (Mondy *et al.* 1986). Human resource planning involves matching the internal and external supply of people with job openings anticipated in the organisation over a specified period of time. However, there is a growing mismatch between emerging jobs and qualified people available to fill them. The labour pool in South Africa is especially important as local companies try to cope with rapid technological change and increasing globalisation of the economy, while facing increasing numbers of highly skilled workers leaving the country in huge numbers. Therefore, this is an important step that is often overlooked within organisations that then find themselves with an inappropriate number of staff.

The human resource planning process is illustrated in Figure 14.2, below. Note that **strategic planning** – which requires consideration of both the external and internal environment – precedes human resource planning.

Human resource planning:
Process of systematically reviewing human resources requirements to ensure that the required number of employees, with the required skills, are available when they are needed.

Strategic planning:
The process by which top management determines the overall purposes and objectives and how they are to be achieved.

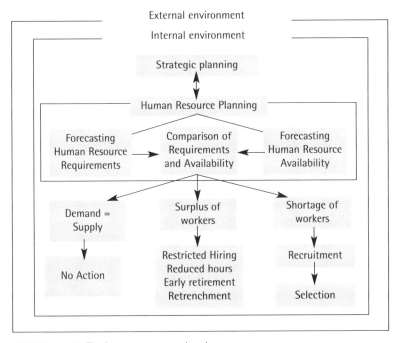

FIGURE 14.2: The human resource planning process

(SOURCE: MONDY & NOE 1996)

Strategic planning is the process by which top management determines
the overall purposes and objectives of an organisation and how they are
to be achieved. There is a growing realisation among professional managers of the importance of including human resource management in the
strategic planning process, where human resource planning is linked to
organisational strategy (Norton 1991).

Those in the profession use several techniques of forecasting human
resource requirements and availability. Some of the techniques are
qualitative in nature, and others are quantitative. The following are
examples of these techniques:

Zero-base forecasting:
Using the organisation's
current level of
employment as the
starting point for the
determination of future
staffing needs.

- **Zero-base forecasting:** This approach uses the organisation's current
level of employment as the starting point for the determination of
future staffing needs. If an employee retires, is retrenched or leaves the
company for any other reason, the position is not automatically filled.
Instead, an analysis is made to determine whether the company can
justify filling it. Equal concern is shown for creating new positions
when they appear to be needed. The key to zero-based forecasting is a
thorough analysis of human resource needs.

Bottom-up approach:
Each successive level in
the organisation – start-
ing with the lowest –
forecasts its requirements,
ultimately providing an
aggregate forecast of
employees needed.

- **Bottom-up approach:** This approach is based on the reasoning
that the manager in each unit is the most knowledgeable about
employment requirements. In the bottom-up approach, each successive level in the organisation – starting with the lowest – forecasts its
requirements, ultimately providing an aggregate forecast of employees
needed. Human resource forecasting is often most effective when
managers periodically project their human resource needs,
comparing their current and anticipated levels and giving the human
resource department adequate lead time to explore internal and
external sources.

Predictor variable:
Using past employment
levels to predict future
requirements.

- **Use of predictor variable:** This technique uses past employment levels
to predict future requirements. Predictor variables are factors known
to have had an impact on employment levels. One of the most useful
predictors of employment levels is sales volume. The relationship
between demand and the number of employees is a positive one.
As can be see in Figure 14.3, on the next page, a firm's sales volume is
depicted on the horizontal axis, and the number of employees actually
required is shown on the vertical axis. This shows that as sales
increase, so does the number of employees. Using such a method,
managers can approximate the number of employees required at
different demand levels.

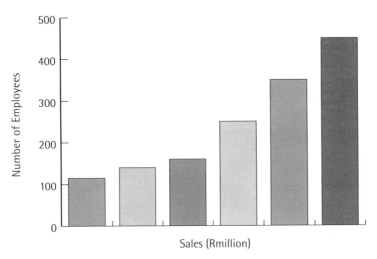

FIGURE 14.3: Graph depicting sales volume and number of employees.

- **Simulation:** This is a technique for experimenting with a real-world situation through a mathematical model representing that situation. A simulation model is an attempt to represent a real-world situation through mathematical logic in order to predict what will occur. Simulation assists the human resource manager by permitting the asking of many 'what if' questions without having to make a decision resulting in real-world consequences.

Simulation:
Experimenting with a real-world situation through a mathematical model in order to predict what will occur.

Downsizing

One consequence of human resource planning and strategic planning could be the decision by an organisation to downsize. This is closely tied to retrenchment and is also known as restructuring and rightsizing, where, typically the organisation and the number of people it employs shrink. In recent years, many South African organisations, both private and public, have undertaken the extremely painful task of downsizing and restructuring. Because of either economic or competitive pressures, organisations have found themselves with too many employees or with employees that have the wrong kinds of skills. In some cases, downsizing is not simply as a result of economic downturn. In many cases, it is part of a longer-term process of restructuring to take advantage of new technologies, corporate partnerships and cost minimisation.

Downsizing:
Also known as restructuring and rightsizing, where, typically, the organisation and the number of people it employs shrinks.

However, downsizing is often unsuccessful. The reason for this is that downsizing has not been able to solve the fundamental causes of the problems. Organisations have developed an appropriate strategy for growth, but have focused on reducing costs, which is merely a symptom of the problem.

One result of downsizing is that many layers are often pulled out of an organisation, making it more difficult for individuals to advance in the organisations. In addition, often when one company downsizes, others must follow if they are to be competitive. Thus, more and more individuals find themselves stagnating in the same job until they retire. To reinvigorate demoralised employees, caused by downsizing, some companies provide additional training, short sabbaticals, and compensation based on a person's contribution, not his or her title (Fierman 1992).

Very often the industrial psychologist or human resource departments are not adequately consulted prior to the downsizing exercise, but are relied upon to implement the decision.

Globalisation

Globalisation: The process of interconnecting the world's people with respect to the cultural, economic, political, technological and environmental aspects of their lives.

Trade between nations has grown from US$308 billion in 1950 to US$3.8 trillion in 1993 (Brown *et al.* 1994). Several factors account for this dramatic growth. Firstly, technology has lowered the cost of transportation and communication drastically, thereby enhancing opportunities for international commerce. Secondly, laws restricting trade have, in general, become liberalised throughout the world. Thirdly, developing nations have sought to expand their economies by promoting exports and opening their doors to foreign companies seeking investments, and this has expanded opportunities for economic growth and competition throughout the world. These factors all contribute to the growing trend toward globalisation, which is the process of interconnecting the world's people with respect to the cultural, economic, political, technological and environmental aspects of their lives (Lodge 1995).

When hiring for the global age, employers have a number of decisions to make. For example, should an expatriate workforce be utilised or should the company rely on local talent? What qualities in individuals lead to success? Regardless of the nature of their business, organisations need to locate a good fit for global operations. Global workers will also become increasingly mobile. They will be recruited, selected and moved with less regard for national boundaries. At some stage in the future, human resources will cross national borders as easily as computer chips and cars (Solomon 1995).

In selecting individuals for overseas assignments, management must recognise that no one style of leadership will be equally effective in all countries. People in various countries have widely divergent backgrounds, education, cultures and religions – and live within a variety of social conditions and economic and political systems. Employees have to consider all these factors, because they can have a rather dramatic effect on the working environment of the person selected. An appropriate approach for the multinational corporation must be based on common sense and informed conjecture. It seems reasonable that a successful international manager should possess the following qualities, among others:

- a basic knowledge of history, particularly in countries with old and homogeneous cultures;
- an understanding of the basic economic and sociological concepts of various countries;
- an interest in the host country and a willingness to learn and use its language; and
- a respect for differing philosophical and ethical approaches to living.
  (FERGUS 1990)

Coping with human resource problems in the global environment is very complex. South African human resource managers must find a way to educate, or re-educate, much of the South African labour force to give them a competitive edge over their global competitors. There is a need to carefully review the human resources situation in host countries and plan to cope with its limitations and take advantage of its strengths. In addition, human resource professionals cannot afford to overlook qualified women for overseas assignments.

Labour relations

The industrial and organisational psychology perspective of industrial relations takes the view of a relationship between workers and their employees. The relationship formed is a human one and, as such, can contain all the elements common to all other relationships (e.g. friendship, marriage). According to Bendix (1996), this relationship has to be nurtured through mutuality of interest, reciprocity of support, understanding and trust. Bendix further states that there are a number of factors that serve to regulate the interaction between the parties to the relationship, namely custom and tradition, legislation, mutual agreement and ethical considerations.

Mention the word 'union' and most people will have some opinion, positive or negative, regarding South African labour organisation. To some, the word evokes images of labour-management conflict – grievances, strikes and boycotts. To others, the word represents industrial democracy, fairness, opportunity and equal representation. Many think of unions as simply creating an adversarial relationship between employees and managers.

Regardless of attitudes toward them, since the late 1970s, when trade unions first enjoyed recognition in South Africa, they have been an important force shaping organisational practices, legislation and political thought. In particular, trade unions played a significant political role during the apartheid years in South Africa in providing a platform to resist the repressive regime of the time. In post-apartheid South Africa, trade unions remain an important role player because of their influence on organisational productivity, business competitiveness, labour law development, and human resources policies and practices. Like business organisations, unions are constantly undergoing changes in operation and philosophies, and have in recent years become involved in joint ventures with various business partners. In South Africa, the business interests of trade unions includes media, mining and agriculture.

Trade union growth in South Africa since 1979 has been phenomenal, especially as it occurred during a period when trade unions in other countries were largely on the decline. During the 1980s, South Africa was reputed to have the fastest-growing union movement in the world.

So, why do people join unions? The decision to join a union is shaped by internal and external factors. Internal factors include an employee's own value system and needs, while external factors include the following:

● the capacity of the union to assist the employees;
● encouragement and even pressure from co-workers to join;
● the support the union enjoys in the broader society;
● the lack of any other alternatives open to employees; and
● political reasons.

The legislative framework that governs the relationship between employer and employee is quite complex and any person working in the human resources area must have knowledge of these laws. In the next section, the most important laws governing this relationship will be discussed.

Legislative framework

The legislative framework that governs the relationship between employer and employee is reflective of the degree of state involvement. This legislative framework should conform to universal standards and the best guidelines are found in the various recommendations of the International Labour Organisation (ILO). However, it is important to note that any legislation passed in South Africa cannot deviate from the Constitution and the most relevant sections in the Constitution. As far as labour legislations is concerned, the sections outlining fundamental human rights, including labour relations rights, are of importance.

The most important acts that govern labour relations include the Labour Relations Act; Basic Conditions of Employment Act; Wage Act; Unemployment Insurance Act; Compensation for Occupational Injuries and Disease Act, Skill Development Act and Employment Equity Act. A brief description will be provided of each act, with emphasis placed on the Skill Development Act and the Employment Equity Act, as they are the most recent and often the most contentious (Finnemore 1999; Nel *et al.* 2001).

The new Labour Relations Act (passed in 1995) provides for bargaining council agreements and arbitration awards. In addition, it further establishes the guidelines for the employer-employee relationship by providing for the rights of the organisation, the registration of employers associations and the formation of **bargaining councils** (i.e. a body that is established when both parties voluntary agree to bargain with each other). Provision is also made for **workplace forums** in an attempt to encourage consultation between employers and employee representatives and a dispute settlement process aimed at conciliation and third party intervention (a strike is not permitted if the proper procedures have not been followed). In addition, the act has introduced the Commission for Mediation and Arbitration and replaced the Industrial Court with a Labour Court that now has more power. Finally, the act prohibits victimisation and any interference with **freedom of association**. See Figure 14.4, overleaf, for an outline of a grievance procedure that could lead to mediation, arbitration, a judicial settlement or a strike.

Bargaining councils: Bodies established when both parties voluntarily agree to bargain with each other.

Workplace forums: System to encourage consultation between employers and employee representatives and a dispute settlement process aimed at conciliation and third party intervention.

Freedom of association: The right of employees to join unions and participate in union activities. It also refers to the rights of employers to join unions.

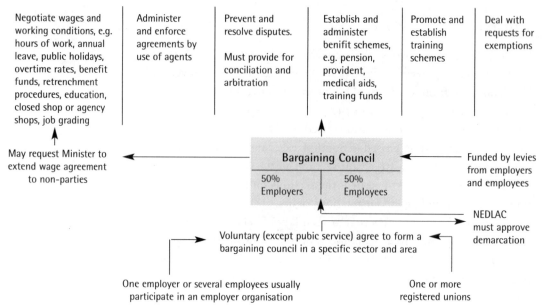

Negotiate wages and working conditions, e.g. hours of work, annual leave, public holidays, overtime rates, benefit funds, retrenchment procedures, education, closed shop or agency shops, job grading

Administer and enforce agreements by use of agents

Prevent and resolve disputes.

Must provide for conciliation and arbitration

Establish and administer benifit schemes, e.g. pension, provident, medical aids, training funds

Promote and establish training schemes

Deal with requests for exemptions

May request Minister to extend wage agreement to non-parties

Bargaining Council

50% Employers | 50% Employees

Funded by levies from employers and employees

NEDLAC must approve demarcation

Voluntary (except pubic service) agree to form a bargaining council in a specific sector and area

One employer or several employees usually participate in an employer organisation

One or more registered unions

(SOURCE: BENDIX 1996: P. 351)

FIGURE 14.4: Grievance procedure within a large, hierarchically structured organisation

In industries where collective bargaining/trade unions are not established, employees are protected by the Basic Conditions of Employment Act and the Wage Act. The Basic Conditions of Employment Act (1998) provides for maximum working hours, payment of overtime and for work on Sundays and public holidays, minimum notice periods, minimum annual leave and sick leave, the regulation of overtime and the prohibition of certain deductions. The Wage Board issues wage determinations on an *ad hoc* basis and it also deals with freedom of association in particular industries, occupations, trades or areas, where there are no bargaining councils. The Occupational Health and Safety Act (1993) provides for the appointment of safety representatives and safety committees.

The Unemployment Insurance Act and the Compensation for Injuries and Disease Act (1993) provide insurance schemes for employers. The first act provides for compulsory payment of unemployment contributions from employers and by employees who earn less than a certain amount per annum. This entitles employees to certain benefits if unemployed. The other fund provides for compulsory levies on employers to compensate employees who suffer disability as a result of an accident or illness that has befallen them in the course of their employment.

Training is of critical importance in South Africa and a number of important legislative initiatives have taken place over the past couple of years. The forerunner to these initiatives was the South African

Qualifications Authority Act No. 58 of 1995. This act put in place the South African Qualifications Authority (SAQA) and its functions, which have been executed by a board since May 1996. The SAQA is required to achieve the objectives of the National Qualifications Framework (NQF). They include the following: to create an integrated national framework for learner achievements; to facilitate access to and progression within education, training and career paths; to enhance the quality of education and training; and to accelerate the redress of past unfair discrimination in education, training and employment opportunities. This became the background for the Skills Development Act, which was passed on 1 February 1999. It replaced the Manpower Training Act and the Guidance and Placement Act. The purposes of the Skills Development Act include the following:

- to develop the skills of the South African workforce;
- to increase the levels of investment in education and training and to improve return on this investment;
- to use the workforce as an active learning environment, to provide employees with opportunities to acquire new skills, and to provide opportunities for new entrants to the labour market;
- to provide employment to people who find it difficult to be employed;
- to encourage workers to participate in leadership and other training programmes; and
- to improve the employment prospects of persons previously disadvantaged by unfair discrimination and to redress these disadvantages through training and education.

The above are to be achieved by:
- establishing a financial and institutional framework consisting of the National Skills Authority, the National Skills Fund, Sector Educational and Training Authorities (SETAs), labour centres and a Skills Development Training Planning Unit. The National Skills Fund is a skills development levy (0.5% of the salary bill per annum) as stipulated by the Skills Development Levies Act;
- encouraging partnerships between the public and private sectors of the economy to provide training and education in the workplace; and
- cooperating with the SAQA.

The Employment Equity Act was implemented in 1999 and passed in October 1998. The overall objective of this act is to achieve equity in employment through implementing affirmative action to redress disadvantages experienced by people from designated groups and

Designated groups:
Women, black people
and the disabled.

promoting equal opportunities. (**Designated groups** refer to women, black people and the disabled; and 'black people' refer to Africans, Coloureds and Indians.) The most important provisions of the act include the following:

- All employees must take steps to end unfair discrimination in the workplace, i.e. in terms of their employment practices and policies.
- Unfair discrimination against employees or job applicants on the grounds of race, gender, sex, pregnancy, marital status, family responsibility, ethnic or racial origin, age disability, religion, conscience, belief, political opinion, culture, language, birth or HIV status is prohibited.
- Medical testing of employees is prohibited unless justified and limitations are placed on the use of psychological testing.
- Employees with more than 50 employees or a total turnover that is equal to or above the required minimum turnover (referred to as designated employers) must prepare and implement employment equity plans.
- Employment Equity Act plans contain employment equity measures to achieve the equitable representation of people from the designated groups in all occupational categories and levels in the workforce.
- All designated employers must report to the Department of Labour on their equity plans.
- A Commission of Employment Equity is established.
- Enforcement of the equity obligations is enforced through the Labour Court and inspectors.

As seen from the above acts, considerable rights and responsibilities have been given to employers and employees. The Bill of Rights had a significant impact on the new labour legislation as well as the policies of the Reconstruction and Development Programme (RDP). Influences of international conventions, standards and norms are also evident. As much of the legislation is relatively new, teething problems will occur and possible amendments may be necessary. Ultimately, the law remains only one of the key factors that influence labour relations. The parties involved as established by the laws hold the key to the success or failure of the above law.

Summary

Industrial psychology is one of the applied areas within the broad field of industrial psychology, and it studies behaviour within the work context. It consists of a number of speciality areas that include personnel psychology, organisational psychology, ergonomics, career psychology, labour relations, consumer psychology, cross-cultural industrial psychology and occupational mental health. The field has a comparatively long history with roots in the turn of the last century, when the field of psychology was still in its infancy. People such as Munsterberg, Scott, and Frank and Lillian Gilbreth promoted the field by applying psychology to industry with success. World Wars I and II were critical in determining the direction of the field. In South Africa, industrial psychology originated as an experimental science in 1946, when the National Institute for Personnel Research was established. To keep abreast of developments in the field, it is important to participate in a number of professional organisations. To practice as an industrial psychologist, registration with the Professional Board for Psychology is necessary. There are a number of strategic issues that face industrial psychologists in this changing world and are critical to manage if an organisation is to prosper and grow. They include human resource planning, human resource forecasting techniques, downsizing and globalisation. The industrial psychology perspective of industrial relations examines the relationship between workers and their employers. This relationship is governed by legislation that has increased since 1994 with the election of the first democratic government. Relevant legislation includes the Labour Relations Act; Basic Conditions of Employment Act; Wage Act; Unemployment Insurance Act; Compensation for Occupational Injuries and Disease Act; Skills Development Act; and Employment Equity Act.

Appendix 1: The Hawthorne studies

The Hawthorne studies took place in 1924 and were named after the place where they took place, Hawthorne, Illinois, in the USA, at the Hawthorne Electrical Plant. This now famous study took industrial psychology beyond just employee recruitment and selection to the more complex problems of interpersonal relations, motivation and organisational issues (Roethlisberger & Dickson 1939). The main aim of the study was to determine the effects of the physical work environment on employee efficiency. The researchers asked the following kinds of questions: What is the effect on productivity when the lighting in the workroom increases? Does temperature and humidity affect production? What will the effect be if workers were allowed rest periods?

The results of the Hawthorne studies surprised the researchers and the plant managers. For example, they found that changing the level of illumination (light) in a room from bright to dim did not diminish the workers' productivity. Thus, it appeared that social and psychological factors in the work environment were of potentially greater importance to workers than physical conditions. With another group of workers, lighting was increased and production level rose. The researchers made other changes: introducing rest periods, free lunches and a shorter working day. With the introduction of each new change, production continued to rise. However, even when the changes were taken away, production continued to increase.

These studies opened up a new area for industrial psychology to explore (which had been ignored up till this point), such as the nature of supervision, the nature of informal groupings amongst workers, communication patterns, employee attitudes towards their job, and the influence of job satisfaction and motivation.

Although these studies were later quite severely critiqued for the flaws in the research process, they remained an important catalyst in expanding the field of industrial psychology (Schultz & Schultz 1998).

Appendix 2: HR issues of a unified Europe

In 1991, *Wall Street Journal* writer Susan Faludi received a Pulitzer Prize for describing the abusive impact of a leverage buyout. Her article sparked a continuing debate over the moral obligations of organisations.

Leverage buyouts (LBO) are a financing method used to generate profits by transferring corporate ownership. While LBOs have been praised for transforming flabby, obsolete corporations into lean, efficient ones, they have also been criticised for eliminating jobs and damaging people's lives.

In a leverage buyout, a small group of investors that usually includes senior management borrows heavily to buy a company from public shareholders and make it a private corporation. The heavy debts must be repaid either by selling some of the assets or by streamlining operations to make the company highly profitable. Both strategies usually result in a loss of jobs, but the owners and investors usually realise a sizeable return on their investment.

The Safeway LBO is often cited as an example of a very profitable buyout. When Safeway faced a hostile takeover by corporate raiders Herbert and Robert Haft, Safeway decided to sell the publicly held company to a group of buyout specialists, Kohlberg, Kravis, Roberts and Company (KKR). When the shareholders sold their shares, they received 82% more than the shares were trading at three months earlier, and the top management team made US$25 million on the sale of their shares. For putting the buyout together, three investment banks received US$65 million, law and accounting firms were paid another US$25 million, and KKR charged Safeway US$60 million in advisory fees.

Not everyone benefited from this financial coup, however. The buyout had a devastating effect on the lives of many former employees. Over 63,000 managers and workers were terminated from Safeway through store sales and layoffs. Those who were rehired generally took a 30% to 50% cut in pay and many could only find part-time employment. Many other, especially those in the Dallas (Texas) area, remained unemployed for an extended time and suffered both financially and psychologically.

Human suffering is difficult to quantify, but the president of Safeway's credit union in Dallas estimated that 80% of the people in that division were devastated by the layoff. Many homes and cars were repossessed. The *Wall Street Journal* article described specific cases of divorce, alcoholism and suicide attributed to the layoff. James White, a Safeway trucker for nearly thirty years in Dallas, is an example. One year after the layoff, while still unemployed, he told his wife he loved her, went into the bathroom, locked the door and shot himself in the head with a hunting rifle.

The flurry of letters to the editor that followed this article included economic justifications by Safeway's president and other business leaders, as well as emotional condemnations by readers who had experienced similar abusive experiences.

Part 2: Recruitment, selection and organisational behaviour

Objectives

After studying this section you should be able to:
- Explain the basic principles of selection
- Describe the steps that might be included in a selection process
- Explain how application blanks can be used in the selection process
- Describe the types of employment interviews and discuss the purposes and limitations of interviewing
- Describe the use of psychometric testing in the selection process
- Describe the process of communication and its role in organisations
- Define leadership, and explain how leading differs from managing
- Define motivation, and explain its importance in the field of organisational behaviour

- Explain the basic characteristics of organisational structure as revealed in an organisational chart
- Explain the concept of diversity management and its organisational implications.

. . . .

As stated in the previous section, people who are lucky enough to find a job most suited to their skills, abilities and education experience a sense of accomplishment and personal satisfaction that is often more important or as important as the salary they receive. If not, it could lead to unhappiness, stress-related illnesses and poor performance on the job. So, it is important both for the company and the individual that the majority of staff hired will work to the ultimate advantage of themselves and of the organisation. To do this, the company needs to gain as much relevant information about the prospective employee as possible (Schultz & Schultz 1998). The recruitment and selection process allows for just that!

Recruitment:
The process whereby an organisation attracts potential employees to apply for jobs.

Job analysis:
Obtaining information about jobs by determining what the duties, tasks or activities are to perform the job successfully.

Job description:
The translation of the information obtained through the job analysis process into a list of job tasks, procedures, responsibilities and outputs.

Job specification:
Information about the physical, experiential and educational qualities required to perform the job.

The recruitment process

What is recruitment? It is the process whereby the organisation attracts potential employees to apply for jobs. However, even before recruitment can take place, it is vital that the requirements and tasks of the job are properly understood. The process to do this is called **job analysis** and it involves obtaining information about jobs by determining what duties, tasks or activities are needed to perform the job successfully (Sherman *et al.* 1996). This produces the **job description**, which translates the information obtained through the job analysis process into a list of job tasks, procedures, responsibilities and outputs. It also produces the **job specification**, which contains information about the physical, experiential and educational qualities required to perform the job.

What sources are used to attract potential resources? Recruitment is usually done by utilising internal and external sources. External sources refer to print and electronic media advertisements, referrals by current employees, executive search firms (also known as head hunters), employment agencies, job fairs, vocational guidance counsellors, university and Technikon campuses, professional publications and 'walk-ins'. Internal recruitment sources include internal notice boards (job posting), which is often a requirement by unions (Gatewood & Field 1998).

The selection process

What is selection? According to Muchinsky (1997), we should rather refer to **personnel selection**, which is the process of identifying who will be hired from a pool of recruited applicants. In other words, it is the process of separating the selected applicants from the rejected ones. This process is actually a data/information gathering process whereby as much information is gathered about the applicants as possible in order to employ the 'best person' or rather the person who best matches the requirements of the job. This process is not solely the domain of the organisations any longer, as it is influenced by anti-discrimination legislation, the aim of which is to ensure that every person who applies for a job should have a fair chance of getting the job.

In South Africa, since the first democratic elections in 1994, legislation such as the Constitution, the new Labour Relations Act (1995) and the Employment Equity Act (1998) now provides protection for workers, unions and individuals against discrimination. Even applicants are now protected by legislation, as they have all the rights of current employers. To be more specific, these laws now protect the employees and applicants against unfair discrimination on any arbitrary ground, including but not limited to race, gender, sex, ethnic or social origin, colour, sexual orientation, age, disability, religion, conscience, belief, political opinion, culture, language, marital status or family responsibilities, including pregnancy. These grounds are not related to the inherent or operational requirements of the job, and as such, if used as a factor in the selection decision, would be deemed discriminatory. However, if an employer can prove that a decision has been taken on the basis of an inherent requirement, the decision cannot be said to be discriminatory.

Now let us look at the steps in the selection process, keeping the legislative framework firmly in our minds! The steps may vary depending on a number of factors, such as the type of organisation and the type and level of job. The steps that typically are taken during the selection process are shown in Figure 14.5, on the next page. Not all applicants will progress through all the steps, as some may be rejected after the preliminary interview, others after psychological tests, and so on (Sherman *et al.* 1996).

Personnel selection:
The process of identifying who will be hired from a pool of recruited applicants.

FIGURE 14.5: Steps in the selection process

(Source: Sherman *et al.* 1996: p. 191)

Application blanks

If you apply for a job, the first step is usually to complete an application form or blank. This is a form that requires biographical information like name, address, education and work experience. It might also cover medical history, specific skills and any criminal convictions. It serves several purposes. Firstly, it provides the information needed to decide whether the applicant meets the minimum requirements in terms of education, experience, etc. Secondly, it will provide a source of questions during the interview, as clarity might be sought about certain information provided in the form. Thirdly, it will provide sources of reference checks. Finally, it will also provide information regarding the employee's conformity with various laws and regulations, e.g. proof of registration as a psychologist (Schultz & Schultz 1998; Sherman *et al.* 1996). It is important to remember, however, that certain information required on the form could fall foul of the legislation referred to earlier if not directly related to the job, e.g. questions asking about age, religion and marital status. The question of race can only be asked if it is used to determine/calculate employment equity targets (Bendix 1996).

Selection interview

Traditionally, the selection interview is the most popular step in the process. In fact, it is very rare to find a situation where someone is employed without an interview. Depending on the kind of job, interviews may be conducted by one person or more than one. They can also be conducted using the telephone and/or television. There are two kinds of interviews that are used in the process, i.e. unstructured and structured interviews. In an **unstructured interview** the applicant is given the freedom to determine the direction of the interview. The interviewer asks broad, open-ended questions such as 'Tell me about your last job' and 'Tell me about your strengths and weaknesses'. The interviewer then asks follow-up questions, allowing the applicant to elaborate. Although information is gained that might be hidden in a more structured interview, it is difficult to compare the responses of different applicants and it is more open to the biases and prejudices of the interviewer. In fact, the reliability and validity of this method is minimal, but it continues to be popular. It is important to remember that the same constraints imposed by legislation are applicable here as well. So the questions asked must be related to the requirements of the job.

Unstructured interview: Interview that allows the applicant the freedom to determine the direction of the interview.

The **structured interview** has a set of standardised questions (based on the job analysis), and is judged or rated against a standard set of answers. This type of interview is more likely to provide the information necessary for making sound appointment decisions and it can reduce the legal charges of discrimination. With the introduction of anti-discrimination legislation, the interview is highly vulnerable to legal attack and more litigation can be expected in this area. Two variations of the structured interview include the situational interview and the behavioural event interview. With the situational interview, the applicant is provided with a hypothetical situation and asked how he or she would respond. With the behavioural event interview, the applicant is asked what he or she actually did in a given situation.

Structured interview: Interview that contains a set of standardised questions (based on the job analysis) and is judged or rated against a standard set of answers.

Psychological tests

Carefully developed and researched psychological tests have several characteristics that set them apart from the tests you read in magazines and newspapers such as 'Are you a good husband', etc. A psychological test must be standardised, objective, based on sound norms, reliable and valid. Let us look briefly at what those descriptors mean. **Standardisation** refers to the fact that the testing conditions and procedures for administering the test must be the same. **Objectivity** refers to the fact

Standardisation: This refers to the fact that the testing conditions and procedures for administering the test must be the same.

Objectivity: This refers to the fact that the scores of the test must be unbiased and if anyone or different scorers mark the same test they should obtain the same results.

Test norms:
These establish a frame of reference, or point of comparison, so that the performance of one person is compared with others.

Reliability:
This refers to the consistency or stability of a response to a test. In other words, a test should give the same score when repeated, if the measured trait has not changed.

Validity:
This refers to the accuracy of the tests, i.e. do they measure what they claim to measure?

Bias:
The systematic error in measurement and prediction in test scores.

Fairness:
A value judgement regarding decisions or actions taken.

that the scores of the test must be unbiased and if different scorers mark the same test they should obtain the same results. With **test norms**, a frame of reference or point of comparison is established, so that the performance of one person is compared with others. **Reliability** refers to the consistency or stability of a response to a test. In other words, a test should give the same score when repeated, if the measured trait has not changed. **Validity** refers to the accuracy of the tests, i.e. do they measure what they purport to measure (Gatewood & Field 1998)?

Another important and often controversial characteristic is that of **bias** and the **fairness** of psychological tests. Although there has been lack of agreement regarding the definition of these terms, Murphy and Davidshofer (1988) define bias as the systematic error in measurement and prediction in test scores, while fairness refers to a value judgment regarding decisions or actions taken.

So, how can psychological tests help in the selection procedure? Proponents argue that the scores of psychological tests are the best predicators of behaviour or performance on the job (better than any other measure) (Schultz & Schultz 1998). Although the testing movement gained ground during the first and World War II, as described in the previous chapter, from about the late 1950s, widespread mistrust and suspicion of tests and testing came to the fore, particularly in the USA. This arose as studies started to reveal that certain tests, particularly intelligence tests, were culturally biased, in other words, they discriminated against blacks (Kaplan & Saccuzzo 1997). In South Africa, although the issue of bias only appeared in 1981, when Owen undertook the first study of bias in intelligence tests, testing was largely influence by the apartheid policies of the Nationalist government. In fact, studies by Abrahams (1996), Owen (1989), and Taylor and Radford (1986) showed that bias existed in South African ability and personality measures as well. As a result, large sections of the population began to reject the tests altogether. However, since the adoption of the anti-discriminatory legislation described earlier, test developers and users are now much more careful to develop and use tests that are for all South Africans. In fact, to ensure that discrimination is addressed in the testing arena, the Employment Equity Act No. 55 of 1998 (Section 8) was passed, which prohibits tests if they have not been proved to be valid and reliable, not biased against any employee or group, and can be applied fairly. So, should we still use tests? Foxcroft (1997) and others such as Plug (1996), Nell (1994) and Shuttleworth-Jordan (1996) contended that there is South African research evidence that supports the continued use of tests information when used with other sources of information to make decisions. In fact, research in South Africa (England & Zietsman 1995) and the USA (Schultz & Schultz 1998) showed that the use of tests is still prevalent in industry, especially within the selection arena.

Psychological tests differ in terms of how they are constructed and administered and in terms of the types of behaviour they measure. On the one hand, categories include group and individual tests, paper and pencil tests, and computer assisted tests. On the other hand, psychological tests can measure cognitive ability, interests, aptitude, motor skills and personality (Schultz & Schultz 1998). In other words, even though it has its problems, testing can still provide useful information about candidates (if it meets all the criteria/characteristics described earlier).

Reference letter

This is a routine and commonly used method to obtain information about a job applicant from persons who know something about his or her background, skills and works history such as employers, co-workers and friends. The aim is to verify information reported by the person/applicant and to determine other people's impressions of them. A major limitation of this step is that referees often present a false picture of the applicant. The reasons for this include the following: applicants choose referees who they think will make them appear exceptional; current employers want to get rid of an employee, hence the glowing letter; and academics write glowing letters of recommendation or standard letters of recommendation as they fear they would jeopardise students' chances of gaining employment (Schultz & Schultz 1998). To increase the validity of this method, it is advocated that the questions asked about the candidates should focus on the job description and requirements of the job, not personal characteristics. Although still the most popular in many countries, including South Africa, the popularity of reference letters is declining in the USA, as organisations are now no longer willing to supply information or letters of references because of the threat of possible legal action. Thousands of lawsuits have already been filed against organisations in the USA when candidates feel they did not get a particular job because of the contents of a referee's report. Organisations are now advised to refuse to reveal any information about employees beyond dates of employment, job title and final salary (Leap & Crino 1993).

Reference letter:
Letter used to obtain information about a job applicant from persons who know something about his or her background, skills and work history such as employers, co-workers and friends.

Performance appraisal

The performance of employees is continually appraised, either informal-
ly or formally. If conducted formally, it is more accurate and fair, and
provides useful information to the employee and employer. So, what
exactly is a performance appraisal system? According to Schultz &
Schultz (1998), it is the periodic, formal evaluation of the performance of
employees on the job. There are a number of benefits for both employees
and employer in conducting formal performance appraisals. They can
improve the quality of decisions in organisations in a number of areas
such as salary increases, promotions and dismissal. They also improve
the quality of individual/employee decision making, ranging from career
choice to the development of future strengths. They can affect the way
employees view the organisation and their loyalty and commitment to
the organisation. In other words, if employees feel that the appraisal
system is unfair or irrational, employee satisfaction and commitment is
undermined. Appraisals also provide a rational, legal, defensible basis for
taking decisions affecting personnel (Muchinsky 1997).

Using the results of performance appraisals

In addition to the above benefits, performance appraisals may be applied
to any other management functions (see Figure 14.6). However, even
before we look at their uses, it is importation to note that criteria must
be established before the process can take place. These are derived from
the job analysis process and form the basis of the performance appraisal
system. So why is it so important for organisations to conduct formal
performance appraisals?

FIGURE 14.6: Application of Performance appraisal

(SOURCE: MUCHINSKY 1997: p. 214)

Training and development

Perhaps the most important function of the information is to provide feedback regarding their job performance to employees. It is important that it highlights the employees' strengths and weaknesses and that the appraisal is related to job-related characteristics only. Deficiencies or weaknesses should then become the targets for training (Muchinsky 1997). In most cases, deficiencies in performance may be attributable to inadequate knowledge and skills, e.g. a secretary may improve her skills by attending a workshop on updated computer software. For supervisory and managerial personnel, a performance appraisal system may indicate that training is required in areas such as interpersonal conflict management, planning and budgeting (Leap & Crino 1993).

Wage and salary administration

Although salary increases are influenced by the increase in the cost of living, productivity, seniority and the financial conditions of the organisations, employee merit/job performance (as measured by the performance appraisal) is also an important factor for the majority of organisations. Information supplied by the performance appraisal method should allow for the comparison of employee performance across different levels (Leap & Crino 1993). It is primarily because of the link with salary increases that many employees and unions are not in favour of the performance appraisal system. Many labour unions insist that seniority (length of service) rather than employee merit be used. They also often question the validity and reliability of the system, as they are skeptical about programmes that are deemed to be poorly designed (Schultz & Schultz 1998).

A study by Malwandla (1995) conducted in the South African public sector showed that many managers also disliked performance appraisals because they result in a great deal of paperwork. Other problems included the unequal standards applied by raters and the delay in providing feedback.

Promotion, transfer and termination of employment

The selection of one employee for promotion over others is primarily a result of the evaluation of past performance on the job. To maintain employee initiative, morale and commitment, decisions around promotion cannot depend on a supervisor's whim or bias but must be based on information gathered through a valid and reliable performance appraisal system. It is also useful in making transfer and termination decisions. Like promotions, job responsibilities often change with transfers, and it is important to identify those employees who are capable of accepting the new responsibility. Performance appraisal results are often an important source of information in disciplinary cases that lead to dismissal. It is important that adequate information is provided through the process that clearly supports the reasons for dismissal (Leap & Crino 1993).

Performance appraisal methods

A wide variety of performance appraisal systems have been designed with the aim of measuring the quality and quantity of performance. However, the major methods used are graphic rating scales, employee comparison methods, and behavioural checklists and scales. Let us take a closer look at these three!

Graphic rating scales

Graphic rating scales: Method of rating individuals on a number of traits or factors using points with either numerical or verbal labels, or both.

This is the most common performance appraisal method, where individuals are rated on a number of traits or factors. Predetermined scales are presented to the supervisor/manager to rate the worker on a number of important aspects of the job, such as quality of the work, dependability, and ability to get along with co-workers. They usually have points with either numerical or verbal labels, or both. These verbal labels can be simple one word descriptors, or they can be more lengthy and specific. See Figure 14.7.

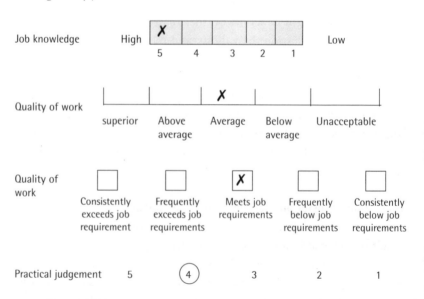

FIGURE 14.7: Examples of graphic scales for various performance dimensions
(SOURCE: MUCHINSKY 1997: p. 224)

An important advantage of this method is that the same basic scales can be used for different jobs, by simply changing the relevant job dimension. However, many organisations make the mistake of changing the dimensions for the different jobs without ensuring that they actually assess the performance of that particular job. The major weakness of this method is that it is more open to biased response patterns (by the rater), such as the tendency to give everyone good or fair ratings (Muchinsky 1997; Riggio 2000).

Employee comparison methods

These methods involve a form of comparison of one employee's performance with the performance of others. The methods are quite easy to adopt and include rankings, paired comparisons and forced distributions. **Rankings** require supervisors/managers to rank order their subordinates from best to worst on an overall comparative ranking or on specific performance dimensions. Although this is a quick and easy method, it has many limitations. The major limitation is that there is no absolute standards of performance, e.g. in a group of exceptional workers, those ranked low could actually be exceptional workers if compared to others in the organisation. **Paired comparison** requires the rater to compare each worker with each other worker in the group and then decide which of the pair is the better individual. This is mostly used to evaluate overall performance rather than on a single dimension, and is used when the number of employees to be rated is small. Although relatively simple to use, the same drawbacks occur as with the ranking method (Riggio 2000).

The **forced distribution** method is most useful when the number of employees to be rated is large. It is based on the normal distribution and the assumption is that employee job performance is also normally distributed. The distribution is divided into five to seven categories, where the rater, using predetermined categories (based on the normal distribution), places the employee into one of the categories. The major limitation of this method is that performance is not compared to a pre-determined standard. Also, the raters feel that performance is not normally distributed but negatively skewed, i.e. they feel that most of their employees perform very well (Riggio 2000; Muchinsky 1997).

Employee comparison methods:
Methods that compare one employee's performance with the performance of others.

Rankings:
Method that requires supervisors/managers to rank order their subordinates from best to worst on an overall comparative ranking or on specific performance dimensions.

Paired comparison:
Method that requires the rater to compare each worker with each other worker in the group and then decide which of the pair is the better individual.

Forced distribution method:
Most useful method when the number of employees to be rated is large. It is based on the normal distribution and the assumption is that employee job performance is also normally distributed.

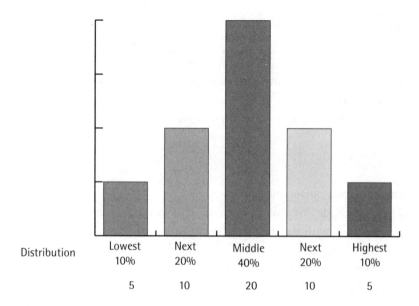

Distribution	Lowest 10%	Next 20%	Middle 40%	Next 20%	Highest 10%
	5	10	20	10	5

FIGURE 14.8: Number of employees to be placed in each category based on 50 employees

(SOURCE: MUCHINSKY 1997: p. 226)

Behavioural checklists and scales

Critical incidents: Behaviours that influence employees' performance on the job.

Weighted checklist: Checklist that quantifies critical incident.

To overcome some of the limitations of the above approaches, behavioural checklists and scales were developed in recent years. These focus on behaviour and all the methods in this cluster have their origins, directly or indirectly, in the **critical incidents** method. The methods include critical incidents, a **weighted checklist**, behaviourally anchored weighted scales and behavioural-observation scales. The critical incidents method was developed by Flanagan in 1954 and it refers to behaviours that result in good or poor performance. Supervisors record behaviours of employees that influence their performance on the job, in other words, they record critical incidents. These incidents are usually grouped by aspects of performance, e.g. job knowledge, leadership and decision-making ability. The weighted checklist is an attempt to quantify the previous method. Once a list has been developed of critical incidents, a group of supervisors ('experts') rate each critical incident in terms of its relative importance to the job. These scale values are usually derived by averaging the ratings made by the supervisor (see Figure 14.9 on the next page).

Instructions: Below you will find a list of behavioral items. Read each item and decide whether it describes the person being evaluated. If you feel the item does describe the person, place a check mark in the space provided. If the item does not describe the person, leave the space next to the icon blank.

1. *Regularly sets vague and unrealistic program goals*
2. *Is concerned only with the immediate problems of the day and sees very little beyond the day-to-day*
3. *Develops work schedules that allow for completion of projects provided no major problems are encountered*
4. *Is aware of needs and trends in area of responsibility and plans accordingly*
5. *Follows up on projects to ensure that intermediate goals are achieved*
6. *Looks for new markets and studies potential declines in current markets*
7. *Anticipates and plans for replacement of key personnel in the event of corporate relocation.*

TABLE 14.9: Checklist for a project manager

(SOURCE: RIGGIO 2000: p. 170)

The **Behaviourally Anchored Rating Scale (BARS)** is a combination of the rating scales and the critical incidents method. With this method, scale labels that are clearly defined as behavioural incidents are used which reflect good, poor and average performance. A BARS scale to appraise supermarket checkout assistants is given in Figure 14.10.

Behaviourally Anchored Rating Scale (BARS): A combination of the rating scales and the critical incidents method. With this method, scale labels that are clearly defined as behavioural incidents are used, which reflect good, poor and average performance.

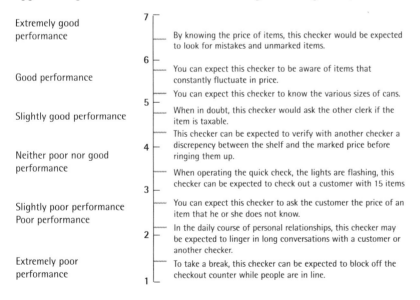

FIGURE 14.10: Critical-incident behaviours associated with job performance for supermarket checkout clerks.

(SOURCE: SCHULTZ & SCHULTZ 1998: p. 145)

**The behavioural
observation scales
(BOS):**
Assessment scales that
focus on how often the
subordinate has been
observed performing key
work-related behaviours.

Although this is a lengthy and tedious process to develop, it focuses on performance on the job, avoiding or minimising rater bias to a large extent. The **behavioural observation scales (BOS)** are related to the BARS, but with this method, raters focus on how often the subordinate has been observed performing key work-related behaviours. While the BARS focuses on expectations that a subordinate would be able to perform critical incidents that are typical of a specific job, the BOS focus on critical incidents that were actually performed. However, it is important to note that this method does not involve the direct observation and appraisal of the subordinate, but rather what the rater can remember. The problem is that the raters may be selective or biased in what they remember (Muchinsky 1997; Schultz & Schultz 1998).

In conclusion, a good performance appraisal system must consist of two important parts: the performance assessment (appraisal) and the performance feedback. This feedback should occur in face-to-face meetings in which the supervisor provides constructive information, encouragement and guidelines for the improvement of the subordinate's future performance. Since performance appraisals are important to employees' livelihood and career advancement, there are legal considerations that have to be taken into account as well. Therefore, the appraisal process must be valid, resulting from a thorough job analysis process that does not discriminate against any individual or group of employees (Riggio 2000).

Organisational behaviour

**Organisational
behaviour:**
The social arrangement of
people in organisations.

A further key aspect in the study of industrial psychology is organisational behaviour. As highlighted in the previous chapter, people remain the key ingredient for the success of any organisation. No matter how good a company's product or service may be, and no matter how technologically advanced the company's equipment may be, there can be no company without people. Therefore, in this section, emphasis will be placed on the key knowledge areas concerning behaviours in organisational settings by reviewing individual, group and organisational processes.

Often referred to as the study of effective behaviour in organisations, the study of organisational behaviour is the study of the social arrangement of people in organisations. In studying these social arrangements, the discipline draws heavily from the behavioural and social sciences such as psychology, sociology, philosophy, politics and economics. However, the study of organisational behaviour is more than just the sum total of these sciences. Because it is the study of human behaviour within specific settings (organisations with a collective purpose), the aspects of common control and performance help to integrate knowledge so that the study of organisational behaviour becomes a study in its own right.

Even a cursory review of any business publication in South Africa reveals an overwhelming emphasis on the development of organisational excellence, where managers continually strive to improve their firm's performance and their own behaviour by subtly benchmarking themselves against so-called 'excellent' firms. The initiators of the 'excellence' industry were Tom Peters and Bob Waterman, Jr. (Peters and Waterman 1982). From their research they emerged with nine organisational properties that 'excellent' companies seem to share:

- staying close to the customer;
- managing ambiguity and paradox;
- sticking to the knitting;
- hands-on, value driven;
- a bias toward action;
- simple form and lean staff;
- autonomy and entrepreneurship;
- simultaneous loose-tight properties; and
- productivity through people.

The resonating theme of excellent companies is their people and their ability to give them just the right amount of responsible autonomy, involvement and commitment. To this end this section will explore the organisational aspects of communication, leadership, motivation, power and organisational structure in this pursuit of excellence.

Communication in organisations

It is no surprise that experts consider communication to be a key process underlying all aspects of organisational activities (Hellriegel *et al.* 2001). Contemporary scholars variously refer to organisational communication as 'the social glue ... that continues to keep the organisation tied together' and as the 'essence of the organisation'. Many years ago, the well-known management theorist and former New Jersey Bell Telephone president Chester Barnard said, 'The structure, extensiveness and scope of the organisation are almost entirely determined by communication techniques' (Barnard 1938). This makes sense considering that supervisors spend as much as 80% of their time engaged in some form of communication, such as speaking or listening to others or writing to and reading material from others (Lengel & Draft 1988).

Communication in organisations:
The process by which a person, group or organisation (the sender) transmits some type of information (the message) to another person, group or organisation (the receiver) and the resultant feedback, if any.

Given the importance of communication in organisations, we closely examine the process here by defining it as the process by which a person, group or organisation (the sender) transmits some type of information (the message) to another person, group or organisation (the receiver) and the resultant feedback, if any.

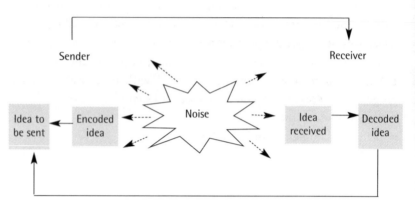

FIGURE 14.11: Transmission of encoded message through media channels

Encoding

Encoding:
The process by which an idea is transformed so that it can be transmitted to and recognised by a receiver, e.g. a written or spoken message.

The communication process begins when one party has an idea it wishes to transmit to another. Either party may be an individual, a group or an entire organisation. The sender's mission is to shape the idea into a form that can be sent to and understood by the receiver. This is the process of encoding, i.e. translating an idea into a form (e.g. written or spoken language) that can be recognised by a receiver. We encode information when we select the words used to write a letter or to speak with someone in person. This process is critical to communicating our ideas clearly. Unfortunately, however, people are far from perfect when it comes to encoding their ideas (although this skill can be improved).

Channels of communication

Channels of communication:
The pathways along which information travels to reach the desired receiver.

An encoded message is ready to be transmitted over one or more channels of communication, i.e. the pathways along which information travels to reach the desired receiver. Telephone lines, radio and television signals, fibre optic cables, mail routes, and even the airwaves carrying the vibrations of our voices all represent potential channels of communication.

Decoding

The message that is received by the recipient is decoded, which involves converting the message back into the sender's original ideas. This can involve different processes such as comprehension and the interpretation of facial expressions. The receiver's ability to comprehend and interpret information received from others may be flawed. As with encoding, therefore, shortcomings in the receiver's ability to decode information represent a further potential weakness in the communication process. These shortcomings can be limited through appropriate training interventions.

Decoding:
The process by which a receiver transforms a message back into the sender's original ideas.

Feedback

After the decoding process, the receiver can transmit a new message to the original sender, which has the intention of informing the sender that the message was either correctly or incorrectly understood. If the sender deems the message to be incorrectly understood by the recipient, it can be either re-sent in its original format or it can be modified to better conform to the recipient's apparent zone of understanding.

Feedback:
The transmission of a new message to the original sender, which has the intention of informing the sender that the message was either correctly or incorrectly understood.

Noise

The communication process may appear to be simple and easily managed, but there may be numerous barriers that may distort the clarity of the message. These distorting influences are referred to as noise. Noise may appear at any stage of the communication process as a result of poor encoding or decoding, or distractions like time pressure and organisational politics affecting the receiver.

Noise:
Barriers that may distort the clarity of a message.

Ways of improving organisational communication

As communication plays a central role in organisational functioning, every effort should be made to improve the communication process, as it holds the key to desirable benefits for the organisation, groups and individuals (Alessandra & Hunksaler 1993). The following steps can be taken to secure the benefits of effective communication:

- **Use simple clear language:** The use of jargon may help communication within professions but should be avoided when used outside the groups within which it has meaning, as it could result in confusion. Thus, the clearest communication entails the use of short, simple language that is to the point.

- **Be an active and attentive listener:** Listening is often seen as a passive process where information sent by others is taken in (Rowe & Baker 1984). However, the process is much more active, where good listeners ask questions when something is not understood or indicate that they understand by nodding their heads. In this way, the listener helps the communication process by letting the sender know whether the message is being correctly received.
- **Avoid overload:** A busy manager may be bombarded with too much information, which can lead to a condition of overload. In a survey of executives from a number of developed industrialised countries, half of them indicated that frequently they are unable to handle the volumes of information they receive (Jones 1997).
- **Give and receive feedback:** Most employees believe the feedback between themselves and their organisations is not that good (McCathrin 1990). This often points to the lack of available channels for upward communication. The implementation of a suggestion system is one way to eliminate this problem.
- **Use technology:** The technological age has brought many tools that managers can use to improve communications. With millions of companies and individuals having access to e-mail, this is an obvious tool in effective communications. The advent of video-mediated communication (VMC) allows for the simultaneous transmission of audio and video signals between two or more computers, allowing an inexpensive link between employees in distant locations.

Leadership

Leadership:
The process through which leaders influence the attitudes, behaviour and values of others.

Managers today are required to supervise large numbers of subordinates who are spread over many locations, and even across continents. In addition, they often must manage people across different functions, such as manufacturing, marketing and finance. They are viewed as agents for change who support the latest organisational theories, even if they do not agree with them (Vecchio 2000). Even with the increasing demands placed on managers, there appears to be very little hesitation from employees to accept such positions (Schellhardt 1997).

Management of functions and people in an organisation is often regarded as being synonymous with leadership. However, leader and manager are not equivalent terms. Someone may be an outstanding manager in terms of the planning, organising and controlling activities of a workgroup, but that alone does not qualify one as a leader. In essence, the primary function of a leader is to create the essential purpose or mission of the organisation and the strategy for attaining it. In contrast, the primary function of a manager is to implement that vision. Essentially, the manager's job is to put into practice the means to achieve the leader's vision. Thus, where managers are primarily concerned with the complexities of the task, leadership is about coping with change. Specifically, managers create plans and monitor results, but leaders establish direction by creating a vision of the future (Kotter 1990).

The differences between managers and leaders may be easy to describe, but the distinction between establishing and implementing a mission is often blurred in practice. See Figure 14.12.

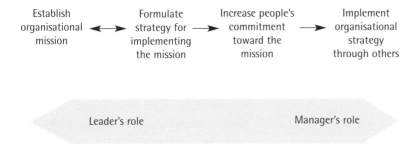

FIGURE 14.12

As indicated in Figure 14.12, this blurring occurs because many leaders (e.g. the CEO) frequently must create a vision, formulate a strategy for implementing it, and also increase people's commitment toward that vision and plan. In contrast, managers are charged with implementing organisational strategy through others. At the same time, however, managers frequently are also involved in helping to formulate strategy and with increasing people's commitment and effort toward implementing that plan. This means that managers and leaders play several overlapping roles in actual practice, which makes distinguishing between them often difficult.

Many people fantasise about being a leader and so being viewed with great awe and respect. However, relatively few individuals become leaders. This then raises the question: What sets effective leaders apart from most others? One of the most widely studied approaches to this question suggests that effective leadership is based on the characteristics people have. Basically, this approach postulates that people become leaders because, in some special way, they are different from others. (Geier 1969). This is known as the trait approach to leadership, further refined as 'The Great Person Theory'. Great leaders like Nelson Mandela (ANC) and Herman Mashaba (Black Like Me) do seem to differ from ordinary human beings in several respects, namely, that they all possess high levels of ambition coupled with clear visions of precisely where they want to go. According to this view, great leaders possess key traits that set them apart from most other human beings, these traits remaining stable over time and across different groups.

Lord *et al.* (1986) spelt out the special abilities of effective leaders in terms of the following characteristics:

Drive:	Desire for achievement, ambition, high energy, tenacity and initiative.
Honesty and integrity:	Trustworthy, reliable and open.
Leadership motivation:	Desire to influence others to reach shared goals.
Self-confidence:	Trust in own abilities.
Cognitive ability:	Intelligence; ability to integrate and interpret large amounts of information.
Knowledge of the business:	Knowledge of an industry and relevant technical matters.
Creativity:	Capacity to come up with original ideas.
Flexibility:	Ability to adapt to needs of followers and the situation.

Change-oriented leadership

The increasing integration of the world economy, often referred to as globalisation, has produced a growing demand for managers skilled in international practices and able to structure their organisations in such a way to ensure survival. South African businesses have also joined this global trend with many public companies moving their primary listing to off-shore stock exchanges like New York and London. Recent examples of this have been the foreign listing of Old Mutual and South African Breweries. The South African Department of Trade and Industry has also made South Africa's entry into the global arena a major focus of its strategic vision by providing numerous incentives to develop world-class manufacturing capacity and to boost exports.

In developing South African organisations as global players, leaders must have clear visions of what they are required to deal with in order to flourish in globalisation. This vision should undoubtedly have a change orientation that can be best achieved through the following approaches or styles: charismatic leadership, transformational leadership and super leadership.

Charismatic leadership

Through the ages, some leaders have had extraordinary success in generating profound changes among their follows. With almost visionary leadership, people like Bill Gates of Microsoft Corporation have changed entire societies through their actions. Individuals who accomplish such feats are referred to as charismatic leaders. Studies of identifiable charismatic individuals indicate that charismatic types often reject formal authority and are willing to take personal risks because of their strong convictions (Podsakoff *et al.* 1996).

Charismatic leadership: Leadership based on referent power and characterised by self-confidence, a sense of purpose and an articulate vision.

Transformational leadership

This encompasses a broader concept than charisma, and implies reshaping the entire strategies of an organisation. Transformational leadership elevates the goals of subordinates and enhances their self-confidence to strive for higher goals. Transformational leadership is potentially strongest at the highest levels of management. This view underscores the importance of vision, intellectual stimulation and individualised consideration in leadership, and the major role that leadership can have during times of change and crisis (Bass 1995).

Transformational leadership: A leadership style that implies reshaping the entire strategy of an organisation.

Super leadership

A super leader is someone who leads others to lead themselves. Super leadership is extremely useful in developing self-managed work teams. Although self-managed work teams are not the focus of this text, the notion of super leadership is equally relevant in any general management situation. Super leaders empower their followers by acting as a teacher and coach rather than as a dictator and autocrat (McDermott 1996). Productive thinking is the cornerstone of super leadership. Specifically, managers are encouraged to teach followers how to engage in productive thinking. This is expected to increase employees' feelings of personal control and intrinsic motivation. Super leadership has the potential to free up a manager's time because employees are encouraged to manage themselves (Manz & Sims 1989).

Super leadership: Leaders lead others to lead themselves.

Motivation, job satisfaction and job involvement

One basic question underpins the theme of this section: How do you go about motivating people in organisations? Generally, managers in organisations may have many interesting ideas about how to motivate employees, which they have accumulated through many years of experience. Some examples often cited refer to weekly pep talks, departmental conferences, money, time off work, etc. These examples are often based on management intuition and are often not always effective.

Job satisfaction: An individual's attitude toward his or her job.

Motivation represents 'those psychological processes that cause the arousal, direction, and persistence of voluntary actions that are goal directed' (Mitchell 1982). Managers need to understand these psychological processes if they are to successfully guide employees toward accomplishing organisational objectives. Mitchell (1997) proposed a broad conceptual model that explains how motivation influences job behaviours and performance. This model is shown in Figure 14.13, which identifies the causes and consequences of motivation.

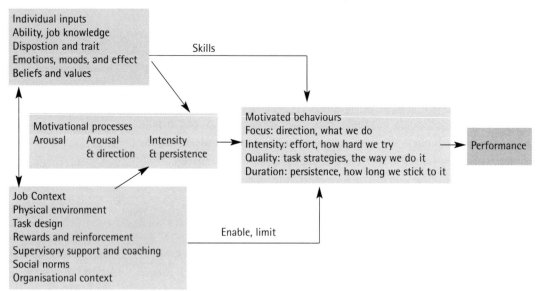

FIGURE 14.13: The causes and consequences of motivation

The above figure shows that individual inputs and job context are the two key categories of factors that influence motivation. Employees bring ability, job knowledge, dispositions and traits, emotions, moods, beliefs and values to the work setting. The job context includes the physical environment, the tasks one completes, the organisation's approach to recognition and rewards, the adequacy of supervisory support and coaching, and the organisation's culture. These two categories of factors influence each other as well as the motivational processes of arousal, direction and persistence.

This model further reveals that motivated behaviours are directly affected by an individual's ability and job knowledge (skills), motivation, and a combination of enabling and limiting job context factors. For instance, it would be difficult to persist in a project if you were working with defective raw materials or broken equipment. In contrast, motivated behaviours are likely to be enhanced when managers supply employees with adequate resources to get the job done and provide effective coaching. This coaching might entail furnishing employees with successful role models, showing employees how to complete tasks, and helping them maintain high self-efficacy and self-esteem. Performance is, in turn, influenced by motivated behaviour.

There are four important conclusions derived from the job performance model of motivation:

- Motivation involves a host of psychological processes that culminate in an individual's desire and intentions to behave in a particular way.
- Behaviour is influenced by more than just motivation. Behaviour is affected by individual inputs, job context factors and motivation.
- Behaviour is different from performance. Performance represents an accumulation of behaviours that occur over time and across contexts and people.
- Motivation is a necessary but insufficient contributor to job performance. This reveals that performance problems are due to a combination of individual inputs, job context factors, motivation and appropriate motivated behaviours.

Organisational structure and design

The way the component parts of organisations are put together and interact toward the achievement of its goals are described as its structure. The concepts of organisational structure and function that are frequently used to describe organisations include the following dimensions: decentralisation versus centralisation, a tall versus a flat structure, and a functional versus a divisional structure.

Decentralisation versus centralisation

Decentralisation is the degree to which decision making occurs lower down in an organisation's hierarchy. In a more **centralised** organisation, there is relatively less participation by employees in a variety of decisions. Decentralised organisations are characterised by less monitoring or checking on decisions made by employees.

The extent of decentralisation that exists in an organisation is extremely difficult to quantify. It would not be prudent to rely on the statements of top management regarding the extent of decentralisation in their organisations. Although top management may endorse the value of decentralisation, it is not always evident in their actions. A useful measure for determining the degree of decentralisation is to examine the amount of expenses employees are permitted to incur without approval by a supervisor. Generally, the greater the amount of latitude allowed employees on expenditures, the greater the extent of decentralisation that may be inferred. In addition, the variety and magnitude of decisions

Organisational design:
The process of coordinating the structural elements of an organisation in the most appropriate manner.

Organisational structure:
The formal configuration between individuals and groups regarding the allocation of tasks, responsibilities and authorities within organisations.

Decentralisation:
The degree to which decision making occurs lower down in an organisation's hierarchy. Decentralised organisations are characterised by less monitoring or checking on decisions made by employees.

Centralisation:
In a centralised organisation, there is relatively less participation by employees in a variety of decisions.

made outside of the top or central office can provide an indication of the degree of decentralisation (Vecchio 2000).

However, it is not reasonable to endorse the notion of decentralisation for all organisations. It is more acceptable to think in terms of an optimal level of decentralisation for any given organisation after due consideration of the particular environment in which it operates. Extreme decentralisation can lead to a lack of necessary integration and coordination. The following are possible drawbacks associated with decentralised organisational structures:

- Because of a lack of coordinated direction, there is a tendency to focus on current problems and functions, and to ignore opportunities for growth and innovation.
- Shared resources (such as computer equipment, staff, and research and development facilities) may pose problems because of the need to allocate their usage. Similarly, shared functions may create coordinating difficulties.
- Internal disputes and conflicts may arise. These conflicts may not be easily resolved, because each department or division operates with relative independence. Also, potential disputes between units are not as likely to be detected, averted or well managed if the actions of units are not coordinated.

As these points imply, extreme decentralisation can lead to a lack of integration and coordination. Nonetheless, decentralisation is often touted as a beneficial organisational attribute because of its anticipated enhancement of employee motivation, performance, satisfaction and creativity. According to this line of reasoning, the greater level of autonomy that decentralisation affords to employees leads to greater employee involvement and commitment (Duncan 1995).

Tall versus flat structures

Tall versus flat structures refers to the number of levels of authority and width (or size) of each level. Tall organisations have more levels, while flat organisations have fewer levels. Figure 14.4, on the next page, provides examples of both types of organisation.

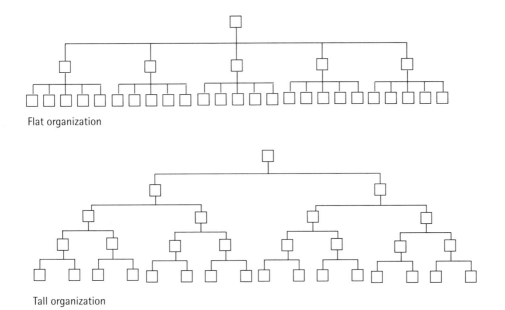

Flat organization

Tall organization

FIGURE 14.14 The structure of a flat and a tall organisation

These figures represent structures that are generally referred to as traditional organisational structures characterised by an authority hierarchy, which is reflected in the **organisational chart**, or **organogram**, above. The organogram depicts graphically the various levels of status or authority in an organisation and the number of workers that report to each level of authority. The chain of command is the number of authority levels in a particular organisation. The **chain of command** follows the lines of authority and status vertically through the organisation. The **span of control** is the number of workers who must report to a single supervisor. An organisation with a wide span of control has many workers reporting to each supervisor; an organisation with a narrow span has few subordinates reporting to each superior. Based on these dimensions of chain of command and span of control, traditional organisations are described as being tall or flat. A tall organisational structure has a long chain of command, i.e. many authority levels and a narrow span of control. A flat organisational structure has a short chain of command but has a wide span of control

Organisational chart:
A diagram representing the connections between the various departments within an organisation.

Organogram:
Graphic despiction of the various levels of status or authority in an organisation and the number of workers that report to each level of authority.

Chain of command
The number of authority levels in a particular organisation. The chain of command follows the lines of authority and status vertically through the organisation.

Span of control:
The number of workers who must report to a single supervisor.

An organisation's shape, either tall or flat, can have important implications for work life in the organisation. In tall organisational structures, workers at the bottom levels may feel cut off from those at the higher levels, because many levels of middle-ranking supervisors separate them. On the positive side, tall organisations may offer lower-level employees many different promotional opportunities throughout their careers. Another advantage of such structures is that there is usually adequate supervision, because the span of control is narrow: each supervisor is only responsible for a few employees. However, tall organisations can become 'top heavy' with administrators and managers, because the ratio of line workers to supervisors is very low. Conversely, in a flat structure few levels separate top-level managers from bottom-level workers, possibly leading to greater interaction between the top and bottom of the organisation. However, flat structures offer few promotional opportunities to workers, and supervision may not always be adequate, because many workers report to the same supervisor.

Although there has been considerable research on how the two types of structures affect important outcomes such as productivity and worker satisfaction, the results have been inconclusive. It is more likely that the shape of the organisation follows from its functions and goals. Flat organisational structures may be more common when the task is routine or repetitive, thus requiring a large number of workers who may need minimal supervision. Organisations with complex and multi-faceted goals or products may have taller structures, with different levels handling the various aspects of the company's goals.

Functional versus divisional structure

Functional structure:
Structure that divides the organisation into departments based on the functions or tasks performed, e.g. sales, finance.

Functional structure divides the organisation into departments based on the functions or tasks performed. A manufacturing firm may be made up of a production department, sales department and finance department. A functional design is especially appropriate when the most important needs of an organisation are collaboration and expertise within a defined set of operations, when the environment is stable and when only one or a few products are designed. However, a functional design suffers from several weaknesses. It tends to be slow to respond to changes in the organisation's environment. It may also result in less innovation and a restricted view of and allegiance to the organisation's broader goals.

Divisional structure:
The form used by many large organisations in which separate, autonomous units deal with entire product lines.

A functional design may also have difficulty in coordinating activities among departments. The measure of the contribution of each department is also problematic, as the end product is a composite result of production, personnel, engineering and marketing efforts. Lastly, the distinct advantage of a functional design (i.e. greater coordination) may become a disadvantage as the organisation becomes larger and more complex (Stebbins & Shani 1995).

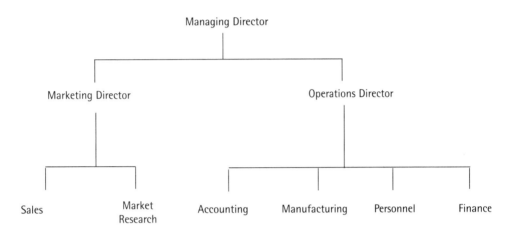

FIGURE 14.15: Example of a functional design

A divisional structure is based on types of products or customers. Each division may perform the same range of functions, but those functions only serve the goals of the particular division. Therefore, each division operates almost as if it were a separate organisation. An organisation that selects a functional design, groups personnel and activities according to organisational output. Each product line is provided with its own production, marketing and development resources as part of the structuring. The primary goals of a functional manager are coordination within product lines and attention to customer desires. Figure 14.16, on the next page, provides an organisational chart of a hypothetical firm with functional design.

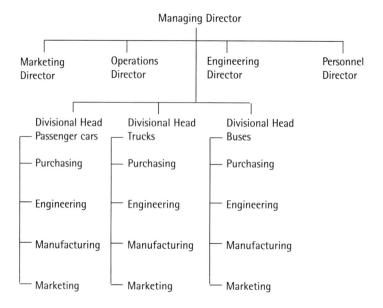

FIGURE 14.16

A functional design is better suited to adapt to changes in the organisation's environment and is especially appropriate for organisations that produce many diverse products or are highly consumer oriented. At the same time, a functional design may lead to tremendous losses in economies of scale, redundancy of effort, and little cooperation across product lines. Sharing of competencies and technical advantages is also limited. Internal competition may also arise. Although competition can be healthy to a point, the structure of the organisation may propel the initial competition into a full-blown power struggle.

(SOURCE: MILES *et al.* 1995)

Organisational development (OD)

Organisational development (OD): A set of social science techniques to plan change in organisational work settings, to enhance the personal development of individuals and to improve the effectiveness of organisational functioning.

In recent years, many organisations have had to cease operating because they were unable to change to keep up with the times. Companies that did not use the latest marketing and production techniques lost out to competitors who took advantage of such state-of-the-art technology. In addition, organisations have to adapt not only to external conditions but also to internal factors (Burke & Litwin 1992). For example, as new generations of employees enter the world of work with different types of skills and different ideas about what they want from their jobs, the organisation must adjust to utilise their skills and to meet their demands. Otherwise, the better employees will leave the organisation, or disgruntled employees may be able to slow down productivity through costly work stoppages and strikes. In addition, the recent trend towards downsizing means that many organisations must produce more with fewer organisational members. In short, the ability to change is critical to an organisation's survival (Greenwood & Hinings 1996). The specific specialty area concerned with helping organisations develop, adapt, and innovate is known as organisational development (OD). OD often involves altering the organisation's work structures or influencing workers' attitudes or behaviours to help the organisation to adapt to fluctuating external and internal conditions.

OD typically takes place in a series of phases. The first phase is usually a diagnosis of the organisation to identify significant problems. In the next phase, appropriate interventions are chosen to try to deal with the problems. The third phase is the implementation of the interventions, or OD techniques. Finally, the results of the interventions are evaluated (Burke 1987). Organisational development does not involve one single theory or approach, but rather a variety of orientations and methods for helping organisations manage change.

Most organisational development programmes are oriented toward long-term organisational improvement rather than focused on solving immediate problems. Generally, OD practitioners believe that their role is not to solve the organisation's problems, but to help improve the organisation's ability to solve its own problems. Typically, employees at all levels collaborate in the development and implementation of the OD programme. It is often found that many OD programmes use team approaches to deal with problems at group and organisational level, rather than focusing on problems associated with individual workers. Often this is done by opening up organisational communication channels and increasing members' involvement in the planning and execution of work activities (Riggio 2000).

Although OD techniques are indicated to improve organisational effectiveness, it requires a considerable amount of time, money and effort. The question is then often asked whether the investment is worthwhile and whether the intervention really works. Given the popularity of OD in organisations, this question is very important, and many relevant studies show the effects of these various interventions to be beneficial – mostly in the area of improving organisational functioning (Porras *et al.* 1992).

Diversity management

Managers are increasingly being asked to boost productivity, quality and customer satisfaction while also reducing costs. These goals can only be met, however, through the cooperation and effort of all employees. This

Diversity management: The management of a multitude of individual differences and similarities that exist among people toward the achievement of the organisation's goals.

cooperation has to be achieved within the context of an increasingly diverse workforce in terms of age, race, ethnicity, gender, sexual orientation and physical ability, to name but a few. The post-apartheid era in South Africa has seen a rapid change in the representation of people from all sectors of society at all levels in organisations. In addition, South Africa's return to the global business environment has required managers to be more aware of especially cultural differences in dealing with their counterparts abroad. Managing diversity is a sensitive, potentially volatile, and sometimes uncomfortable issue. Yet managers are required to deal with it in the name of organisational survival (Kreitner & Kinicki 2001).

Diversity:
The multitude of individual differences and similarities that exist amoung people.

In essence, **diversity** represents the multitude of individual differences and similarities that exist among people (Crocket 1999). This definition underscores three important issues about managing diversity:

- There are many different dimensions or components of diversity. This implies that diversity pertains to everybody. It is not an issue of age, race or gender. It is not an issue of being heterosexual, gay or lesbian. Diversity does not pit white males against other groups of people. Diversity pertains to the host of individual differences that make all of us unique and different from others.
- Diversity is not synonymous with differences. Rather, it encompasses both differences and similarities. This means that managing diversity entails dealing with both simultaneously.
- Diversity includes the collective mixture of differences and similarities, not just pieces of it. Dealing with diversity requires managers to integrate the collective mixture of differences and similarities that exists within organisations.

Academics and business leaders believe that effectively managing diversity is a competitive advantage. This advantage stems from the process in which the management of diversity affects organisational behaviour and effectiveness. Effectively managing diversity can influence an organisation's costs and employee attitudes, recruitment of human resources, sales and market share, creativity and innovation, and group problem solving and productivity.

- **Lower costs and improved employee attitudes:** Effectively managing diversity can lower costs in the following ways. Firstly, if we assume that adhering to equal employment opportunity laws is a prerequisite to managing diversity, then organisations can reduce the chance of experiencing costly discrimination lawsuits. Secondly, savings can occur through reductions in turnover by women and people of colour.

- **Improved recruitment efforts:** Attracting and retaining competent employees is a competitive advantage. Organisations that effectively manage diversity are more likely to meet this challenge because women and people of colour are attracted to such companies. Moreover, recruiting diverse employees helps organisations to provide better customer service because the employees are representative of the communities in which the organisations does business.
- **Increased sales, market share and company profits:** Workforce diversity is the mirror image of consumer diversity. It is thus important for companies to market their products so that they appeal to diverse customers and markets. Diversity promotes the sharing of unique ideas and a variety of perspectives, which, in turn, leads to more effective decision making (Miller *et al.* 1998).
- **Increased productivity and innovation:** Research supports the notion that workforce diversity promotes creativity and innovation. This occurs through the sharing of diverse ideas and perspectives. Larkey (1996) found that innovative companies deliberately used heterogeneous teams to solve problems, and they employed more women and people of colour than less innovative companies. It was also found that innovative companies did a better job of eliminating racism, sexism and classism.
- **Increased group problem solving and productivity:** Because diverse groups possess a broader base of experience and perspectives from which to analyse a problem, they can potentially improve problem solving and performance. Heterogeneous groups produce better quality decisions and demonstrate higher productivity than homogeneous groups (Lau & Murnighan 1998).

In the introduction to this section on the management of diversity, it was noted that it is a sensitive, potentially volatile, and sometimes uncomfortable issue. It is therefore not surprising that organisations encounter significant barriers when trying to move forward with managing diversity. Spragins (1993) presents the most common barriers to implementing successful diversity programmes:

- inaccurate stereotypes and prejudice;
- ethnocentrism;
- poor career planning;
- an unsupportive and hostile working environment for diverse employees;
- lack of political savvy on the part of diverse employees;
- difficulty in balancing career and family issues;
- fears of reverse discrimination;

- diversity not being seen as an organisational priority;
- the need to revamp the organisation's performance appraisal and reward system; and
- resistance to change.

In summary, managing diversity is a critical component of organisational success. However, any such efforts are doomed to failure unless they have the support of top management.

Summary

The selection process should provide as much reliable and valid information as possible about applicants so that their skills can be carefully matched with job specifications. The information that is obtained should be clearly job-related or predictive of success on the job and free from potential discrimination.

The process of communication occurs when a sender of information encodes a message and transmits it over communication channels to a receiver, who decodes it and then sends feedback. Factors interfering with these processes are known as noise. Communication in organisations is used to direct individual action and to achieve coordinated action. The heart of communication is information, but communication is also used to develop friendships and to build interpersonal trust and acceptance in organisations.

Leadership is the process whereby one individual influences other group members toward attaining defined group or organisational goals. Leaders generally use non-coercive forms of influence and, in turn, are influenced by their followers. Whereas leaders create the organisation's mission and outline the strategy for attaining it, managers are responsible for implementing that mission. This distinction is often blurred in practice.

Motivation is concerned with the set of processes that arouse, direct and maintain behaviour toward a goal. It is not equivalent to job performance, but is one of several determinants in job performance. Today's work ethic motivates people to seek interesting and challenging jobs instead of simply money.

Organisational design refers to the formal configuration between individuals and groups regarding allocation of tasks, responsibilities and authority within organisations. An organisational chart can be used to represent this abstract concept.

Most organisational development programmes are oriented toward long-term organisational improvement rather than focused on solving immediate problems. Organisational development does not involve one single theory or approach, but rather a variety of orientations and methods for helping organisations manage change. Typically, employees of all levels collaborate in the development and implementation of the OD programme.

Diversity represents the host of individual differences that make people different from and similar to each other. It is nor simply an issue of age, race, gender or sexual orientation and holds many implications for modern organisational managers.

Appendix 1: The cross–cultural applicability of the16PF

Abrahams' (1996) study focused on the Sixteen Personality Factor Inventory/16PF (SA 92), a popular test that was used extensively in South African organisations within the selection process. It was developed in the USA, and imported and adapted for South African conditions by the Human Sciences Research Council. The main aim of the study was to determine whether scores of the 16PF are comparable in a cross-cultural South African environment. The influences of age, language, socio-economic status and gender on the scores were also determined.

The sample consisted of 983 students drawn from the University of the Western Cape, University of Pretoria, University of Durban-Westville and University of Natal.

To achieve the aims outlined, **construct comparability** studies and **item comparability** studies were conducted. In addition, descriptive statistics were also calculated to provide a general picture of the various sub-samples. A qualitative study was conducted to determine some of the reasons for the occurrence of item comparability of the racial sub-sample.

The results of the qualitative and quantitative students showed that the racial variable had the greatest influence on test scores. Problems existed with the construct and item comparability of the test and significant mean differences were also found between the different racial groups. With the qualitative studies, the results showed that participants whose home language was not English or Afrikaans had difficulty in understanding many of the words and the construction of sentences contained in the 16PF.

The results has implications for test users of the 16PF (SA92) in South African organisations as the Employment Equity Act now specifically forbids the use of psychological tests unless they can be proven to be valid and reliable, and not biased against any group.

Construct comparability: The validity of measures across cultural groups in respect of the same construct.

Item comparability: Situation when performance on all items on a psychological test (particularly a personality test) is found to be comparable between different groups.

Appendix 2: GE is no place for autocrats, Welch decrees

The General Electric Company can no longer tolerate autocratic, tyrannical managers. So said chairman and CEO John Welch, who has cracked his fair share of heads, in his letter to shareholders in GE's annual report: a promising future is 'an easy call' for a leader who 'delivers on commitments – financial or otherwise – and shares the values of our company'. For that person, the prospect is 'onward and upward', he declares.

The second type of leader, one who doesn't meet commitments and doesn't share values, is 'not as pleasant a call, but equally easy', he says. Such personnel are soon gone, is the implication. Leaders who miss commitments but share the values 'usually get a second chance, preferably in a different environment' within the company, Welch declares.

But the fourth type is 'the most difficult for many of us to deal with. That leader delivers on commitments, makes all the numbers, but doesn't share the values we have. This is the individual who typically forces performance out of people rather than inspires it: the autocrat, the big shot, and the tyrant. Too often all of us have looked the other way', tolerating these 'Type 4' managers because 'they always deliver' – at least in the short term.

But these days, in an environment where we must have every good idea from every man and woman in the organisation, we cannot afford management styles that suppress and intimidate, declares Welch.

(HYATT & NAJ 1992)

Further reading

Abrahams, F. (1996) The cross-cultural comparability of the 16 personality factor inventory (16PF). Unpublished doctoral thesis, University of South Africa.

Alessandra, T. & Hunksaker, P. (1993) *Communicating at Work*. New York: Fireside.

Barnard, C.I. (1938) *The Functions of the Executives*. Cambridge, Mass.: Harvard University Press.

Bass, B.M. (1985) *Leadership and Performance beyond Expectations*. New York: Free Press.

Bendix, S. (1996) *Industrial Relations in the New South Africa* (3rd edition). Cape Town: Juta.

Bergh, Z.C. & Theron, A.L. (1999) *Psychology in the Work Context*. Sandton: Oxford.

Berry, L. M. & Houston, J.P. (1993) *Psychology at Work: An Introduction to Industrial and Organisational Psychology*. Dubuque: Brown & Benchmark.

Biesheuvel, S. (1987) Cross-cultural psychology: Its relevance in South Africa. In K.F. Mauer & A. I. Retief (eds), *Psychology in Context. Cross-cultural Research Trends in South Africa*. Pretoria: Human Sciences Research Council.

Brown, L.R., Kane, H. & Ayers, E. (1994) *Vital Sign*. New York: Norton.

Burke, W.W. (1987) *Organizational Development: A Normative View*. Reading, Mass.: Addison-Wesley.

Burke, W. & Litwin, G. (1992) A causal model of organizational performance and change. *Journal of Management*, 18, pp. 523–45.

Cherrington, D.J. (1995) *The Management of Human Resources* (4th edition). Upper Saddle River: Prentice-Hall.

Cloete, N., Muller, J. & Orkin, M. (1986) Neutrale navorsing in diens van die politiek? *Die Suid Afrikaan*, 6, pp. 11–13.

Crockett, J. (1999) Diversity as a business strategy. *Management Review*, May, p. 62.

Dubow, S. (1981) Mental testing and the understanding of race in twentieth century South Africa. In T. Meade & M. Walker (eds), *Science, Medicine and Cultural Imperialism*. London: Macmillan.

Duncan, R. (1995) What is the right organisation structure? *Organisational Dynamics*, 33, p. 66.

England, J. & Zietsman, G. (1995) *The HSRC Stakeholder Survey on Assessment*. Internal report prepared for Human Resources: Assessment and Information Technology, Human Sciences Research Council, South Africa.

Faludi, S.C. (1993) Safeway LBO yields vast profits but exacts a heavy human toll. *The Wall Street Journal*, 16, p. 1.

Fergus, M. (1990) Employees on the move. *HR Magazine*, 36, p. 45.

Fierman, J. (1992) Beating the midlife career crisis. *Fortune*, 128, p. 54.

Finnemore, M. (1999) *Labour Relations in South Africa* (7th edition). Cape Town: Juta.

Foxcroft, C., Roodt, G. & Abrahams, F. (2001a) The practice of psychological assessment: Controlling the use of measures, competing values, and ethical practice standards. In C. Foxcroft & G. Roodt (eds), *Introduction to Psychological Assessment in South Africa*. Sandton: Oxford.

Foxcroft, C., Roodt, G. & Abrahams, F. (2001b) Psychological assessment: A brief retrospective overview. In C. Foxcroft & G. Roodt (eds), *Introduction to Psychological Assessment in South Africa*. Sandton: Oxford.

Foxcroft, C. (1997) Psychological testing in South Africa: Perspectives regarding ethical and fair practice. *European Journal of Psychological Assessment*, 3, pp. 229–35.

Gatewood R.D. & Field, S.H. (1998) *Human Resource Selection* (4th edition). Fort Worth: Dryden.

Geier, J.G. (1969) A trait approach to the study of leadership in small groups. *Journal of Communication*, 17, pp. 316–23.

Greenwood, R. & Hinings, C.R. (1996) Understanding radical organizational change: Bringing together the old and the new institionalism. *Academy of Management Review*, 21, pp. 1022–54.

Gupta, A.K. and Singhal, A. (1993) Managing Human Resources for Innovation and Creativity. *Research-Technology Management*, 36, pp. 41–8.

Hyatt, J.C. & Naj, A.K. (1992) GE is no place for autocrats. *The Wall Street Journal*, 3 March, p. A1

Hellriegel, D., Slocum, J.W & Woodman, R.W. (2001) *Organisational Behaviour* (9th edition). Ohio: South-Western.

Jones, B. (1997) Communication: Dying for information. *Management Review*, July/August, p. 9.

Kamin, L.H. (1974) *The Science and Politics of IQ*. Protomac: Erlbaum.

Kaplan, R.M. & Saccuzzo, D.P. (1989) *Psychological Testing: Principles, Applications, Issues*. Pacific Grove: Brooks/Cole.

Kotter, J.P. (1990) *A Force for Change: How Leadership Differs from Management*. New York: Free Press.

Kreitner, R. & Kinicki, A. (2001) *Organisational Behavior* (5th edition). New York: McGraw-Hill.

Lau, D.C. & Murnighan, J.K. (1998) Demographic diversity and fault lines: The compositional dynamics of organizational groups. *Academy of Management*, 29, pp. 325–40.

Leap, T.L. & Crino, M.D. (1993) *Personnel/Human Resource Management* (2nd edition). New York: Macmillan.

Lengel, R.H. & Draft, R.L. (1988) The selection of communication media as an executive skill. *Academy of Management Executive*, 2, pp. 225–32.

Leonard, B. (1992) HR policies ensure the mirage won't vanish. *HR Magazine*, 37, pp. 85–91.

Lodge, G.C. (1995) *Managing Globalization in the Age of Interdependence*. San Francisco: Pfeifer.

Lord, R.G., De Vader, C.L. & Alliger, G.M. (1986) A meta-analysis of the relationship between personality traits and leadership perceptions: An application of validity generalization procedures. *Journal of Applied Psychology*, 61, pp. 402–10.

Malwandla, M.P. (1995) Performance appraisal systems: A model for the public sector. Unpublished MBA thesis. University of the Witwatersrand.

Manz, C.C. & Sims, H.P. (1989) *Superleadership: Leading Others to Lead Themselves*. New York: Berkley Books.

McCathrin, Z. (1990) The key to employee communication: Small group meetings. *The Professional Communicator*, Spring, pp. 6–7.

McDermott, L. (1996) Toward a feminist understanding of physicality within the context of women's physically active and sporting lives. *Sociology of Sport Journal*, 13(1), pp. 12–30.

Miles, R.E., Coleman, H.J. & Creed, W.E.D. (1995) Keys to success in corporate redesign. *California Management Review*, 37, pp. 128–45.

Miller, C.C., Burke, L.M. & Glick, W.H. (1998) Cognitive diversity among upper-echelon executives: Implications for strategic decision processes. *Strategic Management Journal*, 19, pp. 39–58.

Mitchell, T.R. (1982) Motivation: New direction for theory, research, and practice. *Academy of Management Review*, January, p. 81.

Mitchell, T.R. (1997) Matching motivational strategies with organisational contexts. *Research in Organisational Behaviour*, 19, pp. 57–149.

Mondy, R.W., Noe, R.M. & Edwards, R.E. (1986) What the staffing function entails. *Personnel*, 63, pp. 55–66

Mondy, R.W. & Noe, R.M. (1996) *Human Resource Management* (6th edition). New Jersey: Prentice-Hall.

Muchinsky, P.M. (1997) *Psychology Applied to Work* (5th edition). Pacific Grove: Brooks/Cole.

Muchinsky, P.M., Kriek, H.J. & Schreuder, A.M.J. (1998) *Personnel Psychology*. Halfway House: Thomson.

Murphy, K.R. & Davidshofer, C.O. (1988) *Psychological Testing: Principles and Applications*. Englewood Cliffs: Prentice-Hall.

Nel, P.S., Gerber, P.D., van Dyk, P.S., Haasbroek, G.D., Schultz, H.B. & Sono, T. (2001) *Human Resource Management*. Cape Town: Oxford University Press.

Nell, V. (1994) Interpretation and misinterpretation of the South African Weschler Bellevue Adult Intelligence Scale: A history and prospectus. *South African Journal of Psychology*, 24, pp. 100–9.

Norton, L.A. (1991) Link HR to corporate strategies. *Personnel Journal*, pp. 70, 75.

Owen, K. (1986) *Test and Item Bias: The Suitability of the Junior Aptitude Test as a Common Battery for White, Indian, and Black Pupils in Standard 7*. Pretoria: Human Sciences Research Council.

Peters, T.J. & Waterman, R.H. (1982) *In Search of Excellence*. New York: Harper & Row.

Plug, C. (1996) An evaluation of psychometric test construction and psychological services supported by the HSRC. Unpublished manuscript, University of South Africa.

Podsakoff, P.M., MacKenzie, S.B. & Bommer, W.H. (1996) Meta-analysis of the relationship between Kerr and Jermier's substitutes for leadership and employee job attitudes, role expectations, and performance. *Journal of Applied Psychology*, 81, pp. 380–99.

Poras, J.I., Robertson, P.J. & Goldman, L. (1992) Organizational develop-
    ment: Theory, practice, and research, In *Handbook of
    Industrial/Organizational Psychology*. Palo Alto: Consulting
    Psychologists Press.

Riggio, R.E. (2000) *Introduction to Industrial/Organisational Psychology*
    (3rd edition). Englewood Cliffs: Prentice-Hall.

Rowe, M.P. & Baker, M. (1984) Are you hearing enough employee
    concerns? *Harvard Business Review*, May-June, pp. 127–35.

Schellhardt, T. (1997) Off the ladder: Want to be a manager? *The Wall
    Street Journal*, 4 April.

Schultz, D. & Shultz S.E. (1998) *An Introduction to Industrial and
    Organisational Psychology* (7th edition). Upper Saddle River:
    Prentice-Hall.

Sherman, A., Bohlander, G. & Snell, S. (1996). *Managing Human
    Resources*. Cincinnati: Thomson.

Shuttleworth-Jordan, A.B. (1996) On not re-inventing the wheel: A clinical
    perspective on culturally relevant test-usage. *South African Journal of
    Psychology*, 26, pp. 96–102.

Solomon, C.M. (1995) Staff selection impacts global success. *Personnel
    Journal*, pp. 73–88.

Stebbins, M.W. & Shani, B.R. (1995) Organisation design and the knowl-
    edge worker. *Leadership and Organisation Development Journal*, 16,
    pp. 23–30.

Taylor, T.R. & Radford, E.J. (1986) Psychometric testing as an unfair
    labour practice. *South African Journal of Psychology*, 16, pp. 79–96.

Vecchio, R.P. (2000) *Organisational Behavior: Core Concepts* (4th edition).
    New York: Dryden Press.

15 Health Psychology

T-A. Mashego and K. Peltzer

Objectives

After studying this chapter you should be able to:

- clarify the rationale for the existence of health psychology as a discipline and all it aims to achieve
- define health psychology and all important aspects of the philosophy underlying the discipline
- give a description of the different models used to understand health psychology as a discipline, including to the biopsychological model, the mind-body split dichotomy and the cultural model
- outline people's views of health and illness both at the personal and cultural levels
- see the interconnection between the mind and the body
- define health as opposed to illness
- know about lifestyle diseases associated with health behaviour in the context of the attributions made of such lifestyles to health
- outline the objectives of health psychology as a discipline and its future as a profession.

Introduction

The concept of health is embodied in the everyday talk and thoughts of people with different languages, and from different cultures and religious groups. According to the World Health Organisation (WHO), health is 'the state of complete physical, social and mental well-being, not simply the absence of illness' (WHO 1986).

The WHO (1986) further defined health as a process of enabling people to increase control over and improve their health. In order to reach a state of complete physical, mental and social well-being, an individual or group must be able to identify and to realise aspirations, to satisfy needs and to change or cope with the environment.

Progress in medical science has been impressive over the past years. Knowledge of the body and treatment of disease has been the focus, ignoring possible underlying reasons for illness. Medical treatment does undoubtedly contribute to the decline in infectious diseases as reported in most studies of treatment efficacy, but the contribution of lifestyle changes is in many cases taken for granted. In the 1980s, Goldman estimated that the decline in heart disease mortality observed in the USA between 1968 and 1976 was related to changes in lifestyle, specifically the reduction in both blood cholesterol levels and cigarette smoking (Stroebe & Stroebe 1995).

The burden of chronic disease risk factors is high in South Africa, with its population of about 41 million. Approximately six million people have hypertension, four million have diabetes, seven million smoke and four million have high blood cholesterol. About 56% of the population have at least one of these risk factors and about 20% are at a high level of risk for chronic diseases. The rapid spread of HIV/AIDS in South Africa is changing the health profile and mortality patterns at an unprecedented rate. This multiple burden represents a demand on the health services far beyond their ability to cope. The consequences of these competing priorities are that there is little recognition of the magnitude of the burden of chronic diseases in South Africa, where 48% of reported mortality was due to chronic diseases in 1995 (MRC). According to the WHO Report of 1999, cardiovascular diseases (CVD) accounted for 28.5% of all deaths in low- and middle-income countries in 1998.

In 1996 in South Africa, over 22% of all deaths were due to strokes and heart disease. Half the country's population are under 18 years of age and are exposed to the 'globalisation of risk factors' such as easier access to tobacco products, diets higher in salt and sugar, and the more sedentary lifestyles associated with obesity and type II diabetes mellitus. Many of these influences are known as determinants for socio-economic and behavioural patterns in which the classic risk factors for CVD emerge. The relatively young population is thus exposed to these changing determinants and risk factors for longer periods of time, resulting in CVD at relatively young ages. In South Africa, strokes in 1995 accounted for 4.8% and 2.3% of deaths in women and men respectively in the age group 35–39, and these proportions rose with increasing age.

According to the National Demographic and Health Survey (Department of Health 1999), among a representative sample of the population in South Africa, 2.7% in the age group 15–24 years, 5.1% in the age group 25–34, 12.2% in the age group 35–44, 19.7% in the age group 45–54, 22.2% in the age group 55–64 and 28.5% in the age group 65 years and above measured hypertension (which refers to those with blood pressures greater than or equal to 160/95 mm Hg and those who are taking hypertension medication). In addition, pregnant women are exposed to deficits in nutritional and environmental resources that could result in fetal programming leading to hypertension and obesity in their children later in life, particularly as they are exposed to the increasingly prevalent determinants and risk factors mentioned above (Mbewu 2001).

Definition of health psychology

Marks *et al.* (2000) defined health psychology as an interdisciplinary field concerned with the application of psychological knowledge and techniques to health, illness and health care.

The primary objectives are to promote and maintain the well-being of individuals, communities and populations. At a theoretical level, the objectives are to understand the relationship between the mind and the body that affects the whole individual's well-being. At a practical level, the objectives are to intervene in the interface between the individual, health care and society.

Matarazzo's (1982) definition of health psychology was adopted by professional organisations such as the American Psychological Association (APA), the British Psychological Society (BPS) and other organisations. It stated that:

> *Health psychology is the aggregate of the specific educational, scientific, and professional contributions of the discipline of psychology to the promotion and maintenance of health, the prevention and treatment of illness, the identification of aetiologic and diagnostic correlates of health, illness and related dysfunction and to the analysis and improvement of the health care system and health policy formation*
> (MATARAZZO 1982: P. 4).

Health psychology grew rapidly in the 1980s and 1990s. By the late 1990s, over 6 000 psychologists had become members of APA health psychology division 38 and in the UK the BPS had 1 000 health psychologists as members. Marks *et al.* (2000) attributed this rapid growth in health psychology to three factors.

Firstly, there was increased awareness that vast amounts of illness and mortality are determined by behaviour, i.e. research indicated that all leading causes of death in Western societies had something to do with behaviour, which means many deaths are preventible if effective interventions are put into place. These behaviours were reported to be smoking (active and passive), poor diet, excessive alcohol consumption, lack of exercise, stress, careless driving and speeding, all of which strengthened the belief that individuals are responsible for their own health. Secondly, there was increasing disenchantment with health-care systems. Thirdly, there was poor quality of communication between doctors and other health-care professionals. Such disenchantment led to the other professionals' proposals to look at other ways of conceptualising health and illness, since the psychological factors seemed to have been found to be more important than purely biological causes of well-being.

The health promotion approach advocates that health professionals should be seen as more than just providers of services, but rather as agents of change to facilitate individual and community empowerment towards increased improvement and control of their health (Marks 1999). There are four major approaches to health promotion adopted in South Africa: (1) policy, advocacy and healthy environments; (2) the settings approach, e.g. hospitals and schools; (3) education and information; and (4) re-orienting health services and community participation. In terms of the core package of primary health-care services, health promotion is considered a community service. This implies that health promotion should involve outreach work into health districts (Coulson et al. 1998)

Basic assumptions
Mind-body split

Health psychology provides theories and research to support the notion that the mind and body are one. This discipline aims at providing an integrated model of the individual and to establish a holistic approach to health by challenging the medical model of the mind-body split. There is a consistent suggestion in health psychology that beliefs influence behaviour (which in turn influences health), that stress can cause illness, that illness cognitions relate to recovery and coping relates to longevity.

Epistemologies:
Theories of the methods and ground of knowledge.

Marks et al. (2000) delineated two primary theories of knowledge or epistemologies for studying as well as understanding human behaviour and experience in health psychology. These two epistemologies are the natural science approach or medical approach (with its various offshoots) and the psychosocial approach.

The natural science approach looks at behaviour in the same way as chemists, physicists or biologists do, considering causal relationships to be of primary importance. The basic focus is on questions such as 'Why does such and such a thing happen?' and this question aims at the generation of accurate predictions. This tradition is well represented in the medical model and its recent offshoot, the biopsychosocial model, where illness is regarded as biochemical or physical in nature and the mind as a nervous system activity. However, Engel (1977) challenged the medical model and proposed that health and illness are a consequence of the physical, psychological and cultural variables that make up the 'three Ps' of the psychosocial model: people, prevention and psychology, as contrasted to the 'three Ds' of the medical model: diagnosis, disease and drugs. The new psychosocial theories consider non-physical events as having greater significance in illness and health care. The study of health psychology is concerned with the development of an understanding of the relationship between the psyche and the body (Marks *et al.* 2000).

Different meanings of health

The **cognition model** aims at the examination of the predictors of and precursors to health behaviours. These are derived from subjective expected utility, which suggest that behaviours result from a rational weighing of potential costs and benefits of the behaviour in question. Such demonstrated behaviours result from individual cognitions and not the social context of those cognitions.

Cognition model: Health model that aims at the examination of the predictors of and precursors to health behaviours.

Attitudes to health based on the **health belief model** predict that behaviour is a result of a set of core beliefs, based on the following perceptions by individuals: susceptibility to illness (e.g. 'My chances of getting AIDS are high'); severity of the illness (e.g. 'AIDS is a serious illness'); the cost involved in carrying out a behaviour (e.g. 'Insisting on condom usage will make my partner leave me'); benefits involved in carrying out the behaviour (e.g. diminished concern about becoming infected with an STD); and cues to action that may be internal (e.g. STD symptoms) or external (e.g. information in the form of leaflets about how to deal with partners to avoid contamination).

Health belief model: Health model that predicts that behaviour is a result of a set of core beliefs.

The cognition model has been criticised for its emphasis on the individual, with the exclusion of other factors such as the prediction of behaviour based on outcome expectancy and self-efficacy (Seydel *et al.* 1990; Schwarzer 1992). As such, the model has been recommended for the screening of diseases such as hypertension, cervical cancer, genetic screening, exercise behaviour, etc. (Ogden 2000). Such criticism is based on the premise that beliefs should be looked at in the context of broader societal views, which should also include the individual perceptions described in the cognitive model. The following section deals with the cultural contextualisation of beliefs held about health and illness.

Cultural contextualisation of beliefs about health and illness

Ontology:
Theory of the
nature of being.

Each society has developed its own understanding of health and illness. Shweder *et al.* (1997) described seven general systems, which they termed 'ontologies of suffering'. These are the biomedical, interpersonal, socio-political, psychological, astrophysical, ecological and moral systems. A survey conducted by Murdock (1980) revealed that in sub-Saharan Africa, preference for explanation of illness was based on moral transgressions, while in East Asia it was based on interpersonal explanations, and in the Mediterranean area the preference for the use of witchcraft was more widespread.

With further investigations, Park (1992) found three worldwide explanations for illness: interpersonal, moral and biomedical. Shweder *et al.* (1997) stated that moral discourse was actually found to be the underlying explanation by most societies. They found that the Western discourse was that of autonomy, which focused on the rights of the individual. In health care, this discourse has led to the rights of the individual pervading contemporary medical ethics on a greater scale than any other position (Marks *et al.* 2000). Other moral discourses identified were community discourse, with a focus on community, family, duty and interdependence; as well as divinity discourse, which focuses on divinity and the natural order. This is in line with Hofstede's dimension of individualism versus collectivism, whereby the individualistic groups emphasise the separateness and uniqueness of its members while the collectivists emphasise group needs and interconnectedness (Matsumuto 1996).

Health belief systems

Kleinman (in Stroebe & Stroebe 1995) described three overlapping sectors for health beliefs: the professional, the folk and the popular. The popular sector is the non-professional lay group that first defines illness and later develops health-care activities. The professional sector represents the organised healing sectors, while the folk sector lies somewhere in between the two.

View of health by different groups

The most influential popular lay beliefs about health among Western societies was shown in a study by Herzlich (1973). She found in her study of a French sample that health was conceived as an individual attribute, i.e. a state of harmony and balance. Illness was then attributed to outside

forces in society and its way of life. The ability of an individual to participate in daily activities constituted health, and inactivity was considered
the true criterion of illness.

D'Houtaud and Field (1984) found that perceptions of health and
illness differ according to class distinctions. The upper and middle class
focuses were more **hedonistic** when defining health: they defined it in
terms of their bodies, equilibrium and vitality. Those from lower social
groups preferred defining health in terms of the value of health, psychological well-being, hygiene and absence of sickness. From this it is clear
that health definitions are intimately related to the immediate social
experience of adults (Marks *et al.* 2000). Baxter (1990) found gender
differences in definitions of health, which indicated that females tended
to define health in terms of their personal relationships. This was confirmed in a study by Murray and McMillan (in Marks *et al.* 2000), who
had previously found that a sample of working-class women, when
describing their views of cancer, referred a lot to their families and relationships. Health was not seen as simply a characteristic of their
individual bodies but rather involved their relationships with others.

For non-Western groups, health was found to be defined differently
by different groups. For the Chinese, for example, it was found that health
was defined in terms of destiny, while others defined illness as a form of
retribution for the wrong that one has done to others in the past.

Other definitions include the Buddhist view that sickness and health
lie in the central importance of harmony and balance in one's life.
Equilibrium in a study on Cambodian women referred to the avoidance
of experience of 'internal bad wind'. Equilibrium is retained through
strategies such as 'coin rubbing' and avoidance of individual competitive
behaviour, respect for individuality, nurture of the weak and peaceful
co-existence with the natural environment (Frye 1991). This study illustrated the importance of social balance and interconnectedness, as
opposed to individualism.

In African cultures, ill health may derive from ancestral punishment
for transgressions of norms such as committing incest, non-performance
of prescribed rituals (Mashego 2000) or any unacceptable behaviour.
Also, Africans were found to have definitions of health that centred
around communal beliefs (Marks *et al.* 2000). In a study conducted in
Ethiopia, it was found that illness was seen in terms of four dimensions:
psychological stressors, supernatural retribution, biomedical defects and
social disadvantage (Mulatu 1995). South African blacks have indicated
tendencies towards endorsing Westernised methods of health care, but a
high degree of consultation with traditional healers has been reported
across different class groups (Mahapa & Peltzer 1998). This shows that

Hedonistic:
Believing that pleasure is
the chief aim of life.

there is a high degree of belief that health and sickness have supernatural roots and that witchcraft and sorcery among South African blacks cannot be overlooked in helping them towards effective health care.

It is apparent that people's belief about health and illness are intertwined with broader belief systems. Culture is not just traditional community, but pervades all our lives as cultural beings. The social definition of illness and health should emphasise the individual and the world; we should also bear in mind that alternative belief systems are not fixed, but are systems in a process of constant change.

Lifestyle diseases and health promotion
Smoking

Tobacco-related diseases are among the most avoidable and unnecessary of problems, but which nevertheless seem to continue at pandemic proportions both in developed and developing countries, including South Africa. Evidence show that in countries where smoking is common, for men under 65, 90% of the deaths that resulted from lung cancer, 75% from bronchitis and 25% from ischaemic heart disease were all smoking related (Ram 1986). Overall, however, tobacco use has dropped dramatically in South Africa in the past few years. The prevalence of cigarette smoking among adults has declined from 34% in 1992 to 24% in 1998. About 42% of men and 11% of women smoke cigarettes. Among adolescents aged 15–19 years, 14% of boys and 6% of girls are currently smokers (Department of Health 1999; Saloojee 2000).

Alcohol abuse

In both popular and scientific periodicals, there has been recognition of an accelerated rate of substance use and abuse, particularly of alcohol, in African and other less developed countries (Obot 1989). Several reasons have been posited for this. These include rapid rates of industrial growth and urbanisation, uprooting from familiar environments, disruptions in interpersonal relationships, the need to relieve tension and anxiety as a way of coping with the exigencies of changed social and economic conditions, and the adoption of Western lifestyles, especially by urban populations of professionals and youth.

Superimposed on these related features are the more objective realities of greater availability of the substances, aggressive marketing by indigenous producers and multinational corporations and a general increase in disposable income. In other words, the substances of abuse have become more available, the craving for them has increased and the ability to buy them has improved for more people in African countries.

The modern disease conception of alcoholism holds that alcoholism is a disease like any other disease and should therefore be treated, just like any other disease. According to this model, the disorder develops like any other chronic disease, i.e. insidiously, but follows a predictable course (Jellinek 1952). This occurs as follows: the pre-alcoholic symptomatic phase begins with the use of alcohol to relieve tensions; the second phase, the prodomal phase, is marked by a range of behaviour that includes preoccupation with alcohol, surreptitious drinking and loss of memory; and in the third (crucial) phase the person reaches a stage where he or she loses control over his or her drinking. This loss of control is the beginning of the disease process of addiction. Such a loss of control is seen when the person starts to drink in the early morning, continues to drink the whole day and stays up drinking until late at night. This behaviour leads to impairment in social and occupational functioning, as the person involved loses interest in friends and family and stops working.

Instead of postulating moral decadence as an underlying cause of alcoholism, the medical view insists on biological factors in the etiology of the disorder. This means that alcoholism may be a sign of an underlying biochemical imbalance due to an inherited predisposition to excessive drinking (Goodwin 1971). Research that seeks to unravel the biological determinants has been prolific in recent years. However, doubts have been cast on the argument that the genetic bases of alcoholism exist and can be isolated.

The classic psychoanalytical approach holds that excessive drinking is a sign of fixation at the oral stage of development, where such fixation occurs as a result of unresolved conflict in childhood. Drinking thus becomes a sign of unsuccessfully resolving the conflict. In another view of the psychoanalytic model, alcoholism is regarded as chronic suicide where drinking serves as a means of self-annihilation. This view is supported by the high rate of suicide among alcohol-dependent individuals (Obot 1989). A neo-Freudian view holds that dependence occurs as a result of severe ego impairment and disturbances in the sense of self, involving difficulties with drive and affect, defence, self care, dependency and need satisfaction.

The socio-cultural model, on the other hand, takes into consideration social and environmental factors, which include cultural acceptance of drinking, availability, parental influence and religion. The public health model views these factors as interacting with features of the agent (toxicity, dosage) and host (age, personality, genetic predisposition).

This is a holistic view, which considers the problem of alcohol as an interaction of characteristics of the environment, substance (agent) and individual (host). This model seems more applicable, especially to those interested in the control and preventive approach to alcohol, which is at the core of health promotion.

Factors to be considered in understanding alcoholism

There has been change in patterns of consumption, i.e. the substitution of commercially-brewed Western beverages with high alcohol content for home-brewed traditional beverages.

Alcohol was reported to be associated with spontaneous hypoglycaemia, cirrhosis of the liver and pellagra, as well as a major cause of violence (Geltenal 1966).

Alcohol has been associated with Korsakoff's psychosis, hallucinations, delirium tremens dementia, and paranoid psychosis among patients in East and West Africa (Adomekoh 1976).

There is a lack of sufficient epidemiological studies on alcoholism in Africa. Most studies are conducted on students and hospital patients. Insufficient research leads to inadequate preventive measures aimed at combating alcoholism.

African indigenous churches like the Zion Christian Church (ZCC) and Apostolics have developed a similar self-help approach to Alcoholics Anonymous, i.e. proscription of alcohol use, confession to a Higher Power, peer support, spiritual therapy and counselling (Peltzer 1985).

Chronic diseases and health promotion
Tuberculosis (TB)

The Department of Health has declared TB a top national priority following the discovery that more people in South Africa die of TB than of AIDS. An estimated 140 000 new TB cases occur annually, therefore TB remains a leading cause of mortality and morbidity, despite the fact that it is curable. An estimated 2,9 million people die from TB each year worldwide, making the disease the largest cause of death from a single pathogen (Nichter 1994).

At one time, TB was largely considered a disease of those in poor circumstances, but now it seems to be spreading into more affluent homes and sectors of our community (Sanders 1998). It cannot be over-emphasised that adequate preventive measures, as well as early and aggressive treatment, educating the public about the disease to correct misconceptions and the attainment of patient compliance are paramount in controlling the disease (Grange 1999).

Healthworkers' challenges with TB

Davies (1995) holds that tuberculosis is a contagious disease caused by a mycobacterium bacillus. Infection occurs as a result of tubercle bacilli being inhaled by the host as small airborne droplets. In most cases, the germs are sealed off in the body and they do not multiply, until the body's defences can no longer control the germs and become active, making a person get tuberculosis. The perception of TB as being highly dangerous and infectious meets with contradictory reactions by people, as it is still very highly stigmatised.

Low literacy levels have been regarded as a major factor in lack of knowledge concerning TB treatment. The issue related to TB for health psychology is adherence to treatment: Peltzer (2001) found that of the 219 tuberculosis patients assessed at first diagnosis, 136 were successfully followed up; with 81 (59.6%) showing adherence and 55 (40.4%) showing non-adherence. The factors associated with such behaviour, using a discriminant analysis between adhering and non-adhering groups after six months, were instances where a patient had a supporter, health beliefs, self-efficacy and experiences with taking medication, social support, the quality of the practitioner-patient relationship and the quality and contents of counselling.

Improving knowledge and attitudes do not necessarily lead to changes in behaviour, but provide baseline information for planners of health education programmes (Westaway 1989). Westaway (1989) maintains that many TB patients only seek the help of health authorities when their disease is already at an advanced stage. In South Africa, TB health education programmes have been designed to counteract this state of affairs. Unfortunately, however, many patients suffering from the disease, more especially African hospitalised patients, still seem to lack knowledge about TB.

Coronary heart disease

Coronary heart disease is considered a disease connected to stressful situations. It is thus important that an individual's risk assessment towards coronary heart disease be taken seriously in relation to environmental factors.

Research has indicated that individuals who are more prone to coronary heart diseases are those that have the following stressful situations in their lives:

- experience of extreme situational stressors of either poverty or high-income competitiveness;
- low levels of education;
- isolation and experience of high levels of life stress as compared to those who are better educated with low levels of stress (isolation refers to a work environment where there is less decision latitude and a high level of shiftwork as well as poor social support);
- proneness to anxiety-related disease symptoms, frustration, irritability, sadness and depression;
- fatigue, job dissatisfaction and decreased libido; and
- experience of acute life stress resulting from the sudden death of particular individuals.

The consequences of suffering from coronary heart disease can, from the nature of the disease's onset, be very devastating to the patients. The following are stressors associated with the onset of the disease:

- the speed of events, which does not allow the patient to adjust (this includes the view by the patient that this could be a fatal attack, which brings about drastic changes in the person's daily life and gives very little time to adjust);
- profound physical changes such as chest pain;
- restriction to a hospital bed, which results in inactivity and depression of the major systems, e.g. circulatory, respiratory and gastro-intestinal;
- loss of health;
- discovery of one's own mortality;
- loss of dignity and privacy;
- role change or loss; and
- fear of the unknown (Fullard in Schlebusch 1990).

Patients with coronary heart disease require help in specific ways, as outlined below. Such help includes the following:

- Staff caring for patients should be sensitive.
- Adequate explanations should be provided, which prove useful in reducing anxiety during intervention and treatment of patients.
- Psychological support for both the patient and the family should be provided.
- Initial contact between the patient and the doctors should be well organised.

Prompt attention should be given to deal with anxiety-provoking issues like the sudden onset of the disease, the possibility of death and the display of complicated electronic device. Anxiety provoked by such situations is usually sustained by cognitions of possible death and this leads to depression very easily. Such uncertainties need to be put to rest in good time, to help the patient's ability to respond to treatment.

Patients who respond with denial may find it easy in the beginning, with less possibility of developing depression, but may have difficulties adjusting to the healthier lifestyle demanded by the new condition.

Early introduction of psychological management is important to deal with lessening of the severity of emotional distress, which has important prognostic implications. The explanations and information provided to the patient should match his or her educational and intellectual levels.

Adequate information should be made available as part of a routine for the maximal utilisation of treatment by the patient. Adequate information after discharge is very important, as it lessens anxiety on the part of the patient.

The protective factors found to be more influential are social support, the family (especially a sound marriage), a stable circle of friends, and cultural and religious beliefs (Konig in Schlebusch 1990).

The practice of healthy behaviours

This section will highlight practices regarded as necessary to attain acceptable health status. It will also include practices regarded in psychology as important for healthy living. These practices will be discussed in general, as well as from the perspective of research findings.

Stress control

Stress means many things to different people. To lay people, stress can be defined in terms of pressure, tension, unpleasantness or emotional response. One of the earliest models of stress was developed by Cannon (1932), who referred to stress as anything that triggers the fight-or-flight response, which means that external threats elicit increase in activity and increased arousal. The response to such threats in this mode was seen to be physiological.

The effects of stress can be positive or negative. One example of positive stress is the excitement an experienced actor feels just before a performance. In this case, the fight-or-flight response helps to improve the performance. Another example is the excitement of being in love. Negative stress can be short-term (such as the fear, pressure and need for quick decisions produced when a car suddenly swerves into your path) or long-term (such as the stress you might feel in a complex, high-pressure job). Too much stress, especially over a long period of time, can drain energy, cause undue wear and tear on the body, and make you vulnerable to illness and premature ageing.

Physical stress:
Stress caused by physical demands on the body.

Psychological stress:
Stress caused by mental or emotional demands on the body.

Stress can be divided into two major types: **physical stress** and **psychological stress**. Physical stress is created by physical demands on the body such as those caused by accidents, illness, chemical toxins, a demanding work schedule or prolonged psychological stress. Psychological stress is created by mental or emotional demands on the body. Psychological stress can simply be the result of physical stress. However, psychological stress is more often caused by mental or emotional demands from your personal beliefs, family, work or friends.

Stress management programmes have a greater percentage of focus on psychological stress. The four basic types of psychological stress are defined as follows:

- **Pressure:** An internal or external demand either to complete a task or activity within a limited time or in a specific manner.
- **Frustration:** The blocking of needs or wants.
- **Conflict:** The need to make a choice between two or more competing alternatives.
- **Anxiety/Fear:** One of two basic emotional responses to a perceived threat (the other is anger).

There are three important points about stress that need to be understood in order to develop a complete approach to stress management.

Firstly, distress involves the triggering of the fight-or-flight response and the release of energy, which is not actually needed to cope with an external situation, e.g. when you prepare yourself to escape from a lion, but there is no lion and you do not run. Your body is ready for action that does not happen.

Secondly, your body responds to any thought as though that thought concerns an event occurring in the present. It does not matter whether the thought is about the past, present or future. This is why a vivid thought accompanied by strong emotion about a past negative experience or a possible future problem triggers the fight-or-flight response.

Thirdly, people who experience the prolonged stress of severe anxiety usually have beliefs, attitudes and habitual thinking patterns that tend to perpetuate stress.

Stress management:
The process of reducing daily stress.

The process of reducing daily stress is usually referred to as **stress management**. The word 'management' is of particular importance. Your goal is not to eliminate stress (this is impossible if you are to live a

normal, healthy life), but to manage stress so that it does not prevent
you from living the life you want to live.

Basic stress management principles

- **Accept your body as a machine with a limited supply of energy:**
  The first step in stress management is to treat your body as a
  machine, which needs regular rest, maintenance and care in order
  to work properly. When you wake up each morning you begin your
  day with a limited supply of energy. It is as if your body starts with
  a charged battery and a tank full of fuel. The exact amount of
  energy you have each day varies and is different from that which
  other people have. Once this supply of energy is used up, it can only
  be replaced by taking time to rest and nourish yourself. If you fail
  to do this, your body starts to break down. While almost everyone
  with anxiety-related problems has an intellectual understanding
  of the concept of the body as a machine with a limited supply of
  energy, few actually apply it to their lives. Sometimes, childhood
  training leads to the belief that the body is unimportant. An excessive need for approval, rigid thinking, high expectations of self, or
  a tendency to suppress some or all negative feelings can also cause
  people to ignore the needs of their bodies.
- **Learn to recognise the early signs of stress and what they mean:**
  In order to apply the concept of the body as a machine, you need
  to know when stress is beginning to have a negative effect on you.
  Learning to recognise and pay attention to these early warning signs
  allows you to know when you are running low on energy. The Stress
  Symptom Inventory is designed to help you identify your own
  unique set of warning signs. One of the great lessons you need to
  learn is to assign new meaning to the physical symptoms of stress.
  These symptoms simply mean you have not taken care of yourself in
  one or more important areas. The result is that your body reacts to
  the excessive stress it experiences by producing anxiety symptoms.
  To prevent this, you need to develop skill in both recognising the
  early signs of distress and taking appropriate action at that time. By
  doing this you prevent your body from becoming stressed to the
  point where you experience excessive anxiety.

Why do some people suffer more from stress than others? The answer is
simple. All bodies are not created the same. People with anxiety-related
problems often have highly reactive bodies. For many, this is due to
inherited genetic traits. For others, it is the result of their bodies reaching
breaking point due to excessive stress from physical illness, injury,

relationship or work-related problems, or an unhealthy lifestyle.

The first step in learning how to live with a highly reactive body is to understand that symptoms of anxiety are simply messages that you have not taken care of some important need. This need may be physical, mental, emotional, spiritual or relational in nature. Understanding and accepting this idea helps you avoid exaggerating the importance of anxiety symptoms when they occur. The next step is to identify what that need is and decide on the best way to take care of it.

The physical and psychological responses to stress

The physiology of stress starts in the part of the brain that is used for reasoning, called the new cortex. A message is sent to a deeper brain structure, the pituitary gland, located above the kidneys, which controls the adrenals with a hormone called ACTH. ACTH reaches the adrenals via the bloodstream and causes the release of adrenaline into the bloodstream. Adrenaline activates various other systems to prepare the body for action. Adrenaline is responsible for an increase in heart rate, higher blood pressure and the preparation of muscles for higher functioning.

Selye (1956) who coined the expression 'general adaptation syndrome' (GAS) found that animals exposed to constant stress had smaller adrenals and a burnt-out appearance. Long-term reactions to constant hormonal secretion include stomach ulcers and vascular and coronary diseases. Selye (1956) described the GAS response in three phases. The first phase is the alarm phase, where the sympathetic nervous system is activated as described above. The second phase is resistance, where the body tries to resist the stress. The third stage, exhaustion, will be reached when stress continues for a long time.

The psychological response to stress varies between personal growth and a decrease in psychological well-being. Moderating factors will determine how an individual will perceive stressful events. Personal characteristics that will influence perception will be the perception of a loss of control, a sense of helplessness, chronic anxiety and low self-esteem.

Exercise

There has been an increasing interest in the role of exercise for health promotion. For purposes of health promotion, exercise has been conceptualised in three different ways: (1) the intention of the individual, which include aspects such as the intention to be physically fit, with emphasis on the physical and biological changes that happen as result of intentional bodily movements; (2) the outcome, which differentiates between exercise for physical fitness and for health improvement, which then touches on biological as well as psychological changes in health status; and (3) the location conceptualisation, which refers to the difference between exercise serving as a leisure or an occupational activity.

Physical benefits of exercise

Exercise has been found to affect longevity in that it is able to reduce blood pressure, help manage obesity and diabetes, provide protection against osteoporosis and thinning of bones, and reduce the occurrence of coronary heart disease (Ogden 2000). The effect of exercise on coronary heart disease happens as a result of increased muscular activity to stimulate the muscles that support the heart, an increase in the electrical activity of the heart, an increase in the individual's fibrillation and an increase in the protection of individuals from risk factors that lead to coronary diseases, e.g. hypertension and obesity (Ogden 2000).

Psychological benefits of exercise

Exercise can benefit an individual from a psychological perspective by helping with depression, anxiety and stress and increasing self-esteem and self-confidence. Many theories have reflected on the physiological and psychological approaches to the study of exercise. It has been found that improved psychological well-being is related to social activities associated with exercise and result in increased confidence and self-esteem.

Social and political factors as well as individual versus supervised exercise programmes are important for the prediction of exercise behaviour. In South Africa today, health promotion activities in limiting smoking and the prevention of coronary diseases have increased people's awareness of the need to change their lifestyles for healthy living (Ogden 2000)

Summary

This chapter has attempted to examine the background against which health psychology developed in terms of changes in perspectives on health and illness and by challenging the mind-body split, suggesting in its place a major role for the mind in the cause and treatment of illness. Health psychology attempts to move away from a simple linear model to a notion that illness can be caused by a combination of factors that can be biological, psychological and social. The chapter examined the development of the trend in health that, unlike psychosomatic medicine, focuses on research that is more specific to the discipline of psychology. Different meanings attached to the notion of health, as well as lifestyle diseases, chronic diseases and methods of health promotion and psychological management were presented and discussed in the South African context.

Further reading

Ademakoh, C.C. (1976) Alcoholism: The African scene. *Annals of the New York Academy of Sciences*, 273, 39–46.

Baum, A. & Revenson, T.A. (eds) (2001) *Handbook of Health Psychology.* Mahwah: Erlbaum.

Baxter, M. (1990) *Health and Lifestyles.* London: Routledge

Cannon, W.B. (1932) *The Wisdom of the Body.* New York: Norton.

Coulson, N., Goldstein, S. & Ntuli, A. (1998) *Promoting Health in South Africa.* Sandton: Heinemann.

Davies, P.D.O. (1994) *Clinical Tuberculosis.* London: Chapman & Hall.

De la Cancela, V., Chin, J.L. & Jenkins, Y.M. (1998) *Community Health Psychology.* New York: Routledge.

Department of Health (1999) *South Africa Demographic and Health Survey 1998.* Pretoria: Department of Health.

D'Houtaud, A. & Field, M.G. (1984) The image of health: Variations in perception by social class in a French population. *Sociology of Health and Illness*, 6, 30–60.

Engel, C.L (1977) The need for a new medical model: A challenge for biomedicine. *Science*, 196, 129–36

Forshaw, M. (2002) *Essential Health Psychology.* London: Oxford University Press.

Frye, B.A. (1991) Cultural themes in health care decision making among Cambodian refugee women. *Journal of Community Health Nursing*, 8, 33–44.

Geltenal, M. (1966) Alcoholism in contemporary African society. *Central African Journal of Medicine*, 12, 12–13.

Goodwin, D.W. (1971) Is alcoholism hereditary? *Archives of General Psychiatry*, 25, 545–8.

Goreczny, A.J. & Hersen, M. (eds) (1999) *Handbook of Pediatric and Adolescent Health Psychology.* Needham Heights: Allyn & Bacon.

Grange, J.M. (1999) Doing something about tuberculosis. *British Medical Journal* (South African edition), 10 (7), 341.

Herzlich, C. (1973) *Health and Illness: A Social Psychological Approach.* London: Academic Press.

Jellinek, E.M. (1952) *The Disease Concept of Alcoholism.* New Haven: Hillhouse Press.

Kato, M.P. (1996) *Handbook of Diversity Issues in Health Psychology.* New York: Plenum Press.

Konig, K. (1986) The role of psychological risk factors in coronary rehabilitation. *Bibliotheca Cardiologia*, 40, 74–93.

Mahapa, J.D. & Peltzer, K. (1998) Attitudes of psychiatric nurses towards traditional healers in South Africa. *Journal of Psychology in Africa*, 8, 39–54.

Marks, D.F. (1999) Health psychology as agent of change: Reconstructing health psychology. *Report of the First International on Critical and Qualitative Approaches to Health Psychology.* St John's, New Foundland.

Marks, D.F., Murray, M., Evans B. & Willig, C. (2000) *Health Psychology: Theory, Research and Practice.* London: Sage.

Mashego, T.A.B. (2000) Perceptions of father-daughter incest in African families with special reference to the mothers' role: A cultural contextualisation for intervention. Unpublished doctoral thesis, University of the North.

Matarazzo, J.D. (1982) Behavioral health: A 1990 challenge for the health sciences professions. In J.D. Matarrazzo, N.E. Miller, S.M. Weiss, J.A. Herd & S.M. Weiss (eds), *Behavioral Health: A Handbook of Health Enhancement and Disease Prevention.* New York: John Wiley.

Matsumuto, D. (1996) *Culture and Psychology.* Pacific Grove: Brooks/Cole.

Mbewu, M. (2001) Prevention is both moral and cost-effective. *Bulletin of the World Health Organization*, 79, 988–9.

Medical Research Council of South Africa (MRC). www.mrc.ac.za.

Murdock, G.P. (1980) *Theories of Illness: A World Survey.* Pittsburgh: University of Pittsburgh Press.

Mulatu, M.S. (1995) Lay beliefs about the causes of psychological and physical illness in Ethiopia. *Canadian Health Psychologist*, 3, 38–43.

Nichter, M. (1994) Illness semantics and international health: The weak lungs. *Social Science Medicine*, 38, 649–63.

Obot, I.S. (1989) Alcohol and drug related disorders. In K. Peltzer & P.O. Ebigbo (eds), *Clinical Psychology in Africa.* Frankfurt: IKO Verlag.

Ogden J. (1996) *Health Psychology: A Textbook*. Buckingham: Open University Press.

Park, L. (1992) *Cross-cultural Explanations of Illness: Murdock Revisited*. Chicago: Committee of Human Development, University of Chicago.

Peltzer, K. (1985) The therapy of alcoholics and cannabis smokers in the Zion Christian church in Malawi. *Transcultural Psychiatric Research Review*, 22, 252–5.

Peltzer, K. (2001) Factors at follow-up associated with adherence with directly observed therapy (DOT) for tuberculosis patients in South Africa. *Journal of Psychology in Africa*, 11, 165–85.

Peltzer, K. & Ebigbo, P.O. (1995) *Psychology and Health in African Cultures*. Frankfurt: IKO Verlag.

Ram, N.V. (1986) *Smoking: Third World Alert*. Oxford: Oxford University Press.

Resnick, R.J. & Rozensky, R.H. (eds) (1996) *Health Psychology through the Life Span: Practice and Research Opportunities*. Washington, DC: American Psychological Association.

Saloojee, Y. (2000) Tobacco control. *South African Health Review 2000*, pp. 1–9.

Sanders, F.N. (1998) TB: An ongoing problem. *Continuing Medical Education Journal*, 13(7), 34–7.

Schlebusch, L. (ed.) (1990) *Clinical Health Psychology: A Behavioural Perspective*. Halfway House: Southern.

Schwarzer, R. (1992) Self efficacy in the adoption and maintenance of health behaviours: Theoretical approaches and a new model. In R. Schwarzer (ed.), *Self Efficacy: Thought Control of Action*. Washington, DC: Hemisphere.

Semmes, C.E. (1996) *Racism, Health and Post-Industrialism: A Notion of African American Health*. Wesport: Praeger.

Seydel, E., Taal, E. & Wiegman, O. (1990) Risk appraisal, outcome and self efficacy expectancies: Cognitive factors in preventative behaviour related to cancer. *Psychology and Health*, 4, 99–109.

Seyle, H. (1956) *The Stress of Life*. New York: McGraw-Hill.

Shweder, R.A., Much, N.C., Mahapara, M. & Park, L. (1997) The big three explanations of morality (autonomy, community, divinity) and the big three explanations of suffering. In A.M. Brandt & P. Rozin (eds), *Morality and Health*. London: Routledge.

Stroebe, W. (2000) *Social Psychology and Health* (2nd edition). Buckingham: Open University Press.

Stroebe, W. & Stroebe, M. (1995) *Social Psychology and Health*. Buckingham: Open University Press.

Westaway, M.S. (1989) Knowledge, beliefs and feelings about tuberculosis. *Health Education Research Journal*, 4(2), 205–11.

World Health Organisation (1986) *Ottawa Charter for Health Promotion*. Copenhagen: WHO

Yach, D. & Joubert, G. (2000) Deaths related to smoking in South Africa in 1984 and projected deaths among Coloured and Blacks in the year 2000. *South African Medical Journal*, 73, 400–2.

Yach, D. & Townsend, G.S. (1988) Smoking and health in South Africa. *South African Medical Journal*, 73, 391–9.

16 Research and Statistics

T. B. Pretorius

Objectives

After studying this chapter you should:

- have a broad overview of the research process
- be able to describe the various elements of the process
- be able to use tables, graphs and basic statistics to summarise and describe a data set.

Introduction

The preceding chapters have exposed you to various ideas, theories, explanations and applications in psychology. We call this the 'body of knowledge' of psychology. This 'body of knowledge' represents the research efforts of a multitude of scholars. We would not know or understand certain aspects of human development, how people learn, what contributes to health and so forth, if it was not for the process of continuous renewal of knowledge.

We are faced with rapid social change, with pressing social problems and a complex social environment. Successfully responding to these challenges is only possible through knowledge generation and knowledge revitalisation – which are the primary focuses of research. This chapter briefly exposes you to the essential elements of the research process.

The research process

The various stages in the research process are illustrated in Figure 16.1.

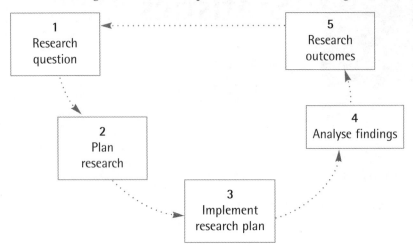

FIGURE 16.1: The research process

The essential elements of each of these stages in the research process are discussed in this chapter.

Research questions

In the course of our everyday lives we often ask questions because we want to learn more about something or someone. The word 'research' comes from the root 'to search'. This search refers to the finding of more information or knowledge that is relevant to some issue or problem. When we do research we are essentially searching for evidence that would answer some questions we have posed. Thus, we understand research to be a process that begins with the asking of questions.

The questions that drive scientific research originate in various ways, for example:

- They can arise out of basic curiosity: Is living in Port Elizabeth less stressful than living in Cape Town?
- They can be suggested by some theory: Does overload in the work situation lead to depression?
- They can be driven by some pressing need: Could medication prevent mother-to-child transmission of HIV/AIDS?
- They can flow from pressing societal problems: What is the relationship between crime and unemployment?

For the rest of this chapter, it will be useful to construct a hypothetical research project to guide us through the various stages of the research process. Support groups have been shown to positively influence addictive behaviours. For example, Alcoholics Anonymous has had some success in helping people cope with addiction to alcohol. Thus the question arises: Does support from others influence cessation of smoking?

Planning the research

Stating the expectations: The hypothesis

In research, a hypothesis is used to indicate the researcher's expectation about the outcome of the research. In other words, we should have some idea of what role support from others could play in giving up smoking. This expectation is normally phrased in terms of a tentative statement in the beginning of the research. This is called a hypothesis. An example in such a statement could be: 'There is a relationship between support from others and cessation of smoking'. We call a hypothesis a tentative statement because it is a prediction rather than a proven fact – we still have to conduct the study to find support for our prediction.

In essence, a hypothesis is our research question rephrased as a statement. Remember we talked about research being a process that starts with the asking of a question. In our example we asked: Is there any relationship between support and cessation of smoking? When this is rephrased as a predictive statement: 'There is a relationship between support from others and cessation of smoking', it is called a hypothesis.

However, such predictive statements should meet some criteria before they actually qualify as hypothesis. Shavelson (1991) suggests three guidelines to determine whether a hypotheses is adequately formulated:

- A hypothesis should predict a particular relationship between two variables (more about variables later).
- A hypothesis should be stated clearly and unambiguously.
- A hypothesis should be testable.

Operationalisation: Specifying the variables

A crucial aspect in planning the research is selecting and defining for research purposes the **variables** to be studied. The word variable comes from the root 'to vary'. In essence therefore a variable is any property of a person, an object or event that can take on different values or different levels, i.e. that can vary from person to person or object to object. For example, eye colour is a variable because it is a property of an object (an eye) that can vary (brown, blue, black). In our example, the

Variable:
Any property of a person, object or event that can take on different values or levels.

two variables are support from others (a lot/very little) and smoking cessation (stopped/did not stop/smoked less).

In the research literature, variables are classified according to how they have been obtained or by virtue of their relationship to one another. If the values of a variable have been obtained through a process of counting using whole numbers (integers) these variables are said to be discrete. Chairs in a lecture room or cars in a parking lot would be examples of discrete variables, since you count chairs or cars in whole numbers (e.g. 10.3 chairs would not be feasible). When the values of a variable are obtained through measurement (for example measuring the height and weight of a person), these variables are said to be continuous variables. Thus a **discrete variable** is a variable that can only be assessed in whole numbers, whereas a **continuous variable** can take on any value, even a fraction of a value.

Discrete variable: Variable that can only be expressed in whole numbers.

Continuous variable: Variable that can take on any value.

Discrete and continuous variables

It is useful to pause briefly to further highlight the difference between discrete and continuous variables. This difference is essential, especially with regard to proper selection of analytical techniques for the different types of variables. Continuous variables, unlike discrete ones often range from low to high. Where there is a definite sense of a continuum (range), they can even assume a decimal value (55.5%) and this type of variable can be used in a range of mathematical calculations. For example, exam results would be an example of a continuous variable, since there is a continuum (30% is less than 50%) and one can calculate the class 'average' by adding all the results together and dividing the total by the number of students in the class. On the other hand, consider street addresses: 10 Mandela Drive, 12 Mandela Drive and 14 Mandela Drive. Although there is a range from low to high, there is no continuum (i.e. 12 Mandela Drive is not less than 14 Mandela Drive) and these values cannot be used in mathematical calculations (i.e. 10 plus 12 Mandela Drive divided by two does not lead to an average of 11 Mandela Drive).

Independent variable: Variable that is manipulated by the researcher to determine its effect on another variable.

Dependent variable: Variable that is influenced by the independent variable.

Intervening variable: Any variable that influences the effect of the independent variable and dependent variable.

Variables may also be classified in terms of the relationship between them. In this regard we distinguish between an **independent** and a **dependent variable**. An independent variable is a variable that is selected, measured or manipulated by the researcher in order to determine what effect this variable has on another variable. In our example, we would be interested in the effect of support from others on smoking behaviour. Thus support from others would constitute our independent variable. The variable that is being influenced is called the dependent variable. In this example it is smoking behaviour.

Given the complexities of human behaviour, the relationship between two variables might be influenced by a third variable, called an **intervening variable**. An intervening variable is any variable that influences the effect of the independent variable on the dependent variable. For example, in our example, the effects of support from others on smoking behaviour might be influenced by self-esteem (i.e. people low in self-esteem might be more likely to benefit from support from others in their attempt to stop smoking).

Roles of intervening variables

In a paper that is under consideration for publication at the time of writing this chapter, I distinguished between four different roles that intervening variables could possibly play in the relationship between the independent and dependent variable (Pretorius, under editorial review):

Direct role: The intervening variable directly affects the dependent variable irrespective of the independent variable. For example, those high in self-esteem would find it easier to stop smoking irrespective of whether they receive support from others.

Moderating role: The intervening variable interacts with the independent variable in affecting the dependent variable. For example, support from others would only influence smoking behaviour for those low in self-esteem. For those high in self-esteem, there would be no relationship between support and smoking behaviour.

Mediating role: The intervening variable operates as a mediator when it transforms the independent variable in some way. In this regard, the intervening variable is the mechanism through which the independent variable influences the dependent variable. For example, support from others provokes feelings of dependence by those high in self-esteem and thus it does not impact on smoking behaviour.

Indirect role: The intervening variable may not be directly related to the dependent variable, but may have an indirect effect by influencing perceptions of the independent variable. Thus people with low self-esteem would perceive support from others positively, which in turn would influence their smoking behaviour.

The major difference between mediating and indirect roles relates to causality. In the mediating effect, the independent variable affects the dependent variable via the intervening variable, whereas in the indirect effect the intervening variable affects the dependent variable via the independent variable.

The 'how of research': Methods and methodology

Methodology refers to the question of how research should be planned, structured and carried out'. Research methods in the social sciences can broadly be classified into two main categories: qualitative and quantitative. Qualitative and quantitative methodologies basically refer to models of how research should be conducted. At a very crude level one can define **quantitative methods** as those that produce numbers that can be analysed with statistics, for example a survey on students' attitudes

Methodology:
The way in which research is planned, structured and carried out.

Qualitative methods:
Methods of research that oroduce numbers that can be analysed statistically.

towards a student radio station would produce a quantitative indication of how many students support such a radio station. Quantitative methods can be divided into two types: (1) those directly eliciting responses from subjects by questioning (questionnaires, schedules and interview guides); and (2) those utilising mechanical observers (cameras, telescopes, microscopes). The sources of quantitative data can be classified into **primary sources** (data gathered and used by the researcher) and **secondary sources** (data used by the researcher but gathered by someone else – for example, census reports, vital statistics records, company files and sales receipts). **Qualitative methods** on the other hand, lead to data that is more textual in nature, i.e. in the form of words rather than numbers. Examples of such qualitative methods include participant observation, discourse analysis and in-depth interviewing.

The qualitative/quantitative distinction is the subject of a huge debate in the social sciences at the moment. At the heart of this debate is the argument that a choice of a methodology reflects a particular view of science or philosophical/theoretical speculation on the nature of science. In this regard it is assumed that the positivist subscribes to a quantitative methodology while the anti-positivist or phenomenologist subscribes to a qualitative methodology. While this is an interesting debate, it is too complex to discuss in detail here. The following represents the main differences between the two approaches:

- Quantitative methodologies result in numerical data, while qualitative methodologies deal primarily with linguistic data.
- Quantitative methodologies are based on viewing reality as an objective phenomenon that lends itself to accurate observation and measurement. Qualitative methodologies, on the other hand are characterised by an emphasis on understanding or the illumination of meanings. They view social reality as created by the participants in a given social context, essentially a construction based upon the actor's frame of reference.
- In quantitative methods, there is a rigid emphasis on a systematic logic of enquiry, based on the assumption that such a systematic method of inquiry enables us to make observations that are independent of opinion, bias and prejudice. On the other hand, the attitudes associated with qualitative modes of enquiry have been described as open and reflexive. The modes of enquiry are supposed to be organic and emergent, allowing for discovery and for decisions to change course. Because the process is open to feedback, it does not encourage artificial closure, as would a pre-planned linear sequence of testing.
- In quantitative methods, the researcher is often detached from the phenomena being studied. In qualitative methods, the researcher's

Primary sources: Data gathered by the researcher.

Secondary sources: Data gathered by someone else.

Qualitative methods: Methods of research that leads to data that is textual in nature.

role is participative with respect to the subject. There is a tendency to treat the subject as a co-investigator engaged in a relationship of collaboration and reciprocity with the researcher. Subjects are consulted as to whether interpretations and conclusions are true to their experience or valid for the setting studied.

Despite the very lively debate surrounding the qualitative/quantitative distinction, I am, however, convinced that qualitative methods are in essence not an alternative to quantitative methods, but that qualitative and quantitative approaches provide complementary evidence. Other methodologists have advised that choice of method should be suited to the nature of the research problem. Thus, the issue of which method to use becomes redefined as a question of when and for what purpose a given method may be most fruitful. The use of multiple research methods within the same research project is referred to as **triangulation**.

    The use of multiple methods (i.e. triangulation) within a single research programme lends itself to either synchronic or diachronic use. In the **synchronic articulation**, qualitative and quantitative data is collected simultaneously. In this synchronic mode of data collection, qualitative and quantitative data is used in a complementary fashion, since they provide different perspectives on the same phenomenon.

    In the **diachronic articulation**, qualitative data is collected either before (called qualitative primary) or after quantitative data (called quantitative primary). When collected after quantitative data, qualitative data is used to supplement, illustrate and highlight quantitative data. When collected before quantitative data, qualitative data is used to generate hypotheses and items for questionnaire construction.

Selecting participants

If a researcher is interested in the effect of support from others on smoking behaviour, it is obvious that in doing research it would be virtually impossible to include all smokers in the research programme. The researcher would normally select a limited number of smokers for inclusion in the research study. All smokers are referred to as the **population**, while the selected group that participates in the research programme is referred to as the **sample**. In other words, a population is the total collection of individuals or objects that forms the focus of the research, while a sample is a selected part or subset of the population.

    Although only a selected group of smokers would form part of the study, it should be obvious that the ultimate aim of the researcher would be to draw some general conclusions about the effect of support from others on smoking behaviour. In other words, ultimately the researcher

Triangulation:
The use of multiple research methods in one research project.

Synchronic articulation:
Method in which qualitative and quantitative data are collected simultaneously.

Diachronic articulation:
Method in which qualitative data are collected after quantitative data, or vice versa.

Population:
Total number of people or objects that forms the subject of research.

Sample:
A selected part of the population.

would want to say something about smokers in general and not only about the smokers that participated in the study. Such general statements can only be made with confidence if the selected group of smokers in some way provides a mirror image of all smokers. In research we say that the selected group (or sample) should be **representative** of the larger group (or the population). For example, if from known data we know that 50% of all smokers are over the age of 21 years and 30% of all smokers are women, a representative sample should also contain the same proportions in terms of age and gender. A sample that is not representative of the population is referred to as a **biased sample**.

In research, we attempt to ensure that a sample is representative through random sampling. **Random sampling** is the process of selecting participants in such a way that: (1) every member of the population has an equal chance of being selected as part of the sample and (2) the selection of any member of the population does not influence the chances of any other member of the population being selected. There are various ways of obtaining a random sample, for example, throwing all the names into a hat and randomly selecting members of the sample from the hat. The selection of the lotto winning numbers is also an example of random selection. Most statistics textbooks include a table of random numbers, which is often used to select a random sample.

Collecting data

In this phase, the researcher enters the research setting and conducts the research in accordance with the planning done in the previous phase. Although the issue of ethics in social science research should be considered at the outset of the research project, it is at this stage that the research actually impacts on participants and therefore ethics should be observed very strictly. Many introductory texts do not deal with the issue of ethics in scientific research and very often it is dealt with (if at all) as an afterthought in more advanced research programmes.

In general, psychological research is guided by ethical principles laid down by the American Psychological Association (1983). These principles emphasise the following:

- It is the responsibility of the individual researcher to evaluate the ethical acceptability of any research project and to observe stringent safeguards to protect the rights of human participants.
- Each researcher remains fully responsible for their work and this responsibility is extended to include not only their own actions but also that of their collaborators, research assistants or students.
- Participants should be fully informed of the details of the research

so that they can make an informed decision as to whether they want to participate.

- Where methodological requirements make the use of concealment or deception necessary and the researcher has established that no alternative procedures are available, then participants need to be debriefed (post research explanation) as soon as possible after the research has been completed.
- The researcher has the responsibility of emphasising the participant's right to decline or discontinue participation in the research study.
- It is the researcher's responsibility to protect subjects from harm, to inform them of any possible risks and to minimise any stress that may be produced by the research.
- The principle should be applied that information obtained about a research participant is confidential unless otherwise agreed upon in advance.

Analysing the research data

Let us assume that in the hypothetical research project on smoking we collected the following information related to the gender of the participants and the number of cigarettes they smoke per day:

Participant number	Gender	No. of cigarettes	Participant number	Gender	No. of cigarettes
1	F	21	21	F	20
2	F	21	22	F	21
3	F	19	23	M	30
4	M	21	24	F	20
5	F	38	25	F	19
6	F	39	26	F	20
7	F	19	27	F	24
8	F	21	28	F	28
9	M	26	29	F	21
10	F	19	30	F	24
11	F	21	31	F	44
12	M	21	32	F	25
13	M	21	33	F	33
14	F	20	34	M	35
15	M	29	35	F	25
16	F	21	36	M	47
17	M	20	37	F	21
18	F	25	38	F	26
19	F	20	39	M	36
20	F	21	40	F	20

In the above table, 'participant number' simply refers to a code assigned to each participant to identify or distinguish them; F refers to female, while M refers to male. Thus, participant number 1 is a female who reported smoking 21 cigarettes per day.

Although the data in the above table is neatly arranged in rows and columns, still they are only meaningless numbers and labels. If properly analysed, however, these numbers or scores can provide us with rich information relating to our research objectives. The tool that we use to analyse these research data is statistics. I emphasised the word tool because so often the study of statistics becomes an end in itself, with the focus entirely on proper calculations, and there is a tendency to forget that statistics are simply a means to an end and not an end in themselves.

Descriptive statistics:
Statistics used to describe and summarise data.

Inferential statistics:
Statistics used to draw inferences based on data collected from a sample.

In the first instance, we should reduce and summarise the above research data so that it becomes more meaningful. This is done using **descriptive statistics**. Once we understand the essential features of our data we would then wish to draw conclusions about our population based on what we know about the sample. This is achieved by means of **inferential statistics**. Descriptive statistics, therefore are used to describe and summarise data, while inferential statistics are used to draw inferences about the population based on data we have collected from a sample. Since this is an introductory chapter, the focus is only on descriptive statistics. Descriptive statistics entail the following:
- the use of tables and graphs to condense and summarise data;
- measures of central tendency, which refer to single numbers that best describe the essential characteristics of the data; and
- measures of variability, which provide an indication of how much scores vary from one another.

The use of tables to summarise data: Frequency distributions

Frequency of occurrence lies at the heart of statistical analysis. It allows us to create order from confusion. Meaningfully arranged, numbers can tell us a story (LAPIN 1980).

Ungrouped frequency distributions

Frequency distribution:
Summary of the frequency that each category of the variable occurs.

A useful way of summarising the above research data would be to list the categories of the variable (for example in the case of gender: Male/Female) and then count the number of times each category occurs. This is referred to as a **frequency distribution**, since it provides a summary of the frequency (the number of times) that each category of the variable occurs.

Below is a frequency distribution of gender:

Categories of gender	f	rf	
		Prop.	Perc.
Male	10	0.25	25
Female	30	0.75	75
	N = 40		

The symbol f is used to denote frequencies. In other words, there were 10 male and 30 women participants. The total number of participants is indicated by the symbol N (i.e. 40). The symbol rf refers to relative frequencies, which is the proportion or percentage of participants falling into a particular category. In other words, 10 out of the 40 participants were male representing a proportion of 0.25 or a percentage of 25%. Relative frequencies are obtained in the following way:

$rf = f \times N$

where: f = frequency in a particular category

N = total number of participants

Thus, to calculate relative frequencies for the category Female: there were 30 women out of 40 participants. The proportion of women therefore was 30/40, which equals 0.75. The percentage of women would be 0.75×100, which equals 75%.

In the preceding example, the variable 'gender' only had two categories (or values), namely male and female. In this case, the actual category is listed together with the frequency with which it occurs. This is referred to as an **ungrouped frequency distribution**, where the values (or categories) of the variable are used separately and not grouped together.

Grouped frequency distribution

Very often, a variable may take on a range of different values. For example, note that 'number of cigarettes' ranges from as low as 19 to as high as 47. In theory, we would therefore have about 29 values listed, which would not lead to an informative or practical frequency distribution. In these instances we would use a **grouped frequency distribution** where the values of the variables are grouped together in classes. For example, we could combine 19, 20, 21, 22 and 23 into the class 19–23.

In constructing a grouped frequency distribution, we are guided by two considerations:

Ungrouped frequency distribution:
Frequency distribution where the values or categories of the variable are not grouped together.

Grouped frequency distribution:
Frequency distribution where the values or categories of the variable are grouped together in classes.

- **The number of classes**: Common sense should prevail with regard to the number of classes. We should not have too many or too few groups, which would make the interpretation of the table difficult. As a rule of thumb, between 5 and 15 groups are recommended. In our example, let us decide on 10 classes or groups.
- **The range of scores that we are dealing with**: The range is simply the highest score minus the lowest score, that is $47 - 19 = 28$.

These two factors determine our **interval size**, which is the number of scores that would be contained in each group. Interval size is obtained by dividing the range by the number of classes. Thus: range/number of classes = $28/10 = 2.8$. Rounded off to the nearest integer, it is 3. Thus, if we use 10 classes or groups of scores, each class would contain 3 scores.

The lowest class should start with a score that is a multiple of the interval size. The lowest value for 'number of cigarettes' is 19. The first score below that which is a multiple of 3 (the interval size) is 18. Thus our first class would be 18–20 (containing 18, 19, 20). The next class would be 21–23 (21, 22, 23). In this way, we would continue until we have constructed all 10 classes. After constructing the 10 classes we would in the normal way determine the frequency of each class interval.

Classes	f	rf			Cumulative		
		Prop.	Perc.		Cum. f	Cum. prop.	Cum. perc.
45–47	1	0.03	3		40	1.00	100
42–44	1	0.03	3		39	0.98	98
39–41	1	0.03	3		38	0.95	95
36–38	2	0.05	5		37	0.93	93
33–35	2	0.05	5		35	0.88	88
30–32	1	0.03	3		33	0.83	83
27–29	2	0.05	5		32	0.80	80
24–26	7	0.18	18		30	0.75	75
21–23	12	0.30	30		23	0.58	58
18–20	<u>11</u>	0.28	28		11	0.28	28
	N = 40						

To illustrate the fundamentals of the above grouped frequency distribution, let us take the category 24–26:

- The f (frequency) column indicates that 7 participants reported that they smoke from 24 to 26 cigarettes a day. According to the rf (relative frequency column), this represents a proportion of 0.18 (7/40) and 18% (7/40 × 100) of the total number of participants.

- The next three columns are called cumulative frequency, cumulative proportion and cumulative percentage. Cumulative frequency indicates the number of scores falling into and below a particular class. The cumulative frequency of the class 24–26 is 30. This means that 30 participants indicated that they smoked 26 or fewer cigarettes a day. This is obtained by taking the frequency of the lowest class (18–20) and adding the frequencies of the second lowest class (21–23): 11 + 12 = 23. Add to that the frequency of the third lowest class (24–26): 23 + 7 = 30, and continue with these successive additions until you reach the highest class. Cumulative proportion is the cumulative frequency divided by the total number of participants and reflects the proportion of participants falling into or below a particular class. Thus, for the class 24–26, the cumulative proportion would be 30/40=0.75. In other words, the proportion of participants that smoked 26 or fewer cigarettes a day is 0.75. Cumulative percentage is cumulative proportion multiplied by 100 and indicates the percentage of participants falling into or below a particular class. For the class 24–26, the cumulative percentage is 75% (0.75 × 100), which means that 75% of the participants smoked 26 or less cigarettes a day.

Bivariate frequency distribution

The frequency tables that we constructed above represent the distribution of scores on one variable (i.e. gender or cigarette consumption). These are referred to as univariate frequency distributions. A **bivariate frequency distribution** is a comparative distribution of two variables. For example, we could take gender and number of cigarettes together and construct one bivariate frequency distribution. Not only would such a distribution give us the same information as the two separate distributions above, it would also tell us how values of one variable are distributed relative to values of another variable. To construct such a bivariate distribution of gender and number of cigarettes we would, for each category of gender, count the number of participants in each category of cigarettes smoked per day.

Bivariate frequency distribution:
A comparative distribution of two variables.

The result would be the following:

Cigarettes per day		Gender		Row total
		Female	Male	
45–47	f		1	1
	Row %		100.0%	100.0%
	Column %	10.0%	2.5%	
	Total %		2.5%	2.5%
42–44	f	1		1
	Row %	100.0%		100.0%
	Column %	3.3%		2.5%
	Total %	2.5%		2.5%
39–41	f	1		1
	Row %	100.0%		100.0%
	Column %	3.3%		2.5%
	Total %	2.5%		2.5%
36–38	f	1	1	2
	Row %	50.0%	50.0%	100.0%
	Column %	3.3%	10.0%	5.0%
	Total %	2.5%	2.5%	5.0%
33–35	f	1	1	2
	Row %	50.0%	50.0%	100.0%
	Column %	3.3%	10.0%	5.0%
	Total %	2.5%	2.5%	5.0%
30–32	f	1		1
	Row %	100.0%		100.0%
	Column %	10.0%		2.5%
	Total %	2.5%		2.5%
27–29	f	1	1	2
	Row %	50.0%	50.0%	100.0%
	Column %	3.3%	10.0%	5.0%
	Total %	2.5%	2.5%	5.0%
24–26	f	6	1	7
	Row %	85.7%	14.3%	100.0%
	Column %	20.0%	10.0%	17.5%
	Total %	15.0%	2.5%	17.5%
21–23	f	9	3	12
	Row %	75.0%	25.0%	100.0%
	Column %	30.0%	30.0%	30.0%
	Total %	22.5%	7.5%	30.0%
18–20	f	10	1	11
	Row %	90.9%	9.1%	100.0%
	Column %	33.3%	10.0%	27.5%
	Total %	25.0%	2.5%	27.5%
	f	30	10	40
	Column%	75.0%	25.0%	100.0%

In the above table, the column totals are similar to the univariate distri-bution for gender, while the row totals are similar to the univariate distribution for cigarettes. The table does, however, also provide us with additional information, for example number of males (1) and females (10) that smoke from 18 to 20 cigarettes per day. Each of the blocks in the table is referred to as a cell. Thus, in the above example we have 20 cells (10 categories for cigarettes × 2 categories for gender). Each cell contains the following:

- The first row of each cell contains the frequencies (f). If one takes the row 18–20, 10 females indicated that they smoke between 18–20 cigarettes a day as opposed to 1 male.
- The second row of each cell contains the row percentage. This refers to the frequencies in each cell as a percentage of the row total. Thus:

$$\text{Row \%} = \frac{\text{cell } f}{\text{row total}} \times 100$$

Taking the 18–20, females it would be:

$$\text{Row \%} = \frac{10}{11} \times 100$$
$$= 90.9\%$$

The row refers to 18–20 cigarettes a day. The total number of people that reported smoking 18–20 cigarettes a day is 11 (row total). Of these, 10 were female. In other words, 90.9% of those that reported smoking 18–20 cigarettes were female.

- The second row in each cell is the column percentages. This refers to the frequencies in each cell as a percentage of the column total. Thus:

$$\text{Column \%} = \frac{\text{cell } f}{\text{column total}} \times 100$$

Taking the 18–20, females it would be:

$$\text{Column \%} = \frac{10}{30} \times 100$$
$$= 33.3\%$$

The column refers to females. The total number of females was 30. Of these, 10 reported smoking 18–20 cigarettes a day. In other words, 33.3% of all females reported smoking 18–20 cigarettes a day.

- The last row in each cell is the total percentage. This refers to the frequency in each cell as a percentage of the total sample. Thus:

$$\text{Total \%} = \frac{\text{cell } f}{\text{total sample (N)}} \times 100$$

Taking the 18–20, females it would be:

$$\text{Total \%} = \frac{10}{40} \times 100$$

$$= 25\%$$

The total sample (N) consisted of 40 participants. Of these, 10 were females who reported smoking 18–20 cigarettes a day. In other words, 25% of the total sample are females who reported smoking 18–20 cigarettes a day.

The various percentages answers different questions. The row percentages provide an answer to the question (using 18–20, females): 'What percentage of those that reported that they smoked 18–20 cigarettes a day is female?' The column percentages provide an answer to the question: 'What percentage of the females reported smoking 18–20 cigarettes a day?' The total percentage provides an answer to the question: 'What percentage of the total sample were females that reported smoking 18–20 cigarettes a day?' Selecting a percentage to use depends on the questions that the researcher wants to answer. In general, it is suggested that the percentages associated with the independent variable are used. In our example, it is more likely that the number of cigarettes smoked is influenced by gender, i.e. that gender is the independent variable. Therefore, since gender is the column variable, the appropriate percentages to use would be the column percentages.

Quick frequency distributions: Stem-and-leaf display

Stem-and-leaf display:
Display in which data are sorted into stems (leading digits) and leaves (trailing digits.

A very quick and useful alternative to the frequency distributions discussed above is what is referred to as a **stem-and-leaf** display. In a stem-and-leaf display, data is sorted into stems (leading digits) and leaves (trailing digits). In such a display, each score is broken down into a leading digit and a trailing digit. For example, a score such as 191 could have a leading digit of 1 (stem) and a trailing digit of 91 (leaf) or a stem of 19 and a leaf of 1. The cigarette smoking data had a range of 19 to 47. Thus our stems could be 1, 2, 3, 4 – representing 10, 20, 30, 40. Using this data, a stem-and-leaf display would look like this:

Stem	Leaf
1	9 9 9 9
2	0 0 0 0 0 0 1 1 1 1 1 1 1 1 1 1 1 4 4 5 5 5 6 6 8 9
3	0 3 5 6 8 9 4
4	7

A stem of 1 and a leaf of 9 represent 19. Thus in the above display we can count four 19s. Similarly a stem of 4 with leaves of 4 and 7 represent 44 and 47 respectively.

In the above display the data appears quite compressed. Note that the stem of 2 has about 28 leaves. A more useful approach would be to repeat stem values twice, once for low-valued leaves (for example, 0–4) and once for high-valued leaves (for example, 5–9). If we use the stem values twice, the stem-and-leaf display would look like this:

Stem	Leaf
1	9 9 9 9
2	0 0 0 0 0 0 1 1 1 1 1 1 1 1 1 1 1 1 4 4
2*	5 5 5 6 6 8 9
3	0 3
3*	5 6 8 9
4	4
4*	7

Note that in the above display, 2 is used for all values from 20 to 24, while 2* is used for all values from 25 to 29. The same is true for all other stems. From this stem-and-leaf display, one can count the occurrence of a value. Thus, we can see that there were four 19s, seven 20s, three 25s etc. The stem-and-leaf display has the advantages of both the grouped and ungrouped frequency distributions. One can see the occurrence of a single score (for example, four 19s) as well as a group of scores (for example, four scores in the category 35–39).

Stem-and-leaf displays are particularly useful in comparing two separate distributions (i.e. bivariate distributions discussed above). For example, a stem-and-leaf display comparing males and females in terms of number of cigarettes would look like this:

Males		Females
Leaf	Stem	Leaf
	1	9 9 9 9
1 1 1 0	2	0 0 0 0 0 1 1 1 1 1 1 1 1 4 4
9 6	2*	5 5 5 6 8
0	3	3
6 5	3*	8 9
	4	4
7	4*	

From this display, one can see that the majority of women are clustered at the lower end of the number of cigarettes consumed.

Graphic presentation of data

One of the unique features of the stem-and-leaf display is that it can also be seen as a pictorial or graphic presentation of scores. The more traditional forms of graphs are the histogram and the frequency polygon. Before discussing these two types of graphs, it is important to highlight some general characteristics of graphs:

- Most graphs use two lines that are perpendicular (placed at right angles) to one another. The horizontal line is called the *x*-axis or **abscissa**, while the vertical line is called the *y*-axis or the **ordinate**.
- In some graphs, two lines (//) are used on either the vertical or horizontal axis to indicate values that are left out.
- When used to summarise the occurrence of scores (i.e. frequencies), the score is listed on the *x*-axis, while the frequencies are listed on the *y*-axis.

Bar charts and histograms

A histogram is a graph in which the frequencies associated with each score (or group of scores) are displayed as a vertical bar. When these vertical bars are used to display the frequencies of discrete categories (such at the categories of gender) the graph is called a bar chart. Using the frequency distribution of gender in our previous example, the bar chart would look like this:

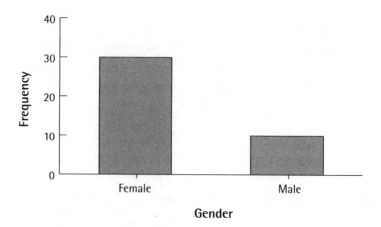

In the bar chart the categories of gender are listed on the *x*-axis and the frequencies on the y-axis. The height of each bar corresponds to the frequency for each category. Also note the gap between the bars that is used to indicate discrete categories. When working with continuous data or data that has been grouped into different classes, the bars would in fact touch each other. In this case, the graph would be called a histogram. A histogram for our data on cigarette smoking would look like this:

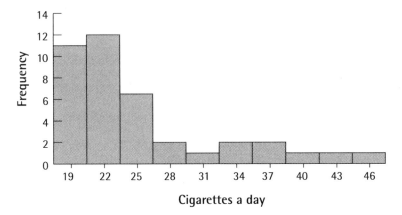

Cigarettes a day

Some characteristics of the histogram include the following:

- Like the bar chart, the frequencies associated with each class (group of scores) are listed on the y-axis.
- However, unlike the bar chart, the x-axis does not denote discrete categories, but is used to indicate groups of scores organised into classes.
- The vertical bars share common boundaries, indicating continuous scores. Compare this with the bar chart, where the bars for the variable gender do not touch.
- Also note that rather than the various classes (for example, 18–20) the midpoint of each class (for example, 19) is listed on the x-axis.

Frequency polygon

An alternative to using bars to indicate frequencies is to use a solid dot and then to join all the dots using a solid line. This is referred to as a frequency polygon (also sometimes called a line graph). A frequency polygon for the data on cigarette smoking is shown below:

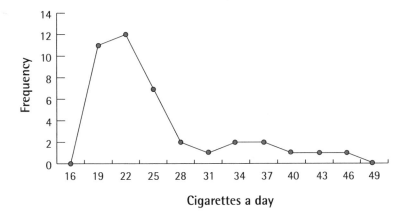

Cigarettes a day

In this polygon, the midpoint of each class is listed on the *x*-axis. Above each midpoint a solid dot is placed corresponding to the frequency of that class. The dots are then joined together with the line. Also note that two additional midpoints were added, one below the lowest class (16) and one above the highest class (49). This is done to anchor the lines of the frequency polygon to the *x*-axis.

Since graphs create a powerful visual impression, there are several tricks that can be used to create misleading impressions. The two graphs below are presentations of the same data set.

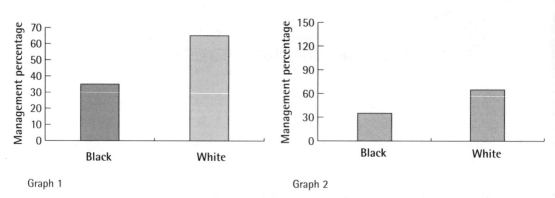

Graph 1   Graph 2

The two graphs relate to the percentage of black and white employees in management positions at a particular company. Both graphs indicate that 35% of management employees are black and 65% are white. The visual effect of the two graphs, however, is quite different. This indicates that simply changing the range of values on the *y*-axis can communicate two quite different pictures. Imagine which graph a company will use in order to convince others that they are doing quite well in terms of employment equity. To prevent graphs from being misleading, psychologists have adopted the 'two-thirds high rule' (APA 1983). This rule states that the *y*-axis should be constructed in such a way that the highest frequency on this axis should be approximately two-thirds the length of the *x*-axis. In our example, it would mean that the highest frequency of 65% should be located at the point where the *y*-axis is approximately two-thirds the length of the *x*-axis.

Shapes of distributions

When data is summarised in graphic form the resulting graph can take on a variety of shapes. The shape of the graph provides important information that is used when deciding on appropriate statistical techniques. There are two important concepts related to the shape of the graph, namely symmetry and modality.

Symmetrical distributions

Symmetrical distributions are distributions shaped in such a way that the left and right halves of the distribution are mirror images of each other.

Symmetrical distribution:
Distribution shaped so that the left and right halves mirror each other.

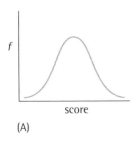
(A)

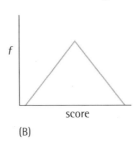
(B)

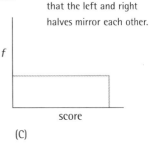
(C)

Figures A, B, and C are all symmetrical distributions, since if the graph is sliced into two halves they would be mirror images of each other. Figure A represents a bell-shaped distribution that is called a **normal distribution**. You will learn about this a lot more in subsequent statistics courses. In the normal distribution, the greater number of frequencies are clustered in the centre and tend to trail off towards both extremes. Social scientists believe that a large number of phenomena (for example, height and weight) are normally distributed in the population. For example, most people would be clustered in the middle range of height, with a few extremely tall people and a few extremely short people.

Normal distribution:
Distribution in which frequencies cluster in the centre.

Bell-shaped distributions may also differ in terms of flatness or peakedness of the distribution. This is referred to as **kurtosis**.

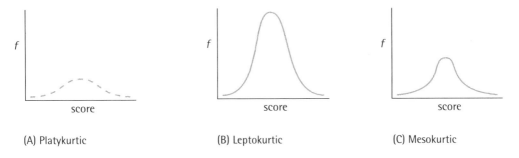

(A) Platykurtic   (B) Leptokurtic   (C) Mesokurtic

Figure B represents a **leptokurtic** distribution, which is characterised by a relatively high peak in comparison with the normal distribution, which results from most scores being clustered around the midpoint of the graph. Figure A represents a **platykurtic** distribution, which appears relatively flat in comparison with the normal distribution as a result of a more evenly distribution of scores. The normal distribution is represented by neither a too flat nor too peaked distribution and is called a **mesokurtic** distribution (Figure C).

A distribution (or graph) that is not symmetrical is referred to as an **asymmetrical distribution**. This occurs when the highest frequency of

Asymmetrical distribution:
Distribution in which the highest frequency of scores is clustered at either end of the distribution.

scores is clustered at either end of the distribution. In this sense, the 'hump' of a distribution that produces a peak is not in the centre but located at either the left or right side of the graph and the distribution is said to be skewed.

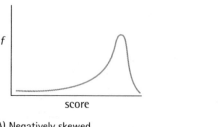

(A) Negatively skewed

(B) Positively skewed

In Figure A, the peak of the distribution is on the right side of the distribution, indicating that most scores are on the higher end of the distribution. The direction of the tail of the distribution (i.e. the lowest frequency) determines the type of skewness. In Figure A, the tail trails off to the left side and this type of distribution is called a **negatively skewed distribution**. In Figure B, the peak of the distribution is on the left side, indicating that most scores are on the lower end of the distribution. The tail trails off to the right side of the distribution, and this type of distribution is called a **positively skewed distribution**. If you go back to our graph on number of cigarettes per day, you will note that the peak is at the lower end of the graph (i.e. most of the scores are clustered at the lower end), while the tail is at the higher end. In other words, this would be indicative of a positively skewed distribution.

Negatively skewed distribution: Distribution in which most scores are on the higher end.

Positively skewed distribution: Distribution in which most scores are on the lower end.

Modality
The concept of modality as it relates to graphs refers to the number of peaks in a graph. The previous figures only had one peak and are therefore referred to as **unimodal distributions**. In the figure below, the distribution has two peaks and is referred to as a **bimodal distribution**.

Unimodal distribution: Distribution with one peak.

Bimodal distribution: Distribution with two peaks.

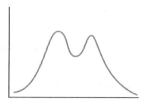

A graph with two peaks simply means that there are two clusters of scores with a high frequency.

Numerical summary measures

Numerical summary measures are single statistics that:

- in some way represent all the values in a distribution – this is called a measure of central tendency; and
- describe the spread (or variability) of scores – measures of variability.

In addition, a comparison of measures of central tendency allows us to draw some conclusions about the shape of the distribution.

Measures of central tendency

A **central tendency** refers to an average, or a score around which other scores tend to cluster. We will consider three of the most common measures of central tendency, namely mode, median and mean. Note that although 'average' has taken on a certain meaning in everyday use, in statistics there are in fact many types of averages.

Central tendency:
A score around which other scores tend to cluster.

Mode

Afrikaans-speaking students would know that the word 'mode' means fashionable in Afrikaans. It has much the same meaning in statistics. The **mode**, crudely put, refers to the score that is most fashionable, i.e. the score that appears most frequently in a set of scores. Consider, for example, the following scores:

Mode:
The score that appears most frequently.

2, 4, 10, 10, 10, 12, 14

The score of 10 occurs three times and thus would be the mode. In the following example, we have two scores with the same frequency:

3, 3, 3, 3, 5, 5, 6, 7, 10, 10, 10, 10

The scores of 3 and 10 both occur four times and both of them would be considered as the mode. This would be a bimodal distribution (see Shapes of distributions, above.).

When scores are arranged in an ungrouped frequency distribution, the mode would be the score/category with the highest frequency. In our frequency table for gender, the score (category) that appears most frequently is Female ($f = 30$).

When scores are arranged in a grouped frequency distribution the mode is the midpoint of the class with the highest frequency. In our example of cigarette smoking, the class with the highest frequency is 21–23 ($f = 12$).

Classes	f	rf		Cumulative		
		Prop.	Perc.	Cum. f	Cum. prop.	Cum. perc.
45–47	1	0.03	3	40	1.00	100
42–44	1	0.03	3	39	0.98	98
39–41	1	0.03	3	38	0.95	95
36–38	2	0.05	5	37	0.93	93
33–35	2	0.05	5	35	0.88	88
30–32	1	0.03	3	33	0.83	83
27–29	2	0.05	5	32	0.80	80
24–26	7	0.18	18	30	0.75	75
21–23	12	0.30	30	23	0.58	58
18–20	11	0.28	28	11	0.28	28
	N = 40					

A note on midpoints

The midpoint of a class is defined as the score that falls halfway between the **upper real limit** and **lower real limit**. This is different from what is called the 'observed limits', which are the actual scores that you can see in the class. For the class 21–23, the observed lower limit is 21, while the observed upper limit is 23. The real limit is obtained by subtracting 0.5 from the observed lower limit and adding 0.5 to the observed upper limit. Thus the lower real limit is 21 – 0.5 = 20.5, while the upper real limit is 23 + 0.5 = 23.5.

To obtain the midpoint: divide interval size in half (3/2 = 1.5) and add this to the lower real limit (20.5 + 1.5 = 22). The midpoint of the class with the highest frequency therefore is 22, which represents the mode of this distribution. (The observant student would note that one could already see that 22 is the midpoint between 21 and 23, without going through this elaborate procedure to calculate the midpoint. This is, however, the correct procedure to calculate the midpoint.)

Median

Median:
The score in the middle of a distribution when scores are arranged in numerical order.

The *Oxford English Dictionary* describes a **median** as (that) 'situated in the middle'. In statistics the median is that score in the middle of the distribution when scores are arranged in numerical order. The median is thus the score above and below which exactly half of the scores fall. If we have an odd number of scores, for example:

16, 18, 20, 26, 30,

the middle score would be 20, since you have two scores on either side of it. If we have an even number of scores, for example:

3, 5, 7, 8, 9, 11, 14, 16,

there is no score exactly in the middle. If we take the two scores 8 and 9, we would have three scores on either side. In this case, the score exactly in the middle of 8 and 9 represents the median. In this case it is 8.5.

When calculating the median for grouped data, we need to firstly determine the class where the middle score would fall. We will use our example:

Classes	f	rf Prop.	Perc.	Cumulative Cum. f	Cum. prop.	Cum. perc.
45–47	1	0.03	3	40	1.00	100
42–44	1	0.03	3	39	0.98	98
39–41	1	0.03	3	38	0.95	95
36–38	2	0.05	5	37	0.93	93
33–35	2	0.05	5	35	0.88	88
30–32	1	0.03	3	33	0.83	83
27–29	2	0.05	5	32	0.80	80
24–26	7	0.18	18	30	0.75	75
21–23	12	0.30	30	23	0.58	58
18–20	11	0.28	28	11	0.28	28
	N = 40					

Since there are 40 scores, we are looking for the 20th score. The column 'cumulative frequencies' indicates where the 20th score is located. The cumulative frequency of the class 21–23 is 23, whereas the cumulative frequency of the class below that is 11. In other words, the first class contains the first 11 scores, while the second class contains scores number 12 to 23. Thus the 20th score would fall into the class 21–23. To obtain the median, apply the following formula:

$$\text{Median} = ll_r + \frac{i \left(\frac{N}{2} - cf \right)}{f}$$

where ll_r = lower real limit of interval containing median

i = interval size

N = number of participants

cf = cumulative frequency below interval containing median

f = frequency of interval containing the median

Although this formula appears intimidating, all you need to do is to follow the instructions below the formula and to replace all the symbols with values. Thus:

ll_r = 20.5 (the lower real limit of class 21–23, which contains the median)

i = 3 (interval size)

N = 40 (number of participants)

cf_{ll} = 11 (cumulative frequency of the class below 21–23)

f = 12 (frequency of class containing median)

Substituting the symbols in the formula with values we have:

$$Median = ll_r + \frac{i\left(\frac{N}{2} - cf_{ll}\right)}{f}$$

$$= 20.5 + \frac{3\left(\frac{40}{2} - 11\right)}{12}$$

$$= 20.5 + \frac{3(9)}{12}$$

$$= 20.5 + 2.25$$

$$= 22.75$$

The median for this distribution would thus be 22.75.

Mean

Mean:
Total of scores divided by the number of observations.

The **mean** is the one measure of central tendency that is most commonly associated with the concept 'average'. It is the most frequently used of all the measures of central tendency and forms the basis of many inferential statistical techniques. The mean is simply all the scores added together divided by the number of observations (N). This is reflected in the formula:

$$\bar{X} = \frac{\Sigma X}{N}$$

where ΣX = sum of scores

N = number of observations

In statistics, the symbol $\bar{X}$ with the bar on top (X) is used to symbolise the mean. The symbol Σ stands for 'the sum of', while X is used to indicate the scores. Thus, ΣX refers to the sum of all the scores.

If we have the following set of scores: 5, 3, 6, 7, 7, 9, 6, we would calculate the mean as follow:

$$\overline{X} = \frac{\Sigma X}{N}$$

$$= \frac{43}{7} \quad (5 + 3 + 6 + 7 + 7 + 9 + 6 = 43)$$

$$= 614$$

When data is arranged in an ungrouped frequency distribution, a slightly revised formula is used:

$$\overline{X} = \frac{\Sigma fX}{N}$$

where ΣfX = sum of frequency

N = number of observations

This formula requires that we need to: (1) multiply each score with the frequency that it occurs (fX); and (2) add these together: ΣfX. The following table of frequencies illustrates this:

Score (X)	f	fX
14	2	28
12	1	12
9	3	27
8	2	16
7	4	28
	N = 12	ΣfX = 111

In the above table, we added the column fX to provide for the multiplication of each score with its associated frequency. The total of this column is ΣfX. Replacing the symbols in the formula with these values we have:

$$\overline{X} = \frac{\Sigma fX}{N}$$

$$= \frac{111}{12}$$

$$= 925$$

We use the same formula for grouped frequency distributions. However, in the case of grouped frequency distributions, we do not have the actual score, since we have grouped scores into classes. In this case we use the midpoint of each class. Note, however, that means (and other statistics like the median) should in general not be computed from grouped frequency distributions. If they are, they should be indicated as approximate means (or other statistics), since they are approximated by using the midpoint of each class. Thus, for our example on cigarette smoking, we would have:

Classes	Midpoint	f	fX
45–47	46	1	46
42–44	43	1	43
39–41	40	1	40
36–38	37	2	74
33–35	34	2	68
30–32	31	1	31
27–29	28	2	56
24–26	25	7	175
21–23	22	12	264
18–20	19	11	209
		N = 40	$\Sigma fX = 1006$

Substituting these values in the formula we have:

$$\text{Approximate } \overline{X} = \frac{\Sigma fX}{N}$$

$$= \frac{1006}{40}$$

$$= 25.15$$

Note that the formula now provides for approximate mean and that in calculating fX we used the midpoint rather then the actual score.

Skewness: Comparing the measures of central tendency

We know that skewness refers to the tendency for scores to cluster at either side of the distribution. This is illustrated below together with the relationship between the various measures of central tendency for the various types of distributions:

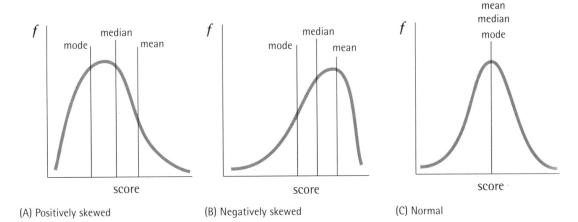

(A) Positively skewed   (B) Negatively skewed   (C) Normal

In a normal distribution (C), the mean, mode and median are exactly the same. On the other hand, in a positively skewed distribution, most scores occur at the lower end of the distribution below the mean, with the median and mode less than the mean. In a negatively skewed distribution, most scores appear above the mean, and the mode and median are also greater than the mean. In our example of cigarette smoking, the mean was 25.15, with the median and mode being 22.75 and 22 respectively. Thus, even if we did not graph the scores, we can conclude by simply comparing the three measures of central tendency that the distribution of number of cigarettes is positively skewed.

Measures of variability

Measures of central tendency only provide us with a partial description of our data. Distributions may have the same central value (i.e. mean) but differ in other ways. Consider three sets of scores with the same mean:

Distribution 1: 20, 30, 40, 50, 60, 70: Mean = 45

Distribution 2: 20, 43, 44, 46, 47, 70: Mean = 45

Distribution 3: 40, 43, 44, 46, 47, 50: Mean = 45

Although these three distributions all have the same mean, it is obvious that they differ in terms of the way that they are spread out. In distribution 1, scores are evenly spread out, while in distribution 2, most of the scores cluster in the centre with two extreme scores at both ends. In distribution 3, all the scores cluster in the centre. Thus, what we also need to fully describe any distribution is an index of the spread of scores or the variability. Indices that measure this spread or variability of scores are called **measures of variability**. When scores are spread out, the variability should be high, while when scores are clustered together, the variability should be low.

Measures of variability: Indices that measure spread of scores.

The most common measures of variability are the range, the sum of squares, the variance and the standard deviation. The range indicates the distance between the highest and lowest scores, whilst the other measures of variability relate to how far scores vary from a typical score (i.e. the mean).

Range

Range:
The difference between the highest score and the lowest score

The **range** is a very basic measure of variability and is simply defined as the highest score minus the lowest score. Given the following data set:

4, 6, 8, 9,

the range would be 9 – 4 = 5.

The range is a very crude measure of variability and is not extensively used in statistics. The basic problem with the range is that it depends on only two extreme scores in a distribution.

Sum of squares, variance, standard deviation

Unlike the range, all the scores in the distribution are used to calculate these three measures of variability. They are based on the extent to which scores in a distribution deviate from the mean. Take the following set of scores:

2, 3, 3, 5, 7, 7, 8,

The mean of these scores is 5 (2 + 3 + 3 + 5 + 7 + 7 + 8/7 = 35/7 = 5). The score 2 would thus deviate from the mean by – 3 (2 – 5), while the score 7 would deviate from the mean by 2 (7 – 5). If we add each score's deviation from the mean together we could derive a single numerical index. The problem is that the sum of the deviation scores will always equal 0. A solution to this is to square each deviation score and then to add these squared deviation scores together. This is called the **sum of squares**, which is defined by the following formula:

$$SS = \sum (\bar{X} - X)^2$$

We can demonstrate this formula by arranging the above scores in the following table:

Scores (X)	X – X̄	(X – X̄)²
2	-3	9
3	-2	4
3	-2	4
5	0	0
7	2	4
7	2	4
8	3	9
$\sum X = 35$	$\sum(X - \bar{X}) = 0$	SS = 34
$\bar{X} = 5$		

As previously indicated, we use the symbol X to symbolise scores. In the second column, the mean is subtracted from each score to obtain the deviation score and in the last column the deviation score is squared. If we add up all the squared deviation scores we obtain the sum of squares.

One difficulty with the sum of squares is that its size is influenced by the number of scores. If we add another 2 to the above distribution, the sum of squares would increase by another 9. An index that takes into account the number of scores is the **variance**, denoted by the symbol s^2. This is simply the sum of squares divided by the number of observations. In fact, we use the number of observations minus 1, since it has been statistically proven that for small samples using $N - 1$ leads to greater accuracy:

$$s^2 = \frac{SS}{N - 1}$$

Variance:
Sum of squares divided by number of observations.

Thus, from the above table we see that ss equals 34 and that the number of observations was 7. The obtained variance would be:

$$s^2 = \frac{SS}{N - 1}$$

$$= \frac{34}{7 - 1}$$

$$= 5.67$$

Both the sum of squares and the variance can be used to compare two different distributions. Thus a distribution with a variance of 7 would have greater variability than a distribution with a variance of 2. However, on its own variance does not have a direct intuitive interpretation, i.e. a variance of 4.86 on its own does not have a direct interpretation. The reason for this is that variance is not directly related to the original scores, but is based on squared deviations. To obtain a measure of variability that is in the same units as the original scores we can use the square root of the variance. This square root of the variance is called the **standard deviation** and is indicated by the symbol s (as opposed to s^2 for the variance):

$$s = \sqrt{\frac{SS}{N - 1}}$$

Standard deviation:
Square root of the variance.

Note that we have simply placed a square root sign over the formula for variance. Working from our table:

$$s = \sqrt{\frac{SS}{N - 1}}$$

$$= \sqrt{\frac{34}{7 - 1}}$$

$$= \sqrt{5.67}$$

$$= 2.38$$

The standard deviation is in the same unit of measurement as the original scores and as the average deviation from the mean. Thus, if the original scores referred to number of children, the standard deviation of 2.38 means that on average scores deviate by 2.38 children from the mean.

Variance and standard deviation for grouped and ungrouped frequency distributions

When scores are arranged in a frequency distribution, we need to take account of the frequencies in calculating the variance or standard deviation. In an ungrouped frequency distribution, the squared deviation of each score is multiplied by the frequency of each score. Thus only the formula for the sum of squares would change to accommodate the frequencies:

$$ss = \sum f (X - \bar{X})^2$$

We have inserted the symbol f (for frequencies) in the above formula. Let us use the previous scores now arranged in the following ungrouped frequency distribution (i.e. score and number of times that each score occurs) to illustrate this formula:

Scores (X)	f	$X - \bar{X}$	$(X - \bar{X})^2$	$f (X - \bar{X})^2$
2	1	-3	9	9
3	2	-2	4	8
5	1	0	0	0
7	2	2	4	8
8	1	3	9	9
	N = 7			
	$\bar{X}$ = 5			ss = 34

Note that since the scores have now been arranged together with the number of times each score occurs (frequency), we have added a new column to provide for the frequency multiplied with the squared deviation score. After this the formulas for the variance and standard deviation are applied in the same way. Note also that the outcome is the same as in the previous example. For the variance:

$$s^2 = \frac{ss}{N - 1}$$

$$= \frac{34}{7 - 1}$$

$$= 5.67$$

For the standard deviation:

$$s = \sqrt{\frac{SS}{N-1}}$$

$$= \sqrt{\frac{34}{7-1}}$$

$$= \sqrt{5.67}$$

$$= 2.38$$

When working with grouped frequency distributions, the same formulas for the variance and standard deviations are used. The only difference is in the calculation of the sum of squares. In grouped frequency distributions we work with groups of scores and therefore we use the *midpoint of the class to represent the score.*

Research outcomes

We undertake research for two primary reasons, namely: (1) to increase our knowledge about a certain subject: and (2) to solve particular problems. Research that is directed towards the accumulation of knowledge is known as knowledge-oriented research. Alternative terms for this in the literature are basic research or theory-driven research. Research directed towards solving problems is known as problem-oriented research, or applied research.

Often there is heated debate about which type of research is more important. Given the huge range of societal problems that face us, there is often an understandable emphasis on problem-oriented research, with scathing attacks on basic research through references like 'pie-in-the-sky' research.

The reality, however, is that both types of research are needed. There is no point in designing an intervention programme for smoking behaviour if the phenomenon itself is not very clearly understood. Gaining knowledge about a particular phenomenon is as important as designing interventions to tackle it. Knowledge-oriented and problem-oriented research should therefore be seen as complementary to each other.

Lastly, I like to view research as a circular (never-ending) process. This is indicated by the dotted line in Figure 16.1. The outcomes of a particular research project very often raise certain questions or identify certain problems that lead to the formulation of a new research project. Also, if the outcome of the research project leads to the design of an intervention, the effects of the intervention programme will have to be determined by means of research.

. . . .

Summary

This chapter has attempted to provide a brief overview of the research process and to expose the student to basic descriptive statistics. In particular, the focus was on planning the research process, distinguishing between qualitative and quantitative methodologies, and analysing the data obtained through the research process. In terms of analysing the data, the focus was on condensing and summarising data by using tables and graphs and determining (calculating) measures of central tendency and of variability.

. . . .

Further reading

American Psychological Association (APA) (1983) *Publication Manual of the American Psychological Association*. Washington, DC: APA.

Pretorius, T.B. (under editorial review Pathways to health: The use of product-term regression analyses to examine third variable influences.

Shavelson, R.J. (1981) *Statistical Reasoning for the Behavioral Sciences*. Boston: Allyn & Bacon.

Index